Lecture Notes in Artificial Intelligence   3717

Edited by J. G. Carbonell and J. Siekmann

Subseries of Lecture Notes in Computer Science

Bernhard Gramlich (Ed.)

Frontiers of Combining Systems

5th International Workshop, FroCoS 2005
Vienna, Austria, September 19-21, 2005
Proceedings

 Springer

Series Editors

Jaime G. Carbonell, Carnegie Mellon University, Pittsburgh, PA, USA
Jörg Siekmann, University of Saarland, Saarbrücken, Germany

Volume Editor

Bernhard Gramlich
Technische Universität Wien
Fakultät für Informatik
Favoritenstrasse 9 - E185/2, 1040 Wien, Austria
E-mail: gramlich@logic.at

Library of Congress Control Number: 2005932552

CR Subject Classification (1998): I.2.3, F.4.1, F.4

ISSN   0302-9743
ISBN-10   3-540-29051-6 Springer Berlin Heidelberg New York
ISBN-13   978-3-540-29051-3 Springer Berlin Heidelberg New York

Springer is a part of Springer Science+Business Media

springeronline.com

© Springer-Verlag Berlin Heidelberg 2005
Printed in Germany

Typesetting: Camera-ready by author, data conversion by Scientific Publishing Services, Chennai, India
Printed on acid-free paper   SPIN: 11559306   06/3142   5 4 3 2 1 0

Preface

This volume contains the proceedings of the 5th International Workshop on Frontiers of Combining Systems (FroCoS 2005) held September 19–21, 2005 in Vienna, Austria. Previously, FroCoS was organized in Munich (1996), Amsterdam (1998), Nancy (2000) and Santa Margherita Ligure near Genoa (2002). In 2004, FroCoS joined IJCAR 2004, the 2nd International Joint Conference on Automated Reasoning. Like its predecessors, FroCoS 2005 offered a common forum for the presentation and discussion of research results and activities on the combination, integration, analysis, modularization and interaction of formally defined systems, with an emphasis on logic-based ones. These issues are important in many areas of computer science, such as logic, computation, program development and verification, artificial intelligence, automated reasoning, constraint solving, declarative programming, and symbolic computation.

There were 28 research papers submitted to FroCoS 2005, authored by researchers from 16 countries. After extensive reviewing and discussion within the Program Committee, 14 papers including two system descriptions were finally accepted for presentation at the conference and publication in this volume. The topics covered by the selected papers include: combinations of logics, theories, and decision procedures; constraint solving and programming; combination issues in rewriting and programming as well as in logical frameworks and theorem proving systems. In addition to the regular accepted papers, this volume also contains papers (three full ones and one abstract) corresponding to four invited talks given by Luca de Alfaro (Univ. of California, Santa Cruz), Silvio Ghilardi (Univ. of Milan), Fausto Giunchiglia (Univ. of Trento) and Eric Monfroy (Univ. of Nantes & UTFSM/Chile).

Many people and institutions contributed to making FroCoS 2005 a success. I would like to thank in particular: the members of the Program Comittee and the additional referees for their careful and thorough reviewing work in a relatively short time; the other members of the FroCoS Steering Committee for their support and encouragement; the invited speakers for their stimulating contributions; the members of the local Organizing Committee for their help with all the local and practical organization issues; Andrei Voronkov for the free use of his efficient EasyChair conference management system and his support; and all institutions that supported FroCoS 2005 either as financial sponsors or by other means: the Vienna University of Technology, Theory and Logic Group (Institute of Computer Languages), the Database and Artificial Intelligence Group (Institute of Information Systems), the Austrian Computer Society (OCG), the European Association for Theoretical Comuter Science (EATCS), the European Association for Programming Languages and Systems (EAPLS), and the Vienna Convention Bureau (VCB).

July 2005   Bernhard Gramlich

Organization

Conference and Program Committee Chair

Bernhard Gramlich (Fakultät für Informatik, TU Wien)

Program Committee

Alessandro Armando	University of Genoa, Italy
Franz Baader	TU Dresden, Germany
Clark W. Barrett	NYU New York, USA
Frédéric Benhamou	LINA, University of Nantes, France
Michel Bidoit	LSV, CNRS & ENS Cachan, France
Jacques Calmet	University of Karlsruhe, Germany
Jürgen Giesl	RWTH Aachen, Germany
Bernhard Gramlich	TU Wien, Austria
Deepak Kapur	UNM Albuquerque, USA
Maarten Marx	University of Amsterdam, The Netherlands
Joachim Niehren	INRIA Futurs, University of Lille, France
Christophe Ringeissen	LORIA-INRIA Nancy, France
Manfred Schmidt-Schauß	University of Frankfurt, Germany
Cesare Tinelli	University of Iowa, USA
Ashish Tiwari	SRI Menlo Park, USA
Frank Wolter	University of Liverpool, UK

Local Organization

Aneta Binder	Bernhard Gramlich
Franziska Gusel	Gernot Salzer
Jana Srna	

Additional Referees

Sergio Antoy	Manuel Clavel	Gilles Dowek
Frederic Blanqui	Jeremy Dawson	Rachid Echahed
Iovka Boneva	Stéphane Demri	Cormac Flanagan
Lucas Bordeaux	Alexander Dikovsky	Vijay Ganesh
Balder ten Cate	Clare Dixon	Thomas Genet

Rajeev Goré

Jean Goubault-Larrecq

Laurent Granvilliers

Ludovic Henrio

Florent Jacquemard

Predrag Janičić

Ulrich Junker

Boris Konev

Marco Kuhlmann

Jordi Levy

Matthias Mann

Marco Maratea

Nicolas Markey

Hans de Nivelle

Silvio Ranise

Yves Roos

David Sabel

Frédéric Saubion

Thomas Schwentick

Helmut Seidl

Aaron Stump

Mateu Villaret

Benjamin Wack

Dirk Walther

Ting Zhang

Table of Contents

Logics, Theories, and Decision Procedures I

Interface Formalisms

Logics, Theories, and Decision Procedures II

Constraint Solving and Programming

Logical Problem Analysis and Encoding I

Combination Issues in Rewriting and Programming

Compositional System Design and Refinement

Logical Problem Analysis and Encoding II

Theorem Proving Frameworks and Systems

A Comprehensive Framework for Combined Decision Procedures

Silvio Ghilardi[1], Enrica Nicolini[2], and Daniele Zucchelli[1,*]

[1] Dipartimento di Scienze dell'Informazione
{ghilardi, zucchelli}@dsi.unimi.it
[2] Dipartimento di Matematica,
Università degli Studi di Milano - Italy

Abstract. We define a general notion of a fragment within higher order type theory; a procedure for constraint satisfiability in combined fragments is outlined, following Nelson-Oppen schema. The procedure is in general only sound, but it becomes terminating and complete when the shared fragment enjoys suitable noetherianity conditions and allows an abstract version of a 'Keisler-Shelah like' isomorphism theorem. We show that this general decidability transfer result covers as special cases, besides applications which seem to be new, the recent extension of Nelson-Oppen procedure to non-disjoint signatures [16] and the fusion transfer of decidability of consistency of A-Boxes with respect to T-Boxes axioms in local abstract description systems [9]; in addition, it reduces decidability of modal and temporal monodic fragments [32] to their extensional and one-variable components.

1 Introduction

Decision procedures for fragments of various logics and theories play a central role in many applications of logic in computer science, for instance in formal methods and in knowledge representation. Within these application domains, relevant data appears to be heterogeneously structured, so that modularity in combining and re-using both algorithms and concrete implementations becomes crucial. This is why the development of meta-level frameworks, accepting as input specialized devices, turns out to be strategic for future advances in building powerful, fully or partially automatized systems. In this paper, we shall consider one of the most popular and simple schemata (due to Nelson-Oppen) for designing a cooperation protocol among separate reasoners; we shall plug it into a higher order framework and show how it can be used to deal with various classes of combination problems, often quite far from the originally intended application domain.

The basic feature of Nelson-Oppen method is simple: constraints involving mixed signatures are transformed into equi-satisfiable pure constraints and then

---

* Work performed within the MIUR Project "Metodi Costruttivi in Topologia, Algebra e Fondamenti dell'Informatica". We wish to thank Manfred Schmidt-Schauss for comments on a preliminary draft of this paper.

B. Gramlich (Ed.): FroCoS 2005, LNAI 3717, pp. 1–30, 2005.

the specialized reasoners try to share all the information they can acquire concerning constraints in the common subsignature, till an inconsistency is detected or till a saturation state is reached.

Nelson-Oppen method was guaranteed to be complete only for disjoint signatures and stably infinite theories, till quite recently, when it was realized [16] that stable infiniteness is just a special case of a compatibility notion, which is related to model completions of shared sub-theories. The above extension of Nelson-Oppen method to combination of theories operating over non disjoint signatures lead to various applications to decision problems in modal logics: such applications (sometimes involving non trivial extensions of the method as well as integration with other work) concerned transfer of decidability of global consequence relation to fusions [16] and to $\mathcal{E}$-connections [4], [5], as well as transfer of decidability of local consequence relation to fusions [8].

Thus, most of previously existing decidability results on fusions of modal logics (for instance those in [33]) were recaptured and sometimes also improved by general automated reasoning methods based on Nelson-Oppen ideas. However, this is far from exhausting all the potentialities of such ideas and further extensions are possible. In fact, the standard approach to decision problems in modal/temporal/description logics is directly based on Kripke models (see for instance [9], [15]), without the intermediation of an algebraic formalism, whereas the intermediation of the formalism of Boolean algebras with operators is essential in the approach of papers like [16], [8], [4], [5]. The appeal to the algebraic formulation of decision problems on one side produces proofs which are much smoother and which apply also to semantically incomplete propositional logics, but on the other side it limits the method to the cases in which such a purely algebraic counterpart of semantic decision problems can be identified.

One of the main reasons for avoiding first-order formalisms in favor of propositional modal logic-style languages lies in the better computational performances of the latter. However, from a purely declarative point of view, first-order formalisms are essential in order to specify in a semantically meaningful language the relevant decision problems. This goal is mainly achieved in the case of modal logic through first-order translations, the role of such translations being simply that of codifying the intended semantics (and not necessarily that of providing computational tools).

If a semantic class $\mathcal{S}$ of Kripke frames is given, relevant decision problems are formulated as satisfiability problems (within members of $\mathcal{S}$) for standard translations of propositional modal formulae. In these formulations, unary predicates occurring in standard translations are considered *in practice* as *second order variables*: in fact, satisfiability requires the existence of suitable Kripke *models* and the latter differ from mere Kripke frames precisely by the specification of a second order assignment. The role played by second order variables becomes even more evident if we analyze the way in which standard translations of modal formulae in fusions are obtained from standard translations of formulae in the component languages. For instance, $ST(\Diamond_1\Diamond_2\mathrm{x}, w)$ is obtained by substituting into $ST(\Diamond_1\mathrm{y}, w) := \exists v(R_1(w, v) \wedge Y(v))$ the 'abstracted' second order term

$\{v \mid ST(\Diamond_2 \mathrm{x}, v)\} := \{v \mid \exists z (R_2(v, z) \wedge X(z))\}$ for Y (a β-conversion should follow the replacement in order to get as normal form precisely $ST(\Diamond_1 \Diamond_2 \mathrm{x}, w)$). Thus, even if we do not 'computationally' trust first-order logic (and consequently not even higher order logic, for much stronger reasons), it makes nevertheless sense to *analyze combination problems in the framework where they arise*, that is in the framework which is the most natural for them.

We shall work within Church's type theory: thus our syntax deals with types and terms, terms being endowed with a (codomain) type. In this higher order context, we shall provide a general definition of a fragment (more specifically of an *interpreted algebraic fragment*, see Definitions 3.2, 3.3) and of a constraint satisfiability problem, in such a way that fragments can be combined into each other and a Nelson-Oppen procedure for constraint satisfiability in combined fragments can be formally introduced.

The general procedure is only sound and specific conditions for guaranteeing termination and completeness are needed. For termination, we rely on *local finiteness* (better, on *noetherianity*) of the shared fragment, whereas for completeness we use heavy model-theoretic tools. These tools (called *isomorphism theorems*) transform equivalence with respect to satisfiability of shared atoms into isomorphism with respect to the shared signature, in such a way that satisfiability of pure constraints is not compromised. The results of this analysis is summarized in our general decidability transfer result (Theorem 5.1).

Of course, isomorphisms theorems are quite peculiar and rare. However, the classical Keisler-Shelah isomorphism theorem based on ultrapowers [11] is sufficient to justify through Theorem 5.1 the recent extension [16] of the Nelson-Oppen results to non disjoint first-order signatures and another isomorphism theorem, based on disjoint unions (better, on disjoint copies), is sufficient to justify in a similar way the decidability transfer result of [9] concerning A-Box consistency with respect to T-Boxes.[1] Having identified the conceptual core of the method, we are now able to apply it to various situations, thus getting further decidability transfer results: these results cover the combination of A-Boxes with a stably infinite first-order theory (Theorem 5.3), the combination of two so-called monadically suitable fragments (Theorem 5.6) and the combination (leading to monodic modal fragments in the sense of [32]) of a one-variable modal fragment with a monadically suitable extensional fragment (Theorem 5.7).

For space reasons, we can only explain here our settings, give examples and state the main results (for proofs and for more information, the reader is referred to the full technical report [17]).

2   Higher-Order Signatures

We adopt a type theory in Church's style (see [2], [3], [21] for introductions to the subject). We use letters $S_1, S_2, \ldots$ to indicate *sorts* (also called *primitive types*)

---

[1] Thus, the difference between the semantically oriented proofs of [9] and the algebraically oriented proofs of papers like [16], [8] seem to be mainly a question of choosing a different isomorphism theorem to justify the combined procedure.

of a signature. Formally, sorts are a set $\mathcal{S}$ and *types over* $\mathcal{S}$ are built inductively as follows: (i) every sort $S \in \mathcal{S}$ is also a type; (ii) Ω is a type (this is called the *truth-values* type); (iii) if τ_1, τ_2 are types, so is $(\tau_1 \rightarrow \tau_2)$.

As usual external brackets are omitted; moreover, we shorten the expression $\tau_1 \rightarrow (\tau_2 \rightarrow \ldots (\tau_n \rightarrow \tau))$ into $\tau_1 \ldots \tau_n \rightarrow \tau$ (in this way, every type τ has the form $\tau_1 \ldots \tau_n \rightarrow \tau$, where $n \geq 0$ and τ is a sort or it is Ω). In the following, we use the notation $\mathcal{T}(\mathcal{S})$ or simply $\mathcal{T}$ to indicate a *types set*, i.e. the totality of types that can be built up from the set of sorts $\mathcal{S}$. We always reserve to sorts the letters $S_1, S_2, \ldots$ (as opposed to the letters τ, υ, etc. which are used for arbitrary types).

A *signature* (or a *language*) is a triple $\mathcal{L} = \langle \mathcal{T}, \Sigma, a \rangle$, where $\mathcal{T}$ is a types set, Σ is a set of constants and a is an *arity map*, namely a map $a : \Sigma \longrightarrow \mathcal{T}$. We write $f : \tau_1 \ldots \tau_n \rightarrow \tau$ to express that f is a *constant of type* $\tau_1 \ldots \tau_n \rightarrow \tau$, i.e. that $a(f) = \tau_1 \ldots \tau_n \rightarrow \tau$. According to the above observation, we can assume that τ is a sort or that $\tau = \Omega$; in the latter case, we say that f is a *predicate* or a *relational* symbol (predicate symbols are preferably indicated with the letters $P, Q, \ldots$).

We require the following *special constants* to be always present in a signature: $\top$ and $\bot$ of type Ω; $\neg$ of type $\Omega \rightarrow \Omega$; $\vee$ and $\wedge$ of type $\Omega\,\Omega \rightarrow \Omega$; $=_\tau$ of type $\tau\tau \rightarrow \Omega$ for each type $\tau \in \mathcal{T}$ (we usually write it as '$=$' without specifying the subscript τ). The *proper symbols* of a signature are its sorts and its non special constants.

A signature is *one-sorted* iff its set of sorts is a singleton. A signature $\mathcal{L}$ is *first-order* if for any proper $f \in \Sigma$, we have that $a(f) = S_1 \ldots S_n \rightarrow \tau$, where τ is a sort or it is Ω. A first-order signature is called *relational* iff any proper $f \in \Sigma$ is a relational constant, that is $a(f) = S_1 \ldots S_n \rightarrow \Omega$. By contrast, a first order signature is called *functional* iff any proper $f \in \Sigma$ has arity $S_1 \ldots S_n \rightarrow S$.

Given a signature $\mathcal{L} = \langle \mathcal{T}, \Sigma, a \rangle$ and a type $\tau \in \mathcal{T}$, we define the notion of an $\mathcal{L}$-*term* (or just *term*) of type τ, written $t : \tau$, as follows (for the definition we need, for every type $\tau \in \mathcal{T}$, a countable supply V_τ of variables of type τ):

- $x : \tau$ (for $x \in V_\tau$) is an $\mathcal{L}$-term of type τ;
- $c : \tau$ (for $c \in \Sigma$ and $a(c) = \tau$) is an $\mathcal{L}$-term of type τ;
- if $t : \upsilon \rightarrow \tau$ and $u : \upsilon$ are $\mathcal{L}$-terms of types $\upsilon \rightarrow \tau$ and υ, respectively, then $val_\tau(t, u) : \tau$ (also written as $t(u) : \tau$) is an $\mathcal{L}$-term of type τ;
- if $t : \tau$ is an $\mathcal{L}$-term of type τ and $x \in V_\upsilon$ is an $\mathcal{L}$-variable of type υ, $\lambda x^\upsilon t : \upsilon \rightarrow \tau$ is an $\mathcal{L}$-term of type $\upsilon \rightarrow \tau$.

In the following, we consider the notation x^τ (c^τ) equivalent to $x : \tau$ ($c : \tau$), where x (resp. c) is a variable (resp. a constant); if it can be deduced from the context, *the specification of the type of a term may be omitted*. Moreover, a term of type τ is also called a *τ-term* and terms of type Ω are also called *formulae*. Given a formula φ, we write $\{x \mid \varphi\}$ for $\lambda x \varphi$. Moreover, we shorten $val_\tau(\cdots (val_{\tau_{n-1}}(t, u_1), \cdots), u_n)$ to $t(u_1, \ldots, u_n)$. Free and bound variables are defined in the usual way; we use the notation $t[x_1, \ldots, x_n]$ (or $fvar(t) \subseteq \{x_1, \ldots, x_n\}$) to mean that the variables occurring freely in t are in-

.cluded in the finite set $\underline{x} = \{x_1, \ldots, x_n\}$. We often indicate finite sets or finite tuples of variables by the letters $\underline{x}, \underline{y}, \ldots$.

Substitutions are defined in the usual way, but α-conversion (that is, bound variables renaming) might be necessary to avoid clashes. We also follow standard practice of considering terms as equivalence classes of terms under α-conversion. β- and η-conversions are defined in the standard way and we shall make use of them whenever needed (for a very brief account on the related definitions and results, the reader is referred to [12]).

For each formula φ, we define the formulae $\forall x^v\, \varphi$ and $\exists x^v\, \varphi$ as $\{x^v \mid \varphi\} = \{x^v \mid \top\}$ and as $\neg \forall x^v\, \neg\varphi$, respectively (the latter can also be defined differently, in an intuitionistically acceptable way, see [21]). For terms φ_1, φ_2 of type Ω, the terms $\varphi_1 \to \varphi_2$ and $\varphi_1 \leftrightarrow \varphi_2$ of type Ω are defined in the usual way.

By the above definitions, first-order formulae *can be considered as a subset* of the higher order formulae defined in this section. More specifically, when we speak of *first-order terms*, we mean variables $x : S$, constants $c : S$ and terms of the kind $f(t_1, \ldots, t_n) : S$, where $t_1, \ldots, t_n$ are (inductively given) first-order terms and $a(f) = S_1 \cdots S_n \to S$. Now *first-order formulae* are obtained from formulae of the kind $\top : \Omega, \bot : \Omega, P(t_1, \ldots, t_n) : \Omega$ (where $t_1, \ldots, t_n$ are first-order terms and $a(P) = S_1 \cdots S_n \to \Omega$) by applying $\exists x^S, \forall x^S, \wedge, \vee, \neg, \to, \leftrightarrow$.

In order to introduce our computational problems, we need to recall the notion of an interpretation of a type-theoretic language. Formulae of higher order type theory which are valid in ordinary set-theoretic models do not form an axiomatizable class, as it is well-known from classical limitative results. We shall nevertheless confine ourselves to standard set-theoretic models, because we are not interested in the whole type theoretic language, but only in more tractable fragments of it.

If we are given a map that assigns to every sort $S \in \mathcal{S}$ a set $[\![S]\!]$, we can inductively extend it to all types over $\mathcal{S}$, by taking $[\![\tau \to \upsilon]\!]$ to be the set of functions from $[\![\tau]\!]$ to $[\![\upsilon]\!]$ (we shall freely refer to such an extension below, without explicitly mentioning it). Given a language $\mathcal{L} = \langle \mathcal{T}, \Sigma, a \rangle$, an $\mathcal{L}$-*structure* (or just a *structure*) $\mathcal{A}$ is a pair $\langle [\![-]\!]_\mathcal{A}, \mathcal{I}_\mathcal{A} \rangle$, where:

(i) $[\![-]\!]_\mathcal{A}$ is a function assigning to a sort $S \in \mathcal{T}$, a (non empty, if you like) set $[\![S]\!]_\mathcal{A}$;
(ii) $\mathcal{I}_\mathcal{A}$ is a function assigning to a constant $c \in \Sigma$ of type τ, an element $\mathcal{I}_\mathcal{A}(c^\tau) \in [\![\tau]\!]_\mathcal{A}$.

In every structure $\mathcal{A}$, we require that $[\![\Omega]\!]_\mathcal{A} = \{0, 1\}$ and that $\top, \bot, \neg, \wedge, \vee$ are given their standard 'truth-table' meaning.

Given an $\mathcal{L}$-structure $\mathcal{A} = \langle [\![-]\!]_\mathcal{A}, \mathcal{I}_\mathcal{A} \rangle$ and a type-conformal assignment α to the variables of $\mathcal{L}$, it is possible to define (in the expected way) the interpretation $\mathcal{I}_\mathcal{A}^\alpha(t)$ of the term t under the assignment α: notice that, if t has type τ, then we have $\mathcal{I}_\mathcal{A}^\alpha(t) \in [\![\tau]\!]_\mathcal{A}$. An $\mathcal{L}$-formula φ is *satisfied* in $\mathcal{A}$ under the assignment α iff $\mathcal{I}_\mathcal{A}^\alpha(\varphi) = 1$ (we usually write $\mathcal{A} \models_\alpha \varphi$ for $\mathcal{I}_\mathcal{A}^\alpha(\varphi) = 1$). A formula is *satisfiable* iff it is satisfied in some structure under some assignment and a set of formulae Γ is satisfiable iff all formulas in Γ are simultaneously satisfied.

For signature inclusions $\mathcal{L}_0 \subseteq \mathcal{L}$, there is an obvious *taking reduct* operation mapping a $\mathcal{L}$-structure $\mathcal{A}$ to a $\mathcal{L}_0$-structure $\mathcal{A}_{|\mathcal{L}_0}$; we can similarly take the $\mathcal{L}_0$-reduct of an assignment, by ignoring the values assigned to variables whose types are not in $\mathcal{L}_0$ (we leave the reader to define these notions properly).

3   Fragments

General type theory is very hard to attack from a computational point of view, this is why we are basically interested only in more tractable fragments and in combinations of them. Fragments are defined as follows:

Definition 3.1. *A* fragment *is a pair* $\langle \mathcal{L}, T \rangle$ *where* $\mathcal{L} = \langle \mathcal{T}, \Sigma, a \rangle$ *is a signature and* T *is a recursive set of* $\mathcal{L}$-terms.

3.1   Algebraic Fragments

We want to use fragments as ingredients of larger and larger combined fragments: a crucial notion in this sense is that of an algebraic fragment.

Definition 3.2. *A* fragment $\langle \mathcal{L}, T \rangle$ *is said to be an* algebraic fragment *iff* T *satisfies the following conditions:*

  (i) T *is closed under composition (that is, it is closed under substitution): if* $u[x_1, \ldots, x_n] \in T$ *and* $t_i \in T$ *for all* $i = 1, \ldots, n$, *then* $u[t_1, \ldots, t_n] \in T$;
  (ii) T *contains domain variables: if* τ *is a type such that some variable of type* τ *occurs free in a term* $t \in T$, *then every variable of type* τ *belongs to* T;
  (iii) T *contains codomain variables: if* $t : \tau$ *belongs to* T, *then every variable of type* τ *belongs to* T.

Observe that from the above definition it follows that T is closed under renaming of terms. Quite often, one is interested in interpreting the terms of a fragment not in the class of all possible structures for the language of the fragment, but only in some selected ones (e.g. when checking satisfiability of some temporal formulae, one might be interested only in checking satisfiability in particular flows of time, those which are for instance discrete or continuous). This is the reason for 'interpreting' fragments:

Definition 3.3. *An* interpreted algebraic fragment *(to be shortened as i.a.f.) is a triple* $\Phi = \langle \mathcal{L}, T, \mathcal{S} \rangle$, *where* $\langle \mathcal{L}, T \rangle$ *is an algebraic fragment and* $\mathcal{S}$ *is a class of* $\mathcal{L}$-structures closed under isomorphisms.

The set of terms T in an i.a.f. $\Phi = \langle \mathcal{L}, T, \mathcal{S} \rangle$ is called the set of Φ-*terms* and the set of types τ such that $t : \tau$ is a Φ-term for some t is called the set of Φ-*types*. A Φ-*variable* is a variable x^τ such that τ is a Φ-type (or equivalently, a variable which is a Φ-term). It is also useful to *identify a (non-interpreted) algebraic fragment* $\langle \mathcal{L}, T \rangle$ with the interpreted algebraic fragment $\Phi = \langle \mathcal{L}, T, \mathcal{S} \rangle$, where $\mathcal{S}$ is taken to be the class of all $\mathcal{L}$-structures.

Definition 3.4. *Given an i.a.f. fragment* Φ*, a* Φ*-atom is an equation* $t_1 = t_2$ *between* Φ*-terms* t_1, t_2 *of the same type; a* Φ*-literal is a* Φ*-atom or a negation of a* Φ*-atom, a* Φ*-constraint is a finite conjunction of* Φ*-literals, a* Φ*-clause is a finite disjunction of* Φ*-literals. Infinite sets of* Φ*-literals (representing an infinite conjunction) are called* generalized Φ*-constraints (provided they contain altogether only finitely many free variables).*

Some Conventions. Without loss of generality, we may assume that $\top$ *is a* Φ*-atom* in every i.a.f. Φ (in fact, to be of any interest, a fragment should at least contain a term t and we can let $\top$ to be $t = t$). As a consequence, $\bot$ will always be a Φ-literal; by convention, however, we shall *include* $\bot$ *among* Φ*-atoms* (hence a Φ-atom is either an equation among Φ-terms - $\top$ included - or it is $\bot$). Since we have $\bot$ as an atom, there is no need to consider the empty clause as a clause, so clauses will be disjunctions of *at least one* literal. The reader should keep in mind these slightly non standard conventions for the whole paper.

A Φ-clause is said *positive* if only Φ-atoms occur in. A Φ-atom $t_1 = t_2$ is closed if and only if t_i is closed ($i \in \{1, 2\}$); the definition of closed Φ-literals, -constraints and -clauses is analogous. For a finite set $\underline{x}$ of variables and an i.a.f. Φ, a $\Phi(\underline{x})$-atom (-term, -literal, -clause, -constraint) is a Φ-atom (-term, -literal, -clause, -constraint) A such that $fvar(A) \subseteq \underline{x}$.

We deal in this paper mainly with the *constraint satisfiability problem* for an i.a.f. $\Phi = \langle \mathcal{L}, T, \mathcal{S} \rangle$: this is *the problem of deciding whether a* Φ*-constraint is satisfiable in some structure* $\mathcal{A} \in \mathcal{S}$. On the other hand, the *word problem* for Φ is the problem of deciding if the universal closure of a given Φ-atom is true in every structure $\mathcal{A} \in \mathcal{S}$.

3.2   Examples

Although there are genuinely intended higher order interpreted algebraic fragments whose word problem is decidable (see for instance Friedman theorem for simply typed λ-calculus) and also whose constraint satisfiability problem is decidable (see Rabin results on monadic second order logic), we shall mainly concentrate on examples providing applications at first-order level. The reader should however notice that we need to use higher order variables and to pay special attention to the types of a fragment in order for fragment combination defined in Subsection 4.1 to cover the desired applications.

Example 3.1 (First-order equational fragments). Let us consider a first-order language $\mathcal{L} = \langle T, \Sigma, a \rangle$ (for simplicity, we also assume that $\mathcal{L}$ is one-sorted). Let T be the set of the first-order $\mathcal{L}$-terms and let $\mathcal{S}$ be an elementary class, i.e. the class of the $\mathcal{L}$-structures which happen to be the models of a certain first-order theory in the signature $\mathcal{L}$. Obviously, the triple $\Phi = \langle \mathcal{L}, T, \mathcal{S} \rangle$ is an i.a.f.. The Φ-atoms will be equalities between Φ-terms, i.e. first-order atomic formulae of the kind $t_1 = t_2$. Word problem in $\Phi = \langle \mathcal{L}, T, \mathcal{S} \rangle$ is standard uniform word problem (as defined for the case of equational theories for instance in [6]), whereas constraint satisfiability problem is the problem of deciding satisfiability of a finite set of equations and inequations.

Example 3.2 (Universal first-order fragments). The previous example disregards the relational symbols of the first-order signature $\mathcal{L}$. To take also them into consideration, it is sufficient to make some slight adjustment: besides first-order terms, also atomic formulae and $\top$, as well as propositional variables (namely variables having type Ω) will be terms of the fragment.[2] The semantic class $\mathcal{S}$ where the fragment is to be interpreted is again taken to be an elementary class. For $\Phi = \langle \mathcal{L}, T, \mathcal{S} \rangle$ so defined, the constraint satisfiability problem becomes essentially the problem of deciding the satisfiability of an arbitrary finite set of literals in the models belonging to $\mathcal{S}$.[3]

We now define different kinds of i.a.f.'s starting from the set F of first-order formulae of a first-order signature $\mathcal{L}$; for simplicity, let's suppose also that $\mathcal{L}$ is relational and one-sorted (call W this unique sort).

Example 3.3 (Full First-Order Language, plain version). We take T to be the union of F with the sets of the individual variables and of the propositional variables. Of course, $\Phi = \langle \mathcal{L}, T \rangle$ so defined is an algebraic fragment, whose types are W and Ω. By Church theorem, both word and constraint satisfiability problem are undecidable here (the two problems both reduce to satisfiability of a first-order formula with equality); they may be decidable in case the fragment is interpreted into some specific semantic class $\mathcal{S}$.

In the next example, we build formulae (out of the symbols of our fixed first order relational one-sorted signature $\mathcal{L}$) by using at most N (free or bound) individual variables; however we are allowed to use also second order variables of arity at most K:

Example 3.4 (Full First-Order Language, NK-version). Fix cardinals $K \leq N \leq \omega$ and consider, instead of F, the set F_{NK} of formulae φ that contains at most N (free or bound) individual variables and that are built up by applying boolean connectives and individual quantifiers to atomic formulae of the following two kinds:

- $P(x_{i_1}, \ldots, x_{i_n})$, where P is a relational constant and $x_{i_1}, \ldots, x_{i_n}$ are individual variables (since at most $x_1, \ldots, x_N$ can be used, we require that $i_1, \ldots, i_n \leq N$);
- $X(x_{i_1}, \ldots, x_{i_n})$, where $i_1, \ldots, i_n \leq N$, and X is a variable of type $W^n \to \Omega$ with $n \leq K$ (here W^n abbreviates $W \cdots W$, n-times).

The terms in the algebraic fragment $\Phi_{NK}^{\mathcal{L}} = \langle \mathcal{L}_{NK}, T_{NK}^{\mathcal{L}} \rangle$ are now the terms t such that $t \sim_{\beta\eta} \{x_1, \ldots, x_n \mid \varphi\}$, for some $n \leq K$ and for some $\varphi \in F_{NK}$,

---

[2] Propositional variables are added here in order to fulfill Definition 3.2(iii).

[3] Notice that, by case splitting, equations $A = B$ among terms of type Ω can be replaced by $A \wedge B$ or by $\neg A \wedge \neg B$ (and similarly for inequations).

with $fvar(\varphi) \subseteq \{x_1, \ldots, x_n\}$.[4] Types in such $\Phi^{\mathcal{L}}_{NK}$ are now $W^n \to \Omega$ $(n \leq K)$ and this fact makes a big difference with the previous example (the difference will be sensible when combined fragments enter into the picture). Constraint satisfiability problems still reduce to satisfiability problems for sentences: in fact, once second order variables are replaced by the names of the subsets assigned to them by some assignment in an $\mathcal{L}$-structure, $\Phi^{\mathcal{L}}_{NK}$-atoms like $\{\underline{x} \mid \varphi\} = \{\underline{x} \mid \psi\}$ are equivalent to the first-order sentences $\forall \underline{x}(\varphi \leftrightarrow \psi)$ and conversely any first-order sentence θ (with at most N bound individual variables) is equivalent to the $\Phi^{\mathcal{L}}_{NK}$-atom $\theta = \top$.

The cases $N = 1, 2$ are particularly important, because in these cases the satisfiability problem for sentences (and hence also constraint satisfiability problems in our fragments) becomes decidable [22],[27], [24], [28].

Further examples can be built by using the large information contained in the textbook [10] (see also [13]). We shall continue here by investigating fragments that arise from research in knowledge representation area, especially in connection to modal and description logics. Before, we introduce a construction that will play a central role in some applications of our results:

Definition 3.5 (Disjoint I-copy). *Consider a first order one-sorted relational signature $\mathcal{L}$ and a (non empty) index set I. The operation $\sum_I$, defined on $\mathcal{L}$-structures and called* disjoint I-copy*, associates with an $\mathcal{L}$-structure $\mathcal{M} = \langle [\![-]\!]_{\mathcal{M}}, \mathcal{I}_{\mathcal{M}} \rangle$ the $\mathcal{L}$-structure $\sum_I \mathcal{M}$ such that $[\![W]\!]_{\sum_I \mathcal{M}}$ is the disjoint union of I-copies of $[\![W]\!]_{\mathcal{M}}$ (here W is the unique sort of $\mathcal{L}$). The interpretation of relational predicates is defined as follows[5]*

$$\sum_I \mathcal{M} \models P(\langle d_1, i_1 \rangle, \ldots, \langle d_n, i_n \rangle) \iff i_1 = \cdots = i_n \text{ and } \mathcal{M} \models P(d_1, \ldots, d_n)$$

(1)

for every n-ary predicate P.

Disjoint I-copy is a special case of a more general disjoint union operation: the latter is defined again by (1) and applies to any I-indexed family of structures (which may not coincide with each other).

Example 3.5 (Modal/Description Logic Fragments, global version). A *modal signature* is a set O_M, whose elements are called unary 'Diamond' modal operators.[6] O_M-modal formulae are built up from a countable set of propositional variables $x, y, z, \ldots$ by applying $\top, \bot, \neg, \wedge, \vee$ as well as the operators $\Diamond_k \in O_M$.

With every modal signature O_M we associate the first-order signature $\mathcal{L}_M$, containing a unique sort W and, for every $\Diamond_k \in O_M$, a relational constant R_k

---

[4] We need to use equivalence up to $\beta\eta$-conversion here to fulfil the properties of Definition 3.2. We recall that $\beta\eta$-equivalence (noted as $\sim_{\beta\eta}$) is decided by the normalization procedure of simply typed lambda calculus.

[5] Elements of the disjoint union of I-copies of a set S are represented as pairs $\langle s, i \rangle$ (meaning that $\langle s, i \rangle$ is the i-th copy of $s \in S$).

[6] The case of n-ary (also non-normal) modal operators does not create special difficulties and it is left to the reader.

of type $WW \rightarrow \Omega$. Suppose we are given a bijective correspondence x $\longmapsto$ X between propositional variables and second order variables of type $W \rightarrow \Omega$. Given an O_M-modal formula φ and a variable w of type W, the *standard translation* $ST(\varphi, w)$ is the $\mathcal{L}_M$-term of type Ω inductively defined as follows:

$$ST(\top, w) = \top; \qquad\qquad\qquad ST(\bot, w) = \bot;$$
$$ST(\mathrm{x}, w) = X(w); \qquad\qquad\quad ST(\neg\psi, w) = \neg ST(\psi, w);$$
$$ST(\psi_1 \circ \psi_2, w) = ST(\psi_1, w) \circ ST(\psi_2, w), \quad \text{where } \circ \in \{\vee, \wedge\};$$
$$ST(\Diamond\psi, w) = \exists v(R(w, v) \wedge ST(\psi, v)),$$

where v is a variable of type W (different from w). Let T_M be the set of those $\mathcal{L}_M$-terms t for which there exists a modal formula φ s.t. $t \sim_{\beta\eta} \{w \mid ST(\varphi, w)\}$. A *modal fragment* is an i.a.f. of the kind $\Phi_M = \langle \mathcal{L}_M, T_M, \mathcal{S}_M \rangle$, where $\mathcal{L}_M, T_M$ are as above and $\mathcal{S}_M$ is a class of $\mathcal{L}_M$-structures closed under isomorphisms and disjoint I-copies (notice that $\mathcal{L}_M$-structures, usually called *Kripke frames* in modal logic, are just sets endowed with a binary relation R_k for every $\Diamond_k \in O_M$).

Φ_M-constraints are (equivalent to) finite conjunctions of equations of the form $\{w \mid ST(\psi_i, w)\} = \{w \mid \top\}$ and of inequations of the form $\{w \mid ST(\varphi_j, w)\} \neq \{w \mid \bot\}$; such constraints are satisfied iff there exists a Kripke model[7] based on a frame in $\mathcal{S}_M$ in which the ψ_i hold globally (namely in any state), whereas the φ_j hold locally (namely in some states s_j). Thus constraint satisfiability problem becomes, in the description logics terminology, just the (simultaneous) relativized satisfiability problem for concept descriptions φ_j wrt to a given T-Box (we call *T-Box* a conjunction of Φ_M-atoms like $\{w \mid ST(\psi_i, w)\} = \{w \mid \top\}$).

Example 3.6 (Modal/Description Logic Fragments, local version). If we want to capture A-Box reasoning too, we need to build a slightly different fragment. The type-theoretic signature $\mathcal{L}_{ML}$ of our fragment is again $\mathcal{L}_M$, but T_{ML} now contains: a) the set of terms which are $\beta\eta$-equivalent to terms of the kind $ST(\varphi, w)$ (these terms are called 'concept assertions'); b) the terms of the kind $R_k(v, w)$ (these terms are called 'role assertions'); c) the variables of type W, Ω and $W \rightarrow \Omega$.

The i.a.f. $\Phi_{ML} = \langle \mathcal{L}_{ML}, T_{ML}, \mathcal{S}_{ML} \rangle$ (where $\mathcal{S}_{ML}$ is again a class of $\mathcal{L}_{ML}$-structures closed under isomorphisms and disjoint I-copies) is called an *A-Box fragment*. By a thorough case analysis [17], it is possible to show that, without loss of generality, constraints in this fragments can be represented as conjunctions of concept assertions and role assertions, plus in addition negations of role assertions and of identities among individual names. We shall call *A-Boxes* these constraints[8] and we reserve the name of *positive A-Boxes* to conjunctions of concept assertions and role assertions.

---

[7] A Kripke model is a Kripke frame together with an assignment of subsets for second order variables of type $W \rightarrow \Omega$.

[8] Standard description logics A-Boxes are just slightly more restricted, because they include only concept assertions, role assertions and also all negations of identities among distinct individual variables (by the so-called 'unique name assumption').

Example 3.7 (Modal/Description Logic Fragments, full version). If we want to deal with satisfiability of an A-Box wrt a T-Box, it is sufficient to join the two previous fragments. More precisely, we can build *full modal fragments* over a modal signature O_M, which are i.a.f.'s of the kind $\Phi_{MF} = \langle \mathcal{L}_{MF}, T_{MF}, \mathcal{S}_{MF} \rangle$, where $\mathcal{L}_{MF} = \mathcal{L}_M$, $\mathcal{S}_{MF}$ is a class of $\mathcal{L}_{ML}$-structures closed under isomorphisms and disjoint I-copies, and $T_{MF} = T_M \cup T_{ML}$. Types in these fragments are W, Ω and $W \to \Omega$; constraints are conjunctions of a T-Box and an A-Box.

Guarded and packed guarded fragments were introduced as generalizations of modal fragments [1], [18], [23]: in fact, they form classes of formulae which are remarkably large but still inherit relevant syntactic and semantic features of the more restricted modal formulae. In particular, guarded and packed guarded formulae are decidable for satisfiability. For simplicity, we give here the instructions on how to build only one kind of guarded fragments with equality (other similar fragments can be built by following the methods we used above).

Example 3.8 (Guarded Fragments). Let us consider a first-order one-sorted relational signature $\mathcal{L}_G$. We define the *guarded formulae* as follows:

- if $X : W \to \Omega$ and $x : W$ are variables, $X(x)$ is a guarded formula;
- if $P : W^n \to \Omega$ is a relational constant and $t_1 : W, \dots, t_n : W$ are variables, $P(t_1, \dots, t_n)$ is a guarded formula;
- if φ is a guarded formula, $\neg\varphi$ is a guarded formula;
- if φ_1 and φ_2 are guarded formulae, $\varphi_1 \wedge \varphi_2$ and $\varphi_1 \vee \varphi_2$ are guarded formulae;
- if φ is a guarded formula and π is an atomic formula such that $fvar_W(\varphi) \subseteq fvar(\pi)$ ($fvar_W(\varphi)$ are the variables of type W which occurs free in φ), then $\forall \underline{y}(\pi[\underline{x}, \underline{y}] \to \varphi[\underline{x}, \underline{y}])$ and $\exists \underline{y}(\pi[\underline{x}, \underline{y}] \wedge \varphi[\underline{x}, \underline{y}])$ are guarded formulae.

Notice that we used second order variables of type $W \to \Omega$ only (and not of type $W^n \to \Omega$ for $n > 1$): the reason, besides the applications to combined decision problems we have in mind, is that we want constraint problems to be equivalent to sentences which are still guarded, see below. Guarded formulae not containing variables of type $W \to \Omega$ are called *elementary* (or first-order) guarded formulae.

Let T_G be the set of $\mathcal{L}_G$-terms t such that t is $\beta\eta$-equivalent to a term of the kind $\{w \mid \varphi(w)\}$ (where φ is a guarded formula such that $fvar_W(\varphi(w)) \subseteq \{w\}$) and let $\mathcal{S}_G$ be a class of $\mathcal{L}_G$-structures closed under isomorphisms and disjoint I-copies: we call the i.a.f. $\Phi_G = \langle \mathcal{L}_G, T_G, \mathcal{S}_G \rangle$ a *guarded fragment*. The only type in this fragment is $W \to \Omega$ and constraint satisfiability problem in this fragment is equivalent to satisfiability of guarded sentences: this is because, in case φ_1, φ_2 are guarded formulae with $fvar_W(\varphi_i) \subseteq \{w\}$ (for $i = 1, 2$), then $\{w \mid \varphi_1\} = \{w \mid \varphi_2\}$ is equivalent to $\forall w(\varphi_1 \leftrightarrow \varphi_2)$ which is guarded (just use $w = w$ as a guard).

3.3 Reduced Fragments and Residues

If $\Phi = \langle \mathcal{L}, T, \mathcal{S} \rangle$ is an i.a.f. and $\underline{x}$ is a finite set of Φ-variables, we let $\Phi(\underline{x})$ denote the Φ-clauses whose free variables are among the $\underline{x}$. If Γ is a set of such $\Phi(\underline{x})$-clauses and $C \equiv L_1 \vee \cdots \vee L_k$ is a $\Phi(\underline{x})$-clause, we say that C is a *Φ-consequence* *of* Γ (written $\Gamma \models_\Phi C$), iff the (generalized, in case Γ is infinite) constraint $\Gamma \cup \{\neg L_1, \ldots, \neg L_k\}$ is not Φ-satisfiable.

The notion of consequence is too strong for certain applications; for instance, when we simply need to delete certain deductively useless data, a weaker notion of redundancy (based e.g. on subsumption) is preferable. Our abstract axiomatization of a notion of redundancy is the following (recall that we conventionally included $\top$ and $\bot$ among Φ-atoms in any i.a.f. Φ):

Definition 3.6. *A redundancy notion for a fragment Φ is a recursive binary relation Red_Φ between a finite set of Φ-clauses Γ and a Φ-clause C satisfying the following properties:*

(i) $Red_\Phi(\Gamma, C)$ implies $\Gamma \models_\Phi C$ (soundness);
(ii) $Red_\Phi(\emptyset, \top)$ and $Red_\Phi(\{\bot\}, C)$ both hold;
(iii) $Red_\Phi(\Gamma, C)$ and $\Gamma \subseteq \Gamma'$ imply $Red_\Phi(\Gamma', C)$ (monotonicity);
(iv) $Red_\Phi(\Gamma, C)$ and $Red_\Phi(\Gamma \cup \{C\}, D)$ imply $Red_\Phi(\Gamma, D)$ (transitivity);
(v) if C is subsumed by some $C' \in \Gamma$,[9] then $Red_\Phi(\Gamma, C)$ holds.

Whenever a redundancy notion Red_Φ is fixed, we say that C is Φ-redundant wrt Γ when $Red_\Phi(\Gamma, C)$ holds.

For example, the *minimum* redundancy notion is obtained by stipulating that $Red_\Phi(\Gamma, C)$ holds precisely when ($\bot \in \Gamma$ or $C \equiv \top$ or $C \equiv \top \vee D$ or C is subsumed by some $C' \in \Gamma$). On the contrary, if the constraint solving problem for Φ is decidable, there is a maximum redundancy notion (called the *full* redundancy notion) given by the Φ-consequence relation.

Let $\Phi = \langle \mathcal{L}, T, \mathcal{S} \rangle$ be an i.a.f. on the signature $\mathcal{L} = \langle \mathcal{T}, \Sigma, a \rangle$ and let $\mathcal{L}_0 = \langle \mathcal{T}_0, \Sigma_0, a_0 \rangle$ be a subsignature of $\mathcal{L}$. The i.a.f. *restricted to* $\mathcal{L}_0$ is the i.a.f. $\Phi_{|\mathcal{L}_0} = \langle \mathcal{L}_0, T_{|\mathcal{L}_0}, \mathcal{S}_{|\mathcal{L}_0} \rangle$ that is so defined:

– $T_{|\mathcal{L}_0}$ is the set of terms obtained by intersecting T with the set of $\mathcal{L}_0$-terms;
– $\mathcal{S}_{|\mathcal{L}_0}$ consists of the structures of the kind $\mathcal{A}_{|\mathcal{L}_0}$, varying $\mathcal{A} \in \mathcal{S}$.

An i.a.f. $\Phi_0 = \langle \mathcal{L}_0, T_0, \mathcal{S}_0 \rangle$ is said to be a $\mathcal{L}_0$-*subfragment* (or simply a subfragment, leaving the subsignature $\mathcal{L}_0 \subseteq \mathcal{L}$ as understood) of $\Phi = \langle \mathcal{L}, T, \mathcal{S} \rangle$ iff $T_0 \subseteq T_{|\mathcal{L}_0}$ and $\mathcal{S}_0 \supseteq \mathcal{S}_{|\mathcal{L}_0}$. In this case, we may also say that Φ is an *expansion* of Φ_0.

Given a set Γ of $\Phi(\underline{x})$-clauses and a redundancy notion Red_{Φ_0} on a subfragment Φ_0 of Φ, we call Φ_0-*basis for* Γ a set Δ of $\Phi_0(\underline{x}_0)$-clauses such that (here $\underline{x}_0$ collects those variables among the $\underline{x}$ which happen to be Φ_0-variables):

(i) all clauses $D \in \Delta$ are positive and are such that $\Gamma \models_\Phi D$;
(ii) for every positive $\Phi_0(\underline{x}_0)$-clause C, if $\Gamma \models_\Phi C$, then C is Φ_0-redundant with respect to Δ.

Since we will be interested in exchange information concerning consequences over shared signatures, we need a notion of a residue, like in partial theory reasoning. Again, we prefer an abstract approach and treat residues as clauses which are recursively enumerated by a suitable device:

---

[9] As usual, this means that every literal of C' is also in C.

Definition 3.7. *Suppose we are given a subfragment Φ_0 of a fragment Φ. A positive residue Φ-enumerator for Φ_0 (often shortened as Φ-p.r.e.) is a recursive function mapping a finite set $\underline{x}$ of Φ-variables, a finite set Γ of $\Phi(\underline{x})$-clauses and a natural number i to a Φ_0-clause $Res_\Phi^{\underline{x}}(\Gamma, i)$ (to be written simply as $Res_\Phi(\Gamma, i)$) in such a way that:*

- *$Res_\Phi(\Gamma, i)$ is a positive clause;*
- *$fvar(Res_\Phi(\Gamma, i)) \subseteq \underline{x}$;*
- *$\Gamma \models_\Phi Res_\Phi(\Gamma, i)$ (soundness).*

Any Φ_0-clause of the kind $Res_\Phi(\Gamma, i)$ (for some $i \geq 0$) will be called a Φ_0-residue of Γ.

Having also a redundancy notion for Φ_0 at our disposal, we can axiomatize the notion of an 'optimized' (i.e. of a non-redundant) Φ-p.r.e. for Φ_0. The Nelson-Oppen combination procedure we give in Subsection 4.2 has *non-redundant* p.r.e.'s as main ingredients and it is designed to be 'self-adaptive' for termination in the relevant cases when termination follows from our results. These are basically the noetherian and the locally finite cases mentioned in Subsection 3.4, where p.r.e.'s which are non redundant with respect to the full redundancy notion usually exist and enjoy the termination property below.

Definition 3.8. *A Φ-p.r.e. Res_Φ for Φ_0 is said to be* non-redundant *(wrt a redundancy notion Red_{Φ_0}) iff it satisfies also the following properties for every $\underline{x}$, for every finite set Γ of $\Phi(\underline{x})$-clauses and for every $i \geq 0$ (we write $\Gamma_{|\Phi_0}$ for the set of clauses in Γ which are Φ_0-clauses):*

- *(i) if $Res_\Phi(\Gamma, i)$ is Φ_0-redundant with respect to $\Gamma_{|\Phi_0} \cup \{Res_\Phi(\Gamma, j) \mid j < i\}$, then $Res_\Phi(\Gamma, i)$ is either $\bot$ or $\top$;*
- *(ii) if $\bot$ is Φ_0-redundant with respect to $\Gamma_{|\Phi_0} \cup \{Res_\Phi(\Gamma, j) \mid j < i\}$, then $Res_\Phi(\Gamma, i)$ is equal to $\bot$;*
- *(iii) if $Res_\Phi(\Gamma, i)$ is equal to $\top$, then $\Gamma_{|\Phi_0} \cup \{Res_\Phi(\Gamma, j) \mid j < i\}$ is a Φ_0-basis for Γ.*

Definition 3.9. *A non-redundant Φ-p.r.e. for Φ_0 is said to be* complete *iff for every $\underline{x}$, for every finite set Γ of $\Phi(\underline{x})$-clauses and for every positive $\Phi_0(\underline{x})$-clause C, we have that $\Gamma \models_\Phi C$ implies that C is Φ_0-redundant wrt $\Gamma_{|\Phi_0} \cup \{Res_\Phi(\Gamma, j) \mid j \leq i\}$ for some i.*

A non-redundant Φ-p.r.e. Res_Φ is said to be terminating *iff for for every $\underline{x}$, for every finite set Γ of $\Phi(\underline{x})$-clauses there is an i such that $Res_\Phi(\Gamma, i)$ is equal to $\bot$ or to $\top$.*

Let us make a few comments on Definition 3.8: first, only non redundant residues can be produced at each step (condition (i)), if possible. If this is not possible, this means that all the relevant information has been accumulated (a Φ_0-basis has been reached). In this case, if the inconsistency $\bot$ is discovered (in the sense that it is perceived as redundant), then the residue enumeration in practice stops, because it becomes constantly equal to $\bot$ (condition (ii)).

The tautology $\top$ has the special role of marking the opposite outcome: it is the residue that is returned precisely when Γ is consistent and a Φ_0-basis has been produced, meaning that all relevant semantic consequences of Γ have been discovered (conditions (ii)-(iii)).

If the redundancy notion we use is trivial (i.e. it is the minimum one), then it is possible to show that only very mild corrections are needed for any Φ-p.r.e. for Φ_0 to become non-redundant. This observation shows that, in practice, any Φ-p.r.e. for Φ_0 can be used as input of our combined decision procedure.

3.4   Noetherian, Locally Finite and Convex Fragments

Noetherianity conditions known from Algebra say that there are no infinite ascending chains of congruences. In finitely presented algebras, congruences are represented as sets of equations among terms, hence noetherianity can be expressed there by saying that there are no infinite ascending chains of sets of atoms, modulo logical consequence. If we translate this into our general setting, we get the following notion.

An i.a.f. Φ_0 is called *noetherian* if and only if for every finite set of variables $\underline{x}$, every infinite ascending chain

$$\Theta_1 \subseteq \Theta_2 \subseteq \cdots \subseteq \Theta_n \subseteq \cdots$$

of sets of $\Phi_0(\underline{x})$-atoms is definitively constant for Φ_0-consequence (meaning that there is an n such that for all m and $A \in \Theta_m$, we have $\Theta_n \models_{\Phi_0} A$).

An i.a.f. Φ_0 is said to be *effectively locally finite* iff

(i) the set of Φ_0-types is recursive and constraint satisfiability problem for Φ_0 is decidable;

(ii) for every finite set of Φ_0-variables $\underline{x}$, there are finitely many computable $\Phi_0(\underline{x})$-terms $t_1, \ldots, t_n$ such that for every further $\Phi_0(\underline{x})$-term u one of the literals $t_1 \neq u, \ldots, t_n \neq u$ is not Φ_0-satisfiable (that is, in the class of the structures in which Φ_0 is interpreted, every $\Phi_0(\underline{x})$-term is equal, as an interpreted function, to one of the t_i).

The terms $t_1, \ldots, t_n$ in (ii) are called the $\underline{x}$-representative terms of Φ_0.

Effective local finiteness is often used in order to make Nelson-Oppen procedures terminating [16], [8], [4]:[10] we shall see however that noetherianity (which is clearly a weaker condition) is already sufficient for that, once it is accompanied by a suitable effectiveness condition.

If Φ_0 is noetherian and Φ is an expansion of it, one can prove [17] that every finite set Γ of $\Phi(\underline{x})$-clauses has a finite full Φ_0-basis (i.e. there is a finite Φ_0-basis for Γ with respect to the full redundancy notion). The following noetherianity requirement for a p.r.e. is intended to be nothing but an effectiveness requirement for the computation of finite full Φ_0-bases.

---

[10] Notice that the above definition of local finiteness becomes slightly redundant in the first order universal case considered in these papers.

A Φ-p.r.e. Res_Φ for a noetherian fragment Φ_0 is said to be *noetherian* iff it is non redundant with respect to the full redundancy notion for Φ_0.

It is possible to prove that a noetherian Φ-p.r.e. Res_Φ for Φ_0 is terminating and also complete. Moreover, if Φ_0 is effectively locally finite and Φ is any extension of it having decidable constraint satisfiability problems, then there always exists a noetherian Φ-p.r.e. for Φ_0 [17].

Noetherianity is the essential ingredients for the termination of Nelson-Oppen combination procedures; on the other hand, for efficiency, convexity is the crucial property, as it makes the combination procedure deterministic [26]. Following an analogous notion introduced in [30], we say that an i.a.f. Φ is Φ_0-*convex* (here Φ_0 is a subfragment of Φ) iff every finite set Γ of Φ-literals having as a Φ-consequence the disjunction of $n > 1$ Φ_0-atoms, actually has as a Φ-consequence one of them.[11] Similarly, a Φ-p.r.e. for Φ_0 is Φ_0-*convex* iff $Res_\Phi(\Gamma, i)$ is always an atom (recall that by our conventions, this includes the case in which it is $\top$ or $\bot$). Any complete non-redundant Φ-p.r.e. for Φ_0 can be turned into a Φ_0-convex complete non-redundant Φ-p.r.e. for Φ_0, in case Φ is Φ_0-convex. Thus the combination procedure of Subsection 4.2 is designed in such a way that it becomes automatically *deterministic* if the component fragments are both convex with respect to the shared fragment.

An example from Algebra may help in clarifying the notions introduced in this section.

Example 3.9 (K-algebras). Given a field K, let us consider the one-sorted language $\mathcal{L}_{Kalg}$, whose signature contains the constants $0, 1$ of type V (V is the unique sort of $\mathcal{L}_{Kalg}$), the two binary function symbols $+, \circ$ of type $VV \to V$, the unary function symbol $-$ of type $V \to V$ and a K-indexed family of unary function symbols g_k of type $V \to V$. We consider the i.a.f. $\Phi_{Kalg} = \langle \mathcal{L}_{Kalg}, T_{Kalg}, \mathcal{S}_{Kalg} \rangle$ where T_{Kalg} is the set of first order terms in the above signature (we shall use infix notation for $+$ and write kv, $v_1 v_2$ for $g_k(v)$, $\circ(v_1, v_2)$, respectively). Furthermore, the class $\mathcal{S}_{Kalg}$ consists of the structures which happen to be models for the theory of (commutative, for simplicity) K-algebras: these are structures having both a commutative ring with unit and a K-vector space structure (the two structures are related by the equations $k(v_1 v_2) = (kv_1)v_2 = v_1(kv_2)$). It is clear that Φ_{Kalg} is an interpreted algebraic fragment, which is also convex and noetherian. Constraint satisfiability problem in this fragment is equivalent to the ideal membership problem and hence it is solved by Buchberger algorithm computing Gröbner bases.

As a subfragment of Φ_{Kalg} we can consider the interpreted algebraic fragment corresponding to the theory of K-vector spaces (this is also convex and noetherian, although still not locally finite). In order to obtain a noetherian Φ_{Kalg}-p.r.e. for Φ_K, we need a condition that is satisfied by common admissible term orderings, namely that membership of a linear polynomial to a finitely generated ideal to be decided only by linear reduction rules. If this happens, we

---

[11] When we say that a fragment Φ is *convex* tout court, we mean that it is Φ-convex. The fragments $\Phi = \langle \mathcal{L}, T, \mathcal{S} \rangle$ analyzed in Example 3.1 are convex in case $\mathcal{S}$ is the class of the models of a first-order Horn theory.

get a noetherian Φ_{Kalg}-p.r.e. for Φ_K *simply by listing the linear polynomials of a Gröbner basis.*

4   Combined Fragments

We give now the formal definition for the operation of combining fragments.

Definition 4.1. *Let $\Phi_1 = \langle \mathcal{L}_1, T_1, \mathcal{S}_1 \rangle$ and $\Phi_2 = \langle \mathcal{L}_2, T_2, \mathcal{S}_2 \rangle$ be i.a.f.'s on the languages $\mathcal{L}_1$ and $\mathcal{L}_2$ respectively; we define the* shared fragment *of Φ_1, Φ_2 as the i.a.f. $\Phi_0 = \langle \mathcal{L}_0, T_0, \mathcal{S}_0 \rangle$, where*

- $\mathcal{L}_0 := \mathcal{L}_1 \cap \mathcal{L}_2$;
- $T_0 := T_{1|\mathcal{L}_0} \cap T_{2|\mathcal{L}_0}$;
- $\mathcal{S}_0 := \mathcal{S}_{1|\mathcal{L}_0} \cup \mathcal{S}_{2|\mathcal{L}_0}$.

Thus the Φ_0-terms are the $\mathcal{L}_0$-terms that are both Φ_1-terms and Φ_2-terms, whereas the Φ_0-structures are the $\mathcal{L}_0$-structures which are reducts either of a Φ_1- or of a Φ_2-structure. According to the above definition, Φ_0 is a subfragment of both Φ_1 and Φ_2.

Definition 4.2. *The* combined fragment *of the i.a.f.'s Φ_1 and Φ_2 is the i.a.f.*

$$\Phi_1 \oplus \Phi_2 = \langle \mathcal{L}_1 \cup \mathcal{L}_2, T_1 \oplus T_2, \mathcal{S}_1 \oplus \mathcal{S}_2 \rangle$$

on the language $\mathcal{L}_1 \cup \mathcal{L}_2$ such that:

- *$T_1 \oplus T_2$ is the smallest set of $\mathcal{L}_1 \cup \mathcal{L}_2$-terms which includes $T_1 \cup T_2$, is closed under composition and contains domain and codomain variables;*
- *$\mathcal{S}_1 \oplus \mathcal{S}_2 = \{ \mathcal{A} \mid \mathcal{A} \text{ is a } \mathcal{L}_1 \cup \mathcal{L}_2\text{-structure s.t. } \mathcal{A}_{|\mathcal{L}_1} \in \mathcal{S}_1 \text{ and } \mathcal{A}_{|\mathcal{L}_2} \in \mathcal{S}_2 \}$.*

$T_1 \oplus T_2$ is defined in such a way that conditions (i)-(ii)-(iii) from Definition 3.2 are matched; of course, since $\Phi_1 \oplus \Phi_2$-types turn out to be just the types which are either Φ_1- or Φ_2-types, closure under domain and codomain variables comes for free.

4.1   The Purification Steps

We say that a $\Phi_1 \oplus \Phi_2$-term is *pure* iff it is a Φ_i-term ($i = 1$ or $i = 2$) and that a $\Phi_1 \oplus \Phi_2$-constraint Γ is *pure* iff it for each literal $L \in \Gamma$ there is $i = 1$ or $i = 2$ such that L is a Φ_i-literal. Constraints in combined fragments can be purified, as we shall see.

One can effectively determine whether a given term $t \in \mathcal{L}_1 \cup \mathcal{L}_2$ belongs or not to the combined fragment: it can be shown [17] that it is sufficient to this aim to check whether it is a pure Φ_i-term and, in the negative case, to split it as $t \equiv u[t_1, \ldots, t_k]$ and to recursively check whether $u, t_1, \ldots, t_k$ are in the combined fragment. [12] The problem however might be computationally hard:

---

[12] This is well defined (by an induction on the size of t), because we do not require our terms to be in $\beta\eta$-normal form (that is, we do not require in Definition 3.2 (i) substitution to be followed by normalization).

since we basically have to guess a subtree of the position tree of the term t, *the procedure we sketched is in NP*. Notice that these complexity complications (absent in the standard Nelson-Oppen case) are due to our level of generality and that they disappear in customary situations where don't know non-determinism can be avoided by looking for 'alien' subterms, see [7] for a thorough discussion of the problem.

Let Γ be any $\Phi_1 \oplus \Phi_2$-constraint: we shall provide finite sets Γ_1, Γ_2 of Φ_1- and Φ_2-literals, respectively, such that Γ is $\Phi_1 \oplus \Phi_2$-satisfiable iff $\Gamma_1 \cup \Gamma_2$ is $\Phi_1 \oplus \Phi_2$-satisfiable. This purification process is obtained by iterated applications of the following:

Purification Rule

$$\frac{\Gamma', A}{\Gamma', A([x]_p),\ x = A_{|p}} \tag{2}$$

where (we use notations like Γ', A for the constraint $\Gamma' \cup \{A\}$)

- p is a non variable position of A;
- $A_{|p}$ is the subterm of A at position p (let τ be its type);
- no free variable in $A_{|p}$ is bound in A;
- x is a fresh variable of type τ;
- the literal $A([x]_p)$ (obtained by replacing in A in the position p the subterm $A_{|p}$ by the variable x) is not an equation between variables;
- $\Gamma', A([x]),\ x = A_{|p}$ is a $\Phi_1 \oplus \Phi_2$-constraint (this means that it still consists of equations and inequations among $\Phi_1 \oplus \Phi_2$-terms).

The *purification process* applies the Purification Rule as far as possible; the rule can be applied in a don't care non deterministic way (however recall that one must take care of the fact that the constraint produced by the rule still consists of $\Phi_1 \oplus \Phi_2$-literals, hence don't know non-determinism may arise inside a single application of the rule).

Proposition 4.1. *The purification process terminates and returns an equi-satisfiable constraint $\Gamma_1 \cup \Gamma_2$, where Γ_i is a set of Φ_i-literals.*

4.2   The Combination Procedure

In this subsection, we develop a procedure which is designed to solve constraint satisfiability problems in combined fragments: the procedure is sound and we shall investigate afterwards sufficient conditions for it to be terminating and complete. Let us fix relevant notation for the involved data.

Assumptions/Notational Conventions. *We suppose that we are given two i.a.f.'s $\Phi_1 = \langle \mathcal{L}_1, T_1, \mathcal{S}_1 \rangle$ and $\Phi_2 = \langle \mathcal{L}_2, T_2, \mathcal{S}_2 \rangle$, with shared fragment $\Phi_0 = \langle \mathcal{L}_0, T_0, \mathcal{S}_0 \rangle$. We suppose also that a redundancy notion Red_{Φ_0} for Φ_0 and two non-redundant Φ_i-p.r.e.'s for Φ_0 (call them Res_{Φ_1}, Res_{Φ_2}) are available.[13] We*

---

[13] Of course, Res_{Φ_1} and Res_{Φ_2} are assumed to be both non-redundant with respect to Red_{Φ_0}.

also fix a purified $\Phi_1 \oplus \Phi_2$-constraint $\Gamma_1 \cup \Gamma_2$ to be tested for $\Phi_1 \oplus \Phi_2$-consistency; we can freely suppose that Γ_1 and Γ_2 contain the same subset Γ_0 of Φ_0-literals (i.e. that $\Gamma_0 := \Gamma_{1|\Phi_0} = \Gamma_{2|\Phi_0}$). We indicate by $\underline{x}_i$ the free variables occurring in Γ_i ($i = 1, 2$); $\underline{x}_0$ are those variables among $\underline{x}_1 \cup \underline{x}_2$ which happen to be Φ_0-variables (again we can freely suppose that $\underline{x}_0 = \underline{x}_1 \cap \underline{x}_2$).

In order to describe the procedure we also need a selection function in the sense of the following definition:

Definition 4.3. A selection function CHOOSE(Λ) is a recursive function accepting as input a set Λ of $\Phi_0(\underline{x}_0)$-atoms and returning a positive $\Phi_0(\underline{x}_0)$-clause C such that:

(i) C is a Φ_i-consequence of $\Gamma_i \cup \Lambda$, for $i = 1$ or $i = 2$;
(ii) if $\perp$ is Φ_0-redundant wrt $\Gamma_0 \cup \Lambda$, then C is $\perp$;
(iii) if C is Φ_0-redundant wrt $\Gamma_0 \cup \Lambda$, then C is $\top$ or $\perp$.

The recursive function CHOOSE(Λ) will be subject also to a fairness requirement that will be explained below.

The Procedure FCOMB. Our combined procedure generates a tree whose internal nodes are labeled by sets of $\Phi_0(\underline{x}_0)$-atoms; leaves are labeled by "unsatisfiable" or by "saturated". The root of the tree is labeled by the empty set and if a node is labeled by the set Λ, then the successors are:

- a single leaf labeled "unsatisfiable", if CHOOSE(Λ) is equal to $\perp$;
- or a single leaf labeled "saturated", if CHOOSE(Λ) is equal to $\top$;
- or nodes labeled by $\Lambda \cup \{A_1\}, \ldots, \Lambda \cup \{A_k\}$, if CHOOSE$(\Lambda)$ is $A_1 \vee \cdots \vee A_k$.

The branches which are infinite or end with the "saturated" message are called *open*, whereas the branches ending with the "unsatisfiable" message are called *closed*. The procedures stops (and the generation of the above tree is interrupted) iff all branches are closed or if there is an open finite branch (of course termination is not guaranteed in the general case).

Fair Selection Functions. The function CHOOSE(Λ) is *fair* iff the following happens for every open branch $\Lambda_0 \subseteq \Lambda_1 \subseteq \cdots$: if C is equal to $Res_{\Phi_i}(\Gamma_i \cup \Lambda_k, l)$ for some $i = 1, 2$ and for some $k, l \geq 0$, then C is Φ_0-redundant with respect to $\Gamma_0 \cup \Lambda_n$ for some n (roughly, *residues wrt Φ_i of an open branch are redundant with respect to the atoms in the branch*). Under the current assumptions/notational conventions, it can be shown that

Proposition 4.2. There always exists a fair selection function.

Next Proposition says that our procedure is always sound and that it terminates under noetherianity assumptions:

Proposition 4.3. (i) If the procedure FCOMB returns "unsatisfiable", then the purified constraint $\Gamma_1 \cup \Gamma_2$ is $\Phi_1 \oplus \Phi_2$-unsatisfiable.
(ii) If Φ_0 is noetherian and Red_{Φ_0} is the full redundancy notion, then the procedure FCOMB terminates on the purified constraint $\Gamma_1 \cup \Gamma_2$.

Algorithm 1 The combination procedure

1: **procedure** FCOMB(Λ)
2:     $C \leftarrow$ CHOOSE(Λ)
3:     **if** $C = \bot$ **then**
4:         **return** *"unsatisfiable"*
5:     **else if** $C = \top$ **then**
6:         **return** *"saturated"*
7:     **end if**
8:     **for all** $A \in C$ **do**
9:         **if** FCOMB($\Lambda \cup \{A\}$) = *"saturated"* **then**
10:             **return** *"saturated"*
11:         **end if**
12:     **end for**
13:     **return** *"unsatisfiable"*
14: **end procedure**

Completeness of the procedure FCOMB cannot be achieved easily, heavy conditions are needed. Since our investigations are taking a completeness-oriented route, it is quite obvious that we must consider from now on only the case in which the input Φ_i-p.r.e.'s are *complete* (see Definition 3.9). In addition we need a compactness-like assumption. We say that an i.a.f. Φ is Φ_0-*compact* (where Φ_0 is a subfragment of Φ) iff, given a Φ-constraint Γ and a generalized Φ_0-constraint Γ_0, we have that $\Gamma \cup \Gamma_0$ is Φ-satisfiable if and only if for all finite $\Delta_0 \subseteq \Gamma_0$, we have that $\Gamma \cup \Delta_0$ is Φ-satisfiable.

Since it can be shown that any extension Φ of a locally finite fragment Φ_0 is Φ_0-compact [17], if we assume effective local finiteness in order to guarantee termination, Φ_0-compactness is guaranteed too.[14]

The following Proposition gives relevant information on the semantic meaning of a run of the procedure that either does not terminate or terminates with a saturation message:

Proposition 4.4. *Suppose that Φ_1, Φ_2 are both Φ_0-compact, that the function* CHOOSE*(Λ) is fair wrt two complete Φ_i-p.r.e.'s and that the procedure* FCOMB *does not return "unsatisfiable" on the purified constraint $\Gamma_1 \cup \Gamma_2$. Then there are $\mathcal{L}_i$-structures $\mathcal{M}_i \in \mathcal{S}_i$ and $\mathcal{L}_i$-assignments α_i ($i = 1, 2$) such that:*

(i) $\mathcal{M}_1 \models_{\alpha_1} \Gamma_1$ and $\mathcal{M}_2 \models_{\alpha_2} \Gamma_2$;
(ii) for every $\Phi_0(\underline{x}_0)$-atom A, we have that $\mathcal{M}_1 \models_{\alpha_1} A$ iff $\mathcal{M}_2 \models_{\alpha_2} A$.

---

[14] Notice that only special kinds of generalized Φ-constraints are involved in the definition of Φ_0-compactness, namely those that contain finitely many proper Φ-literals; thus, Φ_0-compactness is a rather weak condition (that's why it may hold for any extension whatsoever of a given fragment, as shown by the locally finite case). Finally, it goes without saying that, by the compactness theorem for first order logic, Φ_0-compactness is guaranteed whenever Φ is a first-order fragment.

5   Isomorphism Theorems and Completeness

Proposition 4.4 explain what is the main problem for completeness: we would like an open branch to produce Φ_i-structures ($i = 1, 2$) whose $\mathcal{L}_0$-reducts are isomorphic and we are only given Φ_i-structures whose $\mathcal{L}_0$-reducts are $\Phi_0(\underline{x}_0)$-equivalent (in the sense that they satisfy the same $\Phi_0(\underline{x}_0)$-atoms). Hence we need a powerful semantic device that is able to *transform $\Phi_0(\underline{x}_0)$-equivalence into $\mathcal{L}_0$-isomorphism*: this device will be called an isomorphism theorem. The precise formulation of what we mean by an isomorphism theorem needs some preparation. First of all, for the notion of an isomorphism theorem to be useful for us, it should apply to fragments extended with free constants.

Given an i.a.f. $\Phi = \langle \mathcal{L}, T, \mathcal{S} \rangle$, we denote by $\Phi(\underline{c}) = \langle \mathcal{L}(\underline{c}), T(\underline{c}), \mathcal{S}(\underline{c}) \rangle$ the following i.a.f.: (i) $\mathcal{L}(\underline{c}) := \mathcal{L} \cup \{\underline{c}\}$ is obtained by adding to $\mathcal{L}$ finitely many new constants $\underline{c}$ (the types of these new constants must be types of Φ); (ii) $T(\underline{c})$ contains the terms of the kind $t[\underline{c}/\underline{x}, \underline{y}]$ for $t[\underline{x}, \underline{y}] \in T$; (iii) $\mathcal{S}(\underline{c})$ contains precisely the $\mathcal{L}(\underline{c})$-structures whose $\mathcal{L}$-reduct is in $\mathcal{S}$. Fragments of the kind $\Phi(\underline{c})$ are called *finite expansions* of Φ.

Let $\Phi(\underline{c})$ be a finite expansion of $\Phi = \langle \mathcal{L}, T, \mathcal{S} \rangle$ and let $\mathcal{A}, \mathcal{B}$ be $\mathcal{L}(\underline{c})$-structures. We say that $\mathcal{A}$ is *$\Phi(\underline{c})$-equivalent* to $\mathcal{B}$ (written $\mathcal{A} \equiv_{\Phi(\underline{c})} \mathcal{B}$) iff for every closed $\mathcal{L}(\underline{c})$-atom A we have that $\mathcal{A} \models A$ iff $\mathcal{B} \models A$. By contrast, we say that $\mathcal{A}$ is *$\Phi(\underline{c})$-isomorphic* to $\mathcal{B}$ (written $\mathcal{A} \simeq_{\Phi(\underline{c})} \mathcal{B}$) iff there is an $\mathcal{L}(\underline{c})$-isomorphism from $\mathcal{A}$ onto $\mathcal{B}$.

We can now specify what we mean by a structural operation on an i.a.f. $\Phi_0 = \langle \mathcal{L}_0, T_0, \mathcal{S}_0 \rangle$. We will be very liberal here and define *structural operation on Φ_0* any family of correspondences $O = \{O^{\underline{c}_0}\}$ associating with any finite set of free constants $\underline{c}_0$ and with any $\mathcal{A} \in \mathcal{S}_0(\underline{c}_0)$ some $O^{\underline{c}_0}(\mathcal{A}) \in \mathcal{S}_0(\underline{c}_0)$ such that $\mathcal{A} \equiv_{\Phi_0(\underline{c}_0)} O^{\underline{c}_0}(\mathcal{A})$. If no confusion arises, we omit the indication of $\underline{c}_0$ in the notation $O^{\underline{c}_0}(\mathcal{A})$ and write it simply as $O(\mathcal{A})$.

A collection $\mathcal{O}$ of structural operations on Φ_0 *allows a Φ_0-isomorphism theorem* if and only if, for every $\underline{c}_0$, for every $\mathcal{A}, \mathcal{B} \in \mathcal{S}_0(\underline{c}_0)$, if $\mathcal{A} \equiv_{\Phi_0(\underline{c}_0)} \mathcal{B}$ then there exist $O_1, O_2 \in \mathcal{O}$ such that $O_1(\mathcal{A}) \simeq_{\Phi_0(\underline{c}_0)} O_2(\mathcal{B})$.

We shall mainly be interested into operations that can be extended to a preassigned expanded fragment. Here is the related definition. Let an i.a.f. $\Phi = \langle \mathcal{L}, T, \mathcal{S} \rangle$ extending $\Phi_0 = \langle \mathcal{L}_0, T_0, \mathcal{S}_0 \rangle$ be given; a structural operation O on Φ_0 is *Φ-extensible* if and only if for every $\underline{c}$ and every $\mathcal{A} \in \mathcal{S}(\underline{c})$ there exist $\mathcal{B} \in \mathcal{S}(\underline{c})$ such that

$$\mathcal{B}_{|\mathcal{L}_0(\underline{c}_0)} \simeq_{\Phi_0(\underline{c}_0)} O(\mathcal{A}_{|\mathcal{L}_0(\underline{c}_0)}) \quad \text{and} \quad \mathcal{B} \equiv_{\Phi(\underline{c})} \mathcal{A},$$

(where $\underline{c}_0$ denotes the set of those constants in $\underline{c}$ whose type is a Φ_0-type).

Example 5.1 (Ultrapowers). Ultrapowers [11] are basic constructions in the model theory of first-order logic. An ultrapower $\prod_{\mathcal{U}}$ (technically, an ultrafilter $\mathcal{U}$ over a set of indices is needed to describe the operation) transforms a first-order structure $\mathcal{A}$ into a first-order structure $\prod_{\mathcal{U}} \mathcal{A}$ which is elementarily equivalent to it (meaning that $\mathcal{A}$ and $\prod_{\mathcal{U}} \mathcal{A}$ satisfy the same first-order sentences). Hence if we take a fragment $\Phi_0 = \langle \mathcal{L}_0, T_0, \mathcal{S}_0 \rangle$, where $\mathcal{S}_0$ is an elementary class and $\langle \mathcal{L}_0, T_0 \rangle$ is an algebraic fragment of the kind analyzed in Example 3.3, then $\prod_{\mathcal{U}}$

is a structural operation on Φ_0. A deep result in classical model theory (known as the *Keisler-Shelah isomorphism theorem* [11]) says that two $\mathcal{L}_0$-structures $\mathcal{A}$ and $\mathcal{B}$ are elementarily equivalent iff there is an ultrafilter $\mathcal{U}$ such that the ultrapowers $\prod_{\mathcal{U}} \mathcal{A}$ and $\prod_{\mathcal{U}} \mathcal{B}$ are $\mathcal{L}_0$-isomorphic. Thus, if Φ_0 is as above, Keisler-Shelah theorem is a Φ_0-isomorphism theorem in our sense.[15] Notice also that taking the reduct of a first-order structure to a smaller signature commutes with ultrapowers, hence if $\Phi = \langle \mathcal{L}, T, \mathcal{S} \rangle$ is an extension of Φ_0 and $\mathcal{S}$ is elementary and $\langle \mathcal{L}, T \rangle$ is again a fragment of the kind analyzed in Example 3.3, then we have that the Φ_0-structural operation $\prod_{\mathcal{U}}$ is Φ-extensible (the structure $\mathcal{B}$ required in the definition of Φ-extensibility is again $\prod_{\mathcal{U}} \mathcal{A}$, where the ultrapower is now taken at the level of $\mathcal{L}$-structures).

Example 5.2 (Disjoint Copies). Consider a modal fragment Φ_{M_0} based on the empty modal signature O_{M_0} (see Example 3.5); given any non empty set I, taking disjoint I-copy $\sum_I$ is easily seen to be a structural operation on Φ_{M_0}. Moreover, the totality of such operations (varying I) allows a Φ_{M_0}-isomorphism theorem: to show this, it is sufficient to observe that $\Phi_{M_0}(\underline{c}_0)$-equivalent structures becomes isomorphic if a sufficiently large disjoint union is applied to them, because the cardinality of subsets definable through boolean combinations of the $\underline{c}_0$'s are complete invariants for $\mathcal{L}_{M_0}(\underline{c}_0)$-isomorphism (see [17] for details).

Now notice that *a guarded elementary sentence is true in $\mathcal{M}$ iff it is true in $\sum_I \mathcal{M}$*. Hence, taking disjoint I-copies is a Φ-extensible operation, provided Φ is a modal or a guarded fragment (in the sense of Examples 3.5 and 3.8): notice in fact that $\Phi(\underline{c})$-atoms are equivalent to elementary guarded sentences, because the second order variables of type $W \to \Omega$ have been replaced in them by the corresponding free constants $\underline{c}$ (which are constants of type $W \to \Omega$, that is they are unary first-order predicate letters).

Sometimes an isomorphism theorem does not hold precisely for a fragment $\Phi_0 = \langle \mathcal{L}_0, T_0, \mathcal{S}_0 \rangle$, but for an inessential variation (called specialization) of it. A *specialization* of Φ_0 is an i.a.f. $\Phi_0^\star$ which has the same language and the same terms as Φ_0, but whose class of $\mathcal{L}_0$-structures is a smaller class $\mathcal{S}_0^\star \subseteq \mathcal{S}_0$ satisfying the following condition: for every $\underline{c}_0$ and for every $\mathcal{A} \in \mathcal{S}_0(\underline{c}_0)$, there exists $\mathcal{A}^\star \in \mathcal{S}_0^\star(\underline{c}_0)$ such that $\mathcal{A} \equiv_{\Phi_0(\underline{c}_0)} \mathcal{A}^\star$.

Given an i.a.f. $\Phi = \langle \mathcal{L}, T, \mathcal{S} \rangle$ extending Φ_0, we say that Φ is *compatible* with respect to a specialization $\Phi_0^\star$ of Φ_0 if and only if for every $\underline{c}$ and $\mathcal{A} \in \mathcal{S}(\underline{c})$, there exists a $\mathcal{A}' \in \mathcal{S}(\underline{c})$ such that $\mathcal{A} \equiv_{\Phi(\underline{c})} \mathcal{A}'$ and $\mathcal{A}'_{|\mathcal{L}_0} \in \mathcal{S}_0^\star$.

Example 5.3 (Stably Infinite First-Order Theories). The Φ_0-compatibility notion is intended to recapture, in our general setting, T_0-compatibility as introduced in [16]. The latter generalizes, in its turn, the standard stable infiniteness requirement of Nelson-Oppen procedure. Let $\Phi = \langle \mathcal{L}, T, \mathcal{S} \rangle$ be an i.a.f. of the

---

[15] If $\Phi_0 = \langle \mathcal{L}_0, T_0, \mathcal{S}_0 \rangle$ is from Example 3.1-3.2 and quantifier elimination holds in $\mathcal{S}_0$, then the $\prod_{\mathcal{U}}$'s are also structural operations on Φ_0 allowing a Φ_0-isomorphism theorem (this observation is a key point for the proof of Theorem 5.2 below).

kinds considered in Example 3.1 or in Example 3.2: we say that Φ is *stably infinite* iff every satisfiable Φ-constraint is satisfiable in some infinite $\mathcal{L}$-structure $\mathcal{A} \in \mathcal{S}$.

Let now $\Phi_0 = \langle \mathcal{L}_0, T_0, \mathcal{S}_0 \rangle$ be the i.a.f. so specified: (i) $\mathcal{L}_0$ is the empty one-sorted signature; (ii) T_0 contains only the individual variables; (iii) $\mathcal{S}_0$ is the totality of $\mathcal{L}_0$-structures (i.e. the totality of sets). A specialization $\Phi_0^\star$ of Φ_0 is obtained by considering the class $\mathcal{S}_0^\star$ formed by the infinite sets.

By an easy compactness argument (compactness holds because Φ is a first-order fragment and $\mathcal{S}$ is an elementary class), it is easily seen that Φ is stably infinite iff it is compatible with respect to the specialization $\Phi_0^\star$ of Φ_0.

5.1   The Main Combination Result

By assuming the existence of Φ_i-extensible structural operations allowing a Φ_0-isomorphism theorem, it is possible to formulate a sufficient condition for our combined procedure to be complete; if we put together this condition, the termination condition of Proposition 4.3 and various remarks we made in the previous sections, we obtain the following decidability transfer result (see [17] for proof details):

Theorem 5.1. *Suppose that:*

(1) the interpreted algebraic fragments Φ_1, Φ_2 have decidable constraint satisfiability problems;

(2) the shared fragment Φ_0 is effectively locally finite (or more generally, Φ_1, Φ_2 are both Φ_0-compact, Φ_0 is noetherian and there exist noetherian positive residue Φ_1- and Φ_2-enumerators for Φ_0);

(3) Φ_1 and Φ_2 are both compatible with respect to a specialization $\Phi_0^\star$ of Φ_0;

(4) there is a collection $\mathcal{O}$ of structural operations on $\Phi_0^\star$ which are all Φ_1- and Φ_2-extensible and allow a $\Phi_0^\star$-isomorphism theorem.

Then the procedure FCOMB *(together with the preprocessing Purification Rule) decides constraint satisfiability in the combined fragment $\Phi_1 \oplus \Phi_2$.*

Remark. In case the shared fragment Φ_0 is locally finite, a combination procedure can be also obtained simply by guessing a maximal set Θ_0 of $\Phi_0(\underline{x}_0)$-literals and by testing the Φ_i-satisfiability of $\Theta_0 \cup \Gamma_i$. This non-deterministic version of the procedure does not require the machinery developed in Section 3.3 (but it does not apply to noetherian cases and does not yield automatic optimizations in Φ_0-convexity cases).

Remark. Theorem 5.1 cannot be used to transfer decidability of word problems to our combined fragments: the reason is that, in case the procedure FCOMB is initialized with only a single negative literal, constraints containing positive literals are nevertheless generated during the execution (and also by the Purification Rule). However, since negative literals are never run-time generated, Theorem 5.1 can be used to transfer decidability of *conditional word problems*, namely of satisfiability problems for constraints containing just one negative literal.

5.2   Applications: Decidability Transfer Through Ultrapowers

We shall use the Keisler-Shelah isomorphism Theorem of Example 5.1 to get the transfer decidability result of [16] as a special case of Theorem 5.1.

Let $\Phi_1 = \langle \mathcal{L}_1, T_1, \mathcal{S}_1 \rangle$ and $\Phi_2 = \langle \mathcal{L}_2, T_2, \mathcal{S}_2 \rangle$ be i.a.f.'s of the kinds considered in the Example 3.1 or in Example 3.2 and let $\Phi_0 = \langle \mathcal{L}_0, T_0, \mathcal{S}_0 \rangle$ be their shared fragment. The hypothesis for the decidability transfer result of [16] are the following:

(C1) there is a universal theory T_0 in the shared signature $\mathcal{L}_0$ such that every $\mathcal{A} \in \mathcal{S}_0$ is a model of T_0;

(C2) T_0 admits a model-completion $T_0^\star$;[16]

(C3) for $i = 1, 2$, every $\mathcal{A} \in \mathcal{S}_i$ embeds into some $\mathcal{A}' \in \mathcal{S}_i$ which is a model of $T_0^\star$;

(C4) Φ_0 is effectively locally finite.

Theorem 5.2 ([16]). *Suppose that Φ_1 and Φ_2 are i.a.f.'s of the kinds considered in Examples 3.1-3.2, which moreover satisfy conditions (C1)-(C4) above. If constraint satisfiability problems are decidable in Φ_1 and Φ_2, then they are decidable in $\Phi_1 \oplus \Phi_2$ too.*

If we take as T_0 the empty theory (in the one-sorted first-order empty language with equality), then $T_0^\star$ is the theory of an infinite set and condition (C3) is equivalent to stable infiniteness (by a simple argument based on compactness); thus, Theorem 5.2 *reduces to the standard Nelson-Oppen result* [25], [26], [31] *concerning stably infinite theories over disjoint signatures.* We recall from [16] that among relevant examples of theories to which Theorem 5.2 is easily seen to apply, we have Boolean algebras with operators (namely the theories axiomatizing algebraic semantics of modal logic): thus, decidability of conditional word problem transfers from two theories axiomatizing varieties of modal algebras with operators to their union (provided only Boolean operators are shared). This result, proved in [33] by specific techniques, is the algebraic version of the *fusion transfer of decidability of global consequence relation in modal logic.*

We remark that condition (C4) can be weakened to

(C4′) Φ_0 is noetherian and there exist noetherian positive residue Φ_1- and Φ_2-enumerators for Φ_0,

as suggested by Theorem 5.1 (2). As an example of an application of Theorem 5.2 under this weaker condition one can consider the theory of K-algebras endowed with a linear endomorphism: this theory is the combination of the theory of K-algebras and of the theory of K-vector spaces endowed with an endomorphism (positive residue enumerators for the noetherian shared fragment can be obtained in both cases by the method outlined in Example 3.9).

---

[16] We refer the reader to [16] for the definition and to any textbook on model theory like [11] for more information.

As another application of Theorem 5.1 based on Keisler-Shelah isomorphism theorem, we show *how to include a first order equational theory within description logic A-Boxes*. To get a decidability transfer result for the combination of an equational i.a.f. $\Phi = \langle \mathcal{L}, T, \mathcal{S} \rangle$ from Example 3.1 and of an A-Box fragment $\Phi_{ML} = \langle \mathcal{L}_{ML}, T_{ML}, \mathcal{S}_{ML} \rangle$ from Example 3.6, we only need mild additional hypotheses. These are explained in the statement of the following Theorem:

Theorem 5.3. *Suppose that we are given an equational i.a.f. $\Phi = \langle \mathcal{L}, T, \mathcal{S} \rangle$ from Example 3.1 and an A-Box fragment $\Phi_{ML} = \langle \mathcal{L}_{ML}, T_{ML}, \mathcal{S}_{ML} \rangle$ from Example 3.6; suppose also that the signatures $\mathcal{L}$ and $\mathcal{L}_{ML}$ are disjoint, that Φ is stably infinite and that $\mathcal{S}_{ML}$ is an elementary class. Then decidability of constraint satisfiability problems transfers from Φ and Φ_{ML} to $\Phi \oplus \Phi_{ML}$.*

Notice that the fragment $\Phi \oplus \Phi_{ML}$ of Theorem 5.3 is quite peculiar (combined terms all arise from a single composition step).

5.3   Applications: Decidability Transfer Through Disjoint Copies

Disjoint copies are the key tool for transfer decidability results in modal fragments. If O_{M_1} and O_{M_2} are modal signatures, we let $O_{M_1 \oplus M_2}$ indicate their disjoint union ($O_{M_1 \oplus M_2}$ is called the fusion of the modal signatures O_{M_1} and O_{M_2}). Given a modal i.a.f. Φ_{M_1} over O_{M_1} and a modal i.a.f. Φ_{M_2} over O_{M_2} (see Example 3.5), let us define their *fusion* as the modal i.a.f.

$$\Phi_{M_1 \oplus M_2} = \langle \mathcal{L}_{M_1 \oplus M_2}, T_{M_1 \oplus M_2}, \mathcal{S}_1 \oplus \mathcal{S}_2 \rangle.$$

Theorem 5.1 and the considerations in Example 5.2 show that decidability of constraint satisfiability transfers from two modal i.a.f.'s Φ_{M_1} and Φ_{M_2} (operating on disjoint modal signatures) to their combination $\Phi_{M_1} \oplus \Phi_{M_2}$. Since it can be shown that the latter differs from the fusion $\Phi_{M_1 \oplus M_2}$ only by trivial $\beta\eta$-conversions, the following well-known decidability transfer result obtains:

Theorem 5.4 (Decidability transfer for modal i.a.f.'s). *If two modal interpreted algebraic fragments Φ_{M_1} and Φ_{M_2} have decidable constraint satisfiability problems, so does their fusion $\Phi_{M_1 \oplus M_2}$.*

Fragments of the kind examined in Example 3.6 are not interesting for being combined with each other, because the absence of the type $W \to \Omega$ makes such combinations trivial. On the contrary, full modal fragments from Example 3.7 are quite interesting in this respect (we recall that they reproduce both A-Box and T-Box reasoning from the point of view of description logics). Under the obvious definition of fusion for full modal i.a.f.'s, we have the following result (the proof requires just slight modifications to the considerations of Example 5.2):

Theorem 5.5 (Decidability transfer for full modal i.a.f.'s). *If two full modal i.a.f.'s have decidable constraint satisfiability problems, so does their fusion.*

Theorem 5.5 (once completed with the straightforward extension to n-ary non normal modalities) covers the results of [9] on transfer of decidability of A-Box consistency (wrt T-Boxes axioms) in fusions of local abstract description systems.

We now try to extend our decidability transfer results to appropriate combinations of guarded or of two-variable fragments. However, to get positive results, we need to keep shared signatures under control (otherwise undecidability phenomena arise). In addition, we still want to exploit the isomorphism theorem of Example 5.2 and for that we need the shared signature to be empty and second order variables appearing as terms in the fragments to be monadic only. The kind of combination that arise in this way is a form of fusion, that we shall call monadic fusion. We begin by identifying a class of fragments to which our techniques apply.

Let us call $\Phi_{\emptyset} = \langle \mathcal{L}_{\emptyset}, T_{\emptyset}, \mathcal{S}_{\emptyset} \rangle$ the following i.a.f.: (i) $\mathcal{L}_{\emptyset}$ is the empty one-sorted first-order signature (that is, $\mathcal{L}_{\emptyset}$ does not contain any proper symbol, except for its unique sort which is called D); (ii) $T_{\emptyset}$ is equal to $T_{11}^{\mathcal{L}_{\emptyset}}$;[17] (iii) $\mathcal{S}_{\emptyset}$ contains all $\mathcal{L}_{\emptyset}$-structures.

Definition 5.1. *A* monadically suitable[18] *i.a.f.* $\Phi = \langle \mathcal{L}, T, \mathcal{S} \rangle$ *is an i.a.f. such that:*

(i) $\mathcal{L}$ *is a relational one-sorted first-order signature;*
(ii) $T_{11}^{\mathcal{L}_{\emptyset}} \subseteq T \subseteq T_{\omega 1}^{\mathcal{L}}$;
(iii) the $\Phi_{\emptyset}$-structural operation of taking disjoint I-copies is Φ-extensible.

As a first example of a monadically suitable fragment, we can consider the guarded fragments of Example 3.8 (see also the considerations in Example 5.2). To get another family of examples, we introduce an alternative construction for proving extensibility of the operation of taking disjoint I-copies. This construction is nicely behaved only for fragments without identity and is called I-conglomeration:

Definition 5.2 (I-conglomeration). *Consider a first order one-sorted relational signature $\mathcal{L}$ and a (non empty) index set I. The operation $\sum^{I}$, defined on $\mathcal{L}$-structures and called I-conglomeration, associates with an $\mathcal{L}$-structure $\mathcal{M} = \langle [\![-]\!]_{\mathcal{M}}, \mathcal{I}_{\mathcal{M}} \rangle$ the $\mathcal{L}$-structure $\sum^{I} \mathcal{M}$ such that $[\![D]\!]_{\sum^{I} \mathcal{M}}$ is the disjoint union of I-copies of $[\![D]\!]_{\mathcal{M}}$ (here D is the unique sort of $\mathcal{L}$). The interpretation of relational constants is defined in the following way*

$$\sum^{I} \mathcal{M} \models P(\langle d_1, i_1 \rangle, \dots, \langle d_n, i_n \rangle) \quad \Longleftrightarrow \quad \mathcal{M} \models P(d_1, \dots, d_n)$$

for every n-ary relational predicate P different from equality.

---

[17] See Example 3.4 for this notation and for other similar notation used below.
[18] We remark that, despite the fact that the definition of a monadically suitable fragment needs the present paper settings to be formulated, there is some anticipation of it in the literature on monodic fragments (see for instance statements like that of Theorem 11.21 in [15]).

Notice that I-conglomerations and disjoint I-copies *coincide* for relational first order signatures having only unary predicates.

Example 5.4. Let $\mathcal{L}_{2V}$ be a first-order relational one-sorted signature; a *two variables i.a.f.* over $\mathcal{L}_{2V}$ is a fragment of the kind $\Phi_{2V} = \langle \mathcal{L}_{2V}, T_{2V}, \mathcal{S}_{2V} \rangle$, where: (i) T_{2V} contains the terms *without identity* which belongs to the set $T_{NK}^{\mathcal{L}_{2V}}$ of Example 3.4 for $K = 1$ and $N = 2$; (ii) $\mathcal{S}_{2V}$ is a class of $\mathcal{L}_{2V}$-structures closed under isomorphisms and I-conglomerations. To show that Definition 5.1 applies to Φ_{2V}, it is sufficient to check that a first order formula not containing the equality predicate is satisfiable in $\mathcal{M}$ iff it is satisfiable in $\sum^I \mathcal{M}$.

For two monadically suitable i.a.f.'s Φ_1 and Φ_2 operating on disjoint signatures, let us call the combined fragment $\Phi_1 \oplus \Phi_2$ the *monadic fusion* of Φ_1 and Φ_2. For monadic fusions we have the following [17]:

Theorem 5.6 (Decidability transfer for monadically suitable i.a.f.'s). *If two monadically suitable i.a.f.'s Φ_1, Φ_2 operating on disjoint signatures have decidable constraint satisfiability problems, so does their monadic fusion.*

Theorem 5.6 offers various combination possibilities, however notice that: (a) the conditions for a fragment to be monadically suitable are rather strong (for instance, the two variable fragment with identity is not monadically suitable); (b) the notion of monadic fusion is a restricted form of combination, because only unary second order variables are available for replacement when forming formulae of the combined fragment.

5.4   Applications: Decidability Transfer for Monodic Fragments

Fragments in first-order *modal* predicate logic become undecidable quite soon: for instance, classical decidability results for the monadic or the two-variables cases do not extend to modal languages [20], [14], [19]. However there still are interesting modal predicate fragments which are decidable: one-variable fragments are usually decidable [29], [15], as well as many monodic fragments. We recall that a *monodic* formula is a modal first order formula in which modal operators are applied only to subformulae containing at most one free variable. Monodic fragments whose extensional (i.e. non modal) component is decidable seem to be decidable too [32],[15]: we shall give this fact a formulation in terms of a decidability transfer result for monodic fragments which are obtained as combinations of a suitable extensional fragment and of a one-variable first-order modal fragment. Since we prefer, for simplicity, not to introduce a specific formal notion of a modal fragment, we shall proceed through standard translations and rely on our usual notion of an i.a.f..

Constant Domains and Standard Translation. *Modal predicate formulae* are built up from atomic formulae of a given first-order one-sorted relational signature $\mathcal{L}$ and from formulae of the kind $X(x)$ (where X is a unary second order variable), by using boolean connectives, individual quantifiers and a diamond operator $\Diamond$.[19]

There are actually different standard translations for first-order modal languages, we shall concentrate here on the translation corresponding to *constant domain* semantics. The latter is defined as follows. The signature $\mathcal{L}^W$ has, in addition to the unique sort D of $\mathcal{L}$, a new sort W; relational constants of type $D^n \rightarrow \Omega$ have corresponding relational constants in $\mathcal{L}^W$ of type $D^n W \rightarrow \Omega$. We use equal names for corresponding constants: this means for instance that if P has type $D^2 \rightarrow \Omega$ in $\mathcal{L}$, the same P has type $D^2 W \rightarrow \Omega$ in $\mathcal{L}^W$. We shall make the same conventions for second order variables: hence a second order $\mathcal{L}$-variable X of type $D \rightarrow \Omega$ has a corresponding second order variable X of type $DW \rightarrow \Omega$ in $\mathcal{L}^W$.

Notice that a $\mathcal{L}^W$-structure $\mathcal{A}$ is nothing but a $[\![W]\!]_\mathcal{A}$-indexed class of $\mathcal{L}$-structures, all having the same domain $[\![D]\!]_\mathcal{A}$: we indicate by $\mathcal{A}_w$ the structure corresponding to $w \in [\![W]\!]_\mathcal{A}$ and call it the *fiber structure over* w. The signature $\mathcal{L}^{WR}$ is obtained from $\mathcal{L}^W$ by adding it also a binary 'accessibility' relation R of type $WW \rightarrow \Omega$. This is the signature we need for defining the standard translation.

For a modal predicate $\mathcal{L}$-formula $\varphi[x_1^D, \ldots, x_n^D]$ and for a variable $w : W$, we define the (non modal) $\mathcal{L}^{WR}$-formula $ST(\varphi, w)$ as follows:

$$ST(\top, w) = \top; \qquad\qquad ST(\bot, w) = \bot;$$
$$ST(P(x_{i_1}, \ldots, x_{i_m}), w) = P(x_{i_1}, \ldots, x_{i_m}, w); \quad ST(X(x_i), w) = X(x_i, w);$$
$$ST(\neg\psi, w) = \neg ST(\psi, w); \qquad\qquad ST(\exists x^D \psi, w) = \exists x^D ST(\psi, w);$$
$$ST(\psi_1 \circ \psi_2, w) = ST(\psi_1, w) \circ ST(\psi_2, w), \qquad \text{where } \circ \in \{\vee, \wedge\};$$
$$ST(\Diamond\psi, w) = \exists v^W (R(w, v) \wedge ST(\psi, v)).$$

Monodic Fusions for Fragments. Let $\mathcal{F}_{1M}$ be a class of Kripke frames closed under disjoint unions and isomorphisms. We call *one-variable modal fragment* induced by $\mathcal{F}_{1M}$ the i.a.f. $\Phi_{1M} = \langle \mathcal{L}_{1M}, T_{1M}, \mathcal{S}_{1M} \rangle$, where: (i) $\mathcal{L}_{1M} := \mathcal{L}_\emptyset^{WR}$, where $\mathcal{L}_\emptyset$ is the empty one-sorted first-order signature;(ii) T_{1M} contains the terms which are $\beta\eta$-equivalent to terms of the kind $\{w^W, x^D \mid ST(\varphi, w)\}$, where φ is a modal predicate formula having x as the only (free or bound) variable; (iii) $\mathcal{S}_{1M}$ is the class of the $\mathcal{L}_{1M}$-structures $\mathcal{A}$ such that $[\![D]\!]_\mathcal{A}$ is not empty and such that the Kripke frame $([\![W]\!]_\mathcal{A}, \mathcal{I}_\mathcal{A}(R))$ belongs to $\mathcal{F}_{1M}$.

For a *monadically suitable* i.a.f. $\Phi_e = \langle \mathcal{L}_e, T_e, \mathcal{S}_e \rangle$ (recall Definition 5.1), we define the i.a.f. $\Phi_e^W = \langle \mathcal{L}_e^W, T_e^W, \mathcal{S}_e^W \rangle$, as follows: (i) T_e^W contains the terms of the kind $\{w^W, x^D \mid ST(\varphi, w)\}$, for $\{x^D \mid \varphi\} \in T_e$: (ii) $\mathcal{S}_e^W$ contains the $\mathcal{L}_e^W$-structures $\mathcal{A}$ whose fibers $\mathcal{A}_w$ are all in $\mathcal{S}_e$.

Fix a one variable modal fragment Φ_{1M} and a first-order monadically suitable fragment Φ_e; we call *monodic fusion* of Φ_e and Φ_{1M} the combined fragment $\Phi_e^W \oplus \Phi_{1M}$.

---

[19] All the results in this subsection extend to the case of multimodal languages and to the case of n-ary modalities like SINCE, UNTIL, etc.

Thus one may for instance combine guarded or two-variables fragments[20] with one-variables modal fragments to get monodic fusions corresponding to the relevant cases analyzed in [32],[15]. In fact (modulo taking standard translation), in combined fragments like $\Phi_e^W \oplus \Phi_{1M}$ we can begin with formulae $\varphi[x]$ of Φ_e, apply to them a modal operator, then use the formulae so obtained to replace second order variables in other formulae from Φ_e, etc. Fragments of the kind $\Phi_e^W \oplus \Phi_{1M}$ formalize the intuitive notion of a monodic modal fragment whose extensional component is Φ_e. Since Φ_{1M} is also interpreted, constraint satisfiability in $\Phi_e^W \oplus \Phi_{1M}$ is restricted to a desired specific class of modal frames/flows of time.

Theorem 5.7. *If the one variable modal i.a.f. Φ_{1M} and the monadically suitable i.a.f. Φ_e have decidable constraint satisfiability problems, then their monodic fusion $\Phi_e^W \oplus \Phi_{1M}$ also has decidable constraint satisfiability problems.*

The proof of Theorem 5.7 reduces the statement to be proved to Theorem 5.1, after translating our fragments into fragments of a language describing appropriate *descent data* [17] (disjoint I-copies and fiberwise disjoint I-copies then provide the suitable isomorphism theorem).

6   Conclusions

In this paper we introduced a type-theoretic machinery in order to deal with the combination of decision problems of various nature. Higher order type theory has been essentially used as a *unifying specification language*; we have also seen how the *types interplay* can be used in a rather subtle way to design combined fragments and consequently appropriate constraints satisfiability problems.

Decision problems are at the heart of logic and of its applications, that's why they are so complex and irregularly behaved. Given that it is very difficult (and presumably impossible) to get satisfying general results in this area, the emphasis should concentrate on *methodologies* which are capable of solving entire classes of concrete problems. Among methodologies, we can certainly include *methodologies for combination*: these may be very helpful when the solution of a problem can be modularly decomposed or when the problem itself appears to be heterogeneous in its nature.

In this paper, we took into consideration *Nelson-Oppen methodology* (which is probably the simplest combination methodology) and tried to push it as far as possible. Surprisingly, it turned out that it might be quite powerful, when *joined to strong model theoretic results* (the isomorphism theorems). Thus, we tried to give the reader a gallery of different applications that can be solved in a *uniform way* by this methodology. Some of these applications are new, some other summarize recent work by various people. New problems certainly arise now: they concern both further applications of Nelson-Oppen schema and the

---

[20] We recall that two-variable fragments are monadically suitable only if we take out identity.

individuation or more sophisticated schemata, for the problems that cannot be covered by the Nelson-Oppen approach. We hope that the higher order framework and the model theoretic techniques we introduced in this paper may give further contributions within this research perspective.

References

1. H. Andréka, I. Nemeti, and J. VanBenthem. Modal languages and bounded fragments of predicate logics. *Journal of Philosophical Logic*, 27:217–274, 1998.
2. Peter B. Andrews. *An introduction to mathematical logic and type theory: to truth through proof*, volume 27 of *Applied Logic Series*. Kluwer Acad. Publ., 2002.
3. Peter B. Andrews. Classical type theory. In A. Robinson and A. Voronkov, editors, *Handbook of Automated Reasoning*, volume II, pages 966–1007. Elsevier/MIT, 2001.
4. Franz Baader and Silvio Ghilardi. Connecting many-sorted theories. In *Proceedings of the 20th International Conference on Automated Deduction (CADE-05)*, Lecture Notes in Artificial Intelligence, 2005.
5. Franz Baader and Silvio Ghilardi. Connecting many-sorted structures and theories through adjoint functions. In *Proceedings of the 5th International Workshop on Frontiers of Combining Systems (FROCOS-05)*, Lecture Notes in Artificial Intelligence, 2005.
6. Franz Baader and Tobias Nipkow. *Term rewriting and all that*. Cambridge University Press, Cambridge, 1998.
7. Franz Baader and Cesare Tinelli. Deciding the word problem in the union of equational theories. *Information and Computation*, 178(2):346–390, December 2002.
8. Franz Baader, Silvio Ghilardi, and Cesare Tinelli. A new combination procedure for the word problem that generalizes fusion decidability results in modal logics. *Information and Computation*. (to appear).
9. Franz Baader, Carsten Lutz, Holger Sturm, and Frank Wolter. Fusions of description logics and abstract description systems. *Journal of Artificial Intelligence Research*, 16:1–58, 2002.
10. Egon Börger, Erich Grädel, and Yuri Gurevich. *The classical decision problem*. Universitext. Springer-Verlag, Berlin, 2001.
11. Chen-Chung Chang and H. Jerome Keisler. *Model Theory*. North-Holland, Amsterdam-London, IIIrd edition, 1990.
12. G. Dowek. Higher order unification and matching. In A. Robinson and A. Voronkov, editors, *Handbook of Automated Reasoning*, volume II, pages 1009–1062. Elsevier/MIT, 2001.
13. C. Fermüller, A. Leitsch, T. Tammet, and N. Zamov. *Resolution methods for the decision problem*, volume 679 of *Lecture Notes in Computer Science*. Springer-Verlag, 1993. Lecture Notes in Artificial Intelligence.
14. D. M. Gabbay and V.B. Shehtman. Undecidability of modal and intermediate first-order logics with two individual variables. *Journal of Symbolic Logic*, 58:800–823, 1993.
15. D.M. Gabbay, A. Kurucz, F. Wolter, and M. Zakharyaschev. *Many-Dimensional Modal Logics: Theory and Applications*, volume 148 of *Studies in Logic and the Foundations of Mathematics*. Elsevier, 2003.
16. Silvio Ghilardi. Model theoretic methods in combined constraint satisfiability. *Journal of Automated Reasoning*, 33(3-3):221–249, 2005.

17. Silvio Ghilardi, Enrica Nicolini, and Daniele Zucchelli. A comprehensive framework for combined decision procedures. Technical Report 304-05, Dipartimento di Scienze dellInformazione, Università degli Studi di Milano, 2005. URL http://homes.dsi.unimi.it/~ghilardi/allegati/frocos05.zip.

18. E. Grädel. Decision procedures for guarded logics. In *Proceedings of CADE-16*, volume 1632 of *Lecture Notes in Computer Science*, pages 31–51. Springer, 1999.

19. R. Kontchakov, A. Kurucz, and M. Zakharyaschev. Undecidability of first-order intuituionistic and modal logics with two variables. 2004. manuscript.

20. S. Kripke. The undecidability of monadic modal quantificational theory. *Z. Math. Logik Grundlag. Math.*, 8:113–116, 1962.

21. J. Lambek and P. J. Scott. *Introduction to higher order categorical logic*, volume 7 of *Cambridge Studies in Advanced Mathematics*.

22. L. Löwhenheim. Über Möglichkeiten im Relativkalkül. *Math. Annalen*, 76:228–251, 1915.

23. M. Marx. Tolerance logic. *Journal of Logic, Language and Information*, 10:353–374, 2001.

24. M. Mortimer. On languages with two variables. *Z. Math. Logik Grundlag. Math.*, 21:135–140, 1975.

25. Greg Nelson and Derek C. Oppen. Simplification by cooperating decision procedures. *ACM Trans. on Programming Languages and Systems*, 1(2):245–257, October 1979.

26. Derek C. Oppen. Complexity, convexity and combinations of theories. *Theoretical Computer Science*, 12:291–302, 1980.

27. D. Scott. A decision method for for validity of sentences in two variables. *Journal of Symbolic Logic*, 27:477, 1962.

28. K. Segerberg. Two-dimensional modal logic. *Journal of Philosophical Logic*, 2: 77–96, 1973.

29. V.B. Shehtman. On some two-dimensional modal logics. In *8th Congress on Logic Methodology and Philosophy of Science, vol. 1*, pages 326–330. Nauka, Moskow, 1987.

30. Cesare Tinelli. Cooperation of background reasoners in theory reasoning by residue sharing. *Journal of Automated Reasoning*, 30(1):1–31, 2003.

31. Cesare Tinelli and Mehdi T. Harandi. A new correctness proof of the Nelson–Oppen combination procedure. In *Proc. of the 1st Int. Workshop on Frontiers of Combining Systems*, pages 103–120. Kluwer Acad. Publ., 1996.

32. F. Wolter and M. Zakharyaschev. Decidable fragments of first-order modal logics. *Journal of Symbolic Logic*, 66:1415–1438, 2001.

33. Frank Wolter. Fusions of modal logics revisited. In M. Kracht, M. de Rijke, H. Wansing, and M. Zakharyaschev, editors, *Advances in Modal Logic*. CSLI, Stanford, CA, 1998.

Connecting Many-Sorted Structures and Theories Through Adjoint Functions

Franz Baader[1] and Silvio Ghilardi[2]

[1] Institut für Theoretische Informatik, TU Dresden
[2] Dipartimento di Scienze dell'Informazione, Università degli Studi di Milano

Abstract. In a previous paper, we have introduced a general approach for connecting two many-sorted theories through connection functions that behave like homomorphisms on the shared signature, and have shown that, under appropriate algebraic conditions, decidability of the validity of universal formulae in the component theories transfers to their connection. This work generalizes decidability transfer results for so-called $\mathcal{E}$-connections of modal logics. However, in this general algebraic setting, only the most basic type of $\mathcal{E}$-connections could be handled. In the present paper, we overcome this restriction by looking at pairs of connection functions that are adjoint pairs for partial orders defined in the component theories.

1 Introduction

Transfer of decidability from component theories/logics to their combination have been investigated independently in different areas of computer science and logic, and only recently it has turned out that there are close connections between different such transfer results. For example, in modal logics it was shown that in many cases decidability of (relativized) validity transfers from two modal logics to their fusion [14,21,23,3]. In automated deduction, the Nelson-Oppen combination procedure [18,17] and combination procedures for the word problem [20,19,4] were generalized to the case of the union of theories over non-disjoint signatures [7,22,5,8,11,2], and it could be shown that some of these approaches [11,2] actually generalize decidability transfer results for fusions of modal logics from equational theories induced by modal logics to more general first-order theories satisfying certain model-theoretic restrictions. In particular, these generalizations no longer require the shared theory to be the theory of Boolean algebras.

The purpose of this work is to develop similar algebraic generalizations of decidability transfer results for so-called $\mathcal{E}$-connections [15] of modal logics. Intuitively, the difference between fusion and $\mathcal{E}$-connection can be explained as follows. A model of the fusion is obtained from two models of the component logics by identifying their domains. In contrast, a model of the $\mathcal{E}$-connection consists of two separate models of the component logics together with certain connecting relations between their domains. There are also differences in the syntax of the combined logic. In the case of the fusion, the Boolean operators

B. Gramlich (Ed.): FroCoS 2005, LNAI 3717, pp. 31–47, 2005.
© Springer-Verlag Berlin Heidelberg 2005

are shared, and all operators can be applied to each other without restrictions. In the case of the $\mathcal{E}$-connection, there are two copies of the Boolean operators, and operators of the different logics cannot be mixed; the only connection between the logics are new modal operators that are induced by the connecting relations.

In [1], this connection approach was generalized to the more general setting of connecting many-sorted first-order theories. The use of many-sorted theories allowed us to keep the domains separate and to restrict the way function symbols can be applied to each other. To be more precise, let T_1, T_2 be two many-sorted theories that may share some sorts as well as function and relation symbols. We first build the disjoint union $T_1 \uplus T_2$ of these two theories (by using disjoint copies of the shared parts), and then connect them by introducing *connection functions* between the shared sorts. These connection functions must behave like homomorphisms for the shared function and predicate symbols, i.e., the axioms stating this are added to $T_1 \uplus T_2$. This corresponds to the fact that the new modal operators in the $\mathcal{E}$-connection approach interact with the Boolean operators of the component logics. In [1], we started with the simplest case where there is just one connection function, and showed that decidability of the universal fragments of T_1, T_2 transfers to their connection whenever certain model-theoretic conditions are satisfied. The approach was then extended to the case of several connection functions, and to variants of the general combination scheme where the connection function must satisfy additional properties (like being surjective, an embedding, or an isomorphism).

However, in the $\mathcal{E}$-connection approach introduced in [15], one usually considers not only the modal operator induced by a connecting relation, but also the modal operator induced by its inverse. It is not adequate to express these two modal operators by independent connection function going in different directions since this does not capture the relationships that must hold between them. For example, if $\diamond$ is the diamond operator induced by the connecting relation E, and $\square^-$ is the box operator induced by its inverse E^-, then the formulae $x \to \square^- \diamond x$ and $\diamond \square^- y \to y$ are valid in the $\mathcal{E}$-connection. In order to express these relationships in the algebraic setting without assuming the presence of the Boolean operators in the shared theory, we replace the logical implication $\to$ by a partial order $\leq$,[1] and require that $x \leq r(\ell(x))$ and $\ell(r(y)) \leq y$ holds for the corresponding connection functions. If ℓ, r are also order preserving, then this means that ℓ, r is a pair of *adjoint functions* for the partial order $\leq$. We call the connection of two theories obtained this way an *adjoint theory connection*.

In this paper we give an abstract algebraic condition under which the decidability of the universal fragment transfers from the component theories to their adjoint theory connection. In contrast to the conditions in [1], which are compatibility conditions between a shared theory and the component theories, this is a condition that requires the existence of certain subtheories of the component theories, but these subtheories need not be the same for different components.

---

[1] In the presence of (some of) the Boolean operators, this partial order is obtained in the usual way, e.g., by defining $x \leq y$ iff $x \sqcup y = y$, where $\sqcup$ is the join (disjunction) operator. Note that the applications of $\diamond$ and $\square^-$ preserve this order.

We then give sufficient conditions under which our new condition is satisfied. In particular, this shows that the decidability transfer results for $\mathcal{E}$-connection with inverse connection modalities follow from our more general algebraic result.

2 Notation and Definitions

In this section, we fix the notation and give some important definitions, in particular a formal definition of the adjoint connection of two theories. In addition, we show some simple results regarding adjoint functions in partially ordered set.

Basic Model Theory. We use standard *many-sorted first-order logic* (see, e.g., [9]), but try to avoid the notational overhead caused by the presence of sorts as much as possible. Thus, a *signature* Ω consists of a non-empty set of sorts S together with a set of function symbols $\mathcal{F}$ and a set of predicate symbols $\mathcal{P}$. The function and predicate symbols are equipped with arities from S^* in the usual way. For example, if the arity of $f \in \mathcal{F}$ is $S_1 S_2 S_3$, then this means that the function f takes tuples consisting of an element of sort S_1 and an element of sort S_2 as input, and produces an element of sort S_3. We consider logic with equality, i.e., the set of predicate symbols contains a symbol $\approx_S$ for equality in every sort S. Usually, we will just use $\approx$ without explicitly specifying the sort.

Terms and first-order formulae over Ω are defined in the usual way, i.e., they must respect the arities of function and predicate symbols, and the variables occurring in them are also equipped with sorts. An Ω-*atom* is a predicate symbol applied to (sort-conforming) terms, and an Ω-*literal* is an atom or a negated atom. A *ground* literal is a literal that does not contain variables. We use the notation $\phi(\underline{x})$ to express that ϕ is a formula whose free variables are among the ones in the tuple of variables $\underline{x}$. An Ω-*sentence* is a formula over Ω without free variables. An Ω-*theory* T is a set of Ω-sentences (called the axioms of T). If T, T' are Ω-theories, then we write (by a slight abuse of notation) $T \subseteq T'$ to express that all the axioms of T are logical consequences of the axioms of T'. The formula ϕ is called *open* iff it does not contain quantifiers; it is called *universal* iff it is obtained from an open formula by adding a prefix of universal quantifiers. The theory T is a *universal theory* iff its axioms are universal sentences.

From the semantic side, we have the standard notion of an Ω-*structure* $\mathcal{A}$, which consists of non-empty and pairwise disjoint domains A_S for every sort S, and interprets function symbols f and predicate symbols P by functions $f^{\mathcal{A}}$ and predicates $P^{\mathcal{A}}$ according to their arities. By A we denote the union of all domains A_S. Validity of a formula ϕ in an Ω-structure $\mathcal{A}$ ($\mathcal{A} \models \phi$), satisfiability, and logical consequence are defined in the usual way. The Ω-structure $\mathcal{A}$ is a *model* of the Ω-theory T iff all axioms of T are valid in $\mathcal{A}$. The class of all models of T is denoted by $Mod(T)$.

If $\phi(\underline{x})$ is a formula with free variables $\underline{x} = x_1, \ldots, x_n$ and $\underline{a} = a_1, \ldots, a_n$ is a (sort-conforming) tuple of elements of A, then we write $\mathcal{A} \models \phi(\underline{a})$ to express that $\phi(\underline{x})$ is valid in $\mathcal{A}$ under the assignment $\{x_1 \mapsto a_1, \ldots, x_n \mapsto a_n\}$. Note that $\phi(\underline{x})$ is valid in $\mathcal{A}$ iff it is valid under all assignments iff its universal closure is valid in $\mathcal{A}$. An Ω-*homomorphism* between two Ω-structures $\mathcal{A}$ and $\mathcal{B}$ is a mapping $\mu : A \to B$ that is sort-conforming (i.e., maps elements of sort S in $\mathcal{A}$ to elements of sort S in $\mathcal{B}$), and satisfies the condition

$$(*) \qquad \mathcal{A} \models A(a_1, \ldots, a_n) \quad \text{implies} \quad \mathcal{B} \models A(\mu(a_1), \ldots, \mu(a_n))$$

for all Ω-atoms $A(x_1, \ldots, x_n)$ and (sort-conforming) elements $a_1, \ldots, a_n$ of A. In case the converse of $(*)$ holds too, μ is called an *embedding*. Note that an embedding is something more than just an injective homomorphism since the stronger condition must hold not only for the equality predicate, but for all predicate symbols. If the embedding μ is the identity on A, then we say that $\mathcal{A}$ is an *Ω-substructure* of $\mathcal{B}$. An important property of universal theories is that their classes of models are *closed under building substructures*, i.e., if T is a universal Ω-theory and $\mathcal{A}$ is an Ω-substructure of $\mathcal{M}$, then $\mathcal{M} \in Mod(T)$ implies $\mathcal{A} \in Mod(T)$ (see, e.g. [6]).

We say that Σ is a subsignature of Ω (written $\Sigma \subseteq \Omega$) iff Σ is a signature that can be obtained from Ω by removing some of its sorts and function and predicate symbols. If $\Sigma \subseteq \Omega$ and $\mathcal{A}$ is an Ω-structure, then the *Σ-reduct* of $\mathcal{A}$ is the Σ-structure $\mathcal{A}|_\Sigma$ obtained from $\mathcal{A}$ by forgetting the interpretations of sorts, function and predicate symbols from Ω that do not belong to Σ. Conversely, $\mathcal{A}$ is called an *expansion* of the Σ-structure $\mathcal{A}|_\Sigma$ to the larger signature Ω.

Given a set X of constant symbols not belonging to the signature Ω, but each equipped with a sort from Ω, we denote by Ω^X the extension of Ω by these new constants. If $\mathcal{A}$ is an Ω-structure, then we can view the elements of A as a set of new constants, where $a \in A_S$ has sort S. By interpreting each $a \in A$ by itself, $\mathcal{A}$ can also be viewed as an Ω^A-structure. The *diagram* $\Delta_\Omega(\mathcal{A})$ of $\mathcal{A}$ is the set of all ground Ω^A-literals that are true in $\mathcal{A}$. *Robinson's diagram theorem* [6] says that there is an embedding between the Ω-structures $\mathcal{A}$ and $\mathcal{B}$ iff there is an expansion of $\mathcal{B}$ to an Ω^A-structure that is a model of the diagram of $\mathcal{A}$.

Adjoint Functions in Posets. We recall some basic facts about adjoints among posets (see, e.g., [12] for more details). A partially ordered set (*poset*, for short) is a set P equipped with a reflexive, transitive, and antisymmetric binary relation $\leq$. Such a poset is called *complete* if the *meet* $\bigwedge_i a_i \in P$ and the *join* $\bigvee_i a_i \in P$ of a family $\{a_i\}_{i \in I}$ of elements of P always exist. In case I is empty, the meet is the greatest and the join the least element of P.

Let P, Q be posets. A pair of maps $f^* : P \to Q$ and $f_* : Q \to P$ is said to be an *adjoint pair* (written $f^* \dashv f_*$) iff the condition

$$f^*(a) \leq b \qquad \text{iff} \qquad a \leq f_*(b) \tag{1}$$

is satisfied for all $a \in P, b \in Q$. In this case, f^* is called the *left adjoint* to f_*, and f_* is called the *right adjoint* to f^*. The left (right) adjoint to a given map $f : P \to Q$ may not exist, but if it does, then it is unique.

Condition (1) implies that f^*, f_* are *order preserving*. For example, assume that $a_1, a_2 \in P$ are such that $a_1 \leq a_2$. Now, $f^*(a_2) \leq f^*(a_2)$ implies $a_2 \leq f_*(f^*(a_2))$ by (1), and thus by transitivity $a_1 \leq f_*(f^*(a_2))$. By (1), this implies $f^*(a_1) \leq f^*(a_2)$.

Instead of condition (1), we may equivalently require that f^*, f_* are order preserving and satisfy, for all $a \in P, b \in Q$, the conditions

$$a \leq f_*(f^*(a)) \qquad \text{and} \qquad f^*(f_*(b)) \leq b. \qquad (2)$$

If $f^* \dashv f_*$ is an adjoint pair, then the mappings f^*, f_* are inverse to each other on their images, i.e., for all $a \in P, b \in Q$

$$f^*(a) = f^*(f_*(f^*(a))) \qquad \text{and} \qquad f_*(f^*(f_*(b))) = f_*(b). \qquad (3)$$

Adjoint pairs compose in the following sense: if $f^* : P \to Q, f_* : Q \to P$ and $g^* : Q \to R, g_* : R \to Q$ are such that $f^* \dashv f_*$ and $g^* \dashv g_*$, then we also have that $g^* \circ f^* \dashv f_* \circ g_*$ (where composition should be read from right to left).

If P, Q are complete posets, then any pair of adjoints $f^* \dashv f_*$ between P and Q preserves meet and join in the following sense: the left adjoint preserves join and the right adjoint preserves meet. The latter can, e.g., be seen as follows:

$$a \leq f_*(\bigwedge b_i) \text{ iff } f^*(a) \leq \bigwedge b_i \text{ iff } \forall i. f^*(a) \leq b_i \text{ iff } \forall i. a \leq f_*(b_i) \text{ iff } a \leq \bigwedge f_*(b_i).$$

Since a is arbitrary, this shows that $f_*(\bigwedge b_i) = \bigwedge f_*(b_i)$.

Given a mapping $f : P \to Q$ between the posets P, Q, we may ask under what conditions it has a left (right) adjoint. As we have seen above, order preserving is a necessary condition, but it is easy to see that it is not sufficient.

If P, Q are complete, then meet preserving is a necessary condition for f to have a left adjoint f^*, and join preserving is a necessary condition for f to have a right adjoint f_*. These conditions are also sufficient: if f preserves join (meet), then the following mapping f_* (f^*) is a right (left) adjoint to f:

$$f_*(b) := \bigvee_{f(a) \leq b} a \qquad \text{and} \qquad f^*(b) := \bigwedge_{b \leq f(a)} a.$$

Example 1. Let W_1, W_2 be sets, and consider the posets induced by the sub-set relation on their powersets $\wp(W_1)$ and $\wp(W_2)$. Obviously, these posets are complete, where set union is the join and set intersection is the meet operation. Any binary relation $E \subseteq W_2 \times W_1$ yields a join-preserving diamond operator $\Diamond_E : \wp(W_1) \to \wp(W_2)$ by defining for all $a \in \wp(W_1)$:

$$\Diamond_E a := \{ w_2 \in W_2 \mid \exists w_1 \in W_1. (w_2, w_1) \in E \wedge w_1 \in a \}.$$

The right adjoint to this diamond operator is the box operator $\Box_E^- : \wp(W_2) \to \wp(W_1)$, which can be defined as the map taking $b \in \wp(W_2)$ to

$$\Box_E^- b := \{ w_1 \in W_1 \mid \forall w_2 \in W_2. (w_2, w_1) \in E \to w_2 \in b \}.$$

It is easy to see that these two maps indeed form an adjoint pair for set inclusion, i.e., we have $\Diamond_E \dashv \Box_E^-$. Conversely, for any adjoint pair $f^* \dashv f_*$ with

$$f^* : \wp(W_1) \to \wp(W_2) \qquad \text{and} \qquad f_* : \wp(W_2) \to \wp(W_1),$$

there is a *unique* relation $E \subseteq W_2 \times W_1$ such that $f^* = \Diamond_E$ and $f_* = \Box_E^-$. To show this, just take E to consist of the pairs (w_2, w_1) such that $w_2 \in f^*(\{w_1\}))$. This shows that the adjoint pairs among powerset Boolean algebras coincide with the pairs of inverse modal operators on the powersets defined above.

Adjoint Connections. We define adjoint connections first on the semantic side, where we connect classes of structures, and then on the syntactic side, where we connect theories.

Let Ω_1, Ω_2 be two disjoint (many-sorted) signatures.[2] We assume that Ω_1 contains a binary predicate symbol $\sqsubseteq^1$ of arity $S^1 S^1$, and Ω_2 contains a binary predicate symbol $\sqsubseteq^2$ of arity $S^2 S^2$. The combined signature $\Omega_1 +^* \Omega_2$ contains the union $\Omega_1 \cup \Omega_2$ of the signatures Ω_1 and Ω_2. In addition $\Omega_1 +^* \Omega_2$ contains *two new function symbols* ℓ, r of arity $S^1 S^2$ and $S^2 S^1$. Since the signatures Ω_1 and Ω_2 are sorted and disjoint, it is easy to see that $(\Omega_1 +^* \Omega_2)$-structures are formed by 4-tuples of the form $(\mathcal{M}^1, \mathcal{M}^2, \ell^{\mathcal{M}}, r^{\mathcal{M}})$, where $\mathcal{M}^1$ is an Ω_1-structure, $\mathcal{M}^2$ is an Ω_2-structure, and

$$\ell^{\mathcal{M}} : \mathcal{S}^1 \to \mathcal{S}^2 \qquad \text{and} \qquad r^{\mathcal{M}} : \mathcal{S}^2 \to \mathcal{S}^1$$

are functions between the interpretations $\mathcal{S}^1, \mathcal{S}^2$ of the sorts S^1, S^2 in $\mathcal{M}^1, \mathcal{M}^2$.

Let $\mathcal{K}_1$ be a class of Ω_1-structures and $\mathcal{K}_2$ a class of Ω_2-structures such that each of the structures in $\mathcal{K}_i$ interprets $\sqsubseteq^i$ as a partial order on the interpretation $\mathcal{S}^i$ of the sort S^i $(i = 1, 2)$. The combined class of structures $\mathcal{K}_1 +^* \mathcal{K}_2$, called the *adjoint connection* of $\mathcal{K}_1$ and $\mathcal{K}_2$, consists of those $(\Omega_1 +^* \Omega_2)$-structures $(\mathcal{M}^1, \mathcal{M}^2, \ell^{\mathcal{M}}, r^{\mathcal{M}})$ for which $\mathcal{M}^1 \in \mathcal{K}_1$, $\mathcal{M}^2 \in \mathcal{K}_2$, and $\ell^{\mathcal{M}}, r^{\mathcal{M}}$ is an adjoint pair for the posets given by $\mathcal{S}^1, \mathcal{S}^2$ and the interpretations of the predicate symbols $\sqsubseteq^1, \sqsubseteq^2$ in $\mathcal{M}^1, \mathcal{M}^2$, respectively.

Let T_1 be an Ω_1-theory and T_2 an Ω_2-theory such that the axioms of T_i $(i = 1, 2)$ entail the reflexivity, transitivity, and antisymmetry axioms for $\sqsubseteq^i$. The combined theory $T_1 +^* T_2$, called the *adjoint theory connection* of T_1 and T_2, has $\Omega_1 +^* \Omega_2$ as its signature, and the following *axioms*:

$$T_1 \; \cup \; T_2 \; \cup \; \{ \forall x, y. \, (\ell(x) \sqsubseteq^2 y \leftrightarrow x \sqsubseteq^1 r(y)) \}.$$

In the sequel, superscripts 1 and 2 for the partial orders $\sqsubseteq^1, \sqsubseteq^2$ are sometimes omitted. It is easy to see that the adjoint theory connection corresponds to building the adjoint connection of the corresponding classes of models.

Proposition 2. $Mod(T_1 +^* T_2) = Mod(T_1) +^* Mod(T_2)$.

Example 3. We show that basic $\mathcal{E}$-connections of abstract description systems, as introduced in [15], are instances of our approach for connecting classes of structures. A *Boolean-based signature* is a signature Ω including the signature Ω_{BA} of Boolean algebras. Boolean-based signatures correspond to the *abstract description languages* (ADL) introduced in [15], with the exception that we do not consider object variables and relation symbols.[3]

An *algebraic Ω-model* is an Ω-structure whose Ω_{BA}-reduct is a Boolean algebra. As a special case we consider Ω-*frames*, which are algebraic Ω-models

---

[2] If Ω_1, Ω_2 are not disjoint, we can make them disjoint by appropriately renaming the shared sorts and the shared function and predicate symbols.

[3] This means that our approach cannot treat the *relational* object assertions of [15] (see Example 9 below for more details). These object assertions correspond to role assertions of description logic ABoxes, and are usually not considered in modal logic.

$\mathcal{F}(W)$ whose Ω_{BA}-reduct is the Boolean algebra $\wp(W)$, where W is a set (called the set of possible worlds). Ω-frames are the same as the *abstract description models* (ADM) introduced in [15]. An *abstract description system* (ADS) is determined by an ADL together with a class of ADMs for this ADL. Thus, in our setting, an ADS is given by a Boolean-based signature Ω together with a class of Ω-frames.

Let Ω_1, Ω_2 be Boolean-based signatures, and $\mathcal{K}_1, \mathcal{K}_2$ be classes of Ω_1- and Ω_2-frames, respectively. Any element of their adjoint connection $\mathcal{K}_1 +^* \mathcal{K}_2$ is of the form $(\mathcal{F}(W_1), \mathcal{F}(W_2), \ell^{\mathcal{M}}, r^{\mathcal{M}})$, where $\mathcal{F}(W_1) \in \mathcal{K}_1$, $\mathcal{F}(W_2) \in \mathcal{K}_2$, and $\ell^{\mathcal{M}}, r^{\mathcal{M}}$ is an adjoint pair between the powersets $\wp(W_1)$ and $\wp(W_2)$. The considerations in Example 1 show that there is a relation $E \subseteq W_2 \times W_1$ such that $\ell^{\mathcal{M}} = \Diamond_E$ and $r^{\mathcal{M}} = \Box_E^-$. We call such a relation a *connecting relation*. Conversely, assume that $\mathcal{F}(W_1) \in \mathcal{K}_1$, $\mathcal{F}(W_2) \in \mathcal{K}_2$. If $E \subseteq W_2 \times W_1$ is a connecting relation, then $\Diamond_E, \Box_E^-$ is an adjoint pair, and thus $(\mathcal{F}(W_1), \mathcal{F}(W_2), \Diamond_E, \Box_E^-)$ belongs to the adjoint connection $\mathcal{K}_1 +^* \mathcal{K}_2$.

Let $\mathcal{ADS}_1, \mathcal{ADS}_2$ be the ADSs induced by Ω_1, Ω_2 and $\mathcal{K}_1, \mathcal{K}_2$. The above argument shows that the basic $\mathcal{E}$-connection of $\mathcal{ADS}_1$ and $\mathcal{ADS}_2$ (with just one connecting relation) is given by $\Omega_1 +^* \Omega_2$ and the frame class $\mathcal{K}_1 +^* \mathcal{K}_2$.

This example shows that the adjoint connection of frame classes really captures the basic $\mathcal{E}$-connection approach introduced in [15]. On the one hand, our approach is more general in that it can also deal with arbitrary classes of algebraic models (and not just frame classes), and even more generally with signatures that are not Boolean based. On the other hand, in [15], also more general types of $\mathcal{E}$-connections are considered. First, there may be more than one connecting relation in $\mathcal{E}$. In our algebraic setting this means that more than one pair of adjoints is considered. Though we do not treat this case here, it is straightforward to extend our approach to several (independent) pairs of adjoints. Second, in [15] $n \geq 2$ rather than just 2 ADSs are connected. We will show later on how our approach can be extended to deal with this case. Third, [15] considers extensions of the basic connection approach such as applying Boolean operations to connecting relations. These kinds of extensions can currently not be handled by our algebraic approach.

3 The Decidability Transfer Result

We are interested in deciding universal fragments i.e., validity of universal formulae (or, equivalently open formulae) in a theory T or a class of structures $\mathcal{K}$. The formula ϕ is *valid* in the class of structures $\mathcal{K}$ iff ϕ is valid in each element of $\mathcal{K}$. It is valid in the theory T iff it is valid in $Mod(T)$. It is well known that the validity problem for universal formulae is equivalent to the problem of deciding whether a set of literals is satisfiable in some element of $\mathcal{K}$ (some model of T). We call such a set of literals a *constraint*.

By introducing new free constants (i.e., constants not occurring in the axioms of the theory), we can assume without loss of generality that such constraints contain no variables. In addition, we can transform any ground constraint into an equi-satisfiable set of *ground flat literals*, i.e., literals of the form

$$a \approx f(a_1, \ldots, a_n), \quad P(a_1, \ldots, a_n), \quad \text{or} \quad \neg P(a_1, \ldots, a_n),$$

where $a, a_1, \ldots, a_n$ are (sort-conforming) free constants, f is a function symbol, and P is a predicate symbol (possibly also equality).

Before we can formulate the decidability transfer result, we must first define the conditions under which it holds. These conditions are conditions regarding the existence of certain subtheories T_0 of the component theories. Let Ω_0 be a single-sorted signature containing (possibly among other symbols) a binary predicate symbol $\sqsubseteq$, and let T_0 be a universal Ω_0-theory that entails reflexivity, transitivity, and antisymmetry of $\sqsubseteq$.

The *first condition* is that T_0 must be locally finite, i.e., all finitely generated models of T_0 are finite. To be more precise, we need the following restricted version of the effective variant of local finiteness defined in [11,2]. The theory T_0 is called *locally finite with an effective bound* iff there is a computable function B_{T_0} from the non-negative integers into the non-negative integers with the following property: if the model $\mathcal{A}$ of T_0 is generated by a set of generators of size n, then the cardinality of $\mathcal{A}$ is bounded by $B_{T_0}(n)$.

The *second condition* requires the existence of certain adjoint functions. We say that T_0 *guarantees adjoints* iff every Ω_0-embedding $e : \mathcal{A} \to \mathcal{M}$ of a finitely generated model $\mathcal{A}$ of T_0 into a model $\mathcal{M}$ of T_0 has both a left adjoint e^* and a right adjoint e_* for the posets induced by the interpretations of $\sqsubseteq$ in $\mathcal{A}$ and $\mathcal{M}$.

Definition 4. *Let Ω be a (many-sorted) signature, and $\mathcal{K}$ be a class of Ω-structures. We say that $\mathcal{K}$ is adjoint combinable iff there exist a finite single-sorted subsignature Ω_0 of Ω containing the binary predicate symbol $\sqsubseteq$, and a universal Ω_0-theory T_0 such that*

1. *every axiom of T_0 is valid in $\mathcal{K}$;*
2. *the axioms of T_0 entail reflexivity, transitivity, and antisymmetry for $\sqsubseteq$;*
3. *T_0 is locally finite with an effective bound;*
4. *T_0 guarantees adjoints.*

Let T be an Ω-theory. We say that T is adjoint combinable iff the corresponding class of models $Mod(T)$ is adjoint combinable.

For adjoint combinable classes of structures, decidability of the universal fragment transfers from the components to their adjoint connection. It should be noted that the universal theory T_0 ensuring adjoint combinability need not be the same for the component theories.

Theorem 5. *Let $\mathcal{K}_1, \mathcal{K}_2$ be adjoint combinable classes of structures over the respective signatures Ω_1, Ω_2. Then the decidability of the universal fragments of $\mathcal{K}_1$ and $\mathcal{K}_2$ entails the decidability of the universal fragment of $\mathcal{K}_1 +^* \mathcal{K}_2$.*

Proof. Let $T_0^{(1)}$ and $T_0^{(2)}$ be the universal theories over the signatures $\Omega_0^{(1)}$ and $\Omega_0^{(2)}$ ensuring adjoint combinability of $\mathcal{K}_1$ and $\mathcal{K}_2$, respectively. To prove the theorem, we consider a finite set Γ of ground flat literals over the signature $\Omega_1 +^* \Omega_2$ (with additional free constants), and show how it can be tested for satisfiability in $\mathcal{K}_1 +^* \mathcal{K}_2$. Since all literals in Γ are flat, we can divide Γ into three disjoint sets $\Gamma = \Gamma_0 \cup \Gamma_1 \cup \Gamma_2$, where Γ_i $(i = 1, 2)$ is a set of literals over Ω_i (expanded with free constants), and Γ_0 is of the form

$$\Gamma_0 = \{\ell(a_1) \approx b_1, \ldots, \ell(a_n) \approx b_n, r(b_1') \approx a_1', \ldots, r(b_m') \approx a_m'\}$$

for free constants a_j, b_j, a_i', b_i'.

The following procedure decides satisfiability of Γ in $\mathcal{K}_1 +^* \mathcal{K}_2$:

1. Guess a 4-tuple $\mathcal{A}, \mathcal{B}, \mu, \nu$, where:
   (a) $\mathcal{A}$ is a finite $\Omega_0^{(1)}$-structure generated by $\{a_1, \ldots, a_n, a_1', \ldots, a_m'\}$ such that $|A| \leq B_{T_0^{(1)}}(n + m)$ and $\sqsubseteq$ is interpreted as a partial order, and $\mathcal{B}$ is a finite $\Omega_0^{(2)}$-structure generated by $\{b_1, \ldots, b_n, b_1', \ldots, b_m'\}$ such that $|B| \leq B_{T_0^{(2)}}(n + m)$ and $\sqsubseteq$ is interpreted as a partial order.
   (b) $\mu : \mathcal{A} \longrightarrow \mathcal{B}$ and $\nu : \mathcal{B} \longrightarrow \mathcal{A}$ is an adjoint pair for the partial orders induced by the interpretations of $\sqsubseteq$ in $\mathcal{A}, \mathcal{B}$ such that

$$\mu(a_j) = b_j \ (j = 1, \ldots, n) \quad \text{and} \quad \nu(b_i') = a_i' \ (i = 1, \ldots, m).$$

2. Check whether $\Gamma_1 \cup \Delta_{\Omega_0^{(1)}}(\mathcal{A})$ is satisfiable in $\mathcal{K}_1$ (if not, go back to Step 1).
3. Check whether $\Gamma_2 \cup \Delta_{\Omega_0^{(2)}}(\mathcal{B})$ is satisfiable in $\mathcal{K}_2$ (if not, go back to Step 1). If it is satisfiable, return 'satisfiable'.
4. If all guesses fail, return 'unsatisfiable'.

Local finiteness with an effective bound of the theories $T_0^{(i)}$ entails that the functions $B_{T_0^{(i)}}$ are computable. Since the signatures $\Omega_0^{(i)}$ are finite, there are only finitely many guesses in Step 1, and we can effectively generate all of them. Steps 2 and 3 are effective since satisfiability of a finite set of literals in $\mathcal{K}_i$ $(i = 1, 2)$ is decidable by our assumption that the universal fragments of $\mathcal{K}_1$ and $\mathcal{K}_2$ are decidable. Thus, it is sufficient to show that the procedure is sound and complete.

To show *completeness*, suppose that the constraint Γ is satisfiable in $\mathcal{K}_1 +^* \mathcal{K}_2$. Thus, there is a structure $\mathcal{M} = (\mathcal{M}_1, \mathcal{M}_2, \ell^{\mathcal{M}}, r^{\mathcal{M}}) \in \mathcal{K}_1 +^* \mathcal{K}_2$ satisfying Γ. In particular, $\mathcal{M}_1 \in \mathcal{K}_1, \mathcal{M}_2 \in \mathcal{K}_2$, and $\ell^{\mathcal{M}} \dashv r^{\mathcal{M}}$ is an adjoint pair such that

$$\ell^{\mathcal{M}}(a_j) = b_j \quad \text{and} \quad r^{\mathcal{M}}(b_i') = a_i'.^4$$

Let $\mathcal{A}$ be the $\Omega_0^{(1)}$-substructure of $\mathcal{M}_1|_{\Omega_0^{(1)}}$ generated by $\{a_1, \ldots, a_n, a_1', \ldots, a_m'\}$, and $\mathcal{B}$ be the $\Omega_0^{(2)}$-substructure of $\mathcal{M}_2|_{\Omega_0^{(2)}}$ generated by $\{b_1, \ldots, b_n, b_1', \ldots, b_m'\}$. The $\Omega_0^{(i)}$-reduct $\mathcal{M}_i|_{\Omega_0^{(i)}}$ of $\mathcal{M}_i$ $(i = 1, 2)$ is a model of $T_0^{(i)}$. Since $T_0^{(i)}$ is universal, the substructures $\mathcal{A}, \mathcal{B}$ are also models of $T_0^{(1)}, T_0^{(2)}$, respectively. In particular, this implies that $\sqsubseteq$ is interpreted as a partial order in $\mathcal{A}$ and $\mathcal{B}$. Since the

---

[4] Here we identify (for the sake of simplicity) the constants a_j, a_i', b_j, b_i' with their interpretations in $\mathcal{M}_1, \mathcal{M}_2$.

theories $T_0^{(i)}$ are locally finite with an effective bound, the cardinalities of these substructures are bounded by the respective functions $B_{T_0^{(i)}}$.

We know $\mathcal{M}_1 \in \mathcal{K}_1$ satisfies Γ_1. In addition, since $\mathcal{A}$ is an $\Omega_0^{(1)}$-substructure of $\mathcal{M}_1$, Robinson's diagram theorem entails that $\mathcal{M}_1$ satisfies $\Delta_{\Omega_0^{(1)}}(\mathcal{A})$. Thus, $\Gamma_1 \cup \Delta_{\Omega_0^{(1)}}(\mathcal{A})$ is satisfiable in $\mathcal{K}_1$. The fact that $\Gamma_2 \cup \Delta_{\Omega_0^{(2)}}(\mathcal{B})$ is satisfiable in $\mathcal{K}_2$ can be shown in the same way.

To construct the adjoint pair $\mu \dashv \nu$, we consider the $\Omega_0^{(1)}$-embedding e and the $\Omega_0^{(2)}$-embedding f, where

$$e : \mathcal{A} \to \mathcal{M}_1|_{\Omega_0^{(1)}} \quad \text{and} \quad f : \mathcal{B} \to \mathcal{M}_2|_{\Omega_0^{(2)}}$$

are given by the inclusion maps. Since the theories $T_0^{(i)}$ guarantee adjoints, these embeddings have both left and right adjoints. Let us call f^* the left adjoint to f and e_* the right adjoint to e. We define

$$\mu := f^* \circ \ell^{\mathcal{M}} \circ e \quad \text{and} \quad \nu := e_* \circ r^{\mathcal{M}} \circ f.$$

Since adjoints compose, we have indeed $\mu \dashv \nu$. It remains to be shown that $\mu(a_j) = b_j$ and $\nu(b_i') = a_i'$. We restrict the attention to the first identity (as the second one can be proved symmetrically). We know that $\ell^{\mathcal{M}}(a_j) = b_j$, and since e is the inclusion map we have $e(a_j) = a_j$. Thus

$$\mu(a_j) = f^*(\ell^{\mathcal{M}}(e(a_j))) = f^*(\ell^{\mathcal{M}}(a_j)) = f^*(b_j).$$

Since f is the inclusion map, we have $f^*(b_j) = f(f^*(f(b_j)))$ and because $f^* \dashv f$ we know by (3) that $f(f^*(f(b_j))) = f(b_j) = b_j$. If we put all these identities together, we obtain $\mu(a_j) = b_j$.

To show *soundness*, we argue as follows. If $\Gamma_1 \cup \Delta_{\Omega_0^{(1)}}(\mathcal{A})$ is satisfiable in $\mathcal{K}_1$, then there is a structure $\mathcal{M}_1 \in \mathcal{K}_1$ that satisfies Γ_1 and has $\mathcal{A}$ as $\Omega_0^{(1)}$-substructure. The $\Omega_0^{(1)}$-reduct of $\mathcal{M}_1$ is a model of $T_0^{(1)}$, and since $T_0^{(1)}$ is universal this implies that the substructure $\mathcal{A}$ is also a model of $T_0^{(1)}$. Analogously, if $\Gamma_2 \cup \Delta_{\Omega_0^{(2)}}(\mathcal{B})$ is satisfiable in $\mathcal{K}_2$, then there is a structure $\mathcal{M}_2 \in \mathcal{K}_2$ that satisfies Γ_2 and has the model $\mathcal{B}$ of $T_0^{(2)}$ as $\Omega_0^{(2)}$-substructure.

In order to construct a structure $\mathcal{M} = (\mathcal{M}_1, \mathcal{M}_2, \ell^{\mathcal{M}}, r^{\mathcal{M}}) \in \mathcal{K}_1 +^* \mathcal{K}_2$ satisfying $\Gamma = \Gamma_0 \cup \Gamma_1 \cup \Gamma_2$, it is enough to construct the adjoint pair $\ell^{\mathcal{M}}, r^{\mathcal{M}}$ such that it extends the pair μ, ν provided by Step 2b of the procedure. Let

$$e : \mathcal{A} \to \mathcal{M}_1|_{\Omega_0^{(1)}} \quad \text{and} \quad f : \mathcal{B} \to \mathcal{M}_2|_{\Omega_0^{(2)}}$$

be the $\Omega_0^{(1)}$- and $\Omega_0^{(2)}$-embeddings of $\mathcal{A}, \mathcal{B}$ into the reducts of $\mathcal{M}_1, \mathcal{M}_2$, respectively. Without loss of generality we can assume that e, f are inclusion maps. Since the theories $T_0^{(i)}$ guarantee adjoints, these embeddings have both left and right adjoints. Let us call e^* the left adjoint to e and f_* the right adjoint to f. We define

$$\ell^{\mathcal{M}} := f \circ \mu \circ e^* \quad \text{and} \quad r^{\mathcal{M}} := e \circ \nu \circ f_*.$$

Since adjoints compose, we have again $\ell^{\mathcal{M}} \dashv r^{\mathcal{M}}$. It remains to be shown that $\mathcal{M} := (\mathcal{M}_1, \mathcal{M}_2, \ell^{\mathcal{M}}, r^{\mathcal{M}})$ satisfies Γ_0, i.e., $\ell^{\mathcal{M}}(a_j) = b_j$ and $r^{\mathcal{M}}(b_i') = a_i'$.[5]

Again, we restrict the attention to the first identity (as the second one can be proved symmetrically). We have $\mu(a_j) = b_j$, and $\ell^{\mathcal{M}}(a_j) = f(\mu(e^*(a_j))) = \mu(e^*(a_j))$ since f is the inclusion map. Thus, it is enough to show that $e^*(a_j) = a_j$. Since e is the inclusion map, we have $e^*(a_j) = e(e^*(e(a_j)))$ and because $e^* \dashv e$ we know by (3) that $e(e^*(e(a_j))) = e(a_j) = a_j$.   □

Proposition 2 and the above theorem yield the following transfer result for adjoint theory connections.

Corollary 6. *Let T_1, T_2 be adjoint combinable theories over the respective signatures Ω_1, Ω_2. Then the decidability of the universal fragments of T_1 and T_2 entails the decidability of the universal fragment of $T_1 +^* T_2$.*

4 Applications of the Transfer Result

In order to apply Theorem 5, we must find universal theories that extend the theory of posets, guarantee adjoints, and are locally finite with an effective bound. Given such theories $T_0^{(1)}, T_0^{(2)}$, every pair $\mathcal{K}_1, \mathcal{K}_2$ of classes of Ω_1- and Ω_2-structures whose members are models of $T_0^{(1)}, T_0^{(2)}$, respectively, satisfy the conditions of Theorem 5, and hence allow transfer of decidability (of the universal fragment) from $\mathcal{K}_1$ and $\mathcal{K}_2$ to $\mathcal{K}_1 +^* \mathcal{K}_2$.

In order to ensure the existence of adjoints for embeddings, it is enough that meets and joins exist and embeddings preserve them. For this reason, we start with the theory of bounded lattices since it provides us with meet and join. Recall that the theory T_L of *bounded lattices* is the theory of posets endowed with binary meet and join, and a least and a greatest element. In the following, we assume that the signature Ω_L of this theory contains the function symbols $\sqcup, 0$ for the join and the least element, the function symbols $\sqcap, 1$ for the meet and the greatest element, and the relation symbol $\sqsubseteq$ for the partial order. Note, however, that is not really necessary to have $\sqsubseteq$ explicitly in the signature since it can be expressed using meet or join (e.g., $x \sqsubseteq y$ iff $x \sqcup y = y$).

The theory T_L is not locally finite, but we can make it locally finite by adding as extra axioms all the identities that are true in a fixed *finite* lattice $\mathcal{A}$. The theory $T_{\mathcal{A}}$ obtained this way is locally finite: two n-variable terms cannot be distinct modulo $T_{\mathcal{A}}$ in case they are interpreted in $\mathcal{A}$ by the same n-ary function $A^n \to A$, and there are only finitely many such functions. This argument also yields an effective bound: if $|A| = c$, then $B_{T_{\mathcal{A}}}(n) = c^{c^n}$. In addition, $T_{\mathcal{A}}$ guarantees adjoints. To show this, consider an Ω_L-embedding $e : \mathcal{B} \to \mathcal{M}$ of a finitely generated model $\mathcal{B}$ of $T_{\mathcal{A}}$ into a model $\mathcal{M}$ of $T_{\mathcal{A}}$. Since $\mathcal{B}$ is a finite, it is a complete lattice, and the preservation of binary joins, meets, as well as the least

---

[5] As before, we identify (for the sake of simplicity) the constants a_j, a_i', b_j, b_i' with their interpretations in $\mathcal{M}_1, \mathcal{M}_2$.

and greatest element by e implies that e preserves all joins and meets. Thus, it has both a left and a right adjoint.

If we take as $\mathcal{A}$ the two element bounded lattice, then it is well known (see, e.g., [13]) that the theory $T_{\mathcal{A}}$ coincides with the theory T_D of *distributive* lattices, i.e., the extension of T_L by the distributivity axiom $x \sqcup (y \sqcap z) \approx (x \sqcup y) \sqcap (x \sqcup z)$.

Corollary 7. *Let $\mathcal{K}_1, \mathcal{K}_2$ be classes of Ω_1- and Ω_2-structures whose members are models of the theory T_D of distributive lattices. Then the decidability of the universal fragments of $\mathcal{K}_1, \mathcal{K}_2$ implies the decidability of the universal fragment of $\mathcal{K}_1 +^* \mathcal{K}_2$.*

Obviously, any pair of classes of frames over two Boolean-based signatures (see Example 3) satisfies the precondition of the above corollary.

Corollary 8. *Let Ω_1, Ω_2 be Boolean-based signatures, and $\mathcal{K}_1, \mathcal{K}_2$ be classes of Ω_1- and Ω_2-frames. Then the decidability of the universal fragments of $\mathcal{K}_1, \mathcal{K}_2$ implies the decidability of the universal fragment of $\mathcal{K}_1 +^* \mathcal{K}_2$.*

As shown in Example 3, a Boolean-based signature together with a class of frames corresponds to an ADS in the sense of [15]. To show the connection between Corollary 8 and the decidability transfer result proved in [15], we must relate the problem of deciding the universal fragment of a class of frames to the decision problem considered in [15].

Example 9. Consider a Boolean-based signature Ω and a class $\mathcal{K}$ of Ω-frames. Taking into account the Boolean structure and the (implicit or explicit) presence of the partial order $\sqsubseteq$, an Ω-constraint can be represented in the form

$$t_1 \sqsubseteq u_1, \ \ldots, \ t_n \sqsubseteq u_n, \ v_1 \not\approx 0, \ \ldots, \ v_m \not\approx 0.$$

We call such a constraint a *modal constraint*. It is satisfiable in $\mathcal{K}$ whenever there are $\mathcal{F}(W) \in \mathcal{K}$ and $w_1, \ldots, w_m \in W$ such that

$$t_1^{\mathcal{F}(W)} \subseteq u_1^{\mathcal{F}(W)}, \ \ldots, \ t_n^{\mathcal{F}(W)} \subseteq u_n^{\mathcal{F}(W)}, \ w_1 \in v_1^{\mathcal{F}(W)}, \ \ldots, \ w_m \in v_m^{\mathcal{F}(W)}.$$

If one restricts the attention to modal constraints with just one negated equation (i.e., if $m = 1$), then one obtains the traditional relativized satisfiability problem in modal logic. The satisfiability problem introduced in [15] is slightly more general since the set of constraints considered there can also contain object assertions involving relation symbols. As mentioned in Example 3, such assertions can currently not be handled by our approach. Consequently, our transfer result applies to a slightly more restricted satisfiability problem than the one considered in [15]. On the other hand, our result holds for more general theories and classes of structures, i.e., also ones that are not given by classes of frames.

Complexity Considerations. The complexity of the combination algorithm described in the proof of Theorem 5 can be quite high. It is non-deterministic since it guesses finitely generated structures up to a given bound, which may itself be quite large. In addition, the possibly large diagrams of these structures are part of the input for the decision procedures of the component theories.

Depending on the theories $T_0^{(i)}$, specific features of these theories may allow for sensible improvements, due for instance to the possibility of more succinct representations of the diagrams of models of $T_0^{(i)}$. We illustrate this phenomenon by showing how our combination algorithm can be improved in the case of adjoint connections of Boolean-based equational theories, as treated in Corollary 8. With this modified algorithm, we obtain complexity bounds that coincide with the ones shown in [15]. Actually, the algorithm obtained this way is also similar to the one described in [15]. It should be noted, however, that the correctness of this modified algorithm still follows from the proof of our general Theorem 5.

Thus, let Ω_1, Ω_2 be Boolean-based signatures, and $\mathcal{K}_1, \mathcal{K}_2$ be classes of Ω_1- and Ω_2-frames, respectively. As theories $T_0^{(1)}, T_0^{(2)}$ we can then take the theory BA of Boolean algebras. Let $\Gamma = \Gamma_0 \cup \Gamma_1 \cup \Gamma_2$ be a constraint, where Γ_i ($i = 1, 2$) is a set of literals over Ω_i (expanded with free constants), and Γ_0 is of the form

$$\Gamma_0 = \{\ell(a_1) \approx b_1, \dots, \ell(a_n) \approx b_n, r(b'_1) \approx a'_1, \dots, r(b'_m) \approx a'_m\}$$

for free constants a_j, b_j, a'_i, b'_i. If we follow the instructions in the proof of Theorem 5 literally, in order to guarantee the satisfiability of Γ, we must find:

1. a finite Boolean algebra $\mathcal{A}$ generated by $G_1 := \{a_1, \dots, a_n, a'_1, \dots, a'_m\}$ such that $\Gamma_1 \cup \Delta_{\Omega_{BA}}(\mathcal{A})$ is satisfiable in $\mathcal{K}_1$;
2. a finite Boolean algebra $\mathcal{B}$ generated by $G_2 := \{b_1, \dots, b_n, b'_1, \dots, b'_m\}$ such that $\Gamma_2 \cup \Delta_{\Omega_{BA}}(\mathcal{B})$ is satisfiable in $\mathcal{K}_2$;
3. an adjoint pair $\mu : \mathcal{A} \longrightarrow \mathcal{B}$ and $\nu : \mathcal{B} \longrightarrow \mathcal{A}$, such that

$$\mu(a_j) = b_j \ (j = 1, \dots, n) \quad \text{and} \quad \nu(b'_i) = a'_i \ (i = 1, \dots, m). \tag{4}$$

It is well known that a Boolean algebra generated by $n + m$ elements can have cardinality $2^{2^{n+m}}$, and hence its diagram may also be of doubly-exponential size. However, we will show that exponential space is sufficient to represent all the relevant information contained in such a diagram.

Let us call G_1-*minterm* a term τ that is of the form

$$\prod_{g \in G_1} \sigma_\tau(g),$$

where $\sigma_\tau(g)$ is either g or $\overline{g}$. Notice that the G_1-minterm τ is uniquely determined (up to associativity and commutativity of conjunction) by the function σ_τ, and hence there are as many G_1-minterms as there are subsets of G_1. We associate with every finite Boolean algebra $\mathcal{A}$ generated by G_1 the set $W_{\mathcal{A}}$ of the G_1-minterms τ such that $\mathcal{A} \models \tau \neq 0$. The following is not difficult to show:

(i) the map associating with $g \in G_1$ the set $\{\tau \in W_{\mathcal{A}} \mid \sigma_\tau(g) = g\}$ extends to an isomorphism $\iota_{\mathcal{A}} : \mathcal{A} \longrightarrow \wp(W_{\mathcal{A}})$;
(ii) $BA \models \Delta_{\Omega_{BA}}(\mathcal{A}) \Leftrightarrow \delta(\mathcal{A})$, where $\delta(\mathcal{A})$ is the conjunction of the formulas $\tau = 0$ for $\tau \notin W_{\mathcal{A}}$.

Fact (ii) means that $\delta(\mathcal{A})$ can replace $\Delta_{\Omega_{BA}}(\mathcal{A})$ in the consistency test of Step 1 above, and the same consideration obviously applies to $\mathcal{B}$ in Step 2. The size of $\delta(\mathcal{A})$ is singly-exponential, and to guess $\delta(\mathcal{A})$ it is sufficient to guess the set $W_{\mathcal{A}}$ (and not the whole $\mathcal{A}$).

A similar technique can be applied to Step 3. By Fact (i) above, we have $\mathcal{A} \simeq \wp(W_{\mathcal{A}})$ and $\mathcal{B} \simeq \wp(W_{\mathcal{B}})$. Hence, the considerations in Example 1 show that the adjoint pair of Step 3 is uniquely determined by a relation $E \subseteq W_{\mathcal{B}} \times W_{\mathcal{A}}$.

To sum up, the data that we are required to guess are simply a set $W_{\mathcal{A}}$ of G_1-minterms, a set $W_{\mathcal{B}}$ of G_2-minterms, and a relation E among them. All this is an exponential size guess, and thus can be done in non-deterministic exponential time. The decision procedures for the component theories receive exponential size instances of their constraint satisfiability problems as inputs. Finally, Condition (4) can be checked in exponential time. From the considerations in Example 1 and from Fact (ii) above, it follows that $\mu(a_j) = b_j$ is equivalent to the following statement:

$$\forall \tau \in W_{\mathcal{B}}. \ (\tau \in \iota_{\mathcal{B}}(b_j) \ \text{ iff } \ \exists \tau' \in W_{\mathcal{A}}. \ (\tau' \in \iota_{\mathcal{A}}(a_j) \wedge (\tau, \tau') \in E)).$$

Since $W_{\mathcal{A}}$ and $W_{\mathcal{B}}$ are of exponential size, this condition can be tested in exponential time. The same approach can be used to test the conditions $\nu(b_i') = a_i'$.

Overall, the improved combined decision procedure has the following complexity. Its starts with a non-deterministic exponential step that guesses the sets $\delta(\mathcal{A})$ and $\delta(\mathcal{B})$. Then it tests satisfiability in $\mathcal{K}_1$ and $\mathcal{K}_2$ of $\Gamma_1 \cup \delta(\mathcal{A})$ and $\Gamma_2 \cup \delta(\mathcal{B})$, respectively. The complexity of these tests is one exponential higher than the complexity of the decision procedures for $\mathcal{K}_1$ and $\mathcal{K}_2$. Testing Condition (4) needs exponential time. This shows that our combination procedure has the same complexity as the one for $\mathcal{E}$-connections described in [15].

Let us consider the complexity increase caused by the combination procedure in more detail for the complexity class ExpTime, which is often encountered when considering the relativized satisfiability problem in modal logic. Thus, assume that the decision procedures for $\mathcal{K}_1$ and $\mathcal{K}_2$ are in ExpTime. The combined decision procedure then generates doubly-exponentially many decision problems of exponential size for the component procedures. Each of these component decision problems can be decided in doubly-exponential time. This majorizes the exponential complexity of testing Condition (4). Thus, in this case the overall complexity of the combined decision procedure is 2ExpTime, i.e, one exponential higher than the complexity of the component procedures.

5   *N*-Ary Adjoint Connections

We sketch how our results can be extended to the case of n-ary connections by using parametrized notions of adjoints, as suggested in [10]. For simplicity, we limit ourselves to the case $n = 3$, and use a notation inspired by Lambek's syntactic calculus [16]. Let P_1, P_2, P_3 be posets. A triple $(\cdot, /, \backslash)$ of functions

$$\cdot : P_1 \times P_2 \to P_3, \qquad \backslash : P_1 \times P_3 \to P_2, \qquad / : P_3 \times P_2 \to P_1$$

is an *adjoint triple* iff the following holds for all $a_1 \in P_1, a_2 \in P_2, a_3 \in P_3$:

$$a_1 \cdot a_2 \leq a_3 \quad \text{iff} \quad a_2 \leq a_1 \backslash a_3 \quad \text{iff} \quad a_1 \leq a_3 / a_2.$$

To illustrate this definition, we consider a ternary variant of Example 1.

Example 10. Suppose we are given three sets W_1, W_2, W_3 and a ternary relation $E \subseteq W_3 \times W_2 \times W_1$. With two given subsets $a_1 \subseteq W_1, a_2 \subseteq W_2$, we can associate a subset $a_1 \cdot_E a_2 \subseteq W_3$ as follows:

$$a_1 \cdot_E a_2 := \{w_3 \mid \exists (w_2, w_1) \in W_2 \times W_1. \ (w_3, w_2, w_1) \in E \wedge w_1 \in a_1 \wedge w_2 \in a_2\}.$$

If we fix a_1, the function $a_1 \cdot_E (-) : \wp(W_2) \to \wp(W_3)$ preserves all joins, and hence has a right adjoint $a_1 \backslash_E (-) : \wp(W_3) \to \wp(W_2)$, which can be described as follows: for every $a_3 \subseteq W_3$, the subset $a_1 \backslash_E a_3 \subseteq W_2$ is defined as

$$a_1 \backslash_E a_3 := \{w_2 \mid \forall (w_3, w_1) \in W_3 \times W_1. \ (w_3, w_2, w_1) \in E \wedge w_1 \in a_1 \Rightarrow w_3 \in a_3\}.$$

Similarly, if we fix a_2, the function $(-) \cdot_E a_2 : \wp(W_1) \to \wp(W_3)$ preserves all joins, and hence has a right adjoint $(-)/_E a_2 : \wp(W_3) \to \wp(W_1)$, which can be described as follows: for every $a_3 \subseteq W_3$, the subset $a_3 /_E a_2 \subseteq W_1$ is defined as

$$a_3 /_E a_2 := \{w_1 \mid \forall (w_3, w_2) \in W_3 \times W_2. \ (w_3, w_2, w_1) \in E \wedge w_2 \in a_2 \Rightarrow w_3 \in a_3\}.$$

It is easy to see that the three binary operators $(\cdot_E, /_E, \backslash_E)$ fulfill the definition of an adjoint triple (with set inclusion as partial order). Conversely every adjoint triple (for set inclusion) is induced in this way by a unique ternary relation E.

Using the notion of an adjoint triple, we can now define a ternary variant of the notion of an adjoint connection. Let $\Omega_1, \Omega_2, \Omega_3$, be three disjoint signatures containing binary predicate symbols $\sqsubseteq^i$ of arity $S^i S^i$ $(i = 1, 2, 3)$. The combined signature $+^*(\Omega_1, \Omega_2, \Omega_3)$ contains the union $\Omega_1 \cup \Omega_2 \cup \Omega_3$ of the signatures $\Omega_1, \Omega_2, \Omega_3$ and, in addition, three new function symbols $\cdot, \backslash, /$ of arity $S^1 S^2 S^3$, $S^1 S^3 S^2$ and $S^3 S^2 S^1$, respectively. For $i = 1, 2, 3$, let $\mathcal{K}_i$ be a class of Ω_i-structures such that each of the structures in $\mathcal{K}_i$ interprets $\sqsubseteq^i$ as a partial order on the interpretation of S^i. The *ternary adjoint connection* $+^*(\mathcal{K}_1, \mathcal{K}_2, \mathcal{K}_3)$ of $\mathcal{K}_1, \mathcal{K}_2, \mathcal{K}_3$ consists of those $+^*(\Omega_1, \Omega_2, \Omega_3)$-structures $(\mathcal{M}^1, \mathcal{M}^2, \mathcal{M}^3, \cdot^\mathcal{M}, \backslash^\mathcal{M}, /^\mathcal{M})$ for which $\mathcal{M}^1 \in \mathcal{K}_1$, $\mathcal{M}^2 \in \mathcal{K}_2$, $\mathcal{M}^3 \in \mathcal{K}_3$, and $(\cdot^\mathcal{M}, \backslash^\mathcal{M}, /^\mathcal{M})$ is an adjoint triple for the underlying posets.

Using the observations made in Example 10, it is easy to see that the ternary adjoint connection corresponds to the basic $\mathcal{E}$-connection of three ADSs. Under the same conditions as in Theorem 5, and with a very similar proof, we can show that decidability of the universal fragment also transfers to ternary adjoint connections.

Theorem 11. *Let $\mathcal{K}_1, \mathcal{K}_2, \mathcal{K}_3$ be adjoint combinable classes of structures over the respective signatures $\Omega_1, \Omega_2, \Omega_3$. Then decidability of the universal fragments of $\mathcal{K}_1, \mathcal{K}_2, \mathcal{K}_3$ entails decidability of the universal fragment of $+^*(\mathcal{K}_1, \mathcal{K}_2, \mathcal{K}_3)$.*

6   Conclusion

The main motivation of this work was to develop an algebraic generalization of the decidability transfer results for $\mathcal{E}$-connections shown in [15]. On the one hand, our approach is more general than the one in [15] since it also applies to theories and classes of structures that are not given by ADSs (i.e., classes of frames). More generally, since the theories $T_0^{(1)}, T_0^{(2)}$ need not be the theory of Boolean algebras and since $T_0^{(1)}$ need not coincide with $T_0^{(2)}$, we do not require the underlying logic to be classical propositional logic, and the components may even be based on different logics. On the other hand, we currently cannot handle the relational object assertions considered in [15], and we cannot deal with extensions of the basic $\mathcal{E}$-connection approach such as applying Boolean operations to connecting relations. It is the topic of future research to find out whether such extensions and relational object assertions can be expressed in our algebraic setting.

The paper [1] has the same motivation, but follows a different route towards generalizing $\mathcal{E}$-connections. In the present paper, we used as our starting point the observation that the pair $(\Diamond, \Box^-)$ consisting of the diamond operator induced by the connecting relation E, and the box operator induced by its inverse E^- is an adjoint pair for the partial order $\leq$ defined as $x \leq y$ iff $x \sqcup y = y$, where $\sqcup$ is the Boolean disjunction operator. In [1] we used instead the fact that the diamond operator behaves like a homomorphism for $\sqcup$, i.e., $\Diamond(x \sqcup y) = \Diamond(x) \sqcup \Diamond(y)$. This was generalized to the case of connection functions that behave like homomorphisms for an arbitrary shared subsignature of the theories to be combined. The conditions required in [1] for the transfer of decidability are model-theoretic conditions on a shared subtheory T_0 and its algebraic compatibility with the component theories T_1, T_2. There are examples of theories T_0, T_1, T_2 satisfying these requirements that are quite different from theories induced by (modal) logics. However, there is a price to be payed for this generality: since no partial order is required, it is not possible to model pairs of connection functions that are induced by a connecting relation and its inverse. In contrast, the conditions considered in the present paper are abstract algebraic conditions, which do not look at the structure of models. They require the existence of certain adjoint functions for embeddings between models of subtheories of the component theories. These subtheories need not be identical for different component theories, and there is no additional compatibility requirement between the subtheories and the component theories. In order to require adjoints, we must, however, assume that the models are equipped with a partial order. In addition, one possibility to guarantee the existence of adjoints is to assume that the subtheories provide us with meets and joins. In this case, the theories that we obtain are quite close to theories induced by logics, though not necessarily classical propositional logic.

References

1. F. Baader and S. Ghilardi. Connecting many-sorted theories. In *Proc. CADE-20*, Springer LNAI 3632, 2005. Extended version available on-line at `http://lat.inf.tu-dresden.de/research/reports.html`.

2. F. Baader, S. Ghilardi, and C. Tinelli. A new combination procedure for the word problem that generalizes fusion decidability results in modal logics. In *Proc. IJCAR'04*, Springer LNAI 3097, 2004.

3. F. Baader, C. Lutz, H. Sturm, and F. Wolter. Fusions of description logics and abstract description systems. *J. Artificial Intelligence Research*, 16:1–58, 2002.

4. F. Baader and C. Tinelli. A new approach for combining decision procedures for the word problem, and its connection to the Nelson-Oppen combination method. In *Proc. CADE-14*, Springer LNAI 1249, 1997.

5. F. Baader and C. Tinelli. Deciding the word problem in the union of equational theories. *Information and Computation*, 178(2):346–390, 2002.

6. Ch.-Ch. Chang and H. J. Keisler. *Model Theory*. North-Holland, 3rd edition, 1990.

7. E. Domenjoud, F. Klay, and Ch. Ringeissen. Combination techniques for non-disjoint equational theories. In *Proc. CADE-12*, Springer LNAI 814, 1994.

8. C. Fiorentini and S. Ghilardi. Combining word problems through rewriting in categories with products. *Theoretical Computer Science*, 294:103–149, 2003.

9. J. H. Gallier. *Logic for Computer Science: Foundations of Automatic Theorem Proving*. Harper & Row, 1986.

10. S. Ghilardi and G. C. Meloni. Modal logics with n-ary connectives. *Zeitschrift für Mathematische Logik und Grundlagen der Mathematik*, 36(3):193–215, 1990.

11. S. Ghilardi. Model-theoretic methods in combined constraint satisfiability. *J. Automated Reasoning*, 33(3–4): 221–249, 2004.

12. S. Ghilardi and M. Zawadowski. *Sheaves, Games and Model Completions*, volume 14 of *Trends in Logic*. Kluwer Academic Publishers, 2002.

13. G. Grätzer. *General lattice theory*. Birkhäuser Verlag, Basel, second edition, 1998.

14. M. Kracht and F. Wolter. Properties of independently axiomatizable bimodal logics. *J. Symbolic Logic*, 56(4):1469–1485, 1991.

15. O. Kutz, C. Lutz, F. Wolter, and M. Zakharyaschev. $\mathcal{E}$-connections of abstract description systems. *Artificial Intelligence*, 156:1–73, 2004.

16. J. Lambek. The mathematics of sentence structure. *The American Mathematical Monthly*, 65:154–170, 1958.

17. G. Nelson. Combining satisfiability procedures by equality-sharing. In *Automated Theorem Proving: After 25 Years*, volume 29 of *Contemporary Mathematics*, pages 201–211. American Mathematical Society, 1984.

18. G. Nelson and D. C. Oppen. Simplification by cooperating decision procedures. *ACM Trans. on Programming Languages and Systems*, 1(2):245–257, October 1979.

19. T. Nipkow. Combining matching algorithms: The regular case. *J. Symbolic Computation*, 12:633–653, 1991.

20. D. Pigozzi. The join of equational theories. *Colloquium Mathematicum*, 30(1):15–25, 1974.

21. E. Spaan. *Complexity of Modal Logics*. PhD thesis, Department of Mathematics and Computer Science, University of Amsterdam, The Netherlands, 1993.

22. C. Tinelli and Ch. Ringeissen. Unions of non-disjoint theories and combinations of satisfiability procedures. *Theoretical Computer Science*, 290(1):291–353, 2003.

23. F. Wolter. Fusions of modal logics revisited. In *Proc. Advances in Modal Logic*, CSLI, Stanford, 1998.

Combining Data Structures with Nonstably Infinite Theories Using Many-Sorted Logic*

Silvio Ranise[1], Christophe Ringeissen[1], and Calogero G. Zarba[2]

[1] LORIA and INRIA-Lorraine
[2] University of New Mexico

Abstract. Most computer programs store elements of a given nature into container-based data structures such as lists, arrays, sets, and multisets. To verify the correctness of these programs, one needs to combine a theory S modeling the data structure with a theory T modeling the elements. This combination can be achieved using the classic Nelson-Oppen method only if both S and T are stably infinite.

The goal of this paper is to relax the stable infiniteness requirement. To achieve this goal, we introduce the notion of *polite* theories, and we show that natural examples of polite theories include those modeling data structures such as lists, arrays, sets, and multisets. Furthermore, we provide a method that is able to combine a polite theory S with any theory T of the elements, regardless of whether T is stably infinite or not.

The results of this paper generalize to many-sorted logic those recently obtained by Tinelli and Zarba concerning the combination of *shiny* theories with nonstably infinite theories in one-sorted logic.

1 Introduction

In program verification one has often to decide the satisfiability or validity of logical formulae involving data structures such as lists, arrays, sets, and multisets. These data structures can be considered as structured containers of elements of a given nature. For instance, one may want to reason about lists of integers, sets of booleans, or multisets of reals.

One way to reason about data structures over elements of a given nature is to use the Nelson-Oppen method in order to modularly combine a decision procedure for a theory S modeling the data structure with a decision procedure for a theory T modeling the elements. However, this solution requires that both S and T be *stably infinite*. Unfortunately, this requirement is not satisfied by many practically relevant theories such as, for instance, the theory of booleans, the theory of integers modulo n, and the theory of fixed-width bit-vectors [8].

Recently, Tinelli and Zarba [13] introduced a generalization of the one-sorted version of the Nelson-Oppen method in order to combine theories that are not

---

* This work is partly supported by grants NSF ITR CCR-0113611, NSF CCR-0098114, and projects ACI GECCOO, and QSL VALDA-2.

B. Gramlich (Ed.): FroCoS 2005, LNAI 3717, pp. 48–64, 2005.

stably infinite. More precisely, they introduce the notion of *shiny* theories, and prove that a shiny theory S can be combined with any other arbitrary theory T, even if the latter is not stably infinite. They also provide a list of shiny theories which includes the theory of equality, the theory of partial orders, the theory of total orders, and the theory of bounded lattices.

Despite these promising results, Tinelli and Zarba's method has two drawbacks.

First, when combining a shiny theory S, one has to compute a function $mincard_S$. This function takes as input an S-satisfiable conjunction Γ of literals, and returns the minimal cardinality k for which there is a T-model of Γ of cardinality k. Although $mincard_S$ is computable for a wide class of theories, its complexity is in general *NP*-hard. Due to this high complexity, it is natural to study how to avoid the computation of $mincard_S$.

Second, the notion of shininess is too strong, and it may be very difficult to find further examples of practically relevant shiny theories. We believe that this difficulty is due to the fact that the notion of shiny theories was introduced in one-sorted logic.

In this paper we are interested in the problem of combining a theory S modeling a data structure with a nonstably infinite theory T modeling the elements. More in detail, the contributions of this paper are:

1. In order to sidestep the difficulties of finding shiny theories, we operate in many-sorted logic rather than in one-sorted logic.
2. We introduce the notion of *polite* theories, and we prove that natural examples of polite theories are those modeling data structures such as lists, arrays, sets, and multisets.
3. We provide a new combination method that is able to combine a polite theory S with any theory T, regardless of whether T is stably infinite or not.
4. We generalize the notion of shininess from one-sorted logic to many-sorted logic, and we prove that—under rather weak assumptions—shininess is equivalent to politeness in one-sorted logic. The equivalence is less clear in many-sorted logic.

The crux of our combination method is to modify the Nelson-Oppen method. The nondeterministic version of this method consists in guessing an arrangement over the set of shared variables. This arrangement is used to build equalities and disequalities between variables, to constrain simultaneously the inputs of decision procedures for component theories. Our modification is related to the variables involved in an arrangement; precisely:

Modification 1: Guess an arrangement over an extended set of variables, and not just the shared ones. For correctness, the extended arrangement must also contain opportunely introduced fresh variables, whose role is to witness that certain facts hold for the data structure.

Our method does not require the computation of a $mincard_S$ function, and it is therefore easier to implement than the one presented in [13].

Related work. Implicit versions of Modification 1 were already used by Zarba in order to combine the theory of sets [15] and the theory of multisets [14] with any arbitrary theory T of the elements, even if T is not stably infinite.

The first explicit version of Modification 1 is due to Fontaine and Gribomont [6] who combine the theory of arrays with any other nonstably infinite theory T not containing the sort array. Their result applies to conjunctions of literals not containing disequalities between terms of sort array.

The latest explicit version of Modification 1 was used by Fontaine, Ranise, and Zarba [7], in order to combine a nonstably infinite theory T of the elements with the theory T_{length} of lists of elements with length constraints.

Baader and Ghilardi [1,2] have recently introduced a new method for combining theories over nondisjoint signatures using many-sorted logic. Their result for theories over nondisjoint signatures—together with ours for nonstably infinite theories—shows that it is very convenient to combine theories using many-sorted logic.

Organization of the paper. In Section 2 we introduce some preliminary notions, as well as the concept of polite theories. In Section 3 we present our combination method. In Section 4 we compare the notion of polite theories with the notion of shiny theories. In Section 5 we prove that natural examples of polite theories are those modeling data structures. In Section 6 we draw conclusions from our work. For lack of space, most proofs are omitted. They can be found in the extended version of this paper [10].

2   Preliminaries

2.1   Syntax

A *signature* Σ is a triple (S, F, P) where S is a set of sorts, F is a set of function symbols, P is a set of predicate symbols, and all the symbols in F, P have arities constructed using the sorts in S. Given a signature $\Sigma = (S, F, P)$, we write Σ^{S} for S, Σ^{F} for F, and Σ^{P} for P. If $\Sigma_1 = (S_1, F_1, P_1)$ and $\Sigma_2 = (S_2, F_2, P_2)$ are signatures, their *union* is the signature $\Sigma_1 \cup \Sigma_2 = (S_1 \cup S_2, F_1 \cup F_2, P_1 \cup P_2)$.

Given a signature Σ, we assume the standard notions of Σ-*term*, Σ-*literal*, and Σ-*formula*. A Σ-*sentence* is a Σ-formula with no free variables. A literal is *flat* if it is of the form $x \approx y$, $x \not\approx y$, $x \approx f(y_1, \ldots, y_n)$, $p(y_1, \ldots, y_n)$, and $\neg p(y_1, \ldots, y_n)$, where $x, y, y_1, \ldots, y_n$ are variables, f is a function symbol, and p is a predicate symbol.

If t is a term, we denote with $vars_\sigma(t)$ the set of variables of sort σ occurring in t. Similarly, if φ is a formula, we denote with $vars_\sigma(\varphi)$ the set of free variables of sort σ occurring in t. If φ is either a term or a formula, we denote with $vars(\varphi)$ the set $\bigcup_\sigma vars_\sigma(\varphi)$. Finally, if Φ is a set of terms or a set of formulae, we let $vars_\sigma(\Phi) = \bigcup_{\varphi \in \Phi} vars_\sigma(\varphi)$ and $vars(\Phi) = \bigcup_{\varphi \in \Phi} vars(\varphi)$.

In the rest of this paper, we identify conjunctions of formulae $\varphi_1 \wedge \cdots \wedge \varphi_n$ with the set $\{\varphi_1, \ldots, \varphi_n\}$.

2.2 Semantics

Definition 1. Let Σ be a signature, and let X be a set of variables whose sorts are in Σ^S. A Σ-INTERPRETATION $\mathcal{A}$ over X is a map which interprets each sort $\sigma \in \Sigma^S$ as a non-empty domain A_σ, each variable $x \in X$ of sort σ as an element $x^{\mathcal{A}} \in A_\sigma$, each function symbol $f \in \Sigma^F$ of arity $\sigma_1 \times \cdots \times \sigma_n \rightarrow \tau$ as a function $f^{\mathcal{A}} : A_{\sigma_1} \times \cdots \times A_{\sigma_n} \rightarrow A_\tau$, and each predicate symbol $p \in \Sigma^P$ of arity $\sigma_1 \times \cdots \times \sigma_n$ as a subset $p^{\mathcal{A}}$ of $A_{\sigma_1} \times \cdots \times A_{\sigma_n}$.

A Σ-STRUCTURE is a Σ-interpretation over an empty set of variables. □

A Σ-formula φ over a set X of variables is *satisfiable* if it is true in some Σ-interpretation over X. Two Σ-formulae φ and ψ over a set X of variables are *equivalent* if $\varphi^{\mathcal{A}} = \psi^{\mathcal{A}}$, for all Σ-interpretations over X.

Let $\mathcal{A}$ be an Ω-interpretation over some set V of variables. For a signature $\Sigma \subseteq \Omega$ and a set of variables $U \subseteq V$, we denote with $\mathcal{A}^{\Sigma,U}$ the interpretation obtained from $\mathcal{A}$ by restricting it to interpret only the symbols in Σ and the variables in U. Furthermore, we let $\mathcal{A}^{\Sigma} = \mathcal{A}^{\Sigma,\emptyset}$.

2.3 Theories

Following Ganzinger [9], we define theories as sets of structures rather than as sets of sentences. More formally, we give the following definition.

Definition 2. A Σ-THEORY is a pair $(\Sigma, \mathbf{A})$ where Σ is a signature and $\mathbf{A}$ is a class of Σ-structures. Given a theory $T = (\Sigma, \mathbf{A})$, a T-INTERPRETATION is a Σ-interpretation $\mathcal{A}$ such that $\mathcal{A}^{\Sigma} \in \mathbf{A}$. □

Given a Σ-theory T, a Σ-formula φ over a set X of variables is T-*satisfiable* if it is true in some T-interpretation over X. We write $\mathcal{A} \models_T \varphi$ when $\mathcal{A}$ is a T-interpretation satisfying φ. Given a Σ-theory T, two Σ-formulae φ and ψ over a set X of variables are T-*equivalent* if $\varphi^{\mathcal{A}} = \psi^{\mathcal{A}}$, for all T-interpretations over X.

Given a Σ-theory T, the *quantifier-free satisfiability problem* of T is the problem of deciding, for each quantifier-free Σ-formula φ, whether or not φ is T-satisfiable.

Definition 3 (Combination). Let $T_i = (\Sigma_i, \mathbf{A}_i)$ be a theory, for $i = 1, 2$. The COMBINATION of T_1 and T_2 is the theory $T_1 \oplus T_2 = (\Sigma, \mathbf{A})$ where $\Sigma = \Sigma_1 \cup \Sigma_2$ and $\mathbf{A} = \{\mathcal{A} \mid \mathcal{A}^{\Sigma_1} \in \mathbf{A}_1 \text{ and } \mathcal{A}^{\Sigma_2} \in \mathbf{A}_2\}$. □

If Φ is a set of Σ-sentences, we let $Theory^{\Sigma}(\Phi) = (\Sigma, \mathbf{A})$ be the theory such that $\mathbf{A}$ is the class of all Σ-structures satisfying Φ.

Proposition 4. *Let Φ_i be a set of Σ_i-sentences, for $i = 1, 2$. Then*

$$Theory^{\Sigma_1}(\Phi_1) \oplus Theory^{\Sigma_2}(\Phi_2) = Theory^{\Sigma_1 \cup \Sigma_2}(\Phi_1 \cup \Phi_2).$$ □

We introduce below several classes of theories. We will see how they relate in Remark 10.

Definition 5 (Finite model property). Let Σ be a signature, let $S \subseteq \Sigma^S$ be a set of sorts, and let T be a Σ-theory. We say that T has the FINITE MODEL PROPERTY with respect to S if for every T-satisfiable quantifier-free Σ-formula φ there exists a T-interpretation $\mathcal{A}$ satisfying φ such that A_σ is finite, for each sort $\sigma \in S$. □

Definition 6 (Stable infiniteness). Let Σ be a signature, let $S \subseteq \Sigma^S$ be a set of sorts, and let T be a Σ-theory. We say that T is STABLY INFINITE with respect to S if for every T-satisfiable quantifier-free Σ-formula φ there exists a T-interpretation $\mathcal{A}$ satisfying φ such that A_σ is infinite, for each sort $\sigma \in S$. □

Definition 7 (Smoothness). Let Σ be a signature, let $S = \{\sigma_1, \ldots, \sigma_n\} \subseteq \Sigma^S$ be a set of sorts, and let T be a Σ-theory. We say that T is SMOOTH with respect to S if:

- for every T-satisfiable quantifier-free Σ-formula φ,
- for every T-interpretation $\mathcal{A}$ satisfying φ,
- for every cardinal number $\kappa_1, \ldots, \kappa_n$ such that $\kappa_i \geq |A_{\sigma_i}|$, for $i = 1, \ldots, n$,

there exists a T-interpretation $\mathcal{B}$ satisfying φ such that

$$|B_{\sigma_i}| = \kappa_i, \qquad\qquad \text{for } i = 1, \ldots, n.$$ □

Definition 8 (Finite witnessability). Let Σ be a signature, let $S \subseteq \Sigma^S$ be a set of sorts, and let T be a Σ-theory. We say that T is FINITELY WITNESSABLE with respect to S if there exists a computable function *witness* that for every quantifier-free Σ-formula φ returns a quantifier-free Σ-formula $\psi = witness(\varphi)$ such that:

(i) φ and $(\exists \bar{v})\psi$ are T-equivalent, where $\bar{v} = vars(\psi) \setminus vars(\varphi)$;
(ii) if ψ is T-satisfiable then there exists a T-interpretation $\mathcal{A}$ satisfying ψ such that $A_\sigma = [vars_\sigma(\psi)]^{\mathcal{A}}$, for each $\sigma \in S$. □

Definition 9 (Politeness). Let Σ be a signature, let $S \subseteq \Sigma^S$ be a set of sorts, and let T be a Σ-theory. We say that T is POLITE with respect to S if it is both smooth and finitely witnessable with respect to S. □

Remark 10. Let Σ be a signature, let $S \subseteq \Sigma^S$, and let T be a Σ-theory. Then the following holds (cf. Figure 1):

- If T is smooth with respect to S then T is stably infinite with respect to S.
- If T is finitely witnessable with respect to S then T has the finite model property with respect to S. □

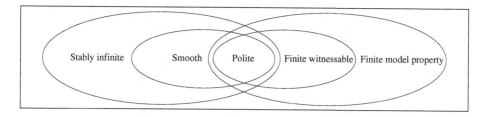

Fig. 1. Relationships between classes of theories

3   The Combination Method

Let T_i be a Σ_i-theory, for $i = 1, 2$, and let $S = \Sigma_1^S \cap \Sigma_2^S$. Assume that:

- the quantifier-free satisfiability problem of T_i is decidable, for $i = 1, 2$;
- $\Sigma_1^F \cap \Sigma_2^F = \emptyset$ and $\Sigma_1^P \cap \Sigma_2^P = \emptyset$;
- T_2 is polite with respect to S.

In this section we describe a method for combining the decision procedures for the quantifier-free satisfiability problems of T_1 and of T_2 in order to decide the quantifier-free satisfiability problem of $T_1 \oplus T_2$. Without loss of generality, we restrict ourselves to conjunctions of literals.

The combination method consists of four phases: *variable abstraction*, *witness introduction*, *decomposition*, and *check*.

First phase: variable abstraction. Let Γ be a conjunction of $(\Sigma_1 \cup \Sigma_2)$-literals. The output of the variable abstraction phase is a conjunction $\Gamma_1 \cup \Gamma_2$ satisfying the following properties:

(a) each literal in Γ_i is a Σ_i-literal, for $i = 1, 2$;
(b) $\Gamma_1 \cup \Gamma_2$ is $(T_1 \oplus T_2)$-satisfiable if and only if Γ is $(T_1 \oplus T_2)$-satisfiable.

Note that properties (a) and (b) can be effectively enforced with the help of fresh variables. We call $\Gamma_1 \cup \Gamma_2$ a conjunction of literals in *separate* form.

Second phase: witness introduction. Let $\Gamma_1 \cup \Gamma_2$ be a conjunction of literals in separate form returned in the variable abstraction phase. In the witness introduction phase we compute $\psi_2 = witness_{T_2}(\Gamma_2)$, and we output $\Gamma_1 \cup \{\psi_2\}$. Intuitively, this phase introduces the fresh variables in $vars(\psi_2) \setminus vars(\Gamma)$, whose role is to witness that certain facts hold for the polite theory T_2.[1]

Third phase: decomposition. Let $\Gamma_1 \cup \{\psi_2\}$ be the conjunction obtained in the witness introduction phase. Let $V_\sigma = vars_\sigma(\psi_2)$ for each $\sigma \in S$, and let $V = \bigcup_{\sigma \in S} V_\sigma$. In the decomposition phase we nondeterministically guess a family E

---

[1] For instance, in the theory of arrays a literal $a \not\approx_{\mathsf{array}} b$ implies that there is an index i such that $\mathsf{read}(a, i) \not\approx \mathsf{read}(b, i)$. Then, i can be thought of as a witness of $a \not\approx_{\mathsf{array}} b$.

of equivalence relations $E = \{E_\sigma \subseteq V_\sigma \times V_\sigma \mid \sigma \in S\}$. Then, we construct the *arrangement* of V induced by E, defined by

$$arr(V, E) = \{x \approx y \mid (x, y) \in E_\sigma \text{ and } \sigma \in S\} \cup$$
$$\{x \not\approx y \mid (x, y) \in (V_\sigma \times V_\sigma) \setminus E_\sigma \text{ and } \sigma \in S\},$$

and we output the conjunction $\Gamma_1 \cup \{\psi_2\} \cup arr(V, E)$.

Fourth phase: check. Let $\Gamma_1 \cup \{\psi_2\} \cup arr(V, E)$ be a conjunction obtained in the decomposition phase. The check phase consists in performing the following steps:

Step 1. If $\Gamma_1 \cup arr(V, E)$ is T_1-satisfiable go to the next step; otherwise output `fail`.

Step 2. If $\{\psi_2\} \cup arr(V, E)$ is T_2-satisfiable go to the next step; otherwise output `fail`.

Step 3. output `succeed`.

3.1   An Example

Let Σ_1 be the signature containing a sort elem, as well as two constant symbols a and b of sort elem. Consider the Σ_1-theory $T_1 = \mathit{Theory}^{\Sigma_1}(\Phi_1)$, where

$$\Phi_1 = \{(\forall_{\mathsf{elem}}\ x)(x \approx a \ \lor \ x \approx b)\}\ .$$

Clearly, for every T_1-interpretation $\mathcal{A}$, we have $|A_{\mathsf{elem}}| \leq 2$. Therefore, T_1 is not stably infinite with respect to {elem}.

Next, consider the Σ_{set}-theory T_{set} of sets of elements. The signature Σ_{set} contains, among other set-theoretical symbols, a sort elem for elements, and a sort set for sets of elements. The theory T_{set} will be defined more formally in Subsection 5.4. For this example, it suffices to know that T_{set} is polite with respect to {elem}.

Next, consider the following conjunction Γ of $(\Sigma_1 \cup \Sigma_{\mathsf{set}})$-literals:

$$\Gamma = \begin{cases} a \approx b, \\ x \not\approx \emptyset, \\ y \not\approx \emptyset, \\ x \cap y \approx \emptyset \end{cases},$$

where x and y are set-variables.

Note that Γ is $(T_1 \oplus T_{\mathsf{set}})$-unsatisfiable. To see this, assume by contradiction that $\mathcal{A}$ is a $(T_1 \oplus T_{\mathsf{set}})$-interpretation such that Γ is true in $\mathcal{A}$. By the first literal in Γ, we have $|A_{\mathsf{elem}}| = 1$. However, by the three last literals in Γ, we have $|A_{\mathsf{elem}}| \geq 2$, a contradiction.

We want to formally detect that Γ is $(T_1 \oplus T_{\mathsf{set}})$-unsatisfiable by using our combination method.

Since all literals in Γ are either Σ_1-literals or Σ_{set}-literals, in the variable abstraction phase we do not need to introduce fresh variables, and we simply return the two conjunctions:

$$\Gamma_1 = \left\{ a \approx b \right\}, \qquad\qquad \Gamma_{\text{set}} = \left\{ \begin{array}{l} x \not\approx \emptyset, \\ y \not\approx \emptyset, \\ x \cap y \approx \emptyset \end{array} \right\}.$$

In the witness introduction phase we need to compute $witness_{\text{set}}(\Gamma_{\text{set}})$. The intuition behind the computation of $witness_{\text{set}}(\Gamma_{\text{set}})$ is as follows.[2]

The literal $x \not\approx \emptyset$ implies the existence of an element w_x in x. Likewise, the literal $y \not\approx \emptyset$ implies the existence of an element w_y in y. The output of $witness_{\text{set}}(\Gamma_{\text{set}})$ is a conjunction Δ_{set} that makes explicit the existence of the elements w_x and w_y. We can do this by letting

$$\Delta_{\text{set}} = \left\{ \begin{array}{l} w_x \in x, \\ w_y \in y, \\ x \cap y \approx \emptyset \end{array} \right\}.$$

Note that Γ_{set} and $(\exists_{\text{elem}}\ w_x)(\exists_{\text{elem}}\ w_y)\Delta_{\text{set}}$ are T_{set}-equivalent.

In the decomposition phase we need to guess an equivalence relation E_{elem} over the variables in $vars_{\text{elem}}(\Delta_{\text{set}})$. Since $vars_{\text{elem}}(\Delta_{\text{set}}) = \{w_x, w_y\}$, there are two possible choices: either we guess $(w_x, w_y) \in E_{\text{elem}}$ or we guess $(w_x, w_y) \notin E_{\text{elem}}$.

If we guess $(w_x, w_y) \in E_{\text{elem}}$ then we have that $\Delta_{\text{set}} \cup \{w_x \approx w_y\}$ is T_{set}-unsatisfiable, and we will output `fail` in step 2 of the check phase. If instead we guess $(w_x, w_y) \notin E_{\text{elem}}$ then we have that $\Gamma_1 \cup \{w_x \not\approx w_y\}$ is T_1-unsatisfiable, and we will output `fail` in step 1 of the check phase.

Since the check phase outputs `fail` for any equivalence relation E_{elem} of $vars_{\text{elem}}(\Delta_{\text{set}})$, our combination method correctly concludes that Γ is $(T_1 \oplus T_{\text{set}})$-unsatisfiable.

3.2   Correctness and Complexity

The correctness of our combination method is based on the following Combination Theorem, which is a particular case of a combination result holding for order-sorted logic [12].

Theorem 11 (Combination). *Let Σ_1 and Σ_2 be signatures such that $\Sigma_1^{\text{F}} \cap \Sigma_2^{\text{F}} = \emptyset$ and $\Sigma_1^{\text{P}} \cap \Sigma_2^{\text{P}} = \emptyset$. Also, let Φ_i be a set of Σ_i-formulae, for $i = 1, 2$. Then $\Phi_1 \cup \Phi_2$ is satisfiable if and only if there exists an interpretation $\mathcal{A}$ satisfying Φ_1 and an interpretation $\mathcal{B}$ satisfying Φ_2 such that:*

(i) $|A_\sigma| = |B_\sigma|$, for every $\sigma \in \Sigma_1^{\text{S}} \cap \Sigma_2^{\text{S}}$;
(ii) $x^{\mathcal{A}} = y^{\mathcal{A}}$ if and only if $x^{\mathcal{B}} = y^{\mathcal{B}}$, for every $x, y \in vars(\Phi_1) \cap vars(\Phi_2)$. □

---

[2] A formal definition of a function $witness_{\text{set}}$ can be found in Subsection 5.4. For this example, we prefer to stick to intuitive arguments.

Proposition 12. *Let T_i be a Σ_i-theory such that $\Sigma_1^F \cap \Sigma_2^F = \emptyset$ and $\Sigma_1^P \cap \Sigma_2^P = \emptyset$, for $i = 1, 2$. Assume that T_2 is polite with respect to $S = \Sigma_1^S \cap \Sigma_2^S$. Also, let $\Gamma_1 \cup \Gamma_2$ be a conjunction of literals in separate form, and let $\psi_2 = witness_{T_2}(\Gamma_2)$. Finally, let $V_\sigma = vars_\sigma(\psi_2)$, for each $\sigma \in S$, and let $V = \bigcup_{\sigma \in S} V_\sigma$. Then the following are equivalent:*

1. *$\Gamma_1 \cup \Gamma_2$ is $(T_1 \oplus T_2)$-satisfiable;*
2. *There exists a family E of equivalence relations*

$$E = \{E_\sigma \subseteq V_\sigma \times V_\sigma \mid \sigma \in S\},$$

such that $\Gamma_1 \cup arr(V, E)$ is T_1-satisfiable and $\{\psi_2\} \cup arr(V, E)$ is T_2-satisfiable. □

PROOF. $(1 \Rightarrow 2)$. Assume that $\Gamma_1 \cup \Gamma_2$ is $(T_1 \oplus T_2)$-satisfiable. Let $\bar{v} = vars(\psi_2) \setminus vars(\Gamma_2)$. Since Γ_2 and $(\exists \bar{v})\psi_2$ are T_2-equivalent, it follows that $\Gamma_1 \cup \{\psi_2\}$ is also $(T_1 \oplus T_2)$-satisfiable. Thus, we can fix a $(T_1 \oplus T_2)$-interpretation $\mathcal{A}$ satisfying $\Gamma_1 \cup \{\psi_2\}$. Next, let $E = \{E_\sigma \mid \sigma \in S\}$ where

$$E_\sigma = \{(x, y) \mid x, y \in V_\sigma \text{ and } x^{\mathcal{A}} = y^{\mathcal{A}}\}, \qquad \text{for } \sigma \in S.$$

By construction, we have that $\Gamma_1 \cup arr(V, E)$ is T_1-satisfiable and $\{\psi_2\} \cup arr(V, E)$ is T_2-satisfiable.

$(2 \Rightarrow 1)$. Let $\mathcal{A}$ be a T_1-interpretation satisfying $\Gamma_1 \cup arr(V, E)$, and let $\mathcal{B}$ be a T_2-interpretation satisfying $\{\psi_2\} \cup arr(V, E)$. Since T_2 is finitely witnessable, we can assume without loss of generality that $B_\sigma = V_\sigma^{\mathcal{B}}$, for each $\sigma \in S$.

Thus, for each $\sigma \in S$, we have

$$|B_\sigma| = |V_\sigma^{\mathcal{B}}| \qquad \text{since } B_\sigma = V_\sigma^{\mathcal{B}}$$
$$= |V_\sigma^{\mathcal{A}}| \qquad \text{since both } \mathcal{A} \text{ and } \mathcal{B} \text{ satisfy } arr(V, E)$$
$$\leq |A_\sigma| \qquad \text{since } V_\sigma^{\mathcal{A}} \subseteq A_\sigma.$$

But then, by the smoothness of T_2, there exists a T_2-interpretation $\mathcal{C}$ satisfying $\{\psi_2\} \cup arr(V, E)$ such that $|C_\sigma| = |A_\sigma|$, for each $\sigma \in S$. We can therefore apply Theorem 11 to $\mathcal{A}$ and $\mathcal{C}$, obtaining the existence of a $(T_1 \oplus T_2)$-interpretation $\mathcal{F}$ satisfying $\Gamma_1 \cup \{\psi_2\} \cup arr(V, E)$. Since Γ_2 and $(\exists \bar{v})\psi_2$ are T_2-equivalent, it follows that $\mathcal{F}$ also satisfies $\Gamma_1 \cup \Gamma_2$. ■

Using Proposition 12 and the fact that our combination method is terminating, we obtain the correctness of our combination method.

Theorem 13 (Correctness and complexity). *Let T_i be a Σ_i-theory, for $i = 1, 2$. Assume that:*

- *the quantifier-free satisfiability problem of T_i is decidable, for $i = 1, 2$;*
- *$\Sigma_1^F \cap \Sigma_2^F = \emptyset$ and $\Sigma_1^P \cap \Sigma_2^P = \emptyset$;*
- *T_2 is polite with respect to $\Sigma_1^S \cap \Sigma_2^S$.*

Then the quantifier-free satisfiability problem of is decidable.

Moreover, if the quantifier-free satisfiability problems of T_1 and of T_2 are in NP, and witness$_{T_2}$ is computable in polynomial time, then the quantifier-free satisfiability problem of $T_1 \oplus T_2$ is NP-complete. □

PROOF. Clearly, the decidability of the quantifier-free satisfiability problem of $T_1 \oplus T_2$ follows by Proposition 12 and the fact that our combination method is terminating.

Concerning NP-hardness, note that if we can solve the quantifier-free satisfiability problem of $T_1 \oplus T_2$, then we can also solve propositional satisfiability.

Concerning membership in NP, assume that the quantifier-free satisfiability problems of T_1 and of T_2 are in NP, and that witness$_{T_2}$ is computable in polynomial time. Without loss of generality, it is enough to show that in nondeterministic polynomial time we can check the $(T_1 \oplus T_2)$-satisfiability of conjunctions of $(\Sigma_1 \cup \Sigma_2)$-literals. To see this, note that the execution of our combination method requires to guess an arrangement over a set of variables whose cardinality is polynomial with respect to the size of the input. This guess can be done in nondeterministic polynomial time. ∎

Theorem 13 can be repeatedly applied to consider the union of n theories $T_1 \oplus \cdots \oplus T_n$, where $T_2, \ldots, T_n$ are polite with respect to the set of shared sorts. This leads to the following generalization of Theorem 13 for n theories.

Theorem 14. *Let $n \geq 2$, and let T_i be a Σ_i-theory, for $1 \leq i \leq n$. Also, let $S = \bigcup_{i \neq j}(\Sigma_i^S \cap \Sigma_j^S)$. Assume that:*

- *the quantifier-free satisfiability problem of T_i is decidable, for $1 \leq i \leq n$;*
- *$\bigcup_{i \neq j}(\Sigma_i^S \cap \Sigma_j^S) = \bigcap_i \Sigma_i^S$;*
- *$\Sigma_i^F \cap \Sigma_j^F = \emptyset$ and $\Sigma_i^P \cap \Sigma_j^P = \emptyset$, for $1 \leq i < j \leq n$;*
- *T_i is polite with respect to S, for $2 \leq i \leq n$.*

Then the quantifier-free satisfiability problem of $T_1 \oplus \cdots \oplus T_n$ is decidable.

Moreover, if the quantifier-free satisfiability problem of T_i is in NP, for $1 \leq i \leq n$, and witness$_{T_i}$ is computable in polynomial time, for $2 \leq i \leq n$, then the quantifier-free satisfiability problem of $T_1 \oplus \cdots \oplus T_n$ is NP-complete. □

PROOF. We proceed by induction on n. If $n = 2$ we can apply our combination method to T_1 and T_2, and the claim follows by Theorem 13. If instead $n > 2$, it suffices to apply our combination method first to T_1 and T_2, and subsequently to $T_1 \oplus T_2, T_3, \ldots, T_n$. ∎

4   Shiny Theories

Shiny theories were introduced by Tinelli and Zarba [13] in order to extend the one-sorted version of the Nelson-Oppen method to the combination of nonstably infinite theories. Shiny theories are interesting because every shiny theory S can be combined with any other theory T, even if the latter is not stably infinite.

The notion of shininess was originally introduced in one-sorted logic, and in this section we generalize it to many-sorted logic. We also prove that, under rather weak assumptions, shininess is equivalent to politeness in one-sorted logic. The equivalence is less clear in many-sorted logic.

Definition 15. Let T be a Σ-theory, let $S \subseteq \Sigma^S$, and let φ be a T-satisfiable quantifier-free Σ-formula. We denote with $mincard_{T,S}(\varphi)$ the minimum of the following set of cardinal numbers:

$$\left\{ \left(\max_{\sigma \in S} |A_\sigma| \right) \mid \mathcal{A} \models_T \varphi \right\}. \qquad \Box$$

Remark 16. Let T be a Σ-theory that has the finite model property with respect to S. Then, for every T-satisfiable quantifier-free Σ-formula φ, we have $mincard_{T,S}(\varphi) \in \mathbb{N}^+$. $\qquad \Box$

Definition 17 (Shininess). Let Σ be a signature, let $S \subseteq \Sigma^S$ be a set of sorts, and let T be a Σ-theory. We say that T is SHINY with respect to S if:

- T is smooth with respect to S;
- T has the finite model property with respect to S;
- $mincard_{T,S}$ is computable. $\qquad \Box$

The following proposition shows that shinineess always implies politeness.

Proposition 18. *Let T be a shiny theory with respect to a set S of sorts. Then T is polite with respect to S.* $\qquad \Box$

The following proposition establishes sufficient conditions under which politeness implies shininess.

Proposition 19. *Let Σ be a signature, let $S \subseteq \Sigma^S$ be a set of sorts, and let T be a Σ-theory. Assume that:*

- *$\Sigma^S = S$;*
- *Σ is finite;*
- *For each Σ-interpretation $\mathcal{A}$ such that $\bigcup_{\sigma \in S} A_\sigma$ is finite, it is decidable to check whether $\mathcal{A}$ is a T-interpretation or not;*
- *T is polite with respect to S.*

Then T is shiny with respect to S. $\qquad \Box$

When $|\Sigma^S| = 1$, Proposition 19 tells us that in the one-sorted case politeness and shininess are the same concept for all practical purposes. When $|\Sigma^S| > 1$, the hypothesis $\Sigma^S = S$ may be too strong. Consequently, the equivalence between politeness and shininess is less clear in the many-sorted case.

5   Polite Theories

In this section we prove that natural examples of polite theories are those modeling data structures such as lists, arrays, sets, and multisets.

For convenience, when proving that a Σ-theory T is polite with respect to a set S of sorts, we will define the function $witness_T$ by restricting ourselves to conjunctions Γ of flat Σ-literals such that $vars_\sigma(\Gamma) \neq \emptyset$, for each sort $\sigma \in S$. The extended version of this paper [10] shows that this can be done without loss of generality.

As a warm up, we start by showing that the theory of equality is polite.

5.1   Equality

Definition 20. The THEORY OF EQUALITY with signature Σ is the theory $T^\Sigma_\approx = \langle \Sigma, \mathbf{A} \rangle$, where $\mathbf{A}$ is the class of all Σ-structures. $\quad\square$

Witness function. A witness function $witness_\approx$ for $T^\Sigma_\approx$ can be defined as follows. Without loss of generality, let Γ be a conjunction of flat Σ-literals such that $vars_\sigma(\Gamma) \neq \emptyset$, for each sort $\sigma \in S$. Then we simply let $witness_\approx(\Gamma) = \Gamma$.

Theorem 21 (Politeness). *For each signature Σ, and for any nonempty set of sorts $S \subseteq \Sigma^S$, the theory $T^\Sigma_\approx$ is polite with respect to S.* $\quad\square$

5.2   Lists

Let A be a nonempty set. A *list* x over A is a sequence $\langle a_1, \ldots, a_n \rangle$, where $n \geq 0$ and $\{a_1, \ldots, a_n\} \subseteq A$. We denote with A^* the set of lists over A.

The theory of lists T_{list} has a signature Σ_{list} containing a sort elem for elements and a sort list for lists of elements, plus the following symbols:

- the constant symbol nil, of sort list;
- the function symbols
    - car, of arity list $\rightarrow$ elem;
    - cdr, of arity list $\rightarrow$ list;
    - cons, of arity elem $\times$ list $\rightarrow$ list.

Definition 22. A STANDARD list-INTERPRETATION $\mathcal{A}$ is a Σ_{list}-interpretation satisfying the following conditions:

- $A_{\mathsf{list}} = (A_{\mathsf{elem}})^*$;
- $\mathsf{nil}^{\mathcal{A}} = \langle \rangle$;
- $\mathsf{car}^{\mathcal{A}}(\langle e_1, \ldots, e_n \rangle) = e_1$, for each $n > 0$ and $e_1, \ldots, e_n \in A_{\mathsf{elem}}$;
- $\mathsf{cdr}^{\mathcal{A}}(\langle e_1, \ldots, e_n \rangle) = \langle e_2, \ldots, e_n \rangle$, for each $n > 0$ and $e_1, \ldots, e_n \in A_{\mathsf{elem}}$;
- $\mathsf{cons}^{\mathcal{A}}(e, \langle e_1, \ldots, e_n \rangle) = \langle e, e_1, \ldots, e_n \rangle$, for each $n \geq 0$ and $e, e_1, \ldots, e_n \in A_{\mathsf{elem}}$.

The THEORY OF LISTS is the pair $T_{\mathsf{list}} = \langle \Sigma_{\mathsf{list}}, \mathbf{A} \rangle$, where $\mathbf{A}$ is the class of all standard list-structures. $\quad\square$

Witness function. A witness function $witness_{\mathsf{list}}$ for the theory T_{list} can be defined as follows. Without loss of generality, let Γ be a conjunction of flat Σ_{list}-literals such that $vars_{\mathsf{elem}}(\Gamma) \neq \emptyset$. We let $witness_{\mathsf{list}}(\Gamma)$ be the result of applying to Γ the following transformations:

- Replace each literal of the form $e \approx \mathsf{car}(x)$ in Γ with the formula $x \not\approx \mathsf{nil} \to x \approx \mathsf{cons}(e, y')$, where y' is a fresh list-variable.
- Replace each literal of the form $x \approx \mathsf{cdr}(y)$ in Γ with the formula $x \not\approx \mathsf{nil} \to y \approx \mathsf{cons}(e', x)$, where e' is a fresh elem-variable.
- For each literal of the form $x \not\approx_{\mathsf{list}} y$ in Γ, generate two fresh elem-variables $w'_{x,y}$ and $w''_{x,y}$, and add the literals $w'_{x,y} \approx w'_{x,y}$ and $w''_{x,y} \approx w''_{x,y}$ to Γ.

Remark 23. Let Γ be a conjunction of flat Σ_{list}-literals, let $\Delta = witness_{\mathsf{list}}(\Gamma)$, and let $\bar{v} = vars(\Delta) \setminus vars(\Gamma)$. Then Γ and $(\exists \bar{v})\Delta$ are T_{list}-equivalent. □

Theorem 24 (Politeness). *The theory* T_{list} *is polite with respect to* $\{\mathsf{elem}\}$. □

A conjecture. We conjecture that a more efficient witness function $witness'_{\mathsf{list}}$ for T_{list} can be defined as follows. Without loss of generality, let Γ be a conjunction of flat Σ_{list}-literals such that $vars_{\mathsf{elem}}(\Gamma) \neq \emptyset$. We let $witness'_{\mathsf{list}}$ be the result of applying to Γ the following transformation:

- Replace each literal of the form $x \approx \mathsf{cdr}(y)$ in Γ with the formula $x \not\approx \mathsf{nil} \to y \approx \mathsf{cons}(e', x)$, where e' is a fresh elem-variable.

We do not have yet a formal proof of this claim.

5.3   Arrays

The theory of arrays T_{array} has a signature Σ_{array} containing a sort elem for elements, a sort index for indices, and a sort array for arrays, plus the following two function symbols:

- read, of sort $\mathsf{array} \times \mathsf{index} \to \mathsf{elem}$;
- write, of sort $\mathsf{array} \times \mathsf{index} \times \mathsf{elem} \to \mathsf{array}$.

Notation. Given $a : I \to E$, $i \in I$ and $e \in E$, we define $a_{i \mapsto e} : I \to E$ as follows: $a_{i \mapsto e}(i) = e$ and $a_{i \mapsto e}(j) = a(j)$, for $j \neq i$.

Definition 25. A STANDARD array-INTERPRETATION $\mathcal{A}$ is a Σ_{array}-interpretation satisfying the following conditions:

- $A_{\mathsf{array}} = (A_{\mathsf{elem}})^{A_{\mathsf{index}}}$;
- $\mathsf{read}^{\mathcal{A}}(a, i) = a(i)$, for each $a \in A_{\mathsf{array}}$ and $i \in A_{\mathsf{index}}$;
- $\mathsf{write}^{\mathcal{A}}(a, i, e) = a_{i \mapsto e}$, for each $a \in A_{\mathsf{array}}$, $i \in A_{\mathsf{index}}$, and $e \in A_{\mathsf{elem}}$.

The THEORY OF ARRAYS is the pair $T_{\mathsf{array}} = \langle \Sigma_{\mathsf{array}}, \mathbf{A} \rangle$, where $\mathbf{A}$ is the class of all standard array-structures. □

Witness Function. A witness function $witness_{array}$ for the theory T_{array} can be defined as follows. Without loss of generality, let Γ be a conjunction of flat Σ_{array}-literals such that $vars_{index}(\Gamma) \neq \emptyset$ and $vars_{elem}(\Gamma) \neq \emptyset$. We let $witness_{array}(\Gamma)$ be the result of applying to Γ the following transformation:

- Replace each literal of the form $a \not\approx_{array} b$ in Γ with a literal of the form $read(a, i') \not\approx read(b, i')$, where i' is a fresh index-variable.

Remark 26. Let Γ be a conjunction of flat Σ_{array}-literals, let $\Delta = witness_{array}$ (Γ), and let $\bar{v} = vars(\Delta) \setminus vars(\Gamma)$. Then Γ and $(\exists \bar{v})\Delta$ are T_{array}-equivalent. $\square$

Theorem 27 (Politeness). *For any nonempty set of sorts $S \subseteq \{elem, index\}$, the theory T_{array} is polite with respect to S.* $\square$

5.4   Sets

The theory of sets T_{set} has a signature Σ_{set} containing a sort elem for elements and a sort set for sets of elements, plus the following symbols:

- the constant symbol $\emptyset$, of sort set;
- the function symbols:
  - $\{\cdot\}$, of sort elem $\rightarrow$ set;
  - $\cup$, $\cap$, and $\setminus$, of sort set $\times$ set $\rightarrow$ set;
- the predicate symbol $\in$, of sort elem $\times$ set.

Definition 28. A STANDARD set-INTERPRETATION $\mathcal{A}$ is a Σ_{set}-interpretation satisfying the following conditions:

- $A_{set} = \mathcal{P}(A_{elem})$;
- the symbols $\emptyset$, $\{\cdot\}$, $\cup$, $\cap$, $\setminus$, and $\in$ are interpreted according to their standard interpretation over sets.

The THEORY OF SETS is the pair $T_{set} = \langle \Sigma_{set}, \mathbf{A} \rangle$, where $\mathbf{A}$ is the class of all standard set-structures. $\square$

Witness Function. A witness function $witness_{set}$ for the theory T_{set} can be defined as follows. Without loss of generality, let Γ be a conjunction of flat Σ_{set}-literals such that $vars_{elem}(\Gamma) \neq \emptyset$. We let $witness_{set}(\Gamma)$ be the result of applying to Γ the following transformation:

- Replace each literal of the form $x \not\approx_{set} y$ in Γ with a literal of the form $e' \in (x \setminus y) \cup (y \setminus x)$, where e' is a fresh elem-variable.

Remark 29. Let Γ be a conjunction of flat Σ_{set}-literals, let $\Delta = witness_{set}(\Gamma)$, and let $\bar{v} = vars(\Delta) \setminus vars(\Gamma)$. Then Γ and $(\exists \bar{v})\Delta$ are T_{set}-equivalent. $\square$

Theorem 30 (Politeness). *The theory T_{set} is polite with respect to $\{elem\}$.* $\square$

5.5   Multisets

Multisets—also known as bags—are collections that may contain duplicate elements. Formally, a multiset x is a function $x : A \rightarrow \mathbb{N}$, for some set A.

We use the symbol $[\![\,]\!]$ to denote the empty multiset. When $n \geq 0$, we write $[\![e]\!]^{(n)}$ to denote the multiset containing exactly n occurrences of e and nothing else. When $n < 0$, we let $[\![e]\!]^n = [\![\,]\!]$.

Let x, y be two multisets. Then:

- their *union* $x \cup y$ is the multiset z such that, for each element e, the equality $z(e) = \max(x(e), y(e))$ holds;
- their *sum* $x \uplus y$ is the multiset z such that, for each element e, the equality $z(e) = x(e) + y(e)$ holds;
- their *intersection* $x \cap y$ is the multiset z such that, for each element e, the equality $z(e) = \min(x(e), y(e))$ holds.

The theory of multisets T_{bag} has a signature Σ_{bag} containing a sort int for integers, a sort elem for elements, and a sort bag for multisets, plus the following symbols:

- the constant symbols:
    - 0 and 1, of sort int;
    - $[\![\,]\!]$, of sort bag;
- the function symbols:
    - $+$, $-$, $\max$, and $\min$, of sort $\mathsf{int} \times \mathsf{int} \rightarrow \mathsf{int}$;
    - $[\![\cdot]\!]^{(\cdot)}$, of sort $\mathsf{elem} \times \mathsf{int} \rightarrow \mathsf{bag}$;
    - $\cup$, $\uplus$, and $\cap$, of sort $\mathsf{bag} \times \mathsf{bag} \rightarrow \mathsf{bag}$;
    - count, of sort $\mathsf{elem} \times \mathsf{bag} \rightarrow \mathsf{int}$;
- the predicate symbol $<$, of sort $\mathsf{int} \times \mathsf{int}$.

Definition 31. A STANDARD bag-INTERPRETATION $\mathcal{A}$ is a Σ_{bag}-interpretation satisfying the following conditions:

- $A_{\mathsf{int}} = \mathbb{Z}$;
- $A_{\mathsf{bag}} = \mathbb{N}^{A_{\mathsf{elem}}}$;
- the symbols 0, 1, $+$, $-$, $\max$, $\min$, and $<$ are interpreted according to their standard interpretation over the integers;
- the symbol $[\![\,]\!]$, $\cup$, $\cap$, $\setminus$, $[\![\cdot]\!]^{(\cdot)}$ are interpreted according to their standard interpretation over multisets;
- $\mathsf{count}^{\mathcal{A}}(e, x) = x(e)$, for each $e \in A_{\mathsf{elem}}$ and $x \in A_{\mathsf{bag}}$.

The THEORY OF MULTISETS is the pair $T_{\mathsf{bag}} = \langle \Sigma_{\mathsf{bag}}, \mathbf{A} \rangle$, where $\mathbf{A}$ is the class of all standard bag-structures. $\square$

Witness Function. A witness function $witness_{\mathsf{bag}}$ for the theory T_{bag} can be defined as follows. Without loss of generality, let Γ be a conjunction of flat Σ_{bag}-literals such that $vars_{\mathsf{elem}}(\Gamma) \neq \emptyset$. We let $witness_{\mathsf{bag}}(\Gamma)$ be the result of applying to Γ the following transformation:

– Replace each literal of the form $x \not\approx_{\mathsf{bag}} y$ in Γ with a literal of the form $\mathsf{count}(e', x) \not\approx \mathsf{count}(e', y)$, where e' is a fresh elem-variable.

Remark 32. Let Γ be a conjunction of flat Σ_{bag}-literals, let $\Delta = witness_{\mathsf{bag}}(\Gamma)$, and let $\bar{v} = vars(\Delta) \setminus vars(\Gamma)$. Then Γ and $(\exists\bar{v})\Delta$ are T_{bag}-equivalent.   □

Theorem 33 (Politeness). *The theory T_{bag} is polite with respect to* {elem}.□

6 Conclusion

We addressed the problem of combining a theory S modeling a data structure containing elements of a given nature with a theory T of the elements. We were particularly interested in the case in which T is not stably infinite.

To solve this problem, we defined the notion of polite theories, and we showed that a polite theory S can be combined with any theory T, regardless of whether T is stably infinite or not. We then proved that natural examples of polite theories are given by the theory of equality, lists, arrays, sets, and multisets.

Our results were developed using many-sorted logic rather than one-sorted logic. In our experience, combining nonstably infinite theories in one-sorted logic is difficult. By moving to many-sorted logic, we were able to find many practically relevant theories (e.g., lists, arrays, sets, and multisets) that can be combined with nonstably infinite theories.

Concerning future research, we wish to study how polite theories relate to observable theories [3] and local theory extensions [11]. We also wish to implement our combination method in **haRVey** [5], and apply it to the verification of set-based specifications of smart-cards [4].

Acknowledgments

We are grateful to Pascal Fontaine, Deepak Kapur, and Cesare Tinelli for pleasant discussions on the problem of combining nonstably infinite theories. We are also grateful to the anonymous reviewers for their constructive feedback. Full credit for the results of Section 4 goes to the reviewers.

References

1. Franz Baader and Silvio Ghilardi. Connecting many-sorted structures and theories through adjoint functions. In Bernhard Gramlich, editor, *Frontiers of Combining Systems*, Lecture Notes in Computer Science. Springer, 2005.
2. Franz Baader and Silvio Ghilardi. Connecting many-sorted theories. In Robert Nieuwenhuis, editor, *Automated Deduction – CADE-20*, volume 3632 of *Lecture Notes in Computer Science*. Springer, 2005.
3. Michel Bidoit and Rolf Hennicker. Behavioural theories and the proof of behavioural properties. *Theoretical Computer Science*, 165(1):3–55, 1996.

4. Jean-François Couchot, David Déharbe, Alain Giorgetti, and Silvio Ranise. Scalable automated proving and debugging of set-based specifications. *Journal of the Brazilian Computer Society*, 9(2):17–36, 2004.
5. David Déharbe and Silvio Ranise. Light-weight theorem proving for debugging and verifying units of code. In *Software Engineering and Formal Methods*, pages 220–228. IEEE Computer Society, 2003.
6. Pascal Fontaine and Pascal Gribomont. Combining non-stably infinite, non-first order theories. In Silvio Ranise and Cesare Tinelli, editors, *Pragmatics of Decision Procedures in Automated Reasoning*, 2004.
7. Pascal Fontaine, Silvio Ranise, and Calogero G. Zarba. Combining lists with non-stably infinite theories. In Franz Baader and Andrei Voronkov, editors, *Logic for Programming, Artificial Intelligence, and Reasoning*, volume 3452 of *Lecture Notes in Computer Science*, pages 51–66. Springer, 2005.
8. Vijay Ganesh, Sergey Berezin, and David L. Dill. A decision procedure for fixed-width bit-vectors. Unpublished, 2005.
9. Harald Ganzinger. Shostak light. In Andrei Voronkov, editor, *Automated Deduction – CADE-18*, volume 2392 of *Lecture Notes in Computer Science*, pages 332–346. Springer, 2002.
10. Silvio Ranise, Christophe Ringeissen, and Calogero G. Zarba. Combining data structures with nonstably infinite theories using many-sorted logic. Technical report, INRIA, 2005. Also published as Technical Report at Department of Computer Science, University of New Mexico. Electronically available at http://www.inria.fr/rrrt/index.en.html or http://www.cs.unm.edu/research/.
11. Viorica Sofronie-Stokkermans. Hierarchic reasoning in local theory extensions. In Robert Nieuwenhuis, editor, *Automated Deduction – CADE-20*, volume 3632 of *Lecture Notes in Computer Science*. Springer, 2005.
12. Cesare Tinelli and Calogero G. Zarba. Combining decision procedures for sorted theories. In José Júlio Alferes and João Alexandre Leite, editors, *Logics in Artificial Intelligence*, volume 3229 of *Lecture Notes in Computer Science*, pages 641–653. Springer, 2004.
13. Cesare Tinelli and Calogero G. Zarba. Combining nonstably infinite theories. *Journal of Automated Reasoning*, 2005. To appear.
14. Calogero G. Zarba. Combining multisets with integers. In Andrei Voronkov, editor, *Automated Deduction – CADE-18*, volume 2392 of *Lecture Notes in Computer Science*, pages 363–376. Springer, 2002.
15. Calogero G. Zarba. Combining sets with elements. In Nachum Dershowitz, editor, *Verification: Theory and Practice*, volume 2772 of *Lecture Notes in Computer Science*, pages 762–782. Springer, 2004.

On a Rewriting Approach to Satisfiability Procedures: Extension, Combination of Theories and an Experimental Appraisal*

Alessandro Armando[1], Maria Paola Bonacina[2],
Silvio Ranise[3], and Stephan Schulz[2]

[1] DIST, Università degli Studi di Genova,
Viale Causa 13, I-16145 Genova, Italy
armando@dist.unige.it
[2] Dipartimento di Informatica, Università degli Studi di Verona,
Strada Le Grazie 15, I-37134 Verona, Italy
mariapaola.bonacina@univr.it, schulz@eprover.org
[3] LORIA & INRIA-Lorraine,
615 Rue du Jardin Botanique, F-54600 Villers-lès-Nancy, France
silvio.ranise@loria.fr

Abstract. The rewriting approach to $\mathcal{T}$-satisfiability is based on establishing termination of a rewrite-based inference system for first-order logic on the $\mathcal{T}$-satisfiability problem. Extending previous such results, including the *quantifier-free theory of equality* and the *theory of arrays with or without extensionality*, we prove termination for the theories of *records with or without extensionality*, *integer offsets* and *integer offsets modulo*. A general theorem for termination on *combinations of theories*, that covers any combination of the theories above, is given next. For empirical evaluation, the rewrite-based theorem prover E is compared with the validity checkers CVC and CVC Lite, on both synthetic and real-world benchmarks, including both valid and invalid instances. Parametric synthetic benchmarks test *scalability*, while real-world benchmarks test ability to handle huge sets of literals. Contrary to the folklore that a general-purpose prover cannot compete with specialized reasoners, the experiments are overall favorable to the theorem prover, showing that the rewriting approach is both elegant and practical.

1 Introduction

Many state-of-the-art verification tools (e.g., [21,11,9,6]) incorporate satisfiability procedures for theories of data types. However, most verification problems involve more than one theory, so that one needs procedures for *combination of theories* (e.g., [14,20]). Combination is complicated: for instance, understanding, formalizing and proving correct the method in [20] required much work (e.g., [16,7,12]). Combining theories by combining algorithms may lead to *ad*

---

* Research supported in part by MIUR grant no. 2003-097383.

hoc procedures, that are hard to modify, extend, integrate into, or even interface with other systems. Satisfiability procedures need to be proved correct and complete, by showing that whenever they report "satisfiable," the ouput represents a model. Model-construction arguments for concrete procedures are specialized for those, so that each new procedure requires a new proof (e.g., [16,22]), while abstract frameworks often focus on combining the theory of equality with at most one other theory (e.g., [12]). Data structures and algorithms for each new procedure are usually implemented from scratch, with little software reuse and high risk of errors.

If one could use *first-order theorem-proving strategies*, combination would become much simpler, because in several cases it would be sufficient to give as input the union of the presentations of the theories. No *ad hoc* correctness and completeness proofs would be needed, because a sound and complete theorem-proving strategy is a *semi-decision procedure* for unsatisfiability. Existing first-order provers could represent a repository of code available for reuse.

The crux is *termination*: to have a *decision procedure*, one needs to prove that a complete theorem-proving strategy is bound to terminate on satisfiability problems in the theories of interest. It was shown in [5] that a standard, (refutationally) complete *rewrite-based inference system*, named $\mathcal{SP}$, is guaranteed to terminate on satisfiability problems in the quantifier-free theories of *equality, lists, arrays with and without extensionality, sets with extensionality* and the combination of lists and arrays. Thus, rewrite-based theorem provers can be used *off the shelf* as validity checkers, as done in, e.g., [10,1].

This paper advances the rewriting approach to satisfiability in several ways. First, we prove termination of $\mathcal{SP}$ for the theories of *records with or without extensionality, integer offsets* and *integer offsets modulo*. Second, we give a *modularity theorem for combination of theories* stating sufficient conditions for $\mathcal{SP}$ to terminate on the combination, if it terminates on each theory separately. Any combination of the theories above, and with the *quantifier-free theory of equality* and *arrays (with or without extensionality)*, is covered. Third, we report on experiments comparing the rewrite-based E prover [17], CVC [21] and CVC Lite [6] on six sets of *parametric synthetic benchmarks*: three on arrays with extensionality, one combining arrays and integer offsets, one combining arrays, records and integer offsets to model *queues*, and one combining arrays, records and integer offsets modulo to model *circular queues*. CVC and CVC Lite seem to be the only state-of-the-art tools implementing a correct and complete procedure for arrays with extensionality.[1] Contrary to expectation, the general first-order prover with the theory presentations in input is, overall, comparable with the validity checkers with the theories built-in, and in many cases even outperforms them. To complete our appraisal, we tested E on sets of literals extracted from real-world problems of the UCLID suite [8], and found it solves them very fast.

An extended abstract of this paper was presented in [3]. Very preliminary experiments with a few of the synthetic benchmarks were reported in [2]. A full

---

[1] Neither Simplify nor ICS 2.0 are complete in this regard: cf. [11], Sec. 5, and a personal communication from H. Rueß to A. Armando in April 2004, respectively.

version of this paper with proofs and a description of the synthetic benchmarks is available in [4].

2   A Rewrite-Based Methodology for $\mathcal{T}$-Satisfiability

$\mathcal{T}$-satisfiability is the problem of deciding satisfiability of sets $\mathcal{T} \cup S$, where $\mathcal{T}$ is a presentation of a (decidable) theory and S a set of ground equational literals on $\mathcal{T}$'s signature (or $\mathcal{T}$-literals). The rewrite-based methodology [5] applies first-order theorem-proving strategies based on the $\mathcal{SP}$ inference system (*superposition/paramodulation, reflection, equational factoring, subsumption, simplification and tautology deletion*, e.g., [15]). A theorem-proving strategy (inference system + search plan) is complete if the inference system is refutationally complete and the search plan is fair. A fundamental feature of $\mathcal{SP}$ is the usage of a *complete simplification ordering (CSO)* on terms and literals, in such a way that only maximal sides of maximal instances of literals are paramodulated into and from. Let $\mathcal{SP}_\succ$ be $\mathcal{SP}$ with CSO $\succ$ and $\mathcal{SP}_\succ$-*strategy* be any strategy with inference system $\mathcal{SP}_\succ$.

In the following, $\simeq$ is (unordered) equality, $=$ is identity, $\bowtie$ is either $\simeq$ or $\not\simeq$, l, r, u, t are terms, v, w, x, y, z are variables, all other lower case letters are constants or functions based on arity, and $Var(t)$ denotes the set of variables occurring in t. For a term t, $depth(t) = 0$, if t is a constant or a variable, and $depth(f(t_1, \ldots, t_n)) = 1 + max\{depth(t_i) : 1 \le i \le n\}$. A term is *flat* if its depth is 0 or 1. For a literal, $depth(l \bowtie r) = depth(l) + depth(r)$. A positive literal is *flat* if its depth is 0 or 1. A negative literal is *flat* if its depth is 0.

The rewrite-based methodology for $\mathcal{T}$-satisfiability consists of:

1. *$\mathcal{T}$-reduction:* specific inferences, depending on $\mathcal{T}$, are applied to remove certain literals or symbols and obtain an equisatisfiable $\mathcal{T}$-*reduced* problem.
2. *Flattening:* all ground literals are flattened by introducing new constants, yielding an equisatisfiable $\mathcal{T}$-reduced *flat* problem.
3. *Ordering selection and termination:* any fair $\mathcal{SP}_\succ$-strategy is shown to terminate when applied to a $\mathcal{T}$-reduced flat problem, provided $\succ$ is "good" for $\mathcal{T}$, or $\mathcal{T}$-*good*. An $\mathcal{SP}_\succ$-strategy will be $\mathcal{T}$-*good*, if $\succ$ is.

This methodology is *fully automated*, except for the proof of termination: the $\mathcal{T}$-reduction inferences are mechanical, flattening is a mechanical operation, and a theorem prover can generate $\mathcal{T}$-good orderings.

Let $\mathcal{E}$ denote the empty presentation, i.e., the presentation of the *quantifier-free theory of equality*. If $\mathcal{T}$ is $\mathcal{E}$, S is a set of ground equational literals built from free symbols, and $\mathcal{SP}_\succ$ reduces to ground completion, which is guaranteed to terminate, so that any fair $\mathcal{SP}_\succ$-strategy is a satisfiability procedure for $\mathcal{E}$.

2.1   The Theory of Arrays with and Without Extensionality

Given sorts INDEX, ELEM and ARRAY, for indices, elements and arrays, respectively, and function symbols select : ARRAY $\times$ INDEX $\rightarrow$ ELEM, and store :

ARRAY × INDEX × ELEM → ARRAY, with the usual meaning, the standard presentation $\mathcal{A}$ consists of axioms (1) and (2), while the presentation $\mathcal{A}^e$ of the theory with extensionality also includes axiom (3) in the following list:

$$\forall x, z, v. \qquad \qquad select(store(x, z, v), z) \simeq v \qquad \qquad (1)$$

$$\forall x, z, w, v. \quad (z \not\simeq w \supset select(store(x, z, v), w) \simeq select(x, w)) \qquad (2)$$

$$\forall x, y. \qquad (\forall z. select(x, z) \simeq select(y, z) \supset x \simeq y) \qquad \qquad (3)$$

with variables x, y of sort ARRAY, w, z of sort INDEX and v of sort ELEM.

Definition 1. *A set of ground $\mathcal{A}$-literals is $\mathcal{A}$-reduced if it contains no literal $l \not\simeq r$, where l and r are terms of sort ARRAY.*

Definition 2. *A CSO $\succ$ is $\mathcal{A}$-good if (1) $t \succ c$ for all ground compound terms t and all constants c, and (2) $a \succ e \succ j$, for all constants a of sort ARRAY, e of sort ELEM and j of sort INDEX.*

$\mathcal{A}$-*reduction* replaces every literal $l \not\simeq r \in S$, with l and r of sort ARRAY, by $select(s, sk_{l,r}) \not\simeq select(t, sk_{l,r})$, where $sk_{l,r}$ is a Skolem constant of sort INDEX. Then (cf. [5], Th. 7.1), $\mathcal{A}^e \cup S$ is satisfiable if and only if $\mathcal{A} \cup Red_{\mathcal{A}}(S)$ is, where $Red_{\mathcal{A}}(S)$ is the $\mathcal{A}$-reduced form of S, and any additional function symbol other than select and store is *array-safe* (i.e., for $f: s_0, \ldots, s_{m-1} \longrightarrow s_m$, with $m \geq 1$, s_k is not ARRAY for all k, $0 \leq k \leq m$).

Theorem 1. *A fair $\mathcal{A}$-good $\mathcal{SP}_\succ$-strategy is guaranteed to terminate on $\mathcal{A} \cup S$, where S is an $\mathcal{A}$-reduced set of ground flat $\mathcal{A}$-literals, and therefore is a satisfiability procedure for $\mathcal{A}$ and $\mathcal{A}^e$ (cf. Theorem 7.2 in [5]).*

2.2   The Theory of Records with and Without Extensionality

Records are data structures that aggregate attribute-value pairs: assuming $Id = \{id_1, \ldots, id_n\}$ is a set of field identifiers and $T_1, \ldots, T_n$ are n types, REC(id_1 : $T_1, \ldots, id_n : T_n$), abbreviated REC, is the sort of records that associate an element of type T_i to the field identifier id_i, for $1 \leq i \leq n$. The signature of the *theory of records* features a pair of function symbols $rselect_i$: REC → T_i and $rstore_i$: REC × T_i → REC for each i, $1 \leq i \leq n$. Its presentations, $\mathcal{R}$, without extensionality, and $\mathcal{R}^e$, with extensionality, are given by the following axioms (only (4) and (5) in $\mathcal{R}$ and all three in $\mathcal{R}^e$):

$$\forall x, v. \qquad rselect_i(rstore_i(x, v)) \simeq v \qquad \text{for all } i, 1 \leq i \leq n \qquad (4)$$

$$\forall x, v. \quad rselect_j(rstore_i(x, v)) \simeq rselect_j(x) \quad \text{for all } i, j, 1 \leq i \neq j \leq n \ (5)$$

$$\forall x, y. \ (\bigwedge_{i=1}^n rselect_i(x) \simeq rselect_i(y) \supset x \simeq y) \qquad \qquad (6)$$

where x, y have sort REC and v has sort T_i.

Definition 3. *A set of ground $\mathcal{R}$-literals is $\mathcal{R}$-reduced if it contains no literal $l \not\simeq r$, where l and r are terms of sort REC.*

Given a set of ground $\mathcal{R}$-literals S, $\mathcal{R}$-*reduction* consists of two phases. First, every literal $l \not\simeq r \in S$, with l and r of sort REC, is replaced by the disjunction $\bigvee_{i=1}^{n}$ rselect$_i(l) \not\simeq$ rselect$_i(r)$. Second, every such disjunction is split into n literals rselect$_i(l) \not\simeq$ rselect$_i(r)$ for $1 \leq i \leq n$, replacing S by n sets $S_i = S \setminus \{l \not\simeq r\} \cup \{$rselect$_i(l) \not\simeq$ rselect$_i(r)\}$ for $1 \leq i \leq n$. Each S_i is $\mathcal{R}$-reduced, and $Red_{\mathcal{R}}(S)$ denotes the class $\{S_i : 1 \leq i \leq n\}$.

Lemma 1. $\mathcal{R}^e \cup S$ *is satisfiable if and only if* $\mathcal{R} \cup S_i$ *is, for some* $S_i \in Red_{\mathcal{R}}(S)$.

Definition 4. *A CSO* $\succ$ *is* $\mathcal{R}$-*good if* $t \succ c$ *for all ground compound terms* t *and all constants* c.

Termination depends on a case analysis showing that only certain clauses can be generated, and the consideration that only finitely many such clauses can be built from a finite signature:

Theorem 2. *A fair* $\mathcal{R}$-*good* $\mathcal{SP}_{\succ}$-*strategy is guaranteed to terminate on* $\mathcal{R} \cup S$, *where* S *is an* $\mathcal{R}$-*reduced set of ground flat* $\mathcal{R}$-*literals, and therefore is a satisfiability procedure for* $\mathcal{R}$ *and* $\mathcal{R}^e$.

2.3   The Theory of Integer Offsets

The *theory of integer offsets* is a fragment of the theory of the integers, often applied in verification (e.g., [8]). Its signature has two unary function symbols s and p (the successor and predecessor functions, respectively) and its presentation $\mathcal{I}$ is given by the following infinite set of formulæ(e.g., [8,13]):

$$\forall x. \quad s(p(x)) \simeq x \tag{7}$$
$$\forall x. \quad p(s(x)) \simeq x \tag{8}$$
$$\forall x. \quad s^i(x) \not\simeq x \quad \text{for } i > 0 \tag{9}$$

where $s^1(x) = s(x)$, $s^{i+1}(x) = s(s^i(x))$ for $i \geq 1$, and the formulæ in (9) are called *acyclicity axioms*. For convenience, let $Ac = \{\forall x. s^i(x) \not\simeq x : i > 0\}$.

Definition 5. *A set of ground flat* $\mathcal{I}$-*literals is* $\mathcal{I}$-*reduced if it does not contain occurrences of* p.

Given a set S of ground flat $\mathcal{I}$-literals, the symbol p may appear only in literals of the form $p(c) \simeq d$, because ground flat literals have the form $c \not\simeq d$ and do not contain p. $\mathcal{I}$-*reduction* consists of replacing every equation $p(c) \simeq d$ in S by $c \simeq s(d)$. The resulting $\mathcal{I}$-reduced form of S is denoted $Red_{\mathcal{I}}(S)$. $\mathcal{I}$-reduction reduces satisfiability with respect to $\mathcal{I}$ to satisfiability with respect to Ac, so that axioms (7) and (8) can be removed:

Lemma 2. *Let* S *be a set of ground flat* $\mathcal{I}$-*literals.* $\mathcal{I} \cup S$ *is satisfiable if and only if* $Ac \cup Red_{\mathcal{I}}(S)$ *is.*

The next step is to bound the number of axioms in Ac needed to solve the problem. Let $Ac(n) = \{\forall x.\, \mathrm{s}^i(x) \not\simeq x : 0 < i \leq n\}$. The intuition is that the bound will be given by the number of occurrences of s in S: since S is flat, having n occurrences of s means that there are n literals $\mathrm{s}(c_i) \simeq c_{i+1}$ for $0 \leq i \leq n$, which means a model must have $n+1$ distinct elements. Thus, it is sufficient to consider $Ac(n + 1)$. From such a model it is possible to build a model for any larger instance of acyclicity by adding elements to the domain:

Lemma 3. *Let S be an $\mathcal{I}$-reduced set of ground flat $\mathcal{I}$-literals with n occurrences of* s*. Then $Ac \cup S$ is satisfiable if and only if $Ac(n + 1) \cup S$ is.*

Termination puts no requirement on the ordering; in other words, any CSO is $\mathcal{I}$-good:

Theorem 3. *A fair $\mathcal{SP}_{\succ}$-strategy is guaranteed to terminate on $Ac(n + 1) \cup S$, where S is an $\mathcal{I}$-reduced set of ground flat $\mathcal{I}$-literals, and n is the number of occurrences of* s *in S, and therefore is a satisfiability procedure for $\mathcal{I}$.*

2.4   The Theory of Integer Offsets Modulo

The above treatment can be extended to the *theory of integer offsets modulo*, useful to describe data structures whose indices range over the integers modulo k, where k is a positive integer. The presentation $\mathcal{I}_k$ is obtained from $\mathcal{I}$ by replacing Ac with the following k axioms

$$\forall x.\quad \mathrm{s}^i(x) \not\simeq x \text{ for } 1 \leq i \leq k - 1 \tag{10}$$

$$\forall x.\quad \mathrm{s}^k(x) \simeq x \tag{11}$$

Let $C(k) = \{\forall x.\, \mathrm{s}^k(x) \simeq x\}$. Definition 5 and Lemma 2 apply also to $\mathcal{I}_k$, whereas Lemma 3 is no longer necessary, because $\mathcal{I}_k$ is finite to begin with. A case analysis of applicable inferences proves the following two results:

Lemma 4. *A fair $\mathcal{SP}_{\succ}$-strategy is guaranteed to terminate when applied to $Ac(k - 1) \cup C(k) \cup S$, where S is an $\mathcal{I}$-reduced set of ground flat $\mathcal{I}$-literals.*

Alternatively, since $\mathcal{I}_k$ is finite, it is possible to omit $\mathcal{I}$-reduction and show termination of $\mathcal{SP}_{\succ}$ on the original problem format:

Lemma 5. *A fair $\mathcal{SP}_{\succ}$-strategy is guaranteed to terminate when applied to $\mathcal{I}_k \cup S$, where S is a set of ground flat $\mathcal{I}$-literals.*

Theorem 4. *A fair $\mathcal{SP}_{\succ}$-strategy is a satisfiability procedure for $\mathcal{I}_k$.*

3   Combination of Theories

The rewrite-based approach is especially suited for combination of theories, because it combines presentations, rather than combining algorithms. Knowing that an $SP_\succ$-strategy is a satisfiability procedure for $T_1, \ldots, T_n$, the combination problem is to show that it also decides satisfiability problems in the union $T = \bigcup_{i=1}^{n} T_i$. Of the rewrite-based methodology, T_i-reduction applies separately for each theory, and flattening is harmless. Thus, one only has to prove termination. The main theorem in this section establishes sufficient conditions for SP to terminate on T-satisfiability problems if it terminates on T_i-satisfiability problems for all i, $1 \leq i \leq n$. A first condition is that the ordering be T-good:

Definition 6. *Let $T_1, \ldots, T_n$ be presentations of theories. A CSO $\succ$ is T-good, where $T = \bigcup_{i=1}^{n} T_i$, if it is T_i-good for all i, $1 \leq i \leq n$.*

A second condition will serve the purpose of excluding paramodulations from variables, when considering inferences across theories. This is key, since a variable may paramodulate into any proper non-variable subterm. A maximal literal $t \simeq x$ such that $x \in Var(t)$ cannot be used to paramodulate from x, since $t \succ x$, because a CSO includes the subterm ordering. Thus, it is sufficient to ensure that literals $t \simeq x$ such that $x \notin Var(t)$ are inactive:

Definition 7. *A clause C is* variable-inactive *for $\succ$, if for all its ground instances $C\sigma$ no maximal literal in $C\sigma$ is instance of an equation $t \simeq x$ where $x \notin Var(t)$. A set of clauses is* variable-inactive *for $\succ$, if all its clauses are.*

Definition 8. *A presentation T is* variable-inactive *for $SP_\succ$, if S_∞ is variable-inactive for $\succ$ whenever $S_0 = T \cup S$ is, where $S_\infty = \bigcup_{j \geq 0} \bigcap_{i \geq j} S_i$ is the limit of any fair $SP_\succ$ derivation $S_0 \vdash_{SP_\succ} S_1 \vdash_{SP_\succ} \ldots S_i \vdash_{SP_\succ} \ldots$ from S_0.*

For satisfiability problems, $S_0 \setminus T$ is ground, so that S_0 is variable-inactive if the clauses in T are variable-inactive.

Last, the signatures of the T_i's may share constants, including constants introduced by flattening, but not function symbols. It follows that paramodulations from compound terms are excluded, and the only inferences across theories are paramodulations from constants into constants, that are finitely many, since there are finitely many constants:

Theorem 5. *Let $T_1, \ldots, T_n$ be presentations of theories, with no shared function symbol, and let $T = \bigcup_{i=1}^{n} T_i$. Assume that for all i, $1 \leq i \leq n$, S_i is a T_i-reduced set of ground flat T_i-literals. If for all i, $1 \leq i \leq n$, a fair T_i-good $SP_\succ$-strategy is guaranteed to terminate on $T_i \cup S_i$, and T_i is variable-inactive for $SP_\succ$, then, a fair T-good $SP_\succ$-strategy is guaranteed to terminate on $T \cup S_1 \cup \ldots \cup S_n$, and therefore is a satisfiability procedure for T.*

All presentations considered in this paper satisfy the requirements of Theorem 5: $\mathcal{E}$ is variable-inactive vacuously, while $\mathcal{A}$, $\mathcal{R}$, $\mathcal{I}$ and $\mathcal{I}_k$ are variable-inactive by inspection of generated clauses in the proofs of their respective termination theorems. Furthermore, an $\mathcal{A}$-good ordering is also $\mathcal{R}$-good.

Corollary 1. *A fair $SP_\succ$-strategy is a satisfiability procedure for any combination of the theories of arrays, with or without extensionality, records, with or* *without extensionality, integer offsets or integer offsets modulo, and the quantifier-free theory of equality, provided (1) $\succ$ is $\mathcal{R}$-good whenever records are included, (2) $\succ$ is $\mathcal{A}$-good whenever arrays are included, and (3) all free function symbols are array-safe whenever arrays with extensionality and equality are included.*

In general, the requirement of being variable-inactive is rather natural for purely equational theories, where $\mathcal{T}$ is a set of equations:

Theorem 6. *If $\mathcal{T}$ is a presentation of a purely equational theory with no trivial models, then $\mathcal{T}$ is variable-inactive for $\mathcal{SP}_\succ$ for any CSO $\succ$.*

For first-order theories, variable-inactivity excludes, for instance, the generation of clauses in the form $a_1 \simeq x \vee \ldots \vee a_n \simeq x$, where the a_i's are constants, for $1 \leq i \leq n$. Such a disjunction may be generated only within a clause that contains at least one greater literal (e.g., involving function symbols). It is well-known (e.g., [7,12]) that the Nelson-Oppen combination method [14] is complete without branching for *convex* theories, i.e., such that $\mathcal{T} \models S \supset \bigvee_{i=1}^{n} l_i \simeq r_i$ implies $\mathcal{T} \models S \supset l_j \simeq r_j$ for some j, $1 \leq j \leq n$, and S a set of $\mathcal{T}$-equations. It was shown in [7] that for a first-order theory with no trivial models convex implies *stably infinite*, i.e., such that any quantifier-free formula A has a $\mathcal{T}$-model only if it has an infinite $\mathcal{T}$-model. By applying this result, we have:

Theorem 7. *Let $\mathcal{T}$ be a presentation of a first-order theory with no trivial models. If $a_1 \simeq x \vee \ldots \vee a_n \simeq x \in S_\infty$, where S_∞ is the limit of any fair $\mathcal{SP}_\succ$-derivation from $S_0 = \mathcal{T} \cup S$, for any CSO $\succ$, then $\mathcal{T}$ is not convex.*

Thus, if $\mathcal{T}$ is not variable-inactive, because it generates some $a_1 \simeq x \vee \ldots \vee a_n \simeq x$, so that Theorem 5 does not apply, then $\mathcal{T}$ is not convex, and the Nelson-Oppen method does not apply either.

4   Experiments

We defined six sets of synthetic benchmarks: three in $\mathcal{A}^e$ (STORECOMM(n), SWAP(n) and STOREINV(n)), one combining $\mathcal{A}$ and $\mathcal{I}$ (IOS(n)), one combining $\mathcal{A}$, $\mathcal{R}$ and $\mathcal{I}$ (QUEUE(n)) and one combining $\mathcal{A}$, $\mathcal{R}$ and $\mathcal{I}_k$ (CIRCULAR_QUEUE(n, k)), with the common property that the set of formulæ grows monotonically with n. They were submitted to E 0.82, CVC 1.0a and CVC Lite 1.1.0. The prover E implements (a variant of) $\mathcal{SP}$ with a choice of search plans [17]. CVC [21] and CVC Lite [6] combine several $\mathcal{T}$-satisfiability procedures in the style of [14], including that of [22] for $\mathcal{A}^e$, and integrate them with a SAT engine. While CVC was superseded by CVC Lite, which is more modular and programmable, CVC is reportedly still faster on many problems.

A generator of pseudo-random instances of the benchmarks was written, producing either $\mathcal{T}$-reduced, flattened input files or plain input files. In the following, *native input* means $\mathcal{T}$-reduced, flattened files for E, and plain files for CVC and CVC Lite. Run times (on a 3.00GHz 512MB RAM Pentium 4 PC, with time and

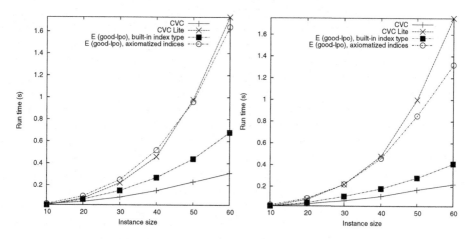

Fig. 1. Performances on valid (*left*) and invalid (*right*) STORECOMM instances, native input

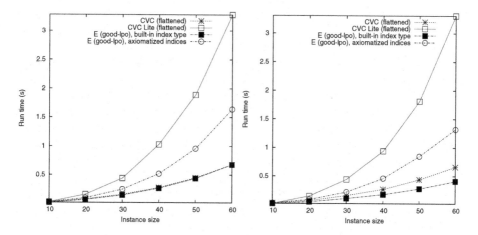

Fig. 2. Performances on valid (*left*) and invalid (*right*) STORECOMM instances, flat input for all

memory limited to 150 sec and 256 MB per run) do not include flattening time, because flattening is a one-time linear time operation, and flattening time is insignificant. For those problems (STORECOMM(n) and SWAP(n)) such that a value of n determines a set of instances of the problem, rather than a single instance, the reported run time is the *median* over all tested instances,[2] because the median is well-defined even when a system fails on some, but not all instances of size n,

---

[2] The figures refer to runs with 9 instances for each value of n. Different numbers of instances (e.g., 5, 20) were tried, but the impact on performance was negligible.

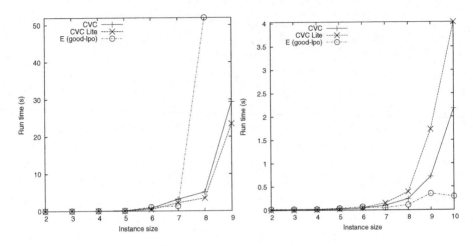

Fig. 3. Performances on valid (*left*) and invalid (*right*) SWAP instances, native input

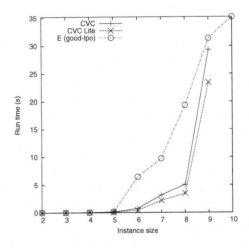

Fig. 4. Performances on valid SWAP instances with added lemma for E

a situation that occurs for all systems. (A failure is considered to be larger than all successful run times.)

The results for E refer to two strategies: $E(good\text{-}lpo)$ features a lexicographic path ordering (LPO), while $E(std\text{-}kbo)$ has a Knuth-Bendix ordering (KBO). $E(good\text{-}lpo)$ is $\mathcal{A}\text{-}good$, whereas $E(std\text{-}kbo)$ is $\mathcal{R}\text{-}good$ but not $\mathcal{A}\text{-}good$. $E(good\text{-}lpo)$ selects clauses by weight (symbol count where functions, constants and $\simeq$ weigh 2 and variables weigh 1), except for ensuring that all input clauses are selected before generated ones. $E(std\text{-}kbo)$ gives ground clauses higher priority than non-ground clauses and ranks clauses of same priority by weight as above.

We begin with the STORECOMM problems (Fig. 1 and 2). These sets include disequalities stating that all indices are distinct. Since many problems involve

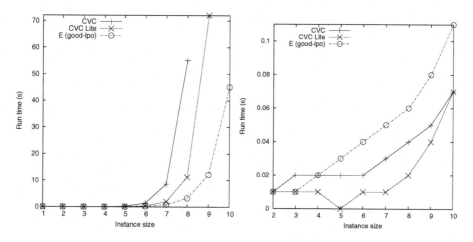

Fig. 5. Performances on valid (*left*) and invalid (*right*) STOREINV instances, native input

distinct objects, that is, constants that name elements known to be distinct in all models, E has a feature to build knowledge of distinct objects into the inference rules [18]. In Fig. 1 and 2, *built-in index type* refers to runs using this feature, while *axiomatized indices* refers to runs with the disequalities included in the input. On valid instances, *E(good-lpo)* with axiomatized indices and CVC Lite show nearly the same performance, with E apparently slightly ahead in the limit. *E(good-lpo)* with built-in indices outperforms CVC Lite by a factor of about 2.5. CVC performs best improving by another factor of 2. Perhaps surprisingly, since theorem provers are optimized for showing *unsatisfiability*, E performs even better on invalid (i.e., satisfiable) instances (Fig. 1, right), where it is faster than CVC Lite, and *E(good-lpo)* with built-in indices comes closer to CVC.

When *all* systems run on flattened input (Fig. 2), both CVC and CVC Lite exhibit run times approximately two times higher than with native format, and CVC Lite turns out to be the slowest system. CVC and E with built-in indices are the fastest: on valid instances, their performances are so close, that the plots are barely separable, but E is faster on invalid instances. Incidentally, it is not universally true that flattening hurt CVC and CVC Lite: on the SWAP problems CVC Lite performed better with flattened input. Although CVC is overall the fastest system on STORECOMM, E is faster than CVC Lite, and can do better than CVC on invalid instances when they are given the same input.

For SWAP (Fig. 3, left) the systems are very close up to instance size 5. Beyond this point, E leads up to size 7, but then is overtaken by CVC and CVC Lite. E can solve instances of size 8, but is much slower than CVC and CVC Lite, which solve instances up to size 9. No system can solve instances of size 10. For invalid instances, E solves easily instances up to size 10 in less than 0.5 sec, while CVC and CVC Lite are slower, taking 2 sec and 4 sec, respectively, and showing worse asymptotic behavior. Fig. 4 displays performances on valid instances, when the input for E includes the lemma $store(store(x, z, select(x, w)), w, select(x, z)) \simeq store(store(x, w, select(x, z)), z, select(x, w))$ that expresses "commutativity" of

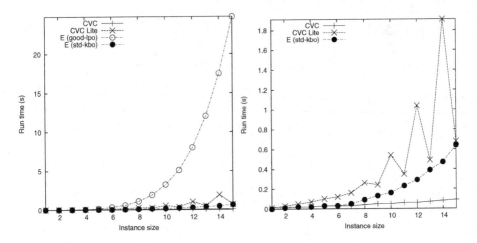

Fig. 6. Performances on IOS instances: on the right a rescaled version, with only the three fastest systems, of the same data on the left

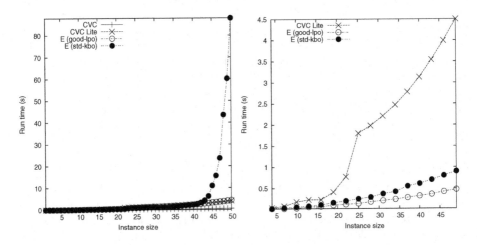

Fig. 7. Performances on QUEUE (*left*) and CIRCULAR_QUEUE with $k = 3$ (*right*)

store. Although this addition means that the theorem prover is no longer a decision procedure,[3] E terminates also on instances of size 9 and 10, and seems to show a better asymptotic behavior.

The comparison becomes even more favorable for the prover on STOREINV (Fig. 5). CVC solves valid instances up to size 8, CVC Lite goes up to size 9, but E solves instances of size 10, the largest generated. A comparison of run times at size 8 (the largest solved by all systems), gives 3.4 sec for E, 11 sec for CVC Lite, and 70 sec for CVC. Furthermore, *E(std-kbo)* (not shown in the figure) solves

---

[3] Theorem 1 does not hold, if this lemma is added to the presentation.

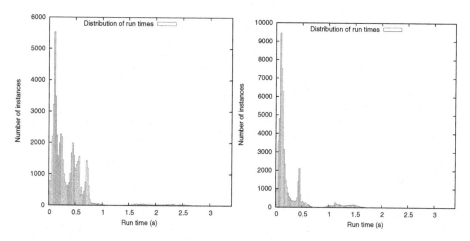

Fig. 8. Distribution of run times for E in automatic mode (*left*) and with optimized strategy (*right*) on the UCLID test set

valid instances in *nearly constant time*, taking less than 0.3 sec for the hardest problem. For invalid instances, E does not do as well, but the run times here are minimal, as the largest, for instances of size 10, is about 0.1 sec.

The IOS problems (all valid) are encoded for CVC and CVC Lite by using built-in linear arithmetic (on the reals for CVC and on the integers for CVC Lite). We tried to use inductive types in CVC, but it performed badly and reported incorrect results.[4] In terms of performance (Fig. 6), CVC clearly wins, as expected from a system with built-in arithmetic. *E(good-lpo)* is no match, although it solves all tried instances (Fig. 6, left). *E(std-kbo)* does much better, because of the ordering, and because, by not preferring initial clauses, it does not consider the axioms early. *E(std-kbo)* also does better than CVC Lite: it scales smoothly, while CVC Lite displays oscillating run times, showing worse performance for even instance sizes than for odd ones (Fig. 6, right).

Fig. 7 (left) shows performances on plain queues: as expected, CVC is the fastest system, but *E(good-lpo)* competes very well with the systems with built-in linear arithmetic. Fig. 7 (right) does not include CVC, because CVC cannot handle arithmetic modulo. Between CVC Lite and E, the latter demonstrates a clear superiority: it shows nearly linear performance, and proves the largest instance in less than 0.5 sec, nine times faster than CVC Lite.

For "real-world" problems, we extracted the satisfiability problems generated by haRVey [10] from various UCLID inputs. This resulted in over 55,000 proof tasks in the *combination of the theories of integer offsets and equality*. These problems (all valid) were easy for E in automatic mode, where the prover chooses ordering and search plan. E could solve all problems, taking less than 4 sec on

---

[4] This is a known bug, that will not be fixed since CVC is no longer supported (personal communication from A. Stump to A. Armando, Feb. 2005). CVC Lite 1.1.0 does not support inductive types.

the hardest one, with average 0.372 sec and median 0.25 sec (on three 2.4GHz Pentium-4 PC's, all other parameters unchanged). Fig 8 shows a histogram of run times: the vast majority of problems is solved in less than 1 sec and very few need between 1.5 and 3 sec. An optimized search plan was found by testing on a random sample of 500 problems, or less than 1% of the full set. With this search plan, similar to *E(std-kbo)*, the performance improved by about 40% (Fig 8, right): the average is 0.249 sec, the median 0.12 sec, the longest time 2.77 sec, and the vast majority of problems is solved in less than 0.5 sec.

5   Discussion

The application of automated reasoning to verification has long shown the importance of $\mathcal{T}$-satisfiability procedures. The most common approach, popularized as the *"little proof engines"* paradigm [19], works by building each theory into a dedicated inference engine. By symmetry with "little proof engines," one may use *"big proof engines"* for theorem-proving strategies for first-order logic. Although there has always been a continuum between big and little engines of proof (viz., the research on *reasoning modulo a theory*), these two paradigms have also grown apart from each other to some extent. The *rewriting approach to satisfiability* aims at replacing the apparent dichotomy ("little engines *versus* big engines") by a cross-fertilization ("big engines *as* little engines"). The general idea is to explore how big-engine technology (e.g., orderings, inference rules, search plans, algorithms, data structures, implementation techniques) may be applied selectively and efficiently "in the small."

The crucial point to use a first-order strategy as a $\mathcal{T}$-satisfiability procedure is to prove termination. We showed that a typical, complete, rewrite-based inference system for first-order logic, named $\mathcal{SP}$, is guaranteed to terminate on three new theories: *records, with and without extensionality, integer offsets*, and *integer offsets modulo*. For *combination of theories*, we gave a modularity theorem, stating sufficient conditions for $\mathcal{SP}$ to terminate on the combination, provided it terminates on each theory, and applied it to all theories under consideration.

Our experimental comparison of E with CVC and CVC Lite is the first of this kind. An analysis of E's traces showed that these $\mathcal{T}$-satisfiability problems behave very differently compared to more classical theorem-proving problems.

Table 1. Performance characteristics of array and TPTP problems

Problem Name	Initial clauses	Generated clauses	Processed clauses	Remaining clauses	Unnecessary inferences
STORECOMM(60)/1	1896	2840	4323	7	26.4%
STOREINV(5)	27	22590	7480	31	95.5%
SWAP(8)/3	62	73069	21743	56	98.2%
SET015-4	15	39847	7504	16219	99.90%
FLD032-1	31	44192	3964	31642	99.96%
RNG004-1	20	50551	4098	26451	99.90%

The latter usually involve large presentations, with rich signatures and many universal variables, rewrite rules, and mixed positive/negative literal clauses. The search space is typically infinite and only a very small part of it can ever be explored. In $\mathcal{T}$-satisfiability, presentations are usually small, there is only one goal clause, and a large number of ground rewrite rules generated by flattening. The search space is finite, but nearly all of it has to be explored. Table 1 compares the behavior of E in automatic mode on medium-difficulty unsatisfiable array problems and representative TPTP problems of similar difficulty for the prover.[5] Considering these differences, the theorem prover turned out to be very competitive with the "little engines" systems, although it was optimized for different search problems. Thus, further improvements might be obtained by studying search plans and implementation techniques of first-order inferences that target $\mathcal{T}$-satisfiability.

The prover terminated also beyond known termination results (e.g., Fig. 4, and the runs with $E(std\text{-}kbo)$), suggesting that theorem provers are not so brittle with respect to termination, and offer the flexibility of adding useful lemmata. Future directions for theoretical research include stronger termination theorems, and upper bounds on the number of generated clauses, assuming either blind saturation, or a fixed search plan, or a search plan of a given family. More general open issues are the integration with approaches to handle theories such as full linear arithmetics or bitvectors, and the application of "big engines" to more general $\mathcal{T}$-decision problems (arbitrary quantifier-free formulæ), whether by integration with a SAT solver (as explored first in [10]), or by using the prover's ability to handle first-order clauses.

Acknowledgements. We thank Stefano Ferrari, former student of the second author, for running preliminary experiments, and Paolo Fiorini, colleague of the second author, for access to the computers of the robotics laboratory.

References

1. K. Arkoudas, K. Zee, V. Kuncak, and M. Rinard. Verifying a File System Implementation. In *Proc. ICFEM 2004*, volume 3308 of *LNCS*. Springer, 2004.
2. A. Armando, M. P. Bonacina, S. Ranise, M. Rusinowitch, and A. K. Sehgal. High-Performance Deduction for Verification: a Case Study in the Theory of Arrays. In *Notes of the 2nd VERIFY Workshop, 3rd FLoC*, number 07/2002 in Technical Reports, pages 103–112. DIKU, U. Copenhagen, 2002.
3. A. Armando, M. P. Bonacina, S. Ranise, and S. Schulz. Big Proof Engines as Little Proof Engines: New Results on Rewrite-Based Satisfiability Procedures. In *Notes of the 3rd PDPAR Workshop, CAV-17*, Technical Reports. U. Edinburgh, 2005.
4. A. Armando, M. P. Bonacina, S. Ranise, and S. Schulz. On a Rewriting Approach to Satisfiability Procedures: Theories of Data Structures, Combination Framework and Experimental Appraisal. Technical Report 36/2005, Dip. di Informatica, U. Verona, May 2005. http://www.sci.univr.it/~bonacina/verify.html.

---

[5] TPTP 3.0.0: TPTP or "Thousands of Problems for Theorem Provers" is a standard library. See http://www.tptp.org/.

5. A. Armando, S. Ranise, and M. Rusinowitch. A Rewriting Approach to Satisfiability Procedures. *Information and Computation*, 183(2):140–164, 2003.
6. C. W. Barrett and S. Berezin. CVC Lite: A New Implementation of the Cooperating Validity Checker. In *Proc. CAV-16*, volume 3114 of *LNCS*, pages 515–518. Springer, 2004.
7. C. W. Barrett, D. L. Dill, and A. Stump. A Generalization of Shostak's Method for Combining Decision Procedures. In *Proc. FroCoS-4*, volume 2309 of *LNCS*. Springer, 2002.
8. R. E. Bryant, S. K. Lahiri, and S. A. Seshia. Modeling and Verifying Systems Using a Logic of Counter Arithmetic with Lambda Expressions and Uninterpreted Functions. In *Proc. CAV-14*, volume 2404 of *LNCS*. Springer, 2002.
9. L. de Moura, S. Owre, H. Rueß, J. Rushby, and N. Shankar. The ICS Decision Procedures for Embedded Deduction. In *Proc. IJCAR-2*, volume 3097 of *LNAI*, pages 218–222. Springer, 2004.
10. D. Déharbe and S. Ranise. Light-Weight Theorem Proving for Debugging and Verifying Units of Code. In *Proc. SEFM03*. IEEE, 2003.
11. D. L. Detlefs, G. Nelson, and J. B. Saxe. Simplify: a Theorem Prover for Program Checking. Technical Report 148, HP Labs, 2003.
12. H. Ganzinger. Shostak Light. In *Proc. CADE-18*, volume 2392 of *LNAI*, pages 332–347. Springer, 2002.
13. H. Ganzinger, G. Hagen, R. Nieuwenhuis, A. Oliveras, and C. Tinelli. DPLL(T): Fast Decision Procedures. In *Proc. CAV-16*, volume 3114 of *LNCS*, pages 175–188. Springer, 2004.
14. G. Nelson and D. C. Oppen. Simplification by Cooperating Decision Procedures. *ACM TOPLAS*, 1(2):245–257, 1979.
15. R. Nieuwenhuis and A. Rubio. Paramodulation-Based Theorem Proving. In *Handbook of Automated Reasoning*, volume 1. Elsevier Science, 2001.
16. H. Rueß and N. Shankar. Deconstructing Shostak. In *Proc. LICS-16*. IEEE, 2001.
17. S. Schulz. E – A Brainiac Theorem Prover. *J. of AI Comm.*, 15(2–3):111–126, 2002.
18. S. Schulz and M. P. Bonacina. On Handling Distinct Objects in the Superposition Calculus. In *Notes of the 5th Int. Workshop on Implementation of Logics, LPAR-11*, pages 66–77, March 2005.
19. N. Shankar. Little Engines of Proof, 2002. Invited talk, 3rd FLoC, Copenhagen; http://www.csl.sri.com/users/shankar/LEP.html.
20. R. E. Shostak. Deciding Combinations of Theories. *J. ACM*, 31(1):1–12, 1984.
21. A. Stump, C. W. Barrett, and D. L. Dill. CVC: a Cooperating Validity Checker. In *Proc. CAV-14*, LNCS. Springer, 2002.
22. A. Stump, C. W. Barrett, D. L. Dill, and J. Levitt. A Decision Procedure for an Extensional Theory of Arrays. In *Proc. LICS-16*. IEEE, 2001.

Sociable Interfaces[*]

Luca de Alfaro[1], Leandro Dias da Silva[1,2], Marco Faella[1,3], Axel Legay[1,4],
Pritam Roy[1], and Maria Sorea[5]

[1] School of Engineering, Universitity of California, Santa Cruz, USA
[2] Electrical Engineering Department, Federal University of Campina Grande, Paraiba, Brazil
[3] Dipartimento di Scienze Fisiche, Università di Napoli "Federico II", Italy
[4] Department of Computer Science, University of Liège, Belgium
[5] School of Computer Science, University of Manchester, United Kingdom

Abstract. Interface formalisms are able to model both the input requirements
and the output behavior of system components; they support both bottom-up
component-based design, and top-down design refinement. In this paper, we propose "sociable" interface formalisms, endowed with a rich compositional semantics that facilitates their use in design and modeling. Specifically, we introduce
interface models that can communicate via both actions and shared variables, and
where communication and synchronization covers the full spectrum, from one-to-
one, to one-to-many, many-to-one, and many-to-many. Thanks to the expressive
power of interface formalisms, this rich compositional semantics can be realized
in an economical way, on the basis of a few basic principles. We show how the
algorithms for composing, checking the compatibility, and refining the resulting
sociable interfaces can be implemented symbolically, leading to efficient implementations.

1 Introduction

Interface theories are formal models of communicating systems. Compared to traditional models, the strength of interface theories lies in their ability to model both the
input requirements, and the output behavior, of a system. This gives rise to a *compatibility* test when interface models are composed: two interfaces are compatible if there
is a way to use them (an environment) in which their input assumptions are simultaneously satisfied. This ability to model input assumptions and provide a compatibility test
makes interface models useful in system design. In particular, interface models support
both bottom-up, and top-down, design processes [6,7]. In a bottom-up direction, the
compatibility test can be used to check that portions of the design work correctly, even
before all the components are assembled in the final design. In a top-down direction,
interface models enable the hierarchical decomposition of a design specification, while
providing a guarantee that if the components satisfy their specifications, then they will
interact correctly in the overall implementation.

---

[*] This research was supported in part by the NSF CAREER award CCR-0132780, by the ONR
grant N00014-02-1-0671, by the ARP award TO.030.MM.D., by awards from the Brazilian
government agencies CNPq and CAPES, and by a F.R.I.A Grant

B. Gramlich (Ed.): FroCoS 2005, LNAI 3717, pp. 81–105, 2005.

In this paper we present interfaces models that can communicate via both actions and variables, and that provide one-to-one, many-to-one, one-to-many, and many-to-many communication and synchronization. We show that this rich communication semantics can be achieved by combining a small number of basic concepts, thanks to the expressive power of interface models. This leads to an uniform, and conceptually simple, communication model. We call this model *sociable interfaces,* underlining the ease with which these interfaces can be composed into models of design. While sociable interfaces do not break new ground in the conceptual theory of interface models, we hope that they constitute a useful step towards a practical, interface-based design methodology.

In sociable interfaces, synchronization and communication are based on two main ideas. The first idea is that the same action can appear as a label of both input and output transitions: when the action labels output transitions, it means that the interface can emit the action; when the action labels an input transition, it means that the action can be accepted if sent from other components. Depending on whether the action labels only input transitions, only output transitions, or both kind of transitions, we have different synchronization schemes. For instance, if an action a is associated only with output transitions, it means that the interface can emit a, but cannot receive it, and thus it cannot be composed with any other interface that emits a. Conversely, if a is associated only with input transitions, it means that the interface accepts a from other interfaces, but will not emit a. Finally, if a is associated both with input and output transitions, it means that the interface can both emit a, and accept a when emitted by other interfaces.

The second idea is that global variables do not belong to specific interfaces: the same global variable can be updated by multiple interfaces. In an interface, the output transitions associated with an action specifies how global variables can be updated when the interface emits the action; the input transition associated with an action specifies constraints on how other interfaces can update the global variables when emitting the action. By limiting the sets of variables whose value must be tracked by the interfaces, and by introducing appropriate non-interference conditions among interfaces, we can ensure that interfaces can participate in complex communication schemes with limited knowledge about the other participants. In particular, interfaces do not need to know in advance the number or identities of the other interfaces that take part in communication schemes. This facilitates component reuse, as the same interface model can be used in different contexts.

We show that the compatibility and refinement of sociable interfaces can be checked via efficient symbolic algorithms. We have implemented these algorithms in a tool called TIC (Tool for Interface Compatibility); the tool is written in Ocaml [10], and the symbolic algorithms for interface compatibility and refinement are built on top of the MDD/BDD Glue and Cudd packages [13,12].

The paper is organized as follows. First, we introduce *sociable interface automata,* which include actions, but not variables, and which are a more "sociable" version of the interface automata of [6,8]. After illustrating the various synchronization and communication features for sociable interface automata, we endow them with variables in Section 3, obtaining *sociable interface modules.* We describe the communication mechanisms of sociable interface modules via examples, and we show how the examples can

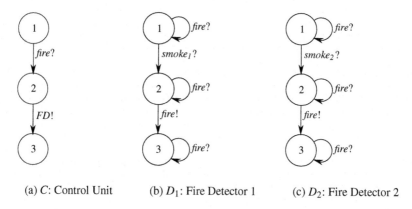

(a) C: Control Unit   (b) D_1: Fire Detector 1   (c) D_2: Fire Detector 2

Fig. 1. Sociable interface automata for a fire detection and reporting system

be encoded in the input language of the tool TIC. The refinement of sociable interfaces is discussed Section 4, and the symbolic implementation of the composition and refinement algorithms is in Section 5. We conclude with a comparison between sociable interfaces and previous interface formalisms.

2   Sociable Interface Automata

Social interfaces communicate via both actions and variables. We first illustrate how sociable interfaces communicate via actions; in the next section, we will augment them with variables, obtaining the model implemented in the tool TIC. We begin with an informal, intuitive preview, which will motivate the definitions.

2.1   Preview

To provide some intuition on sociable interfaces, we present an example: a very simple model of a fire detection and reporting system. The sociable interfaces for this example are depicted in Figure 1: D_1 and D_2 are the fire detectors (there could be more), and C is the control unit. When the fire detectors D_1 and D_2 detect smoke (input events $smoke_1?$, $smoke_2?$), they generate an output event $fire!$. The control unit, upon receiving the input event $fire?$, issues a call for the fire department (output event $FD!$). Similar to the original interface model [6,8], the input and output transitions departing from a state of a sociable interface denote the inputs that can be received, and the outputs that can be generated, from that state. For instance, the sociable interface C (Figure 1(a)) specifies that input event $fire?$ can be accepted at state 1, but not at state 2.

Product and composition. To compose two sociable interfaces, we first form their automata product. In the product, shared output/input events (such as the pair $fire!$–$fire?$ in Figure 1) synchronize: this models communication, or synchronization, initiated by the interface issuing the output transition. Similarly, two interfaces can also synchronize on shared inputs: when the environment generates an input, both interfaces will receive it

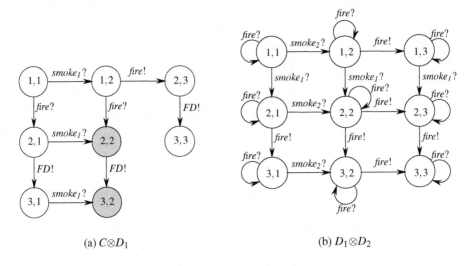

(a) $C \otimes D_1$ (b) $D_1 \otimes D_2$

Fig. 2. Product of the automata D_1, D_2, and C

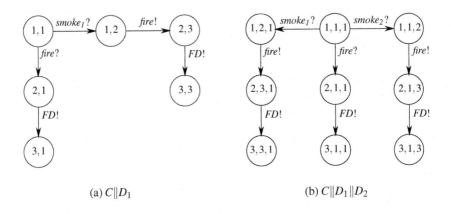

(a) $C \| D_1$ (b) $C \| D_1 \| D_2$

Fig. 3. Composition of the automata D_1, D_2, and C

and take the corresponding input transition. However, interfaces do not synchronize on shared outputs: as an example, D_1 and D_2 do not synchronize on the output event *fire!* in their product $D_1 \otimes D_2$ (Figure 2(b)). The idea is that, in an asynchronous model, independent components issue their output asynchronously, so that synchronization cannot happen. As usual, interfaces do not synchronize on non-shared actions.

In the product of two interfaces, we distinguish between *good* and *bad* states. A state is *good* if all the outputs produced by one component can be accepted as inputs by the other component; a state is bad otherwise. For instance, in the product $C \otimes D_1$ (Figure 2(a)), the states $\langle 2, 2 \rangle$ and $\langle 3, 2 \rangle$ are *bad*, since from state 2 the detector D_1 can issue *fire!*, and this cannot be matched by an input transition *fire?* neither from state 2 nor from state 3 of the control unit.

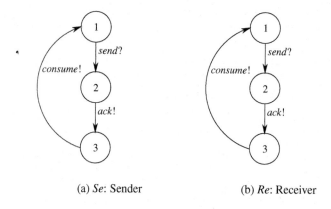

(a) *Se*: Sender   (b) *Re*: Receiver

Fig. 4. A simple communication protocol

A state of the product is *compatible* if there is an Input strategy that can avoid all bad states: this means that starting from that state, there is an environment under which the component interfaces interact correctly. The composition of two interfaces is obtained by removing all incompatible states from the product. The composition $C \| D_1$ of C and D_1 is depicted in Figure 3(a), and the composition of $C \| D_1 \| D_2$ is depicted in Figure 3(b). Notice that in the composition $C \| D_1 \| D_2$, once $smoke_1$ (resp. $smoke_2$) is received, $smoke_2$ (resp. $smoke_1$) is not allowed. This behavior results from the design of the control unit which cannot accept more than one "smoke-input" before issuing *FD!*.

Multi-way communication. In a sociable interface, the same action can label both input and output transitions: this is illustrated, for instance, by action *fire* in Figures 1(b) and 1(c). Indeed, sociable interfaces do not have separate input and output transition alphabets: rather, they have a single *action alphabet*, and actions in this alphabet can label edges both as inputs, giving rise to *input transitions*, and as outputs, giving rise to *output transitions*. For example, the action *fire* at state 2 of D_1 corresponds to both an output, and to an input transition: this indicates that D_1 can generate output *fire*, while at the same time being composable with other interfaces that generate *fire* as output (such as D_2). Thus, if an action a is in the alphabet of an interface, there are four cases:

– If a is not associated with any transition, then the interface neither outputs a, nor can it be composed with other interfaces that do.
– If a is associated with output transitions only, then the interface can generate a, but it cannot be composed with interfaces that also output a.
– If a is associated with input transitions only, then the interface can receive a, but not output it.
– If a is associated with both input and output transitions, then the interface can generate a, and it can be composed with other interfaces that do.

We notice how these four cases all arise in an uniform way from our interpretation of input and output edges. All of these cases have a use in system modeling: the fire detector example illustrated the non-exclusive generation of outputs, the next example illustrates exclusive generation.

Figure 4 depicts a simple communication protocol. In this protocol, the sender *Se*, after receiving information from the environment (label *produce?*), sends this information to the receiver (label *send!*), and awaits for an acknowledge (label *ack?*). The lack of input edges labeled with *send* in *Se*, and the lack of input edges labeled with *ack* in *Re* indicate that the communication channel between *Se* and *Re* is not shared: only *Se* can generate *send* actions, and only *Re* can generate *ack* actions.

2.2 Definitions

Given two sets A and B, we denote with $A \rightrightarrows B$ the set of *nondeterministic functions* from A to B, that is: $A \to 2^B$.

Definition 1 (Sociable Interface Automaton). A *sociable interface automaton* (automaton for short) is a tuple $M = (Act, S, \tau^I, \tau^O, \varphi^I, \varphi^O)$, where:

- *Act* is a set of *actions*.
- S is a set of *states*.
- $\tau^I : Act \times S \rightrightarrows S$ is the *input transition function*.
- $\tau^O : Act \times S \rightrightarrows S$ is the *output transition function*.
- $\varphi^I \subseteq S$ is the *input invariant*.
- $\varphi^O \subseteq S$ is the *output invariant*.

We require τ^I to be deterministic, that is: for all $s \in S$ and $a \in Act$, $|\tau^I(a,s)| \leq 1$.

For all $s \in S$ and $a \in Act$, we define $\widehat{\tau}^I(a,s) = \tau^I(a,s) \cap \varphi^I$, and $\widehat{\tau}^O(a,s) = \tau^O(a,s) \cap \varphi^O$. Together, S, τ^I and τ^O define a graph whose edges are labeled with actions in *Act*. As it was already informally done in the examples of Section 2.1, we therefore depict interface automata as graphs. To distinguish input from output transitions, we add a tag at the end of the name of the action: as in process algebra notation, we add "?" for input transitions and "!" for output transitions. In all examples, it holds $\varphi^I = \varphi^O = S$.

Example 1. Figure 1(b) is a graphical representation of a 3-state automaton whose actions are *fire*, and *smoke$_1$*. For instance, from state 2, the automaton can take an input transition *fire?*, as well as an output transition *fire!*.

The semantics of a sociable interface automaton can be described in terms of a game between two players, Input and Output, played over the graph representation of the automaton. At each round, from the current state in the graph, the Input player chooses an outgoing input edge, and the Output player chooses an outgoing output edge. In order to ensure that both players always have an enabled move, we introduce a special move Δ_0 which, when played, gives rise to a *stuttering step*, that is, a step that does not change the current state of the automaton. Furthermore, we postulate that player Output (resp. Input) can choose only edges that lead to states where the output (resp. input) invariant holds. Thus, input and output invariants are used to restrict the set of moves available to the players; their true usefulness will become clearer when considering interfaces with variables, i.e. *modules*.

In the remaining of this section, we consider a fixed sociable interface automaton $M = (Act_M, S_M, \tau_M^I, \tau_M^O, \varphi_M^I, \varphi_M^O)$. The sets of enabled moves can be defined as follows.

Definition 2 (Moves). For all $s \in S_M$, the set of moves for player Input at s is given by:

$$\Gamma^I(M,s) = \{\Delta_0\} \cup \{\langle a,s'\rangle \in Act_M \times S_M \mid s' \in \widehat{\tau}^I_M(a,s)\}.$$

Similarly, the set of moves for player Output at s is given by:

$$\Gamma^O(M,s) = \{\Delta_0\} \cup \{\langle a,s'\rangle \in Act_M \times S_M \mid s' \in \widehat{\tau}^O_M(a,s)\}.$$

Example 2. Consider the automaton D_1 of Example 1, we have that $\Gamma^I(D_1,1) = \{\Delta_0, \langle fire,1\rangle, \langle smoke_1,2\rangle\}$, and $\Gamma^O(D_1,2) = \{\Delta_0, \langle fire,3\rangle\}$.

At each game round, both players choose a move from the corresponding set of enabled moves. The outcome of their choice is defined as follows.

Definition 3 (Move Outcome). For all states $s \in S_M$ and moves $m^I \in \Gamma^I(M,s)$ and $m^O \in \Gamma^O(M,s)$, the *outcome* $\delta(M,s,a^I,a^O) \in S_M$ of playing m^I and m^O at s can be defined as follows, according to whether m^I and m^O are Δ_0 or a move of the form $\langle a,s'\rangle$.

$$\delta(M,s,\Delta_0,\Delta_0) = \{s\}, \qquad\qquad \delta(M,s,\Delta_0,\langle a,s'\rangle) = \{s'\},$$

$$\delta(M,s,\langle a,s'\rangle,\Delta_0) = \{s'\}, \qquad\qquad \delta(M,s,\langle a,s'\rangle,\langle b,t'\rangle) = \{s',t'\}.$$

A *strategy* represents the behavior of a player in the game. A strategy is a function that, given the history of the game, i.e., the sequence of states visited in the course of the game, yields one of the player's enabled moves.

For $s \in S_M$, we define the set of *finite runs* starting from s as the set $Runs(M,s) \subseteq S^*_M$ of all finite sequences $s_0s_1s_2\ldots s_n$, such that $s_0 = s$, and for all $0 \le i < n$, $s_{i+1} \in \delta(M,s_i,m^I,m^O)$, for some $m^I \in \Gamma^I(M,s_i)$, $m^O \in \Gamma^O(M,s_i)$. We also set $Runs(M) = \bigcup_{s \in S_M} Runs(M,s)$.

Definition 4 (Strategy). A *strategy* for player $p \in \{I,O\}$ in an automaton M is a function $\pi^p : Runs(M) \to Act_M \cup \{\Delta_0\}$ that associates, with every run $\sigma \in Runs(M)$ whose final state is s, a move $\pi^p(\sigma) \in \Gamma^p(M,s)$. We denote by Π^I_M and Π^O_M the set of input and output strategies for M, respectively.

An input and an output strategy jointly determine a *set* of *outcomes* in $Runs(M)$.

Definition 5 (Strategy Outcome). Given a state $s \in S_M$, an input strategy $\pi^I \in \Pi^I_M$ and an output strategy $\pi^O \in \Pi^O_M$, the set *outcomes* $\widehat{\delta}(M,s,\pi^I,\pi^O)$ of π^I and π^O from s consists of all finite runs $\sigma = s_0s_1s_2\ldots s_n$ such that $s = s_0$, and for all $0 \le i < n$, $s_{i+1} \in \delta(M,s_i,\pi^I(\sigma_{0:i}),\pi^O(\sigma_{0:i}))$, where $\sigma_{0:i}$ denotes the prefix $s_0s_1s_2\ldots s_i$ of σ.

Definition 6 (Winning States). Given a state $s \in S_M$ and a goal $\gamma \subseteq Runs(M,s)$, we say that s is *winning* for input with respect to γ, and we write $s \in Win^I(M,\gamma)$, iff there is $\pi^I \in \Pi^I_M$ such that for all $\pi^O \in \Pi^O_M$, $\widehat{\delta}(M,s,\pi^I,\pi^O) \subseteq \gamma$. Similarly, we say that s is *winning* for output with respect to γ, and we write $s \in Win^O(M,\gamma)$, iff there is $\pi^O \in \Pi^O_M$ such that for all $\pi^I \in \Pi^I_M$, $\widehat{\delta}(M,s,\pi^I,\pi^O) \subseteq \gamma$.

A state of an automaton is *well-formed* if both players have a strategy to always satisfy their own invariant. Following temporal logic notation, for all $X \subseteq S_M$, we denote by $\Box X$ the set of all runs in $Runs(M)$ all whose states belong to X. Formally, $\Box X = \{s_0 s_1 s_2 \ldots s_n \in Runs(M) \mid \forall 0 \le i \le n . s_i \in X\}$.

Definition 7 (Well-formed State). We say that a state $s \in S_M$ is *well-formed* iff $s \in Win^I(M, \Box\varphi_M^I) \cap Win^O(M, \Box\varphi_M^O)$.

Notice that if s is well-formed, then $s \in \varphi_M^I \cap \varphi_M^O$.

Definition 8 (Normal Form). We say that M is in *normal form* iff $\varphi_M^I = Win^I(M, \Box\varphi_M^I)$, and $\varphi_M^O = Win^O(M, \Box\varphi_M^O)$.

Given an automaton M_1, we can define an automaton M_2 such that the well-formed portion of M_1 coincides with the one of M_2, and M_2 is in normal form. Let $M_1 = (Act_1, S_1, \tau_1^I, \tau_1^O, \varphi_1^I, \varphi_1^O)$, we set $M_2 = (Act_1, S_1, \tau_2^I, \tau_2^O, \varphi_2^I, \varphi_2^O)$, where, $\varphi_2^I = Win^I(M_1, \Box\varphi_1^I)$ and $\varphi_2^O = Win^I(M_1, \Box\varphi_1^O)$. Thus, in the following, unless differently specified, we only consider automata in normal form.

Definition 9 (Well-formed Automaton). We say that M is *well-formed* iff it is in normal form, and $\varphi_M^I \cap \varphi_M^O \ne \emptyset$.

Lemma 1. *If M is in normal form, then it holds:*

$$\forall s \in \varphi_M^I . \forall a \in \Gamma^O(M,s) . \widehat{\tau}_M^O(a,s) \subseteq \varphi_M^I$$
$$\forall s \in \varphi_M^O . \forall a \in \Gamma^I(M,s) . \widehat{\tau}_M^O(a,s) \subseteq \varphi_M^O.$$

Proof. For the first statement, by contradiction, suppose there is $s \in \varphi_M^I$ and $a \in \Gamma^O(M,s)$ such that $\widehat{\tau}_M^O(a,s) \not\subseteq \varphi_M^I$. Then $s \notin Win^I(M, \Box\varphi_M^I)$, because there is no way for the Input player to prevent output a to be carried out (see Definition 3). This contrasts with the assumption that M is in normal form. The second statement can be proven along similar lines.

2.3 Compatibility and Composition

In this subsection, we define the composition of two automata $M_1 = (Act_1, S_1, \tau_1^I, \tau_1^O, \varphi_1^I, \varphi_1^O)$ and $M_2 = (Act_2, S_2, \tau_2^I, \tau_2^O, \varphi_2^I, \varphi_2^O)$. We first define the product between $M_1 \otimes M_2$ as the classical automata-theoretic product, where M_1 and M_2 synchronize on shared actions and evolve independently on non-shared ones. We then identify a set of incompatible states where M_1 can do an output transition that is not accepted by M_2 or vice-versa. Finally, we obtain the composition $M_1 \| M_2$ from $M_1 \otimes M_2$ by strengthening the input assumptions of $M_1 \otimes M_2$ in such a way that M_1 and M_2 mutually satisfy their input assumptions.

Definition 10. We define the set of shared actions of M_1 and M_2 by:

$$Shared(M_1, M_2) = Act_1 \cap Act_2.$$

The product of two automata M_1 and M_2 is an automaton $M_1 \otimes M_2$, representing the joint behavior of M_1 and M_2. Similarly to other interface models, for each shared action, the output transitions of M_1 synchronize with the input transitions of M_2, and symmetrically, the output transitions of M_2 are synchronized with the input transitions of M_1. This models communication, and gives rise to output transitions in the product. The input transitions of M_1 and M_2 corresponding to shared actions are also synchronized, and lead to input transitions in the product. Output transitions, on the other hand, are not synchronized. If both M_1 and M_2 can emit a shared action a, they do so asynchronously, so that their output transitions interleave. As usual, the automata interleave asynchronously on transitions labeled by non-shared actions.

Definition 11 (Product). The *product* $M_1 \otimes M_2$ is the automaton $M_{12} = (Act_{12}, S_{12}, \tau_{12}^I, \tau_{12}^O, \varphi_{12}^I, \varphi_{12}^O)$, consisting of the following components.

- $Act_{12} = Act_1 \cup Act_2$; $S_{12} = S_1 \times S_2$.
- $\varphi_{12}^I = \varphi_1^I \times \varphi_2^I$; $\varphi_{12}^O = \varphi_1^O \times \varphi_2^O$.
- For $a \in Shared(M_1, M_2)$,

$$\langle s', t' \rangle \in \tau_{12}^O(a, \langle s, t \rangle) \text{ iff } \begin{cases} s' \in \tau_1^O(a, s) \text{ and } t' \in \tau_2^I(a, t) \text{ or} \\ t' \in \tau_2^O(a, t) \text{ and } s' \in \tau_1^I(a, s) \end{cases}$$

$$\langle s', t' \rangle \in \tau_{12}^I(a, \langle s, t \rangle) \text{ iff } s' \in \tau_1^I(a, s) \text{ and } t' \in \tau_2^I(a, t).$$

- For $a \in Act_1 \setminus Act_2$,

$$\langle s', t \rangle \in \tau_{12}^O(a, \langle s, t \rangle) \text{ iff } s' \in \tau_1^O(a, s)$$

$$\langle s', t \rangle \in \tau_{12}^I(a, \langle s, t \rangle) \text{ iff } s' \in \tau_1^I(a, s).$$

- For $a \in Act_2 \setminus Act_1$,

$$\langle s, t' \rangle \in \tau_{12}^O(a, \langle s, t \rangle) \text{ iff } t' \in \tau_2^O(a, t)$$

$$\langle s, t' \rangle \in \tau_{12}^I(a, \langle s, t \rangle) \text{ iff } t' \in \tau_2^I(a, t).$$

Example 3. The sociable interface automaton depicted in Figure 2(a) is the product $C \otimes D_1$ of the automata depicted in Figures 1(a) and 1(b). For instance, the input transition *fire?* from state $\langle 1, 1 \rangle$ to state $\langle 2, 1 \rangle$ is obtained by combining the input transition *fire?* from state 1 to state 2 in C with the input transition *fire?* from state 1 to state 1 in D_1. The output transition *FD!* from state $\langle 1, 2 \rangle$ to state $\langle 2, 3 \rangle$ is obtained by combining the input transition *fire?* from state 1 to state 2 in C with the output transition *fire!* from state 2 to state 3 in D_1.

We have the following theorem.

Theorem 1. *The product is a commutative and associative operation, up to isomorphism.*

The product $M_{12} = M_1 \otimes M_2$ may contain states in which one of the components, say M_1, can do an output transition labeled by a shared action while the other component cannot do the corresponding input transition. This constitutes a violation of the input assumptions of M_2. We formalize such notion by introducing a *local compatibility* condition. To this end, for $p \in \{I, O\}$, we denote by $En^p(M, a)$ the set of states of M where the action a is enabled as input if $p = I$, and as output if $p = O$. Formally,

$$En^p(M, a) = \{s \in S_M \mid \widehat{\tau}_M^p(a, s) \neq \emptyset\}.$$

Definition 12 (Local Compatibility). Given $\langle s, t \rangle \in S_{12}$, $\langle s, t \rangle \in good(M_1, M_2)$ iff, for all $a \in Shared(M_1, M_2)$ the following conditions hold:

$$s \in En^O(M_1, a) \Rightarrow t \in En^I(M_2, a)$$
$$t \in En^O(M_2, a) \Rightarrow s \in En^I(M_1, a).$$

Example 4. Consider the product $C \otimes D_1$ of Example 4. The state $\langle 3, 2 \rangle$ does not satisfy the Local Compatibility condition because, from state 2, D_1 can issue an output transition *fire!*, and this cannot be matched by an input transition *fire?* from state 3 of the control unit.

The composition of M_1 and M_2 is obtained from the product $M_1 \otimes M_2$ by strengthening the input assumptions of $M_1 \otimes M_2$ to avoid states that are not in $good(M_1, M_2)$. This is done by restricting the input invariant φ_{12}^I as shown in the next definition. The reason for restricting only the input behavior is that, when composing automata, only their input assumptions can be strengthened to ensure that no incompatibility arises, while their output behavior cannot be modified.

Definition 13 (Composition). Assume M_1 and M_2 are compatible. The *composition* $M_1 \| M_2$ is a sociable interface automaton identical to $M_1 \otimes M_2$, except that $\varphi_{M_1 \| M_2}^I = \varphi_{12}^I \cap Win^I(M_{12}, \square(\varphi_{12}^I \cap good(M_1, M_2)))$.

Definition 14 (Compatibility). We say that M_1 and M_2 are *compatible* if $\varphi_{M_1 \| M_2}^I \cap \varphi_{M_1 \| M_2}^O \neq \emptyset$.

The following theorem states that once the input transition relations have been strengthened, the automaton is in normal form: it is not necessary to also strengthen the output transition relations. This result thus provides a sanity check, since strengthening the output transitions means restricting the output behavior of the interfaces, which is not reasonable.

Theorem 2. *If M_1 and M_2 are compatible, and they are in normal form, then $M_1 \| M_2$ is in normal form.*

The following result implies that the automata can be composed in any order.

Theorem 3. *The composition is a commutative and associative operation, up to isomorphism.*

3   Sociable Interfaces with Variables

3.1   Preview

In modeling systems and designs, it is often valuable to have a notion of global state, which can be read and updated by the various components of the system. A common, and flexible, paradigm consists in having the global state consist of a value assignment to a set of global variables. Once the global state is represented by global variables, it is natural to encode also the local state of each component via (local) variables.

Previous interface models, such as interface automata [6,8] and interface modules [7,3] were based on either actions, or variables, but not both. In sociable interfaces, however, we want to have both: actions to model synchronization, and variables to encode the global and local state of components. In this, sociable interfaces are closely related to the *I/O Automata Language* (IOA) of [11].

Interface models are games between Input and Output, and in the models, it is essential that Input and Output are able to choose their moves independently from one another. To this end, in previous interface formalisms with variables, the variables were partitioned into *input* and *output* variables [7,3]. A move of Input consisted in choosing the next value of the input variables, and a move of Output consisted in choosing the next value of the output variables: this ensured the independence of the moves. Consequently, interfaces sharing output variables could not be composed, and in a composite system, every variable that was not input from the environment was essentially "owned" by one of the component interfaces, which was the only one allowed to modify its value.

In sociable interface modules, we can leverage the presence of actions in order to achieve a more general setting, in which variables can be modified by more than one module. Informally, the model is as follows. With each action, we associate a set of variables that can be modified by the action, as well as an output and an input transition relation that describe the ways in which the variables can be modified when the component, or its environment, output the action. When the Output player takes an action a, the output transition relation associated with a specifies how the player can update the variables associated with a. Symmetrically, when the Input player takes an action a, the input transition relation associated with a specifies what changes to the variables associated with a can be accepted by the module.

When modules are composed, actions synchronize in the same way as they do in sociable interface automata. When an output event $a!$ of module M synchronizes with an input event $a?$ of module N, we must check that all variable updates that can accompany $a!$ from M are acceptable to N, that is, that the output transition relation associated with a in M respects the constraints specified by the input transition relation associated with a in N. Empty transition relations are used to rule out the possibility of taking an action as output or input.

3.2   An Example: Modeling a Print Server

We illustrate the main features of sociable interface modules through a very simple example: a model of a shared print server. The model consists of modules representing the print server, as well as user processes that communicate with the server to print

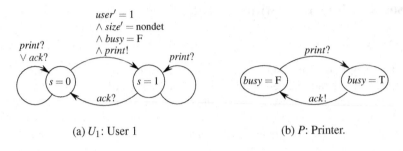

(a) U_1: User 1   (b) P: Printer.

Fig. 5. Informal depiction of the user process and printer interface modules

jobs. The modules composing this example are depicted in an intuitive fashion in Figure 5; the actual input to the tool TIC for this model is given in Figure 6, and it will be described later.

The user module U_1 (Figure 5(a)) communicates via two actions: an action *print*, whose output represents a print request, and an action *ack*, whose input represents an acknowledgment. When generating *print* as an output, U_1 updates the global variables *user* and *size*, which indicate the user who issued the request, and the size of the request. The print server P (Figure 5(b)) synchronizes on *ack* and *print*, and also updates a global state variable *busy*, indicating whether the printer is busy. To ensure compatibility, the user module checks that *busy* = F before printing. In addition, to ensure compatibility in presence of multiple user modules, the user module ignores inputs *ack* when idle ($s = 0$), as these acknowledgments are directed to other users, and ignores all inputs *print*, as these correspond to input requests from other users.

3.3 Definitions

We assume a fixed set $\mathcal{V}$ of variables. All variables in $\mathcal{V}$ are interpreted over a given domain $\mathcal{D}$. Given $V \subseteq \mathcal{V}$, a *state* over V is a mapping $s : V \to \mathcal{D}$ that associates with each $x \in V$ a value $s(x) \in \mathcal{D}$. For a set of variables $U \subseteq V$, and a state $s \in [\![V]\!]$, the restriction of s to U is a state $t \in [\![U]\!]$ denoted as $s[U]$. For two disjoint sets of variables V_1 and V_2, and two states $s_1 \in [\![V_1]\!]$ and $s_2 \in [\![V_2]\!]$, the operation $(s_1 \circ s_2)$ composes the two states resulting in a new state $s = s_1 \circ s_2 \in [\![V_1 \cup V_2]\!]$, such that $s(x) = s_1(x)$ for all $x \in V_1$ and $s(x) = s_2(x)$ for all $x \in V_2$.

Our formal model with variables is called a *sociable interface module*. It is convenient to define sociable interface modules with respect to a predicate representation. Given a set V of variables, we denote by $Preds(V)$ the set of first-order predicate formulas with free variables in V; we assume that these predicates are written in some specified first-order language with interpreted function symbols and predicates; in our tool, the language contains some arithmetic operators, relational symbols, and boolean connectives. Given a set of variables V, we let $V' = \{x' \mid x \in V\}$ be the set consisting of primed versions of variables in V. A variable $x' \in V'$ represents the *next value* of $x \in V$. Given a formula $\psi \in Preds(V)$ and a state $s \in [\![V]\!]$, we write $s \models \psi$ if the predicate formula ψ is true when its free variables are interpreted as specified by s. Given a formula

$\rho \in Preds(V \cup V')$ and two states $s, s' \in [\![V]\!]$, we write $\langle s, s' \rangle \models \rho$ if the formula ρ holds when its free variables $x \in V$ are interpreted as $s(x)$, and its free variables $x' \in V'$ are interpreted as $s'(x)$. Given a set U of variables, we define the formula:

$$Unchgd(U) = \bigwedge_{x \in U} (x' = x),$$

which states that the variables in U do not change their value in a transition. Given a predicate $\psi \in Preds(V)$, we denote by ψ' the predicate obtained by substituting x with x' in ψ, for all $x \in V$.

With these definitions, we can define sociable interface modules as follows.

Definition 15 (Sociable Interface Module). A *sociable interface module* (*module*, for short) is a tuple $M = (Act, V^G, V^L, V^H, W, \rho^{IL}, \rho^{IG}, \rho^O, \psi^I, \psi^O)$, where:

- *Act* is a set of *actions*.
- V^G is a set of *global variables*, V^L is a set of *local variables*, and $V^H \subseteq V^G$ is a set of *history variables*. We require $V^L \cap V^G = \emptyset$. We set $V^{\text{all}} = V^L \cup V^G$ and $V = V^L \cup V^H$.
- $W : Act \rightrightarrows V^{\text{all}}$ associates with each $a \in Act$ the set of variables $W(a) \subseteq V^{\text{all}}$ that can be modified by a.
- For each $a \in Act$, the predicate $\rho^{IL}(a) \in Preds(V^{\text{all}} \cup (V^{\text{all}})')$ is the *input local transition predicate* for a. We require this transition predicate to be *deterministic* w.r.t. variables in V^L, that is, for all $a \in Act$, all $s \in [\![V^{\text{all}}]\!]$, and all $t \in [\![(V^G)']\!]$, there is a unique $u \in [\![(V^L)']\!]$ such that $s \circ t \circ u \models \rho^{IL}(a)$.
- For each $a \in Act$, the predicate $\rho^{IG}(a) \in Preds(V^{\text{all}} \cup (V^G)')$ is the *input global transition predicate* for a.
- For each $a \in Act$, the predicate $\rho^O(a) \in Preds(V^{\text{all}} \cup W(a)')$ is the *output transition predicate* for a.
- $\psi^I \in Preds(V^{\text{all}})$ is the *input invariant predicate*.
- $\psi^O \in Preds(V^{\text{all}})$ is the *output invariant predicate*.

A *state* is a value assignment to V^{all}; we denote the set of states of the module by $S = [\![V^{\text{all}}]\!]$. The invariant predicates define invariants

$$\varphi^I = \{s \in S \mid s \models \psi^I\}, \qquad\qquad \varphi^O = \{s \in S \mid s \models \psi^O\}.$$

As a shorthand, for all $a \in Act$ we let $\rho^I(a) = \rho^{IL}(a) \wedge \rho^{IG}(a)$, and we define

$$\widehat{\rho}^I(a) = \rho^I(a) \wedge (\psi^I)'$$

$$\widehat{\rho}^O(a) = \rho^O(a) \wedge (\psi^O)' \wedge Unchgd(V^{\text{all}} \setminus W(a)).$$

Notice that $\widehat{\rho}^I(a)$ and $\widehat{\rho}^O(a)$ are predicates over $V^{\text{all}} \cup (V^{\text{all}})'$.

In our model, each module owns a set of local variables, that describe the internal state of a component. We distinguish a set V^H of *history* variables, and a set $V^G \setminus V^H$ of *history-free* variables. A module must be aware of all actions that can modify its history variables (see, in the following, the *non-interference* condition in Definition 19). On the other hand, history-free variables can be modified by environment actions that are not known to the module. The distinction between the history and history-free global variables is thus used to limit the amount of actions a module should include; this point will be clarified when we will discuss module composability.

The definitions of the input and output transition relations are similar to those of Section 2. We require the input transition relation to be deterministic on local variables. This assumption corresponds to the assumption, in the model without variables, that input transitions are deterministic. In fact, we will see that when an output and an input transitions synchronize, it is the output transition that selects the next value of the global variables, and the input transition is used only to determine the next value of the local variables.

In the remainder of this section we consider a fixed module $M = (Act_M, V_M^G, V_M^L, V_M^H, W_M, \rho_M^{IL}, \rho_M^{IG}, \rho_M^O, \psi_M^I, \psi_M^O)$, and we set $V_M = V_M^L \cup V_M^H$, $V_M^{all} = V_M^L \cup V_M^G$, and correspondingly for the shorthands $\widehat{\rho}_M^I$ and $\widehat{\rho}_M^O$.

Definition 16 (Set of States). The set of states of the sociable interface module M is given by $S_M = [\![V_M^{all}]\!]$.

The sets of moves for players Input and Output are defined as follows. Note that, when Input plays the move Δ_0, Input can also choose a new assignment to the history-free variables. This models the fact that history-free variables can be modified by environment actions that are not known to the module.

Definition 17 (Moves). The sets $\Gamma^I(M,s)$ and $\Gamma^O(M,s)$ of Input and Output moves at $s \in S_M$ are defined as follows:

$$\Gamma^I(M,s) = \{\Delta_0\} \times \{s' \in [\![V_M^{all}]\!] \mid s'[V_M] = s[V_M]\} \cup$$
$$\{\langle a,s' \rangle \in Act_M \times [\![V_M^{all}]\!] \mid \langle s,s' \rangle \models \widehat{\rho}_M^I(a)\}$$

$$\Gamma^O(M,s) = \{\Delta_0\} \cup \{\langle a,s' \rangle \in Act_M \times [\![V_M^{all}]\!] \mid \langle s,s' \rangle \models \widehat{\rho}_M^O(a)\}.$$

The outcome of the moves are as follows.

Definition 18 (Move Outcome). For all states $s \in S_M$ and moves $m^I \in \Gamma^I(M,s)$ and $m^O \in \Gamma^O(M,s)$, the *outcome* $\delta(M,s,m^I,m^O) \subseteq S_M$ of playing m^I and m^O at s can be defined as follows.

$$\delta(M,s,\langle \Delta_0,s' \rangle, \Delta_0) = \{s'\}, \qquad \delta(M,s,\langle \Delta_0,s' \rangle, \langle a,t' \rangle) = \{s',t'\},$$
$$\delta(M,s,\langle a,s' \rangle, \Delta_0) = \{s'\}, \qquad \delta(M,s,\langle a,s' \rangle, \langle b,t' \rangle) = \{s',t'\}.$$

The definitions of run, strategy, strategy outcome, winning state and well-formedness are similar to the ones given in Section 2.

3.4 The Printer Example, Continued

Figure 6 presents our print-server example, encoded in the actual input language of the tool TIC. The system consists of the global variables *busy*, *size*, *user*, of a printer module, and of two user modules. In each module, we give the set of history-free variables

```
var busy: bool;    // global variable indicating a printer busy
var size: [0..10]; // size of the print job
var user: [0..5];  // user who requested the job

module Printer:

  output ack   { busy ==> not busy'; }
                              // ack? is not allowed

  input  print { global: not busy ==> busy'; }

endmodule


module User1:
  var s: [0..1];
  stateless size, user;

  output print { s = 0 & not busy ==>
                              s' = 1 & user' = 1 & nondet size'; }

  input  print { } // print? is allowed and ignored

  input  ack   { local: s = 1 ==> s' := 0;
                 else  s = 0 ==> ;        } // ignore ack? when s=0

endmodule


module User2:
  var s: [0..1];
  stateless size, user;

  output print { s = 0 & not busy ==>
                              s' = 1 & user' = 2 & nondet size'; }

  input  print { } // print? is allowed and ignored

  input  ack   { local: s = 1 ==> s' := 0;
                 else  s = 0 ==> ;        } // ignore ack? when s=0

endmodule
```

Fig. 6. TIC input modeling a simple print server

(called *stateless* in the language of the tool); the set of global variables of the module is simply inferred as the set of global variables that appear anywhere in the module.

The module `Printer` communicates via two actions, *ack* and *print*. The transition predicates of these actions are specified using a guarded-commands syntax, similar to [4,1]. Each guarded command has the form *guard* $\Rightarrow$ *command*, where *guard* and *command* are formulas written over the set of primed and unprimed variables. A guarded command *guard* $\Rightarrow$ *command* can be taken when its guard is true; when taken, *command* specify how the variables are updated. For instance, the output transition *print* in module `User1` can be taken when $s = 0$ and *busy* $= F$, and it leads to a state where $s = 1$ and *user* $= 1$. The value of *size* in the destination state is nondeterministic.

When specifying sociable interface modules in the tool TIC, we use several short-hands to make the notation more pleasant:

- When we do not specify the input or output transition relation for an action, the omitted transition relations are assumed to be false. For example, the action *ack* has no input transition relation in the printer: this specifies that no other module should be able to emit it. Similarly, the action *ack* has no output transition relation in the user modules, specifying that modules do not generate it.
- When we specify a transition relation via an empty guarded command, the guard is assumed to be always true, and the command is as follows:
  - *Output transition relations, and local part of input transitions:* no variables are changed.
  - *Global part of input transitions:* the transition relation is considered to be *true*, so that all state changes are accepted.
- In a guarded command *guard* $\Rightarrow$ *command*, when *guard* is missing, it is assumed to be true. If *command* is missing, then:
  - *Output transitions, and local part of input transitions:* no variables are changed.
  - *Global part of input transitions:* the transition relation is considered to be *true*, so that all state changes are accepted.
- In output transitions, and in the local part of input transitions, variables that are not mentioned primed in the *command* portion of a guarded command *guard* $\Rightarrow$ *command* do not change their value.

As a more elaborate example, in Figure 7 we present the code of a print server that can accept or reject jobs, depending on their length.

3.5 Compatibility and Composition

We now describe the composition of two modules. Due to the presence of variables, this process is more involved than the one presented in Section 2.

The composition of two modules M_1 and M_2 is defined in four steps, in a similar way as stated in [9]. First, we define when M_1 and M_2 are *composable*, and in the affirmative case, we define their *product* $M_1 \otimes M_2$. On the resulting product module, we identify a set of *bad states:* these are the states where M_1 (resp. M_2) can produce an output that is not accepted by M_2 (resp. M_1). Finally, the *composition* $M_1 \| M_2$ of M_1 and

```
var busy: bool;     // global variable indicating a printer busy
var size: [0..10]; // size of the print job
var user: [0..5];   // user who requested the job

module Printer:
  output ack   { busy & size < 5 ==> not busy'; } // accept if size < 5
                              // ack? is not allowed

  output nack  { busy & size > 4 ==> not busy'; } // reject if size > 4
                              // nack? is not allowed

  input  print { global: not busy ==> busy'; }
endmodule

module User1:
  var s: [0..1];
  stateless size, user;

  output print { s = 0 & not busy ==>
                                    s' = 1 & user' = 1 & nondet size'; }
  input  print { } // print? is allowed and ignored

  input  ack   { local: s = 1 ==> s' := 0;
                  else  s = 0 ==> ;           } // ignore ack? when s=0

  input  nack  { local: s = 1 ==> s' := 0;
                  else  s = 0 ==> ;           } // ignore nack? when s=0
  endmodule

module User2:
  var s: [0..1];
  stateless size, user;

  output print { s = 0 & not busy ==>
                                    s' = 1 & user' = 2 & nondet size'; }
  input  print { } // print? is allowed and ignored

  input  ack   { local: s = 1 ==> s' := 0;
                  else  s = 0 ==> ;           } // ignore ack? when s=0

  input  nack  { local: s = 1 ==> s' := 0;
                  else  s = 0 ==> ;           } // ignore nack? when s=0
endmodule
```

Fig. 7. TIC input modeling a print server that rejects large jobs

M_2 is obtained from the product $M_1 \otimes M_2$ by strengthening the input transition relations of $M_1 \otimes M_2$ in such a way that all bad states are avoided.

In the following, we consider two modules M_1 and M_2, where $M_i = (Act_i, V_i^G, V_i^L, V_i^H, W_i, \rho_i^{IL}, \rho_i^{IG}, \rho_i^O, \psi_i^I, \psi_i^O)$, for $i = 1, 2$, and we let $V_i = V_i^L \cup V_i^H$ and $V_i^{all} = V_i^L \cup V_i^G$.

We say that two modules M_1 and M_2 are *composable* if they have disjoint sets of local variables, and if they satisfy a *non-interference* condition, stating that if an action of a module can modify a state variable of the other, then the action is shared. This condition ensures that the set of actions of a module includes all the actions that can modify its state variables. This condition is essential for modular reasoning. It ensures that composition does not add behaviors: all changes in the state of M_1 caused by modules with which M_1 is composable can be already explained by the input transitions associated with actions of M_1.

Definition 19 (Composability). Two sociable interface modules M_1 and M_2 are *composable* iff $V_1^L \cap V_2^L = \emptyset$ and if the following *non-interference* conditions hold:

$$\forall a \in Act_2 . \ W_2(a) \cap V_1 \neq \emptyset \implies a \in Act_1$$
$$\forall a \in Act_1 . \ W_1(a) \cap V_2 \neq \emptyset \implies a \in Act_2.$$

The non-interference condition is the main justification for distinguishing between the sets of history and history-free variables. The non-interference condition states that a module should know all actions of other modules that modify its history variables. If we dropped the distinction, requiring that a module knows all actions of other modules that can change any of its variables (history or history-free), we could greatly increase the number of actions that must be known to the module.

As an example, consider a set of modules $\{N_i\}_{i \in \{1..100\}}$. Each module has an action a_i whose output transition relation sets *index* to i, and x to some content, where *index* and x are global variables shared among all $N_1, \ldots, N_{100}$. If module N_i does not need to keep track of the value of *index* and x, as these variables are used as outputs only, then we can let *index* $\notin V_{N_i}$ and $x \notin V_{N_i}$, even though of course *index*, $x \in V_{N_i}^{all}$. The non-interference condition for N_i, stated in terms of V_{N_i}, will not require N_i to know about a_j for $i \neq j$. This keeps the model of N_i simple and concise and, even more importantly, enables us to model N_i before we know exactly how many other modules there are that can modify *index* and x. Dropping the distinction between V_{N_i} and $V_{N_i}^{all}$, on the other hand, would force each N_i to have all the actions $a_1, \ldots, a_{100}$ in its set of actions, greatly complicating the model, and forcing us to know in advance how many components there are, before each of the components can be modeled. Similarly, if a module reads a variable x, but does not need to know how and when the value of x is changed, then the variable x can be declared to be history-free, so that the module does not have to know all the actions that can modify x. Hence, the distinction between history and history-free variables is at the heart of our "sociable" approach to compositional modeling.

We define the product of two sociable interface modules M_1 and M_2 as follows.

Definition 20 (Product). Assume that M_1 and M_2 are composable. The *product* $M_1 \otimes M_2$ is the interface $M_{12} = (Act_{12}, V_{12}^G, V_{12}^L, V_{12}^H, W_{12}, \rho_{12}^{IL}, \rho_{12}^{IG}, \rho_{12}^O, \psi_{12}^I, \psi_{12}^O)$, defined as follows.

– $Act_{12} = Act_1 \cup Act_2$.

– $V_{12}^G = V_1^G \cup V_2^G; \quad V_{12}^L = V_1^L \cup V_2^L; \quad V_{12}^H = V_1^H \cup V_2^H; \quad V_{12}^{\text{all}} = V_1^{\text{all}} \cup V_2^{\text{all}}.$

– $W_{12}(a) = \begin{cases} W_1(a) \cup W_2(a) \cup V_1^L \cup V_2^L & \text{for } a \in Shared(M_1, M_2) \\ W_i(a) & \text{for } a \in Act_i \setminus Act_{3-1}, i \in \{1,2\}. \end{cases}$

– $\psi_{12}^I = \psi_1^I \wedge \psi_2^I; \quad \psi_{12}^O = \psi_1^O \wedge \psi_2^O.$

– For $a \in Shared(M_1, M_2)$, we let:

$\rho_{12}^O(a) =$
$$= \begin{pmatrix} \exists (V_{12}^G)' \setminus W_{12}(a)' . \rho_1^O(a) \wedge \rho_2^{IL}(a) \wedge \rho_2^{IG}(a) \wedge Unchgd(V_{12}^{\text{all}} \setminus (W_1(a) \cup V_2^L)) \\ \vee \\ \exists (V_{12}^G)' \setminus W_{12}(a)' . \rho_2^O(a) \wedge \rho_1^{IL}(a) \wedge \rho_1^{IG}(a) \wedge Unchgd(V_{12}^{\text{all}} \setminus (W_2(a) \cup V_1^L)) \end{pmatrix}$$

$\rho_{12}^{IL}(a) = \rho_1^{IL}(a) \wedge \rho_2^{IL}(a)$

$\rho_{12}^{IG}(a) = \rho_1^{IG}(a) \wedge \rho_2^{IG}(a).$

– For $i \in \{1,2\}$ and $a \in Act_i \setminus Act_{3-i}$ we let:

$$\rho_{12}^O(a) = \rho_i^O(a)$$
$$\rho_{12}^{IL}(a) = \rho_i^{IL}(a) \wedge Unchgd(V_{3-i}^L)$$
$$\rho_{12}^{IG}(a) = \rho_i^{IG}(a) \wedge Unchgd(V_{3-i}^H).$$

We have the following result.

Theorem 4. *Product between modules is a commutative and associative operation.*

Similarly to Definition 12, we identify a set of locally incompatible states of the product $M_1 \otimes M_2$.

Definition 21 (Local Compatibility). Given $s \in [\![V_{12}^{\text{all}}]\!]$, we say that s is *good* iff it satisfies the predicate $good(M_1, M_2)$, defined as follows:

$good(M_1, M_2) =$
$$= \bigwedge_{a \in Shared(M_1, M_2)} \begin{pmatrix} \forall (V_{12}^{\text{all}})' . \left((\widehat{\rho}_1^O(a) \wedge Unchgd(V_2^G \setminus W_1(a))) \implies \widehat{\rho}_2^{IG}(a) \right) \\ \wedge \\ \forall (V_{12}^{\text{all}})' . \left((\widehat{\rho}_2^O(a) \wedge Unchgd(V_1^G \setminus W_2(a))) \implies \widehat{\rho}_1^{IG}(a) \right) \end{pmatrix}.$$

Using this condition, the composition $M_1 \| M_2$ is obtained from $M_1 \otimes M_2$ by restricting the input invariant of M_{12} to the set of well-formed states from where input has a strategy to always stay in the good states $good(M_1, M_2)$, in analogy with Definition 13.

Theorem 5. *Composition between modules is a commutative and associative operation.*

4 Refinement

We wish to define a refinement relation between modules, such that when M_1 refines M_2, M_1 can be used as a replacement for M_2 in any context. First, some conditions should hold on the set of variables that the modules manipulate. In the following, M_1 and M_2 are two modules in normal form. For $i \in \{1,2\}$, let $M_i = (Act_i, V_i^G, V_i^L, V_i^H, W_i, \rho_i^{IL}, \rho_i^{IG}, \rho_i^O, \psi_i^I, \psi_i^O)$, $V_i = V_i^H \cup V_i^L$ and $S_i = \llbracket V_i \rrbracket$. The sets Act_i, V_i^G, V_i^H, and W_i jointly define the *signature* of a module M_i.

Definition 22 (Signature). The signature $Sign(M_i)$ of a module $M_i = (Act_i, V_i^G, V_i^L, V_i^H, W_i, \rho_i^{IL}, \rho_i^{IG}, \rho_i^O, \psi_i^I, \psi_i^O)$, is the tuple $(Act_i, V_i^G, V_i^H, W_i)$.

The following result shows that signature equality preserves composability. It can be proved by inspecting Definition 19.

Theorem 6. *Let N_1, N_2, and N_3 be three modules, such that the $Sign(N_1) = Sign(N_2)$, and N_2 and N_3 are composable. For $i \in \{1,2,3\}$, let V_i^L be the set of local variables of N_i. If $V_1^L \cap V_3^L = \emptyset$, then N_1 and N_3 are composable.*

To replace M_2, M_1 should also behave like it, from the point of view of the environment. As usual in a game-theoretic setting such as ours, this constraint is captured by *alternating simulation* [2]. Intuitively, M_1 must be willing to accept at least all the inputs that M_2 accepts, and it should emit a subset of the outputs emitted by M_2.

Definition 23 (Alternating Simulation). Assume that $Sign(M_1) = Sign(M_2)$. A relation $\preceq \subseteq S_1 \times S_2$ is an *alternating simulation* iff $s \preceq t$ implies:

1. $s[V_1^G] = t[V_1^G]$;

2. for all $a \in Act_1$ and for all $t' \in S_2$ such that $\langle t, t' \rangle \models \hat{\rho}_2^I(a)$ there exists $s' \in S_1$ such that $\langle s, s' \rangle \models \hat{\rho}_1^I(a)$ and $s' \preceq t'$;

3. for all $a \in Act_1$ and for all $s' \in S_1$ such that $\langle s, s' \rangle \models \hat{\rho}_1^O(a)$ there exists $t' \in S_2$ such that $\langle t, t' \rangle \models \hat{\rho}_2^O(a)$ and $s' \preceq t'$.

We say that s is similar to t, and we write $s \sqsubseteq t$, if there exists an alternating simulation $\preceq$ such that $s \preceq t$. Similarity is itself a simulation (the coarsest one). For M_1 to refine M_2, M_1 and M_2 should have the same signature, and each well-formed state of M_2 must be similar to some well-formed state of M_1.

Definition 24 (Refinement). We say that M_1 *refines* M_2 iff (i) $Sign(M_1) = Sign(M_2)$, and (ii) for all $t \models \psi_2^I \wedge \psi_2^O$ there is $s \models \psi_1^I \wedge \psi_1^O$ such that $s \sqsubseteq t$.

Theorem 7. *Let N_1, N_2, and N_3 be three modules, such that N_1 refines N_2, and N_2 and N_3 are compatible. For $i \in \{1,2,3\}$, let V_i^L be the set of local variables of N_i. If $V_1^L \cap V_3^L = \emptyset$, then N_1 and N_3 are compatible.*

We now introduce the related concept of *bisimilarity*. Bisimilarity between two modules captures the intuitive concept that the environment cannot distinguish the two modules.

Definition 25 (Alternating Bisimulation). Assume that $Sign(M_1) = Sign(M_2)$. A relation $\approx\, \subseteq S_1 \times S_2$ is an *alternating bisimulation* iff it is a *symmetrical* alternating simulation.

We say that s and t are *bisimilar*, and we write $s \cong t$, if there exists an alternating bisimulation $\approx$ such that $s \approx t$.

Definition 26 (Bisimilarity). We say that M_1 and M_2 are *bisimilar* iff *(i)* $Sign(M_1) = Sign(M_2)$, and *(ii)* for all $t \models \psi_2^I \wedge \psi_2^O$ there is $s \models \psi_1^I \wedge \psi_1^O$ such that $s \cong t$, and for all $s \models \psi_1^I \wedge \psi_1^O$ there is $t \models \psi_2^I \wedge \psi_2^O$ such that $s \cong t$.

Theorem 8. *Let* N_1, N_2, *and* N_3 *be three modules, such that* N_1 *is bisimilar to* N_2. *For* $i \in \{1, 2, 3\}$, *let* V_i^L *be the set of local variables of* N_i. *If* $V_1^L \cap V_3^L = \emptyset$ *and* $V_2^L \cap V_3^L = \emptyset$, *then* N_1 *and* N_3 *are compatible iff* N_2 *and* N_3 *are compatible.*

5   Symbolic Implementation

In this section, we examine the problem of efficiently implementing the following operations: *(i)* module composition, *(ii)* verification of safety properties of modules (such as well-formedness), and *(iii)* refinement and bisimilarity checking between modules.

Consider the module $M = (Act_M, V_M^G, V_M^L, V_M^H, W_M, \rho_M^{IL}, \rho_M^{IG}, \rho_M^O, \psi_M^I, \psi_M^O)$, and set $V_M^{\text{all}} = V_M^L \cup V_M^G$.

A well-established technique for efficiently implementing finite transition systems is based on MDDs [12,14]. MDDs are graph-like data structures that allow us to represent and manipulate functions of the type $A \to \{T, F\}$, for a finite set A (i.e. predicates over A). Therefore, we assume that the variable domain $\mathscr{D}$ is finite, and we represent the predicates $\rho_M^{IL}, \rho_M^{IG}, \rho_M^O, \psi_M^I$, and ψ_M^O as MDDs. We now show that all the operations involved in computing the composition of modules, checking their well-formedness, checking safety properties, and checking refinement are computable on MDDs.

5.1   Safety Games

A basic operation on modules is computing the set of winning states for a player $p \in \{I, O\}$ w.r.t. a safety goal, that is $Win^p(M, \Box\varphi)$, for some set $\varphi \subseteq [\![V_M^{\text{all}}]\!]$. The operations of checking well-formedness, putting a module in normal form, and computing the composition of two modules, are all reducible to solving safety games.

By abuse of notation, we denote by $Win^p(M, \Box\varphi)$ both the set of states it denotes, and its characteristic function, which is a predicate over V_M^{all}.

It is well known that such set of winning states can be characterized as a fix-point of an equation involving the so-called *controllable predecessors operators*. For a player $p \in \{I, O\}$ and a predicate $X \in Preds(V_M^{\text{all}})$, the operator $Cpre^p(X)$ returns the set of states from which player p can force the game into X in one step, regardless of the opponent's moves. Formally, we have the following definition.

Definition 27 (Controllable Predecessor Operator). For a predicate $X \in Preds(V_M^{all})$, we have:

$$Cpre^I(X) = \exists m^I \in \Gamma^I(M,s).\forall m^O \in \Gamma^O(M,s).\forall t \in \delta(M,s,m^I,m^O).t \models X$$
$$Cpre^O(X) = \exists m^O \in \Gamma^O(M,s).\forall m^I \in \Gamma^I(M,s).\forall t \in \delta(M,s,m^I,m^O).t \models X.$$

Intuitively, $Cpre^I(X)$ (resp. $Cpre^O(X)$) holds true for the states from which the Input (resp. Output) player has a move that leads to X for each possible counter-move of the Output (resp. Input) player. For all $\varphi \in Preds(V_M^{all})$, we have:

$$Win^I(M,\square\varphi) = \nu X.[\varphi \wedge Cpre^I(X)]$$
$$Win^O(M,\square\varphi) = \nu X.[\varphi \wedge Cpre^O(X)],$$

where $\nu X.f(X)$ denotes the greatest fixpoint of the operator f. Since $Cpre^I(\cdot)$ is monotonic, the above fixpoints exist and can be computed by Picard iteration:

$$X_0 = \varphi, \qquad X_{i+1} = \varphi \wedge Cpre^I(X_i), \qquad \ldots \qquad X_n = X_{n+1} = Win^I(M,\square\varphi). \qquad (1)$$

We now show how to compute $Cpre^I(X)$ starting from the MDD representation of M. Considering Definition 18, in order for a state s to satisfy $Cpre^I(X)$, two conditions must hold. First, every output transition should lead to X. Second, either $s \models X$, in which case Input can play $\langle \Delta_0,s \rangle$, or there must be an input transition that leads to X. This observation allows us to express $Cpre^I(X)$ as follows:

$$Cpre^I(X) = \forall Pre^O(X) \wedge \exists Pre^I(X),$$

where

$$\forall Pre^O(X) = \bigwedge_{a \in Act_M} \forall(V_M^{all})'.(\hat{\rho}_M^O(a) \Rightarrow X')$$
$$\exists Pre^I(X) = X \vee (\exists(V_M^{all})'.X' \wedge Unchgd(V_M^H \cup V_M^L)) \vee \bigvee_{a \in Act_M} \exists(V_M^{all})'.(\hat{\rho}_M^I(a) \wedge X').$$

Since boolean operations and quantifications of variables are computable on MDDs, the operators above are computable. In a dual fashion, $Cpre^O(X)$ can be computed from the non-game operators $\forall Pre^I(\cdot)$ and $\exists Pre^O(\cdot)$.

We can improve the efficiency of computing $Win^I(M,\square\varphi)$, by observing that, since (1) is a decreasing sequence, it holds that $\nu X.[\varphi \wedge Cpre^I(X)] = \nu X.[\varphi \wedge X \wedge Cpre^I(X)]$. Since $X \wedge Cpre^I(X) = X \wedge \forall Pre^O(X)$, we obtain

$$Win^I(M,\square\varphi) = \nu X.[\varphi \wedge X \wedge \forall Pre^O(X)] = \nu X.[\varphi \wedge \forall Pre^O(X)].$$

In conclusion, we can then compute $Win^I(M,\square\varphi)$ by iterating $\forall Pre^O(\cdot)$ instead of the more complicated $Cpre^I(\cdot)$. A similar argument holds for the computation of $Win^O(M,\square\varphi)$.

5.2   Composition

By inspecting Definition 20, it is clear that computing the product of two modules M_1 and M_2 only involves simple boolean operations on the predicates that define the modules. Such operations are computable on MDDs.

To obtain the composition $M_1 \| M_2$, according to Definition 13, the input invariant ψ_{12}^I of the product must be conjoined with the predicate $Win^I(M_1 \otimes M_2, \Box(\psi_{12}^I \wedge good(M_1, M_2)))$. To compute the above winning set, we first compute the predicate $good(M_1, M_2)$ following Definition 21, and then solve the safety game as explained in Section 5.1.

5.3   Refinement

Let M_1 and M_2 be two modules in normal form, such that $Sign(M_1) = Sign(M_2)$. For $i \in \{1, 2\}$, let $M_i = (Act, V^G, V_i^L, V^H, W, \rho_i^{IL}, \rho_i^{IG}, \rho_i^O, \psi_i^I, \psi_i^O)$, $V_i^{all} = V^G \cup V_i^L$ and $S_i = [\![V_i^{all}]\!]$. Assume for simplicity that $V_1^L \cap V_2^L = \emptyset$. We wish to compute the coarsest alternating simulation $\sqsubseteq$ between S_1 and S_2. Consider the predicate $\psi_{\sqsubseteq}$ over the set of variables $V_1^{all} \cup V_2^{all}$, defined as the greatest fixpoint of the operator $SimPre(\cdot)$, defined as follows. For all $X \in Preds(V_1^{all} \cup V_2^{all})$, we have

$$SimPre(X) = X \wedge \bigwedge_{a \in Act} \forall (V_2^{all})' . \exists (V_1^L)' . \left(\widehat{\rho}_2^I(a) \implies \widehat{\rho}_1^I(a) \wedge X' \right)$$

$$\wedge \bigwedge_{a \in Act} \forall (V_1^{all})' . \exists (V_2^L)' . \left(\widehat{\rho}_1^O(a) \implies \widehat{\rho}_2^O(a) \wedge X' \right).$$

The operator $SimPre(\cdot)$, and consequently its fixpoint $\psi_{\sqsubseteq}$, can be computed from the MDD representation of M_1 and M_2. The following result states that $\psi_{\sqsubseteq}$ can be used to trivially obtain $\sqsubseteq$. The result can be proven by induction, observing that $SimPre(\cdot)$ represents conditions 2 and 3 of Definition 23.

Theorem 9. *Given $s \in S_1$ and $t \in S_2$, $s \sqsubseteq t$ iff $s[V^G] = t[V^G]$ and $s \circ t[V_2^L] \models \psi_{\sqsubseteq}$.*

A similar algorithm can be used to compute the coarsest bisimulation $\cong$.

6   Comparison with Previous Interface Models

The sociable interface model presented in this paper is closely related to the *I/O Automata Model* (IOA) of [11]: sociable interfaces synchronize on actions and use variables to encode the state of components. However, sociable interfaces diverge from *I/O Automata* in several ways. Unlike *I/O Automata*, where every state must be receptive to every possible input event, sociable interfaces allow states to forbid some input events. By not accepting certain inputs, sociable interfaces express the assumption that the environment never generates these inputs: hence, sociable interfaces (like other interface models) model both the output behavior, and the input assumptions, of a component. This approach implies a notion of composition (based on synthesizing the weakest environment assumptions that guarantee compatibility) which is not present in the I/O Automata Model.

Interface models are the subject of many recent works. Previous interface models, such as interface automata [6,8] and interface modules [7,3] were based on either actions, or variables, but not both. Sociable interfaces do not break new ground in the conceptual theory of interface models. However, by allowing both actions and variables, they take advantage of the existing models and try to avoid their deficiencies. The rest of this section is devoted to a quick presentation of existing interface models.

Variable-based interface formalisms. In variable-based interface formalisms, such as the formalisms of [7,3], communication is mediated by input and output variables, and the system evolves in synchronous steps. It is well known that synchronous, variable-based models can also encode communication via actions [1]: the generation of an output $a!$ is translated into the toggling of the value of an (output) boolean variable x_a, and the reception of an input $a?$ is encoded by forcing a transition to occur whenever the (input) variable x_a is toggled. This encoding is made more attractive by syntactic sugar [1]. However, this encoding prevents the modeling of many-to-one and many-to-many communication.

In fact, due to the synchronous nature of the formalism, a variable can be modified at most by one module: if two modules modified it, there would be no simple way to determine its updated value.[1] Since the generation of an output $a!$ is modeled by toggling the value of a boolean variable x_a, this limitation indicates that an output action can be emitted at most by one module. As a consequence, we cannot write modules that can accept inputs from multiple sources: every module must know precisely which other modules can provide inputs to it, so that distinct communication actions can be used. The advance knowledge of the modules involved in communication hampers module re-use.

Action-based interface formalisms. Action-based interfaces, such as the models of [6,5,8], enable a natural encoding of asynchronous communication. In previous proposal, however, two interfaces could be composed only if they did not share output actions — again ruling out many-to-one communication.

Furthermore, previous action-based formalisms lacked a notion of global variables which are visible to all the modules of a system. Such global variables are a very powerful and versatile modeling paradigm, providing a notion of global, shared state. Mimicking global variables in purely action-based models is rather inconvenient: it requires encapsulating every global variable by a module, whose state corresponds to the value of the variable. Read and write accesses to the variable must then be translated to appropriate sequences of input and output actions, leading to cumbersome models.

References

1. R. Alur and T.A. Henzinger. Reactive modules. *Formal Methods in System Design*, 15:7–48, 1999.
2. R. Alur, T.A. Henzinger, O. Kupferman, and M.Y. Vardi. Alternating refinement relations. In *CONCUR 98: Concurrency Theory. 9th Int. Conf.*, volume 1466 of *Lect. Notes in Comp. Sci.*, pages 163–178. Springer-Verlag, 1998.

---

[1] A possible way out would be to define that, in case of simultaneous updates, only one of the updates occurs nondeterministically. This choice, however, would lead to a complex semantics, and to complex analysis algorithms.

3. A. Chakrabarti, L. de Alfaro, T.A. Henzinger, and F.Y.C. Mang. Synchronous and bidirectional component interfaces. In *CAV 02: Proc. of 14th Conf. on Computer Aided Verification*, volume 2404 of *Lect. Notes in Comp. Sci.*, pages 414–427. Springer-Verlag, 2002.
4. K.M. Chandy and J. Misra. *Parallel Program Design: A Foundation.* Addison-Wesley Publishing Company, 1988.
5. L. de Alfaro. Game models for open systems. In *Proceedings of the International Symposium on Verification (Theory in Practice)*, volume 2772 of *Lect. Notes in Comp. Sci.* Springer-Verlag, 2003.
6. L. de Alfaro and T.A. Henzinger. Interface automata. In *Proceedings of the 8th European Software Engineering Conference and the 9th ACM SIGSOFT Symposium on the Foundations of Software Engineering (ESEC/FSE)*, pages 109–120. ACM Press, 2001.
7. L. de Alfaro and T.A. Henzinger. Interface theories for component-based design. In *EMSOFT 01: 1st Intl. Workshop on Embedded Software*, volume 2211 of *Lect. Notes in Comp. Sci.*, pages 148–165. Springer-Verlag, 2001.
8. L. de Alfaro and T.A. Henzinger. Interface-based design. In *Engineering Theories of Software Intensive Systems, proceedings of the Marktoberdorf Summer School*. Kluwer, 2004.
9. L. de Alfaro and M. Stoelinga. Interfaces: A game-theoretic framework to reason about open systems. In *FOCLASA 03: Proceedings of the 2nd International Workshop on Foundations of Coordination Languages and Software Architectures*, 2003.
10. Xavier Leroy. Objective caml. http://caml.inria.fr/ocaml/index.en.html.
11. N.A. Lynch. *Distributed Algorithms*. Morgan-Kaufmann, 1996.
12. R.I. Bahar, E.A. Frohm, C.M. Gaona, G.D. Hachtel, E. Macii, A. Pardo, and F. Somenzi. Algebraic Decision Diagrams and Their Applications. In *IEEE/ACM International Conference on CAD*, pages 188–191, Santa Clara, California, 1993. IEEE Computer Society Press.
13. Fabio Somenzi. Cudd: Cu decision diagram package. http://vlsi.colorado.edu/˜fabio/CUDD/cuddIntro.html.
14. A. Srinivasan, T. Kam, S. Malik, and R. Brayton. Algorithms for discrete function manipulation. In *Proceedings International Conference CAD (ICCAD-91)*, 1990.

About the Combination of Trees and Rational Numbers in a Complete First-Order Theory

Khalil Djelloul

Laboratoire d'Informatique Fondamentale de Marseille,
Parc scientifique et technologique de Luminy,
163 avenue de Luminy - Case 901,
13288 Marseille, cedex 9. France

Abstract. Two infinite structures (sets together with operations and relations) hold our attention here: the trees together with operations of construction and the rational numbers together with the operations of addition and substraction and a linear dense order relation without endpoints. The object of this paper is the study of the *evaluated trees*, a structure mixing the two preceding ones.

First of all, we establish a general theorem which gives a sufficient condition for the completeness of a first-order theory. This theorem uses a special quantifier, primarily asserting the existence of an infinity of individuals having a given first order property. The proof of the theorem is nothing other than the broad outline of a general algorithm which decides if a proposition or its negation is true in certain theories.

We introduce then the theory T_E of the evaluated trees and show its completeness using our theorem. From our proof it is possible to extract a general algorithm for solving quantified constraints in T_E.

1 Introduction

Recall that a tree built on a set E is essentially a hierarchized set of nodes labelled by the elements of E. To each element e of E corresponds an operation f, called *construction operation*, which, starting from a sequence $a_1, \ldots, a_n$ of trees, builds the tree whose top node is labelled e and whose sequence of immediate daughters is $a_1, \ldots, a_n$.

The algebra of (possibly) infinite trees plays a fundamental act in computer science: it is a model for composed data known as *record* in Pascal or *structure* in C. The construction operation corresponds to the creation of a new record, i.e. of a cell containing an elementary information possibly followed by n cells, each one pointing to a record. Infinite trees correspond to a circuit of pointers.

As early as 1976, Gerard Huet proposed an algorithm for unifying infinite terms, that is solving equations in that algebra [10]. Bruno Courcelle has studied the properties of infinite trees in the scope of recursive program schemes [8,7]. Alain Colmerauer has described the execution of Prolog II, III and IV programs in terms of solving equations and disequations in that algebra [5,4,2]. Michael Maher has proposed and justified complete axiomatizations of different sets of trees equipped with construction operations [11]: for each of these sets, he has presented a complete theory, i.e. a set of first-order properties which entails all the other first-order properties of this set.

As for us, we give and justify here a complete axiomatization of the set of (possibly) infinite trees built on a superset of the set of the rational numbers and equipped not only with construction operations but with the operations of addition and substraction and a linear order relation (dense, without endpoints). It is this set with its operations and relations, i.e. this model, that we call *evaluated trees*.

The paper is organized in five sections followed by a conclusion. This introduction is the first section. The second one introduces the needed elements of first-order logic and ends with a basic sufficient condition for the completeness of a theory. It is a variant of the one given in section 1.5 of [3].

The third section is devoted to a much more elaborated sufficient condition for the completeness of a theory. The idea behind this condition comes from a decomposition algorithm introduced by Thi-Bich-Hanh Dao in her dissertation [9]. The idea consists in decomposing a sequence of existential quantifications preceding a conjunction of formulas, in three embedded sequences of quantifications having very particular properties, which can be expressed with the help of three special quantifiers denoted by $\exists?$, $\exists!$, $\exists_{o\,\infty}^{\Psi(u)}$ and called *at-most-one, exactly-one, zero-infinite*. These special quantifiers, together with their properties, are described at the beginning of the section. While the quantifiers $\exists?$, $\exists!$ are just convenient notations, the quantifier $\exists_{o\,\infty}^{\Psi(u)}$, one of the essential contribution of this paper, expresses a property which is not expressible at the first-order level.

The fourth section introduces the theory T_E of the evaluated trees and its standard model E. Particular formulas called *blocks* are also studied there. They are used for building all needed formulas.

The fifth section shows the completeness of T_E by using the completeness theorem of the third section. The general theorem, the zero-infinite quantifier and the proof of the completeness of T_E are our contribution in this paper. Due to lack of space, we give here only the main proofs, nevertheless, we can find a complete version with full proofs at http://www.lif.univ-mrs.fr/~djelloul.

2   Formal Preliminaries

2.1   Expressions

We are given once for all, an infinite countable set **V** of *variables* and the set L of *logical* symbols:

$$=, true, false, \neg, \wedge, \vee, \rightarrow, \leftrightarrow, \forall, \exists, (,).$$

We are also given once for all, a *signature* S, i.e. a set of symbols partitioned into two subsets: the set of *function* symbols and the set of *relation* symbols. To each element s of S is linked a non-negative integer called *arity* of s. An n-ary symbol is a symbol with arity n. An 0-ary function symbol is called *constant*.

As usual, an *expression* is a word on $L \cup S$ which is either a *term*, i.e. of the one of the two forms:

$$x, ft_1 \ldots t_n, \tag{1}$$

or a *formula*, i.e. of the one of the eleven forms:

$$s = t, \ rt_1 \ldots t_n, \ true, \ false,$$
$$\neg\varphi, \ (\varphi \wedge \psi), \ (\varphi \vee \psi), \ (\varphi \rightarrow \psi), \ (\varphi \leftrightarrow \psi), \tag{2}$$
$$(\forall x \, \varphi), \ (\exists x \, \varphi).$$

In (1), x is taken from $\mathbf{V}$, f is an n-ary function symbol taken from S and the t_i's are shorter terms. In (2), s, t and the t_i's are terms, r is an n-ary relation symbol taken from S and φ and ψ are shorter formulas.

The formulas of the first line are known as *atomic*, and *flat* if they are of one of the forms:

$$true, \ false, \ x_0 = x_1, x_0 = fx_1 \ldots x_n, \ rx_1 \ldots x_n,$$

where the x_i's are taken from $\mathbf{V}$, f is an n-ary function symbol taken from S and r is an n-ary relation symbol taken from S.

Recall that an occurrence of a variable x in a formula is *bound* if it occurs in a sub-formula of the form $(\forall x \, \varphi)$ or $(\exists x \, \varphi)$. It is *free* in the contrary case. The *free variables of a formula* are those which have at least a free occurrence in this formula. A *proposition* or a *sentence* is a formula without free variables.

We do not distinguish two formulas which can be made equal using the following transformations of the sub-formulas:

$$(\varphi \wedge \psi) \wedge \phi \Longrightarrow \varphi \wedge (\psi \wedge \phi), \ \varphi \wedge \psi \Longrightarrow \psi \wedge \varphi,$$
$$\varphi \wedge true \Longrightarrow \varphi, \ \varphi \vee false \Longrightarrow \varphi.$$

If I is the set $\{i_1, \ldots, i_n\}$, we write respectively $\bigwedge_{i \in I} \varphi_i$ and $\bigvee_{i \in I} \varphi_i$ for $\varphi_{i_1} \wedge \varphi_{i_2} \wedge \ldots \wedge \varphi_{i_n} \wedge true$, and $\varphi_{i_1} \vee \varphi_{i_2} \vee \ldots \vee \varphi_{i_n} \vee false$. In particular, for $I = \emptyset$, the formulas $\bigwedge_{i \in I} \varphi_i$ and $\bigvee_{i \in I} \varphi_i$ are reduced respectively to *true* and to *false*. We denote by $Card(I)$, the cardinality of the set I.

2.2   Model

A *model* is a couple $M = (\mathcal{M}, \mathcal{F})$, where:

- $\mathcal{M}$, the *universe* or *domain* of M, is a nonempty set disjoint from S, its elements are called *individuals* of M;
- $\mathcal{F}$ is a family of operations and relations in the set $\mathcal{M}$, subscripted by the elements of S and such that:
  - for every n-ary function symbol f taken from S, f^M is an n-ary operation in $\mathcal{M}$, i.e. an application from $\mathcal{M}^n$ in $\mathcal{M}$. In particular, when f is a constant, f^M belongs to $\mathcal{M}$;
  - for every n-ary relation symbol r taken from S, r^M is an n-ary relation in $\mathcal{M}$, i.e. a subset of $\mathcal{M}^n$.

Let $M = (\mathcal{M}, \mathcal{F})$ be a model. An M-*expression* φ is an expression built on the signature $S \cup \mathcal{M}$ instead of S, by considering the elements of $\mathcal{M}$ as 0-ary function symbols. If for each free variable x of φ, we replace each free occurrence of x by the same element of $\mathcal{M}$, we get an M-expression called *instantiation* of φ by individuals of M.

If φ is a M-formula, we say that φ *is true in* M and we write

$$M \models \varphi, \tag{3}$$

iff for any instantiation φ' of φ by individuals of M, the set $\mathcal{M}$ has the property expressed by $\varphi\prime$, when we interpret the function and relation symbols of $\varphi\prime$ by the corresponding functions and relations of M and when we give to the logical symbols their usual meaning.

Let us finish this sub-section by a convenient notation . Let $\bar{x} = x_1...x_n$ be a word on $\mathbf{V}$ and let $\bar{i} = i_1...i_n$ be a word on $\mathcal{M}$ or $\mathbf{V}$ of the same length as $\bar{x}$. If $\varphi(\bar{x})$ is a M-formula, then we denote by $\varphi(\bar{i})$, the M-formula obtained by replacing in $\varphi(\bar{x})$ each free occurrence of x_j by i_j.

2.3   Theory

A *theory* is a (possibly infinite) set of propositions. A set T^* of propositions is said to be a *set of axioms* for a theory T iff T^* and T have the same consequences. We say that the model M is a *model of* T, iff for each element φ of T, $M \models \varphi$. If φ is a formula, we write

$$T \models \varphi,$$

iff for each model M of T, $M \models \varphi$. We say that the formulas φ and ψ are *equivalent in* T iff $T \models \varphi \leftrightarrow \psi$.

2.4   Complete Theory

In what follows we use the abbreviation wfva for *"without free variables added"*. A formula φ is equivalent to a wfva formula ψ in T means that $T \models \varphi \leftrightarrow \psi$ and ψ does not contain other free variables than those of φ.

Definition 2.4.1 *A theory T is* complete *iff for every proposition φ, one and only one of the following properties holds: $T \models \varphi$, $T \models \neg\varphi$.*

Property 2.4.2 *A theory T is complete if there exists a set of formulas, called* basic formulas, *such that:*

1. *every flat atomic formula is equivalent in T to a wfva Boolean combination of basic formulas,*
2. *every basic formula without free variables is equivalent in T, either to true or to false,*
3. *every formula of the form*

$$\exists x \left(\bigwedge_{i \in I} \varphi_i \right) \wedge \left(\bigwedge_{i \in I'} \neg\varphi_i \right), \tag{4}$$

where the φ_i's are basic formulas, is equivalent in T to a wfva Boolean combination of basic formulas.

3   A General Theorem for the Completeness of a First Order Theory

3.1   Vectorial Quantifiers

Let M be a model and let T be a theory. Let $\bar{x} = x_1 \ldots x_n$ and $\bar{y} = y_1 \ldots y_n$ be two words on $\mathbf{V}$ of the same length. Let ψ, ϕ, φ and $\varphi(\bar{x})$ be M-formulas.

Notation 3.1.1 *We write*

$$
\begin{array}{ll}
\exists \bar{x}\, \varphi & \text{for } \exists x_1 \ldots \exists x_n\, \varphi, \\
\forall \bar{x}\, \varphi & \text{for } \forall x_1 \ldots \forall x_n\, \varphi, \\
\exists ? \bar{x}\, \varphi(\bar{x}) & \text{for } \forall \bar{x} \forall \bar{y}\, \varphi(\bar{x}) \wedge \varphi(\bar{y}) \rightarrow \bigwedge_{i \in \{1,\ldots,n\}} x_i = y_i, \\
\exists ! \bar{x}\, \varphi & \text{for } (\exists \bar{x}\, \varphi) \wedge (\exists ? \bar{x}\, \varphi).
\end{array}
$$

The word $\bar{x}$, which can be the empty word ε, is called *vector of variables*. Note that the formulas $\exists ? \varepsilon \varphi$ and $\exists ! \varepsilon \varphi$ are respectively equivalent to *true* and to φ in any model M.

Property 3.1.2 *If $T \models \exists ? \bar{x}\, \varphi$ then*

$$T \models (\exists \bar{x}\, \varphi \wedge \neg \phi) \leftrightarrow (\exists \bar{x} \varphi) \wedge \neg (\exists \bar{x}\, \varphi \wedge \phi).$$

Property 3.1.3 *If $T \models \psi \rightarrow (\exists ! \bar{x}\, \varphi)$ then*

$$T \models (\psi \wedge (\exists \bar{x}\, \varphi \wedge \neg \phi)) \leftrightarrow (\psi \wedge \neg (\exists \bar{x}\, \varphi \wedge \phi)).$$

Property 3.1.4 *If $T \models \exists ? \bar{y} \phi$ and if each variable of $\bar{y}$ does not have free occurrences in φ then*

$$T \models (\exists \bar{x}\, \varphi \wedge \neg (\exists \bar{y}\, \phi \wedge \psi)) \leftrightarrow \left[\begin{array}{l} (\exists \bar{x}\, \varphi \wedge \neg (\exists \bar{y}\, \phi)) \vee \\ (\exists \overline{xy}\, \varphi \wedge \phi \wedge \neg \psi) \end{array} \right].$$

3.2   Quantifier Zero-Infinite

Let M be a model. Let T be a theory. Let φ_i and $\varphi(\bar{x})$ be M-formulas and let $\Psi(u)$ be a set of formulas having at most u as a free variable.

Definition 3.2.1 *We write*

$$M \models \exists_{o\,\infty}^{\Psi(u)} x\, \varphi(x), \tag{5}$$

iff for any instantiation $\exists x\, \varphi'(x)$ of $\exists x\, \varphi(x)$ by individuals of M one of the following properties holds:

- *the set of the individuals i of M such that $M \models \varphi'(i)$, is empty,*
- *for all finite sub-set $\{\psi_1(u), .., \psi_n(u)\}$ of elements of $\Psi(u)$, the set of the individuals i of M such that*
  $M \models \varphi'(i) \wedge \bigwedge_{j \in \{1,\ldots,n\}} \neg \psi_j(i)$ *is infinite.*

We write $T \models \exists_{o}^{\Psi(u)} {}_{\infty} x \, \varphi(x)$, iff for each model M of T we have (5).

Property 3.2.2 *If $T \models \exists_{o}^{\Psi(u)} {}_{\infty} x \, \varphi(x)$ and if for each φ_i, at least one of the following properties holds:*

- *$T \models \exists? x \, \varphi_i$,*
- *there exists $\psi_i(u) \in \Psi(u)$ such that $T \models \forall x \, \varphi_i \to \psi_i(x)$,*

then

$$T \models (\exists x \, \varphi(x) \wedge \bigwedge_{i \in I} \neg \varphi_i) \leftrightarrow (\exists x \, \varphi(x))$$

3.3 The General Theorem for the Completeness of a Theory

Theorem 3.3.1 *A theory T is complete if there exists a set $\Psi(u)$ of formulas, having at most u as free variable, a set A of formulas, closed under conjunction and renaming, a set A' of formulas of the form $\exists \bar{x} \alpha$ with $\alpha \in A$, and a sub-set A'' of A such that:*

1. *every flat atomic formula is equivalent in T to a wfva Boolean combination of basic formulas of the form $\exists \bar{x} \alpha$ with $\alpha \in A$,*
2. *every formula without free variables of the form $\exists \bar{x}' \alpha' \wedge \alpha''$ with $\exists \bar{x}' \alpha' \in A'$ and $\alpha'' \in A''$ is equivalent either to false or to true in T,*
3. *every formula of the form $\exists \bar{x} \, \alpha \wedge \psi$, with $\alpha \in A$ and ψ any formula, is equivalent in T to a wfva formula of the form:*

$$\exists \bar{x}' \, \alpha' \wedge (\exists \bar{x}'' \, \alpha'' \wedge (\exists \bar{x}''' \, \alpha''' \wedge \psi)),$$

   with $\exists \bar{x}' \, \alpha' \in A'$, $\alpha'' \in A''$, $\alpha''' \in A$ and $T \models \forall \bar{x}'' \alpha'' \to \exists! \bar{x}''' \alpha'''$,
4. *if $\exists \bar{x}' \alpha' \in A'$ then $T \models \exists? \bar{x}' \, \alpha'$ and for each free variable y in $\exists \bar{x}' \alpha'$, at least one of the following properties holds:*
   - *$T \models \exists? y \bar{x}' \alpha'$,*
   - *there exists $\psi(u) \in \Psi(u)$ such that $T \models \forall y \, (\exists \bar{x}' \, \alpha') \to \psi(y)$,*
5. *if $\alpha'' \in A''$ then*
   - *the formula $\neg \alpha''$ is equivalent in T to a wfva formula of the form $\bigvee_{i \in I} \alpha_i$ with $\alpha_i \in A$,*
   - *for each x'', the formula $\exists x'' \alpha''$ is equivalent in T to a wfva formula which belongs to A'',*
   - *for each x'', $T \models \exists_{o}^{\Psi(u)} {}_{\infty} x'' \, \alpha''$.*

Let us first make some remarks on the five conditions of Theorem 3.3.1. If T is a theory which satisfies the five conditions of this theorem then the following three properties hold:

Property 3.3.2 *Every formula of the form*

$$\exists \bar{x} \, \alpha,$$

with $\alpha \in A$, is equivalent in T to a wfva formula of the form

$$\exists \bar{x}' \, \alpha' \wedge \alpha'',$$

with $\exists \bar{x}' \alpha' \in A'$ and $\alpha'' \in A''$.

Property 3.3.3 *Every formula of the form*

$$\exists \bar{x}\, \alpha \wedge \bigwedge_{i \in I} \neg(\exists \bar{y}_i \beta_i),$$

with $\alpha \in A$ and $\beta_i \in A$, is equivalent in T to a wfva formula of the form

$$\exists \bar{x}'\, \alpha' \wedge (\exists \bar{x}''\, \alpha'' \wedge \bigwedge_{j \in J} \neg(\exists \bar{y}'_j\, \beta'_j \wedge \beta''_j)),$$

with $\exists \bar{x}' \alpha' \in A'$, $\alpha'' \in A''$, $\exists \bar{y}'_j \beta'_j \in A'$, $\beta''_j \in A''$ and $Card(I) = Card(J)$.

Corollary 3.3.4 *Every formula of the form*

$$\exists \bar{x}\, \alpha \wedge \bigwedge_{i \in I} \neg(\exists \bar{y}_i \beta_i),$$

with $\alpha \in A$ and $\beta_i \in A$, is equivalent in T to a disjunction of wfva formulas of the form

$$\exists \bar{x}'\, \alpha' \wedge (\exists \bar{x}''\, \alpha'' \wedge \bigwedge_{j \in J} \neg(\exists \bar{y}'_j\, \beta'_j)),$$

with $\exists \bar{x}' \alpha' \in A'$, $\alpha'' \in A''$ and $\exists \bar{y}'_j\, \beta'_j \in A'$.

To prove the Properties 3.3.2 and 3.3.3 we use Property 3.1.3 and the conditions 3 and 5 of Theorem 3.3.1. To prove Corollary 3.3.4 we use several times Properties 3.3.3 and 3.1.4 and the conditions 4 and 5 of Theorem 3.3.1.

Proof of Theorem 3.3.1 Let T be a theory which satisfies the five conditions of Theorem 3.3.1. Let us show that T is complete by using Property 2.4.2 and by taking the formulas of the form $\exists \bar{x} \alpha$ with $\alpha \in A$, as basic formulas.

Let us show that the first condition of Property 2.4.2 is satisfied. If φ is a flat atomic formula, then according to the first condition of Theorem 3.3.1, φ is equivalent in T to a wfva Boolean combination of basic formulas. Thus, the first condition of Property 2.4.2 holds.

Let us show that the second condition of Property 2.4.2 is satisfied. If φ is a basic formula without free variables, then according to Property 3.3.2 and the second condition of Theorem 3.3.1, φ is equivalent in T, either to *true*, or to *false*. Thus, the second condition of Property 2.4.2 holds.

Let us show now that the third condition of Property 2.4.2 is satisfied. Let be a formula of the form

$$\exists x\, (\bigwedge_{i \in I}(\exists \bar{x}_i\, \alpha_i)) \wedge (\bigwedge_{j \in J} \neg(\exists \bar{y}_j\, \beta_j)),$$

with $\alpha_i \in A$ and $\beta_j \in A$. We must prove that this formula is equivalent in T to a wfva Boolean combination of basic formulas, i.e. to a wfva Boolean combination of formulas of the form $\exists \bar{x} \alpha$ with $\alpha \in A$. By lifting the quantifications $\exists \bar{x}_i$ after having possibly renamed some variables of the $\bar{x}_i$'s, we get a wfva formula equivalent in T of the form

$$\exists \bar{x}\, \alpha \wedge \bigwedge_{j \in J} \neg(\exists \bar{y}_j \beta_j),$$

with $\alpha \in A$ and $\beta_j \in A$ because A is closed under conjunction and renaming. According to Corollary 3.3.4, the preceding formula is equivalent in T either to false, which is clearly a Boolean combination of basic formulas, or to a wfva disjunction of formulas of the form

$$\exists \bar{x}' \, \alpha' \wedge (\exists \bar{x}'' \alpha'' \wedge \bigwedge_{i \in I} \neg(\exists \bar{y}'_i \beta'_i)). \tag{6}$$

with $\exists \bar{x}' \alpha' \in A'$, $\alpha'' \in A''$ and $\exists \bar{y}'_i \beta'_i \in A'$. Let us show now that each formula of this disjunction is equivalent in T to a wfva Boolean combination of basic formulas. Let φ be a formula of the form (6). We denote by I_1, the set of the $i \in I$ such that x''_n does not have free occurrences in the formula $\exists \bar{y}'_i \beta'_i$, thus, φ is equivalent in T to the following wfva formula

$$\exists \bar{x}' \alpha' \wedge (\exists x''_1 ... \exists x''_{n-1} \left[\begin{matrix} (\bigwedge_{i \in I_1} \neg(\exists \bar{y}'_i \beta'_i)) \wedge \\ (\exists x''_n \alpha'' \wedge \bigwedge_{i \in I - I_1} \neg(\exists \bar{y}'_i \beta'_i)) \end{matrix} \right]). \tag{7}$$

Since $\alpha'' \in A''$ and $\exists \bar{y}'_i \beta'_i \in A'$ and according to Property 3.2.2 and the conditions 4 and 5 (more exactly the third point of the condition 5) of Theorem 3.3.1, the formula (7) is equivalent in T to the following wfva formula

$$\exists \bar{x}' \alpha' \wedge (\exists x''_1 ... \exists x''_{n-1} (\bigwedge_{i \in I_1} \neg(\exists \bar{y}'_i \beta'_i)) \wedge (\exists x''_n \alpha'')). \tag{8}$$

Since $\alpha'' \in A''$ and according to the condition 5 (more precisely the second point of the condition 5) of Theorem 3.3.1, the formula (8) is equivalent in T to a wfva formula of the form

$$\exists \bar{x}' \alpha' \wedge (\exists x''_1 ... \exists x''_{n-1} (\bigwedge_{i \in I_1} \neg(\exists \bar{y}'_i \beta'_i)) \wedge \alpha''_n),$$

with $\exists \bar{x}' \alpha' \in A'$, $\alpha''_n \in A''$ and $\exists \bar{y}'_i \beta'_i \in A'$. Which is equivalent in T to the wfva formula

$$\exists \bar{x}' \alpha' \wedge (\exists x''_1 ... \exists x''_{n-1} \alpha''_n \wedge \bigwedge_{i \in I_1} \neg(\exists \bar{y}'_i \beta'_i)).$$

By repeating the three preceding steps $(n-1)$ times and by denoting by I_k the set of the $i \in I_{k-1}$ such that $x''_{(n-k+1)}$ does not have free occurrences in $\exists \bar{y}'_i \beta'_i$, the preceding formula is equivalent in T to the following wfva formula

$$\exists \bar{x}' \alpha' \wedge \alpha''_1 \wedge \bigwedge_{i \in I_n} \neg(\exists \bar{y}'_i \beta'_i),$$

with $\exists \bar{x}' \alpha' \in A'$, $\alpha''_1 \in A''$ and $\exists \bar{y}'_i \beta'_i \in A'$. Since $\exists \bar{x}' \alpha' \in A'$ and according to the condition 4 of Theorem 3.3.1, we get $T \models \exists? \bar{x}' \alpha'$, thus, $T \models \exists? \bar{x}' \alpha' \wedge \alpha''_1$. According to Property 3.1.2, the preceding formula is equivalent in T to the following wfva formula

$$(\exists \bar{x}' \alpha' \wedge \alpha''_1) \wedge \bigwedge_{i \in I_n} \neg(\exists \bar{x}' \alpha' \wedge \alpha''_1 \wedge \exists \bar{y}'_i \beta'_i).$$

By lifting the quantifications $\exists \bar{y}'_i$ after having possibly renamed some variables of the $\bar{y}'_i$'s, the preceding formula is equivalent in T to a wfva formula of the form

$$(\exists \bar{x}' \alpha' \wedge \alpha''_1) \wedge \bigwedge_{i \in I_n} \neg(\exists \bar{x}' \bar{y}'_i \alpha' \wedge \alpha''_1 \wedge \beta'_i), \tag{9}$$

with $\alpha' \in A$, $\alpha''_1 \in A$ and $\beta'_i \in A$ (because A is closed under renaming, A'' is a sub-set of A and $\exists \bar{x}' \alpha' \in A'$). Since the formulas α', α''_1, β'_i belong to A and since A is closed under conjunction, the formula (9) is equivalent in T to a wfva formula of the form

$$(\exists \bar{x}\, \alpha) \wedge \bigwedge_{i \in I} \neg(\exists \bar{y}_i\, \beta_i),$$

with $\alpha \in A$ and $\beta_i \in A$. This formula is clearly a Boolean combination of basic formulas. The third condition of Property 2.4.2 holds. Thus T, is a complete theory. □

4   The Theory T_E of the Evaluated Trees

Notation 4.0.5 *Let a be a positive integer and let $t_1, ..., t_n$ be terms. We denote by*

- *N, the set of the integer numbers.*
- *Q, the set of the rational numbers together with its usual operations of addition "$+$" and substraction "$-$" and its usual linear order relation "$<$" (dense and without endpoints).*
- *$t_1 < t_2$, the term $< t_1 t_2$.*
- *$t_1 + t_2$, the term $+t_1 t_2$.*
- *$t_1 + t_2 + t_3$, the term $+t_1(+t_2 t_3)$.*
- *$-at_1$, the term $\underbrace{(-t_1) + \cdots + (-t_1)}_{a}$.*
- *$0t_1$, the term 0.*
- *at_1, the term $\underbrace{t_1 + \cdots + t_1}_{a}$,*
- *$\sum_{i=1}^{n} t_i$, the term $\overline{t_1 + t_2 + ... + t_n} + 0$, where $\overline{t_1 + t_2 + ... + t_n}$ is the term $t_1 + t_2 + ... + t_n$ in which we have removed all the t_i's which are equal to 0.*

4.1   The Axiomatization of T_E

The signature S of the theory T_E of the *evaluated trees* is composed of:

- an infinite set $\mathbf{F}$ of function symbols disjoint from $\mathbf{Q}-\{0,1\}$ and containing at least the following function symbols: $-, +, 0, 1$ of respective arities $1, 2, 0, 0$,
- the 1-ary relation symbol *num*,
- the 2-ary relation symbol "$<$".

The axioms of T_E are the propositions of one of the twenty one following forms:

1 $\forall \bar{x} \forall \bar{y} \left((\neg num\ f\bar{x}) \wedge f\bar{x} = f\bar{y} \right) \rightarrow \bigwedge_i x_i = y_i,$
2 $\forall \bar{x} \forall \bar{y}\ f\bar{x} = g\bar{y} \rightarrow num\ f\bar{x},$
3 $\forall \bar{x} \forall \bar{y} \left(\bigwedge_{i \in I} num\ x_i \right) \wedge \left(\bigwedge_{j \in J} \neg num\ y_j \right) \rightarrow$
   $(\exists! \bar{z}\ \bigwedge_{k \in K} (\neg num\ z_k \wedge z_k = t_k(\bar{x}, \bar{y}, \bar{z}))),$

4 $\forall x \forall y \left(num\ x \wedge num\ y \right) \rightarrow x + y = y + x,$
5 $\forall x \forall y \forall z \left(num\ x \wedge num\ y \wedge num\ z \right) \rightarrow x + (y + z) = (x + y) + z,$
6 $\forall x\ num\ x \rightarrow x + 0 = x,$
7 $\forall x\ num\ x \rightarrow x + (-x) = 0,$
8_n $\forall x\ num\ x \rightarrow (\underbrace{x + \cdots + x}_{n} = 0 \rightarrow x = 0),$

9_n $\forall x\ num\ x \rightarrow \exists! y \underbrace{y + \cdots + y}_{n} = x,$

10 $\forall x\ num\ x \rightarrow \neg x < x,$
11 $\forall x \forall y \forall z\ num\ x \wedge num\ y \wedge num\ z \rightarrow ((x < y \wedge y < z) \rightarrow x < z),$
12 $\forall x \forall y \left(num\ x \wedge num\ y \right) \rightarrow (x < y \vee x = y \vee y < x),$
13 $\forall x \forall y \left(num\ x \wedge num\ y \right) \rightarrow (x < y \rightarrow (\exists z\ num\ z \wedge x < z \wedge z < y)),$
14 $\forall x\ num\ x \rightarrow (\exists y\ num\ y \wedge x < y),$
15 $\forall x\ num\ x \rightarrow (\exists y\ num\ y \wedge y < x),$
16 $\forall x \forall y \forall z \left(num\ x \wedge num\ y \wedge num\ z \right) \rightarrow (x < y \rightarrow (x + z < y + z)),$

17 $\forall x \forall y\ num\ x + y \leftrightarrow num\ x \wedge num\ y,$
18 $\forall x\ num\ -x \leftrightarrow num\ x,$
19 $\forall x \forall y\ x < y \rightarrow (num\ x \wedge num\ y),$
20 $\forall \bar{x}\ \neg num\ h\bar{x},$
21 $0 < 1,$

where f and g are two distinct function symbols taken from $\mathbf{F}$, $h \in \mathbf{F} - \{+, -, 0, 1\}$, x, y, z are variables, $\bar{x}$ is a vector of distinct variables x_i, $\bar{y}$ is a vector of distinct variables y_i and where $t_k(\bar{x}, \bar{y}, \bar{z})$ is a term which begins by a function symbol f_k element of $\mathbf{F} - \{0, 1\}$ followed by variables taken from $\bar{x}$ or $\bar{y}$ or $\bar{z}$, moreover, if $f_k \in \{+, -\}$ then $t_k(\bar{x}, \bar{y}, \bar{z})$ contains at least a variable taken from $\bar{y}$ or $\bar{z}$.

4.2   The Standard Model E of T_E

Definition 4.2.1 *If each n-ary element of $\mathbf{F} - \{0, 1\}$ is considered as an n-ary label and each element of $\mathbf{Q}$ is considered as an 0-ary label, then we call:*

- *tree, a tree* [1] *(possibly infinite) labelled by $\mathbf{F} \cup \mathbf{Q}$,*
- *numerical tree, a tree labelled by $\mathbf{Q} \cup \{+, -\}$,*

---

[1] More precisely we define formally a tree a built on a set E of elements of different arities as follow: We define first a node to be a word constructed on the set of strictly positive integers. A tree a, is then a mapping of type $N \rightarrow E$ where N is a non-empty set of nodes, each one of the $i_1 \ldots i_k$ (with $k \geq 0$) satisfying the two conditions: (1) if $k > 0$ then $i_1 \ldots i_{k-1} \in N$, (2) if the arity of $a(i_1 \ldots i_k)$ is n, then the set of nodes of N of the form $i_1 \ldots i_k i_{k+1}$ is obtained by giving to i_{k+1} the values $1, \ldots, n$.

– evaluated numerical tree, *a tree labelled by* Q *(thus, it is a tree reduced to a leaf labelled by* Q *)*
– evaluated tree, *a tree whose all numerical sub-trees are evaluated.*

The theory T_E has as standard model the model E of *the evaluated trees,* defined as follows:

The signature of E: Both T_E and E have the same signature.

The domain of E: The domain $\mathcal{E}$ of E is the set of the evaluated trees.

The relations of E: To the relation symbol num we associate the set num^E of the evaluated numerical trees. To the binary relation symbol $<$ we associate the set of the couples (x, y) such that $x \in num^E$, $y \in num^E$ and the value of x is lower (according to the order " $<$ ") than the value of y.

The operations of E: To each n-ary symbol $f \in \mathbf{F}$ we associate the operation $f^E : \mathcal{E}^n \to \mathcal{E}$, defined as follow:

$$fa_1 \ldots a_n = \begin{cases} 0, & \text{if } f \text{ is the function symbol "0" and } n = 0. \\ 1, & \text{if } f \text{ is the function symbol "1" and } n = 0. \\ (-a_1), & \text{if } f \text{ is the function symbol "}-\text{" and} \\ & a_1 \in num^E \text{ and } n = 1. \\ (a_1 + a_2), & \text{if } f \text{ is the function symbol "}+\text{" and} \\ & a_1 \in num^E \text{ and } a_2 \in num^E \text{ and } n = 2. \\ \text{The tree whose top node is labelled } f \text{ and whose sequence of} \\ \text{immediate daughters is } a_1, \ldots, a_n, \text{ otherwise.} \end{cases}$$

The main difficulty to prove that E is a model of T_E, is to show that the axiom 3 of the unique solution is satisfied in E. For this, we can use a proof given by Dao in [9].

4.3   The Blocks of T_E

Definition 4.3.1 *Let* $f \in \mathbf{F}$, $a_0 \in \mathbf{N}$ *and* $a_i \in \mathbf{N}$. *We call* block *every conjunction* α *of formulas of the form:*

– *true,*
– *false,*
– $num\, x_0$,
– $\neg num\, x_0$,
– $x_0 = x_1$,
– $x_0 = f x_1 \ldots x_n$
– $\sum_{i=1}^{n} a_i x_i = a_0 1$,
– $\sum_{i=1}^{h} a_i x_i < a_0 1$,

such that each variable x *in* α *has at least an occurrence in a sub-formula of* α *of the form* $num\, x$ *or* $\neg num\, x$. *A block* α *without occurrences of the relation symbol* " $=$ " *is called* relational *block. A block* α *without occurrences of the relation symbol* " $<$ " *and where each variable has an occurrence in at least one of the equations of* α *is called* equational.

Definition 4.3.2 *If the block α has a sub-formula of the form*

$$x_0 = t_0(x_1) \wedge x_1 = t_1(x_2) \wedge ... \wedge x_{n-1} = t_{n-1}(x_n) \wedge \bigwedge_{i=0}^{n-1} \neg num\, x_i$$

where x_{i+1} occurs in the term $t_i(x_{i+1})$, then the variable x_n and the equation $x_{n-1} = t_{n-1}(x_n)$ are called reachable *in α from x_0.*

According to the axioms 1 and 2 of T_E we have the following property

Property 4.3.3 *Let α be a block. If all the variables of $\bar{x}$ are reachable in α from the free variables of $\exists \bar{x}\alpha$, then*

$$T_E \models \exists?\bar{x}\alpha.$$

4.4   The Solved Blocks

Suppose that the variables of V are ordered by a linear strict order relation, denoted by " $\succ$ ".

Definition 4.4.1 *A block α is called* well-typed *iff α does not contain sub-formulas of one of the following forms:*

- $num\, x \wedge \neg num\, x$,
- $x = h\bar{y} \wedge num\, x$,
- $x = 0 \wedge \neg num\, x$,
- $x = 1 \wedge \neg num\, x$,
- $x = y \wedge num\, x \wedge \neg num\, y$,
- $x = y \wedge \neg num\, x \wedge num\, y$,
- $x = -y \wedge \neg num\, x \wedge num\, y$
- $x = -y \wedge num\, x \wedge \neg num\, y$
- $x = y + z \wedge num\, x \wedge \neg num\, y$,
- $x = y + z \wedge num\, x \wedge \neg num\, z$,
- $x = y + z \wedge \neg num\, x \wedge num\, y \wedge num\, z$,
- $\sum_{i=1}^{n} a_i x_i = a_0 1 \wedge \neg num\, x_k$, with $a_k \neq 0$,
- $\sum_{i=1}^{n} a_i x_i < a_0 1 \wedge \neg num\, x_k$, with $a_k \neq 0$,

with $h \in F - \{0, 1, +, -\}$, $k \in \{1, ..., n\}$, $a_0 \in N$ and $a_i \in N$.

Definition 1. *Let $f \in F - \{0, 1\}$. We call* leader *of the equation $x_0 = f x_1 ... x_n$ or $x_0 = x_1$ according to the order $\succ$, the variable x_0. We call* leader *of the formula $\sum_{i=1}^{n} a_i x_i = a_0 1$ or $\sum_{i=1}^{n} a_i x_i < a_0 1$ according to the order $\succ$, the greater variable x_k such that $a_k \neq 0$.*

Definition 4.4.2 *A block α is called $(\succ)$-solved in T_E, iff:*

1. *α is well-typed,*
2. *α does not contain sub-formulas of the form $\beta \wedge false$, where β is a formula different from the formula true,*

3. if $x = y$ is a sub-formula of α, then $x \succ y$,
4. all the leaders of the equations of α are distinct and do not occur in any inequation of α,
5. α does not contain sub-formulas of one of the following forms
   - $0 = a_0 1$ (with $a_0 \in \mathbf{N}$),
   - $x = y \wedge num\, x \wedge num\, y$,
   - $x = y + z \wedge num\, x \wedge num\, y \wedge num\, z$,
   - $x = -y \wedge num\, x \wedge num\, y$.

Property 4.4.3 *Every block is equivalent in T_E to a $(\succ)$- block.*

Property 4.4.4 *Let α be a $(\succ)$-solved equational block different from the formula false and let $\bar{x}$ be the set of the leaders of the equations of α. We have:*

$$T_E \models \exists! \bar{x} \alpha.$$

5   Proof of the Completeness of T_E

Theorem 5.0.5 *The theory T_E is a complete theory.*

Let us show this theorem by using Theorem 3.3.1. Let us start by choosing the sets $\Psi(u)$, A, A' and A''.

5.1   Choice of the Sets $\Psi(u)$, A, A' and A''

- $\Psi(u)$ is the set of the formulas of the form $\exists \bar{y}\, u = f\bar{y} \wedge \neg num\, u$, with $f \in \mathbf{F} - \{0,1\}$,
- A is the set of the blocks.
- A' is the set of the formulas of the form $\exists \bar{x}' \alpha'$, where:
  - all the variables of $\bar{x}'$ are reachable in α' from the free variables of $\exists \bar{x}' \alpha'$,
  - α' is a $(\succ)$-solved equational block, different from the formula *false*, and where the order $\succ$ is such that all the variables of $\bar{x}'$ are greater than the free variables of $\exists \bar{x}' \alpha'$,
  - all the equations of α' of the form $x_0 = x_1$ or $x_0 = f x_1 ... x_n$ with $f \in \mathbf{F} - \{0,1\}$ are reachable in α' from the free variables of $\exists \bar{x}' \alpha'$,
  - if $\sum_{i=1}^{n} a_i x_i = a_0 1$ is a sub-formula of α' then, each variable x_i such that $a_i \neq 0$ is either reachable in α' from the free variables of $\exists \bar{x}' \alpha'$, or free in $\exists \bar{x}' \alpha'$.
- A'' is the set of the $(\succ)$-solved relational blocks.

Note 5.1.1 *Note that, A is closed under conjunction and renaming and A'' is a sub-set of A.*

We show - without too many difficulties - by induction on the structure of the $(\succ)$-solved blocks that T_E satisfies the first four conditions of Theorem 3.3.1. On the other hand, the fifth condition - and more exactly the third point of the fifth condition - is much less obvious. This proof deserves to be detailed.

5.2 T_E Satisfies the Third Point of the Condition 5 of Theorem 3.3.1

First, we present two properties which hold in any model M of T_E. These properties result from the axiomatization of T_E and introduce the notion of *zero-infinite* in T_E.

Property 5.2.1 *Let M be a model of T_E and let $f \in \mathbf{F} - \{0,1\}$. The set of the individuals i of M, such that $M \models \neg num\, i$ and the set of the individuals i of M, such that $M \models \exists \overline{x}\, i = f\overline{x}$, are infinite.*

Property 5.2.2 *Let M be a model of T_E, let $\{m_1, ..., m_n\}$ be a finite set of individuals of M and let $\varphi'(x)$ be the following M-formula:*

$$num\, x \wedge \bigwedge_{j=1}^{n} \left(b_j x + \sum_{k=1}^{n} a_{jk} m_{jk} < a_{j0} 1 \right). \tag{10}$$

The set of the individuals i of M such that $M \models \varphi'(i)$ is empty or infinite.

Let $\varphi(x)$ be a formula which belongs to A'', let us show that, for every variables x we have $T_E \models \exists_0^{\Psi(u)} {}_\infty x\, \varphi(x)$. Let M be a model of T_E and let $\exists x\, \varphi'(x)$ be an any instantiation of $\exists \overline{x}\, \varphi(x)$ by individuals of M such that $M \models \exists x\, \varphi'(x)$. Having an any condition of the form

$$M \models \varphi'(i) \wedge \neg\psi_1(i) \wedge \cdots \wedge \neg\psi_n(i),$$

with $\psi_j(u) \in \Psi(u)$, it is enough to show that there exists an infinity of individuals i of M which satisfy this condition. This condition can be replaced by the following stronger condition

$$M \models \begin{pmatrix} num\, i\ \vee \\ \psi_{n+1}(i) \end{pmatrix} \wedge \varphi'(i) \wedge \neg\psi_1(i) \wedge \cdots \wedge \neg\psi_n(i),$$

where $\psi_{n+1}(u)$ is an element of $\Psi(u)$ which has been chosen different from $\psi_1(u), \ldots, \psi_n(u)$, (always possible because the set $\mathbf{F}$ is infinite). Since for every k between 1 and n, we have:

- $T_E \models num\, x \rightarrow \neg\psi_k(x)$
- $T_E \models \psi_{n+1}(x) \rightarrow \neg\psi_k(x)$ (axiom 2).

The preceding condition is simplified to

$$M \models (num\, i \wedge \varphi'(i)) \vee (\psi_{n+1}(i) \wedge \varphi'(i))$$

and thus, knowing that $M \models \exists x\, \varphi'(x)$, it is enough to show that there exists an infinity of individuals i of M such that

$$M \models num\, i \wedge \varphi'(i) \quad \text{or} \quad M \models \psi_{n+1}(i) \wedge \varphi'(i). \tag{11}$$

Two cases arise:

Either the formula $num\,x$ occurs in $\varphi'(x)$. Since $\varphi'(x)$ is an instantiation of a $(\succ)$-solved relational block and $M \models \exists x\,\varphi'(x)$, the formula $num\,x \wedge \varphi'(x)$ is equivalent in M to a M-formula of the form (10). According to Property 5.2.2 and since $M \models \exists x\,num\,x \wedge \varphi'(x)$, there exists an infinity of individuals i of M such that $M \models num\,i \wedge \varphi'(i)$ and thus, such that (11).

Or, the formula $num\,x$ does not occur in $\varphi'(x)$. Since $\varphi'(x)$ is an instantiation of a $(\succ)$-solved relational block and $M \models \exists x\,\varphi'(x)$, the M-formula $\psi_{n+1}(x) \wedge \varphi'(x)$ is equivalent in M to $\psi_{n+1}(x)$. According to Property 5.2.1 there exists an infinity of individuals i of M such that $M \models \psi_{n+1}(i)$, thus, such that $M \models \psi_{n+1}(i) \wedge \varphi'(i)$ and thus such that (11). $\qquad\square$

6   Conclusion

We have established a general theorem which gives a sufficient condition for the completeness of a first-order theory and we have used it to show the completeness of the theory T_E of the evaluated trees. We have built this hybrid theory starting from two theories: the theory of the trees and the theory of the rational numbers together with the operations of addition and substraction and a linear dense order relation without endpoints.

To simplify our proof, and more exactly the last condition of our theorem, we need to establish a sufficient condition which makes it possible to show the completeness of a theory which is a combination of two complete theories. Nevertheless, our theorem enabled us to show the completeness of many other theories such as: the theory of intervals, the theory of concatenation, the theory of lists and many others hybrid theories.

Currently, we are working on a complete axiomatization of the combination of trees together with construction operations and real numbers together with the operations of addition " $+$ ", substraction " $-$ ", multiplication " $*$ " and a dense linear order relation without endpoints. We have also recently developed - starting from our proof - an algorithm for solving general first-order constraints in T_E. We are in the process of studying its complexity and the expressiveness of the first-order constraints in T_E [6].

Acknowledgements. I thank Alain Colmerauer for our many discussions and its help in the organization and the drafting of this paper. I thank him too, for the definitions and proof of his course of DEA. I dedicate to him this paper with my best wishes for a speedy recovery.

References

1. Baader F, Nipkow T. Term rewriting and all that. Cambridge university press 1998. ISBN 0-521-45520-0.
2. Benhamou F, Bouvier P, Colmerauer A, Garetta H, Giletta B, Massat J, Narboni G, N'dong S, Pasero R, Pique J, Touraivane, Van caneghem M, Vetillard E. Le manuel de Prolog IV , PrologIA, Marseille, France, 1996.

3. Chang C, Keisler H. *Model theory*. Section 1.4 Theories and examples of theories. Elsevier, fifth impression, 1988.

4. Colmerauer A. An introduction to Prolog III. *Communication of the ACM*, 33(7):68–90,1990.

5. Colmerauer A. Equations and inequations on finite and infinite trees. Proceeding of the International conference on the fifth generation of computer systems Tokyo, 1984. P. 85–99.

6. Colmerauer A, Dao T. Expressiveness of full first order constraints in the algebra of finite and infinite trees. In 6th International Conference of Principles and Practice of Constraint Programming, CP'2000, LNCS 1894, pages 172–186. Springer, 2000.

7. Courcelle B. Equivalences and Transformations of Regular Systems applications to Program Schemes and Grammars, Theretical Computer Science, vol. 42, 1986, p. 1–122.

8. Courcelle B. Fundamental Properties of Infinite Trees, Theoretical Computer Science, vol. 25, n o 2, 1983, p. 95–169.

9. Dao T. *Resolution de contraintes du premier ordre dans la theorie des arbres finis ou infinis*. These d'informatique, Universite de la mediterranee, decembre 2000.

10. Huet G. Resolution d'equations dans les langages d'ordre 1, 2,...ω. These d'Etat, Universite Paris 7. France,1976.

11. Maher M. Complete axiomatization of the algebra of finite, rational and infinite trees. *Technical report, IBM - T.J.Watson Research Center*, 1988.

A Complete Temporal and Spatial Logic for Distributed Systems*

Dirk Pattinson[1] and Bernhard Reus[2]

[1] LMU München, Institut für Informatik, 80538 München
[2] University of Sussex, Informatics, Brighton BN1 9QH

Abstract. In this paper, we introduce a spatial and temporal logic for reasoning about distributed computation. The logic is a combination of an extension of hybrid logic, that allows us to reason about the spatial structure of a computation, and linear temporal logic, which accounts for the temporal aspects. On the pragmatic side, we show the wide applicability of this logic by means of many examples. Our main technical contribution is completeness of the logic both with respect to spatial/temporal structures and a class of spatial transition systems.

1 Introduction

With the advent of the Internet, mobility and spatial distribution of information systems have established themselves as a new computational paradigm.

Distributed and mobile systems, however, require new specification and verification methodologies. Program logics have to account for space *and* time in a single, unified framework, stating where and when certain computations happen. A further challenge consists of the fact that these systems run on heterogeneous platforms using various different programming languages.

The formal modelling of distributed and mobile systems has traditionally been the domain of process calculi. Several approaches can be found in the literature, for example the π-calculus [22], the ambient calculus [9], and Klaim [12]. In all of these approaches, distributed processes are represented as terms in the language of the underlying calculus. For each of these calculi, corresponding formal logics have been proposed to reason about the behaviour of distributed computation. For example, see [23,7,4,5] for the π-calculus, [9] for the Ambient-calculus, and [24] for Klaim, to name but a few. From a practical perspective, it seems unrealistic to assume that all entities participating in a distributed (or mobile) system can be specified in a single *syntactic* framework: by its very nature, distributed computation integrates various different platforms, operating systems, and programming languages.

A single *semantic* framework is, however, desirable as it supports the analysis and comparison of different logics and calculi. This paper bridges the gap between theory and practice and introduces syntax-independent models of distributed and mobile systems together with an associated logic, that allows to reason about the behaviour of

---

* This work was partially sponsored by the DAAD and the British Council in the ARC project 1205 "Temporal and Spatial Logic for Mobile Systems".

B. Gramlich (Ed.): FroCoS 2005, LNAI 3717, pp. 122–137, 2005.

such systems. On a semantical level, we consider *spatial transition systems*, which encapsulate the behaviour of individual components without the need of expressing the behaviour of the component in a particular syntactic formalism. The properties of the systems under consideration are expressed using *linear spatial temporal logic ($\mathcal{LSTL}$)*, a new logic that we introduce and study in this paper. It arises as a combination of two logics that reflect the two aspects of distributed computation. The first is an extension of both hybrid logic [1,3] and combinatory dynamic logic [25]. This logic, which we call $\mathcal{HL}^*$, is used to reason about the spatial (e.g. network) structure present at one particular point in time. The second is linear temporal logic [20,19] to capture the temporal aspect. This linear spatial temporal logic is independent of any concrete programming or process language. By means of examples, we show that our models and our logic capture many situations that naturally arise in distributed computation.

Our main technical contribution is the completeness of our logic, both with respect to spatio-temporal structures (which are introduced later in the paper) and a class of spatial transition systems. In more detail, we first introduce the spatial component $\mathcal{HL}^*$ of our logic, which can be viewed either as extension of hybrid logic [3,2] with iteration (Section 2) or of combinatory dynamic logic [25] with satisfaction operators. We show that the resulting logic is weakly complete with respect to named models, that is, Kripke models where every location can be referenced by a (not necessarily unique) name. We then use local formulas, a subset of hybrid formulas that only describe properties of one specific node of the distributed structure, in place of propositional atoms in a linear temporal logic. As names provide the only handle to distinguish different nodes of the system, we have to insist that names do not change over time, that is, we consider names as *physical entities* rather than logical ones. Consequently, we have to extend the technique of [14] to account for this interference between the temporal and spatial dimension of the logic. This is achieved by considering sequences with *consistent naming* as models for the combined logic, which is reflected by an additional axiom. The second main result is the completeness of linear spatial temporal logic (Section 3) w.r.t. spatio-temporal structures. This completeness result is then extended to spatial transition systems (Section 4), which can be thought of as machine models for distributed computation. In a nutshell, we obtain a new and complete logical formalism, that is capable of reasoning about distributed computation and applicable to many situations that naturally arise in distributed computation.

Related Work. We have already mentioned the work on spatial logics interpreted over process calculi, notably the π-calculus and the ambient calculus [7,4,5], where the completeness of the logic is in general neglected; however [18] proves a Hennessy-Milner property. In [23,24], modal logics with primitive modal operators for process communication are proposed, but these are also tailored towards their specific process calculi. Finally, spatial logics that are structurally similar to ours have been proposed in the context of semi-structured data, e.g. Ghelli et al.'s work on query languages for XML documents [7]. Completeness is not addressed there. An intuitionistic hybrid logic is investigated in [10] including a completeness result, but w.r.t. Kripke structures that define intuitionistic models and places having no structure at all. A temporal and spatial logic is also used in [21,26] on the basis of a less flexible model of tree sequences. There is no completeness result so far.

2   Spatial Reasoning with Hybrid Logic

This section introduces the purely spatial part of our logic in isolation. To capture the whereabouts of a computation, two ingredients are essential: names for locations where computation takes place and the topological structure that connects these locations. We use a combination of hybrid logic [1] and combinatory dynamic logic [25] that reflects precisely these criteria. Our logic is an extension of modal logic, with a name attached to each world; this feature is present both in hybrid logic and in combinatory dynamic logic. This basic setup is extended with satisfaction operators (borrowed from hybrid logic), that allow us to assert that a formula holds at a specific point of the model. Combinatory dynamic logic contributes a modality for transitive closure, which provides the linguistic means to reason about reachable nodes in a model.

While modalities for transitive closure (i.e. the $*$ of dynamic logic) is needed to have enough expressive power in the language, satisfaction operators are crucial when it comes to combining spatial and temporal aspects. A satisfaction operator $@_i$ shifts the evaluation context the node of the model that has name i. As a consequence, satisfaction operators give rise to formulas $@_i\phi$ that that are either true or false at every node of the model.

A model of our logic is a Kripke Model, where additionally every name is assigned to a unique node. In view of our intended application, we view the worlds of the model as the locations where computation happens and call them *places*. Following the hybrid tradition, place names are referred to as *nominals*. If two places p_1 and p_2 of the model are related, then we interpret this as "from p_1 one can see p_2", or "p_1 has a network connection to p_2", depending on the particular context. In particular, as we require that every node has a name, and names are drawn from a countably infinite set of nominals, all of our models will have an at most countable carrier.

We now introduce the syntax and semantics of our extension $\mathcal{HL}^*$ of hybrid logic.

Definition 1 (Syntax of $\mathcal{HL}^*$). *Suppose that* A *is a set of atomic propositions and* Nom *is a set of nominals. The language of the logic* $\mathcal{HL}^*(\mathsf{A}, \mathsf{Nom})$ *is defined to be the least set of formulas according to the grammar*

$$\phi, \psi \in \mathcal{HL}^* ::= a \mid i \mid \Diamond\phi \mid \Diamond^*\phi \mid \phi \wedge \psi \mid \neg\phi \mid @_i\phi$$

where $a \in \mathsf{A}$ *ranges over the atomic propositions and and* $i \in \mathsf{Nom}$ *is a nominal. We use standard abbreviations for the propositional connectives* $\vee$, $\rightarrow$ *and put* $\Box = \neg \Diamond \neg$, $\Box^* = \neg \Box^* \neg$. *We call a formula* $\phi \in \mathcal{HL}^*$ *local, if* $\phi = @_i\psi$ *for some* $i \in \mathsf{Nom}$ *and* $\psi \in \mathcal{HL}^*$; *the set of local formulas is denoted by* $L(\mathcal{HL}^*)$.

As it is common in Hybrid Logics, proposition $@_i\phi$ represents a local property, i.e. the fact that ϕ holds at at the unique place with name i. Moreover, $\Diamond\phi$ means that ϕ holds at some place directly reachable from here, whereas $\Diamond^*\phi$ means that ϕ holds somewhere reachable from here.

Our notion of model is standard; for notational convenience, we distinguish between the valuation of propositional variables and that of nominals. The semantics of $\mathcal{HL}^*$ is as follows:

Definition 2 (Semantics of $\mathcal{HL}^*$). *A named hybrid model is a tuple $(P, \rightarrow, V, N)$ where P is a set of* places, $\rightarrow \subseteq P \times P$ *is an adjacency relation, $V : A \rightarrow \mathcal{P}(P)$ and $N :$ Nom $\rightarrow P$ are a valuation of propositional variables and nominals, respectively, with N a surjection.*

Given a named model $S = (P, \rightarrow, V, N)$, satisfaction at a point $p \in P$ is given inductively by

$$(S, p) \models a \text{ iff } p \in V(a)$$
$$(S, p) \models i \text{ iff } p = N(i)$$
$$(S, p) \models \Diamond \phi \text{ iff } \exists p'. \, p \rightarrow p' \wedge (S, p') \models \phi$$
$$(S, p) \models \Diamond^* \phi \text{ iff } \exists n \in \mathbb{N}. \, (S, p) \models \Diamond^n \phi$$
$$(S, p) \models @_i \phi \text{ iff } (S, N(i)) \models \phi$$

where the semantics of propositional connectives is as usual. We write $S \models \phi$ iff $(S, p) \models \phi$ for all $p \in P$ and $\mathcal{HL}^* \models \phi$ if $S \models \phi$ for all named models S. If there is danger of confusion, we make the logic explicit in the satisfaction relation and write $(S, p) \models_{\mathcal{HL}^*} \phi$ to say that S is a named hybrid model and $\phi \in \mathcal{HL}^*$ and similarly for $S \models_{\mathcal{HL}^*} \phi$.

With the intuition that the places $p \in P$ of the Kripke frame $(P, \rightarrow)$ represent network nodes and the transition relation $p \rightarrow p'$ represents the possibility of transferring data from p to p', we can formulate assertions on the network topology:

Example 1. 1. The fact that node j is reachable from everywhere is described by the formula $\Diamond^* j$.
2. The fact that network node i is transitively connected to node j is captured in the formula $@_i(\Diamond^* j)$. Note the use of the satisfaction operator $@_i$ to shift the evaluation of the formula $\Diamond^* j$ to the node with name i.
3. If every node of a connected component of a Kripke model is connected to every other node of this component, the model will satisfy the formula $\Diamond^* i \rightarrow \Diamond i$.
4. Finally, we can force connections to be bidirectional by means of the formula $@_i(\Diamond^* j) \rightarrow @_j(\Diamond^* i)$.

Note that only the formula in 2 is *local*.

Our key concern in this section is to analyse the relationship between syntax and semantics of $\mathcal{HL}^*$, and our main result is completeness of the axiom system that we introduce now.

2.1   The Axioms of $\mathcal{HL}^*$

Note that we cannot expect $\mathcal{HL}^*$ to be strongly complete w.r.t. named models. For example, consider the set of formulas $\{\neg i \mid i \in \text{Nom}\}$. This set is consistent, as all its finite subsets are, but not satisfiable in a named model with name set Nom. We therefore have to content ourselves with weak completeness of $\mathcal{HL}^*$, stating that validity of $\phi \in \mathcal{HL}^*$ in all models implies derivability of ϕ. The deducibility predicate $\vdash \subseteq \mathcal{HL}^*$, is given by the following axioms and rules.

(taut) all propositional tautologies

(K$_@$) $@_i(\phi \to \psi) \to (@_i\phi \to @_i\psi)$

(intro) $i \wedge \phi \to @_i\phi$

(sym) $@_i j \leftrightarrow @_j i$

(agree) $@_j @_i \phi \leftrightarrow @_i \phi$

(iter) $\boxminus^* \phi \to \phi \wedge \boxminus\boxminus^* \phi$

(K$_\boxminus$) $\boxminus(\phi \to \psi) \to (\boxminus\phi \to \boxminus\psi)$

(self-dual) $@_i\phi \leftrightarrow \neg@_i\neg\phi$

(ref) $@_i i$

(nom) $@_i j \wedge @_j \phi \to @_i \phi$

(back) $\Diamond@_i p \to @_i p$

(ind) $(\phi \to \boxminus\phi) \wedge \phi \to \boxminus^* \phi$

The proof rules of $\mathcal{HL}^*$ are summarised as follows.

$$(mp) \frac{\phi \to \psi \quad \phi}{\psi} \quad (gen) \frac{\phi}{\boxminus\phi} \quad (gen_@) \frac{\phi}{@_i\phi} \quad (subst) \frac{\phi}{\phi[\theta/x]}(x \in \mathsf{Nom} \cup \mathsf{A})$$

$$(name) \frac{j \to \phi}{\phi}(j \notin \mathrm{nom}(\phi)) \quad (paste) \frac{(@_i \Diamond j) \wedge (@_j \phi) \to \psi}{@_i \Diamond\phi \to \psi} \ (j \notin \mathrm{nom}(\phi, \psi))$$

where $\mathrm{nom}(\phi)$ (resp. $\mathrm{nom}(\phi, \psi)$) denotes the set of nominals occurring in the formula ϕ (resp. in ϕ or ψ) and in the substitution rule it is silently understood to be type correct, i.e. formulas will be substituted for atomic propositions and nominals for nominals only.

Definition 3. *If $\Phi \subseteq \mathcal{HL}^*$ is a set of formulas of $\mathcal{HL}^*$, then $\phi \in \mathcal{HL}^*$ is derivable from Φ, if ϕ is contained in the least set of formulas that contains Φ and the above axioms and is closed under the proof rules of $\mathcal{HL}^*$. This is denoted by $\Phi \vdash_{\mathcal{HL}^*} \phi$. We write $\mathcal{HL}^* \vdash \phi$, if ϕ is a theorem of $\mathcal{HL}^*$, i.e. $\emptyset \vdash_{\mathcal{HL}^*} \phi$.*

It is straightforward to check the following proposition.

Proposition 1. *$\mathcal{HL}^*$ is sound, that is, if $\mathcal{HL}^* \vdash \phi$, then $\mathcal{HL}^* \models \phi$ for all $\phi \in \mathcal{HL}^*$.*

2.2   Completeness of $\mathcal{HL}^*$

We now establish completeness of $\mathcal{HL}^*$. The proof follows a standard argument using a canonical model, existence lemma, and truth lemma. We just elaborate on those issues that are specific to our logic. We begin with the construction of our model.

Definition 4 (see also [1]). *Suppose $\Phi \subseteq \mathcal{HL}^*$ is maximally consistent. Φ is named, if $i \in \Phi$ for some nominal $i \in \mathsf{Nom}$, and Φ is pasted, if $@_i \Diamond\phi \in \Phi$ implies that for some $j \in \mathsf{Nom}$, $@_i \Diamond j \wedge @_j \phi \in \Phi$.*

If Φ is a named and pasted maximally $\mathcal{HL}^*$-consistent set, or a named and pasted $\mathcal{HL}^*$-MCS for short, then the model induced by Φ is given by $M_\Phi = (P, \to_c, V, N)$, where

- $P = \{\Delta_i \mid i \in \mathsf{Nom}\}$ *with* $\Delta_i = \{\phi \mid @_i\phi \in \Phi\}$;
- $\to_c$ *is the canonical relation defined by $u \to_c u'$ iff $\{\Diamond\phi \mid \phi \in u'\} \subseteq u$;*
- $V(a) = \{p \in P \mid a \in p\}$ *is the canonical valuation of propositional variables,*
- $N(i) = $ *the unique $p \in P$ with $i \in P$.*

The following lemma justifies the above definition.

Lemma 1. *Suppose $M_\Phi = (P, \to_c, V, N)$ is the model induced by a named and pasted $\mathcal{HL}^*$-MCS Φ. Then p is named for every $p \in P$, and moreover $i \in p \cap q$ implies $p = q$ for all $p, q \in P$ and all $i \in$ Nom.*

Our desire for a named model dictates that we only use named MCS-s, and the condition that the MCS-s be pasted ensures the validity of an existence lemma; see [1, Section 7.3] for more on this issue. The following is an adaptation of the classical Lindenbaum lemma guaranteeing the existence of named and pasted MCS's.

Lemma 2. *Suppose $\phi \in \mathcal{HL}^*$ is consistent. Then there exists a named and pasted $\mathcal{HL}^*$-MCS containing ϕ and $@_i \neg j$ for all $i \neq j \in M$, for some countable subset $M \subseteq$ Nom with $M \cap \mathrm{nom}(\phi) = \emptyset$.*

Consequently, a model induced by a MCS of the sort described in Lemma 2 is named and countable. Note that we extend a single formula to a maximally consistent set. This allows us to avoid having to enrich the language with new nominals (cf. [1, Section 7.3]). The proof for the existence lemma now works as for the basic hybrid case, and we move straight to the truth lemma.

Lemma 3 (Truth Lemma). *Suppose $M_\Phi = (P, \to_c, V, N)$ is the model induced by a named and pasted $\mathcal{HL}^*$-MCS Φ. Then, for all $\phi \in \mathcal{HL}^*$ and all $p \in P$, we have $(M_\Phi, p) \models \phi$ iff $\phi \in p$.*

Our completeness result follows from Lemma 3 as usual:

Theorem 1. *$\mathcal{HL}^*$ is weakly complete w.r.t. countable, named models.*

There are two points to note here. First, unlike the classical case, we do not have strong completeness w.r.t. named models, as the Lindenbaum Lemma 2 would fail. Second, the preceding theorem asserts that $\mathcal{HL}^*$ is complete for models with countable carrier. This will be important for the completeness of the combined logic with respect to spatial transition systems. We conclude the section with a trivial corollary to the completeness theorem, which will be of fundamental importance later.

Corollary 1. *Suppose $\phi \in L(\mathcal{HL}^*)$ is local. Then ϕ is consistent iff $M \models \phi$ for some countable, named model M.*

This claim follows from the very nature of local formulas: a formula $@_i \phi$ is valid in a place iff it is valid in the place named i, hence local formulas are either globally true or globally false.

3 Temporalising Hybrid Logics

After having studied $\mathcal{HL}^*$ in isolation, we now add a temporal dimension to $\mathcal{HL}^*$. The logic $\mathcal{HL}^*$ allows us to reason about *where* a distributed computation happens; the temporal extension will furthermore furnish us with the expressive power to say *when* this will be the case.

The idea is quite simple: We consider linear temporal logic, but with atomic propositions replaced by local $\mathcal{HL}^*$-formulas. This is as in [15, Section 14], but with one important exception: In *loc.cit.*, the logic being temporalised is completely independent from the added temporal layer. In our case, spatial information needs to be propagated over time, leading to an entanglement of both dimensions. Semantically, this is reflected by or notion of model, which enforces consistency of names, and accounted for by an additional axiom in the proof calculus.

We call the resulting logic $\mathcal{LSTL}$. This logic naturally incorporates a temporal and a spatial aspect: the formulas of $\mathcal{HL}^*$ specify spatial properties *at a given point in time*, and temporal logic allows one to reason about the evolution of the spatial structure over time.

3.1   Linear Temporal Logic (A reminder)

Before we introduce $\mathcal{LSTL}$, let us briefly re-capitulate the syntax and semantics of propositional linear temporal logic. For a clear distinction between the propositional variables of the spatial and temporal logics, we denote the latter by T.

Definition 5. *Suppose* $\mathsf{T} = \{a_0, a_1, \dots\}$ *is a set (of atomic propositions). Then the language* $\mathcal{LTL}(\mathsf{T})$ *of linear temporal logic over* T *is the least set according to the grammar*

$$\phi, \psi \in \mathcal{LTL}(\mathsf{T}) ::= \mathsf{ff} \mid \phi \rightarrow \psi \mid \bigcirc\phi \mid \phi\,\mathcal{U}\,\psi \mid a$$

where $a \in \mathsf{T}$ *ranges over the set of propositional variables. As usual, the other connectives,* tt, $\vee$, $\wedge$, $\neg$ *can be defined from* ff *and* $\rightarrow$, *and we abbreviate* $\Diamond\phi = \mathsf{tt}\,\mathcal{U}\,\phi$ *and* $\Box\phi = \neg\Diamond\neg\phi$.

We call a sequence of valuations $V = (V_n)_{n\in\mathbb{N}}$ *of* T *a temporal structure. Given such a* $V = (V_n)_{n\in\mathbb{N}}$, *i.e. each* V_n *is of type* $\mathsf{T} \rightarrow \{\mathsf{tt}, \mathsf{ff}\}$, *the satisfaction relation is inductively given by*

$$\begin{array}{lll} (V, n) \models a & \textit{iff} & V_n(a) = \mathsf{tt} \\ (V, n) \models \bigcirc\phi & \textit{iff} & (V, n+1) \models \phi \\ (V, n) \models \phi\,\mathcal{U}\,\psi & \textit{iff} & \exists j \geq i.(V, j) \models \psi \text{ and } \forall i \leq k < j.\,(V, k) \models \phi \end{array}$$

where the semantics of propositional connectives is defined as usual. Finally, we put $V \models \phi$ *if* $(V, n) \models \phi$ *for all* $n \in \mathbb{N}$ *and* $\mathcal{LTL} \models \phi$ *if* $V \models \phi$ *for all temporal structures* V. *To distinguish satisfaction w.r.t. linear temporal logic, we sometimes write* $(V, n) \models_{\mathcal{LTL}} \phi$, *and similarly* $V \models_{\mathcal{LTL}} \phi$.

The formula $\bigcirc\phi$ is usually read as "ϕ is true in the next point in time", and $\phi\,\mathcal{U}\,\psi$ reads "ϕ is true until ψ becomes true". Similarly, $\Diamond\phi$ means that "ϕ will eventually become true", and finally $\Box\phi$ expresses that ϕ will be true in all future states. It is well known that the axioms

(taut)	all propositional tautologies	(ltl1)	$\bigcirc\phi \wedge \bigcirc(\phi \rightarrow \psi) \rightarrow \bigcirc\psi$
(ltl2)	$\phi\,\mathcal{U}\,\psi \leftrightarrow \psi \vee (\phi \wedge \bigcirc(\phi\,\mathcal{U}\,\psi))$	(ltl3)	$\bigcirc(\neg\phi) \rightarrow \neg\bigcirc\phi$

together with the inference rules

$$(\text{mp})\ \frac{\phi, \phi \to \psi}{\psi} \qquad (\text{nex})\ \frac{\phi}{\bigcirc\phi} \qquad (\text{ind})\ \frac{\phi' \to \neg\psi \wedge \bigcirc\phi'}{\phi' \to \neg(\phi\,\mathcal{U}\,\psi)}$$

provide a complete axiomatisation of propositional linear temporal logic. We write $\mathcal{LTL} \vdash \phi$ if ϕ can be derived using the above axioms and rules. It is easy to check soundness of the above axioms and rules, and we have the following well-known completeness theorem [17,13,19]:

Theorem 2. *A formula* $\phi \in LTL$ *is valid in all temporal structures iff* ϕ *is derivable, i.e.* $\mathcal{LTL} \models \phi \iff \mathcal{LTL} \vdash \phi$ *for all* $\mathcal{LTL}$*-formulas* ϕ.

3.2   The Logic $\mathcal{LSTL}$

We now embark on the programme of temporalising $\mathcal{HL}^*$, which essentially amounts to replacing (temporal) propositions in $\mathcal{LTL}$-formulas by local $\mathcal{HL}^*$-formulas and the addition of an axiom that represents that names do not change over time. The resulting logic is called $\mathcal{LSTL}$, and the formal definition is as follows:

Definition 6. *The* language *of the logic* $\mathcal{LSTL}$ *is the language of linear temporal logic over the set* $L(\mathcal{HL}^*) = \{\phi \in \mathcal{HL}^* \mid \phi \text{ local }\}$ *of atoms, i.e.* $\mathcal{LTL}(L(\mathcal{HL}^*))$. *Note that propositional combinations of local formulas are not local anymore, but this does not matter as the propositional connectives are in* $\mathcal{LTL}$ *as well.*

A spatio-temporal structure *is a sequence* $(S_n)_{n\in\mathbb{N}}$ *of named* $\mathcal{HL}^*$*-models. The structure* $(S_n)_{n\in\mathbb{N}}$ *has* consistent naming, *if* $S_0 \models @_{ij}$ *iff* $S_n \models @_{ij}$ *for all* $i, j \in$ Nom *and all* $n \in \mathbb{N}$.

Every spatio-temporal structure $(S_n)_{n\in\mathbb{N}}$ *gives rise to a sequence of valuations*

$$S_n^\sharp : L(\mathcal{HL}^*) \to \{\text{tt}, \text{ff}\}, \quad \phi \mapsto \begin{cases} \text{tt} & S_n \models \phi \\ \text{ff} & \text{otherwise.} \end{cases}$$

Validity of a $\mathcal{LSTL}$ *formula* ϕ *in a spatio-temporal structure is can now be defined by* $(S_n)_{n\in\mathbb{N}} \models_{\mathcal{LSTL}} \phi$ *iff* $(S_n^\sharp)_{n\in\mathbb{N}} \models_{\mathcal{LTL}} \phi$, *where the latter is the standard validity in linear temporal logic (Definition 5).*

Finally, $\mathcal{LSTL} \models \phi$ *iff* $S \models_{\mathcal{LSTL}} \phi$ *for all spatio-temporal structures* S *with consistent naming.*

The reason for introducing structures with consistent naming is that in our view "names are physical", which in particular means that they do not change over time (like an IP address for example compared to a domain name that may change). Moreover, those names will provide the only glue between the models in a spatio-temporal structure. Consistent naming ensures that we can address the same physical location at different times via the same (physical) name. We conclude the section on syntax and semantics of $\mathcal{LSTL}$ with some examples.

Example 2 (Network routing). If we let places denote the nodes of a network and the spatial structure reflect the network topology, we are able to formulate assertions on the network and its routing of packets. We are only interested in a finite number of such nodes K. The packet with destination r is encoded as atomic proposition of $\mathcal{HL}^*$, denoted $\underline{r}$. We want to send it from s and thus assume that there is a spatial connection between nodes s and r (Reach). It is also assumed that the network does not change its spatial topology (Static) – and thus in particular does never lose any connections. Packet $\underline{r}$, wherever it may be, will always be broadcast to neighbour nodes (Broadcast). Finally, we have to ensure that – as messages are only broadcasted to neighbours in K – that $\underline{r}$ can reach its destination via a path that only visits nodes in K, which is implied by (Connect). In $\mathcal{LSTL}$ this reads as follows:

Reach $= @_s \Diamond^* r$
Static $= \bigwedge_{p,q \in K} @_p \Diamond q \;\to\; \Box @_p \Diamond q$
Broadcast $= \bigwedge_{p,q \in K} (@_p \underline{r} \wedge @_p \Diamond q) \;\to\; \bigcirc @_q \underline{r}$
Connect $= \bigwedge_{i \in K} @_i \boxminus \bigvee_{j \in K} j$

In such a situation one can derive that message $\underline{r}$ will eventually arrive, ie. $@_s \underline{r} \to \Diamond\, @_r \underline{r}$.

Example 3. Agents can be specified by describing the computation at various places in terms of state transitions. If agent A runs at place i and agent B runs at place j, and their state change is described by functions $\delta_A : S_A \to S_A$ and $\delta_B : S_B \to S_B$, respectively, then the system obtained by running A and B concurrently can be specified by

$$\bigwedge_{s \in S_A} @_i \varphi(s) \to \bigcirc @_i \varphi(\delta_A(s)) \wedge \bigwedge_{s \in S_B} @_i \varphi(s) \to \bigcirc @_j \varphi(\delta_B(s))$$

where $\varphi(\cdot)$ is a logical formula that characterises the respective state. If agent B "moves into" agent A after performing a state change from s_{mv} to s_e then this can be specified by

$$@_j \varphi(s_{mv}) \wedge \neg @_i \Diamond j \wedge \neg @_j \Diamond i \to \bigcirc @_i \Diamond j \wedge @_j \varphi(s_e)$$

This movement is accounted for by the change of the spatial structure. This can be extended to describe behaviours of ambient like agents [8].

Example 4 (Leader election protocol). The following example is an adaptation of the IEEE 1394 Leader election protocol (see e.g. [26]). Let places again denote a finite number of network nodes. The network topology is described by a fixed *acyclic* (and finite) neighbourhood relation R. The network nodes are supposed to elect a leader.

Let the spatial structure represent the election results, i.e. how "local leaders" were chosen between each pair of connected nodes. Hence, we have $p \to q$ if p has chosen q to be its leader (and p and q are neighbours).

The protocol can be specified as follows: Initially, there are no connections between places (Init). Next$_{p,q}$ describes the situation where two nodes, p and q have not determined a leader between each other yet, and p is the only neighbour of q with that property. In such a case, q can become a subordinate of p, which is specified on the second line of Next. The first line specifies a "frame"-condition, namely that connections between places are always maintained, and for places who are not neighbours, do not even change. Goal states that for any two places in the neighbourhood relation one is the leader of the other. This implies that there is a leader for all nodes. Finally, Live axiomatises that if Goal is not (yet) true, there are places p and q that decide leadership amongst them in the next step.

The specification of the overall system then is: Init $\wedge$ Next $\wedge$ Live $\rightarrow$ Goal.

$\begin{aligned}
\text{Init} \quad &= \bigwedge_p @_p \neg \diamondsuit\text{tt} \\
\text{Next}_{p,q} &= @_p \neg \diamondsuit\text{tt} \wedge @_q \neg \diamondsuit\text{tt} \wedge \bigwedge_{r \neq p, R(q,r)} @_r \diamondsuit\text{tt} \\
\text{Next} \quad &= \bigwedge_{p,q} @_q \diamondsuit p \rightarrow \bigcirc @_q \diamondsuit p \wedge \bigwedge_{p,q, \neg R(p,q)} @_q \diamondsuit p \iff \bigcirc @_q \diamondsuit p \; \wedge \\
&\quad \bigwedge_{R(p,q)} (\bigcirc @_q \diamondsuit p) \wedge @_q \neg \diamondsuit p \rightarrow \text{Next}_{p,q} \\
\text{Goal} \quad &= \bigwedge_{p \neq q, R(p,q)} @_p \diamondsuit q \vee @_q \diamondsuit p \\
\text{Live} \quad &= \text{Goal} \vee \bigvee_{p,q} @_q \neg \diamondsuit p \wedge \bigcirc @_q \diamondsuit p
\end{aligned}$

We deem this formulation in $\mathcal{LSTL}$ more natural than the one given in [26].

Example 5 (XML documents). Let us specify an XML document with an active component. The spatial structure mirrors the XML document tree-structure, such that places correspond to *occurrences* of pairs of matching tags, i.e. $i \rightarrow j$ means that the XML-component at j is defined inside the one at i. The tags used and the text contained inside these tag are expressed as spatial propositions. As documents are finite, we are only interested in a finite set of places F. The document specified below has a *root* component (1), and a weather component somewhere under the root node (2). Moreover, if the weather component contains a temperature component, it will eventually fill in a valid integer representing the temperature in degrees (3).

1. $\bigwedge_{p \in F} @_{root} \diamondsuit^* p \wedge \neg @_p \diamondsuit^* root$
2. $@_{root} \diamondsuit^* \langle \text{weather} \rangle$
3. $\bigwedge_{p \in F} @_p(\langle \text{weather} \rangle \wedge \diamondsuit^* \langle \text{temp} \rangle) \rightarrow \diamond @_p(\langle \text{weather} \rangle \wedge \diamondsuit^*(\langle \text{temp} \rangle \wedge \text{valid\_int}))$

Note that the basic set of inference rules accounts for loops and self-reference in the structure of XML documents. While this is possible in some dialects of XML, e.g. Xlink [11] and other tree based query languages [6], it is easy to axiomatise special properties of trees in $\mathcal{LSTL}$. For example, the formula $\neg @_i \diamondsuit^* i$ ensures that there are no cycles in the structure of the document.

3.3   Proof Rules of $\mathcal{LSTL}$

This section describes a complete axiomatisation of $\mathcal{LSTL}$. Extending [14], we enrich a standard and complete axiomatisation of $\mathcal{LTL}$ with the following rule and axiom scheme:

$$(\text{emb}) \quad \frac{\mathcal{LTL} \vdash \phi}{\mathcal{LSTL} \vdash \phi} \qquad (\text{cn}) \quad @_i j \leftrightarrow \bigcirc @_i j$$

to import spatial deduction into $\mathcal{LSTL}$ and to account for the fact that we are axiomatising structures with consistent naming, which is the main difference to [14], which presumes complete independence of the temporal component and the logic being temporalised.

Definition 7. *Suppose $\phi \in \mathcal{LSTL}$. Then $\mathcal{LSTL} \vdash \phi$ if ϕ is in the least set of formulas closed under (emb), (cn) and the axioms and rules of any complete axiomatisation of $\mathcal{LTL}$.*

It is straightforward to verify soundness of $\mathcal{LSTL}$.

Proposition 2 (Soundness of $\mathcal{LSTL}$). *Suppose* $\phi \in \mathcal{LSTL}$. *Then* $\mathcal{LSTL} \models \phi$ *if* $\mathcal{LSTL} \vdash \phi$.

3.4   Completeness of $\mathcal{LSTL}$

We now tackle completeness of $\mathcal{LSTL}$. Our construction is an extension of the construction presented in [14] that accounts for the fact that the rule (cn) axiomatises consistent naming, which is a property of spatio-temporal structures that cuts across time.

The proof of completeness fixes a fixed enumeration of a set $\mathsf{T} = \{p_0, p_1, p_2, \dots\}$ of propositional variables, that is used to encode sentences of $\mathcal{LSTL}$ in $\mathcal{LTL}$. We need the following technical terminology.

Definition 8. *For a fixed enumerations* $L(\mathcal{HL}^*) = \{\phi_0, \phi_1, \phi_2 \dots\}$ *we define the correspondence mapping* $\sigma : \mathcal{LTL}(L(\mathcal{HL}^*)) \to \mathcal{LTL}(\mathsf{T})$ *as the mapping* $\phi_i \mapsto a_i$.

Because we replace propositional reasoning when substituting $L(\mathcal{HL}^*)$-formulas for atoms in linear temporal logic, we need to encode the relations between the atoms on a purely propositional level in order to make use of completeness of $\mathcal{LTL}$. This is the purpose of the next definition.

Definition 9. *We inductively define the set* $\mathrm{Lit}(\phi) \subseteq \mathcal{HL}^*$ *of literals of* $\phi \in \mathcal{LSTL}$ *as follows:*

$$\mathrm{Lit}(\mathrm{ff}) = \emptyset \qquad \mathrm{Lit}(\phi \to \psi) = \mathrm{Lit}(\phi) \cup \mathrm{Lit}(\psi) \qquad \mathrm{Lit}(\bigcirc\phi) = \mathrm{Lit}(\phi)$$
$$\mathrm{Lit}(a) = \{a, \neg a\} \qquad \mathrm{Lit}(\phi\,\mathcal{U}\,\psi) = \mathrm{Lit}(\phi) \cup \mathrm{Lit}(\psi)$$

where $p \in \mathcal{HL}^*$ *in the last line above. If* $\phi \in \mathcal{LSTL}$, *the set of* inconsistencies *of* ϕ *is given as*

$$\mathrm{Inc}(\phi) = \{\bigwedge \Phi \mid \Phi \subseteq \mathrm{Lit}(\phi) \text{ and } \Phi \vdash_{\mathcal{HL}^*} \mathrm{ff}\}.$$

Theorem 3. *The logic $\mathcal{LSTL}$ is weakly complete.*

Proof. Suppose $\phi \in \mathcal{LSTL}$ is consistent; we show that ϕ has a model, which is equivalent to the claim by contraposition. Let $\mathrm{nom}(\phi) = \bigcup\{\mathrm{nom}(\psi) \mid \psi \in \mathrm{Lit}(\phi)\}$ denote the set of nominals occurring in ϕ making use of nom for $\mathcal{HL}^*$- formulas (see Section 2). We now let

$$\hat{\phi} = \phi \wedge \bigwedge_{\psi \in \mathrm{Inc}(\phi)} \Box\neg\psi \wedge \bigwedge_{i,j \in \mathrm{nom}(\phi)} @_{ij} \leftrightarrow \bigcirc @_{ij}$$

Note that consistency of ϕ implies consistency of $\hat{\phi}$, which in turn implies consistency of $\sigma(\hat{\phi})$. Hence there exists a sequence $V = (V_n)$ of valuations of the propositional variables T s.t. $V \models_{\mathcal{LTL}} \sigma(\hat{\phi})$. The intuition behind the definition of $\hat{\phi}$ is that $\hat{\phi}$ encodes not only ϕ, but also all relations between its literals on a purely propositional level. This encoding ensures that propositionally valid literals are actually consistent in the logic $\mathcal{HL}^*$, a fact that is crucial for completeness, which we now address.

By construction, this valuation satisfies

$$V_0 \models \sigma(@_i j) \iff V_n \models \sigma(@_i j)$$

for all $n \in \mathbb{N}$ and all $i, j \in \mathrm{nom}(\phi)$. Take

$$G_n(\phi) = \{\psi \in \mathrm{Lit}(\phi) \mid V_n \models \sigma(\psi)\}.$$

Then all G_n are $\mathcal{HL}^*$-consistent (Lemma 14.2.17 of [15]). Moreover, we have $@_i j \in G_0(\phi) \iff @_i j \in G_n(\phi)$ for all $i, j \in \mathrm{nom}(\phi)$ and all $n \in \mathbb{N}$ by construction. As $G_n(\phi)$ consists of local formulas only, we can invoke Corollary 1 to obtain a countable named model S_n with $S_n \models G_n(\phi)$ for all $n \in \mathbb{N}$.

We can assume without loss of generality that the sequence (S_n) has constant naming, as $S_n \models @_i j \iff S_0 \models @_i j$ for $i, j \in \mathrm{Nom}(\phi)$ and $n \in \mathbb{N}$ and we can always change the valuation of nominals not occurring in ϕ (and hence G_n) without changing the validity of formulas.

Now $V \models \sigma(\hat{\phi})$ implies that $V \models \sigma(\phi)$ which implies $M \models \phi$ where the latter can be shown by induction on the structure of ϕ.

4   Spatial Transition Systems

The spatio-temporal structures of Def. 6 have one significant drawback, they are just arbitrary sequences of spatial models and there are no rules on how one spatial model evolves from its predecessors. As a remedy, and to bridge the gap between spatio-temporal structures and programming languages, spatial transition systems are introduced below. They are an abstraction of distributed programs. Completeness of $\mathcal{LSTL}$ with respect to these transitions systems will follow from the fact that every spatio-temporal structure arises as a run of a spatial transition system.

Definition 10. *A spatial transition system (STS) Θ consists of an enumerable set of physical places P, a surjective map $\eta : \mathrm{Nom} \to P$ mapping nominals – ie. (non-unique) place names – to physical places, and a P-indexed set of transition systems $(X_p, \to_p, \lambda_p, \mu_p, s_p^0)_{p \in P}$ such that*

- *X_p is the set of states of computations happening at place p,*
- *$\to_p \subseteq X_p \times X_p$ is the (possibly non-deterministic) state transition relation of the computation at place p. Transitions in $(X_p \times X_p)$ are autonomous transitions that can happen at place p.*
- *$\lambda_p : X_p \to \mathcal{P}(P)$ describes the spatial structure in terms of all connected neighbours of p at any state during the computation,*
- *$\mu_p : X_p \to \mathcal{P}(\mathrm{A})$ characterises the states of the computation at p by stating which (spatial) propositions hold in each state,*
- *s_p^0 is the initial state for the computation in p.*

A system state s of Θ is then a place indexed vector of states, i.e. $s \in \Pi_{p \in P}. X_p$. We write $s(p)$ for the component of s belonging to place p. A spatial transition system

$\Theta = (P, \eta, (X_p, \to_p, \lambda_p, \mu_p, s_p^0)_{p \in P})$ *induces a transition relation* $\to_\Theta$ *on system states* $s, s' \in \Pi_{p \in P}. X_p$ *as follows:*

$$s \to_\Theta s' \iff \exists Q \subseteq P (\forall p \in Q. s(p) \to_p s'(p) \text{ and } \forall p \notin Q. s(p) = s'(p))$$

with $s^\Theta = (s_p^0)_{p \in P}$ *as initial state.*

Runs of an STS are always infinite, as all the computations may be idle (choosing Q to be $\emptyset$). This provides us with a unified setting for finite and infinite computations. Moreover, the computations at different places may proceed in different speeds, reflected by the fact that at every tick of the synchronous clock describing the progress of a system state $s \in \Pi_{p \in P}. X_p$, some of the computations, precisely those in $P \setminus Q$, are idle. This is supposed to reflect the fact that the computations are actually running independently. Any computation in $p \in P$ can be non-deterministic if $\to_p$ is not the graph of a function.

Definition 11. *Every system state s for a STS Θ as described above gives rise to a named spatial model $Sp(s) = (P, \to_s, V_s, N_s)$ setting*

$$p \to_s q \iff q \in \lambda_p(s(p)), \quad V_s(a) = \{p \in P \mid a \in \mu_p(s(p))\}, \quad N_s = \eta.$$

The set of spatio-temporal structures generated by the STS Θ, called Run(Θ), *contains all sequences of models generated by possible runs of Θ, i.e.*

$$\text{Run}(\Theta) = \{(Sp(s_n))_{n \in \mathbb{N}} \mid s_0 = s^\Theta \wedge s_n \to_\Theta s_{n+1} \text{ for all } n \in \mathbb{N}\}.$$

As η in the definition of STS does not depend on the states of the STS, all spatio-temporal structures in Run(Θ) *have consistent naming. Validity for an STS is defined via a detour through the spatio-temporal structures:*

$$\Theta \models \phi \iff \forall (S_n) \in \text{Run}(\Theta). (S_n) \models \phi.$$

Due to the independent definition of the computations at places P, there cannot be any communication between them. Therefore, we will refine the notion of an STS shortly, but the present definition is sufficient to prove a completeness result.

Before we embark on completeness, we need one little technical lemma on consistent naming, which uses the following terminology: For a function $f : X \to Y$, the *kernel* of f is the set $\text{Ke}(f) = \{(x, x') \in X \times X \mid f(x) = f(x')\}$. Note that $\text{Ke}(f)$ is an equivalence relation.

Lemma 4. *Suppose $(S_n)_{n \in \mathbb{N}}$ is a spatio-temporal structure with consistent naming and $S_n = (P_n, \to_n, V_n, N_n)$. Then $\text{Ke}(N_k) = \text{Ke}(N_l)$ for all $k, l \in \mathbb{N}$ and $P \cong$ Nom$/\text{Ke}(N_k)$ for all $k \in \mathbb{N}$.*

Lemma 5. *For an $\mathcal{LSTL}$ formula ϕ, if $\Theta \models \phi$ for all STS Θ, then $S \models \phi$ for all spatio-temporal structures S with consistent naming (according to Def. 6).*

Proof. Assume $\Theta \models \phi$ for all STS Θ and let a spatio-temporal structure S with consistent naming be given. Assume $S = (S_n, \to_n, V_n, P_n)$. By the last lemma, we can assume without loss of generality that $S_0 = $ Nom$/\text{Ke}(N_0) = S_k$ for all $k \in \mathbb{N}$. We now show that S can be generated by a spatial transition system. We let $P = S_0$ and put $\eta(i) = N_0(i)$ for $i \in$ Nom. The components at each place $p \in P$ are given by:

- $X_p = \mathbb{N}$
- $n \to_p m$ iff $m = n + 1$
- $\lambda_p(n) = \{q \in S_n \mid p \to_n q\}$
- $\mu_p(n) = \{a \in \mathsf{A} \mid p \in V_n(a)\}$
- $s_p^0 = 0$.

Clearly $S \in \mathsf{Run}(\Theta)$, hence $S \models \phi$ by assumption.

Corollary 2. *The logic $\mathcal{LSTL}$ is weakly complete w.r.t. spatial transition systems.*

The transition systems defined above still do not provide means for programming synchronisation between computations (which can be used to program communication). Therefore we define *synchronised* spatial transition system as a superset of the spatial ones, ensuring that the completeness result above is not jeopardised. The main idea of a synchronised spatial transition system is the following. We equip the transition systems $(X_p, \to_p, \lambda_p, \mu_p, s_p^0)$ that model the system behaviour at place p with a *labelled transition relation* $\to_p \subseteq X_p \times \sigma \times X_p$, where σ is a set of labels that contains the distinguished label τ. We now stipulate that the system state s can evolve into a system state s' if either some of the processes make an internal transition (labelled with τ) or all processes capable of performing ℓ transitions participate in a synchronous transition, labelled with $\ell \neq \tau$. The formal definition reads as follows.

Definition 12. *A synchronised spatial transition system (SSTS) Σ is defined like a STS with an additional enumerable set of synchronisation labels σ with distinguished element $\tau \in \sigma$ and slightly changed transition systems $\to_p \subseteq (X_p \times \sigma \times X_p)$. We write $x \xrightarrow{\ell}_p y$ to indicate the $(x, \ell, y) \in \to_p$. For all $p \in P$ define labels $: P \to \mathcal{P}(\sigma)$ by $\mathrm{labels}(p) = \{\ell \in \sigma \mid \ell \neq \tau \wedge \exists s, t \in X_p. \ s \xrightarrow{\ell}_p t\}$ to denote all labels for which there are synchronised transitions for the computation at p. The system transitions for such a SSTS are now defined below, making sure that ℓ-synchronised transitions (for $\ell \neq \tau$) can only be performed if all processes with ℓ-labelled transitions actually fire ℓ-transitions synchronously. We stipulate $s \to_\Sigma s'$ if one of the following two conditions are satisfied:*

1. $\exists Q \subseteq P(\forall p \in Q. \ s(p) \xrightarrow{\tau}_p s'(p)$ and $\forall p \notin Q. s(p) = s'(p))$, or
2. $\exists \ell \neq \tau \in \sigma(\forall p \in P_\ell. s(p) \xrightarrow{\ell}_p s'(p)$ and $\forall p \notin P_\ell. s(p) = s'(p))$.

where $P_\ell = \mathrm{labels}^{-1}(\{\ell\})$ denotes the set $\{p \in P \mid \ell \in \mathrm{labels}(p)\}$ of places that can fire an ℓ-transition.

Example 6 (Leader Election Protocol IEEE 1394). We present an SSTS that fulfils the specification given in Example 4. The SSTS is defined as follows: Set $P = \mathsf{Nom}$ and $\eta = id$. For $p \in \mathsf{Nom}$ let $X_p = (\mathbb{N}, \mathcal{P}(\mathsf{Nom}))$ such that $\lambda_p(\_, x) = x$. The first component keeps track of the number of neighbours with which p has yet to decide about the leadership. Let σ contain a label $\ell_{\{i,j\}}$ for each pair of names, such that $R(i, j)$. Remember that R is the fixed neighbourhood relation describing the topology of an acyclic network. The initial state for each p is now $(\mathrm{card}\{j \in \mathsf{Nom} \mid R(j, p)\}, \emptyset)$.

For every $i, j \in \mathsf{Nom}$ such that $R(i, j)$ we have transitions

$$(1, x) \xrightarrow{\ell_{\{i,j\}}}_i (0, x \cup \{j\}) \qquad (n + 1, x) \xrightarrow{\ell_{\{i,j\}}}_j (n, x)$$

According to this definition, any node i can only chose j to be its leader if j is a neighbour, and j is the only neighbour that has not yet become a subordinate to another node.

Corollary 3. *The logic $\mathcal{LSTL}$ is weakly complete w.r.t. synchronised spatial transition system.*

This follows from Corollary 2 and the fact that every STS is also an SSTS.

5   Conclusions

By blending well-known ingredients, hybrid logic and linear temporal logic, extending a recipe from [14], we obtained a logic for reasoning about time and space for distributed computations that we proved to be complete. Our model is capable of representing many situations that naturally arise in distributed computing, including the behaviour of distributed agents (Example 3). Further research is necessary to investigate whether the spatial formulas can be extended, e.g. by hybrid quantifiers that could replace the finite conjunctions in our examples; this work will be guided by [16]. On the spatio-temporal side the question remains how to reflect synchronisation on the logical level.

References

1. Patrick Blackburn, Maarten de Rijke, and Yde Venema. *Modal Logic*. Number 53 in Cambridge Tracts in Theoretical Computer Science. Cambridge University Press, 2001.
2. Patrick Blackburn and Miroslava Tzakova. Hybrid completeness. *Logic Journal of the IGPL*, 6(4):625–650, 1998.
3. Patrick Blackburn and Miroslava Tzakova. Hybrid languages and temporal logic. *Logic Journal of the IGPL*, 7(1):27–54, 1999.
4. Luís Caires and Luca Cardelli. A spatial logic for concurrency (part I). *Inf. Comput.*, 186(2):194–235, 2003.
5. Luís Caires and Luca Cardelli. A spatial logic for concurrency - II. *Theor. Comput. Sci.*, 322(3):517–565, 2004.
6. Cristiano Calcagno, Philippa Gardner, and Uri Zarfaty. Context logic and tree update. In *POPL '05: Proceedings of the 32nd symposium on Principles of programming languages*, pages 271–282, New York, NY, USA, 2005. ACM Press.
7. Luca Cardelli, Philippa Gardner, and Giorgio Ghelli. A spatial logic for querying graphs. In Peter Widmayer, Francisco Triguero Ruiz, Rafael Morales Bueno, Matthew Hennessy, Stephan Eidenbenz, and Ricardo Conejo, editors, *Automata, Languages and Programming, 29th International Colloquium, ICALP 2002, Proceedings*, volume 2380 of *Lecture Notes in Computer Science*, pages 597–610. Springer, 2002.
8. Luca Cardelli and Andrew D. Gordon. Anytime, anywhere: Modal logics for mobile ambients. In *POPL*, pages 365–377, 2000.
9. Luca Cardelli and Andrew D. Gordon. *Mobile ambients*, pages 198–229. Cambridge University Press, New York, NY, USA, 2001.
10. Rohit Chadha, Damiano Macedonio, and Vladimiro Sassone. A distributed Kripke semantics. Technical Report 2004:04, University of Sussex, 2004.
11. W3C consortium. Xlink language version 1.0.
12. Rocco de Nicola, Gian Luigi Ferrari, and Rosario Pugliese. Klaim: A kernel language for agents interaction and mobility. *IEEE Trans. Softw. Eng.*, 24(5):315–330, 1998.

13. Ronald Fagin, Joseph Y. Halpern, Yoram Moses, and Moshe Y. Vardi. *Reasoning about Knowledge*. MIT Press, 1995.

14. Marcelo Finger and Dov Gabbay. *Adding a Temporal Dimension to a Logic System*, chapter 14, pages 524–552. Volume 1 of *Oxford Logic Guides* [15], 1994.

15. Dov Gabbay, Ian Hodkinson, and Mark Reynolds. *Temporal Logic: Mathematical Foundations and Computational Aspects: Volume I*. Number 28 in Oxford Logic Guides. Oxford University Press, 1994.

16. Dov Gabbay, Agi Kurucz, Frank Wolter, and Michael Zakharyaschev. *Many-dimensional Modal logics: Theory and Applications*. Elsevier, 2003.

17. Dov Gabbay, Amir Pnueli, Saharon Shela, and Johnatan Stavi. On the temporal analysis of fairness. In *Proc. of the 7th ACM Symp. on Principles of Programming Languages*, pages 163–173. ACM press, 1980.

18. Daniel Hirschkoff. An extensional spatial logic for mobile processes. In Philippa Gardner and Nobuko Yoshida, editors, *Proc. of 15th Int. Conf. CONCUR 2004*, volume 3170 of *Lecture Notes in Computer Science*, pages 325–339. Springer, 2004.

19. Fred Kröger. *Temporal Logic of Programs*, volume 8 of *EATCS Monographs on Theoretical Computer Science*. Springer-Verlag, 1987.

20. Zohar Manna and Amir Pnueli. *The Temporal Logic of Reactive and Concurrent Systems*. Springer, 1992.

21. Stephan Merz, Martin Wirsing, and Júlia Zappe. A spatio-temporal logic for the specification and refinement of mobile systems. In Mauro Pezzè, editor, *Proc. of 6th Int. Conf. Fundamental Approaches to Software Engineering (FASE) 2003*, volume 2621 of *Lecture Notes in Computer Science*, pages 87–101. Springer, 2003.

22. Robin Milner, Joachim Parrow, and David Walker. A calculus of mobile processes. *Inf. Comput.*, 100(1):1–40, 1992.

23. Robin Milner, Joachim Parrow, and David Walker. Modal logic for mobile processes. *Theoretical Computer Science*, 1(114):149–171, 1993.

24. Rocco De Nicola and Michele Loreti. A modal logic for mobile agents. *ACM Trans. Comput. Logic*, 5(1):79–128, 2004.

25. Solomon Passy and Tinko Tinchev. An essay in combinatory dynamic logic. *Information and Computation*, 93, 1991.

26. Júlia Zappe. Towards a mobile TLA. In M. Nissim, editor, *ESSLI Student Workshop on Logic*, 2002.

Hybrid CSP Solving

Eric Monfroy[1,3], Frédéric Saubion[2], and Tony Lambert[2,3]

[1] Universidad Técnica Federico Santa María, Valparaíso, Chile
Firstname.Name@inf.utfsm.cl
[2] LERIA, Université d'Angers, France
Firstname.Name@univ-angers.fr
[3] LINA, Université de Nantes, France
Firstname.Name@univ-nantes.fr

Abstract. In this paper, we are concerned with the design of a hybrid resolution framework. We develop a theoretical model based on chaotic iterations in which hybrid resolution can be achieved as the computation of a fixpoint of elementary functions. These functions correspond to basic resolution techniques and their applications can easily be parameterized by different search strategies. This framework is used for the hybridization of local search and constraint propagation, and for the integration of genetic algorithms and constraint propagation. Our prototype implementation gave experimental results showing the interest of the model to design such hybridizations.

1 Introduction

The resolution of constraint satisfaction problems (CSP) appears nowadays as a very active and growing research area. Indeed, constraint modeling allows both scientists and practitioners to handle various industrial or academic applications (e.g., scheduling, timetabling, boolean satisfiability, ...). In this context, CSP are basically represented by a set of decision variables and a set of constraints among these variables. The purpose of a resolution process is therefore to assign a value to each variable such that the constraints are satisfied. We focus here on discrete CSP in which variables take their values over finite sets of integers. Discrete CSP are widely used to model combinatorial problems, and, by extension, combinatorial optimization problems, where the purpose is to find a solution of the problem which optimizes (minimizes or maximizes) a given criterion, usually encoded by an objective function.

The resolution of CSP involves many different techniques issued from different scientific communities: computer science, operation research or applied mathematics. Therefore, the principles and purposes of the proposed resolution approaches are very diverse. But, one may classified these methods in two families, which differ on a fundamental aspect of the resolution: complete methods whose purpose is to provide the whole set of solutions and incomplete methods which aim at finding one solution. On the one hand, complete methods, thanks to an exhaustive exploration of the search space, are able to demonstrate that a

B. Gramlich (Ed.): FroCoS 2005, LNAI 3717, pp. 138–167, 2005.

given problem is not satisfiable while incomplete methods will be ineffective in that case. On the other hand, incomplete methods, which explore only some parts of the search space with respect to specific heuristics, are often more efficient to obtain a solution and, moreover, for large instances with huge search space they appear as the only usable methods since resolution becomes intractable for complete methods.

A common idea to get more efficient and robust algorithms consists in combining several resolution paradigms in order to take advantage of their respective assets. Such combinations are now more and more studied in the constraint programming community [21,30,31,32].

Complete solvers usually build a search tree by applying domain reduction, splitting and enumeration. Local consistency mechanisms [24,27] allow the algorithms to prune the search space by deleting inconsistent values from variables domains. Such solvers have been embedded in constraint programming languages (Chip [2], Ilog Solver [19], CHOCO [22], ...) which provide a general framework for constraint modeling and resolution. Unfortunately, this approach requires an important computational effort and therefore encounters some difficulties with large scale problems. These performances can be improved by adding more specific techniques such as efficient constraint propagation algorithms, global constraints, ... We refer the reader to [5,12,25,9] for an introduction to constraint programming.

Incomplete methods mainly rely on the use of heuristics providing a more efficient exploration of interesting areas of the search space in order to find some solutions. Unfortunately, these approaches do not ensure to collect all the solutions nor to detect inconsistency. This class of methods, known as metaheuristics, covers a very large panel of resolution paradigms from evolutionary algorithms to local search techniques. We refer the reader to [1,29,18] for an overview of these different algorithms and their applications to combinatorial optimization problems. [11] presents an overview of possible uses of local search in constraint programming.

Due to their different algorithmic process, these approaches often differ in their representation of the search space and in the benefit they get from the structure of the problem. Therefore, hybridizations of these techniques have often been tackled through heterogeneous combinations of coexisting resolution processes, with a master-slave like management, and are often related to specific problems or class of problems. Such designs lead to intricate solvers whose behavior is sometimes hard to analyze and which offer few flexibility in order to handle other problems.

Our purpose is to present in this paper a general hybridization framework in order to combine usual complete constraint programming resolution techniques, namely constraint propagation and splitting, together with metaheuristics optimization techniques, namely local search and genetic algorithms. This framework is based on the original mathematical framework proposed by K.R. Apt in [4]. In this framework, basic resolution processes are abstracted by functions over an ordered structure. This allows us to consider the different resolution agents at a same level and to study more precisely various hybridization strategies.

In this paper, we first focus on hybridization of constraint propagation techniques (CP) and local search (LS) for constraint satisfaction problems, based on preliminary results [28,23], and then we present a new hybridization of CP and genetic algorithms (GA) for constraint optimization problems. As mentioned above, the main difference between these two classes of problems will consist of different evaluation or fitness function which have to take into account the satisfaction problem (minimization of the number of violated constraint) and eventually an optimization criterion.

This paper is organized as follows. In Section 2 we recall the basic notions related to CSPs, to complete methods (more especially constraint propagation based methods) and incomplete methods (local search and genetic algorithms) for solving CSPs. In Section 3, we present the uniform computational framework that we extend later for hybridization of CP and LS (Section 4) and hybridization of CP and GA (Section 5). Section 6 shows some experimental results of hybridization, obtained with our generic constraint system. Finally, we conclude and propose some perspectives in Section 7.

2   Constraint Satisfaction Problems

In this section, we first recall the basic notions related to Constraint Satisfaction Problems (CSP) [34]. We describe then, three important resolution approaches that we will use in our hybridization framework: complete resolution techniques based on constraint propagation, local search methods, and genetic algorithms.

A CSP is a tuple (X, D, C) where $X = \{x_1, \cdots, x_n\}$ is a set of variables that takes their values in their respective domains $D_1, \cdots, D_n$. A constraint $c \in C$ is a relation $c \subseteq D_1 \times \cdots \times D_n$. D denotes the Cartesian product of $D_1 \times \cdots \times D_n$ and C the union of its constraints.

A tuple $d \in D$ is a solution of a CSP (X, D, C) if and only if $\forall c \in C, d \in c$.

Note that, without any loss of generality, we consider that each constraint is over all the variables $x_1, \ldots, x_n$. However, one can consider constraints over some of the x_i. Then, the notion of scheme [4,3] or projections can be used to denote sequences of variables.

2.1   Solving CSP with Complete Resolution Techniques

Complete resolution techniques generally perform a systematic exploration of the search space which obviously corresponds to the set of possible tuples D. To avoid and reduce the combinatorial grow up of this extensive exploration, these methods use particular techniques to prune the search space. Constraint propagation, one of the most popular of these pruning techniques, is based on local consistency properties. A local consistency (e.g., [24,27]) is a property of the constraints and variables which is used by the search mechanisms to delete values from variables domains which violate constraints and thus, cannot lead to solutions. There are several levels of local consistencies that consider one or several constraints at a time: we may mention node consistency and arc consistency [24] as famous examples of local consistencies.

But constraint propagation is not sufficient for fully defining a complete solver and split techniques are added to obtain a complete search algorithm. Constraint propagation consists in examining a subset C' of C (generally C' is restricted to one constraint) to delete some inconsistent values (from a local consistency point of view) of the domains of variables appearing in C'. These domain reductions are then used to reduce variables appearing in $C \setminus C'$. Hence, reductions are propagated to the entire CSP. When no more propagation is possible and the solutions are not reached, the CSP is split into sub-CSPs on which propagation is applied again, and so on until the solutions are reached. Generally, the domain of a variable is split into two sub-domains leading to two sub-CSPs. One of the most popular strategy of splitting is enumeration that consists in restricting one of the sub-domain to one value, the other sub-domain being the initial domain without this value.

```
solve(CSP):
            while not solved do
                    constraint propagation
                    if not solved
                        then split
                                search
                    endif
            endwhile
```

Fig. 1. A simple constraint solving algorithm

Figure 1 shows a simple but generic solve algorithm based on constraint propagation. The "search" function consists in calls to the solve function: search manages the sub-CSPs created by split. Usual search is depth or breadth first search. "solved" is a Boolean that is set to true when the CSP is found inconsistent, or when the wish of the user is reached: one solution, all solutions, or an optimum solution have been computed.

2.2 Solving CSP with Local Search

Local search techniques usually aim at solving optimization problems and have been widely used for combinatorial problems [1,29,18]. In the particular context of constraint satisfaction, these methods are applied in order to minimize the number of violated constraints and thus to find a solution of the CSP. A local search algorithm, starting from a given configuration, explores the search space by a sequence of moves. At each iteration, the next move corresponds to the choice of one of the so-called neighbors of the current state. This neighborhood often corresponds to small changes of the current configuration. Moves are guided by a fitness function which evaluates their benefit from the optimization point of view, in order to reach a local optimum. In the next sections, we attempt to generalize the definition of local search.

For the resolution of a CSP (X, D, C), the search space can be usually defined as the set of possible tuples of $D = D_1 \times \cdots \times D_n$ and the neighborhood is a mapping $\mathcal{N} : D \to 2^D$. This neighborhood function defines indeed possible moves and therefore fully defines the exploration landscape. The fitness (or evaluation) function $eval$ is related to the notion of solution and can be defined as the number of constraints c such that $d \notin c$ (d being a tuple from D).

As mentioned above, in the context of constraint satisfaction problems, the evaluation function corresponds to the minimization of the number of violated constraint. Therefore, given a configuration $d \in D$, representing an assignment, a basic local search move can either lead to an increase of the number of satisfied constraints (i.e., choose $d' \in \mathcal{N}(d)$ such that $eval(d') < eval(d)$) or to any other configuration which does not improve the evaluation function. These two possible steps can be interpreted as intensification or diversification of the search and local search algorithms are often based on the management of these basic heuristics by introducing specific control features. Therefore, a local search algorithm can be considered as a sequence of moves on a structure ordered according to the evaluation function.

2.3   Genetic Algorithms

Evolutionary algorithms are mainly based on the notion of adaptation of a population of individuals to a criterion using evolution operators like crossover [15].

Based on the principle of natural selection, *Genetic Algorithms* [17,20] have been quite successfully applied to combinatorial problems such as scheduling or transportation problems. The key principle of this approach states that, species evolve through adaptations to a changing environment and that the gained knowledge is embedded in the structure of the population and its members, encoded in their chromosomes. If individuals are considered as potential solutions to a given problem, applying a genetic algorithm consists in generating better and better individuals with respect to the problem by selecting, crossing, and mutating them. This approach reveals very useful for problems with huge search spaces. We had to adapt some basic techniques and slightly modify some definitions to fit our context but we refer the reader to [26] for a survey.

A genetic algorithm consists of the following components:

- a representation of the potential solutions: in most cases, individuals will be strings of bits representing its *genes*,
- a way to create an initial population,
- an *evaluation function eval*: the evaluation function rates each potential solution with respect to the given problem,
- genetic operators that define the composition of the children: two different operators will be considered: *Crossover* allows to generate new individuals(the offsprings) by crossing individuals of the current population

(the parents), *Mutation* arbitrarily alters one or more genes of a selected individual,

- parameters: population size p_{size} and probabilities of crossover p_c and mutation p_m.

In the context of GA, for the resolution of a given CSP (X, D, C), the search space can be usually defined with the set of tuples $D = D_1 \times \cdots \times D_n$. We consider a populations g, which is a subset of D, such that its cardinality is i. An element $s \in g$ is an individual and represents a potential solution to the problem.

Here, we will use the hybridization CP+GA in the context of constraint optimization problems. Therefore, evaluation functions (related to previous *eval* function but extended to optimization problems) provide information about the quality of an individual and so, of a population. Thus, these functions have to handle both the constraints of the problem and the optimization criterion.

A tuple in D is evaluated on an ordered set E whose lower bound corresponds indeed to the evaluation of an optimal solution. Therefore a fitness function $eval_{ind}: D \to E$ is such that $eval_{ind}(s)$ takes into account the number of unsatisfied constraints and the optimization criterion (abstraction of the objective function) for an individual s. We consider that E is ordered such that if s is a feasible solution (i.e. all constraints are satisfied) then $eval_{ind}(s)$ is restricted to its optimization evaluation. We denote $s <_{eval} s'$ the fact that $eval_{ind}(s) <_E eval_{ind}(s')$. When solving optimization problems we have to isolate the best solution yet found. Thus, s is the current solution for a population g if $\forall s' \in g, s \leq_{eval} s'$.

We extend this notion of fitness to population by $eval_{gen}: 2^D \to F$ such that $eval_{gen}(g)$ represents the evaluation of the individuals of the population g. The set F is ordered such that: g is a population solution if it contains an individual solution (i.e at least one of the components of g has an evaluation restricted to its optimization evaluation).

This $eval_{gen}(g)$ function, can represent for example, the sum of all the fitness of each individual, the sum of squares, or can be restricted to the best individual in the population. Furthermore, we denote $g <_{eval} g'$ the fact that $eval_{gen}(g) <_F eval_{gen}(g')$.

3   A Uniform Computational Framework

As described in the previous section, different techniques may be used to solve CSP (and many others which are not recalled here since they are out of the scope of this paper). Our purpose is to integrate the various involved computation processes in a uniform description framework. Since we want to combine all our resolution technique at a same level, the chaotic iterations model of K.R. Apt particularly fits our requirements. Therefore, the purpose of this section is to formalize the general computation scheme presented in Section 2.1, and to prepare it for hybridization of techniques.

In [4,3] K.R. Apt proposed a general theoretical framework for modeling constraint propagation. In this context, domain reduction corresponds to the computation of a fixpoint of a set of functions over a partially ordered set.

These *domain reduction functions* are monotonic and inflationary functions; they abstract the notion of constraint.

Example 1 (Domain reduction functions). Consider three Boolean variables X, Y, and Z and the Boolean constraint $and(X, Y, Z)$ such that $and(X, Y, Z)$ represents the Boolean relation $X \wedge Y = Z$. An example of reduction function for the constraint $and(X, Y, Z)$ can be defined by: if the domain of Z is $\{1\}$, then the domains of X and Y must be reduced to $\{1\}$.

Here is another example of reduction functions for linear equalities over integer numbers:

$$\text{if } x < y, x \in [l_x..r_x], y \in [l_y..r_y]$$
$$\text{we can reduce the domain of } x \text{ and } y \text{ as follows:}$$
$$x \in [l_x..min(r_x, r_y - 1)], y \in [max(l_y, l_x + 1)..r_y]$$

The computation of the least common fixpoint of a set of functions F can be achieved by the Generic Iteration algorithm (GI) described in Figure 2. In the GI algorithm, G represents the current set of functions still to be applied ($G \subseteq F$), d is a partially ordered set (the domains in case of CSP).

GI: Generic Iteration Algorithm

$d := \perp$;
$G := F$;
While $G \neq \emptyset$ do
        choose $g \in G$;
        $G := G - \{g\}$;
        $G := G \cup update(G, g, d)$;
        $d := g(d)$;
endwhile
where for all G, g, d, the set of functions $update(G, g, d)$ from F is such that:

- $\{f \in F - G \mid f(d) = d \wedge f(g(d)) \neq g(d)\} \subseteq update(G, g, d)$.
- $g(d) = d$ implies that $update(G, g, d) = \emptyset$.
- $g(g(d)) \neq g(d)$ implies that $g \in update(G, g, d)$

Fig. 2. The Generic Iteration Algorithm

Suppose that all functions in F are inflationary ($x \sqsubseteq f(x)$ for all x) and monotonic ($x \sqsubseteq y$ implies $f(x) \sqsubseteq f(y)$ for all x, y) and that $(D, \sqsubseteq)$ is finite. Then, every execution of the **GI** algorithm terminates and computes in d the least common fixpoint of the functions from F (see [4]).

Note that in the following we consider only partial orderings.

Constraint propagation is now achieved by instantiating and "feeding" the **GI** algorithm:

- the $\sqsubseteq$ partial ordering is instantiated by $\supseteq$, the usual set inclusion,
- $d := \perp$ corresponds to $d := D_1 \times \ldots \times D_n$, the Cartesian product of the domains of the variables from the initial CSP to be solved,
- F is a set of domain reduction functions which abstract the constraints in order to reduce domains of variables.

This algorithm allows us to compute the smallest box (i.e., Cartesian product of domains) with respect to the given domain reduction functions that contains the solutions of the initial CSP.

At this point, as shown in Figure 1, the exploration of the reduced domains is continued by interleaving splitting and again propagation phases.

In order to obtain a more uniform and generic framework, our purpose is to integrate the splitting process as a reduction function inside the **GI** algorithm. This is motivated by the fact that we want to manage constraint propagation, split and local search (respectively genetic algorithms) at the same level. To this end, we will extend the notion of CSP to sampled CSP (respectively CSP with genetic factor) on which an other type of reduction functions will be applied to mimic basic operations of local search algorithms (respectively basic operations of genetic algorithms).

Therefore, we have to introduce new functions in the generic iteration algorithm including splitting operators and local search strategies (respectively a genetic algorithm process). Then, these search methods can be viewed as the computation of a fixpoint of a set of functions on an ordered set. But, these new operators require also a new computation structure and the first step of our work consists in defining this main structure.

4   CP+LS

Extending the framework described above (Section 3), we propose here a computational structure taking into account both constraint programming and local search basic resolution processes. CSPs and search paths are embedded in this new computation structure. Some reduction functions that achieve constraint propagation, split, and local search are then introduced to compute over this structure.

4.1   Sampling the Search Space

Domain reductions and splits apply on domains of values: they transform Cartesian product of the domains. Local search acts on a different structure which usually corresponds to points of the search space. Here, we propose a more general and abstract definition based on the notion of sample.

Definition 1 (Sample). *Consider a CSP (X, D, C). A sample function ε is a function $\varepsilon : D \rightarrow 2^D$. By extension, $\varepsilon(D)$ denotes the set $\bigcup_{d \in D} \varepsilon(d)$.*

Generally, $\varepsilon(d)$ is restricted to d and the set of samples is thus the search space D $(\varepsilon(D) = D)$. However, $\varepsilon(d)$ can also be defined as a scatter of tuples around d, an approximation covering d, or a box covering d (e.g., for continuous domains). Moreover, it is reasonable to impose that $\varepsilon(D)$ contains all the solutions. Indeed, the search space D is abstracted by $\varepsilon(D)$ to be used by LS.

In this context, a local search can be fully defined by:

- a neighborhood function on $\varepsilon(D)$ which computes the neighbors (i.e., a set of samples) for each sample of $\varepsilon(D)$;
- and the set of local search paths. Each path is composed of a sequence of visited samples and represents moves from neighbors to neighbors.

Given a neighborhood function $\mathcal{N}: \varepsilon(D) \to 2^{\varepsilon(D)}$, we define the set of possible local search paths as $\mathcal{LS}_D =$

$$\bigcup_{i>0} \{p = (s_1, \cdots, s_i) \in \varepsilon(D)^i \mid \forall j,\, 1 \le j < i - 1,\, s_{j+1} \in \mathcal{N}(s_j) \text{ and } s_1 \in \varepsilon(D)\}$$

The fundamental property of local search relies on its exploration based on the neighborhood relation.

From a practical point of view, a local search is limited to finite paths with respect to a stopping criterion: this can be a fixed maximum number of iterations (i.e., the length of the path) or, in our context of CSP resolution, the fact that a solution has been reached.

For this concern, according to Section 2.2, we consider an evaluation function $eval: \varepsilon(D) \to \mathbb{N}$ such that $eval(s)$ represents the number of constraints unsatisfied by the sample s. Moreover, we impose that $eval(s)$ is equal to 0 iff s is a solution. We denote $s <_{eval} s'$ the fact that $eval(s) < eval(s')$.

Therefore, from a LS point of view, a result is either a search path leading to a solution or a search path of a maximum given size. According to this fact, we define an order on local search paths as follows:

Definition 2 (local search ordering). *We consider an order $\sqsubseteq_{ls}$ on $\mathcal{LS}_D$ defined by:*

$(s_1, \ldots, s_n) \sqsubseteq_{ls} (s_1, \ldots, s_n)$

$(s'_1, \ldots, s'_m) \sqsubseteq_{ls} (s_1, \ldots, s_n)$ *if $n > m$ and $\forall j, 1 \le j \le m, eval(s'_j) \ne 0$ and $\forall i, 1 \le i \le n, eval(s_i) \ne 0$*

$(s'_1, \ldots, s'_m) \sqsubseteq_{ls} (s_1, \ldots, s_n)$ *if $eval(s_n) = 0, \forall i, 1 \le i \le n - 1, eval(s_i) \ne 0$ and $\forall j, 1 \le j \le m, eval(s'_j) \ne 0$*

The following example illustrates the notion of results from a LS process.

Example 2 (LS paths). Consider $p_1 = (a, b)$, $p_2 = (a, c)$ and $p_3 = (b)$ three elements of $\mathcal{LS}_D$ such that $eval(b) = 0$ (i.e., b is a solution). Then, these three paths correspond to possible results of a local search of size 2, they are not comparable with respect to Definition 2.

4.2   Computation Structure

We can now define the structure required for the hybridization of local search and constraint solving. To this end, we instantiate the abstract framework of K.R. Apt described in Section 2.1.

Definition 3 (Sampled CSP). *A sampled CSP (sCSP) is defined by a triple (D, C, p), a sample function ε, and a local search ordering $\sqsubseteq_{ls}$ where*

- $D = D_1 \times ... \times D_n$
- $\forall c \in C, c \subseteq D_1 \times ... \times D_n$
- $p \in \mathcal{LS}_D$

Note that, in our definition, the local search path p should be included in the box defined by $\varepsilon(D)$. We denote $SCSP$ the set of $sCSP$. We can now define an ordering relation on the sampled structure $(SCSP, \sqsubseteq)$.

Definition 4 (Order over sampled CSPs). *Given two sCSPs $\psi = (D, C, p)$ and $\psi' = (D', C, p')$,*

$$\psi \sqsubseteq \psi' \quad iff \quad D' \subseteq D \ or \ (D' = D \ and \ p \sqsubseteq_{ls} p').$$

This relation is extended on 2^{SCSP} as follows:

$$\{\phi_1, \ldots, \phi_k\} \sqsubseteq \{\psi_1, \ldots, \psi_l\} \quad iff \quad \forall \phi_i, (\exists \psi_j, \phi_i \sqsubseteq \psi_j \ and \ \not\exists \psi_j, \psi_j \sqsubset \phi_i)$$

where $i \in [1..k], j \in [1..l]$.

Note that this partial ordering on sCSPs could also be extended by considering an order on constraints; this would enable constraint simplifications. But this is out of the scope of our hybridization.

We denote ΣCSP the set 2^{SCSP} which constitutes the key set of our computation structure. We denote σCSP an element of ΣCSP. A σCSP is thus a set of sCSPs. As in [4], we define the least element $\bot$ as $\{(D, C, p)\}$, i.e., the initial σCSP to be solved.

4.3   Solutions

Since our framework is dedicated to CSP solving, we must define precisely the notion of solution accordingly to the previous computation structure. These notions are well defined for complete methods and incomplete methods.

From the complete resolution point of view, a solution of a CSP is a tuple from the search space which satisfies all the constraints. For local search, the notion of solution is related to the evaluation function *eval* which defines a solution as an element s of $\varepsilon(D)$ such that $eval(s) = 0$.

Definition 5 (Solutions). *Given a sCSP $\psi = (D, C, p)$, the set of solutions of ψ is defined by:*

- *for constraint propagation (CP) based solvers:*

$$Sol_D(\psi) = \{d \in D | \forall c \in C, d \in c\}$$

- *for local search (LS):*

$$Sol_{\mathcal{LS}_D}(\psi) = \{(s_1, \cdots, s_n) \in \mathcal{LS}_D \,|\, eval(s_n) = 0\}$$

– for a LS/CP hybrid solver:

$$Sol(\psi) = \{(d, C, p)|d \in Sol_D(\psi) \text{ or } p \in Sol_{\mathcal{L}S_D}(\psi)\}$$

This notion is extended to any σCSP Ψ by:

$$Sol(\Psi) = \bigcup_{\psi \in \Psi} Sol(\psi)$$

4.4   Reduction Functions Definitions and Properties

The computation structure ΣCSP has been defined for integrating CP and LS and we have now to define our hybrid functions which will be used in the GI algorithm. Given a σCSP $\Psi = \{\psi_1, \cdots, \psi_n\}$ of ΣCSP, we need to define functions on Ψ which correspond to domain reduction, split, and local search. These functions may apply on several sCSPs ψ_i of Ψ, and for each ψ_i on some of its components. Since we consider here finite initial CSPs, note that our structure is a finite partial ordering.

Definition 6 (Domain reduction function). *A domain reduction function red is a function:*

$$red: \Sigma CSP \rightarrow \Sigma CSP$$
$$\{\psi_1, \cdots, \psi_n\} \mapsto \{\psi'_1, \cdots, \psi'_n\}$$

such that $\forall i \in [1 \cdots n]$:

- *either $\psi_i = \psi'_i$*
- *or $\psi_i = (D, C, p)$, $\psi'_i = (D', C, p')$ and $D \supseteq D'$ and $Sol_D(\psi_i) = Sol_D(\psi'_i)$.*

Note that this definition insures that $\{\psi_1, \cdots, \psi_n\} \sqsubseteq red(\{\psi_1, \cdots, \psi_n\})$ and that the function is inflationary and monotonic on $(\Sigma CSP, \sqsubseteq)$. Note also that by definition $p' \in \mathcal{L}S_{D'}$. This definition allows one to specify a function that reduces several domains of several $sCSPs$ of a σCSP at the same time. From a constraint programming point of view, a reduction function preserves the solution set of the initial CSP: no solution of the initial CSP is lost by a domain reduction function. This is also the case for domain splitting as defined below.

Definition 7 (Domain splitting). *A domain splitting function sp on ΣCSP is a function such that for all $\Psi = \{\psi_1, \ldots, \psi_n\} \in \Sigma CSP$:*

a. *$sp(\Psi) = \{\psi'_1, \ldots, \psi'_m\}$ with $n \le m$,*
b. *$\forall i \in [1..n]$,*
   - *either $\exists j \in [1..m]$ such that $\psi_i = \psi'_j$*
   - *or there exist $\psi'_{j_1}, \ldots, \psi'_{j_h}$, $j_1, \ldots, j_h \in [1..m]$ such that*

$$Sol_D(\psi_i) = \bigcup_{k=1..h} Sol_D(\psi'_{j_k})$$

c. *and,* $\forall j \in [1..m]$,
  - *either* $\exists i \in [1..n]$ *such that* $\psi_i = \psi'_j$
  - *or* $\psi'_j = (D', C, p')$ *and there exists* $\psi_i = (D, C, p)$, $i \in [1..n]$ *such that* $D \supset D'$.

Conditions a. and b. ensure that some sCSPs have been split into sub-sCSPs by splitting some of their domains (one or several variable domains) into smaller domains without discarding solutions (defined by the union of solutions of the ψ_i). Condition c. ensures that the search space does not grow: every domain of the sCSPs composing Ψ' is included in one of the domain of some sCSP composing Ψ. Note that the domain of several variables of several sCSPs can be split at the same time.

Definition 8 (Local Search). *A local search function* λ_N *is a function*

$$\lambda_N: \Sigma CSP \to \Sigma CSP$$
$$\{\psi_1, \cdots, \psi_n\} \mapsto \{\psi'_1, \cdots, \psi'_n\}$$

where

- N *is the maximum number of consecutive moves*
- $\forall i \in [1..n]$
  - *either* $\psi_i = \psi'_i$
  - *or* $\psi_i = (D, C, p)$ *and* $\psi'_i = (D, C, p')$ *with* $p = (s_1, \cdots, s_k)$ *and* $p' = (s_1, \cdots, s_k, s_{k+1})$ *such that* $s_{k+1} \in \mathcal{N}(s_k) \cap D$ *and* $k + 1 \leq N$.

The parameter N represents the maximum length of a local search path, i.e., the number of moves allowed in a usual local search process. A local search function may try to improve the sample of one or several sCSPs at once. Even when λ_N tries to reduce ψ_i, note that $\psi_i = \psi'_i$ may happen when:

1. $p \in Sol_{\mathcal{LS}_D}(\psi)$: the last sample s_n of the current local search path cannot be improved using λ_N,
2. the length n of the search path is such that $n = N$: the maximum allowed number of moves has been reached,
3. λ_N is the identity function on ψ_i, i.e., λ_N does not try to improve the local search path of the sCSP ψ_i. This might happen when no possible move can be performed (e.g., a descent algorithm has reached a local optimum or all neighbors are tabu in a tabu search algorithm [14]).

4.5 σCSPs Resolution

For the complete solving of a σCSP $\{(D_1 \times \ldots \times D_n, C, p)\}$ the **GI** algorithm must now be instantiated as follows:

- the $\sqsubseteq$ ordering is instantiated by the ordering given in Definition 4,
- $d := \perp$ corresponds to $d := \{(D_1 \times \ldots \times D_n, C, p)\}$,

— F is a set of given monotonic and inflationary functions as defined in Section 4.4: domain reduction functions (extensions of common domain reduction functions for CSPs), domain splitting functions (usual split mechanisms integrated as reduction functions), and local search functions (e.g., functions for descent, tabu search, ...).

We now propose an instantiation of the function schemes presented in the previous section. From an operational point of view, reduction functions have to be applied on some selected $sCSPs$ of a given σCSP. More practically, we build the functions on sCSPs and then extend them on $\sigma CSPs$. Thus, a function on ΣCSP will be driven by an operator selecting the sCSPs of a σCSP.

We now define these selection operators. Given a selection function $select$: $A \to 2^B$ let us consider a function $f^{select} \colon A \to C$ such that $f^{select}(x) = g(y), y \in select(x)$ where $g \colon B \to C$. Therefore, f^{select} can be viewed as a non deterministic function. Formally, we may associate to any function f^{select} a family of deterministic functions $(f^i)_{i>0}$ such that $\forall x \in A, \forall y \in select(x), \exists k > 0, f^k(x) = g(y)$. If we consider finite sets A and B then this family is also finite.

Indeed, each σCSP that can result from the application of some functions on the initial σCSP requires all reduction functions (defined for the initial σCSP) to model the different possible executions of the resolution process. In other terms, consider an sCSP ψ_i of a σCSP Ψ; a set F' of functions can apply on ψ_i through Ψ (through the sCSP selection process). If a new sCSP ψ_j can be created (e.g., by split), then the functions of F' are also required to be applied on ψ_j through Ψ (again, through the sCSP selection process). However, ψ_j will may be not be created. Note that in theory, it is necessary to consider all possible σCSP (and thus, all possible sets of all possible sCSP); however, in practice, only required functions are fed in the **GI** algorithm, induced by the σCSP under consideration in the resolution process.

We first define functions on $SCSP$ with respect to selection functions to select the domains on which the functions apply. In order to extend operations on $SCSP$ to ΣCSP, we introduce a selection process which allows us to extract particular $sCSPs$ of a given σCSP (see Figure 3).

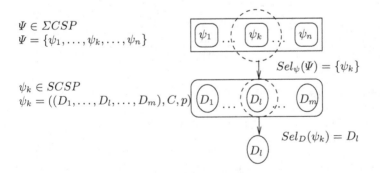

$\Psi \in \Sigma CSP$
$\Psi = \{\psi_1, \ldots, \psi_k, \ldots, \psi_n\}$

$Sel_\psi(\Psi) = \{\psi_k\}$

$\psi_k \in SCSP$
$\psi_k = ((D_1, \ldots, D_l, \ldots, D_m), C, p)$

$Sel_D(\psi_k) = D_l$

Fig. 3. Selection functions

Let us consider a domain selection function $Sel_D \colon SCSP \to 2^D$ and a $sCSP$ selection function $Sel_\psi \colon \Sigma SCSP \to \Sigma SCSP$.

Domain Reduction. We may first define a domain reduction operator on a single sCSP as:

$$red^{Sel_D} : SCSP \to SCSP$$
$$\psi = (D, C, p) \mapsto (D', C, p')$$

such that

1. $D = D_1 \times \cdots \times D_n, D' = D'_1 \times \cdots \times D'_n$ and $\forall i, 1 \le i \le n$
   - $D_i \notin Sel_D(\psi) \Rightarrow D'_i = D_i$
   - $D_i \in Sel_D(\psi) \Rightarrow D'_i \subseteq D_i$
2. $p' = p$ if $p \in \mathcal{LS}_{D'}$ otherwise p' is set to any sample chosen in $\varepsilon(D')$

Note that Condition 2. insures that the local search path associated to the sCSP stays in $\varepsilon(D')$. Note that we could keep $p' = (s_i)$ where s_i is the latest element of p which belongs to D' or we could keep a suitable sub-path of p. We have chosen to model here a restart from a randomly chosen sample after each reduction or split. The function red^{Sel_D} is extended to ΣCSP as:

$$red^{Sel_\psi, Sel_D} : \Sigma CSP \to \Sigma CSP$$
$$\Psi \mapsto (\Psi \setminus Sel_\psi(\Psi)) \bigcup_{\psi \in Sel_\psi(\Psi)} red^{Sel_D}(\psi)$$

Split. We first define a split operator on a single sCSP as follows:

$$sp_k^{Sel_D} : SCSP \to \Sigma CSP$$
$$\psi \mapsto \Psi'$$

with $\psi = (D_1 \times \ldots \times D_h \times \ldots \times D_n, C, p)$ where $\{D_h\} = Sel_D(\psi)$ and
$\Psi' = \{(D_1 \times \ldots \times D_{h_1} \times \ldots \times D_n, C, p_1), \cdots, (D_1 \times \ldots \times D_{h_k} \times \ldots \times D_n, C, p_k)\}$
such that

1. $D_h = \bigcup_{i=1}^{k} D_{h_i}$
2. for all $i \in [1..k]$, $p_i = p$ if $p \in \mathcal{LS}_{(D_1 \times \cdots \times D_{h_i} \times \cdots \times D_n)}$ otherwise, p_i is set to any sample chosen in $\varepsilon(D_1 \times \ldots \times D_{h_i} \times \ldots \times D_n)$.

For the sake of readability we present a function that splits only one domain of the sCSP. But this can obviously be extended to split several domains at once. The last condition is needed to comply with the sCSP definition: it corresponds to the fact that, informally, the samples associated to any sCSP belong to the box induced by their domains. The function is extended to ΣCSP as follows:

$$sp_k^{Sel_\psi, Sel_D} : \Sigma CSP \to \Sigma CSP$$
$$\Psi \mapsto (\Psi \setminus Sel_\psi(\Psi)) \bigcup_{\psi \in Sel_\psi(\Psi)} sp_k^{Sel_D}(\psi)$$

Local Search. As mentioned above, local search is viewed as the definition of a partial ordering $\sqsubseteq_{ls}$; this order is then used to define the ordering $\sqsubseteq$ on our hybrid structure ΣCSP. The components that remain to be defined are: 1) the strategy to compute a local search path p' of length $n+1$ from a local search path p of length n, and 2) the stop criterion which is commonly based on a fixed limited number of moves and, in our particular context of CSP resolution, the notion of computed solution.

First, we define a local search operator on $SCSP$ as a function $strat$: $SCSP \rightarrow 2^{\varepsilon(D)}$. This function specifies the choice strategy of a given local search heuristics for moving from a sample to one of its neighbors.

$$\lambda_N^{strat}: SCSP \rightarrow SCSP$$
$$\psi \mapsto \psi'$$

where

- N is the maximum allowed number of moves
- $\psi = (C, D, p)$ and $\psi' = (C, D, p')$ with $p = (s_1, \cdots, s_n)$
  1. $p' = p$ if $p \in Sol_{\mathcal{L}S_D}$
  2. $p' = p$ if $n = N$
  3. $p' = (s_1, \cdots, s_n, s_{n+1})$ such that $s_{n+1} = strat(\psi)$ otherwise

Using this schema, we present here some examples of well known "move" heuristics. Consider a sCSP $\psi = (D, C, (s_1, \cdots, s_n))$. Each function consists in selecting one feasible neighbor (i.e., a sample of the neighborhood which is also in the current reduced search space D to comply with Definition 8) of a sample:

- **Random Walk:** the function $strat_{rw}$ randomly selects one sample of the neighborhood of the current sample

$$strat_{rw}(\psi) = s \;\; \text{s.t.} \;\; s \in D \cap \mathcal{N}(s_n)$$

- **Descent:** the function $strat_d$ selects a neighbor improving the current sample with respect to the fitness function

$$strat_d(\psi) = s \;\; \text{s.t.} \;\; s \in D \cap \mathcal{N}(s_n) \text{ and } s <_{eval} s_n$$

- **Strict Descent:** $strat_{sd}$ is similar to $strat_d$ but selects the best improving neighbor; $strat_{sd}(\psi) = s$ s.t.

$$s \in D \cap \mathcal{N}(s_n), \; s <_{eval} s_n, \text{ and } \forall s' \in D \cap \mathcal{N}(s_n), s \leq_{eval} s'$$

- **Tabu of length l:** selects the best neighbor not visited during the past l moves; $strat_{tabu_l}(\psi) = s$ s.t.

$$s \in \varepsilon(D) \cap \mathcal{N}(s_n) \text{ and } \forall j \in [n - l..n], s \neq s_j \text{ and } \forall s' \in D \cap \mathcal{N}(s_n), s \leq_{eval} s'$$

Note that, again, these functions satisfy the properties (inflationary and monotonic) required to be fed in the GI algorithm. Then, this function is extended to ΣCSP as:

$$\lambda_N^{Sel_\psi, strat} : \Sigma CSP \rightarrow \Sigma CSP$$
$$\Psi \mapsto (\Psi \setminus Sel_\psi(\Psi)) \bigcup_{\psi \in Sel_\psi(\Psi)} \lambda_N^{strat}(\psi)$$

Combination. The "choose function" of the **GI** algorithm now totally manages the hybridization/combination strategy; different scheduling of functions lead to the same result (in term of least common fixpoint), but not with the same efficiency.

Note that in practice, we are not always interested in reaching the fixpoint of the **GI** algorithm. We can also be interested in solutions such as sCSPs which contain a solution for local search or a solution for constraint propagation. In this case, various runs of the **GI** algorithm with different strategies ("choose function") can lead to different solutions (e.g., in case of problems with several solutions, or several local minima).

Result of the GI Algorithm. We now compare the result of the GI algorithm with respect to Definition 5 for solution of a σCSP.

Since we are in chaotic iteration framework (concerning orderings and functions), given a σCSP Ψ and a set F of reduction functions (as defined above) the GI algorithm computes a common least fixpoint of the functions in F. Note that, this result is insured by the fact that our LS functions, which limit the size of search paths, induce a finite partial ordering in our computation structure. Clearly, this fixpoint $lfp(\Psi)$ abstracts all the solutions of $Sol(\Psi)$:

- $\bigcup_{(d,C,p)\in Sol(\Psi)} d \supseteq \bigcup_{(d,C,p)\in glfp(\Psi)} d$
- for all $(D, C, p) \in Sol(\Psi)$ s.t. $p = (s_1, \ldots, s_n) \in Sol_{\mathcal{LS}_D}(\Psi)$ there exists a $(d, C, p') \in glfp(\Psi)$ s.t. $s_n \in \varepsilon(d)$.

The first item states that all domain reduction and split functions used in GI preserve solutions. The second item ensures that all solutions computed by LS functions are in the fixpoint of the GI algorithm.

In practice, one can stop the GI algorithm before the fixpoint is reached. For example, one can compute the fixpoint of the LS functions; in this case, the search space may be reduced (and thus, the possible moves) by applying only some of the CP functions. This corresponds to the hybrid nature of the resolution process and the tradeoff between a complete and incomplete exploration of the space.

5   CP+GA

In this section, we describe the hybridization of a propagation based solver and genetic algorithms. We use the same approach as the one for local search. Thus, we try to keep the same progress, notations, and structure for this section.

5.1   Populations

Genetic algorithms aim at generating new populations using genetic operators, selection [6], (e.g. proportional selection [17], roulette-wheel selection [15], tournament selection, linear ranking [7], ...), recombination (e.g., elitist recombination [33], multiparent recombination like [10]), and mutation.

A new population is called an offspring and formally it is a mapping $\mathcal{O}$: $2^D \rightarrow 2^D$. We define the set of possible genetic descendants, i.e., the set of sequences of populations as follows:

$$\mathcal{GA} = \bigcup_{k>0} \{p = (g_1, \cdots, g_k) \mid \forall j \in [1..k],\ g_j \in 2^D \text{ and } \forall j \in [2..k], g_j \in \mathcal{O}(g_{j-1})\}$$

where g_1 represents the initial population and k the length of the process. Note that, in practice, the size of th epopulation is fixed.

From a practical point of view, genetic algorithms are stopped by a criterion which is usually a fixed maximum number of iterations. Therefore, from a GA point of view, a result is either a population g which contains solutions or a genetic process of a maximum given size. Based on a fitness function (as presented in Section 2.3), we introduce the following order on sequences of populations of $\mathcal{GA}$:

Definition 9 (Order on sequences of populations). *Consider a fitness function eval together with its associate order. The order $\sqsubseteq_{ga}$ on $\mathcal{GA}$ is defined by:*

$$(g_1, \ldots, g_n) \sqsubseteq_{ga} (g'_1, \ldots, g'_m) \quad \textit{iff} \quad g'_m \leq_{eval} g_n$$

We have now to define the computation structure on which reduction functions will be applied and which includes the new component corresponding to the introduction of GA.

5.2   Computation Structure

In order to handle the different data structures associated to each technique of the hybrid resolution, we complete CSPs with *genetic factors*. Such a factor corresponds indeed to a GA process, and optimization will be done using them.

The resolution will be achieved according to the generic algorithm recalled in Section 2.3. We have here to define the computation structure devoted to this hybridization CP+GA.

Definition 10 (CSP with genetic factor). *A CSP with genetic factor (gcsp) for optimization is defined by a sequence (D, C, p, f) where*

- $D = D_1 \times ... \times D_n$
- $\forall c \in C, c \subseteq D_1 \times ... \times D_n$
- $p \in \mathcal{GA}$
- f: objective function.

GCSP denotes the set of gcsp, and $\Sigma GCSP$ denotes the set 2^{GCSP}

Note that, in the definition, the genetic algorithm process p should be included in the search space defined by D. Recall that the objective function f is taken into account in the *eval* function (see Section 2.3), and thus is also taken into account in the $\leq_{eval}$ and $\sqsubseteq_{ga}$ orderings (see above), and consequently in the ordered structure $(GCSP, \sqsubseteq)$ that we define below.

Definition 11 (Order on $GCSP$). *Given two gcsps $\psi = (D, C, p, f)$ and $\psi' = (D', C, p', f)$, $\psi \sqsubseteq \psi'$ iff*

- $D' \subseteq D$
- *or $(D' = D$ and $p \sqsubseteq_{ga} p')$.*

This relation is extended on 2^{GCSP}: $\{\phi_1; ...; \phi_k\} \sqsubseteq \{\psi_1; ...; \psi_l\}$, iff

$$\forall \phi_i, (\exists \psi_j, \phi_i \sqsubseteq \psi_j \text{ and } \not\exists \psi_j, \psi_j \sqsubset \phi_i)$$

where $i \in [1..k], j \in [1..l]$.

$\Sigma GCSP$ (i.e., the set 2^{GCSP}) constitutes the key set of our computation structure. We use here σCSP to denote an element of $\Sigma GCSP$. The least element $\perp$ is $\{(D, C, p, f)\}$, i.e., the initial σCSP to be solved.

5.3   Solution

From the CP point of view, a solution of an gcsp $\psi = (D, C, p, f)$ is a tuple which satisfies all the constraints. From the GA point of view, the notion of solution is related to the evaluation function: a solution is defined as an element s of a population g of the sequence p such that s is the minimum (or maximum) of the objective function with respect to all such s' appearing in p. Given an gcsp $\psi = (D, C, p, f)$, these two points of view induce two sets of solutions:

- Feasible solutions: $Sol_{CP}(\psi) = \{d \in D \mid \forall c \in C, d \in c\}$
- Optimum solutions (minimization): $Sol_{\mathcal{G}\mathcal{A}}(\psi) = \{s \mid p = (g_1, \ldots, g_m)$ and $\forall i \in [1..m], \forall s' \in g_i, s \leq_{eval} s'\}$.
- Optimum solutions (maximization): $Sol_{\mathcal{G}\mathcal{A}}(\psi) = \{s \mid p = (g_1, \ldots, g_m)$ and $\forall i \in [1..m], \forall s' \in g_i, s' \leq_{eval} s\}$.

Based on this, we define the set of solutions in the hybrid model for a given gcsp ψ as:

$$Sol(\psi) = Sol_{CP}(\psi) \cap Sol_{\mathcal{G}\mathcal{A}}(\psi)$$

Hence a solution of a given gcsp is a tuple d such that d satisfies the constraints and minimizes (respectively maximizes) the objective function. This notion of solution is generalized to the computation structure $\Sigma GCSP$.

Definition 12. *Given a σCSP $\Psi = \{\psi_1, \ldots, \psi_k\}$ according to*

- *a minimization problem: $Sol(\Psi) = Min(\{s_i\} \mid s_i \in sol(\psi_i))$*
- *a maximization problem: $Sol(\Psi) = Max(\{s_i\} \mid s_i \in sol(\psi_i))$*

5.4   A Function-Based Solving Process

At this step, we have to define the reduction functions on $\Sigma GCSP$. They describe the different components of the resolution process: constraint propagation by domain reduction and splitting, combined with genetic algorithms.

Given an element $\Psi = \{\psi_1, \cdots, \psi_n\}$ of $\Sigma GCSP$, we have to apply functions on Ψ which correspond to domain reduction, domain splitting, and genetic algorithm. These functions may operate on elements ψ_i of Ψ, and for each ψ_i on some of its components. We should note that since we consider here finite sets as initial gcsps, the structure is a finite partial ordering.

The following definitions introduce the fundamental properties of the different operators and their general purpose.

The definitions of a reduction function and of a split for the hybridization CP+GA are similar to the ones of CP+LS (Definitions 6 and 7) but this time they apply on $\Sigma GCSP$. The same remark is also valid concerning Definition 15 and Definition 8.

Definition 13 (Domain reduction function). *A domain reduction function red is a function:*

$$red: \Sigma GCSP \to \Sigma GCSP$$
$$\{\psi_1, \cdots, \psi_n\} \mapsto \{\psi'_1, \cdots, \psi'_n\}$$

such that $\forall i \in [1 \cdots n]$:

- *either* $\psi_i = \psi'_i$,
- *or* $\psi_i = (D, C, p, f)$, $\psi'_i = (D', C, p', f)$ *and* $D \supseteq D'$ *and* $Sol(\psi_i) = Sol(\psi'_i)$.

This definition ensures that $\{\psi_1, \cdots, \psi_n\} \sqsubseteq red(\{\psi_1, \cdots, \psi_n\})$ and that the function is inflationary and monotonic on $(\Sigma GCSP, \sqsubseteq)$. From a constraint programming point of view, no solution of the initial $\sigma GCSP$ is lost by a domain reduction function. This is also the case for domain splitting as defined below.

Definition 14 (Domain splitting). *A domain splitting function sp on $\Sigma GCSP$ is a function such that for all $\Psi = \{\psi_1, \ldots, \psi_n\} \in \Sigma GCSP$:*

a. $sp(\Psi) = \{\psi'_1, \ldots, \psi'_m\}$ *with* $n \leq m$,
b. $\forall i \in [1..n]$,
   - *either* $\exists j \in [1..m]$ *such that* $\psi_i = \psi'_j$
   - *or there exist* $\psi'_{j_1}, \ldots, \psi'_{j_h}$, $j_1, \ldots, j_h \in [1..m]$ *such that*

$$Sol_D(\psi_i) = \bigcup_{k=1..h} Sol_D(\psi'_{j_k})$$

c. *and,* $\forall j \in [1..m]$,
   - *either* $\exists i \in [1..n]$ *such that* $\psi_i = \psi'_j$
   - *or* $\psi'_j = (D', C, p', f)$ *and there exists* $\psi_i = (D, C, p, f)$, $i \in [1..n]$ *such that* $D \supseteq D'$.

Conditions a. and b. ensure that some gcsps have been split without discarding solutions. Condition c. ensures that the search space does not grow (each new search space is included in one of the initial search space).

Finally we define genetic algorithm as a reduction function on $\Sigma GCSP$.

Definition 15 (Genetic algorithms). *A genetic algorithm function Γ_N is a function:*

$$\Gamma_N : \Sigma GCSP \to \Sigma GCSP \ ,$$
$$\{\psi_1, \cdots, \psi_n\} \mapsto \{\psi'_1, \cdots, \psi'_n\}$$

where N is the maximum number of consecutive offsprings, and $\forall i \in [1..n]$

- *either $\psi_i = \psi'_i$*
- *or $\psi_i = (D, C, p, f)$ and $\psi'_i = (D, C, p', f)$ with $p = (g_1, \cdots, g_k)$ and $p' = (g_1, \cdots, g_k, g_{k+1})$ such that*
  $g_{k+1} \in \mathcal{O}(g_k) \cap D^m$ and $k + 1 \leq N$, where m is the size of the population .

N is the maximum length of a genetic algorithm, i.e., the number of offsprings allowed in a usual genetic search process. Note that $\psi_i = \psi'_i$ can happen when:

1. $n = N$: the maximum allowed number of operations has been reached,
2. Γ_N is the identity function on ψ_i, i.e., Γ_N does not try to improve the generation of the GCSP ψ_i. This might happen when no possible move can be performed (e.g., all individuals are equal and no mutation are allowed).

We now give some properties on some possible genetic algorithm functions.

Definition 16 (elitism). *A genetics algorithm is called elitist if at every step the current best individual survives, the best solution is never lost during the search. Formally consider a search path $p = (g_1, \ldots, g_k)$:*

$$\forall j \in [1..k-1], \text{if there exists } s \in g_j \text{ s.t. } \forall s' \in g_j, s \leq_{eval} s', \text{ then } s \in g_{j+1}$$

Property 1 (Convergence). Suppose that the genetic algorithm is elitist. Suppose that for every population g there is a nonzero probability P that in the next generation the population is better:

$$\forall s \in g_k, \exists s' \in g_{k+1} \text{ s.t. } s' \leq_{eval} s$$

Then the fitness of the population at time t converges to the optimal value, for $t \to \infty$.

Thus, with the previous properties, GA optimizes the objective function, taking its values in a search space which is becoming locally consistent using CP. With successive constraint propagations and splits, the search space is progressively restricted to feasible solution, therefore GA finds the optimum.

5.5 $\sigma GCSP$s Resolution

As in the previous section, the **GI** algorithm is fed with the ordering on $\Sigma GCSP$; the least element $\bot$ is $\{(D, C, p, f)\}$, i.e., the initial $\sigma GCSP$ to be solved; and monotonic and inflationary functions: domain reduction, split, and genetic algorithms.

Similarly to Section 4, reduction functions can first be built over GCSP before being extended over $\Sigma GCSP$. In this case, a selection process is also needed in order to take into account each $\sigma GCSP$ that could be created during resolution. We do not detail here this process, since it is the same as for local search hybridization.

Result of the GI Algorithm. The result of the **GI** algorithm can be defined similarly as before. Given a $\sigma GCSP$ Ψ and a set F of reduction functions the GI algorithm computes a common least fixpoint of the functions in F. This fixpoint $glfp(\Psi)$ abstracts all the solutions of $Sol(\Psi)$:

- $\bigcup_{(d,C,p) \in Sol(\Psi)} d \supseteq \bigcup_{(d,C,p) \in glfp(\Psi)} d$
- for all $(D, C, p, f) \in Sol(\Psi)$ s.t. $p = (g_1, \ldots, g_n) \in Sol_{\mathcal{G}\mathcal{A}_D}(\Psi)$ there exists a $(d, C, p', f) \in glfp(\Psi)$ s.t. $\exists i \in [1..n], d \in g_i$.

The first item states that all domain reduction and split functions used in GI preserve solutions. The second item ensures that in all sequences of populations that are solution of the GA functions, there is a population containing a tuple which is in the fixpoint of the GI algorithm.

6 Experimentations

In this section, hybridizations CP+LS and CP+GA are tested using our constraint system (developed in C++). The purpose of this section is to highlight the benefit of our framework for hybridization and the benefit of hybrid resolution; note that our purpose is not to test a high performance implementation on large scale benchmarks. All tests are performed on a cluster with 22 processors running sequentially at 2.2 GHz with 1 Go of RAM each.

6.1 CP+LS for Constraint Satisfaction Problems

Problem Instances. We consider various classic CSP problems: $S+M=M$ (Send + More = Money), *Magic Square*, *Langford numbers*, the *Zebra* puzzle, *Golomb ruler*, and the *Uzbekian problem*, issued from the CSPlib [13].

Experimental Process. Our basic functions are stored into three sets: a set of domain reduction functions dr, a set of split functions sp, and a set of local search functions ls. The *choose* function of the **GI** algorithm is defined as follows: we consider a tuple (α, β, γ) such that α, β, and γ represent respectively the percentage of reduction functions, split functions, and local search functions, that are applied; functions are fairly selected with respect to these ratios.

The reduction functions are defined as follows. A domain reduction corresponds either to a bound consistency operator or a global constraint filtering operator (e.g., $alldifferent$). A split function cuts the selected domain into two subdomains. A local search function is a basic LS move; LS functions are then instantiated by a tabu search strategy which selects the best neighbor not currently in a tabu list of length 10 (see Section 4.5).

In the following, we consider three types of strategies corresponding to selection function of sCSP (to select one $sCSP$ in a σCSP, i.e., Sel_ψ function as defined in Section 4.5), and selection function of domain (to select one domain in a CSP, i.e., Sel_D function as defined in Section 4.5) for domain reduction and split functions. Here, we do not formalize these functions, but we just describe their strategies:

- **random:** Sel_ψ selects any $sCSP$, and Sel_D selects any domain of the selected $sCSP$.
- **depth-first:** Sel_ψ selects the $sCSP$ containing the smallest domain, and Sel_D selects the smallest domain of the selected $sCSP$.
- **LS-forward checking:** forward checking consists in instantiating variables (split by enumeration) in a given order and to prevent future conflicts by reducing variables directly linked to the one freshly enumerated. Our LS-forward checking strategy is similar; ls functions will apply on the $sCSP$ that has just been split.
- **width-first:** Sel_ψ selects the $sCSP$ containing the largest domain, and Sel_D selects the largest domain of the selected $sCSP$.

Combining our reduction functions and the three above mentioned strategies, we obtain three packs (one for each strategy) of sets of functions (dr, sp, and ls).

Experimental Results. The evaluation and comparison criterion corresponds to the number of basic functions applied to reach a first solution. Such an application of function is either a step of local search, a split, or a domain reduction (reduction of one domain using one constraint). We focus here on small problems: thus, computation times represents less than one minute of CPU time (e.g., a solution for the Langford Number is found in one sec.).

Interaction between CP and LS. We study here the benefit of the hybridization CP+LS. Using various strategies we highlight the effect of different cooperations on solving efficiency.

We first focus on the problems Langford Number and S+M=M; the tests are performed by increasing the percentage α of propagation from 0 to 100%. To insure to reach a solution, we set the split ratio to $\beta = \alpha * 0.1$. For example, if $\alpha = 0.4$, we set β to 4% of split, and thus 56% of LS. These tests use the depth-first strategy above-mentioned.

Figure 4 shows that the best results for the Langford Number problem correspond to a range of propagation rate between 35% and 45%. As a matter of fact, when local search represents less than 10% of the search effort, reaching a solution means computing the fixpoint for constraint propagation (i.e., applying all

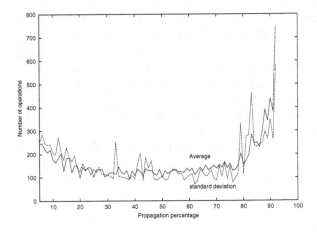

Fig. 4. Cost of a solution Langford Number (Depth-First)

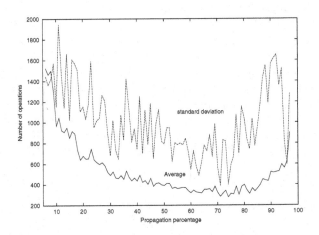

Fig. 5. Cost of a solution Send+More=Money (Depth-First)

propagation functions). Note that, for this problem, tabu search alone (Figure 4, left) provides better results than propagation with split (Figure 4, right).

Figure 5 shows the above-mentioned depth-first strategy to solve the S+M= M problem. The standard deviation is important: indeed, although sCSPs and domains are selected by the strategy, the choice of functions to apply is not fixed (random). However, the average performances are more regular, and the best range corresponds to 70%– 80% of propagation. Here, LS alone (Figure 5, right) appears less efficient than CP (Figure 5, left).

Thus, choosing the best settings for hybridization depends on the problem and on the strategies that are applied. Table 1 presents the best ranges using the LS-Forward-checking strategy for different problems.

Table 1. Best range of propagation rate (α) to compute a solution

Problem	S+M	LN42	Zebra	M. square	Golomb
Rate FC	70-80	15 - 25	60-70	30-45	30 - 40

These results point out that the incremental introduction of CP in LS (the same remark is valid for LS in CP) improves the general efficiency of resolution. These ratios of hybridization can thus be tuned to optimize performances.

Benefit of Hybridization with respect to LS and CP alone. In Table 2 we present a comparative study of the hybridization CP+LS, CP alone, and LS alone:

- the three strategies above-mentioned (random, depth-first, LS forward checking)
- CP+LS: the ratios (α, β, γ) are the best ratios selected in Table 1,
- CP (alone): the ratios are (90%, 10%, 0),
- LS (alone): the ratios are (0, 0, 100%).

Table 2. Average number of operations to compute a first solution

Strategy	Method	S+M	LN42	M. square	Golomb
Random	LS	1638	383	3328	3442
	CP+LS	1408	113	892	909
	CP	3006	1680	1031	2170
D-First	LS	1535	401	3145	3265
	CP+LS	396	95	814	815
	CP	1515	746	936	1920
FC	LS	1635	393	3240	3585
	CP+LS	22	192	570	622
	CP	530	425	736	1126

Again, these results show that hybridization benefits from the interaction between the solving methods. Improvements occur on problems for which LS performs better than CP but also on problems for which CP is better than LS. Moreover, the improvement is strongly related to the problem structure (such as the density of solutions) and to the chosen strategy. Experiments with the Width-First strategy above-mentioned are not presented here but provided similar results.

6.2   CP+GA for Constraint Optimization Problems

Problem Instances. The BACP (Balanced Academic Curriculum Problem) is a problem class issued from the CSPlib [13]: it consists in organizing courses in order to balance the work load of students for each period of their curriculum. We

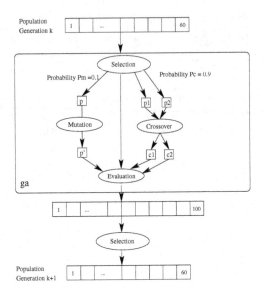

Fig. 6. *ga* functions

consider here various instantiations of the BACP: the bacp8, bacp10, and bacp12 problems issued from the CSPlib [13]; and finally data of this three curriculum are used to form a new problem (bacpall) for which some courses are shared by several curriculums.

Experimental Process. Similarly to CP+LS, our basic functions are organized into three sets: the set of domain reduction functions dr, the set of split functions sp, and the set of GA functions ga. In the following, the strategy is the depth-first strategy presented in the previous section.

Here, reduction functions correspond to arc consistency operators and reduction of global constraints (e.g., $period, load$) used to model the problems and to prune the search tree by detecting inconsistencies. The global constraint $period(i, \delta, \epsilon)$ computes the number of domains within the value i. If less than j occurrences of i are present in the m different domains, then the current CSP is locally inconsistent: $\delta \leq (\sum_{k=1}^{m} 1 \mid x_k = i) \leq \epsilon$. The global constraints $load(i, \beta, \gamma)$ counts the charge for a given period i of the current CSP: $\beta \leq (\sum_{k=1}^{m} c_k \mid x_k = j) \leq \gamma$.
sp are split operators which cut the selected domain into two subdomains.
ga are basic GA operators (see figure 6) which are instantiated by our genetic algorithm: from a population k, our genetic algorithm generates a new population k+1 of 60 individuals selected among 100 issued from k. When ga is called by the main algorithm, the following different cases may occur:

- the population $k + 1$ has less than 100 individuals: an individual is selected randomly; then, either it is coupled with another parent to create 2 children

in the population $k + 1$, either it is submitted to mutation, or it remains unchanged in the population $k + 1$.
- the population $k + 1$ has 100 individuals: the 60 best ones are selected according to the evaluation function which takes into account the objective function.

Experimental Results. For these experimentations, we integrated the GA module (i.e., *ga* functions) in our constraint based solving system for hybridization. We also added the notion of optimization to the single notion of solution.

In order to compare our results, we present the results of [8] using the linear programming solver lp_solve for the bacp8 and bacp10 problems (Table 3 shows the progress of the cost –evaluation– of the objective function w.r.t. the computation time). The results with our hybrid solver CP+GA are shown in Table 4. If lp_solve is able to find the optimal solution for the first problem, it is not the case for the second one.

Table 3. Results in seconds using lp_solve

Sol quality	bacp 8	Sol quality	bacp 10
24	137.08	33	9.11
23	218.23	32	25.38
21	218.43	30	25.65
20	712.84	29	1433.18
19	1441.98	27	1433.48
18	1453.73	26	1626.49
17 (optimum)	1459.73	24	1626.84

As mentioned above, we control the rates of each family of functions dr, sp and ga by defining the strategy (completing the depth-first strategy) as a tuple $(\%_{dr}, \%_{sp}, \%_{ga})$ of application rates. These values correspond indeed to a probability of application of a function from each family. In practice, we measure in Figure 7 the rate of effective applications, i.e., we only count the functions which are chosen according to the strategy and having a real impact on the resolution.

The most interesting in such an hybridization is the completeness of the association GA-CP, and the roles played by GA and CP in the search process (see Figures 7): GA optimizes the solutions in a search space progressively becoming locally consistent (and thus smaller and smaller) using constraints propagation and split. To evaluate the benefits of each of the methods we have measured:

- for CP: the number of effective reductions that are performed and the number of split,
- and for GA: the fact that the next generation is globally better than the previous one.

First of all, splits are limited to 1% of the total number of basic operations (reduction functions) because of the space complexity they generate.

Table 4. Results using GA+CP

Sol quality	bacp 8	bacp 10	bacp 12
24	0.47	4.71	2.34
23	0.54	4.67	2.40
22	0.61	3.68	2.48
21	0.61	4.36	2.76
20	0.69	4.63	3.20
19	0.83	4.95	4.25
18	1.20	5.13	35.20
17	15.05 (optimum)	5.60	
16		6.39	
15		8.53	
14		34.84 (optimum)	

Concerning the single problems (bacp8, bacp10, bacp12). At the beginning, CP represents 70% of the effort: constraint propagation narrows the search space. On the contrary, GA represents about 30%. During this period, not enough local consistency is enforced by constraint propagation, and GA only finds solutions (satisfying all constraints) with costs greater than 21. Then, at the beginning of the second half of the search process, CP and GA converge in terms of efficiency: most of the sub-GCSP have reach the local consistency and tests over constraints do not improve domain reduction. At the end, GA performs 70% of the search effort to find the optimal solution.

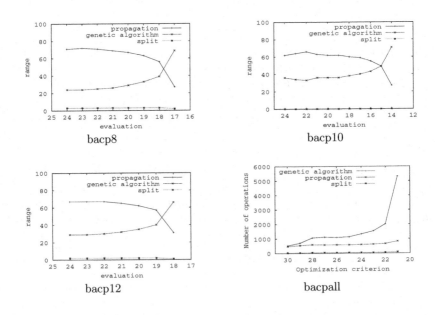

Fig. 7. Evolution of CP vs GA during the optimization process

Concerning strategies using GA and CP alone. In this implementation, CP is unable to find a feasible solution in 10 minutes cpu time. *GA* can find alone the optimal value but is 10 times slower than the hybrid resolution $GA + CP$. Therefore, we did not include these results in the tables.

In the figure for the all-period problem, CP and GA start searching with the same efficiency; but while CP seems to be stable, most of the operations are performed by the genetic process to improve the solution. This could be explained by the fact that, in this problem, constraints are too weak with respect to the number of variables and the size of the generated search space. But, in our hybrid resolution system, GA appears as a powerful method even if most of the constraint operators have not reached their fixpoints.

7   Perspectives and Conclusion

Most of hybrid approaches are ad-hoc algorithms based on a master-slave combination: they favor the development of systems whose efficiency is strongly related to a given class of CSPs. In this paper, we have used a more suitable general framework to model hybrid solving algorithms. We have shown that this work can serve as a basis for the integration of LS and CP methods, and the integration of GA and CP methods in order to highlight the connections between complete and incomplete techniques and their main properties.

We have shown how to integrate two techniques in the framework of chaotic iterations: CP+LS and CP+GA. However, this requires defining a new computation structure and orders on these structures. Moreover, the reduction functions have to be adapted to the new structures. Thus, integrating a new technique requires modifying the current structures and functions. We plan to modify our framework in order to be able to add a new technique without modifying the structure, simply by extending the existing structure. We also plan to modify function definition so that they can be defined independently. Some new types of functions operating the cooperation between the techniques. The first use of this new framework will be an hybrid solver CP+LS+GA.

A future extension will consists in providing "tools" to help designing and testing finer strategies in the GI algorithm in our particularly suitable uniform framework. To this end, we plan to extend works of [16] where strategies are built using some composition operators in the GI algorithm. Moreover, this will also open possibilities of concurrent and parallel applications of reduction functions inside the model.

At last, we plan to extend our prototype implementation (Section 6) into a complete generic implementation of our framework.

Acknowledgements. We would like to thank the program committee who gave us the opportunity of writing this paper and more especcially Christophe Ringeissen for his interesting remarks and useful comments.

References

1. E. Aarts and J.K. Lenstra, editors. *Local Search in Combinatorial Optimization.* John Wiley and Sons, 1997.
2. A. Aggoun and N. Beldiceanu. Overview of the chip compiler system. In K. Furukawa, editor, *Logic Programming, Proceedings of the Eigth International Conference*, pages 775–789. MIT Press, 1991.
3. K. Apt. The rough guide to constraint propagation. In *Proceedings of the 5th International Conference on Principles and Practice of Constraint Programming (CP'99)*, volume 1713 of *Lecture Notes in Computer Science*, pages 1–23, Springer, 1999. (Invited lecture).
4. K. Apt. From chaotic iteration to constraint propagation. In *Proceedings of ICALP '97*, volume 1256 of Lecture Notes in Computer Science, pages 36–55. Springer, 1997.
5. K. Apt. *Principles of Constraint Programming.* Cambridge University Press, 2003.
6. T. Bäck, J. M. de Graaf, J. N. Kok, and W. A. Kosters. Theory of genetic algorithms. In *Current Trends in Theoretical Computer Science*, pages 546–578. 2001.
7. J. E. Baker. *Adaptive Selection Methods for Genetic Algorithms.* ICGA, pages 101-111, 1985.
8. C. Castro and S. Manzano. Variable and value ordering when solving balanced academic curriculum problems. In *Proceedings of 6th Workshop of the ERCIM WG on Constraints. CoRR cs.PL/0110007*, 2001.
9. R. Dechter. *Constraint Processing.* Morgan Kaufmann, 2003.
10. A. E. Eiben, P-E. Raué and Z. Ruttkay. Genetic algorithms with multi-parent recombination. In *PPSN III: Proceedings of the International Conference on Evolutionary Computation*, volume 866 of Lecture Notes in Computer Science, pages 78-87, Springer, 1994.
11. F. Focacci, F. Laburthe, and A. Lodi. Local search and constraint programming. In *Handbook of Metaheuristics*, volume 57 of International Series in Operations Research and Management Science, Kluwer, 2002.
12. T. Fruewirth and S. Abdennadher. *Essentials of Constraint Programming.* Springer, 2003.
13. I. Gent, T. Walsh, and B. Selman. http://www.csplib.org, funded by the UK Network of Constraints.
14. F. Glover and M. Laguna. *Tabu Search.* Kluwer Academic Publishers, 1997.
15. D. E. Goldberg. *Genetic Algorithms in Search, Optimization and Machine Learning.* Addison-Wesley Longman Publishing Co., Inc., 1989.
16. L. Granvilliers and E. Monfroy. Implementing Constraint Propagation by Composition of Reductions. *Proceedings of International Conference on Logic Programming*, volume 2916 of Lecture Notes in Computer Science, pages 300-314. Springer, 2003.
17. J. H. Holland. *Adaptation in Natural and Artificial Systems.* 1975.
18. H. Hoos and T. Stülze. *Stochastic local search : foundations and applications.* Morgan Kaufmann, Elsevier, 2004.
19. ILOG. *ILOG Solver 5.0 User's Manual and Reference Manual*, 2000.
20. K. A. D. Jong. *An analysis of the behavior of a class of genetic adaptive systems.* Phd thesis, University of Michigan, 1975.
21. N. Jussien and O. Lhomme. Local search with constraint propagation and conflict-based heuristics. *Artificial Intelligence*, 139(1):21-45, 2002.
22. F. Laburthe. CHOCO: implementing a cp kernel. In *CP'00 Post Conference Workshop on Techniques for Implementing Constraint Programming Systems - TRICS*, 2000.

23. T. Lambert and E. Monfroy and F. Saubion. Solving Strategies using a Hybridization Model for Local Search and Constraint Propagation. In *Proceedings of ACM SAC'2005*, pages 398-403, ACM Press 2005.

24. A. Mackworth. *Encyclopedia on Artificial Intelligence*, chapter Constraint Satisfaction. John Wiley, 1987.

25. K. Mariott and P. Stuckey. *Programming with Constraints, An introduction*. MIT Press, 1998.

26. Z. Michalewicz. *Genetic algorithms + data structures = evolution programs (3rd, extended ed.)*. Springer, New York, 1996.

27. R. Mohr and T.C. Henderson. Arc and path consistency revisited. *Artificial Intelligence*, 28:225–233, 1986.

28. E. Monfroy, F. Saubion and T. Lambert. On Hybridization of Local Search and Constraint Propagation. In *Proceedings of ICLP'2004*, pages 299-313, volume 3132 of Lecture Notes in Computer Science, Springer, 2004.

29. P. Pardalos and M. Resende. *Handbook of Applied Optimization*. Oxford University Press, 2002.

30. G. Pesant and M. Gendreau. A view of local search in constraint programming. In *Proceedings of the Second International Conference on Principles and Practice of Constraint Programming*, volume 1118 in Lecture Notes in Computer Science, pages 353–366. Springer, 1996.

31. S. Prestwich. A hybrid search architecture applied to hard random 3-sat and low-autocorrelation binary sequences. In *Principle and Practice of Constraint Programming - CP 2000*, volume 1894 in Lecture Notes in Computer Science, pages 337–352. Springer, 2000.

32. P. Shaw. Using constraint programming and local search methods to solve vehicle routing problems. In *Principles and Practice of Constraint Programming - CP98*, volume 1520 of Lecture Notes in Computer Science, pages 417–431. Springer, 1998.

33. D. Thierens and D. E. Goldberg. Convergence Models of Genetic Algorithm Selection Schemes. In *PPSN III: Proceedings of the International Conference on Evolutionary Computation*, volume 866 of Lecture Notes in Computer Science, pages 119-129,Springer, 1994.

34. E. Tsang. *Foundations of Constraint Satisfaction*. Academic Press, London, 1993.

An Efficient Decision Procedure for UTVPI Constraints

Shuvendu K. Lahiri and Madanlal Musuvathi

Microsoft Research
{shuvendu, madanm}@microsoft.com

Abstract. A unit two variable per inequality (UTVPI) constraint is of the form $a.x + b.y \leq d$ where x and y are integer variables, the coefficients $a, b \in \{-1, 0, 1\}$ and the bound d is an integer constant. This paper presents an efficient decision procedure for UTVPI constraints. Given m such constraints over n variables, the procedure checks the satisfiability of the constraints in $O(n.m)$ time and $O(n+m)$ space. This improves upon the previously known $O(n^2.m)$ time and $O(n^2)$ space algorithm based on transitive closure. Our decision procedure is also equality generating, proof generating, and model generating.

1 Introduction

A unit two variable per inequality (UTVPI) constraint is of the form $a.x + b.y \leq d$ where x and y are integer variables, the coefficients $a, b \in \{-1, 0, 1\}$ and the bound d is an integer constant. This is a useful fragment of integer linear arithmetic as many hardware and software verification queries are naturally expressed in this fragment.

For example, Ball et al. [1] note that most queries that arise during the predicate abstraction refinement process in SLAM [2] fit into this fragment. Others, including Pratt [18] and Seshia et al. [19] have observed that significant portion of linear arithmetic queries are restricted to difference logic (a fragment of UTVPI constraints of the form $x \leq y + c$.).

The fragment UTVPI is also important because it is the most expressive fragment of linear arithmetic that enjoys a polynomial decision procedure [11]. Namely, extending this fragment to contain three variables (with just unit coefficients) per inequality or adding non-unit coefficients for two variable inequalities make the decision problem NP-complete [12]. Having an integer solver is often useful when dealing with variables for which rational solutions are unacceptable. Such examples often arise when modeling indices of an array or queues in hardware or software [7,13].

In this paper, we present an efficient decision procedure for UTVPI constraints. Given m such constraints over n variables, the procedure checks the satisfiability of the constraints in $O(n.m)$ time and $O(n + m)$ space. This improves upon the previously known $O(n^2.m)$ time and $O(n^2)$ space algorithm provided by Jaffar et al. [11] based on transitive closure. The space improvement of our algorithm is particularly evident when m is $O(n)$, which occurs

B. Gramlich (Ed.): FroCoS 2005, LNAI 3717, pp. 168–183, 2005.

very frequently in practice, as the number of constraints that arise in typical verification queries have a sparse structure. In fact, the actual complexity of our algorithm is $O(\mathcal{NCD})$, which is the complexity of an algorithm that can determine if there is a negative weight cycle in a directed graph. [1] Accordingly, the time bound of our algorithm can be further improved by using a more efficient negative cycle detection algorithm [4].

In addition to checking satisfiability of a set of UTVPI constraints, the decision procedure is also *equality* generating, *proof* producing and generates models for satisfiable formulas. The decision procedure generates equalities between variables implied by a set of UTVPI constraints in $O(n.m)$ time. The algorithm can generate a proof of unsatisfiability and equalities implied in $O(n.m)$ time. Both these algorithms use a linear $O(n + m)$ space. The model generation algorithm run in $O(n.m + n^2.logn)$ time and $O(n^2)$ space.

Finally, we conclude the paper by showing that the problem of finding *diverse* models for UTVPI constraints is NP-complete. A diverse model ρ for a set of UTVPI constraints ϕ is an assignment from the set of variables of ϕ to integers, such that $\rho(x) = \rho(y)$ if and only if $x = y$ is implied by ϕ. We also relate the problem of generating disjunctions of equalities from the theory to the problem of diverse model generation.

2   Background

2.1   Requirements from a Decision Procedure

For a given theory T, a decision procedure for T checks if a formula ϕ in the theory is *satisfiable*, i.e. it is possible to assign values to the symbols in ϕ that are consistent with T, such that ϕ evaluates to `true`.

Decision procedures, nowadays, do not operate in isolation, but form a part of a more complex system that can decide formulas involving symbols shared across multiple theories. In such a setting, a decision procedure has to support the following operations efficiently:

1. *Satisfiability Checking*: Checking if a formula ϕ is satisfiable in the theory.
2. *Model Generation*: If a formula in the theory is satisfiable, find values for the symbols that appear in the theory that makes it satisfiable. This is crucial for applications that use theorem provers for test-case generation.
3. *Equality Generation*: The Nelson-Oppen framework for combining decision procedures [17] requires that each theory (at least) produces the set of equalities over variables that are implied by the constraints.
4. *Proof Generation*: Proof generation can be used to certify the output of a theorem prover [16]. Proofs are also used to construct conflict clauses efficiently in a lazy SAT-based theorem proving architecture [6].

---

[1] The traditional Bellman-Ford algorithm for negative cycle detection runs in $O(n.m)$ time.

2.2 Negative Cycle Detection

Let $G(V, E)$ be a directed graph with vertices V and edges E. For each edge $e \in E$, we denote $s(e)$, $d(e)$ and $w(e)$ to be the source, destination and the weight of the edge. A *path* P in G is a sequence of edges $[e_1, \ldots, e_n]$ such that $d(e_i) = s(e_{i+1})$, for all $1 \le i \le n - 1$. For a path $P \doteq [e_1, \ldots, e_n]$, $s(P)$ denotes $s(e_1)$, $d(P)$ denotes $d(e_n)$ and $w(P)$ denotes the sum of the weights on the edges in the path, i.e. $\sum_{1 \le i \le n} w(e_i)$. A cycle C is a sequence of edges $[e_1, \ldots, e_n]$ where $s(e_1) = d(e_n)$. We use $u \rightsquigarrow v$ in E to denote that there is a path from u to v through edges in E.

Given a graph $G(V, E)$, the problem of determining if G has a cycle C, such that $w(C) < 0$ is called the *negative cycle detection* problem. Various algorithms can be used to determine the existence of negative cycles in a graph [4]. Negative cycle detection (NCD) algorithms have two properties:

1. The algorithm determines if there is a negative cycle in the graph. In this case, the algorithm produces a particular negative cycle as a witness.
2. If there are no negative cycles, then the algorithm generates a *feasible* solution $\delta : V \to \mathcal{Z}$, such that for every $(u, v) \in E$, $\delta(v) \le \delta(u) + w(u, v)$.

For example, the Bellman-Ford [3,8] algorithm for single-source shortest path in a graph can be used to detect negative cycles in a graph. If the graph contains n vertices and m edges, the Bellman-Ford algorithm can determine in $O(n.m)$ time and $O(n+m)$ space, if there is a negative cycle in G, and a feasible solution otherwise.

In this paper, we assume that we use one such NCD algorithm. We will define the complexity $O(\mathcal{NCD})$ as the complexity of the NCD algorithm under consideration. This allows us to leverage all the advances in NCD algorithms in recent years [4], that have complexity better than the Bellman-Ford algorithm.

3   UTVPI Constraints

The unit two variables per inequality (UTVPI) constraints are a fragment of linear arithmetic constraints of the form $a.x + b.y \le d$ where x and y are integer variables, the coefficients $a, b \in \{-1, 0, 1\}$ and the bound d is an integer constant. The fragment also includes single variable per inequality (SVPI) constraints $a.x \le d$.

Figure 1 describes the set of inference rules that is sound and complete for this fragment. Jaffar et al. [11] showed that a set of UTVPI constraints C is unsatisfiable if and only if the closure of C with respect to the transitive and the tightening rule in Figure 1, contains a constraint $0 \le d$, where $d < 0$.

3.1   Existing Decision Procedures for UTVPI

The only algorithms known for solving a set of UTVPI constraints are based on transitive (and tightening) closure.

$$\frac{a.x + b.y \leq c \qquad - a.x + b'.z \leq d}{b.y + b'.z \leq c + d} \qquad \text{(TRANSITIVE)}$$

$$\frac{a.x + b.y \leq c \qquad a.x - b.y \leq d \qquad a \in \{-1, 1\}}{a.x \leq \lfloor (c + d)/2 \rfloor} \qquad \text{(TIGHTENING)}$$

$$\frac{a.x + b.y \leq c \qquad - a.x - b.y \leq d \qquad c + d < 0}{\bot} \qquad \text{(CONTRADICTION)}$$

Fig. 1. Inference rules for UTVPI. The constants a, b, b' range over $\{-1, 0, 1\}$, and c, d range over $\mathcal{Z}$.

Jaffar et al. [11] provided the first decision procedure for UTVPI. The algorithm was based on incrementally processing a set of constraints C and maintaining a transitive and tight closure C^* of the set of constraints seen so far. After the addition of a new constraint $a.x + b.y \leq d$, the algorithm computes the set of new UTVPI constraints as follows:

1. For every $-a.x + b'.z \leq d' \in C^*$, and for every $-b.y + b''.w \leq d'' \in C^*$, compute the closure of $\{-a.x + b'.z \leq d', a.x + b.y \leq d, -b.y + b''.w \leq d''\}$ using the transitive rule in Figure 1.
2. For any constraint $2a'.w \leq d'$ produced in step 1, we add the tightening constraint $a'.w \leq \lfloor d'/2 \rfloor$ to the closure.
3. For each *new* tightening constraint $a'.w \leq d'$ produced in step 2, and for every constraint $b'.z - a'.w \leq d''$, we add the transitive constraint $b'.z \leq d + d''$ to the closure, and compute the transitive closure.

The runtime of the algorithm is $O(m.n^2)$ and the space requirement is $O(n^2)$.

Harvey et al. [9] improved on this algorithm by showing that the transitive and tightening steps can be combined together in a single step (i.e. step 1) without the need for the subsequent steps. The asymptotic complexity of the algorithm (both time and space), however, remains unchanged.

In this paper, we provide an $O(\mathcal{NCD})$ time algorithm based on negative cycle detection that strictly improves upon the previous decision procedures for UTVPI constraints. Also, our algorithm has an $O(n + m)$ space complexity that performs better when m is $O(n)$. On the downside, our algorithm is not incremental and requires all the constraints to be provided at once. Currently, we are using this decision procedure in a lazy SAT-based theorem proving framework [6], where nonincremental decision procedures suffice. However, we hope to make this algorithm incremental in our future work.

3.2 Constraint Graph

Given a set of UTVPI constraints, our algorithm reduces the problem of checking the satisfiability of the constraints to finding negative cycles in an appropriate graph. This transformation is a simple extension of a similar transformation for

Table 1. Edges in $\text{cons}(x^+, x^-, y^+, y^-)$traint graphs

UTVPI	Assoc. Difference Constraints	Graph Edges
$x - y \le k$	$x^+ - y^+ \le k$, $y^- - x^- \le k$	$y^+ \xrightarrow{k} x^+$, $x^- \xrightarrow{k} y^-$
$x + y \le k$	$x^+ - y^- \le k$, $y^+ - x^- \le k$	$y^- \xrightarrow{k} x^+$, $x^- \xrightarrow{k} y^+$
$-x - y \le k$	$x^- - y^+ \le k$, $y^- - x^+ \le k$	$y^+ \xrightarrow{k} x^-$, $x^+ \xrightarrow{k} y^-$
$x \le k$	$x^+ - x^- \le 2.k$	$x^- \xrightarrow{2.k} x^+$
$-x \le k$	$x^- - x^+ \le 2.k$	$x^+ \xrightarrow{2.k} x^-$

difference constraints [5] and has been previously used by Miné [15], for solving UTVPI constraints over rationals.

Let ϕ be a set of UTVPI constraints. One can construct the *constraint graph* $G_\phi(V, E)$ as follows. For each variable x in ϕ, the vertex set V contains two vertices x^+ and x^- that respectively represent the terms x and $-x$. We use $\mathcal{T}(v)$ to denote the representing term for a vertex v. Also, for any vertex $v \in V$, we define $-v$ to be the vertex such that $\mathcal{T}(v) = -\mathcal{T}(-v)$. That is, $-x^+$ is x^-, and $-x^-$ is x^+. To avoid confusion, we will use $x, y, z, \ldots$ to represent variables in ϕ and $u, v, w, \ldots$ to represent vertices in V.

Each UTVPI constraint in ϕ can be transformed to a set of difference constraints over vertices as shown in Table 1. For each such difference constraint $u - v \le k$, the graph $G_\phi(V, E)$ contains a directed edge (v, u) with weight k. It is obvious that if ϕ contains m UTVPI constraints in n variables then $G_\phi(V, E)$ will contain at most $2.n$ vertices and $2.m$ edges. The following propositions are obvious.

Proposition 1. *For every edge $(u, v) \in E$, the constraint graph $G_\phi(V, E)$ contains an edge $(-v, -u)$ with equal weight.*

Proposition 2. *If there is a path P from u to v in the constraint graph, then there is a path P' from $-v$ to $-u$ such that $w(P) = w(P')$.*

For vertices $u, v \in V$, let $SP(u, v)$ denote any of the shortest paths from u to v in G_ϕ. Let $wSP(u, v)$ represent $w(SP(u, v))$.

Proposition 3. *Let u and v be two vertices in G_ϕ such that $u \leadsto v$. Then ϕ implies $\mathcal{T}(y) - \mathcal{T}(x) \le wSP(u, v)$.*

The proof follows by transitivity of constraints in ϕ.

Lemma 1. *A set of UTVPI constraints ϕ is unsatisfiable in $\mathcal{Q}$ if and only if the constraint graph $G_\phi(V, E)$ contains a negative weight cycle [15].*

The proof of the lemma simply follows from a similar proof for the satisfiability of difference constraints [5].

Lemma 1 essentially solves the satisfiability problem for rationals. However, this lemma is not sufficient for integers. For instance, Figure 3.2 shows a set of constraints which is unsatisfiable in integers but the corresponding constraint

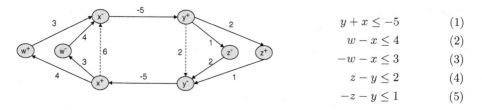

$$y + x \leq -5 \qquad (1)$$
$$w - x \leq 4 \qquad (2)$$
$$-w - x \leq 3 \qquad (3)$$
$$z - y \leq 2 \qquad (4)$$
$$-z - y \leq 1 \qquad (5)$$

Fig. 2. A set of UTVPI constraints that are unsatisfiable in $\mathcal{Z}$ and the corresponding constraint graph. The dotted edges are the tightening edges. Note that the vertices of the negative-weight cycle (x^+, x^-, y^+, y^-) in $G_{\phi \cup T}$ are contained in a zero-weight cycle $(x^+, w^+, x^-, y^+, z^+, y^-)$ in G_ϕ.

graph has no negative cycles. In this example, Equations (2) and (3) imply $-2.x \leq 7$ which for integers can be tightened to $-x \leq 3$. Similarly, Equations (4) and (5) imply $-y \leq 1$. These bounds on $-x$ and $-y$ contradict Equation (1).

4 Efficient Decision Procedure for UTVPI Constraints

As described in the previous section, the constraint graph G_ϕ of a set of constraints ϕ contains a negative cycle only if the ϕ are unsatisfiable in $\mathcal{Q}$. To extend this result for $\mathcal{Z}$, this section describes a method to extend the constraint graph by adding *tightening* edges. The resulting graph contains a negative cycle exactly when the constraints are unsatisfiable in $\mathcal{Z}$.

4.1 Tightening Edges

Given a constraint graph $G_\phi(V, E)$, our goal is to capture the tightening rule in Figure 1. For a constraint graph G_ϕ, define the set of tightening edges T as follows:

$$T = \{(u, -u) \mid wSP(u, -u) \text{ is odd}\}$$

For each edge in T, the weight of the edge is defined as follows

$$w_T(u, -u) = wSP(u, -u) - 1, \text{ for all edges } (u, -u) \in T$$

Now, whenever ϕ implies the tightest bound $2.x \leq k$ where k is odd, then by Proposition 3, $wSP(x^-, x^+) = k$ in G_ϕ. By the Tightening Rule in Figure 1, ϕ implies $2.x \leq k - 1$. This "tightened" constraint is captured by the tightening edge (x^-, x^+) in T. Note, that the weight of such an edge in T is even.

Given a constraint graph G_ϕ, define the graph $G_{\phi \cup T}$ as the one obtained by adding all edges in T to G_ϕ. The following lemma describes a way to check if the input constraints ϕ is satisfiable in $\mathcal{Z}$.

Lemma 2. *A set of UTVPI constraints ϕ is unsatisfiable in $\mathcal{Z}$ if and only if the graph $G_{\phi \cup T}$ has a negative weight cycle.*

Lemma 2 leads to the following naive algorithm

Proposition 4. *Naive Algorithm: The set of UTVPI constraints can be decided in $O(nm + n^2 log n)$ time and $O(n + m)$ space.*

This algorithm uses a minor modification of Johnson's *All Pair Shortest Paths* algorithm to identify the edges in T in $O(nm + n^2 log n)$ time and $O(n + m)$ space. Then, negative cycles in $G_{\phi \cup T}$ can be found in $O(\mathcal{NCD})$. Note that this is an improvement over the Harvey and Stuckey's algorithm.

4.2 Efficient Decision Procedure

Our goal is to improve upon the naive algorithm to decide a set of UTVPI constraints in $O(\mathcal{NCD})$ time. The crucial insight is to notice that the naive algorithm is computing *all* edges in T while only some of them might potentially lead to negative cycles. Our algorithm precisely identifies those edges in T by looking for *zero-weighted* cycles in G_{ϕ}.

We present the algorithm below:

Algorithm 1 NCD-UTVPI *Algorithm:*

1. Given a set of UTVPI constraints ϕ, construct the constraint graph $G_{\phi}(V, E)$.
2. Run a negative cycle detection algorithm.
   (a) If G_{ϕ} contains a negative cycle, return UNSAT.
   (b) Otherwise, the negative cycle detection algorithm returns a feasible solution δ [2] , such that $\delta(v) - \delta(u) \leq w(u, v)$ for all edges $(u, v) \in E$.
3. Let E' be set of edges in G such that an edge $(u, v) \in E'$ if and only if $\delta(v) - \delta(u) = w(u, v)$
4. Create the induced subgraph $G'_{\phi}(V, E')$ from $G_{\phi}(V, E)$.
5. Group the vertices in G'_{ϕ} into *strongly connected components* (SCCs). Vertices u and v are in the same SCC if and only if $u \leadsto v$ and $v \leadsto u$ in E'. This can be done in linear time [20].
6. For each vertex $u \in V$,
   (a) if $-u$ is in the same SCC as u and if $\delta(u) - \delta(-u)$ is odd, then return UNSAT.
7. return SAT

In the algorithm above, all steps except step 2 can be done in linear time. Thus the algorithm has $O(\mathcal{NCD})$ time complexity and $O(n+m)$ space complexity. To prove the soundness and completeness of this algorithm, we need the following definitions and lemmas.

Given a feasible solution δ for the constraint graph G_{ϕ}, define the *slack* of an edge as: $sl_{\delta}(u, v) = \delta(u) - \delta(v) + w(u, v)$. When the feasible solution δ is obvious from the context, $sl(u, v)$ refers to $sl_{\delta}(u, v)$. From the definition of feasibility of δ, we have the fact that $sl(u, v) \geq 0$ for all edges (u, v) in G_{ϕ}. Note that the step 3 of the algorithm above identifies E' to be the set of edges with slack zero. Also, the slack of a path P is defined as $sl(P) = \Sigma_{e \in P} sl(e)$.

---

[2] Note, δ is a mapping from V to $\mathcal{Z}$.

Proposition 5. *Let P be a path from u to v in G_ϕ. Then, $w(P) = sl(P) + \delta(v) - \delta(u)$.*

The proof follows from a simple induction on the length of the path P.

Proposition 6. *For any cycle C in G_ϕ, $w(C) = sl(C)$.*

The proof follows from Proposition 5 when P forms a cycle.

Proposition 7. *If P is a path from u to v and all edges in P have a slack zero, then $wSP(u, v) = \delta(v) - \delta(u)$.*

Proof. We have $sl(P) = 0$. Thus $w(P) = \delta(v) - \delta(u)$ from Proposition 5. However, as slacks of all edges are nonnegative, $sl(SP(u, v)) \geq 0$. From Proposition 5, we have $wSP(u, v) = sl(SP(u, v)) + \delta(v) - \delta(u) \geq w(P)$, which can be possible only when the inequality is tight. Thus, the proposition is true.

Theorem 1. *The NCD-UTVPI algorithm is sound.*

Proof. The algorithm returns UNSAT at two places. In step 2a, the graph G_ϕ contains a negative cycle and thus by Lemma 1, ϕ is unsatisfiable in $\mathcal{Q}$ and thus in $\mathcal{Z}$. If the algorithm returns UNSAT in step 6a, then we show that ϕ is unsatisfiable in $\mathcal{Z}$ (but satisfiable in $\mathcal{Q}$). We have two vertices u and $-u$ that are in the same SCC in G'_ϕ such that $\delta(-u) - \delta(u)$ is odd. Since the vertices are in the same SCC, we have a path in from u to $-u$ in G'_ϕ. By Proposition 7, $wSP(u, -u)$ is odd, and thus T contains an edge $(u, -u)$ of weight $\delta(-u) - \delta(u) - 1$. Similarly, T contains an edge $(-u, u)$ of weight $\delta(u) - \delta(-u) - 1$. These two edges form a negative cycle (of weight -2) in $G_{\phi \cup T}$. Thus, ϕ is unsatisfiable by Lemma 2.

To prove the completeness, we have to show that given a set of UTVPI constraints ϕ that is unsatisfiable, the *NCD-UTVPI* algorithm returns UNSAT. The proof of this theorem is more involved, and requires the following two lemmas.

Lemma 3. *If C is a cycle in $G_{\phi \cup T}$, then there is a cycle C' in $G_{\phi \cup T}$ with at most two edges from T such that either $w(C') < 0$ or $w(C') \leq w(C)$.*

Proof. The lemma is trivially true if $G_{\phi \cup T}$ only contains cycles with at most two edges from T. Otherwise, let C be a cycle in $G_{\phi \cup T}$ such that C contains n tightening edges with $n > 2$. For $0 \leq i < n$, let $t_i = (v_i, -v_i)$ be the tightening edges in the order they appear in C. Also, the fragment P_i of C denotes a path from $-v_i$ to v_{i+1} in G_ϕ, where the addition is performed modulo n. From Proposition 2, there is a path P'_i from $-v_{i+1}$ to v_i in G_ϕ, such that $w(P'_i) = w(P_i)$. Define C_i as the cycle consisting of t_i, P_i, t_{i+1}, P'_i. Obviously, C_i contains only two tightening edges, for $0 \leq i < n$.

We can show that at least one of the C_i satisfies the conditions of the lemma. Suppose this is not the case, then $w(C_i) \geq 0$ and $w(C_i) > w(C)$, for all $0 \leq i < n$. We have,

$$\begin{aligned}
\textstyle\sum_{i=0}^{n-1} w(C_i) &= \textstyle\sum_{i=0}^{n-1} w(t_i) + w(P_i) + w(t_{i+1}) + w(P'_i) \\
&= \textstyle\sum_{i=0}^{n-1} w(t_i) + 2.w(P_i) + w(t_{i+1}) && \text{as } w(P) = w(P') \\
&= \textstyle\sum_{i=0}^{n-1} 2.w(t_i) + 2.w(P_i) && \text{by reordering the sum} \\
&= 2.w(C)
\end{aligned}$$

By assumption, the left hand side $\Sigma_{i=0}^{n-1} w(C_i) \geq 0$, which implies that $w(C) \geq 0$. Also by assumption, $2.w(C) = \Sigma_{i=0}^{n-1} w(C_i) > n.w(C)$. However, this contradicts with the fact that $n > 2$. Thus, at least there is a C_i that satisfies the requirements of the lemma.

The above lemma essentially restricts negative cycle detection to those cycles with at most two tightening edges.

Corollary 1. $G_{\phi \cup T}$ *contains a negative cycle if and only if when it contains a negative cycle with at most most two edges from T.*

This corollary simply follows from Lemma 3 when the cycle C has a negative weight.

Lemma 4. *Suppose G_ϕ contains no negative cycles but $G_{\phi \cup T}$ contains a negative cycle. Then there is a zero weight cycle in G_ϕ containing vertices u and $-u$ such that $wSP(u, -u)$ is odd.*

Proof. Let C be a negative cycle in $G_{\phi \cup T}$. By Corollary 1, C has at most two tightening edges without loss of generality. Since G_ϕ contains no negative cycles, C contains at least one tightening edge. Thus, there are the following two cases:
*Case 1: C contains exactly one tightening edge $(u, -u)$. Define P as the fragment of C from $-u$ to u. Consider the cycle C' formed by P along with $SP(u, -u)$ (in G_ϕ). By definition of the tightening edge, $w(C) = wSP(u, -u) - 1 + w(P) = w(C') - 1 < 0$. Also, as C' is a cycle in G_ϕ, we have $w(C') \geq 0$. These constraints imply that $w(C') = 0$ and is the cycle required by the lemma.
*Case 2: C contains two tightening edges. Let $(u, -u)$ and $(v, -v)$ be the tightening edges in order they appear in C. Define P_u as the fragment of C from $-u$ to v and define P_v as the fragment of C from $-v$ to u. Without loss of generality, $w(P_u) \leq w(P_v)$. Also, by Proposition 2, there is a path P'_u from $-v$ to u, such that $w(P_u) = w(P'_u)$. Consider the cycle C' consisting of $SP(u, -u), P_u,$ $SP(v, -v), P'_u$. By definition of tightening edges both $wSP(u, -u)$ and $wSP(v, -v)$ are odd. Thus, $w(C')$ is even. Also,

$$
\begin{aligned}
w(C) &= wSP(u, -u) - 1 + w(P_u) + wSP(v, -v) - 1 + w(P_v) \\
&\geq wSP(u, -u) - 1 + w(P_u) + wSP(v, -v) - 1 + w(P_u) \quad \text{by assumption} \\
&= w(C') - 2 \qquad\qquad\qquad\qquad\qquad\qquad\qquad\quad \text{as } w(P_u){=}w(P'_u)
\end{aligned}
$$

Thus, $w(C') \leq w(C) + 2$. Since C is a negative cycle, we have $w(C') \leq 1$. However, we can tighten this constraint as $w(C')$ is even. Thus, we have $w(C') \leq 0$. Since, C' is a cycle in G_ϕ $w(C') \geq 0$. Thus, C' is the cycle required by the lemma.

The proof of completeness of the *NCD-UTVPI* algorithm follows from the above lemma.

Theorem 2. *The* NCD-UTVPI *algorithm is complete.*

Proof. Let ϕ be a set of UTVPI constraints. If ϕ is unsatisfiable in $\mathcal{Q}$, then the constraint graph G_ϕ has a negative cycle by Lemma 1. The NCD-UTVPI algorithm returns UNSAT in step 2a. Suppose ϕ is satisfiable in $\mathcal{Q}$ but unsatisfiable in $\mathcal{Z}$. Then, by Lemma 2, $G_{\phi \cup T}$ contains a negative cycle, while G_ϕ does not. Thus, by Lemma 4, G_ϕ contains a zero weight cycle with a vertex u such that $SP(u, -u)$ is odd. By Proposition 6, all edges in C have a slack equal to zero. Thus u and $-u$ are in the same SCC in the graph G' defined in step 5 of the NCD-UTVPI algorithm. Finally, $SP(u, -u) = \delta(-u, u)$ by Proposition 7. Thus, the NCD-UTVPI algorithm will detect the vertex u in step 6a.

5   Equality Generation

This section describes how to generate variable equalities implied by a set of UTVPI constraints. This is essential when the UTVPI decision procedure is combined with other theories in a Nelson-Oppen framework. Given a set of m UTVPI constraints ϕ over n variables, we show how to infer implied variable equalities from G_ϕ in $O(n.m)$ time and $O(n + m)$ space.

5.1   Naive Algorithm

Akin to the decision procedure described in Section 4, we first provide a naive algorithm for generating equalities in $O(nm + n^2 log n)$ time to capture the main intuition, and then improve to a $O(nm)$ algorithm. Though m can be n^2 in the worst case, this improvement is motivated by the fact that in practice m is often $O(n)$.

The naive algorithm proceeds as in Proposition 4 by explicitly constructing $G_{\phi \cup T}$ by identifying all tightening edges in $O(nm + n^2 log n)$ time. Given $G_{\phi \cup T}$ with no negative cycles (§2), the following lemma provides a way to generate variable equalities in $O(\mathcal{NCD})$ time

Lemma 5. *Let* $\delta_{\phi \cup T}$ *be a feasible solution produced by a negative cycle detection algorithm for* $G_{\phi \cup T}$. *The set of constraints* ϕ *implies* $x = y$ *if and only if the following is true:*

1. $\delta_{\phi \cup T}(x^+) = \delta_{\phi \cup T}(y^+)$, *and*
2. *there is a zero weight cycle in* $G_{\phi \cup T}$ *that contains both* x^+ *and* y^+.

This lemma directly follows from the equality generation algorithm for difference constraints [14].

The conditions in this lemma can be checked by performing a SCC computation on the subgraph of $G_{\phi \cup T}$ induced by edges with slack zero, similar to the *NCD-UTVPI* algorithm. Now, ϕ implies $x = y$ whenever x and y are in the same SCC with the same $\delta_{\phi \cup T}$ values. This can be done in average linear time using a hashtable, or in $O(n. \log n)$ time by sorting all vertices in the same SCC according to their $\delta_{\phi \cup T}$ values.

We state the naive algorithm below.

Algorithm 2 *EqGen-Naive Algorithm:*

1. Starting with $G_{\phi \cup T}$, run a negative cycle detection algorithm to produce a feasible solution $\delta_{\phi \cup T}$.
2. Let E_0 be the set of edges such that $e \in E_0$ if and only if $sl(e) = 0$.
3. Create the subgraph G_0 induced by E_0.
4. Group the vertices of G_0 into strongly connected components.
5. If vertices x^+ and y^+ are in the same SCC and $\delta_{\phi \cup T}(x^+) = \delta_{\phi \cup T}(y^+)$, then report the variable equality $x = y$.

5.2   Efficient Equality Generation

In this section, we improve the naive algorithm by precisely inferring those tightening edges that can result in a zero-weighted cycle in $G_{\phi \cup T}$. We do this by using the following lemma, similar to Lemma 4.

Lemma 6. *Assuming $G_{\phi \cup T}$ has no negative cycles and if C is a zero weight cycle in $G_{\phi \cup T}$ containing a tightening edge $(u, -u)$, then there is a cycle C' in G_ϕ containing u and $-u$, and such that $w(C') \leq 2$.*

Proof. By Lemma 3, we can assume that C has at most two tightening edges. Let P be the fragment of C from $-u$ to u. Consider the cycle C_1 formed by $SP(u, -u), P$. By definition of the tightening edge, this cycle has weight $w(C_1) = wSP(u, -u) + w(P) = w(C) + 1 = 1$. If C contains no other tightening edge, then C_1 is a cycle in G_ϕ proving the lemma. Otherwise, C contains at most one other tightening edge, which can be removed like before to obtain C_2 such that $w(C_2) = 2$. Now, C_2 is the required cycle in G_ϕ.

By Lemma 6, we only need to add tightening edges whose endpoints are in cycles of weight less than or equal to two. Moreover, under any feasible solution δ, any edge e in such a cycle will have $sl(e) \leq 2$. By identifying such edges, the following algorithm generates all variable equalities implied by ϕ in $O(n.m)$ time.

Algorithm 3 *EqGen Algorithm:*

1. Given a set of UTVPI constraints ϕ, construct the constraint graph $G_\phi(V, E)$.
2. Assume *NCD-UTVPI* algorithm returns SAT. Also, assume that a feasible solution δ exists for G_ϕ.
3. Let $E_2 = \{(u, v) | sl(u, v) \leq 2\}$, and let $G_2(V, E_2)$ be the subgraph of G_ϕ induced by E_2.
4. Let T_2 be the set of tightening edges, initially set to the empty set.
5. For each vertex v
   (a) Find P_v the path in G_2 from v to $-v$ with the smallest slack, if any. This can be done in $O(m)$ by using a modified breadth-first-search.
   (b) If P_v exists,
      i. Let $wSP(v, -v) = \delta(-v) - \delta(v) + sl(P_v)$.

ii. If $wSP(v, -v)$ is odd, then add the edge $(v, -v)$ to T_2 and assign a weight $w_{T_2}(v, -v) = wSP(v, -v) - 1$.
6. Consider the graph $G_{\phi \cup T_2}$ obtained by adding all the edges in T.
7. Now proceed as in the EqGen-Naive algorithm with $G_{\phi \cup T_2}$ instead of $G_{\phi \cup T}$.

Proposition 8. *When the EqGen algorithm computes $wSP(v, -v)$ in step 5(b)i, the value computed is equal to the weight of the shortest path between v and $-v$.*

Lemma 7. *$G_{\phi \cup T}$ contains a zero weight cycle exactly when $G_{\phi \cup T_2}$ contains a zero weight cycle.*

Proof. Since $G_{\phi \cup T_2}$ is a subgraph of $G_{\phi \cup T}$, one way of the proof is trivial. Suppose $G_{\phi \cup T}$ contains a zero weight cycle C. If C has no tightening edges, then C is a cycle in $G_{\phi \cup T_2}$. Otherwise, let $(u, -u)$ be a tightening edge in C. By Lemma 6, there is a cycle C' in G_ϕ such that $w(C') \leq 2$ and C' contains u and $-u$. Since $sl(C') \leq 2$, all edges in C' have a slack less than or equal to 2, and thus are in E_2. Thus, the EqGen algorithm will add the tightening edge in T_2.

6 Proof Generation

Using the UTVPI decision procedure in a lazy-proof-explication framework requires the procedure to produce proofs whenever it reports the input constraints as unsatisfiable, or whenever it propagates an implied variable equality. This section describes how to generate the proofs for the decision procedure described in this paper.

Both the *NCD-UTVPI* algorithm and the EqGen algorithm rely on two vertices u and v (say) being in the same SCC in an appropriate graph. As a witness for this fact, we need a path from u to v and a path from v to u. We assume that the standard SCC algorithm can be modified to provide this witness [14].

The *NCD-UTVPI* algorithm returns UNSAT in two cases. In the first case, the constraint graph G_ϕ has a negative cycle. By assumption, the negative cycle detection algorithm produces a witness which is the proof of unsatisfiability of the input constraints. In the second case, the algorithm produces a vertex u and $-u$ in the same SCC of G'_ϕ. Applying the transitivity rule along the path from u to $-u$, we have $-2.a.x \leq k$ where $a.x$ is the variable corresponding to u and $k = \delta(-v) - \delta(v)$ is an odd number. By applying the tightening rule, we get $-2.a.x \leq k - 1$. Using the path from $-u$ to u we have $2.a.x \leq -k$ which by tightening we get $2.a.x \leq -k - 1$. This is the proof of the contradiction.

The EqGen algorithm detects zero-weight cycles in the graph $G_{\phi \cup T_2}$. First, every tightening edge in $G_{\phi \cup T_2}$ has a proof involving transitivity along a particular path of odd length, followed by a tightening rule. Also, whenever the EqGen algorithm reports an equality $x = y$, x^+ and y^+ are in the same SCC. The proof of this equality can be inferred along the proof of Lemma 5.

7   Model Generation

In this section, we describe how to generate models for a set of constraints C, when C is satisfiable.

Let ρ be a function that maps each variable to an integer. Let $\preceq$ be a linear order of the variables that appear in C. The assignment ρ is constructed using the following algorithm that assigns values to the variables in the order $\preceq$:

1. Construct the set of UTVPI constraints C^* that is the closure of C under transitivity and tightening.
2. $V_\rho \leftarrow \{\}$.
3. For each variable $x \in V$ in the order $\preceq$:
   (a) Let B_x be the set of constraints of the form $x \leq c$ or $x \geq c$ obtained after evaluating C^* under the current partial assignment ρ.
   (b) Assign $\rho(x)$ to be a value that satisfies all the bounds in B_x.
   (c) $V_\rho \leftarrow V_\rho \cup \{x\}$.
4. Return ρ.

At any point in the above algorithm, ρ has assigned a subset of the variables (V_ρ) in C^* values over integers. For all the variables for which ρ is undefined, $\rho(x) = x$. If ρ be such a partial assignment, let us define C_ρ to be the set of constraints $C \cup \{y = \rho(y) \mid y \in V_\rho\}$. It is easy to see that at any point in the above algorithm, C_ρ implies $x \neq c$ for any $x \in V$ if and only if C_ρ implies either $x < c$ or $x > c$.

Lemma 8. *A set of UTVPI constraints C implies $x \neq d$ for some $d \in \mathcal{Z}$ if and only if C implies $x < d$ or C implies $x > d$.*

Proof. We only prove the "if" direction of this lemma. The proof relies on the following two claims:

1. The set of constraints $C' \doteq C \cup \{x = d\}$ is unsatisfiable (or equivalently $C \Rightarrow x \neq d$) if and only if there is negative cycle in the constraint graph (described in Section 4.1) after adding all the difference constraints for each constraint in C' and all the resulting tightening edges to the graph.
2. Adding $x = d$ to the set C does not imply any new tightening constraints.

The property 1 follows from Lemma 2. Since any tightening constraint for a variable y_1 can only result from two constraints $y_1 - y_2 \leq c_1$ and $y_1 + y_2 \leq c_2$ and the constraint $x = d$ can't give rise to a constraint with two variables (under transitive and tightening steps), the property 2 holds.

Therefore, adding the edges $x^+ - x^- \leq 2.d$ and $x^- - x^+ \leq -2.d$ for the constraint $x = d$ can result in a negative cycle in the difference graph, if and only there is a path from x^- to x^+ of length less than $-2.d$ (that implies $x > d$) or there is a path from x^+ to x^- of length less than $2.d$ (that implies $x < d$).

Lemma 9. *During the step 3a of the above algorithm, the set of constraints C_ρ implies $x \neq c$ if and only if B_x contains either $x \leq d$ with $d < c$ or $x \geq d$ with $d > c$.*

The proof of this lemma follows from Lemma 8.

Theorem 3. *The assignment ρ generated by the algorithm above satisfies all the constraints in C.*

The proof follows from a simple induction on the size of V_ρ. At each point in the algorithm, the assignment ρ and the set of constraints C are consistent.

An easy implementation of the above algorithm can be obtained in $O(n^3)$ time and $O(n^2)$ space by using the algorithm for computing the transitive and tight closure [15,11]. The time complexity can further be improved to $O(n.m + n^2.lg(n))$ by using Johnson's [5] algorithm for performing the all-pair shortest path.

7.1   Model Generation in Nelson-Oppen Framework

For a conjunction of UTVPI constraints C, the assignment ρ computed above satisfies all the constraints in C. However, this is not sufficient to produce a model in the Nelson-Oppen combination framework. We assume that the user is familiar with the high-level description of the Nelson-Oppen combination method [17]. Consider the following example where a formula involves the logic of equality with uninterpreted functions (EUF) and UTVPI constraints.

Let $\psi = (f(x) \neq f(y) \land x \leq y)$ be a formula in the combined theory. Nelson-Oppen framework will add $\psi_1 \doteq f(x) \neq f(y)$ to the EUF theory (T_1) and $\psi_2 \doteq x \leq y$ to the UTVPI theory (T_2). Since there are no equalities implied by either theory, and each theory T_i is consistent with ψ_i, the formula ψ is satisfiable. Now, the UTVPI theory generates the model $\rho \doteq \langle x \mapsto 0, y \mapsto 0 \rangle$ for ψ_2. However, this is not a model for ψ.

To generate an assignment for the variables that are shared across two theories, each theory T_i needs to ensure that the variable assignment ρ for T_i assigns two shared variables x and y equal values if and only if the equality $x = y$ is implied by the constraints in theory T_i.

Definition 1. *For a set of UTVPI constraints C, an assignment ρ for the variables in C is called* diverse, *if for any two variables x and y in $vars(C)$, $\rho(x) = \rho(y)$ if and only if $x = y$ is implied by C.*

We will show that the problem of checking if a set of UTVPI constraints has a diverse model is NP-complete. Clearly, the problem is in NP. We will reduce the following (NP-complete) pipeline scheduling problem to this problem to show NP-hardness.

Theorem 4 (Minimum precedence constrained sequencing with delays [10]). *Given a set T of tasks, a directed acyclic graph $G(T, E)$ defining precedence constraints for the tasks, a positive integer D, and for each task t an integer delay $0 \leq d(t) \leq D$. The problem of determining a one-processor schedule for T that obeys the precedence constraints and delays, within a deadline k, is NP-complete. That is, checking if there exists an injective function for the start times $S : T \rightarrow \mathcal{Z}$ such that for every $(t_i, t_j) \in E$, $S(t_j) - S(t_i) > d(t_i)$, and $S(t_i) \leq k$ for all $t_i \in T$ is NP-complete.*

It is easy to construct a set of UTVPI constraints C such that C has a diverse model if and only if a one-processor schedule for tasks in T exists. Observe that the problem can be mapped to the fragment of UTVPI that contains only $x - y < c$ constraints with positive c.

Corollary 2. *For a given set of constraints $C \doteq \{x_i - y_i < c_i \mid c_i \geq 0\}$, finding a diverse model for C is NP-complete.*

We now show an interesting consequence of Corollary 2 for combining the UTVPI theory with other theories in Nelson-Oppen setting.

7.2   Generating Disjunction of Equalities

To combine the decision procedures of a non-convex theory T_1 (such as UTVPI) with a convex theory T_2 (e.g. EUF) in Nelson-Oppen framework, T_1 needs to infer the *strongest* disjunction of equalities between variables that is implied by the set of T_1 constraints. That is, if C_1 is a set of UTVPI constraints, then we need to generate a disjunction of equalities $\{e_1, \ldots, e_k\}$ over variables such that $C_1 \Rightarrow e_1 \vee \ldots \vee e_k$, and the disjunction of no proper subset of $\{e_1, \ldots, e_k\}$ is implied by C_1.

Theorem 5. *For a set of UTVPI constraints C that does not imply any equality between variables in vars(C), C has a diverse model ρ if and only if C does not imply any disjunction of equalities $\{e_1, \ldots, e_k\}$ (for $k > 1$) over pairs of variables in vars(C).*

Proof. First, let us assume that C implies a disjunction over a minimal set of equalities $\{u_1 = v_1, \ldots, u_k = v_k\}$, for $k > 1$. This means that any model ρ for C is also a model for $C \wedge (u_1 = v_1 \vee \ldots u_k = v_k)$, and therefore must satisfy at least one of the equalities. Hence ρ can't be diverse.

For the other direction, assume that C does not have any diverse models. This implies that for any model ρ of C, there is at least a pair of variables u and v such that $\rho(u) = \rho(v)$. Thus the formula $C \wedge \bigwedge\{u \neq v \mid u \in vars(C), v \in vars(C), u \not\equiv v\}$ does not have any models or is unsatisfiable. Therefore C implies $\bigvee\{u = v \mid u \in vars(C), v \in vars(C), u \not\equiv v\}$. Since none of the equalities in this set (in isolation) is implied by C, there has to be a minimal subset of equalities whose disjunction is implied by C.

The above theorem illustrates that the problem of checking if a set of UTVPI constraints imply a disjunction of equalities over the variables is NP-complete.

References

1. T. Ball, B. Cook, S. K. Lahiri, and L. Zhang. Zapato: Automatic Theorem Proving for Software Predicate Abstraction Refinement. In *Computer Aided Verification (CAV '04)*, LNCS 3114. Springer-Verlag, 2004.
2. T. Ball, R. Majumdar, T. Millstein, and S. K. Rajamani. Automatic predicate abstraction of C programs. In *Programming Language Design and Implementation (PLDI '01)*, Snowbird, Utah, June, 2001. *SIGPLAN Notices*, 36(5), May 2001.

3. R. Bellman. On a routing problem. *Quarterly of Applied Mathematics*, 16(1):87–90, 1958.
4. B. V. Cherkassky and A. V. Goldberg. Negative-cycle detection algorithms. In *European Symposium on Algorithms*, pages 349–363, 1996.
5. T. H. Cormen, C. E. Leiserson, and R. L. Rivest. *Introduction to Algorithms*. MIT Press, 1990.
6. C. Flanagan, R. Joshi, X. Ou, and J. Saxe. Theorem Proving usign Lazy Proof Explication. In *Computer-Aided Verification (CAV 2003)*, LNCS 2725, pages 355–367. Springer-Verlag, 2003.
7. C. Flanagan, K. R. M. Leino, M. Lillibridge, G. Nelson, J. B. Saxe, and R. Stata. Extended static checking for java. In *ACM SIGPLAN Conference on Programming Language Design and Implementation (PLDI'02)*, pages 234–245, 2002.
8. L. R. Ford, Jr., and D. R. Fulkerson. *Flows in Networks*. Princeton University Press, 1962.
9. W. Harvey and P. J. Stuckey. A unit two variable per inequality integer constraint solver for constraint logic programming. In *Proceedings of the 20th Australasian Computer Science Conference (ACSC '97)*, pages 102–111, 1997.
10. J. L. Hennessy and T. R. Gross. Postpass code optimization of pipeline constraints. *ACM Trans. Program. Lang. Syst.*, 5(3):422–448, 1983.
11. J. Jaffar, M. J. Maher, P. J. Stuckey, and H. C. Yap. Beyond Finite Domains. In *Proceedings of the Second International Workshop on Principles and Practice of Constraint Programming, PPCP'94*.
12. J. C. Lagarias. The computational complexity of simultaneous diophantine approximation problems. *SIAM Journal of Computing*, 14(1):196–209, 1985.
13. S. K. Lahiri and R. E. Bryant. Deductive verification of advanced out-of-order microprocessors. In *Computer-Aided Verification (CAV 2003)*, LNCS 2725, pages 341–354. Springer-Verlag, 2003.
14. S. K. Lahiri and M. Musuvathi. An efficient nelson-oppen decision procedure for difference constraints over rationals. Technical Report MSR-TR-2005-61, Microsoft Research, 2005.
15. A. Miné. The octagon abstract domain. In *AST 2001 in WCRE 2001*, IEEE, pages 310–319. IEEE CS Press, October 2001.
16. G. C. Necula and P. Lee. Proof generation in the touchstone theorem prover. In *Conference on Automated Deduction*, LNCS 1831, pages 25–44, 2000.
17. G. Nelson and D. C. Oppen. Simplification by cooperating decision procedures. *ACM Transactions on Programming Languages and Systems (TOPLAS)*, 2(1):245–257, 1979.
18. V. Pratt. Two easy theories whose combination is hard. Technical report, Massachusetts Institute of Technology, Cambridge, Mass., September 1977.
19. S. A. Seshia and R. E. Bryant. Deciding quantifier-free presburger formulas using parameterized solution bounds. In *19th IEEE Symposium of Logic in Computer Science(LICS '04)*. IEEE Computer Society, July 2004.
20. R. E. Tarjan. Depth first search and linear graph algorithms. *SIAM Journal of Computing*, 1(2):146–160, 1972.

Declarative Constraint Programming with Definitional Trees

Rafael del Vado Vírseda*

Dpto. de Sistemas Informáticos y Programación,
Universidad Complutense de Madrid, Spain
rdelvado@sip.ucm.es

Abstract. The new generic scheme $CFLP(\mathcal{D})$ has been recently proposed in [14] as a logical and semantic framework for lazy Constraint
Functional Logic Programming over a parametrically given constraint
domain $\mathcal{D}$. Further, [15] presented a Constrained Lazy Narrowing Calculus $CLNC(\mathcal{D})$ as a convenient computation mechanism for solving
goals for $CFLP(\mathcal{D})$-programs, which was proved sound and strongly
complete with respect to $CFLP(\mathcal{D})$'s semantics. Now, in order to provide a formal foundation for an efficient implementation of goal solving
methods in existing systems such as *Curry* [8] and $\mathcal{TOY}$ [13,6], this paper enriches the $CFLP(\mathcal{D})$ framework by presenting an optimization of
the $CLNC(\mathcal{D})$ calculus by means of definitional trees to efficiently control the computation. We prove that this new Constrained Demanded
Narrowing Calculus $CDNC(\mathcal{D})$ preserves the soundness and completeness properties of $CLNC(\mathcal{D})$ and maintains the good properties shown
for needed and demand-driven narrowing strategies [4,11,17].

1 Introduction

The effort to combine the main lines of research in multiparadigm declarative
programming, namely *Constraint Logic Programming* (*CLP*) [10] and *Functional Logic Programming* (*FLP*) [7], in a unified and suitable framework called
Constrained Functional Logic Programming (*CFLP*), arose around 1990 and has
grown in the last years. Recently, a new generic scheme called $CFLP(\mathcal{D})$ has
been proposed in [14] as a logical and semantic framework for lazy Constraint
Functional Logic Programming over a parametrically given constraint domain $\mathcal{D}$,
which provides a clean and rigorous declarative semantics for *CFLP* languages
as in the $CLP(\mathcal{D})$ scheme, but overcoming some limitations of older *CFLP*
schemes [12,16]. In this setting, $CFLP(\mathcal{D})$-programs are presented as sets of
constrained rewrite rules that define the behavior of possible higher-order and/or
non-deterministic lazy functions over $\mathcal{D}$. The main novelties in [14] were a new
formalization of constraint domains for *CFLP* and a new *Constraint ReWriting
Logic CRWL(\mathcal{D})* parameterized by a constraint domain $\mathcal{D}$, which provides a logical characterization of program semantics. Further, [15] has extended [14] with a

---

* The work of this author has been partially supported by the Spanish National Project
MELODIAS (TIC2002-01167).

B. Gramlich (Ed.): FroCoS 2005, LNAI 3717, pp. 184–199, 2005.

suitable operational semantics, which relies on a new formal notion of constraint solver and a new *Constrained Lazy Narrowing Calculus* $CLNC(\mathcal{D})$ for solving goals for $CFLP(\mathcal{D})$-programs, which can be proved sound and strongly complete w.r.t. $CRWL(\mathcal{D})$'s semantics. These properties qualify $CLNC(\mathcal{D})$ as a convenient computation mechanism for declarative constraint programming languages.

However, efficiency is a major concern for the implementation of $CFLP(\mathcal{D})$ systems, since non-deterministic computations often generate huge search spaces with their associated overheads both in terms of time and space. In the field of functional logic programming languages using lazy narrowing as operational model, *needed narrowing strategies* [4,2,9] and *demand-driven narrowing strategies* [11,17] are known to provide a sound and complete goal solving mechanism while avoiding unneeded computation steps. These strategies are based on *definitional trees*, first introduced in [1], and they have led to efficient implementations of lazy narrowing in existing systems such as *Curry* [8] and $\mathcal{TOY}$ [13,6].

Although *Curry* and $\mathcal{TOY}$ support constraint programming over a few specific domains, general results on the combination of demand/needed lazy narrowing with goal solving are still missing. The aim of the present paper is to provide such results. More precisely, this paper uses definitional trees to design a combination of the *Constrained Lazy Narrowing Calculus* $CLNC(\mathcal{D})$ from [15] and the *Demand-driven Narrowing Calculus* DNC from [17], yielding a new *Constrained Demanded Narrowing Calculus* $CDNC(\mathcal{D})$ over a parametrically given constraint domain $\mathcal{D}$ which can be proved sound and strongly complete w.r.t. $CRWL(\mathcal{D})$'s semantics, contracts needed positions, and maintains the efficiency properties shown for existing demand/needed narrowing strategies.

The organization of this paper is as follow: Section 2 is devoted to summarize the presentation of the $CFLP(\mathcal{D})$ scheme [14,15] and the technical preliminaries need to formalize the notion of definitional tree. Section 3 introduces a refined representation of definitional trees that deals properly with constraints and defines the subclass of $CFLP(\mathcal{D})$-programs used in this work. In Section 4 we give a formal presentation of the calculus $CDNC(\mathcal{D})$, proving soundness and completeness results and sketching optimality. Finally, some conclusions and plans for future work are drawn in Section 5.

2 The Generic Scheme $CFLP(\mathcal{D})$

In this section we introduce some technical preliminaries regarding the basis of the $CFLP(\mathcal{D})$ scheme [14,15] for lazy Constraint Functional Logic Programming over a parametrically given constraint domain $\mathcal{D}$. We will use this scheme as the logical and semantic framework to define our declarative constraint programs and our new Constrained Demanded Narrowing Calculus with definitional trees.

2.1 Expressions and Patterns

We briefly introduce the syntax of applicative expressions and patterns, which is needed for understanding the construction of constraint domains and solvers.

We assume a *universal signature* $\Sigma = \langle DC, FS \rangle$, where $DC = \bigcup_{n \in \mathbb{N}} DC^n$ and $FS = \bigcup_{n \in \mathbb{N}} FS^n$ are families of countably infinite and mutually disjoint sets of *data constructors* resp. *evaluable function symbols*, each one with an associated arity. Evaluable functions can be further classified into domain dependent *primitive functions* $PF^n \subseteq FS^n$ and user *defined functions* $DF^n = FS^n \setminus PF^n$ for each $n \in \mathbb{N}$. We write $\Sigma_\perp$ for the result of extending DC^0 with the special symbol $\perp$, intended to denote an undefined data value. As notational conventions, we use $c, d \in DC$, $f, g \in FS$ and $h \in DC \cup FS$, and we define the *arity* of $h \in DC^n \cup FS^n$ as $ar(h) = n$. We also assume that DC^0 includes the three constants *true*, *false* and *success*, which are useful for representing the results returned by various primitive functions. Next we assume a countably infinite set $\mathcal{V}$ of *variables* $X, Y, \ldots$ and a set $\mathcal{U}$ of *primitive elements* $u, v, \ldots$ (as e.g. the set $\mathbb{R}$ of the real numbers) mutually disjoint and disjoint from $\Sigma_\perp$. *Partial expressions* $e \in Exp_\perp(\mathcal{U})$ have the following syntax:

$$e ::= \perp \mid u \mid X \mid h \mid (e \, e_1)$$

where $u \in \mathcal{U}$, $X \in \mathcal{V}$, $h \in DC \cup FS$. Following a usual convention, we assume that application associates to the left, and we use the notation $(e \, \overline{e}_n)$ to abbreviate $(e \, e_1 \ldots e_n)$. The set of variables occurring in e is written $var(e)$. An expression e is called *linear* iff there is no $X \in var(e)$ having more than one occurrence in e. The following classification of expressions is also useful: $(X \, \overline{e}_m)$, with $X \in \mathcal{V}$ and $m \geq 0$, is called a *flexible expression*, while $u \in \mathcal{U}$ and $(h \, \overline{e}_m)$ with $h \in DC \cup FS$ are called *rigid expressions*. Moreover, a rigid expression $(h \, \overline{e}_m)$ is called *active* iff $h \in FS$ and $m \geq ar(h)$, and *passive* otherwise. The occurrence of a symbol is *passive* iff is a primite element $u \in \mathcal{U}$ or is the root symbol h of a passive expression (a symbol, as used in this sense, is called a *passive symbol*). Some interesting subsets of $Exp_\perp(\mathcal{U})$ are: $GExp_\perp(\mathcal{U})$, the set of the *ground* expressions e such that $var(e) = \emptyset$ and $Exp(\mathcal{U})$, the set of the *total* expressions e with no occurrences of $\perp$. Another important subclass of expressions is the set of *partial patterns* $s, t \in Pat_\perp(\mathcal{U})$, whose syntax is defined as follows:

$$t ::= \perp \mid u \mid X \mid c \, \overline{t}_m \mid f \, \overline{t}_m$$

where $u \in \mathcal{U}$, $X \in \mathcal{V}$, $c \in DC^n$, $m \leq n$, $f \in FS^n$, $m < n$. The subsets $Pat(\mathcal{U})$, $GPat_\perp(\mathcal{U}) \subseteq Pat_\perp(\mathcal{U})$ consisting of the *total* and *ground* patterns, respectively, are defined in the natural way. We define the *information ordering* $\sqsubseteq$ as the least partial ordering over $Pat_\perp(\mathcal{U})$ satisfying the following properties: $\perp \sqsubseteq t$ for all $t \in Pat_\perp(\mathcal{U})$, and $(h \, \overline{t}_m) \sqsubseteq (h \, \overline{t'}_m)$ whenever these two expressions are patterns and $t_i \sqsubseteq t'_i$ for all $1 \leq i \leq m$.

2.2   Substitutions

As usual, we define *substitutions* $\sigma \in Sub_\perp(\mathcal{U})$ as mappings $\sigma : \mathcal{V} \to Pat_\perp(\mathcal{U})$ extended to $\sigma : Exp_\perp(\mathcal{U}) \to Exp_\perp(\mathcal{U})$ in the natural way. By convention, we write ε for the identity substitution, $e\sigma$ instead of $\sigma(e)$, and $\sigma\theta$ for the composition of σ and θ, such that $e(\sigma\theta) = (e\sigma)\theta$ for any $e \in Exp_\perp(\mathcal{U})$. We define the *domain* and the *variable range* of a substitution in the usual way, namely: $dom(\sigma) = \{X \in \mathcal{V} \mid \sigma(X) \neq X\}$ and $ran(\sigma) = \bigcup_{X \in dom(\sigma)} var(\sigma(X))$. As usual, a substitution σ such that $dom(\sigma) \cap ran(\sigma) = \emptyset$ is called *idempotent*. For any set of variables $\mathcal{X} \subseteq \mathcal{V}$ we define the *restriction* $\sigma \lceil_{\mathcal{X}}$ as the substitution σ' such that $dom(\sigma') = \mathcal{X}$ and $\sigma'(X) = \sigma(X)$ for all $X \in \mathcal{X}$. We use the notation $\sigma =_{\mathcal{X}} \theta$ to indicate that $\sigma \lceil_{\mathcal{X}} = \theta \lceil_{\mathcal{X}}$, and we abbreviate $\sigma =_{\mathcal{V} \backslash \mathcal{X}} \theta$ as $\sigma =_{\backslash \mathcal{X}} \theta$. An expression e' is an *instance* of e if there is a substitution σ with $e' = e\sigma$. In this case we write $e \preceq e'$. An expression e' is a *variant* of e if $e \preceq e'$ and $e' \preceq e$.

2.3   Positions

To manipulate expressions and patterns we give the following definitions. An *occurrence* or *position* is a sequence p of positive integers identifying a subexpression in an expression. For every expression e, the set $Pos(e)$ of *positions* in e is inductively defined as follow: the empty sequence denoted by ϵ, identifies e itself. For every expression of the form $h\overline{e}_m$, the sequence $i \cdot q$, where i is a positive integer not greater than n and q is a position, identifies the subexpression of e_i at q. The subexpression of e at p is denoted by $e|_p$ and the result of *replacing* $e|_p$ with e' in e is denoted by $e[e']_p$. The expression $p \cdot q$ denotes the position resulting from the concatenation of the positions p and q. If e is a linear expression, $pos(X, e)$ will be used for the position of the variable X occurring in e.

2.4   Constraints over a Given Constraint Domain

Now we are ready to give a short summary of the generic $CFLP(\mathcal{D})$ scheme by introducing the essential notions of constraint domain $\mathcal{D}$, constraints and constraint solver over $\mathcal{D}$ which are needed for this work. Additional explanations and examples can be found in [14].

Definition 1 (constraint domain). *A constraint domain is any structure* $\mathcal{D} = \langle D_{\mathcal{U}}, \{p^{\mathcal{D}} \mid p \in PF\}, Solve^{\mathcal{D}} \rangle$ *such that the carrier set* $D_{\mathcal{U}} = GPat_{\perp}(\mathcal{U})$ *coincides with the set of ground patterns for some set of primitive elements* $\mathcal{U}$, *the interpretation* $p^{\mathcal{D}} \subseteq D_{\mathcal{U}}^n \times D_{\mathcal{U}}$ *of each* $p \in PF^n$ *(we use the notation* $p^{\mathcal{D}} \overline{t}_n \rightarrow t$ *to indicate that* $(\overline{t}_n, t) \in p^{\mathcal{D}}$ *) satisfies* monotonicity, antimonotonicity *and* radicality *requirements (see [14] for details) and* $Solve^{\mathcal{D}}$ *is a constraint solver, whose expected behavior will be explained in Definition 4 below.*

Assuming an arbitrarily fixed constraint domain $\mathcal{D}$ built over a certain set of primitive elements $\mathcal{U}$ (as e.g. the set $\mathbb{R}$ of the real numbers), we will now define the syntax and semantics of constraints over $\mathcal{D}$ used in this work.

Definition 2 (constraints over a constraint domain).

1. *Primitive Constraints have the syntactic form* $p\overline{t}_n \rightarrow! t$, *with* $p \in PF^n$, $\overline{t}_n \in Pat_{\perp}(\mathcal{U})$ *and* $t \in Pat(\mathcal{U})$ *(for example, addition constraints* $X + Y \rightarrow!$ R *or comparison constraints* $X > 0 \rightarrow!$ *true over* $\mathbb{R}$). *The special constants* $\triangle$ *and* $\blacktriangle$ *are also primitive constraints.*

2. *Constraints have the syntactic form* $p\overline{e}_n \rightarrow! t$, *with* $p \in PF^n$, $\overline{e}_n \in Exp_{\perp}(\mathcal{U})$ *and* $t \in Pat(\mathcal{U})$ *(i.e. possibly including occurrences of user defined function symbols). The special constants* $\triangle$ *and* $\blacktriangle$ *are also constraints.*

In the sequel we use the notation $PCon_\perp(\mathcal{D})$ for the set of all the primitive constraints π over $\mathcal{D}$ and we reserve the capital letters Π and S for sets of primitive constraints, often interpreted as conjunctions. The semantics of primitive constraints depends on the notion of solution, presented in the next definition.

Definition 3 (primitive semantic notions).

1. *The set of* valuations *over $\mathcal{D}$ is defined as the set of ground substitutions $Val_\perp(\mathcal{D}) = GSub_\perp(\mathcal{U})$. The set of* solutions *of $\pi \in PCon_\perp(\mathcal{D})$ is a subset $Sol_\mathcal{D}(\pi) \subseteq Val_\perp(\mathcal{D})$ defined as follows: $Sol_\mathcal{D}(\triangle) = Val_\perp(\mathcal{D})$, $Sol_\mathcal{D}(\blacktriangle) = \emptyset$ and $Sol_\mathcal{D}(p\,\bar{t}_n \rightarrow!\,t) = \{\eta \in Val_\perp(\mathcal{D}) \mid t\eta \text{ is total and } p^\mathcal{D}\,\bar{t}_n\eta \rightarrow t\eta\}$. The set of* solutions *of $\Pi \subseteq PCon_\perp(\mathcal{D})$ is defined as $Sol_\mathcal{D}(\Pi) = \bigcap_{\pi \in \Pi} Sol_\mathcal{D}(\pi)$.*

2. *Π is called* satisfiable *in $\mathcal{D}$ (in symbols, $Sat_\mathcal{D}(\Pi)$) iff $Sol_\mathcal{D}(\Pi) \neq \emptyset$. Otherwise Π is called* unsatisfiable *(in symbols, $Unsat_\mathcal{D}(\Pi)$).*

3. *π is a* consequence *of Π in $\mathcal{D}$ (in symbols, $\Pi \models_\mathcal{D} \pi$) iff $Sol_\mathcal{D}(\Pi) \subseteq Sol_\mathcal{D}(\pi)$. In particular, $p\,\bar{t}_n \rightarrow!\,t$ is a consequence of Π in $\mathcal{D}$ (in symbols, $\Pi \models_\mathcal{D} p\,\bar{t}_n \rightarrow!\,t$) iff $p^\mathcal{D}\,\bar{t}_n\eta \rightarrow t\eta$ with $t\eta$ total holds for all $\eta \in Sol_\mathcal{D}(\Pi)$.*

Finally, we describe the behavior of the constraint solver $Solve^\mathcal{D}$ introduced in *Definition 1* as the basis of our new goal solving mechanism. This notion of solver was first introduced in [15] w.r.t the semantics given in the previous definition.

Definition 4 (constraint solver over $\mathcal{D}$).

1. *We say that a variable $X \in \mathcal{V}$ is* demanded *by a set of total primitive constraints $\Pi \subseteq PCon(\mathcal{D})$ iff $\mu(X) \neq \perp$ holds for every $\mu \in Sol_\mathcal{D}(\Pi)$. We write $dvar_\mathcal{D}(\Pi)$ for the set of the variables demanded by Π. For practical constraint domains, $dvar_\mathcal{D}(\Pi)$ is expected to be computable (see [15]).*

2. *A constraint solver over a constraint domain $\mathcal{D}$ is formalized by a function $Solve^\mathcal{D}$ expecting as parameters a finite set $S \subseteq PCon(\mathcal{D})$ of total primitive constraints (called the* constraint store*) and a finite set of variables $\chi \subseteq \mathcal{V}$ (called the set of* protected variables*). The solver is expected to return a finite disjunction of alternatives $Solve^\mathcal{D}(S,\chi) = \bigvee_{i=1}^{k}(S_i \,\square\, \sigma_i)$, where $\square$ must be interpreted as conjunction, and satisfying the following requirements:*

   (a) *Each $S_i \subseteq PCon(\mathcal{D})$ is in χ-solved form (i.e. $Solve^\mathcal{D}(S_i,\chi) = S_i\,\square\,\varepsilon$). Furthermore, either all the protected variables disappear or some protected variable becomes demanded (i.e. $var(S_i) \cap \chi = \emptyset$ or else $dvar_\mathcal{D}(S_i) \cap \chi \neq \emptyset$).*

   (b) *Each $\sigma_i \in Sub(\mathcal{U})$ is an idempotent total substitution that cannot bind protected variables (i.e. $dom(\sigma_i) \cap var(S_i) = \emptyset$ and $\chi \cap (dom(\sigma_i) \cup ran(\sigma_i)) = \emptyset$).*

   (c) *No solution is lost by the constraint solver and the solution space associated to each alternative is included in the one of the input constraint store (i.e. $Sol_\mathcal{D}(S) = \bigcup_{i=1}^{k} Sol_\mathcal{D}(S_i\,\square\,\sigma_i)$).*

   In the case $k = 0$, $\bigvee_{i=1}^{k}(S_i\,\square\,\sigma_i)$ is understood as $\blacktriangle$. In this case, $Sol_\mathcal{D}(S) \subseteq Sol_\mathcal{D}(\blacktriangle) = \emptyset$ means failure detection. More details on the working of constraint solvers will be given in Section 4.

Example 1 (The constraint domain $\mathcal{H}_{seq}$). We consider the simple constraint domain $\mathcal{H}_{seq}$, analogous to the extension of the Herbrand Domain with equality and disequality constraints, built over an empty set of primitive elements and having the strict equality seq as its only primitive, interpreted to behave as follows: $seq^{\mathcal{H}_{seq}} t\ t \to true$ for all total $t \in GPat(\emptyset)$; $seq^{\mathcal{H}_{seq}} t\ s \to false$ for all $t, s \in GPat_{\perp}(\emptyset)$ such that t, s have no common upper bound w.r.t. the information ordering $\sqsubseteq$; $seq^{\mathcal{H}_{seq}} t\ s \to \perp$ otherwise. In the sequel, $t == s$ abbreviates the equality constraint $seq\ t\ s \to!\ true$ and $t\ /= s$ abbreviates the disequality constraint $seq\ t\ s \to!\ false$. A constraint solver $Solve^{\mathcal{H}_{seq}}$ for this domain can be found in [15]. Further examples of other interesting constraint domains known for their practical value in constraint programming (real numbers, finite domains, etc) can be found in [14]. All the results of this paper are valid for any arbitrary constraint domain $\mathcal{D}$ satisfying *Definition 1*.

3 $CFLP(\mathcal{D})$-Programs with Definitional Trees

The class of so-called $COISS(\mathcal{D})$-programs with constraints and definitional trees used in this work is a proper subclass of the generic $CFLP(\mathcal{D})$-programs presented in [14,15]. In this section we discuss $COISS(\mathcal{D})$-programs and their intended semantics.

3.1   Overlapping Definitional Trees with Constraints

In the sequel we assume an arbitrarily fixed constraint domain $\mathcal{D}$ built over a set of primitive elements $\mathcal{U}$. In this setting, $CFLP(\mathcal{D})$-*programs* are presented as sets of constrained rewrite rules that define the behavior of possibly higher-order and/or non-deterministic lazy functions over $\mathcal{D}$, called *program rules*. More precisely, a program rule R for $f \in DF^n$ has the form $R : f\ \bar{t}_n \to r \Leftarrow P \,\square\, C$ (abbreviated as $f\ \bar{t}_n \to r$ if P and C are both empty) and is required to satisfy the three conditions listed below:

1. The *left-hand side* $f\ \bar{t}_n$ is a linear expression, and for all $1 \leq i \leq n$, $t_i \in Pat(\mathcal{U})$ are total patterns. The *right-hand side* $r \in Exp(\mathcal{U})$ is also total.
2. P is a finite sequence of so-called *productions* of the form $e_i \to R_i$ $(1 \leq i \leq k)$, intended to be interpreted as conjunction of local definitions, and fulfilling the following two *admissibility conditions*:
   (a) For all $1 \leq i \leq k$, $e_i \in Exp(\mathcal{U})$ is a total expression, R_i is a different variable, and $R_i \notin var(f\ \bar{t}_n)$.
   (b) It is possible to reorder the productions of P in the form $P \equiv e_1 \to R_1, \ldots, e_k \to R_k$ where $R_j \notin var(e_i)$ for all $1 \leq i \leq j \leq k$ *(no cycles)*.
3. C is a finite set of total constraints, also intended to be interpreted as conjunction, and possibly including occurrences of defined function symbols.

Example 2. The following $CFLP(\mathcal{D})$-program can be used over the constraint domain $\mathcal{H}_{seq}$ presented in *Example 1*. We use the constructors $0 \in DC^0$, $s \in DC^1$, and a Prolog-like syntax for list constructors (i.e. [ ] denotes the empty list

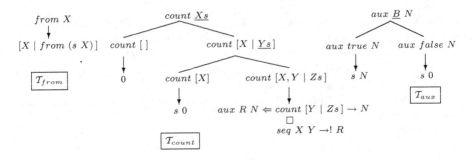

Fig. 1. Constrained definitional trees for *from*, *count* and *aux*

and $[X|Xs]$ denotes a non-empty list consisting of a first element X and a remaining list Xs). More examples of $CFLP(\mathcal{D})$-programs can be found in [14,15].

$$from\ X \to [X\ |\ from\ (s\ X)] \qquad \text{\% increasing infinite list } from \text{ starting value } X$$

$$
\begin{aligned}
count\ [] &\to 0 &&\text{\% } counting \text{ consecutive and repetitive values from}\\
count\ [X] &\to s\ 0 &&\text{\% the head of a list until finding a different value}\\
count\ [X,Y|Zs] &\to aux\ R\ N \quad \Leftarrow\quad count\ [Y|Zs] \quad\to\quad N\ \square\ seq\ X\ Y \quad\to!\ R
\end{aligned}
$$

$$
\begin{aligned}
aux\ true\ \ N &\to s\ N\\
aux\ false\ N &\to s\ 0
\end{aligned}
$$

The class of $COISS(\mathcal{D})$-programs is defined as the subclass of $CFLP(\mathcal{D})$-programs whose defining rules can be organized in a hierarchical structure called *definitional tree* [1]. More precisely, we choose to reformulate the notions presented in [2,3,17] about *overlapping definitional trees* and *conditional overlapping inductively sequential systems*, including now constrained rules over a generic constraint domain $\mathcal{D}$.

Definition 5 (definitional trees with constraints).
Let $\mathcal{P}$ be a $CFLP(\mathcal{D})$-program over a given constraint domain $\mathcal{D}$. A call pattern is any linear pattern of the form $f\bar{t}_n$, where $f \in DF^n$ and $\bar{t}_n \in Pat_\perp(\mathcal{U})$. $\mathcal{T}$ is a constrained Definitional Tree over $\mathcal{D}$ (cDT($\mathcal{D}$) for short) with call pattern τ iff its depth is finite and one of the following cases holds:

- *$\mathcal{T} \equiv \underline{rule}(\tau \to r_1 \Leftarrow P_1 \,\square\, C_1| \ldots |r_m \Leftarrow P_m \,\square\, C_m)$, where $\tau \to r_i \Leftarrow P_i \,\square\, C_i$ for all $1 \le i \le m$ is a variant of a program rule in $\mathcal{P}$.*

- *$\mathcal{T} \equiv \underline{case}(\tau, X, [\mathcal{T}_1, \ldots, \mathcal{T}_k])$, where X is a variable in τ, $h_1, \ldots, h_k$ $(k > 0)$ are pairwise different passive symbols of $\mathcal{P}$, and for all $1 \le i \le k$, $\mathcal{T}_i$ is a cDT($\mathcal{D}$) with call pattern $\tau\sigma_i$, where $\sigma_i = \{X \mapsto h_i\overline{Y}_{m_i}\}$ with $\overline{Y}_{m_i}$ new distinct variables such that $h_i\overline{Y}_{m_i} \in Pat(\mathcal{U})$.*

We represent a cDT($\mathcal{D}$) $\mathcal{T}$ with call pattern τ using the notation $\mathcal{T}_\tau$. A cDT($\mathcal{D}$) of a function symbol $f \in DF^n$ defined by $\mathcal{P}$ is a cDT($\mathcal{D}$) $\mathcal{T}$ with call pattern $f\overline{X}_n$, where $\overline{X}_n$ are new variables. We represent it using the notation $\mathcal{T}_f$.

Definition 6 ($COISS(\mathcal{D})$-programs).

1. *A function symbol $f \in DF^n$ is called* constrained overlapping inductively sequential *w.r.t. a $CFLP(\mathcal{D})$-program $\mathcal{P}$ iff there exists a $cDT(\mathcal{D})$ $\mathcal{T}_f$ of f such that the collection of all the program rules $\tau \to r_i \Leftarrow P_i \,\square\, C_i$ ($1 \le i \le m$) obtained from the different nodes $\underline{rule}(\tau \to r_1 \Leftarrow P_1 \,\square\, C_1 | \ldots | r_m \Leftarrow P_m \,\square\, C_m)$ occurring in $\mathcal{T}_f$ equals, up to variants, the collection of all the program rules in $\mathcal{P}$ whose left hand side has the root symbol f.*

2. *A $CFLP(\mathcal{D})$-program $\mathcal{P}$ is called a* Constrained Overlapping Inductively Sequential System over $\mathcal{D}$ *(shortly, $COISS(\mathcal{D})$) iff each function defined by $\mathcal{P}$ is constrained overlapping inductively sequential.*

As a concrete example, we consider the $CFLP(\mathcal{H}_{seq})$-program given in *Example 2*. From the definitional trees illustrated by the pictures given in *Figure 1*, it is easy to check that this program is a $COISS(\mathcal{H}_{seq})$. For example, the defined function symbol *count* has the following definitional tree $\mathcal{T}_{count}$:

$\underline{case}\ (count\ Xs, Xs, [$
 $\underline{rule}\ (count\ [\,] \to 0),$
 $\underline{case}\ (count\ [X|Ys], Ys, [$
  $\underline{rule}\ (count\ [X] \to s\ 0),$
  $\underline{rule}\ (count\ [X, Y|Zs] \to aux\ R\ N \Leftarrow count\ [Y|Zs] \to N \,\square\, seq\ X\ Y \to!\ R)\,]\,)\,]\,)$

3.2   The Constraint ReWriting Logic $CRWL(\mathcal{D})$

The *Constraint ReWriting Logic $CRWL(\mathcal{D})$*, parameterized by a constraint domain $\mathcal{D}$ over a set of primitive elements $\mathcal{U}$ and formalized by means of a constrained rewriting calculus, was introduced in [14] in order to provide a declarative semantic for $CFLP(\mathcal{D})$-programs. Now, in order to use $CRWL(\mathcal{D})$ as a logical framework for the semantics of $COISS(\mathcal{D})$-programs, we must first introduce the two possible kinds of constrained statements (*c-statements*) that we intend to derive from a given $COISS(\mathcal{D})$-program:

- *c-productions* of the form $e \to t \Leftarrow \Pi$, where $e \in Exp_\perp(\mathcal{U})$, $t \in Pat_\perp(\mathcal{U})$ and $\Pi \subseteq PCon_\perp(\mathcal{D})$.

- *c-constraints* of the form $p\,\bar{e}_n \to!\,t \Leftarrow \Pi$, with $p \in PF^n$, $\bar{e}_n \in Exp_\perp(\mathcal{U})$, $t \in Pat(\mathcal{U})$ and $\Pi \subseteq PCon_\perp(\mathcal{D})$.

The purpose of the calculus $CRWL(\mathcal{D})$ is to infer the semantic validity of arbitrary c-statements φ from the program rules in $\mathcal{P}$. We write $\mathcal{P} \vdash_\mathcal{D} \varphi$ to indicate that the c-statement φ can be derived from $\mathcal{P}$ in the constrained rewriting calculus $CRWL(\mathcal{D})$ using the set of inference rules given in [14,15]. Useful properties and correctness results relating $CRWL(\mathcal{D})$-derivability to a suitable model-theoretic semantics are also given in [14].

4   Constrained Lazy Narrowing with Definitional Trees

In this section we present a *Constrained Demanded Narrowing Calculus* (shortly, $CDNC(\mathcal{D})$) over $COISS(\mathcal{D})$-programs. For our discussion of this new calculus with definitional trees we are going to combine the ideas and techniques underlying the $CLNC(\mathcal{D})$ calculus in [15] (with generic constraints but no definitional trees) and the DNC calculus in [17] (with definitional trees but no generic constraints). The general idea is to ensure the computation of answers from goals which are correct with respect to $CRWL(\mathcal{D})$'s semantics, while using definitional trees in a similar way to [4] to ensure that all the constrained lazy narrowing steps performed during the computation are needed ones. We give first a precise definition for the class of admissible goals and answers that we are going to use.

4.1   Admissible Goals and Answers

A *goal* for a $COISS(\mathcal{D})$-program must have the form $G \equiv \exists \overline{U}.P \,\square\, C \,\square\, S \,\square\, \sigma$, where the symbol $\square$ must be interpreted as conjunction, and:

- $\overline{U} =_{def} evar(G)$ is the set of so-called *existential variables* of the goal G. These are intermediate variables, whose bindings may be partial patterns.
- $P \equiv e_1 \rightarrow R_1, \ldots, e_n \rightarrow R_n$ is a finite conjunction of productions where each R_i is a distinct variable and e_i is an expression or a pair of the form $< \tau, \mathcal{T} >$, where τ is an instance of the pattern in the root of a $cDT(\mathcal{D})$ $\mathcal{T}$. Those productions $e \rightarrow R$ whose left hand side e is simply an expression are called *suspensions*, while those whose left hand side is of the form $< \tau, \mathcal{T} >$ are called *demanded productions*. The set of *produced variables* of G is defined as $pvar(P) =_{def} \{R_1, \ldots, R_n\}$ and we define the *production relation* $X \gg_P Y$ iff there is some $1 \leq i \leq n$ such that $X \in var(e_i)$ and $Y \equiv R_i$.
- $C \equiv \delta_1, \ldots, \delta_k$ is a finite conjunction of total constraints (possibly including occurrences of defined function symbols).
- $S \equiv \pi_1, \ldots, \pi_l$ is a finite conjunction of total primitive constraints, called *constraint store*.
- σ is an idempotent substitution called *answer substitution* such that $dom(\sigma) \cap var(P \,\square\, C \,\square\, S) = \emptyset$.

Additionally, any *admissible goal* must satisfy the same admissibility conditions given in [15] about produced variables plus a new admissibility condition for definitional trees:

DT *For each demanded production* $< \tau, \mathcal{T} > \rightarrow R$ *in* P, *the variable* R *is demanded (i.e.* $R \in dvar_{\mathcal{D}}(G)$ *in the sense of* Definition 7*), and the variables in* $\mathcal{T}$ *not occur in other place of the goal.*

Similarly to [17,15], $CDNC(\mathcal{D})$ uses a notion of *demanded variable* to deal with lazy evaluation, but now in this work w.r.t. a constraint store, higher-order and definitional trees.

Definition 7. *Let* $G \equiv \exists \overline{U}.\ P \,\square\, C \,\square\, S \,\square\, \sigma$ *be an admissible goal for a given* $COISS(\mathcal{D})$-*program and* $X \in var(G)$. *We say that* X *is a* demanded variable *in* G *iff one of the following cases holds:*

- $X \in dvar_{\mathcal{D}}(S)$ *(see item 1 in* Definition 4*).*
- *there exists some suspension* $(X\overline{a}_k \to R) \in P$ *such that* $k > 0$ *and* R *is a demanded variable in* G.
- *there exists some demanded production* $(< e, \underline{case}\ (\tau, Y, [\mathcal{T}_1, \ldots, \mathcal{T}_k]) > \to R) \in P$ *such that* $X = e|_{pos(Y,\tau)}$ *and* R *is a demanded variable in* G.

We write $dvar_{\mathcal{D}}(G)$ *(or more precisely* $dvar_{\mathcal{D}}(P \square S)$*) for the set of demanded variables in the goal* G.

An admissible goal $G \equiv \exists \overline{U}.\ P \square C \square S \square \sigma$ is called a *solved goal* iff P and C are empty and S is in $\emptyset$-solved form in the sense of item 2.(a) in *Definition 4*. An *initial goal* can be any admissible goal.

Definition 8. *An* answer *for an admissible goal* $G \equiv \exists \overline{U}.\ P \square C \square S \square \sigma$ *and a given* $COISS(\mathcal{D})$-*program* $\mathcal{P}$, *must have the form* $\Pi \square \theta$, *where* $\Pi \subseteq PCon(\mathcal{D})$ *is a finite conjunction of total primitive constraints,* $\theta \in Sub_{\perp}(\mathcal{U})$ *is an idempotent substitution such that* $dom(\theta) \cap var(\Pi) = \emptyset$, *and there is some substitution* $\theta' =_{\backslash evar(G)} \theta$ *fulfilling the following three conditions:*

- $\mathcal{P} \vdash_{\mathcal{D}} (P \square C)\theta' \Leftarrow \Pi$ *in* $CRWL(\mathcal{D})$ *(for demanded productions* $(< \tau, \mathcal{T} > \to R) \in P$, *we consider just* $\mathcal{P} \vdash_{\mathcal{D}} \tau\theta' \to \theta'(R) \Leftarrow \Pi$, *because definitional trees are only used to control the computation),*
- $\Pi \models_{\mathcal{D}} S\theta'$ *(i.e.,* $Sol_{\mathcal{D}}(\Pi) \subseteq Sol_{\mathcal{D}}(S\theta')$*) according to item 3 in* Definition 3*),*
- $X\theta' \equiv t\theta'$ *for each binding* $X \mapsto t \in \sigma$, *abbreviated as* $\theta' \in Sol(\sigma)$.

We write $Ans_{\mathcal{P}}(G)$ *for the set of all answers for* G. *An answer* $\Pi \square \theta \in Ans_{\mathcal{P}}(G)$ *is called* trivial *iff* $Unsat_{\mathcal{D}}(\Pi)$ *and* non-trivial *otherwise. Moreover, we can relate goals and answers by extending the notion of solution introduced in* Definition 3.

Definition 9. *Let* $G \equiv \exists \overline{U}.\ P \square C \square S \square \sigma$ *be an admissible goal for a given* $COISS(\mathcal{D})$-*program* $\mathcal{P}$. *We say that a valuation* $\mu \in Val_{\perp}(\mathcal{D})$ *is a solution of* G *iff* $(\emptyset \square \mu) \in Ans_{\mathcal{P}}(G)$. *We write* $Sol_{\mathcal{P}}(G)$ *for the set of all solutions for* G. *Analogously, we define the set of solutions for an answer* $\Pi \square \theta$ *as* $Sol_{\mathcal{D}}(\Pi \square \theta) =_{def} \{\mu \in Val_{\perp}(\mathcal{D}) \mid \mu \in Sol_{\mathcal{D}}(\Pi) \cap Sol(\theta)\}$.

The next new result is useful to prove the main properties about $CDNC(\mathcal{D})$ and shows that $CRWL(\mathcal{D})$'s semantics does not accept an undefined value for demanded variables, identifying demanded and needed computation steps in derivations.

Lemma 1 (Demand Lemma).
If $\Pi \square \theta$ *is a non-trivial answer of an admissible goal* G *for a* $COISS(\mathcal{D})$-*program and* $X \in dvar_{\mathcal{D}}(G)$ *then* $\theta'(X) \neq \perp$ *for all* $\theta' =_{\backslash evar(G)} \theta$ *given by* Definition 8.

Proof. Let $\Pi \square \theta \in Ans_{\mathcal{P}}(G)$ non-trivial (i.e., $Sol_{\mathcal{D}}(\Pi) \neq \emptyset$). By *Definition 8*, there exits $\Pi \square \theta' \in Ans_{\mathcal{P}}(G)$ such that $\theta =_{\backslash evar(G)} \theta'$. We prove that $\theta'(X) \neq \perp$ reasoning by induction on the order $\gg_P^+$ (the transitive closure of the production relation (see [15] for details) is well-founded due to the property of non-cycles between produced variables in admissible goals). We consider three cases for $X \in dvar_{\mathcal{D}}(G)$ according to *Definition 7*:

- $X \in dvar_{\mathcal{D}}(S)$:
  We suppose that $\theta'(X) = \bot$ and let $\mu \in Sol_{\mathcal{D}}(\Pi)$. By *Definition 8*, $\Pi \models_{\mathcal{D}} S\theta'$, and then $\theta'\mu \in Sol_{\mathcal{D}}(S)$ and $\mu(\theta'(X)) = \mu(\bot) = \bot$. However, since $X \in dvar_{\mathcal{D}}(S)$ and according to item 1 in *Definition 4*, it follows that $\mu(\theta'(X)) \neq \bot$. Therefore, $\theta'(X) \neq \bot$.

- $(X\overline{a}_k \to R) \in P$ with $k > 0$ and $R \in dvar_{\mathcal{D}}(G)$:
  Since $X \gg_P^+ R$ and $R \in dvar_{\mathcal{D}}(G)$, by *induction hypothesis* $\theta'(R) \neq \bot$. By *Definition 8*, $\mathcal{P} \vdash_{\mathcal{D}} \theta'(X)\overline{a_k\theta'} \to \theta'(R) \Leftarrow \Pi$. However, since $k > 0$, it is only possible in $CRWL(\mathcal{D})$ if $\theta'(X) \neq \bot$.

- $X = e|_{pos(Y,\tau)}$, $(< e, \underline{case}(\tau, Y, [\mathcal{T}_1, \ldots, \mathcal{T}_k]) > \to R) \in P$ and $R \in dvar_{\mathcal{D}}(G)$:
  In this case, $e = f\overline{e}_n$ with $f \in DF^n$. Since $X = e|_{pos(Y,\tau)}$, it follows that $X \gg_P^+ R$. Moreover, since $R \in dvar_{\mathcal{D}}(G)$, by *induction hypothesis* $\theta'(R) \neq \bot$. By *Definition 8* and the rule $\mathbf{DF}_{\mathcal{P}}$ of the $CRWL(\mathcal{D})$ calculus [14], $\mathcal{P} \vdash_{\mathcal{D}} f\ \overline{e_n\theta'} \to \theta'(R) \Leftarrow \Pi$ using $(f\overline{t'}_n \to r \Leftarrow P \sqcap C) \in [\mathcal{P}]_{\bot}$ and deductions $\mathcal{P} \vdash_{\mathcal{D}} e_i\theta' \to t_i' \Leftarrow \Pi$ for all $1 \leq i \leq n$. On the other hand, $pos(Y,\tau) = i \cdot p$ with $1 \leq i \leq n$ and $p \in Pos(e_i)$ because $\tau \preceq e$. Due to the form of the definitional tree $\underline{case}$ (see *Definition 5*), t_i' has a passive symbol h_j $(1 \leq j \leq k)$ in the position p. Moreover, there must be only passive symbols above h_j in t_i'. Hence, $t_i' \neq \bot$. Moreover, since $\tau \preceq e$ with $X = e_i|_p$, there must be the same passive symbols and in the same order above $\theta'(X)$ in the position p of $e_i\theta'$. It follows that $\mathcal{P} \vdash_{\mathcal{D}} e_i\theta' \to t_i' \Leftarrow \Pi$ applies the $CRWL(\mathcal{D})$-rule of decomposition $\mathbf{DC}$ in the $CRWL(\mathcal{D})$ calculus [14] to yield $\mathcal{P} \vdash_{\mathcal{D}} \theta'(X) \to h_j \ldots \Leftarrow \Pi$. We conclude that $\theta'(X) \neq \bot$. □

4.2　The $CDNC(\mathcal{D})$ Calculus

The calculus $CDNC(\mathcal{D})$ consists of a set of transformation rules for admissible goals. Each transformation takes the form $G \Vdash G'$, specifying one of the possible ways of performing one step of goal solving. We write $G \Vdash_R G'$ to indicate that $G \Vdash G'$ by means of the $CDNC(\mathcal{D})$ transformation rule R. Derivations are sequences of $\Vdash$-steps. As in the case of constrained SLD derivations for $CLP(\mathcal{D})$ programs [10], successful derivations will eventually end with a solved goal. Failing derivations (ending with an obviously inconsistent goal ■) and infinite derivations are also possible. Similarly to [15,17], all the goal transformation rules are applied by viewing P and C as sets, rather than sequences.

- The goal transformation rules concerning suspensions $e \to R$ (see *Figure 2*) are designed with the aim of modelling the behavior of constrained lazy narrowing with *sharing* as in the $CLNC(\mathcal{D})$ calculus [15], involving primitive functions, possibly higher-order defined functions and functional variables.
- The goal transformation rules for demanded productions $< e, \mathcal{T} > \to R$ (see *Figure 3*) encode the *needed narrowing strategy* guided by the tree $\mathcal{T}$, in a vein similar to [9,17]: if $\mathcal{T}$ is a *rule* tree, then the transformation $\mathbf{RRA}$ chooses one of the available rules for rewriting e, introducing appropriate suspensions and constraints in the new goal so that lazy evaluation is ensured. If $\mathcal{T}$ is a *case* tree, one of the transformations $\mathbf{CSS}$, $\mathbf{DI}$ or $\mathbf{DN}$ can be

SS Simple Suspension $\exists X, \overline{U}.\ t \to X, P \,\square\, C \,\square\, S \,\square\, \sigma \Vdash_{\mathbf{SS}}$
$$\exists \overline{U}.\ (P \,\square\, C \,\square\, S)\sigma_0 \,\square\, \sigma \quad \text{if } t \in Pat(\mathcal{U}) \text{ and } \sigma_0 = \{X \mapsto t\}.$$

IM Imitation $\exists X, \overline{U}.\ h\overline{e}_m \to X, P \,\square\, C \,\square\, S \,\square\, \sigma \Vdash_{\mathbf{IM}}$
$$\exists \overline{X}_m, \overline{U}.\ \overline{(e_m \to X_m}, P \,\square\, C \,\square\, S)\sigma_0 \,\square\, \sigma$$
if $h\overline{e}_m \notin Pat(\mathcal{U})$ is passive, $X \in dvar_{\mathcal{D}}(P \,\square\, S)$ and $\sigma_0 = \{X \mapsto h\overline{X}_m\}$ with $\overline{X}_m$ new variables such that $h\overline{X}_m \in Pat(\mathcal{U})$.

EL Elimination $\exists X, \overline{U}.\ e \to X, P \,\square\, C \,\square\, S \,\square\, \sigma \Vdash_{\mathbf{EL}}$
$$\exists \overline{U}.\ P \,\square\, C \,\square\, S \,\square\, \sigma \quad \text{if } X \notin var(P \,\square\, C \,\square\, S \,\square\, \sigma).$$

PF Primitive Function $\exists X, \overline{U}.\ p\overline{e}_n \to X, P \,\square\, C \,\square\, S \,\square\, \sigma \Vdash_{\mathbf{PF}}$
$$\exists \overline{X}_q, X, \overline{U}.\ \overline{e_q \to X_q}, P \,\square\, C \,\square\, p\overline{t}_n \to! X, S \,\square\, \sigma$$
if $p \in PF^n$, $X \in dvar_{\mathcal{D}}(P \,\square\, S)$, and $\overline{X}_q$ are new variables ($0 \le q \le n$ is the number of $e_i \notin Pat(\mathcal{U})$) such that $t_i \equiv X_j$ ($0 \le j \le q$) if $e_i \notin Pat_{\perp}(\mathcal{U})$ and $t_i \equiv e_i$ otherwise for each $1 \le i \le n$.

DT Definitional Tree $\exists X, \overline{U}.\ f\overline{e}_n \to X, P \,\square\, C \,\square\, S \,\square\, \sigma \Vdash_{\mathbf{DT_1}}$
$$\exists X, \overline{U}.\ <f\overline{e}_n, \mathcal{T}_{f\overline{X}_n}> \to X, P \,\square\, C \,\square\, S \,\square\, \sigma$$
$\exists X, \overline{U}.\ f\overline{e}_n\overline{a}_k \to X, P \,\square\, C \,\square\, S \,\square\, \sigma \Vdash_{\mathbf{DT_2}}$
$$\exists X, X', \overline{U}.\ <f\overline{e}_n, \mathcal{T}_{f\overline{X}_n}> \to X', X'\overline{a}_k \to X, P \,\square\, C \,\square\, S \,\square\, \sigma$$
if $f \in DF^n$ ($k > 0$), $X \in dvar_{\mathcal{D}}(P \,\square\, S)$, and both X' and all variables in $\mathcal{T}_{f\overline{X}_n}$ are new variables.

FV Functional Variable $\exists X, \overline{U}.\ F\overline{e}_q \to X, P \,\square\, C \,\square\, S \,\square\, \sigma \Vdash_{\mathbf{FV}}$
$$\exists \overline{X}_p, X, \overline{U}.\ (h\overline{X}_p\overline{e}_q \to X, P \,\square\, C \,\square\, S)\sigma_0 \,\square\, \sigma\sigma_0$$
if $F \notin pvar(P)$, $q > 0$, $X \in dvar_{\mathcal{D}}(P \,\square\, S)$, $\sigma_0 = \{F \mapsto h\overline{X}_p\}$ and $\overline{X}_p$ are new variables such that $h\overline{X}_p \in Pat(\mathcal{U})$.

Fig. 2. $CDNC(\mathcal{D})$-rules for suspensions

applied, according to the kind of symbol occurring in e at the case-distinction position. Otherwise, we fail using **CC** or the computation must be delayed.
- The goal transformation rules concerning constraints (see *Figure 4*) are designed to combine (primitive or user defined) constraints with the action of a constraint solver that fulfill the requirements given in *Definition 4*. Failure rule **SF** is used for failure detection in constraint solving.

The following simple example of goal solving is intended to illustrate the main properties of the $CDNC(\mathcal{D})$ calculus. At each goal transformation step, we underline which subgoal is selected.

Example 3. We compute all the answers from the user defined constraint $N \mathrel{/=} s\ (count\ (from\ M))$ using the $COISS(\mathcal{H}_{seq})$-program given in *Example 2* and the definitional trees given in *Figure 1*. This example illustrates the use of productions to achieve the effect of a *demand-driven* evaluation with infinite lists and the use of definitional trees for ensuring the efficient choice of demanded redexes.

$\square\ \underline{N \mathrel{/=} s\ (count\ (from\ M))}\ \square\,\square\ \varepsilon \Vdash_{\mathbf{AC}}$ (*non-primitive constraint*)
$\exists L.\ \underline{s\ (count\ (from\ M)) \to L}\ \square\,\square\ N \mathrel{/=} L\ \square \Vdash_{\mathbf{IM}\{L \,\mapsto\, s\,K\}}$ (*L is necessary and demanded*)
$\exists K.\ count\ (from\ M) \to K\ \square\,\square\ \underline{N \mathrel{/=} s\ K}\ \square \Vdash_{\mathbf{CS}\{K\}}$ (*K is necessary but not demanded*)

CSS Case Selection

$$\exists R, \overline{U}. \ < e, \underline{case}(\tau, X, [\mathcal{T}_1, \ldots, \mathcal{T}_k]) > \rightarrow R, P \,\square\, C \,\square\, S \,\square\, \sigma \Vdash_{\mathbf{CSS}}$$
$$\exists R, \overline{U}. \ < e, \mathcal{T}_i > \rightarrow R, P \,\square\, C \,\square\, S \,\square\, \sigma$$

if $e|_{pos(X,\tau)} = h_i \ldots$, with $1 \le i \le k$ given by e, where h_i is the passive symbol associated to $\mathcal{T}_i$.

DI Demand Instantiation

$$\exists R, \overline{U}. \ < e, \underline{case}(\tau, X, [\mathcal{T}_1, \ldots, \mathcal{T}_k]) > \rightarrow R, P \,\square\, C \,\square\, S \,\square\, \sigma \Vdash_{\mathbf{DI}}$$
$$\exists \overline{Y}_{m_i}, R, \overline{U}. \ (< e, \mathcal{T}_i > \rightarrow R, P \,\square\, C \,\square\, S)\sigma_0 \,\square\, \sigma\sigma_0$$

if $e|_{pos(X,\tau)} = Y$, $Y \notin pvar(P)$, $\sigma_0 = \{Y \mapsto h_i \overline{Y}_{m_i}\}$ with h_i $(1 \le i \le k)$ the passive symbol associated to $\mathcal{T}_i$ and $\overline{Y}_{m_i}$ are new variables.

DN Demand Narrowing

$$\exists R, \overline{U}. \ < e, \underline{case}(\tau, X, [\mathcal{T}_1, \ldots, \mathcal{T}_k]) > \rightarrow R, P \,\square\, C \,\square\, S \,\square\, \sigma \Vdash_{\mathbf{DN}}$$
$$\exists R', R, \overline{U}. \ e|_{pos(X,\tau)} \rightarrow R',$$
$$< e[R']_{pos(X,\tau)}, \underline{case}(\tau, X, [\mathcal{T}_1, \ldots, \mathcal{T}_k]) > \rightarrow R, P \,\square\, C \,\square\, S \,\square\, \sigma$$

if $e|_{pos(X,\tau)} = g \ldots$ with $g \in FS$ active (primitive or defined function symbol) and R' new variable.

RRA Rewrite Rule Application

$$\exists R, \overline{U}. \ < e, \underline{rule}(\tau \rightarrow r_1 \Leftarrow P_1 \,\square\, C_1 | \ldots | r_k \Leftarrow P_k \,\square\, C_k) > \rightarrow R, P \,\square\, C \,\square$$
$$S \,\square\, \sigma \Vdash_{\mathbf{RRA}}$$
$$\exists \overline{X}, R, \overline{U}. \ \sigma_f(R_1) \rightarrow R_1, \ldots, \sigma_f(R_m) \rightarrow R_m, r_i \sigma_c \rightarrow R, P_i \sigma_c, P \,\square\, C_i \sigma_c,$$
$$C \,\square\, S \,\square\, \sigma$$

- $\sigma_0 = \sigma_c \uplus \sigma_f$ with $dom(\sigma_0) = var(\tau)$ and $\tau\sigma_0 = e$.
- $\sigma_c =_{def} \sigma \upharpoonright_{dom_c(\sigma_0)}$, where $dom_c(\sigma_0) = \{X \in dom(\sigma_0) \mid \sigma_0(X) \in Pat(\mathcal{U})\}$.
- $\sigma_f =_{def} \sigma \upharpoonright_{dom_f(\sigma_0)}$, where $dom_f(\sigma_0) = \{X \in dom(\sigma_0) \mid \sigma_0(X) \notin Pat(\mathcal{U})\}$ $= \{R_1, \ldots, R_m\}$.
- $\overline{X} \equiv var(\tau \rightarrow r_i \Leftarrow P_i \,\square\, C_i)\backslash dom_c(\sigma_0)$.

CC Case non-Cover

$$\exists R, \overline{U}. \ < e, \underline{case}(\tau, X, [\mathcal{T}_1, \ldots, \mathcal{T}_k]) > \rightarrow R, P \,\square\, C \,\square\, S \,\square\, \sigma \Vdash_{\mathbf{CC}} \blacksquare$$

if $e|_{pos(X,\tau)} = h \ldots$ is a passive symbol and $h \notin \{h_1, \ldots, h_k\}$, where h_i is the passive symbol associated to $\mathcal{T}_i$ $(1 \le i \le k)$.

Fig. 3. $CDNC(\mathcal{D})$-rules for demanded productions and failure detection

At this point, a constraint solver over $\mathcal{H}_{seq}$ (see for example [15]) gives two possible alternatives: $Solve^{\mathcal{H}_{seq}}(\{N \,/\!\!= s\ K\}, \{K\}) = (\square \ \{N \mapsto 0\}) \vee (\{N' \,/\!\!= K\} \,\square\, \{N \mapsto s\ N'\})$, and there are two possible continuations of the computation, where the use of definitional trees $\mathcal{T}_{from}$, $\mathcal{T}_{count}$ and $\mathcal{T}_{aux}$ in demanded productions guides and avoids *don't know* choices of program rules and failure computations w.r.t. the previous calculus $CLNC(\mathcal{D})$ [15]:

$$\exists K. \ \underline{count}\ (from\ M) \rightarrow K \ \square\,\square\,\square\ \{N \mapsto 0\} \Vdash_{\mathbf{EL}} \ (K \text{ is now unnecessary!})$$
$$\square\,\square\,\square\ \{N \mapsto 0\} \ \mathbf{computed\ answer:} \ S_1 \,\square\, \sigma_1 \equiv \ \square\ \{N \mapsto 0\}$$

CS Constraint Solving $\exists \overline{U}.\ P \,\square\, C \,\square\, S \,\square\, \sigma \Vdash_{\mathbf{CS}\{\chi\}}$
$$\exists \overline{Y}_i, \overline{U}.\ (P \,\square\, C)\sigma_i \,\square\, S_i \,\square\, \sigma\sigma_i$$
if $\chi = pvar(P)$, S is not χ-solved, $Solve^{\mathcal{D}}(S, \chi) = \bigvee_{i=1}^{k}(S_i \,\square\, \sigma_i)$, and $\overline{Y}_i$ are the new variables introduced by the solver in $S_i \,\square\, \sigma_i$, for each $1 \le i \le k$.

AC Atomic Constraint $\exists \overline{U}.\ P \,\square\ p\bar{e}_n \to!\ t, C \,\square\, S \,\square\, \sigma \Vdash_{\mathbf{AC}}$
$$\exists \overline{X}_q, \overline{U}.\ \overline{e_q \to X_q}, P \,\square\, C \,\square\ p\bar{t}_n \to!\ t, S \,\square\, \sigma$$
if $p \in PF^n$, $p\bar{e}_n \to!\ t$ is a constraint, $\overline{X}_q$ are new variables ($0 \le q \le n$ is the number of $e_i \notin Pat_\perp(\mathcal{U})$) such that $t_i \equiv X_j$ ($0 \le j \le q$) if $e_i \notin Pat_\perp(\mathcal{U})$ and $t_i \equiv e_i$ otherwise for each $1 \le i \le n$.

SF Solving Failure $\exists \overline{U}.\ P \,\square\, C \,\square\, S \,\square\, \sigma \Vdash_{\mathbf{SF}\{\chi\}} \blacksquare$
if $\chi = pvar(P)$, S is not χ-solved, and $Solve^{\mathcal{D}}(S, \chi) = \blacktriangle$.

Fig. 4. $CLNC(\mathcal{D})$-rules for constraint solving and failure detection

$\exists K, N'.\ \underline{count\ (from\ M) \to K} \,\square\ \square\ N'\ /= K \,\square\ \{N \mapsto s\ N'\} \Vdash_{\mathbf{DT}}$ (K is now demanded!)

$\exists K, N'.\ \underline{< count\ (from\ M), \mathcal{T}_{count} > \to K} \ \square\ \square\ N'\ /= K \,\square\ \{N \mapsto s\ N'\} \Vdash_{\mathbf{DN}}$

$\exists K', K, N'.\ \underline{from\ M \to K'}, < count\ K', \mathcal{T}_{count} > \to K \ \square\ \square\ N'\ /= K \,\square\ \{N \mapsto s\ N'\} \Vdash_{\mathbf{DT}}$

$\exists K', K, N'.\ \underline{< from\ M, \mathcal{T}_{from} > \to K'}, < count\ K', \mathcal{T}_{count} > \to K \ \square\ \square$ (K' is demanded)
$\qquad N'\ /= K \,\square\ \{N \mapsto s\ N'\} \Vdash_{\mathbf{RRA}}$ ('from' rule application)

$\exists K', K, N'.\ \underline{[M|from\ (s\ M)] \to K'}, < count\ K', \mathcal{T}_{count} > \to K \ \square\ \square$
$\qquad N'\ /= K \,\square\ \{N \mapsto s\ N'\} \Vdash^3_{\mathbf{IM}\{K' \mapsto [A|As]\},\ \mathbf{SS}\{A \mapsto M\},\ \mathbf{CSS}}$

$\exists As, K, N'.\ \underline{from\ (s\ M) \to As}, < count\ [M|As], \mathcal{T}_{count\ [\cdot|\cdot]} > \to K \ \square\ \square$
$\qquad N'/= K \,\square\ \{N \mapsto s\ N'\} \Vdash_{\mathbf{DT}}$ (As is demanded by the definitional tree)

$\exists As, K, N'.\ \underline{< from\ (s\ M), \mathcal{T}_{from} > \to As}, < count\ [M|As], \mathcal{T}_{count\ [\cdot|\cdot]} > \to K \ \square\ \square$
$\qquad N'/= K \,\square\ \{N \mapsto s\ N'\} \Vdash_{\mathbf{RRA}}$ ('from' rule application)

$\exists As, K, N'.\ \underline{[s\ M|from\ (s\ (s\ M))] \to As}, < count\ [M|As], \mathcal{T}_{count\ [\cdot|\cdot]} > \to K \ \square\ \square$
$\qquad N'\ /= K \,\square\ \{N \mapsto s\ N'\} \Vdash^3_{\mathbf{IM}\{As \mapsto [B|Bs]\},\ \mathbf{SS}\{B \mapsto s\ M\},\ \mathbf{CSS}}$

$\exists Bs, K, N'.\ \underline{from\ (s\ (s\ M)) \to Bs}, < count\ [M, s\ M|Bs], \mathcal{T}_{count\ [\cdot,\cdot|\cdot]} > \to K \ \square\ \square$
$\qquad N'/= K \,\square\ \{N \mapsto s\ N'\} \Vdash_{\mathbf{RRA}}$ ('count' rule application)

$\exists R, N'', Bs, K, N'.\ from\ (s\ (s\ M)) \to Bs, \underline{aux\ R\ N'' \to K}, count\ [s\ M|Bs] \to N'' \,\square$
$\qquad seq\ M\ (s\ M) \to!\ R \,\square\, N'/= K \,\square\ \{N \mapsto s\ N'\} \Vdash_{\mathbf{DT}}$ (Bs, N'' are not demanded)

$\exists R, N'', Bs, K, N'.\ from\ (s\ (s\ M)) \to Bs, \underline{< aux\ R\ N'', \mathcal{T}_{aux} > \to K}, count\ [s\ M|Bs] \to N'' \,\square$
$\qquad seq\ M\ (s\ M) \to!\ R \,\square\, N'\ /= K \,\square\ \{N \mapsto s\ N'\} \Vdash_{\mathbf{DI}\{R \mapsto \mathbf{false}\}}$

$\exists N'', Bs, K, N'.\ from\ (s\ (s\ M)) \to Bs, \underline{< aux\ false\ N'', \mathcal{T}_{aux, false} > \to K},$
$\qquad count\ [s\ M|Bs] \to N''\ \square\, \underline{M/= s\ M} \,\square\, N'/= K \,\square\ \{N \mapsto s\ N'\} \Vdash_{\mathbf{RRA}, \mathbf{SS}\{K \mapsto s\ 0\}}$

$\exists N'', Bs, N'.\ \underline{from\ (s\ (s\ M)) \to Bs}, count\ [s\ M|Bs] \to N''\ \square\ M\ /= s\ M \,\square$
$\qquad N'\ /= s\ 0 \,\square\ \{N \mapsto s\ N'\} \Vdash^2_{\mathbf{EL}}$ (N'' is unnecessary and then Bs is unnecessary!)

$\exists N'.\ \square\ \underline{M/= s\ M} \,\square\, N'/= s\ 0 \square\ \{N \mapsto s\ N'\} \Vdash^2_{\mathbf{AC}, \mathbf{CS}\{\}}$ (we have again two possibilities)
$\quad \exists N'.\ \square\ \square\ N'\ /= s\ 0 \,\square\ \{M \mapsto 0, N \mapsto s\ N'\}$
$\quad$ **computed answer:** $S_2 \,\square\, \sigma_2 \equiv N'\ /= s\ 0 \,\square\ \{M \mapsto 0, N \mapsto s\ N'\}$
$\quad \exists M', N'.\ \square\ \square\ M'\ /= M, N'\ /= s\ 0 \,\square\ \{M \mapsto s\ M', N \mapsto s\ N'\}$
$\quad$ **computed answer:** $S_3 \,\square\, \sigma_3 \equiv M'\ /= M, N'\ /= s\ 0 \,\square\ \{M \mapsto s\ M', N \mapsto s\ N'\}$

4.3   Properties of the $CDNC(\mathcal{D})$ Calculus

In this last subsection, the relationship between the logic $CRWL(\mathcal{D})$ and our goal solving mechanism $CDNC(\mathcal{D})$ is established in the main results of the paper, namely *soundness* and *completeness* of the $CDNC(\mathcal{D})$ calculus w.r.t. $CFLP(\mathcal{D})$'s semantics. To prove both properties we use techniques similar to those used for the $CLNC(\mathcal{D})$ calculus presented in [15]. The following soundness result ensures that computed answers for a goal G are indeed correct answers.

Theorem 1 (Soundness of $CDNC(\mathcal{D})$).
If G_0 is an initial goal and $G_0 \Vdash^*_{CDNC(\mathcal{D})} G_n$, where $G_n \equiv \exists \overline{U}. \,\square\,\square\, S \,\square\, \sigma$ is a solved goal, then $S \,\square\, \sigma \in Ans_\mathcal{P}(G_0)$.

Completeness of $CDNC(\mathcal{D})$ is based on the following idea: whenever $\Pi \,\square\, \theta \in Ans_\mathcal{P}(G)$ and G is not yet solved, there are finitely many local choices for a first computation step $G \Vdash G_j$ $(1 \le j \le l)$ so that the new goals G_j are "closer to be solved" and "cover all the solutions of $\Pi \,\square\, \theta$". The following completeness result reveals that $CDNC(\mathcal{D})$ is *strongly complete*, i.e. the local choice of the goal transformation rule applied at each step can be a *don't care* choice.

Theorem 2 (Completeness of $CDNC(\mathcal{D})$).
Let G_0 an initial admissible goal and $\Pi_0 \,\square\, \theta_0 \in Ans_\mathcal{P}(G_0)$ non-trivial. Then there exist a finite number of derivations ending in solved goals $G_0 \Vdash^*_{CDNC(\mathcal{D})} G_i$ $(1 \le i \le k)$ such that $Sol_\mathcal{D}(\Pi_0 \,\square\, \theta_0) \subseteq \bigcup_{i=1}^{k} Sol_\mathcal{P}(G_i)$.

Finally, from the viewpoint of efficiency, and according to our *Demand Lemma*, definitional trees in demanded productions are used for ensuring only needed narrowing steps in the line of [4,2,17]. Then, computations in $CDNC(\mathcal{D})$ are in essence needed narrowing derivations modulo non-deterministic choices between overlapping and constrained program rules. Therefore, our efficient mechanism maintains the optimality properties shown in [4,2,17] guiding (and avoiding) *don't know* choices of constrained program rules by means of definitional trees.

5   Conclusions

We have presented an effective computational model for the integration of constraint logic and functional logic programming by means of a new Constrained Demanded Narrowing Calculus $CDNC(\mathcal{D})$ parameterized by a constraint domain $\mathcal{D}$ and using definitional trees to guide the choice of demanded redexes. We have proved soundness and completeness of the new narrowing calculus, and we have argued that the use of definitional trees leads to efficiency improvements w.r.t. our previous calculus $CLNC(\mathcal{D})$ [15]. These properties renders $CDNC(\mathcal{D})$ adequate as a concrete specification for the implementation of the computational behavior in existing $CFLP(\mathcal{D})$ systems such as *Curry* [8] and $\mathcal{TOY}$ [13,6].

In the near future, we plan to investigate both improvements and applications of the $CFLP(\mathcal{D})$ scheme. Since $CFLP(\mathcal{D})$ assumes only free data constructors, planned improvements include enriching the scheme with algebraic data constructors. Planned applications will focus on practical instances of the $CFLP(\mathcal{D})$

scheme, supporting arithmetic constraints over the real numbers and finite domain ($\mathcal{FD}$) constraints. In particular, we plan to investigate practical constraint solving methods and applications of our resulting language in $\mathcal{TOY}(\mathcal{FD})$ [6].

Last but not least, we are working on *declarative debugging* techniques for $CFLP(\mathcal{D})$-programs, following previous work for functional logic programs [5].

References

1. S. Antoy. Definitional trees. In *Proc. Int. Conf. on Algebraic and Logic Programming (ALP'92)*, volume 632 of Springer LNCS, pp. 143–157, 1992.
2. S. Antoy. Optimal non-deterministic functional logic computations. In *Proc. of ALP'97*, pages 16-30. Springer LNCS 1298, 1997.
3. S. Antoy. Constructor-based conditional narrowing. In *Proc. PPDP'01*, ACM Press, pp. 199-206, 2001.
4. S. Antoy, R. Echahed, M. Hanus. A needed narrowing strategy. *Journal of the ACM*, 47(4): 776-822, 2000.
5. R. Caballero, M. Rodríguez-Artalejo. $\mathcal{DDT}$: A Declarative Debugging Tool for Functional Logic Languages. In *Proc. of the 7th International Symposium on FLOPS'04*, volume 2998 of Springer LNCS, pp. 70–84, 2004.
6. A. J. Fernández, M. T. Hortalá-González and F. Sáenz Pérez. $\mathcal{TOY}(\mathcal{FD})$. *User's Manual*, October 27, 2003. System available at http://www.lcc.uma.es/~afdez/cflpfd/.
7. M. Hanus. The Integration of Functions into Logic Programming: From Theory to Practice. *Journal of Logic Programming* 19&20, pp. 583–628, 1994.
8. M. Hanus (ed.), *Curry: an Integrated Functional Logic Language*, Version 0.8, April 15, 2003. http://www-i2.informatik.uni-kiel.de/~curry/.
9. M. Hanus, C. Prehofer. Higher-Order Narrowing with Definitional Trees. *Journal of Functional Programming*, 9(1):33-75, 1999.
10. J. Jaffar, M.J. Maher, K. Marriott and P.J. Stuckey. The Semantics of Constraint Logic Programs. *Journal of Logic Programming*, 37 (1-3) pp. 1–46, 1998.
11. R. Loogen, F.J. López-Fraguas, M. Rodríguez-Artalejo. A demand driven computation strategy for lazy narrowing. In Proc. *Int. Symp. on PLILP'93*, volume 714 of Springer LNCS pp. 184–200, 1993.
12. F.J. López-Fraguas. A General Scheme for Constraint Functional Logic Programming. In *Proc. Int. Conf. on ALP'92*, Springer LNCS 632, pp. 213–227, 1992.
13. F.J. López-Fraguas, J. Sánchez-Hernández. $\mathcal{TOY}$: A Multiparadigm Declarative System. Proc. RTA'99, Springer LNCS 1631, pp 244–247, 1999. System available at http://toy.sourceforge.net.
14. F.J. López-Fraguas, M. Rodríguez-Artalejo and R. del Vado-Vírseda. Constraint Functional Logic Programming Revisited. In *International Workshop on Rewriting Logic and its Applications WRLA'04*, Elsevier ENTCS series, vol. 117, pp. 5–50, 2005.
15. F.J. López-Fraguas, M. Rodríguez-Artalejo and R. del Vado-Vírseda. A lazy narrowing calculus for declarative constraint programming. In *Prof of the 6th International Conference on PPDP'04*, ACM Press, pp. 43–54, 2004.
16. M. Marin, T. Ida and T. Suzuki. Cooperative Constraint Functional Logic Programming. In *Int. Symposium on IPSE'2000*, pp. 223–230, November 1–2, 2000.
17. R. del Vado Vírseda. A Demand-driven Narrowing Calculus with Overlapping Definitional Trees. *5th Int. Conference on PPDP'03*, ACM Press, pp. 213–227, 2003.

Logical Analysis of Hash Functions

Dejan Jovanović[1] and Predrag Janičić[2]

[1] Mathematical Institute,
Kneza Mihaila 35, 11000 Belgrade, Serbia and Montenegro
dejan@mi.sanu.ac.yu
[2] Faculty of Mathematics,
Studentski trg 16, 11000 Belgrade, Serbia and Montenegro
janicic@matf.bg.ac.yu

Abstract. In this paper we report on a novel approach for uniform encoding of hash functions (but also other cryptographic functions) into propositional logic formulae, and reducing cryptanalysis problems to the satisfiability problem. The approach is general, elegant, and does not require any human expertise on the construction of a specific cryptographic function. By using this approach, we developed a technique for generating *hard and satisfiable* propositional formulae and *hard and unsatisfiable* propositional formulae. In addition, one can finely tune the hardness of generated formulae. This can be very important for different applications, including testing (complete or incomplete) SAT solvers. The uniform logical analysis of cryptographic functions can be used for comparison between different functions and can expose weaknesses of some of them (as shown for MD4 in comparison with MD5).

1 Introduction

Hash functions have wide and important role in cryptography. They produce hash values, which concisely represent longer messages or documents from which they were computed. Examples of hash functions are MD4, MD5, and SHA. The main role of cryptographic hash functions is in the provision of message integrity checks and digital signatures.

The subject of research presented in this paper is analysis of hash functions in terms of propositional reasoning.[1] We will try to shed a new light on hash functions and to address several important issues concerning hash functions and SAT problem. First question considered is whether the problem of inverting a hash function can be reduced to a SAT problem; if yes, how it can be done effectively. Section 4.1 gives one methodology for this.

Another question of interest is: *can hash functions be used for generating hard instances of* SAT *problem?* The need for hard instances of SAT problem is well-explained in [1]:

---

[1] The work presented in this paper is, in a sense, parallel to [12], as it investigates hash functions in a similar manner the work reported in [12] investigates DES algorithm.

B. Gramlich (Ed.): FroCoS 2005, LNAI 3717, pp. 200–215, 2005.

"A major difficulty in evaluating incomplete local search style algorithms for constraint satisfaction problems is the need for a source of hard problem instances that are guaranteed to be satisfiable. A standard approach to evaluate incomplete search methods has been to use a general problem generator and a complete search method to filter out the unsatisfiable instances. Unfortunately, this approach cannot be used to create problem instances that are beyond the reach of complete search methods. So far, it has proven to be surprisingly difficult to develop a direct generator for satisfiable instances only."

In [1], it is claimed that cryptographic algorithms cannot be used for generating interesting hard SAT instances, as the problems are too hard (require exhaustive search) and cannot be fine-grained. In this paper, we question these claims and show how hash functions can be used for generating satisfiable SAT instances of finely tuned hardness. We will also consider generating unsatisfiable SAT instances. Namely, while satisfiable instances are required for testing completeness, unsatisfiable instances are required for testing soundness[2] of complete SAT solvers.

Why it is difficult to randomly generate hard satisfiable instances of SAT problem is also discussed in [8]. A survey [4] points that generating hard *solved* instances of SAT problem is equivalent to computing an one-way function, which in turn is equivalent to generating pseudo-random numbers and private-key cryptography. The work [4] also discusses how a fixed-length one-way function can be used to generate hard solved instances of 3SAT. We are not aware that this proposal has been used in practice and it seems that it would be very difficult to apply it to real-world hash functions. We believe that the approach we present in this paper is more elegant and applicable to state-of-the-art hash functions, provided their implementations. In addition, our approach can be used for producing both *satisfiable* SAT *instances of finely tuned hardness* and *unsatisfiable* SAT *instances of finely tuned hardness*.

It is interesting whether logical analysis could expose weaknesses of some hash functions. Finding such a weakness often relies on a human expertise and is most often specific for a certain sort of problems. Therefore, it would be good if a (uniform) logical analysis could provide a deeper understanding of nature of hash functions and expose their potential weaknesses. Experimental results, given in §6, based on uniform logical analysis, show that MD4 function is much weaker than MD5 (as expected).

Another very interesting question is whether such SAT formulae are the hardest SAT formulae (within the class of formulae with the same number of variables). We will briefly comment on this question and possible ways for investigating it within our plans for future work.

---

[2] Since SAT solvers are becoming a standard tool in many critical industrial applications, testing the solver for soundness is of uttermost importance.

2   Background

Hash Functions. A hash function *hash* is a transformation that takes an input sequence of bits m (the message) and returns a fixed-size string, which is called the *hash value* (also the *message digest*, the *digital fingerprint*). The basic requirement for a cryptographic hash function is that the hash value does not reveal any information about the message itself, and moreover that it is hard to find other messages that produce the same hash value. If only a single bit of the message is changed, it is expected that the new hash value is dramatically different from the original one. A hash function is required to have the following features:

Preimage resistant. A hash function *hash* is said to be *preimage resistant* if it
   is hard to invert, where "hard to invert" means that given a hash value h,
   it is computationally infeasible to find some input x such that $hash(x) = h$.
Second preimage resistant. If, given a message x, it is computationally infeasible
   to find a message y different from x such that $hash(x) = hash(y)$, then *hash*
   is said to be *second preimage resistant*.
Collision-resistant. A hash function *hash* is said to be *collision-resistant* if it is
   computationally infeasible to find two distinct messages x and y such that
   $hash(x) = hash(y)$.

A hash function must be able to produce a fixed-length output for an arbitrary-length message. This is usually achieved by breaking the input into series of equal-sized blocks, and then operating on these blocks in a sequence of steps, using compression functions. Often, the last block processed also contains the message length, which improves the properties of the hash. This construction is known as the Merkle-Demagård structure [5,13], and the majority of hash functions in use are of this form, including MD4, MD5 and the SHA family.

MD4 and MD5 are message-digest algorithms developed by Ron Rivest [16,17]. These two algorithms take a message of arbitrary length and produce a 128-bit message digest. Attacks on versions of MD4 with either the first or the last rounds missing were developed very quickly. Also, it was shown how collisions for the full version of MD4 can be found in under a minute on a typical PC. MD5 algorithm is basically an improved version of MD4. The algorithm consists of four distinct rounds, which have a slightly different design from that of MD4. Collisions for the full MD5 were announced in 2004 [19], and the attack was reported to take only one hour on an IBM P690 cluster. This year it was demonstrated that using the methodology of previous attacks it is possible to construct two X.509 certificates with different public keys and the same MD5 hash value [11]. However, this still does not mean that the properties preimage resistant and second preimage resistant for MD5 are completely compromised.

SAT **Problem.** Boolean satisfiability problem (SAT) is the problem of deciding if there is a truth assignment under which a given propositional formula (in conjunctive normal form) evaluates to true. It was shown by Cook [3] that SAT is NP-complete. This was the first problem shown to be NP-complete, and it still holds a central position in the study of computational complexity as the canonical NP-complete problem. The importance of the SAT problem is also grounded in practical applications, since many real-world problems (or their components) in areas such as AI planning, circuit satisfiability and software verification can be efficiently reformulated as instances of SAT. Therefore, good SAT solvers are of great importance and significant research effort has been devoted to finding efficient SAT algorithms.

Due to a general belief that a polynomial time algorithm for SAT is not likely to be found[3] (i.e., it is generally believed that P $\neq$ NP), the only way to evaluate a solver is by its performance on the average, in the worst case, or on a class of SAT instances one is interested in. Also, SAT instances on which the algorithms perform poorly, characterize the weaknesses of these algorithms and can direct further research on improving them.

Experiments suggest that there is a phase transition in SAT problems between satisfiability and unsatisfiability as the ratio of the number of clauses and the number of variables is increased [14]. It is conjectured that, for different types of problem sets, there is a value c_0 of L/N, which is called a *phase transition point* such that:

$$\lim_{N \to \infty} s(N, [cN]) = \begin{cases} 1, \text{ for } c < c_0 \\ 0, \text{ for } c > c_0 \end{cases},$$

where $s(N, L)$ is a *satisfiability function* that maps sets of propositional formulae (of L clauses over N variables) into the segment $[0, 1]$ and corresponds to a percentage of satisfiable formulae. Experimental results also suggest that in all SAT problems there is a typical easy-hard-easy pattern as the ratio L/N is increased, while the most difficult SAT formulae for all decision procedures are those in the crossover region.

zChaff SAT Solver. Majority of the state-of-the-art complete SAT solvers are based on the branch and backtracking algorithm called Davis-Logemann-Loveland algorithm (DLL) [6]. Some of the algorithms also use heuristic local search techniques, but this makes them incomplete (they don't guarantee to find a satisfying assignment if one exists). In addition to DLL, these complete algorithms use a pruning technique called learning. Learning extracts and memorises information from the previously searched space to prune the search in the future. Also, in order to improve the efficiency of the system, techniques as preprocessing, sophisticated branching heuristics, data structures, and random restarts are used (for a survey, see e.g. [20]). There are many SAT packages available, both proprietary and public domain. It is considered that one of the best complete SAT solvers nowadays is the zChaff solver [15]. Besides its smart pruning techniques, zChaff is highly optimised, and achieves remarkably good results in practice. For that reason we chose it as the main SAT solver for our experiments.

---

[3] Clay Institute for Mathematical Sciences is offering a one million dollar prize for a complete polynomial-time SAT solver or a proof that such an algorithm does not exist (the P vs NP problem).

3   Transforming Cryptanalysis of Hash Functions into SAT Problem

Let *hash* be a hash function generating a hash value of a fixed length N. We assume that *hash* is a hash function with a good distribution of output values. This means that for every (or almost every) N-bit sequence h, there is an N-bit message m having h as the hash value, i.e. $hash(m) = h$). In other words, we assume that the hash function is a good approximation of a permutation on N-bit strings. This holds for hash functions MD4 and MD5, and is important for our investigation. Since the problem of inverting a hash value is highly intractable, in order to scale down the problem hardness we also consider input sequences of length less than N. Let $p_1 p_2 \ldots p_M$ denote the bits of an input message (of length M, $M \leq N$). The hash function takes this input sequence and transforms it into a sequence of of bits $h_1 h_2 \ldots h_N$. For hash functions we are interested in, this transformation is computable and, moreover, expressible in propositional logic, i.e., the resulting hash bits h_i can theoretically be expressed as formulae with $p_1, p_2, \ldots, p_M$ as variables. These formulae are very complex as they reflect the inherent complexity of the hash function, but obtaining them effectively is still possible (one method for doing it is described in §4). Let us denote the formula that corresponds to the computation of the bit h_i of the hash value as $H_i(p_1, p_2, \ldots, p_M)$.

Preimage Resistance. When analysing preimage resistance of a hash function, the goal is, given a sequence $h_1 h_2 \ldots h_N$ (the hash value) and the length of the input message M to determine values $p_1, p_2, \ldots, p_M$ that generate this hash value. In other words, we are searching for a valuation v such that $I_v(H_i(p_1, p_2, \ldots, p_M)) = h_i$ $(i = 1, 2, \ldots, N)$, where I_v is the interpretation induced by v. Thus, the valuation v must fulfill

$$I_v(H_i(p_1, p_2, \ldots, p_M)) = \begin{cases} 1 & \text{if } h_i = 1 \\ 0 & \text{if } h_i = 0 \end{cases} .$$

Further, let $\overline{H}_i$ be defined as

$$\overline{H}_i(p_1, p_2, \ldots, p_M) = \begin{cases} H_i(p_1, p_2, \ldots, p_M) & \text{if } h_i = 1 \\ \neg(H_i(p_1, p_2, \ldots, p_M)) & \text{if } h_i = 0 . \end{cases}$$

Obviously, formula $\overline{H}_i$ is true under valuation v if and only if the hash function *hash* transforms the message corresponding to v into a hash with the i-th bit equal to h_i. The formula $\mathcal{H}$ is defined as follows:

$$\mathcal{H}(p_1, p_2, \ldots, p_M) \quad = \quad \bigwedge_{j=1,2,\ldots,N} \overline{H}_j(p_1, p_2, \ldots, p_M) .$$

In order to invert the sequence $h_1, \ldots, h_N$, we have to determine a valuation that satisfies the formula $\mathcal{H}(p_1, p_2, \ldots, p_M)$. Practically, finding such a valuation is of the same difficulty as to determining whether $\mathcal{H}(p_1, p_2, \ldots, p_M)$ is satisfiable.

Hence, we have reduced finding the preimage of a hash function to SAT problem. This reduces the problem of finding the preimage of a hash function to SAT.

Assuming that the hash function is preimage resistant, it is very likely that the formula $\mathcal{H}(p_1, p_2, \ldots, p_M)$ (for large M) is hard to test for satisfiability (otherwise, we would have an effective mechanism for computing the preimage, contradicting the generally accepted assumption of preimage resistance for functions such as MD5). This gives us a method for generating *hard and satisfiable* SAT instances:

1. select a random sequence m of length M;
2. compute the hash value $h_1 h_2 \ldots h_N$ of m;
3. using the above construction, generate the propositional formula $\mathcal{H}$.

Having that valuation induced by m satisfies $\mathcal{H}$ by the construction, it is guaranteed that $\mathcal{H}$ is satisfiable. In addition, it is sound to assume that $\mathcal{H}$ is hard to test for satisfiability. So, this way we can generate *hard and satisfiable* SAT instances for different values of M. Obviously, the bigger M, the harder instance generated.

Second Preimage Resistance. For this property, we assume we are given a sequence $h_1 h_2 \ldots h_N$ (the hash value), the length M of the input message, and also the input bits $p_1, p_2, \ldots, p_M$ that generated this hash value. Our goal is to determine another values $q_1, q_2, \ldots, q_M$ that generate the same hash value. Similarly as above, this reduces to satisfiability of the following formula[4]:

$$\mathcal{H}'(q_1, q_2, \ldots, q_M) \quad = \quad \mathcal{H}(q_1, q_2, \ldots, q_M) \wedge (q_1^{p_1} \vee q_2^{p_2} \vee \ldots \vee q_M^{p_M})$$

where

$$q_i^{p_i} = \begin{cases} \neg q_i & \text{if } p_i = 1 \\ q_i & \text{if } p_i = 0 \end{cases} .$$

The additional clause forces the messages $p_1 p_2 \ldots p_M$ and $q_1 q_2 \ldots q_M$ to differ in at least one bit.

Assuming that the hash function is second preimage resistant, it is very likely that the formula $\mathcal{H}'(q_1, q_2, \ldots, q_M)$ is hard to test for satisfiability for large M. Also, for a good hash function, it is highly unlikely that there is a collision with the length of colliding input messages being less then N. So, it is extremely likely that the formula $\mathcal{H}'(q_1, q_2, \ldots, q_M)$ is unsatisfiable for $M < N$.

This gives us a method for generating *hard and unsatisfiable* SAT instances:

1. select a random sequence m of length M ($M < N$);
2. compute the hash value $h_1 h_2 \ldots h_N$ of m;
3. using the above construction, generate the propositional formula $\mathcal{H}'$.

This way we can generate *hard and unsatisfiable* SAT instances for different values of M. Obviously, the hardness of generated SAT instances grows with M.

---

[4] Note that this condition is stronger than the condition given in §2 — namely, the above condition requires that two messages (with the same hash value) have the same length. However, our intention is to use $\mathcal{H}'$ to generate hard unsatisfiable SAT instances and this additional restriction can actually only bring us some good.

Collision Resistance. To check the collision resistance property, one is looking for two different sequences $p_1p_2 \ldots p_M$ and $p'_1p'_2 \ldots p'_M$, with the same hash value. Collision resistance of the hash function can be reduced to satisfiability of the formula

$$\bigwedge_{i=1,\ldots,N} (H_i(p_1, p_2, \ldots, p_M) \Leftrightarrow H_i(p'_1, p'_2, \ldots, p'_M)) \ \wedge \ \neg \bigwedge_{i=1,\ldots,M} (p_i \Leftrightarrow p'_i) \ .$$

In this case, the only parameter of the formula is M, the length of the colliding messages we are searching for. The number of variables in the given formula, and hence the complexity of search, doubles with M. This makes these feature too hard and we restricted our investigation only to formulae $\mathcal{H}$ and $\mathcal{H}'$ (described as above).

4   Encoding of Hash Functions into Instances of SAT Problem

It is clear from the previous section how the properties of hash functions can be encoded into SAT instances. In this section we introduce a general framework for such encoding based on existing implementations of hash algorithms. Further, we discuss how to transform the acquired propositional formula into CNF.

4.1   Uniform Encoding on the Basis of Hash Function Implementation

Since a good hash algorithm doesn't depend on the secrecy of the algorithm, all of the popular hash algorithms are available both in a descriptive form and in form of implementations in all popular programming languages. Most of the hash algorithms include thousands of logical operation on input bits. This makes any handcrafting of the propositional formulae we are interested in practically an impossible task. Here we present a framework that allows easy generation of propositional formula of a hash transformation, based entirely on an existing implementation of the algorithm in C/C++[5]. This methodology for encoding cryptographic functions into logical formulae is general and can be applied not only to hash functions, but also other algorithms (e.g., DES). Our approach is considerably simpler, faster and more reliable than one used in [12] where a special hand-crafted program was designed to simulate DES for the same purpose. Also, this approach is independent of a concrete hash algorithm, which makes it readily reusable for further investigations on other cryptographic functions.

The implementation relies on a feature of the C++ language called *operator overloading*. Operator overloading is a specific case of polymorphism, in which

---

[5] Due to a requirement that hash algorithms must be extremely fast, C/C++ is the most common programming language for implementing hash functions. All available hash functions used in practice are coded in C/C++, so this does not restrict applicability of the method.

operators commonly used in programming such as +, * or =, are treated as polymorphic function, and as such, they can have different behaviours depending on the types of its operators. This feature is usually only a syntactic sugar, and can be emulated by function calls. For example, x + y * z can be rewritten as add(x, multiply(y, z)). Operator overloading is a common place of criticism when comparing programming languages, since it allows programmers to give to the same operators completely different semantics. This can lead to code that is extremely hard to read, and more important, can lead to errors that are hard to trace. It is considered a good practice to use operator overloading only when necessary and with much care.

We take advantage of offered ambiguous semantics in the following way. Instead of using the algorithm to actually compute the numerical hash value, we change the behaviour of all the arithmetic and logical operators that the algorithm uses, in such a way that each operator produces a propositional formula corresponding to the operation performed. This way one can run the algorithm on general logic variables and produce a formula representing the computation of the algorithm. Afterwards, if needed, one can evaluate the formula obtained by this process, with a specific input message as an argument and get the explicit hash value of the message.

Redefining operators does not (and must not) affect the flow of the algorithm. Since the aim is to record the complete computation of the hash algorithm in one run, this construction can work only if no data-flow dependent conditional structures exist in the code. This restricts the class of the hash functions the approach can handle to the class of linear algorithms (with most, or all, hash functions falling into that category). Some branching and conditional algorithmic structures could also be handled automatically, but it would require more sophisticated interventions in the code together with compiler-like tools that would be able to augment the code appropriately.

Implementation and Overloading of Operators. In the standard implementations of hash functions, 32-bit integers are usually used to represent sequences of 32 bits. To represent a longer bit-array, the array is divided into 32-bit integers, and the computation is entirely performed on these integers. For instance, to represent a sequence of 128 bits of output for MD4 and MD5, four such integers are used. The first step is to create a Word data type that would simulate the functionality of 32-bit unsigned integers. The integers in the original implementation will then be replaced by objects of the new Word data type. With this data type, each bit of an integer is represented by a propositional formula. These formulae represent a complete logical equivalent of the original computation that produced the value of the integer, one formula per bit. Having this representation, the next step is to define the operators that are used in the hash algorithm for the new data type, so that they consistently represent the propositional counterpart of the expected computation.

Implementation of bitwise logical operators + (AND), | (OR), ^ (XOR) and ~ (NOT) is straightforward. For example, the overloaded & operator takes two Word objects and creates a new Word object with every bit being an and-formula of the formulae on the corresponding bits of the input objects. These subformulae represent the logic behind the original & operator — each output formula is an and-formula of the two corresponding input formulae. For both space and time efficiency, subformulae are not copied into the new formulae, but just linked. See Fig. 1 for our implementation of the ~ operator.

```
Word Word::operator ~ () const {
    Word notWord;  // The not of the word

    /* Compute the not */
    for(int i = 0; i < bitArray.size(); i ++) {
        Formula *f = new FormulaNot(bitArray[i]);
        notWord.setFormulaAt(i, f);
    }

    return notWord; // Return the calculated not
}
```

Fig. 1. Implementation of the ~ operator

For the arithmetic operators the same logic as for logical operators is applied, but the things are a bit more complicated. This complexity arises from the fact that the value of a bit in the result depends on all the previous bits of the operands. See Fig. 2 for our implementation of the += operator.

```
Word& Word::operator += (const Word &w) {
    Formula* c = new FormulaNT;     // The carry bit

    /* Compute the sum, starting from the least significant bit */
    for(int i = bitArray.size() - 1; i >= 0; i --) {
        Formula *andF = new FormulaAnd(bitArray[i], w.bitArray[i]);
        Formula *orF  = new FormulaOr(bitArray[i], w.bitArray[i]);
        Formula *xorF = new FormulaXor(bitArray[i], w.bitArray[i]);

        Formula* sumF = new FormulaXor(xorF, c);  // Sum of the bits and the carry bit
        c = new FormulaOr(andF, new FormulaAnd(c, orF)); // New carry bit of the sum

        setFormulaAt(i, sumF);                    // Set the sum formula at i-th bit
    }

    delete c;      // Delete the last carry
    return *this;  // Return the calculated sum
}
```

Fig. 2. Implementation of the += operator

Combining the Implementation with Existing Hash Algorithms. We now have a C++ library that defines the new Word data type and implements all the operators that the hash procedure uses. Combining this library with an existing C/C++ implementation of a hash procedure is an easy task. All that is needed is to take the source files and replace the definitions of all integer objects that are used in computation by the newly defined Word type. This should suffice to get a running implementation that generates a formula corresponding to the computation of the hash function. One should be careful to avoid replacing the auxiliary objects in the source file, since we are not interested in them, and this would only complicate the computation. Example of such objects are constants, indexes and counters in simple counting loops. Although replacing them will not do any harm to the process, the transformation will be much faster if they retain their original type. See Fig. 3 for example how we modified a part of MD5 implementation to fit our needs. The original MD5 source had unsigned int type in places of Word type. We tested our implementation and a range of tests (including the original test cases from [16,17]) confirmed its correctness.

```
inline Word MD5Coder::F(const Word &x, const Word &y, const Word &z) {
    return (((x) & (y)) | ((~x) & (z)));
}

inline void MD5Coder::FF(Word& a, const Word& b, const Word& c, const Word& d,
                         const Word& x, unsigned int s, unsigned int ac)
{
    a += F(b, c, d); a += x; a += ac; a <<= s; a += b;
}

void MD5Coder::encodeBlock(int block) {
    ...
    FF (a, b, c, d, message[blockStart + 4], S11, 0xf57c0faf);
    ...
}
```

Fig. 3. Application of the implemented Word class on a part of the MD5 algorithm

4.2   Generating Conjunctive Normal Form

In the previous section, we showed how to generate a formula $\mathcal{H}$ corresponding to computation of the hash algorithm. In order to test this formula for satisfiability, one first needs to transform $\mathcal{H}$ into conjunctive normal form (CNF). A propositional formula is said to be in CNF if it is a conjunction of one or more disjunctions of literals. Computing an CNF equivalent of a simple formula is a straightforward but exponential task[6]. There is no unique CNF of a formula, and one can apply several different algorithms to make the CNF transformation (trivial recursive transformation, term-rewriting based, sequent calculus based, etc.). The main problem with these algorithms is that large real world formulae tend to be extremely huge. This, together with exponential complexity of the transformation, makes efficient transformation almost an impossible task.

We tried several standard approaches for computing the CNF equivalent of the formula $\mathcal{H}$, but all of them failed even for relatively small message lengths.

---

[6] An example of a formula that requires exponential space, and thus also time, is $(p_1 \wedge q_1) \vee (p_2 \wedge q_2) \vee \ldots \vee (p_n \wedge q_n)$.

Either they did not terminate in a reasonable amount of time, or they failed due to high memory requirements. Therefore, we chose a more reasonable approach, which in turn has some other downsides.

Tseitin Definitional Normal Form. If one drops the requirement of equivalence with the original formula, and only keeps SAT-*equivalence*[7], any formula F can be transformed efficiently into a SAT-equivalent CNF. This translation (due to Tseitin [18]) is linear in both the size of the resulting CNF and the complexity of the translation procedure. Since our formulae contain only negation, standard binary logical connectives and, additionally, XOR, the resulting CNF is in $\leq$3CNF form. That is, every clause has at most 3 literals. Generally, any logical formula that contains at most n-ary logical operators can be transformed to $\leq(n+1)$CNF form. This is achieved by introducing a new variable for every logical operation, and then imposing constraints that preserve the semantics of the operation.

We describe the transformation briefly. Let Φ be an arbitrary formula, and let $Sub(\Phi)$ denote the set of all sub-formulae of Φ. For each non-atomic sub-formula $\psi \in Sub(\phi)$, we add a new propositional variable p_ψ. In case ψ is itself atomic, we take $p_\psi = \psi$. Now, consider the formula

$$p_\Phi \wedge \bigwedge_{\substack{\phi \in Sub(\Phi) \\ \phi = \phi_1 \otimes \phi_2}} (p_\phi \Leftrightarrow (p_{\phi_1} \otimes p_{\phi_2})) \wedge \bigwedge_{\substack{\phi \in Sub(\Phi) \\ \phi = \neg \phi_1}} (p_\phi \Leftrightarrow \neg p_{\phi_1}) \ . \tag{1}$$

It is not hard to see that formula (1) is SAT-equivalent to Φ. The variable p_Φ imposes that Φ is true by propagating the actual evaluation of the formula further up the formula tree using the introduced equivalences.

Transforming formula (1) into CNF is straightforward (see Table 4.2 for transformation rules). Every conjunct in (1) is transformed into CNF with at most 4 clauses, each with at most 3 literals. Thus, the transformation is linear in the size of the formula.

Table 1. Tseitin definitional form transformation rules

Type of formula	Corresponding clauses
$\phi = \neg\phi_1$	$(p_\phi \vee p_{\phi_1}) \wedge (\neg p_\phi \vee \neg p_{\phi_1})$
$\phi = \phi_1 \wedge \phi_2$	$(p_\phi \vee \neg p_{\phi_1} \vee \neg p_{\phi_2}) \wedge (\neg p_\phi \vee p_{\phi_1}) \wedge (\neg p_\phi \vee p_{\phi_2})$
$\phi = \phi_1 \vee \phi_2$	$(\neg p_\phi \vee p_{\phi_1} \vee p_{\phi_2}) \wedge (p_\phi \vee \neg p_{\phi_1}) \wedge (p_\phi \vee \neg p_{\phi_2})$
$\phi = \phi_1 \veebar \phi_2$	$(\neg p_\phi \vee p_{\phi_1} \vee p_{\phi_2}) \wedge (\neg p_\phi \vee \neg p_{\phi_1} \vee \neg p_{\phi_2})$ $\wedge (p_\phi \vee \neg p_{\phi_1} \vee p_{\phi_2}) \wedge (p_\phi \vee p_{\phi_1} \vee \neg p_{\phi_2})$

The main weakness of the definitional CNF transformation is that the number of clauses and variables that are used is quite big. The size of a this CNF form can be reduced significantly by using implications instead of equivalences for

---

[7] Two formulae F and G are said to be SAT-equivalent when it holds that F is satisfiable iff G is satisfiable (for example p and $p \wedge q$).

subformulae that occur in one polarity only [7]. Applying such optimization here does not yield a considerable decrease, since the vast majority of operations is based on XOR operations, and this makes the subformulae bipolar.

In our case, when analyzing a hash function of fixed length N, since $\mathcal{H}$ is a conjunction of the formulae $\overline{H}_j$, we transform each $\overline{H}_j$ into a CNF, and combine them together into a CNF for $\mathcal{H}$. This yields a CNF with M unit clauses corresponding to each $\overline{H}_j$. These can be eliminated by unit propagation, but we decided to leave this to the SAT solver.

4.3   The HashSAT Formula Generator

We implemented a program that uses the modified implementations of MD4 and MD5 hash algorithms and transforms the formulae $\mathcal{H}$ and $\mathcal{H}'$ to definitional CNF. This program takes various parameters, including a hash function to be used, the length of a message to encode, the number of rounds of the selected hash function to encode (we use this parameter to allow more flexibility on the hardness of SAT instances we generate), etc. The program produces output in the standard DIMACS CNF format[8]. It is a simple textual representation, with one line for each clause. The literals in the clauses are represented as numbers, positive or negative depending on the polarity of the literal. This is a common format for SAT solvers, so the files the program generates can be used as benchmarks for SAT solvers other than zChaff. It is worth noting that this process for generating the formulae is very efficient. For instance, a full MD5 SAT problem for a 128-bit message is generated in under 1.2s with using about 16MB of memory on a Linux 2.60GHz Pentium 4 workstation.

5   Experimental Results

In this section we present our experimental results with SAT formulae generated on the basis of the hash functions MD4 and MD5. We used the methods described in §3 and §4 to generate benchmarks according to the first two properties of hash functions (preimage resistance and second preimage resistance). For each message length M we generated 50 formulae in the way described in §3; bits of starting messages m were generated randomly, each bit taking value 0 or 1 with equal probability.

For the maximal message length the generated problems proved to be too hard to test for satisfiability, so we had to scale down the hardness of the problems. One way is to decrease the message lengths (value M) and hence — decrease the search space. The other approach relies on the inner structure of hash functions: most of hash functions work on equal size block, applying basic transformations grouped in rounds. Both MD4 and MD5 transformations have 4 rounds. By reducing the number of rounds the hash functions become simpler, so the corresponding SAT instances become easier.

---

[8] For description see <http://www.satlib.org/Benchmarks/SAT/satformat.ps>.

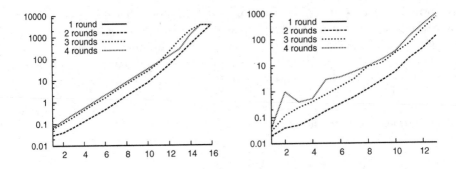

Fig. 4. Preimage resistance (left) and second preimage resistance (right) for MD5. Time scale is logarithmic, CPU time is given is seconds. Separate lines are given for weakened versions with number of rounds from 1 to 3.

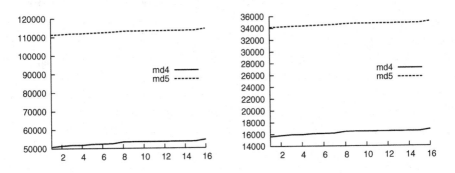

Fig. 5. Growth of clauses (left) and variables (right) in the CNF with size of the input messages for MD4 and MD5

Our results show that, in the worst case, the hash properties, as expected, behave exponentially (against M) when analysed using the described translation to SAT (see Fig. 4). The problems for $M > 16$ needed more time than we set as the time limit (10000s), but we believe that the exponential growth for the CPU time spent, continues for $M > 16$. Note that the restriction to one round gives only trivial problems.

In contrast to the exponential growth for satisfiability testing (in M), the number of clauses grows rather by some small linear factor (see Fig. 5). This means that the we are able to scale the hardness of the formulae arbitrary (for M from 1 to 128), without a significant increase in size of the formula itself.

Figure 6 (left) shows that the function MD4 is more vulnerable to inverting based on the uniform logical analysis. This is expected, as MD5 is generally believed to be of better quality compared to MD4.

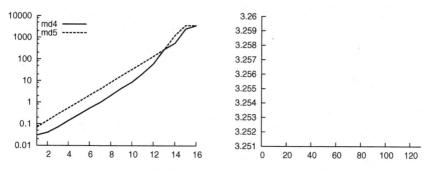

Fig. 6. Comparison of MD5 and MD4 preimage resistance with logarithmic scale for time (left) and L/N ratio with the message length for MD5 (right)

6   Future Work

In the previous sections, we analysed propositional formulae obtained from the input sequences of length M, where $M \leq N$. The value M was used to control the hardness of the problems generated. Alternatively, we could control the problem hardness by the size of the used part of the output: for the preimage resistance feature, we can analyse the following formulae (for the fixed size of the input sequences — the same as the size of the output — N): $\mathcal{H}_i(p_1, p_2, \ldots, p_N) = \bigwedge_{j=1,2,\ldots,i} \overline{H}_j(p_1, p_2, \ldots, p_N)$. Note that the functions $\mathcal{H}_i$ take into account only first i bits of the output. Assuming that the hash function analysed is permutation, for any hash value $h_1 h_2 \ldots h_N$ there is an input of size N that produces it. So, this gives us another method for generating hard and satisfiable SAT instances: (1) select a random bit sequence of length N and use it as a hash value; (2) using the above, construct the propositional formula $\Phi_i = \mathcal{H}_i(p_1, p_2, \ldots, p_N)$. Formulae Φ_i are hard and satisfiable. The bigger i ($i \leq N$), the harder formulae. In a similar manner we could generate unsatisfiable SAT instances. Analysis based on such formulae is the subject of our future research. We will also look at the combinations of these two approaches — controlling problem hardness via both the size of input and the size of output.

One of our motivating ideas for the research presented here was to investigate whether SAT instances generated on the basis of (good) hash functions are among the *hardest instances* (in terms of the phase transition phenomenon in the SAT problem [14]). Unfortunately, we are still unable to answer this question as the generated formulae do not fit the pattern of some class of randomly generated SAT instances, i.e., variables in the clauses are not distributed uniformly. For the generated formulae, the values L/N (number of clauses ratio number of variables) for MD5 are shown in Fig. 6 (right) — these values for $M = 1, \ldots, 128$ are rather stable and range between 3.25 and 3.26 (both with the unit propagation performed or not). Recall that, for some SAT model, the value L/N for the hardest instances is equal to the phase transition point for that SAT model. So, if the variables in our generated formulae were distributed uniformly, and if they indeed the hardest instances (among the formulae with the same distribution on clause length), then the phase transition point for this SAT model would be around 3.25. However, when the unit propagation is performed, in our generated formulae there are around 40% clauses of length 2 and around 60% clauses of length 3 (for $M = 1, \ldots, 128$). For such distribution of clause length (and for uniform distribution of variables), [9] approximates the phase transition point at 1.8, and [2] approximates the phase transition point between 2.1 and 2.4, both lower than 3.25. These issues will be subject of our future research — we will try to further investigate the class of generated SAT instances (with non-uniform variable distribution) and whether the instances that correspond to MD5 are indeed the hardest among them. We will try to answer these questions following the ideas from [10].

We are planning to further investigate alternative ways for transforming obtained formulae to CNF (apart from Tseitin's approach) and investigate a possible impact of this on the hardness of generated formulae.

We are also planning to apply the approach presented here to other cryptographic functions (not only the hash functions). For instance, the cryptographic algorithm DES also falls into a category of transformations that can be encoded into propositional formulae by the methodology we propose in this paper.

7   Conclusions

In this paper we presented a novel approach for uniform encoding of hash functions (but also other cryptographic functions) into propositional logic formulae. The approach is general, elegant, and does not require any human expertise on the construction of a specific cryptographic function. The approach is based on the operator overloading feature of the C++ programming language and it uses existing C implementations of cryptographic functions (and needs to alter them only very slightly). By using this approach, we developed a technique for generating *hard and satisfiable* propositional formulae and *hard and unsatisfiable* propositional formulae. Using this technique, one can finely tune the hardness of generated formulae. This can be very important for different applications, including testing (complete or incomplete) SAT solvers. The uniform logical analysis of cryptographic functions can be used for comparison between different functions and can expose weaknesses of some of them (as shown for MD4 in comparison with MD5). We are planning to further develop and apply the technique presented in this paper.

Acknowledgments. We are grateful to anonymous reviewers for useful comments on the first version of this paper.

References

1. D. Achlioptas, C.P. Gomes, H.A. Kautz, and B. Selman. Generating satisfiable problem instances. In *Proceedings of the 17th National Conference on AI and 12th Conference on Innovative Applications of AI.* AAAI Press / The MIT Press, 2000.

2. D. Achlioptas, L. M. Kirousis, E. Kranakis, and D. Krizanc. Rigorous results for random $2 + p$-SAT. Theoretical Computer Science, 265:109–129, 2001.
3. Stephen A. Cook. The complexity of theorem-proving procedures. In *STOC '71*. ACM Press, 1971.
4. Stephen A. Cook and David G. Mitchell. Finding hard instances of the satisfiability problem: A survey. In *Satisfiability Problem: Theory and Applications*, volume 35 of *DIMACS*. American Mathematical Society, 1997.
5. Ivan Bjerre Damgård. A design principle for hash functions. In *CRYPTO '89*. Springer-Verlag New York, Inc., 1989.
6. Martin Davis, George Logemann, and Donald Loveland. A machine program for theorem-proving. *Communications of the ACM*, 5(7):394–397, 1962.
7. Uwe Egly. On different structure-preserving translations to normal form. *Journal of Symbolic Computation*, 22(2):121–142, 1996.
8. Ian Gent. On the stupid algorithm for satisfiability. Technical Report APES-03-1998, Department of Computer Science, University of Strathclyde, 1998.
9. Ian P. Gent and Toby Walsh. The SAT phase transition. In *Proceedings of ECAI-94*, pages 105–109, 1994.
10. I.P. Gent, E. Macintyre., P. Prosser, and T. Walsh. The constraidness of search. In *Proceedings of AAAI-96*, pages 246–252, Menlo Park, AAAI Press/MIT Press., 1996.
11. A. Lenstra, X. Wang, and B. de Weger. Colliding X.509 certificates. Cryptology ePrint Archive, Report 2005/067, 2005. URL: http://eprint.iacr.org/.
12. Fabio Massacci and Laura Marraro. Logical cryptanalysis as a SAT problem. *Journal of Automated Reasoning*, 24(1-2):165–203, 2000.
13. Ralph C. Merkle. One way hash functions and DES. In Gilles Brassard, editor, *CRYPTO '89*. Springer-Verlag New York, Inc., 1989.
14. G. David Mitchell, Bart Selman, and J. Hector Levesque. Hard and easy distributions of sat problems. In *AAAI-92*. AAAI Press/The MIT Press, 1992.
15. Matthew W. Moskewicz, Conor F. Madigan, Ying Zhao, Lintao Zhang, and Sharad Malik. Chaff: engineering an efficient SAT solver. In *DAC '01*. ACM Press, 2001.
16. Ronald L. Rivest. The MD4 message digest algorithm. RFC 1320, The Internet Engineering Task Force, April 1992.
17. Ronald L. Rivest. The MD5 message digest algorithm. RFC 1321, The Internet Engineering Task Force, April 1992.
18. G. S. Tseitin. On the complexity of derivations in propositional calculus. In *The Automation of Reasoning*. Springer-Verlag, 1983.
19. Xiaoyun Wang, Dengguo Feng, Xuejia Lai, and Hongbo Yu. Collisions for hash functions MD4, MD5, HAVAL-128 and RIPEMD. Cryptology ePrint Archive, Report 2004/199, 2004. URL: http://eprint.iacr.org/.
20. Lintao Zhang and Sharad Malik. The quest for efficient Boolean satisfiability solvers. In *CAV '02*. Springer-Verlag, 2002.

Proving and Disproving Termination of Higher-Order Functions*

Jürgen Giesl, René Thiemann, and Peter Schneider-Kamp

LuFG Informatik II, RWTH Aachen, Ahornstr. 55, 52074 Aachen, Germany
{giesl, thiemann, psk}@informatik.rwth-aachen.de

Abstract. The dependency pair technique is a powerful modular method for automated termination proofs of term rewrite systems (TRSs). We present two important extensions of this technique: First, we show how to prove termination of *higher-order* functions using dependency pairs. To this end, the dependency pair technique is extended to handle (untyped) applicative TRSs. Second, we introduce a method to prove *non-termination* with dependency pairs, while up to now dependency pairs were only used to verify termination. Our results lead to a framework for combining termination and non-termination techniques for first- and higher-order functions in a very flexible way. We implemented and evaluated our results in the automated termination prover AProVE.

1 Introduction

One of the most powerful techniques to prove termination or innermost termination of TRSs automatically is the *dependency pair approach* [4,12,13]. In [16], we recently showed that dependency pairs can be used as a general framework to combine arbitrary techniques for termination analysis in a modular way. The general idea of this framework is to solve termination problems by repeatedly decomposing them into sub-problems. We call this new concept the "dependency pair *framework*" ("DP framework") to distinguish it from the old "dependency pair *approach*". In particular, this framework also facilitates the development of new methods for termination analysis. After recapitulating the basics of the DP framework in Sect. 2, we present two new significant improvements: in Sect. 3 we extend the framework in order to handle *higher-order* functions and in Sect. 4 we show how to use the DP framework to prove *non-termination*. Sect. 5 summarizes our results and describes their empirical evaluation with the system AProVE. All proofs can be found in [17].

2 The Dependency Pair Framework

We refer to [5] for the basics of rewriting and to [4,13,16] for motivations and details on dependency pairs. We only regard finite signatures and TRSs. $\mathcal{T}(\mathcal{F}, \mathcal{V})$ is the set of terms over the signature $\mathcal{F}$ and the infinite set of variables $\mathcal{V} = \{x, y, z, \ldots, \alpha, \beta, \ldots\}$. $\mathcal{R}$ is a *TRS over* $\mathcal{F}$ if $l, r \in \mathcal{T}(\mathcal{F}, \mathcal{V})$ for all rules $l \to r \in \mathcal{R}$.

---

* Supported by the Deutsche Forschungsgemeinschaft DFG under grant GI 274/5-1.

B. Gramlich (Ed.): FroCoS 2005, LNAI 3717, pp. 216–231, 2005.

We will present a method for termination analysis of untyped higher-order functions which do not use λ-abstraction. Due to the absence of λ, such functions can be represented in curried form as *applicative* first-order TRSs (cf. e.g., [22]). A signature $\mathcal{F}$ is *applicative* if it only contains nullary function symbols and a binary symbol $'$ for function application. Moreover, any TRS $\mathcal{R}$ over $\mathcal{F}$ is called *applicative*. So instead of a term $\mathsf{map}(\alpha, x)$ we write $'('(\mathsf{map}, \alpha), x)$. To ease readability, we use $'$ as an infix-symbol and we let $'$ associate to the left. Then this term can be written as $\mathsf{map}'\alpha'x$. This is very similar to the usual notation of higher-order functions where application is just denoted by juxtaposition (i.e., here one would write $\mathsf{map}\,\alpha\,x$ instead of $\mathsf{map}'\alpha'x$).

Example 1. The function map is used to apply a function to all elements in a list. Instead of the higher-order rules $\mathsf{map}(\alpha, \mathsf{nil}) \to \mathsf{nil}$ and $\mathsf{map}(\alpha, \mathsf{cons}(x, xs)) \to \mathsf{cons}(\alpha(x), \mathsf{map}(\alpha, xs))$, we encode it by the following first-order TRS.

$$\mathsf{map}'\alpha'\mathsf{nil} \to \mathsf{nil} \tag{1}$$

$$\mathsf{map}'\alpha'(\mathsf{cons}'x'xs) \to \mathsf{cons}'(\alpha'x)'(\mathsf{map}'\alpha'xs) \tag{2}$$

A TRS is terminating if all reductions are finite, i.e., if all applications of functions encoded in the TRS terminate. So intuitively, the TRS $\{(1), (2)\}$ is terminating iff map terminates whenever its arguments are terminating terms.

For a TRS $\mathcal{R}$ over $\mathcal{F}$, the *defined symbols* are $\mathcal{D} = \{\mathrm{root}(l) \mid l \to r \in \mathcal{R}\}$ and the *constructors* are $\mathcal{C} = \mathcal{F} \setminus \mathcal{D}$. For every $\mathsf{f} \in \mathcal{F}$ let $\mathsf{f}^\sharp$ be a fresh *tuple symbol* with the same arity as f, where we often write F for $\mathsf{f}^\sharp$. The set of tuple symbols is denoted by $\mathcal{F}^\sharp$. If $t = \mathsf{g}(t_1, \ldots, t_m)$ with $\mathsf{g} \in \mathcal{D}$, we let $t^\sharp$ denote $\mathsf{g}^\sharp(t_1, \ldots, t_m)$.

Definition 2 (Dependency Pair). *The set of* dependency pairs *for a TRS $\mathcal{R}$ is $DP(\mathcal{R}) = \{l^\sharp \to t^\sharp \mid l \to r \in \mathcal{R}, t$ is a subterm of r, $\mathrm{root}(t) \in \mathcal{D}\}$.*

Example 3. In the TRS of Ex. 1, the only defined symbol is $'$ and map, cons, and nil are constructors. Let AP denote the tuple symbol for $'$. Then we have the following dependency pairs where s is the term $\mathsf{AP}(\mathsf{map}'\alpha, \mathsf{cons}'x'xs)$.

$$s \to \mathsf{AP}(\mathsf{cons}'(\alpha'x), \mathsf{map}'\alpha'xs) \quad (3) \qquad\qquad s \to \mathsf{AP}(\mathsf{map}'\alpha, xs) \quad (6)$$

$$s \to \mathsf{AP}(\mathsf{cons}, \alpha'x) \quad (4) \qquad\qquad\qquad\qquad s \to \mathsf{AP}(\mathsf{map}, \alpha) \quad (7)$$

$$s \to \mathsf{AP}(\alpha, x) \quad (5)$$

For termination, we try to prove that there are no infinite *chains* of dependency pairs. Intuitively, a dependency pair corresponds to a function call and a chain represents a possible sequence of calls that can occur during a reduction. We always assume that different occurrences of dependency pairs are variable disjoint and consider substitutions whose domains may be infinite. In the following definition, $\mathcal{P}$ is usually a set of dependency pairs.

Definition 4 (Chain). *Let $\mathcal{P}, \mathcal{R}$ be TRSs. A (possibly infinite) sequence of pairs $s_1 \to t_1, s_2 \to t_2, \ldots$ from $\mathcal{P}$ is a $(\mathcal{P}, \mathcal{R})$-chain iff there is a substitution σ with $t_i\sigma \to_\mathcal{R}^* s_{i+1}\sigma$ for all i. It is an* innermost $(\mathcal{P}, \mathcal{R})$-chain *iff $t_i\sigma \xrightarrow{i}_\mathcal{R}^* s_{i+1}\sigma$ and $s_i\sigma$ is in normal form w.r.t. $\mathcal{R}$ for all i. Here, "$\xrightarrow{i}_\mathcal{R}$" denotes innermost reductions.*

Example 5. "(6), (6)" is a chain: an instance of (6)'s right-hand side $\mathsf{AP}(\mathsf{map}'\alpha_1, xs_1)$ can reduce to an instance of its left-hand side $\mathsf{AP}(\mathsf{map}'\alpha_2, \mathsf{cons}'x_2'xs_2)$.

Theorem 6 (Termination Criterion [4]). *A TRS $\mathcal{R}$ is (innermost) terminating iff there is no infinite (innermost) $(DP(\mathcal{R}), \mathcal{R})$-chain.*

The idea of the DP framework [16] is to treat a set of dependency pairs $\mathcal{P}$ together with the TRS $\mathcal{R}$ and to prove absence of infinite $(\mathcal{P}, \mathcal{R})$-chains instead of examining $\to_{\mathcal{R}}$. Formally, a *dependency pair problem* ("DP problem")[1] consists of two TRSs $\mathcal{P}$ and $\mathcal{R}$ (where initially, $\mathcal{P} = DP(\mathcal{R})$) and a flag $e \in \{\mathbf{t}, \mathbf{i}\}$ standing for "<ins>t</ins>ermination" or "<ins>i</ins>nnermost termination". Instead of "$(\mathcal{P}, \mathcal{R})$-chains" we also speak of "$(\mathcal{P}, \mathcal{R}, \mathbf{t})$-chains" and instead of "innermost $(\mathcal{P}, \mathcal{R})$-chains" we speak of "$(\mathcal{P}, \mathcal{R}, \mathbf{i})$-chains". Our goal is to show that there is no infinite $(\mathcal{P}, \mathcal{R}, e)$-chain. In this case, we call the problem *finite*.

A DP problem $(\mathcal{P}, \mathcal{R}, e)$ that is not finite is called *infinite*. But in addition, $(\mathcal{P}, \mathcal{R}, \mathbf{t})$ is already *infinite* whenever $\mathcal{R}$ is not terminating and $(\mathcal{P}, \mathcal{R}, \mathbf{i})$ is already *infinite* whenever $\mathcal{R}$ is not innermost terminating. Thus, there can be DP problems which are both finite and infinite. For example, the DP problem $(\mathcal{P}, \mathcal{R}, \mathbf{t})$ with $\mathcal{P} = \{\mathsf{F}(\mathsf{f}(x)) \to \mathsf{F}(x)\}$ and $\mathcal{R} = \{\mathsf{f}(\mathsf{f}(x)) \to \mathsf{f}(x), \mathsf{a} \to \mathsf{a}\}$ is finite since there is no infinite $(\mathcal{P}, \mathcal{R}, \mathbf{t})$-chain, but also infinite since $\mathcal{R}$ is not terminating. Such DP problems do not cause any difficulties, cf. [16]. If one detects an infinite problem during a termination proof attempt, one can abort the proof, since termination has been disproved (if all proof steps were "complete", i.e., if they preserved the termination behavior).

A DP problem $(\mathcal{P}, \mathcal{R}, e)$ is *applicative* iff $\mathcal{R}$ is a TRS over an applicative signature $\mathcal{F}$, and for all $s \to t \in \mathcal{P}$, we have $t \notin \mathcal{V}$, $\{\mathrm{root}(s), \mathrm{root}(t)\} \subseteq \mathcal{F}^{\sharp}$, and all function symbols below the root of s or t are from $\mathcal{F}$. We also say that such a problem is an applicative DP problem *over* $\mathcal{F}$. Thus, in an applicative DP problem $(\mathcal{P}, \mathcal{R}, e)$, the pairs $s \to t$ of $\mathcal{P}$ must have a shape which is similar to the original dependency pairs (i.e., the roots of s and t are tuple symbols which do not occur below the root). This requirement is needed in Sect. 3.3 in order to transform applicative terms back to ordinary functional form.

Termination techniques should now operate on DP problems instead of TRSs. We refer to such techniques as *dependency pair processors* ("DP processors"). Formally, a DP processor is a function *Proc* which takes a DP problem as input and returns a new set of DP problems which then have to be solved instead. Alternatively, it can also return "no". A DP processor *Proc* is *sound* if for all DP problems d, d is finite whenever $Proc(d)$ is not "no" and all DP problems in $Proc(d)$ are finite. *Proc* is *complete* if for all DP problems d, d is infinite whenever $Proc(d)$ is "no" or when $Proc(d)$ contains an infinite DP problem.

Soundness of a DP processor *Proc* is required to prove termination (in particular, to conclude that d is finite if $Proc(d) = \varnothing$). Completeness is needed to prove non-termination (in particular, to conclude that d is infinite if $Proc(d) = \mathsf{no}$).

So termination proofs in the DP framework start with the initial DP problem $(DP(\mathcal{R}), \mathcal{R}, e)$, where e depends on whether one wants to prove termination or innermost termination. Then this problem is transformed repeatedly by sound DP processors. If the final processors return empty sets of DP problems, then

---

[1] To ease readability we use a simpler definition of *DP problems* than [16], since this simple definition suffices for the new results of this paper.

termination is proved. If one of the processors returns "no" and all processors used before were complete, then one has disproved termination of the TRS $\mathcal{R}$.

Example 7. If d_0 is the initial DP problem $(DP(\mathcal{R}), \mathcal{R}, e)$ and there are sound processors $Proc_0$, $Proc_1$, $Proc_2$ with $Proc_0(d_0) = \{d_1, d_2\}$, $Proc_1(d_1) = \varnothing$, and $Proc_2(d_2) = \varnothing$, then one can conclude termination. But if $Proc_1(d_1) = $ no, and both $Proc_0$ and $Proc_1$ are complete, then one can conclude non-termination.

3   DP Processors for Higher-Order Functions

Since we represent higher-order functions by first-order applicative TRSs, all existing techniques and DP processors for first-order TRSs can also be used for higher-order functions. However, most termination techniques rely on the outermost function symbol when comparing terms. This is also true for dependency pairs and standard reduction orders. Therefore, they usually fail for applicative TRSs since here, all terms except variables and constants have the same root symbol $'$. For example, a direct termination proof of Ex. 1 is impossible with standard reduction orders and difficult[2] with dependency pairs.

Therefore, in Sect. 3.1 and Sect. 3.2 we improve the most important processors of the DP framework in order to be successful on applicative TRSs. Moreover, we introduce a new processor in Sect. 3.3 which removes the symbol $'$ and transforms applicative TRSs and DP problems into ordinary (functional) form again. Sect. 5 shows that these contributions indeed yield a powerful termination technique for higher-order functions. Sect. 3.4 is a comparison with related work.

3.1   A DP Processor Based on the Dependency Graph

The *dependency graph* determines which pairs can follow each other in chains.

Definition 8 (Dependency Graph). *Let $(\mathcal{P}, \mathcal{R}, e)$ be a DP problem. The nodes of the $(\mathcal{P}, \mathcal{R}, e)$-dependency graph are the pairs of $\mathcal{P}$ and there is an arc from $s \to t$ to $u \to v$ iff $s \to t, u \to v$ is an $(\mathcal{P}, \mathcal{R}, e)$-chain.*

Example 9. For Ex. 1, we obtain the following $(\mathcal{P}, \mathcal{R}, e)$-dependency graph for both $e = \mathbf{t}$ and $e = \mathbf{i}$. The reason is that the right-hand sides of (3), (4), and (7) have cons$'(\alpha' x)$, cons, or map as their first arguments. No instance of these terms reduces to an instance of map$'\alpha$ (which is the first argument of s).

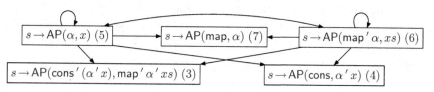

A set $\mathcal{P}' \neq \varnothing$ of dependency pairs is a *cycle* iff for all $s \to t$ and $u \to v$ in $\mathcal{P}'$, there is a path from $s \to t$ to $u \to v$ traversing only pairs of $\mathcal{P}'$. A cycle $\mathcal{P}'$ is a *strongly connected component* (SCC) if $\mathcal{P}'$ is not a proper subset of another cycle.

---

[2] It needs complex DP processors or base orders (e.g., non-linear polynomial orders).

As absence of infinite chains can be proved separately for each SCC, termination proofs can be modularized by decomposing a DP problem into sub-problems.

Theorem 10 (Dependency Graph Processor [16]). *For a DP problem* $(\mathcal{P}, \mathcal{R}, e)$, *let Proc return* $\{(\mathcal{P}_1, \mathcal{R}, e), \ldots, (\mathcal{P}_n, \mathcal{R}, e)\}$, *where* $\mathcal{P}_1, \ldots, \mathcal{P}_n$ *are the SCCs of the* $(\mathcal{P}, \mathcal{R}, e)$-*dependency graph. Then Proc is sound and complete.*

For Ex. 1, we start with the initial DP problem $(\mathcal{P}, \mathcal{R}, e)$, where $\mathcal{P} = \{(3), \ldots, (7)\}$. The only SCC of the dependency graph is $\{(5), (6)\}$. So the above processor transforms $(\mathcal{P}, \mathcal{R}, e)$ into $(\{(5), (6)\}, \mathcal{R}, e)$, i.e., (3), (4), and (7) are deleted.

Unfortunately, the dependency graph is not computable. Therefore, for automation one constructs an *estimated* graph containing at least all arcs of the real graph. The existing estimations that are used for automation [4,18] assume that all subterms with defined root could possibly be evaluated. Therefore, they use a function CAP, where CAP(t) results from replacing all subterms of t with defined root symbol by different fresh variables. To estimate whether $s \to t$ and $u \to v$ form a chain, one checks whether CAP(t) unifies with u (after renaming their variables). Moreover, if one regards termination instead of innermost termination, one first has to linearize CAP(t), i.e., multiple occurrences of the same variable in CAP(t) are renamed apart. Further refinements of this estimation can be found in [18]; however, they rely on the same function CAP.

These estimations are not suitable for applicative TRSs. The problem is that there, *all* subterms except variables and constants have the defined root symbol $'$ and are thus replaced by variables when estimating the arcs of the dependency graph. So for Ex. 1, the estimations assume that (3) could be followed by any dependency pair in chains. The reason is that the right-hand side of (3) is AP$(\mathsf{cons}'\,(\alpha'\,x), \mathsf{map}'\,\alpha'\,xs)$ and CAP replaces both arguments of AP by fresh variables, since their root symbol $'$ is defined. The resulting term AP(y, z) unifies with the left-hand side of every dependency pair. Therefore, the estimated dependency graph contains additional arcs from (3) to every dependency pair.

The problem is that these estimations do not check whether subterms with defined root can really be reduced further when being instantiated. For example, the first argument $\mathsf{cons}'\,(\alpha'\,x)$ of (3)'s right-hand side can never become a redex for any instantiation. The reason is that all left-hand sides of the TRS have the form $\mathsf{map}'\,t_1\,'t_2$. Thus, one should not replace $\mathsf{cons}'\,(\alpha'\,x)$ by a fresh variable.

Therefore, we now refine CAP's definition. If a subterm can clearly never become a redex, then it is not replaced by a variable anymore. Here, ICAP is used for innermost termination proofs and TCAP differs from ICAP by renaming multiple occurrences of variables, which is required when proving full termination.

Definition 11 (ICAP, TCAP). *Let* $\mathcal{R}$ *be a TRS over* $\mathcal{F}$, *let* $f \in \mathcal{F} \cup \mathcal{F}^{\sharp}$.

(i)   ICAP$(x) = x$ *for all* $x \in \mathcal{V}$
(ii) ICAP$(f(t_1, \ldots, t_n)) = f(\text{ICAP}(t_1), \ldots, \text{ICAP}(t_n))$ *iff* $f(\text{ICAP}(t_1), \ldots, \text{ICAP}(t_n))$
       does not unify with any left-hand side of a rule from $\mathcal{R}$
(iii) ICAP$(f(t_1, \ldots, t_n))$ *is a fresh variable, otherwise*

We define TCAP *like* ICAP *but in (i),* TCAP(x) *is a different fresh variable for every occurrence of* x. *Moreover in (ii), we use* TCAP(t_i) *instead of* ICAP(t_i).

Now one can detect that (3) should not be connected to any pair in the dependency graph, since $\text{ICAP}(\text{AP}(\text{cons}'(\alpha'x), \text{map}'\alpha'xs)) = \text{AP}(\text{cons}'y, z)$ does not unify with left-hand sides of dependency pairs. Similar remarks hold for TCAP. This leads to the following improved estimation.[3]

Definition 12 (Improved Estimated Dependency Graph). *In the estimated $(\mathcal{P}, \mathcal{R}, \mathbf{t})$-dependency graph there is an arc from $s \to t$ to $u \to v$ iff TCAP(t) and u are unifiable. In the estimated $(\mathcal{P}, \mathcal{R}, \mathbf{i})$-dependency graph there is an arc from $s \to t$ to $u \to v$ iff ICAP(t) and u are unifiable by an mgu μ (after renaming their variables) such that $s\mu$ and $u\mu$ are in normal form w.r.t. $\mathcal{R}$.*

Now the estimated graph is identical to the real dependency graph in Ex. 9.

Theorem 13 (Soundness of the Improved Estimation). *The dependency graph is a subgraph of the estimated dependency graph.*

Of course, the new estimation of dependency graphs from Def. 12 is also useful for non-applicative TRSs and DP problems. The benefits of our improvements (also for ordinary TRSs) is demonstrated by our experiments in Sect. 5.

3.2   DP Processors Based on Orders and on Usable Rules

Classical techniques for automated termination proofs try to find a *reduction order* $\succ$ such that $l \succ r$ holds for all rules $l \to r$. In practice, most orders are *simplification orders* [10]. However, termination of many important TRSs cannot be proved with such orders directly. Therefore, the following processor allows us to use such orders in the DP framework instead. It generates constraints which should be satisfied by a *reduction pair* [23] $(\succsim, \succ)$ where $\succsim$ is reflexive, transitive, monotonic, and stable and $\succ$ is a stable well-founded order compatible with $\succsim$ (i.e., $\succsim \circ \succ \subseteq \succ$ and $\succ \circ \succsim \subseteq \succ$). Now one can use existing techniques to search for suitable relations $\succsim$ and $\succ$, and in this way, classical simplification orders can prove termination of TRSs where they would have failed otherwise.

For a problem $(\mathcal{P}, \mathcal{R}, e)$, the constraints require that at least one rule in $\mathcal{P}$ is strictly decreasing (w.r.t. $\succ$) and all remaining rules in $\mathcal{P}$ and $\mathcal{R}$ are weakly decreasing (w.r.t. $\succsim$). Requiring $l \succsim r$ for $l \to r \in \mathcal{R}$ ensures that in chains $s_1 \to t_1, s_2 \to t_2, \dots$ with $t_i\sigma \to_{\mathcal{R}}^* s_{i+1}\sigma$, we have $t_i\sigma \succsim s_{i+1}\sigma$. Hence, if a reduction pair satisfies these constraints, then the strictly decreasing pairs of $\mathcal{P}$ cannot occur infinitely often in chains. Thus, the following processor deletes these pairs from $\mathcal{P}$. For any TRS $\mathcal{P}$ and any relation $\succ$, let $\mathcal{P}_\succ = \{s \to t \in \mathcal{P} \mid s \succ t\}$.

Theorem 14 (Reduction Pair Processor [16]). *Let $(\succsim, \succ)$ be a reduction pair. Then the following DP processor Proc is sound and complete. For a DP problem $(\mathcal{P}, \mathcal{R}, e)$, Proc returns*

- *$\{(\mathcal{P} \setminus \mathcal{P}_\succ, \mathcal{R}, e)\}$, if $\mathcal{P}_\succ \cup \mathcal{P}_{\succsim} = \mathcal{P}$ and $\mathcal{R}_{\succsim} = \mathcal{R}$*
- *$\{(\mathcal{P}, \mathcal{R}, e)\}$, otherwise*

---

[3] Moreover, TCAP and ICAP can also be combined with further refinements to approximate dependency graphs [4,18].

DP problems $(\mathcal{P}, \mathcal{R}, i)$ for *innermost* termination can be simplified by replacing the second component $\mathcal{R}$ by those rules from $\mathcal{R}$ that are *usable* for $\mathcal{P}$ (i.e., by the *usable rules* of $\mathcal{P}$). Then by Thm. 14, a weak decrease $l \gtrsim r$ is not required for all rules but only for the usable rules. As defined in [4], the *usable rules* of a term t contain all f-rules for all function symbols f occurring in t. Moreover, if f's rules are usable and there is a rule $f(\ldots) \to r$ in $\mathcal{R}$ whose right-hand side r contains a symbol g, then g is usable, too. The *usable rules* of a TRS $\mathcal{P}$ are defined as the usable rules of its right-hand sides.

For instance, after applying the dependency graph processor to Ex. 1, we have the remaining dependency pairs (5) and (6) with the right-hand sides $\mathsf{AP}(\alpha, x)$ and $\mathsf{AP}(\mathsf{map}'\,\alpha, xs)$. While $\mathsf{AP}(\alpha, x)$ has no usable rules, $\mathsf{AP}(\mathsf{map}'\,\alpha, xs)$ contains the defined function symbol $'$ and therefore, all $'$-rules are usable.

This indicates that the definition of usable rules has to be improved to handle applicative TRSs successfully. Otherwise, whenever $'$ occurs in the right-hand side of a dependency pair, then *all* rules (except rules of the form $f \to \ldots$) would be usable. The problem is that the current definition of "usable rules" assumes that all $'$-rules can be applied to any subterm with the root symbol $'$.

Thus, we refine the definition of usable rules. Now a subterm starting with $'$ only influences the computation of the usable rules if some suitable instantiation of this subterm would start new reductions. To detect this, we again use the function ICAP from Def. 11. For example, $\mathsf{map}'\,\alpha$ can never be reduced if α is instantiated by a normal form, since $\mathsf{map}'\,\alpha$ does not unify with the left-hand side of any rule. Therefore, the right-hand side $\mathsf{AP}(\mathsf{map}'\,\alpha, xs)$ of (6) should not have any usable rules.[4]

Definition 15 (Improved Usable Rules). *For a DP problem* $(\mathcal{P}, \mathcal{R}, i)$, *we define the* usable rules $\mathcal{U}(\mathcal{P}) = \bigcup_{s \to t \in \mathcal{P}} \mathcal{U}(t)$. *Here* $\mathcal{U}(t) \subseteq \mathcal{R}$ *is the smallest set with:*

- *If* $t = f(t_1, \ldots, t_n)$, $f \in \mathcal{F} \cup \mathcal{F}^{\sharp}$, *and* $f(\mathrm{ICAP}(t_1), \ldots, \mathrm{ICAP}(t_n))$ *unifies with a left-hand side* l *of a rule* $l \to r \in \mathcal{R}$, *then* $l \to r \in \mathcal{U}(t)$.
- *If* $l \to r \in \mathcal{U}(t)$, *then* $\mathcal{U}(r) \subseteq \mathcal{U}(t)$.
- *If* t' *is a subterm of* t, *then* $\mathcal{U}(t') \subseteq \mathcal{U}(t)$.

Theorem 16 (Usable Rule Processor). *For a DP problem* $(\mathcal{P}, \mathcal{R}, e)$, *let Proc return* $\{(\mathcal{P}, \mathcal{U}(\mathcal{P}), i)\}$ *if* $e = i$ *and* $\{(\mathcal{P}, \mathcal{R}, e)\}$ *otherwise. Then Proc is sound.*[5]

Example 17. In Ex. 1, now the dependency pairs in the remaining DP problem $(\{(5), (6)\}, \mathcal{R}, i)$ have no usable rules. Thus, Thm. 16 transforms this DP problem into $(\{(5), (6)\}, \varnothing, i)$. Then with the processor of Thm. 14 we try to find a reduction pair such that (5) and (6) are decreasing. Any simplification order $\succ$ (even the embedding order) makes both pairs strictly decreasing: $s \succ \mathsf{AP}(\alpha, x)$ and $s \succ \mathsf{AP}(\mathsf{map}'\,\alpha, xs)$ for $s = \mathsf{AP}(\mathsf{map}'\,\alpha, \mathsf{cons}'\,x'\,xs)$. Thus, both dependency pairs are removed and the resulting DP problem $(\varnothing, \mathcal{R}, i)$ is transformed

---

[4] Our new definition of usable rules can also be combined with other techniques to reduce the set of usable rules [14] and it can also be applied for dependency graph estimations or other DP processors that rely on usable rules [16,18].

[5] Incompleteness is due to our simplified definition of "DP problems". With the full definition of "DP problems" from [16], the processor is complete [16, Lemma 12].

into the empty set by the dependency graph processor of Thm. 10. So innermost termination of the map-TRS from Ex. 1 can now easily be proved automatically. Note that this TRS is non-overlapping and thus, it belongs to a well-known class where innermost termination implies termination.

Similar to the improved estimation of dependency graphs in the previous section, the new improved definition of usable rules from Def. 15 is also beneficial for ordinary non-applicative TRSs, cf. Sect. 5.

In [32], we showed that under certain conditions, the usable rules of [4] can also be used to prove full instead of just innermost termination (for arbitrary TRSs). Then, even for termination, it is enough to require $l \succsim r$ just for the usable rules in Thm. 14. This result also holds for the new improved usable rules of Def. 15, provided that one uses TCAP instead of ICAP in their definition.

3.3 A DP Processor to Transform Applicative to Functional Form

Some applicative DP problems can be transformed (back) to ordinary functional form. In particular, this holds for problems resulting from first-order functions (encoded by currying). This transformation is advantageous: e.g., the processor in Thm. 14 is significantly more powerful for DP problems in functional form, since standard reduction orders focus on the root symbol when comparing terms.

Example 18. We extend the map-TRS by the following rules for minus and div. Note that a direct termination proof with simplification orders is impossible.

$$\mathsf{minus}\,'x\,'0 \to x \qquad (8) \qquad \mathsf{div}\,'0\,'(\mathsf{s}\,'y) \to 0 \qquad (10)$$
$$\mathsf{minus}\,'(\mathsf{s}\,'x)\,'(\mathsf{s}\,'y) \to \mathsf{minus}\,'x\,'y\,(9) \quad \mathsf{div}\,'(\mathsf{s}\,'x)\,'(\mathsf{s}\,'y) \to \mathsf{s}\,'(\mathsf{div}\,'(\mathsf{minus}\,'x\,'y)\,'(\mathsf{s}\,'y))\,(11)$$

While map is really a higher-order function, minus and div correspond to first-order functions. It again suffices to verify innermost termination, since this TRS $\mathcal{R}$ is non-overlapping. The improved estimated dependency graph has three SCCs corresponding to map, minus, and div. Thus, by the dependency graph and the usable rule processors (Thm. 10 and 16), the initial DP problem $(DP(\mathcal{R}), \mathcal{R}, \mathbf{i})$ is transformed into three new problems. The first problem $(\{(5), (6)\}, \varnothing, \mathbf{i})$ for map can be solved as before. The DP problems for minus and div are:

$$(\{\mathsf{AP}(\mathsf{minus}\,'(\mathsf{s}\,'x), \mathsf{s}\,'y) \to \mathsf{AP}(\mathsf{minus}\,'x, y)\}, \varnothing, \mathbf{i}) \qquad (12)$$
$$(\{\mathsf{AP}(\mathsf{div}\,'(\mathsf{s}\,'x), \mathsf{s}\,'y) \to \mathsf{AP}(\mathsf{div}\,'(\mathsf{minus}\,'x\,'y), \mathsf{s}\,'y)\}, \{(8), (9)\}, \mathbf{i}) \quad (13)$$

Since (12) and (13) do not contain map anymore, one would like to change them back to conventional functional form. Then they could be replaced by the following DP problems. Here, every (new) function symbol is labelled by its arity.

$$(\{\mathsf{MINUS}^2(\mathsf{s}^1(x), \mathsf{s}^1(y)) \to \mathsf{MINUS}^2(x, y)\}, \varnothing, \mathbf{i}) \qquad (14)$$
$$(\{\mathsf{DIV}^2(\mathsf{s}^1(x), \mathsf{s}^1(y)) \to \mathsf{DIV}^2(\mathsf{minus}^2(x, y), \mathsf{s}^1(y))\},$$
$$\{\mathsf{minus}^2(x, 0^0) \to x, \mathsf{minus}^2(\mathsf{s}^1(x), \mathsf{s}^1(y)) \to \mathsf{minus}^2(x, y)\}, \mathbf{i}) \qquad (15)$$

These DP problems are easy to solve: for example, the constraints of the reduction pair processor (Thm. 14) are satisfied by the polynomial order which maps $s^1(x)$ to $x+1$, $minus^2(x,y)$ to x, and every other symbol to the sum of its arguments. Thus, termination could immediately be proved automatically.

Now we characterize those applicative TRSs which correspond to first-order functions and can be translated into functional form. In these TRSs, for any function symbol f there is a number n (called its *arity*) such that f only occurs in terms of the form $f' t_1' \ldots ' t_n$. So there are no applications with too few or too many arguments. Moreover, there are no terms $x' t$ where the first argument of $'$ is a variable. Def. 19 extends this idea from TRSs to DP problems.

Definition 19 (Arity and Proper Terms). *Let $(\mathcal{P}, \mathcal{R}, e)$ be an applicative DP problem over $\mathcal{F}$. For each $f \in \mathcal{F} \setminus \{'\}$ let $arity(f) = max\{ n \mid f' t_1' \ldots ' t_n$ or $(f' t_1' \ldots ' t_n)^\sharp$ occurs in $\mathcal{P} \cup \mathcal{R} \}$. A term t is proper iff $t \in \mathcal{V}$ or $t = f' t_1' \ldots ' t_n$ or $t = (f' t_1' \ldots ' t_n)^\sharp$ where in the last two cases, $arity(f) = n$ and all t_i are proper. Moreover, $(\mathcal{P}, \mathcal{R}, e)$ is proper iff all terms in $\mathcal{P} \cup \mathcal{R}$ are proper.*

The DP problems (12) and (13) for minus and div are proper. Here, minus and div have arity 2, s has arity 1, and 0 has arity 0. But the problem $(\{(5), (6)\}, \varnothing, \mathbf{i})$ for map is not proper as (5) contains the subterm $AP(\alpha, x)$ with $\alpha \in \mathcal{V}$.

The following transformation translates proper terms from applicative to functional form. To this end, $f' t_1' \ldots ' t_n$ is replaced by $f^n(\ldots)$, where n is f's arity (as defined in Def. 19) and f^n is a new n-ary function symbol. In this way, (12) and (13) were transformed into (14) and (15) in Ex. 18.

Definition 20 (Transformation $\mathcal{A}$). *$\mathcal{A}$ maps every proper term from $\mathcal{T}(\mathcal{F} \cup \mathcal{F}^\sharp, \mathcal{V})$ to a term from $\mathcal{T}(\{f^n, F^n \mid f \in \mathcal{F} \setminus \{'\}, arity(f) = n\}, \mathcal{V})$:*

- $\mathcal{A}(x) = x$ *for all* $x \in \mathcal{V}$
- $\mathcal{A}(f' t_1' \ldots ' t_n) = f^n(\mathcal{A}(t_1), \ldots, \mathcal{A}(t_n))$ *for all* $f \in \mathcal{F} \setminus \{'\}$
- $\mathcal{A}((f' t_1' \ldots ' t_n)^\sharp) = F^n(\mathcal{A}(t_1), \ldots, \mathcal{A}(t_n))$ *for all* $f \in \mathcal{F} \setminus \{'\}$

For any TRS $\mathcal{R}$ with only proper terms, let $\mathcal{A}(\mathcal{R}) = \{\mathcal{A}(l) \to \mathcal{A}(r) \mid l \to r \in \mathcal{R}\}$.

We now define a DP processor which replaces proper DP problems $(\mathcal{P}, \mathcal{R}, e)$ by $(\mathcal{A}(\mathcal{P}), \mathcal{A}(\mathcal{R}), e)$. Its soundness is due to the fact that every $(\mathcal{P}, \mathcal{R}, e)$-chain results in an $(\mathcal{A}(\mathcal{P}), \mathcal{A}(\mathcal{R}), e)$-chain, i.e., that $t_i \sigma \to_{\mathcal{R}}^* s_{i+1} \sigma$ implies $\mathcal{A}(t_i)\sigma' \to_{\mathcal{A}(\mathcal{R})}^* \mathcal{A}(s_{i+1})\sigma'$ for some substitution σ'. The reason is that t_i and s_{i+1} are proper and while σ may introduce non-proper terms, every chain can also be constructed with a substitution $\bar{\sigma}$ where all $\bar{\sigma}(x)$ are proper. Thus, while soundness and completeness of the following processor might seem intuitive, the formal proof including this construction is quite involved and can be found in [17].

Theorem 21 (DP Processor for Transformation in Functional Form). *For any DP problem $(\mathcal{P}, \mathcal{R}, e)$, let Proc return $\{(\mathcal{A}(\mathcal{P}), \mathcal{A}(\mathcal{R}), e)\}$ if $(\mathcal{P}, \mathcal{R}, e)$ is proper and $\{(\mathcal{P}, \mathcal{R}, e)\}$ otherwise. Then Proc is sound and complete.*

With the processor of Thm. 21 and our new improved estimation of dependency graphs (Def. 12), it does not matter anymore for the termination proof whether first-order functions are represented in ordinary functional or in applicative form: in the latter case, dependency pairs with non-proper right-hand sides are not in SCCs of the improved estimated dependency graph. Hence, after applying the dependency graph processor of Thm. 10, all remaining DP problems are proper and can be transformed into functional form by Thm. 21.

As an alternative to the processor of Thm. 21, one can also couple the transformation $\mathcal{A}$ with the reduction pair processor from Thm. 14. Then a DP problem $(\mathcal{P}, \mathcal{R}, e)$ is transformed into $\{(\mathcal{P} \setminus \{s \to t \mid \mathcal{A}(s) \succ \mathcal{A}(t)\}, \mathcal{R}, e)\}$ if $(\mathcal{P}, \mathcal{R}, e)$ is proper, if $\mathcal{A}(\mathcal{P})_{\succ} \cup \mathcal{A}(\mathcal{P})_{\succsim} = \mathcal{A}(\mathcal{P})$, and if $\mathcal{A}(\mathcal{R})_{\succsim} = \mathcal{A}(\mathcal{R})$ holds for some reduction pair $(\succsim, \succ)$. An advantage of this alternative processor is that it can be combined with our results from [32] on applying usable rules for termination instead of innermost termination proofs, cf. Sect. 3.2.

3.4   Comparison with Related Work

Most approaches for higher-order functions in term rewriting use *higher-order TRSs*. While there exist powerful termination criteria for higher-order TRSs (e.g., [7,29]), the main *automated* termination techniques for such TRSs are *simplification orders* (e.g., [20]) which fail on functions like div in Ex. 18.

Exceptions are the *monotonic higher-order semantic path order* [8] and the existing variants of dependency pairs for higher-order TRSs. However, these variants require considerable restrictions (e.g., on the TRSs [31] or on the orders that may be used [3,24,30].) So in contrast to our results, they are less powerful than the original dependency pair technique when applied to first-order functions.

Termination techniques for higher-order TRSs often handle a richer language than our results. But these approaches are usually difficult to automate (there are hardly any implementations of these techniques available). In contrast, it is very easy to integrate our results into existing termination provers for ordinary first-order TRSs using dependency pairs (and first-order reduction orders).

Other approaches represent higher-order functions by first-order TRSs [1,2,19,25,33], similar to us. However, they mostly use *monomorphic* types (this restriction is also imposed in some approaches for higher-order TRSs [8]). In other words, there the types are only built from basic types and type constructors like $\to$ or $\times$, but there are no *type variables*, i.e., no polymorphic types. Then terms like "map' minus' xs" and "map' (minus' x)' xs" cannot both be well typed, but one needs different map-symbols for arguments of different types. In contrast, our approach uses untyped term rewriting. Hence, it can be applied for termination analysis of polymorphic or untyped functional languages. Moreover, [25] and [33] only consider extensions of the lexicographic path order, whereas we can also handle non-simply terminating TRSs like Ex. 18.

4   A DP Processor for Proving Non-termination

Almost all techniques for automated termination analysis try to *prove termination* and there are hardly any methods to *prove non-termination*. But detecting non-termination automatically would be very helpful when debugging programs.

We show that the DP framework is particularly suitable for combining both termination and *non*-termination analysis. We introduce a DP processor which tries to detect infinite DP problems in order to answer "no". Then, if all previous processors were complete, we can conclude non-termination of the original TRS. As shown by our experiments in Sect. 5, our new processor also successfully handles non-terminating higher-order functions if they are represented by first-order TRSs. An important advantage of the DP framework is that it can couple the search for a proof and a disproof of termination: Processors which try to prove termination are also helpful for the non-termination proof because they transform the initial DP problem into sub-problems, where most of them can easily be proved finite. So they detect those sub-problems which could cause non-termination. Therefore, the non-termination processors should only operate on these sub-problems and thus, they only have to regard a subset of the rules when searching for non-termination. On the other hand, processors that try to disprove termination are also helpful for the termination proof, even if some of the previous processors were incomplete. The reason is that there are many indeterminisms in a termination proof attempt, since usually many DP processors can be applied to a DP problem. Thus, if one can find out that a DP problem is infinite, one knows that one has reached a "dead end" and should backtrack.

To prove non-termination within the DP framework, in Sect. 4.1 we introduce *looping* DP problems and in Sect. 4.2 we show how to detect such DP problems automatically. Finally, Sect. 4.3 is a comparison with related work.

4.1   A DP Processor Based on Looping DP Problems

An obvious approach to find infinite reductions is to search for a term s which evaluates to a term $C[s\mu]$ containing an instance of s. A TRS with such reductions is called *looping*. Clearly, a naive search for looping terms is very costly.

In contrast to "looping TRSs", when adapting the concept of *loopingness* to DP problems, we only have to consider terms s occurring in dependency pairs and we do not have to regard any contexts C. The reason is that such contexts are already removed by the construction of dependency pairs. Thm. 23 shows that in this way one can indeed detect all looping TRSs.

Definition 22 (Looping DP Problems). *A DP problem* $(\mathcal{P}, \mathcal{R}, \mathsf{t})$ *is looping iff there is a* $(\mathcal{P}, \mathcal{R})$-*chain* $s_1 \to t_1, s_2 \to t_2, \ldots$ *with* $t_i \sigma \to^*_\mathcal{R} s_{i+1}\sigma$ *for all* i *such that* $s_1\sigma$ *matches* $s_k\sigma$ *for some* $k > 1$ *(i.e.,* $s_1\sigma\mu = s_k\sigma$ *for a substitution* μ*).*

Theorem 23. *A TRS* $\mathcal{R}$ *is looping iff the DP problem* $(DP(\mathcal{R}), \mathcal{R}, \mathsf{t})$ *is looping.*

Example 24. Consider Toyama's example $\mathcal{R} = \{\mathsf{f}(0, 1, x) \to \mathsf{f}(x, x, x), \mathsf{g}(y, z) \to y, \mathsf{g}(y, z) \to z\}$ and $\mathcal{P} = DP(\mathcal{R}) = \{\mathsf{F}(0, 1, x) \to \mathsf{F}(x, x, x)\}$. We have the $(\mathcal{P}, \mathcal{R})$-chain $\mathsf{F}(0, 1, x_1) \to \mathsf{F}(x_1, x_1, x_1), \mathsf{F}(0, 1, x_2) \to \mathsf{F}(x_2, x_2, x_2)$, since $\mathsf{F}(x_1, x_1, x_1)\sigma \to^*_\mathcal{R} \mathsf{F}(0, 1, x_2)\sigma$ for $\sigma(x_1) = \sigma(x_2) = \mathsf{g}(0, 1)$. As the term $\mathsf{F}(0, 1, x_1)\sigma$ matches $\mathsf{F}(0, 1, x_2)\sigma$ (they are even identical), the DP problem $(\mathcal{P}, \mathcal{R}, \mathsf{t})$ is looping.

Our goal is to detect looping DP problems. In the termination case, every looping DP problem is infinite and hence, if all preceding DP processors were complete, then termination is disproved. However, the definition of "looping" from Def. 22 cannot be used for innermost termination: in Ex. 24, $(DP(\mathcal{R}), \mathcal{R}, \mathbf{t})$ is looping, but $(DP(\mathcal{R}), \mathcal{R}, \mathbf{i})$ is finite and $\mathcal{R}$ is innermost terminating.[6]

Nevertheless, for *non-overlapping* DP problems, $(\mathcal{P}, \mathcal{R}, \mathbf{i})$ is infinite whenever $(\mathcal{P}, \mathcal{R}, \mathbf{t})$ is infinite. So here loopingness of $(\mathcal{P}, \mathcal{R}, \mathbf{t})$ indeed implies that $(\mathcal{P}, \mathcal{R}, \mathbf{i})$ is infinite. We call $(\mathcal{P}, \mathcal{R}, e)$ *non-overlapping* if $\mathcal{R}$ is non-overlapping and no left-hand side of $\mathcal{R}$ unifies with a non-variable subterm of a left-hand side of $\mathcal{P}$.

Lemma 25 (Looping and Infinite DP Problems).

(a) If $(\mathcal{P}, \mathcal{R}, \mathbf{t})$ is looping, then $(\mathcal{P}, \mathcal{R}, \mathbf{t})$ is infinite.
(b) If $(\mathcal{P}, \mathcal{R}, \mathbf{t})$ is infinite and non-overlapping, then $(\mathcal{P}, \mathcal{R}, \mathbf{i})$ is infinite.

Now we can define the DP processor for proving non-termination.

Theorem 26 (Non-termination Processor). *The following DP processor Proc is sound and complete. For a DP problem $(\mathcal{P}, \mathcal{R}, e)$, Proc returns*

- *"no", if $(\mathcal{P}, \mathcal{R}, \mathbf{t})$ is looping and ($e = \mathbf{t}$ or $(\mathcal{P}, \mathcal{R}, e)$ is non-overlapping)*
- $\{(\mathcal{P}, \mathcal{R}, e)\}$, *otherwise*

4.2   Detecting Looping DP Problems

Our criteria to detect looping DP problems automatically use *narrowing*.

Definition 27 (Narrowing). *Let $\mathcal{R}$ be a TRS which may also have rules $l \to r$ with $\mathcal{V}(r) \not\subseteq \mathcal{V}(l)$ or $l \in \mathcal{V}$. A term t narrows to s, denoted $t \leadsto_{\mathcal{R}, \delta, p} s$, iff there is a substitution δ, a (variable-renamed) rule $l \to r \in \mathcal{R}$ and a non-variable position p of t where $\delta = mgu(t|_p, l)$ and $s = t[r]_p \delta$. Let $\leadsto_{\mathcal{R}, \delta}$ be the relation which permits narrowing steps on all positions p. Let $\leadsto_{(\mathcal{P}, \mathcal{R}), \delta}$ denote $\leadsto_{\mathcal{P}, \delta, \varepsilon} \cup \leadsto_{\mathcal{R}, \delta}$, where ε is the root position. Moreover, $\leadsto^*_{(\mathcal{P}, \mathcal{R}), \delta}$ is the smallest relation containing $\leadsto_{(\mathcal{P}, \mathcal{R}), \delta_1} \circ \dots \circ \leadsto_{(\mathcal{P}, \mathcal{R}), \delta_n}$ for all $n \geq 0$ and all substitutions where $\delta = \delta_1 \dots \delta_n$.*

Example 28. Let $\mathcal{R} = \{\mathsf{f}(x, y, z) \to \mathsf{g}(x, y, z), \mathsf{g}(\mathsf{s}(x), y, z) \to \mathsf{f}(z, \mathsf{s}(y), z)\}$ and $\mathcal{P} = DP(\mathcal{R}) = \{\mathsf{F}(x, y, z) \to \mathsf{G}(x, y, z), \mathsf{G}(\mathsf{s}(x), y, z) \to \mathsf{F}(z, \mathsf{s}(y), z)\}$. The term $\mathsf{G}(x, y, z)$ can only be narrowed by the rule $\mathsf{G}(\mathsf{s}(x'), y', z') \to \mathsf{F}(z', \mathsf{s}(y'), x')$ on the root position and hence, we obtain $\mathsf{G}(x, y, z) \leadsto_{\mathcal{P}, [x/\mathsf{s}(x'), y'/y, z'/z], \varepsilon} \mathsf{F}(z', \mathsf{s}(y), z)$.

To find loops, we narrow the right-hand side t of a dependency pair $s \to t$ until one reaches a term s' such that $s\delta$ *semi-unifies* with s' (i.e., $s\delta\mu_1\mu_2 = s'\mu_1$ for some substitutions μ_1 and μ_2). Here, δ is the substitution used for narrowing. Then we indeed have a loop as in Def. 22 by defining $\sigma = \delta\mu_1$ and $\mu = \mu_2$. Semi-unification encompasses both matching and unification and algorithms for semi-unification can for example be found in [21,27].

Theorem 29 (Loop Detection by Forward Narrowing). *Let $(\mathcal{P}, \mathcal{R}, e)$ be a DP problem. If there is an $s \to t \in \mathcal{P}$ such that $t \leadsto^*_{(\mathcal{P}, \mathcal{R}), \delta} s'$ and $s\delta$ semi-unifies with s', then $(\mathcal{P}, \mathcal{R}, \mathbf{t})$ is looping.*

---

[6] One can adapt "loopingness" to the innermost case: $(\mathcal{P}, \mathcal{R}, \mathbf{i})$ is *looping* iff there is an *innermost* $(\mathcal{P}, \mathcal{R})$-chain $s_1 \to t_1, s_2 \to t_2, \dots$ such that $t_i\sigma\mu^n \xrightarrow{i}^*_\mathcal{R} s_{i+1}\sigma\mu^n$, $s_1\sigma\mu = s_k\sigma$, and $s_i\sigma\mu^n$ is in normal form for all i and all $n \geq 0$. Then loopingness implies that the DP problem is infinite, but now one has to examine *infinitely* many instantiations $s_i\sigma\mu^n$ and $t_i\sigma\mu^n$. Nevertheless, one can also formulate sufficient conditions for loopingness in the innermost case which are amenable to automation.

Example 30. We continue with Ex. 28. We had $G(x, y, z) \rightsquigarrow_{(\mathcal{P}, \mathcal{R}), \delta} F(z, \mathsf{s}(y), z)$ where $\delta = [x/\mathsf{s}(x'), y'/y, z'/z]$. Applying δ to the left-hand side $s = F(x, y, z)$ of the first dependency pair yields $F(\mathsf{s}(x'), y, z)$. Now $F(\mathsf{s}(x'), y, z)$ semi-unifies with $F(z, \mathsf{s}(y), z)$, since $F(\mathsf{s}(x'), y, z)\mu_1\mu_2 = F(z, \mathsf{s}(y), z)\mu_1$ for the substitutions $\mu_1 = [z/\mathsf{s}(x')]$ and $\mu_2 = [y/\mathsf{s}(y)]$. (However, the first term does not match or unify with the second.) Thus, $(\mathcal{P}, \mathcal{R}, \mathbf{t})$ is looping and $\mathcal{R}$ does not terminate.

However, while the DP problem of Toyama's example (Ex. 24) is looping, this is not detected by Thm. 29. The reason is that the right-hand side $F(x, x, x)$ of the only dependency pair cannot be narrowed. Therefore, we now introduce a "backward" variant[7] of the above criterion which narrows with the reversed TRSs $\mathcal{P}^{-1}$ and $\mathcal{R}^{-1}$. Of course, in general $\mathcal{P}^{-1}$ and $\mathcal{R}^{-1}$ may also have rules $l \to r$ with $\mathcal{V}(r) \not\subseteq \mathcal{V}(l)$ or $l \in \mathcal{V}$. However, the usual definition of narrowing can immediately be extended to such TRSs, cf. Def. 27.

Theorem 31 (Loop Detection by Backward Narrowing). *Let* $(\mathcal{P}, \mathcal{R}, e)$ *be a DP problem. If there is an* $s \to t \in \mathcal{P}$ *such that* $s \rightsquigarrow^*_{(\mathcal{P}^{-1}, \mathcal{R}^{-1}), \delta} t'$ *and* t' *semi-unifies with* $t\delta$, *then* $(\mathcal{P}, \mathcal{R}, \mathbf{t})$ *is looping.*

Example 32. To detect that Toyama's example (Ex. 24) is looping, we start with the left-hand side $s = F(0, 1, x)$ and narrow 0 to $\mathsf{g}(0, z)$ using $y \to \mathsf{g}(y, z) \in \mathcal{R}^{-1}$. Then we narrow 1 to $\mathsf{g}(y', 1)$ by $z' \to \mathsf{g}(y', z')$. Therefore we obtain $F(0, 1, x)$ $\rightsquigarrow^*_{(\mathcal{P}^{-1}, \mathcal{R}^{-1}), [y/0, z'/1]} F(\mathsf{g}(0, z), \mathsf{g}(y, 1), x)$. Now $t' = F(\mathsf{g}(0, z), \mathsf{g}(y, 1), x)$ (semi-) unifies with the corresponding right-hand side $t = F(x, x, x)$ using $\mu_1 = [x/\mathsf{g}(0, 1), y/0, z/1]$. Thus, $(DP(\mathcal{R}), \mathcal{R}, \mathbf{t})$ is looping and the TRS is not terminating.

However, there are also TRSs where backward narrowing fails and forward narrowing succeeds.[8] Note that Ex. 24 where forward narrowing fails is not right-linear and that the example in Footnote 8 where backward narrowing fails is not left-linear. In fact, our experiments show that most looping DP problems $(\mathcal{P}, \mathcal{R}, \mathbf{t})$ can be detected by forward narrowing if $\mathcal{P} \cup \mathcal{R}$ is right-linear and by backward narrowing if $\mathcal{P} \cup \mathcal{R}$ is left-linear. Therefore, we use the non-termination processor of Thm. 26 with the following heuristic in our system AProVE [15]:

- If $\mathcal{P} \cup \mathcal{R}$ is right- and not left-linear, then use forward narrowing (Thm. 29).
- Otherwise, we use backward narrowing (Thm. 31). If $\mathcal{P} \cup \mathcal{R}$ is not left-linear, then moreover we also permit narrowing steps in variables (i.e., $t|_p \in \mathcal{V}$ is permitted in Def. 27). The reason is that then there are looping DP problems which otherwise cannot be detected by forward or backward narrowing.[9]
- Moreover, to obtain a finite search space, we use an upper bound on the number of times that a rule from $\mathcal{P} \cup \mathcal{R}$ can be used for narrowing.

---

[7] Thus, non-termination can be investigated both by forward and by backward analysis. In that sense, non-termination is similar to several other properties of programs for which both forward and backward analysis techniques are used. A well-known such property is *strictness* in lazy functional languages. Here, classical forward and backward analysis techniques are [26] and [35], respectively.

[8] An example is $\mathcal{R} = \{f(x, x) \to f(0, 1), 0 \to \mathsf{a}, 1 \to \mathsf{a}\}$, $\mathcal{P} = DP(\mathcal{R}) = \{F(x, x) \to F(0, 1)\}$.

[9] An example is the well-known TRS of Drosten [11]. Nevertheless, then there are also looping DP problems which cannot even be found when narrowing into variables.

4.3 Comparison with Related Work

We use narrowing to identify looping DP problems. This is related to the concept of *forward closures* of a TRS $\mathcal{R}$ [10]. However, our approach differs from forward closures by starting from the rules of another TRS $\mathcal{P}$ and by also allowing narrowings with $\mathcal{P}$'s rules on root level. (The reason is that we prove non-termination within the DP framework.) Moreover, we also regard backward narrowing.

There are only few papers on automatically proving *non-termination* of TRSs. An early work is [28] which detects TRSs that are not *simply* terminating (but they may still terminate). Recently, [36,37] presented methods for proving non-termination of *string rewrite systems* (i.e., TRSs where all function symbols have arity 1). Similar to our approach, [36] uses (forward) narrowing and [37] uses ancestor graphs which correspond to (backward) narrowing. However, our approach differs substantially from [36,37]: our technique works within the DP framework, whereas [36,37] operate on the whole set of rules. Therefore, we can benefit from all previous DP processors which decompose the initial DP problem into smaller sub-problems and identify those parts which could cause non-termination. Moreover, we regard full term rewriting instead of string rewriting. Therefore, we use semi-unification to detect loops, whereas for string rewriting, matching is sufficient. Finally, we also presented a condition to disprove *innermost* termination, whereas [36,37] only try to disprove full termination.

5 Experiments and Conclusion

The DP framework is a general concept for combining termination techniques in a modular way. We presented two important improvements: First, we extended the framework in order to handle higher-order functions, represented as applicative first-order TRSs. To this end, we developed three new contributions: a refined approximation of dependency graphs, an improved definition of usable rules, and a new processor to transform applicative DP problems into functional form. The advantages of our approach, also compared to related work, are the following: it is simple and very easy to integrate into any termination prover based on dependency pairs (e.g., AProVE [15], CiME [9], TTT [19]). Moreover, it encompasses the original DP framework, e.g., it is at least as successful on ordinary first-order functions as the original dependency pair technique. Finally, our approach treats untyped higher-order functions, i.e., it can be used for termination analysis of polymorphic and untyped functional languages.

As a second extension within the DP framework, we introduced a new processor for disproving termination automatically (an important problem which was hardly tackled up to now). A major advantage of our approach is that it combines techniques for proving and for disproving termination in the DP framework, which is beneficial for both termination and non-termination analysis.

We implemented all these contributions in the newest version of our termination prover AProVE [15]. Due to the results of this paper, AProVE 1.2 was the most powerful tool for both termination and non-termination proofs of TRSs at the *Annual International Competition of Termination Tools 2005* [34]. In the following table, we compare AProVE 1.2 with its predecessor AProVE 1.1d-γ, which was the winning tool for TRSs at the competition in 2004. While AProVE 1.1d-γ already contained our results on non-termination analysis, the contributions on handling applicative TRSs from Sect. 3 were missing. For the experiments, we used the same setting as in the competition with a timeout of 60 seconds for each example (where however most proofs take less than two seconds).

	higher-order (61 TRSs)		non-term (90 TRSs)		TPDB (838 TRSs)	
	t	n	t	n	t	n
AProVE 1.2	43	8	25	61	639	95
AProVE 1.1d-γ	13	7	24	60	486	92

Here, "*higher-order*" is a collection of untyped versions of typical higher-order functions from [2,3,6,24,25,33] and "*non-term*" contains particularly many non-terminating examples. "*TPDB*" is the *Termination Problem Data Base* used in the annual termination competition [34]. It consists of 838 (innermost) termination problems for TRSs from different sources. In the tables, **t** and **n** are the numbers of TRSs where termination resp. non-termination could be proved.

AProVE 1.2 solves the vast majority of the examples in the "*higher-order*"- and the "*non-term*"-collection. This shows that our results for higher-order functions and non-termination are indeed successful in practice. In contrast, the first column demonstrates that previous techniques for automated termination proofs often fail on applicative TRSs representing higher-order functions. Finally, the last two columns show that our contributions also increase power substantially on ordinary non-applicative TRSs (which constitute most of the TPDB). For further details on our experiments and to download AProVE, the reader is referred to http://www-i2.informatik.rwth-aachen.de/AProVE/.

References

1. T. Aoto and T. Yamada. Termination of simply typed term rewriting systems by translation and labelling. In *Proc. RTA '03*, LNCS 2706, pages 380–394, 2003.
2. T. Aoto and T. Yamada. Termination of simply typed applicative term rewriting systems. In *Proc. HOR '04*, Report AIB-2004-03, RWTH, pages 61–65, 2004.
3. T. Aoto and T. Yamada. Dependency pairs for simply typed term rewriting. In *Proc. RTA '05*, LNCS 3467, pages 120–134, 2005.
4. T. Arts and J. Giesl. Termination of term rewriting using dependency pairs. *Theoretical Computer Science*, 236:133–178, 2000.
5. F. Baader and T. Nipkow. *Term Rewriting and All That*. Cambridge, 1998.
6. R. Bird. *Introduction to Functional Prog. using* Haskell. Prentice Hall, 1998.
7. F. Blanqui. A type-based termination criterion for dependently-typed higher-order rewrite systems. In *Proc. RTA '04*, LNCS 3091, pages 24–39, 2004.
8. C. Borralleras and A. Rubio. A monotonic higher-order semantic path ordering. In *Proc. LPAR '01*, LNAI 2250, pages 531–547, 2001.
9. E. Contejean, C. Marché, B. Monate, and X. Urbain. CiME. http://cime.lri.fr.
10. N. Dershowitz. Termination of rewriting. *J. Symb. Comp.*, 3:69–116, 1987.
11. K. Drosten. *Termersetzungssysteme: Grundlagen der Prototyp-Generierung algebraischer Spezifikationen*. Springer, 1989.
12. J. Giesl and T. Arts. Verification of Erlang processes by dependency pairs. *Appl. Algebra in Engineering, Communication and Computing*, 12(1,2):39–72, 2001.

13. J. Giesl, T. Arts, and E. Ohlebusch. Modular termination proofs for rewriting using dependency pairs. *Journal of Symbolic Computation*, 34(1):21–58, 2002.
14. J. Giesl, R. Thiemann, P. Schneider-Kamp, and S. Falke. Improving dependency pairs. In *Proc. LPAR '03*, LNAI 2850, pages 165–179, 2003.
15. J. Giesl, R. Thiemann, P. Schneider-Kamp, and S. Falke. Automated termination proofs with AProVE. In *Proc. RTA '04*, LNCS 3091, pages 210–220, 2004.
16. J. Giesl, R. Thiemann, and P. Schneider-Kamp. The DP framework: Combining techniques for autom. termination proofs. In *Proc. LPAR '04*, LNAI 3452, 2005.
17. J. Giesl, R. Thiemann, and P. Schneider-Kamp. Proving and disproving termination of higher-order functions. Technical Report AIB-2005-03, RWTH Aachen, 2005. Available from http://aib.informatik.rwth-aachen.de.
18. N. Hirokawa and A. Middeldorp. Automating the DP method. In *Proc. CADE '03*, LNAI 2741, pages 32–46, 2003. Full version in *Information and Computation*.
19. N. Hirokawa and A. Middeldorp. Tyrolean Termination Tool. In *Proc. RTA '05*, LNCS 3467, pages 175–184, 2005.
20. J.-P. Jouannaud and A. Rubio. Higher-order recursive path orderings. In *Proc. LICS '99*, pages 402–411, 1999.
21. D. Kapur, D. Musser, P. Narendran, and J. Stillman. Semi-unification. *Theoretical Computer Science*, 81(2):169–187, 1991.
22. R. Kennaway, J. W. Klop, R. Sleep, and F.-J. de Vries. Comparing curried and uncurried rewriting. *Journal of Symbolic Computation*, 21(1):15–39, 1996.
23. K. Kusakari, M. Nakamura, and Y. Toyama. Argument filtering transformation. In *Proc. PPDP '99*, LNCS 1702, pages 48–62, 1999.
24. K. Kusakari. On proving termination of term rewriting systems with higher-order variables. *IPSJ Transactions on Programming*, 42(SIG 7 (PRO 11)):35–45, 2001.
25. M. Lifantsev and L. Bachmair. An LPO-based termination ordering for higher-order terms without λ-abstraction. In *Proc. TPHOLs '98*, LNCS 1479, 1998.
26. A. Mycroft. The theory and practice of transforming call-by-need into call-by-value. In *Proc. 4th Int. Symp. on Programming*, LNCS 83, pages 269–281, 1980.
27. A. Oliart and W. Snyder. A fast algorithm for uniform semi-unification. In *Proc. CADE '98*, LNCS 1421, pages 239–253, 1998.
28. D. A. Plaisted. A simple non-termination test for the Knuth-Bendix method. In *Proc. CADE '86*, LNCS 230, pages 79–88, 1986.
29. J. van de Pol. Termination of higher-order rewrite systems. PhD, Utrecht, 1996.
30. M. Sakai, Y. Watanabe, and T. Sakabe. An extension of dependency pair method for proving termination of higher-order rewrite systems. *IEICE Transactions on Information and Systems*, E84-D(8):1025–1032, 2001.
31. M. Sakai and K. Kusakari. On dependency pair method for proving termination of higher-order rewrite systems. *IEICE Trans. on Inf. & Sys.*, 2005. To appear.
32. R. Thiemann, J. Giesl, and P. Schneider-Kamp. Improved modular termination proofs using dependency pairs. In *Proc. IJCAR '04*, LNAI 3097, pages 75–90, 2004.
33. Y. Toyama. Termination of S-expression rewriting systems: Lexicographic path ordering for higher-order terms. In *Proc. RTA '04*, LNCS 3091, pages 40–54, 2004.
34. TPDB web page. http://www.lri.fr/~marche/termination-competition/.
35. P. Wadler and J. Hughes. Projections for strictness analysis. In *Proc. 3rd Int. Conf. Functional Prog. Lang. & Comp. Arch.*, LNCS 274, pages 385–407, 1987.
36. J. Waldmann. Matchbox: A tool for match-bounded string rewriting. In *Proc. 15th RTA*, LNCS 3091, pages 85–94, 2004.
37. H. Zantema. TORPA: Termination of string rewriting proved automatically. *Journal of Automated Reasoning*, 2005. To appear.

Proving Liveness with Fairness Using Rewriting

Adam Koprowski and Hans Zantema

Technical University of Eindhoven,
Department of Computer Science,
P.O. Box 513, 5600 MB, Eindhoven, The Netherlands
{A.Koprowski, H.Zantema}@tue.nl

Abstract. In this paper we combine rewriting techniques with verification issues. More precisely, we show how techniques for proving relative termination of term rewrite systems (TRSs) can be applied to prove liveness properties in fair computations. We do this using a new transformation which is stronger than the sound transformation from [5] but still is suitable for automation. On the one hand we show completeness of this approach under some mild conditions. On the other hand we show how this approach applies to some examples completely automatically, using the TPA tool designed for proving relative termination of TRSs. In particular we succeed in proving liveness in the classical readers-writers synchronization problem.

1 Introduction

Usually, *liveness* is roughly defined as: *"something will eventually happen"* and it is often remarked that *"termination is a particular case of liveness"*. In [5] the relationship between liveness and termination was investigated in more detail, and it was observed that conversely liveness can be seen as termination of a modified relation. Since various techniques have been developed to prove termination automatically, an obvious goal is to apply these techniques in order to prove liveness properties. In [5] a method for transforming a class of liveness problems to problems of termination of term rewrite systems (TRSs) has been proposed. For a slightly different setting in [6] another approach was proposed.

Two transformations were given in [5]. The first one, sound and complete, even for extremely simple liveness problems results in complicated TRSs for which proving termination, especially in an automated way, is very difficult. That was the motivation for another, much simpler, transformation, which is sound but not complete.

In this paper this approach is extended in two ways. First we extend the basic framework to fair computations. That means that we do not restrict to the basic notion of liveness stating that any infinite computation eventually reaches a good state, but we do this for infinite fair computations, being infinite computations containing some essential computation steps infinitely often. Fairness has been studied extensively in [4]. In applications one is often interested in the behavior of infinite fair computations rather than of arbitrary infinite computations. For instance, in a waiting line protocol one may want to prove that

B. Gramlich (Ed.): FroCoS 2005, LNAI 3717, pp. 232–247, 2005.

eventually all old clients will be served. If it is allowed that infinitely many new clients come in, one may think of an infinite computation in which this does not hold: infinitely many new clients come in but no client is ever served. However, if serving of clients is defined to be the essential computation step, in a corresponding fair computation it can be proved that eventually all old clients will be served. It turns out that just like liveness corresponds to termination, liveness in fair computations corresponds to *relative termination*. So combining liveness and fairness is a main issue of this paper.

The second extension is the following. It turns out that the simple transformation presented in [5] often results in non-terminating TRSs, and therefore is not applicable, also in liveness problems not involving fairness. Therefore we propose a new transformation. Our new transformation is slightly more complicated than the simple transformation from [5], but much simpler than the sound and complete transformation from [5]. However, assuming some mild conditions, in this paper we show that our new transformation is sound and complete too. Moreover, we show in two examples that our new transformation results in TRSs for which (relative) termination can be proved fully automatically. In particular we consider the classical readers-writers synchronization problem, in which the priority of access is controlled in an obvious way. The desired liveness property states that every process in the system eventually gets access to the resource. Using our technique we succeed in automatically proving this liveness property. Both examples involve infinite state spaces and hence the standard model checking techniques are not applicable to them.

To this end a tool — TPA (*Termination Proved Automatically*, http://www.win.tue.nl/tpa) — was developed for proving relative termination of TRSs automatically, based on polynomial interpretations [9], semantic labelling with booleans and with natural numbers [13], recursive path ordering [3] and a simple version of dependency pairs [1]. Most of those well-known termination techniques, except dependency pairs, were extended in a straightforward way to deal also with relative termination. TPA took part in the annual termination competition in 2005 (http://www.lri.fr/~marche/termination-competition/2005) where it got 3rd place out of 6 participating tools.

This paper is organized as follows. In Section 2 the general framework from [5] is extended in order to deal with liveness with fairness. Next in Section 3 the new transformation is introduced and the corresponding theorems on soundness and completeness are given. Finally in Section 4 two examples are presented in which this new approach has been applied.

2   Liveness with Fairness Conditions

2.1   Liveness in Abstract Reduction

First we present the framework as described in [5] with no more than necessary details to understand its extension given later. For a more elaborate description we refer to the original article.

We give the model of the system that should be verified in the framework of abstract reduction. We assume a set of states S and a binary relation on states expressing computation steps, $\rightarrow \subseteq S \times S$. As usual we write $\rightarrow^*$ for its reflexive transitive closure and $\rightarrow^+$ for its transitive closure. We define a set of states in *normal form* as $\mathrm{NF} \equiv \{s \in S \mid \neg\exists s' \in S : s \rightarrow s'\}$ and a set of terms in normal form reachable from a given set of states I as $\mathrm{NF}(I) \equiv \{s \in \mathrm{NF} \mid \exists t \in I : t \rightarrow^* s\}$. We call a reduction sequence *maximal* if it is either infinite or its last element is in NF. By $\mathrm{SN}(I, \rightarrow)$ we denote termination of reduction sequences starting in I and by $\mathrm{SN}(\rightarrow)$ termination of arbitrary sequences. That is: $\mathrm{SN}(I, \rightarrow) \equiv \neg\exists t_1, t_2, \ldots : t_1 \in I \wedge \forall i : t_i \rightarrow t_{i+1}$ and $\mathrm{SN}(\rightarrow) \equiv \mathrm{SN}(S, \rightarrow)$.

With respect to a set of initial states $I \subseteq S$ and a set of good states $G \subseteq S$, we say that the liveness property $\mathrm{Live}(I, \rightarrow, G)$ holds if all maximal $\rightarrow$-reductions starting in I contain an element from G. More precisely:

Definition 1 (Liveness). *Let S be a set of states, $\rightarrow \subseteq S \times S$; $G, I \subseteq S$. Then* $\mathrm{Live}(I, \rightarrow, G)$ *holds iff*

$$- \;\forall t_1, t_2, \ldots : \left\{ \begin{array}{c} t_1 \in I \\ \forall i : t_i \rightarrow t_{i+1} \end{array} \right\} \implies \exists i : t_i \in G, \text{ and}$$

$$- \;\forall t_1, \ldots, t_n : \left\{ \begin{array}{c} t_1 \in I \\ t_n \in \mathrm{NF} \\ \forall i \in \{1, \ldots, n-1\} : t_i \rightarrow t_{i+1} \end{array} \right\} \implies \exists i \in \{1, \ldots, n\} : t_i \in G.$$

We define the restricted computation relation $\rightarrow_G \equiv \{(s, t) \mid s \rightarrow t \wedge s \notin G\}$. The following theorem from [5] relates liveness to termination of $\rightarrow_G$.

Theorem 2. *If* $\mathrm{NF}(I) \subseteq G$ *then* $\mathrm{Live}(I, \rightarrow, G)$ *iff* $\mathrm{SN}(I, \rightarrow_G)$.

2.2   Liveness with Fairness in Abstract Reduction

In liveness we are mainly interested in the behavior of infinite reduction sequences, or shortly, infinite reductions. However, in many applications one is not interested in arbitrary infinite reductions but in infinite fair reductions, defined as follows. Instead of a single rewrite relation $\rightarrow$ we have two relations $\rightarrow, \xrightarrow{=} \subseteq S \times S$ [1]. An infinite reduction in $\rightarrow \cup \xrightarrow{=}$ is called *fair* (with respect to $\rightarrow$) if it contains infinitely many $\rightarrow$-steps. Finally we say that liveness for fair reductions starting in I with respect to $\rightarrow, \xrightarrow{=}$ and G holds, denoted as $\mathrm{Live}(I, \rightarrow, \xrightarrow{=}, G)$, if any fair $\rightarrow \cup \xrightarrow{=}$ reduction starting in I contains an element of G. Note that all fair reductions are infinite, hence in investigating liveness with fairness we are only interested in systems with infinite behavior.

Definition 3 (Liveness with fairness). *Let S be a set of states, $\rightarrow, \xrightarrow{=} \subseteq S \times S$; $G, I \subseteq S$. Then liveness for fair reductions with respect to $I, \rightarrow, \xrightarrow{=}$ and G, $\mathrm{Live}(I, \rightarrow, \xrightarrow{=}, G)$, holds iff*

---

[1] The notation for $\rightarrow$ and $\xrightarrow{=}$ is chosen to be consistent with the notation for relative termination problems as used in TPDB (Termination Problem Database, http://www.lri.fr/~marche/tpdb/). The database serves as a base of problems for Termination Competitions.

$$- \forall t_1, t_2, \dots : \left\{ \begin{array}{c} t_1 \in I \\ \forall i : t_i \to t_{i+1} \vee t_i \stackrel{=}{\to} t_{i+1} \\ \forall i \exists j > i : t_j \to t_{j+1} \end{array} \right\} \implies \exists i : t_i \in G$$

Our definition is based on the notion of relative termination. We define that $\to$ terminates relatively to $\stackrel{=}{\to}$ if every (possibly infinite) $\to \cup \stackrel{=}{\to}$ computation contains only finitely many $\to$ steps. We introduce the relation $\to / \stackrel{=}{\to} \equiv \stackrel{=}{\to}^* \cdot \to \cdot \stackrel{=}{\to}^*$ and observe that relative termination of $\to$ to $\stackrel{=}{\to}$ is equivalent to $SN(\to / \stackrel{=}{\to})$. Also observe that $SN(\to / \emptyset) \equiv SN(\to)$ so termination is a special case of relative termination.

The result of the next theorem gives us a method of verifying liveness with fairness requirements.

Theorem 4. Live$(I, \to, \stackrel{=}{\to}, G)$ *holds iff* $SN(I, \to_G / \stackrel{=}{\to}_G)$.

Proof. ($\Rightarrow$) Assume that Live$(I, \to, \stackrel{=}{\to}, G)$ holds and $SN(I, \to_G / \stackrel{=}{\to}_G)$ does not hold. From the latter we get that there is an infinite, fair reduction sequence $t_1, t_2, \dots$ with $t_1 \in I$ and $\forall i : t_i \to_G t_{i+1} \vee t_i \stackrel{=}{\to}_G t_{i+1}$. From the definition of $\to_G$ all $t_i \notin G$. But then this reduction sequence is a counter-example for Live$(I, \to, \stackrel{=}{\to}, G)$.

($\Leftarrow$) Since $SN(I, \to_G / \stackrel{=}{\to}_G)$ then in every infinite, fair $\to \cup \stackrel{=}{\to}$ reduction starting in I there is an element from G (which blocks further $\to_G \cup \stackrel{=}{\to}_G$ reductions) and that is exactly what the definition of Live$(I, \to, \stackrel{=}{\to}, G)$ calls for. $\square$

2.3   Liveness with Fairness in Term Rewriting

In previous sections we described the transition relation by means of abstract reductions, and related liveness of $\to$ to termination of $\to_G$. Our goal is to employ techniques for proving termination of rewriting in order to prove liveness properties. To that end a transformation is required since usually $\to_G$ is not a rewrite relation even if $\to$ is a rewrite relation.

For a signature Σ and a set $\mathcal{V}$ of variables, we denote the set of terms over Σ and $\mathcal{V}$ by $\mathcal{T}(\Sigma, \mathcal{V})$. Now we represent the computation states by terms, so S becomes $\mathcal{T}(\Sigma, \mathcal{V})$ and $I, G \subseteq \mathcal{T}(\Sigma, \mathcal{V})$. Abstract reduction relations $\to$ and $\stackrel{=}{\to}$ now correspond to two TRSs over the same signature Σ: R and $R^=$, respectively. As a shorthand for $\to_R$ we write $\to$ and for $\to_{R^=}$ we simply write $\stackrel{=}{\to}$. Just like it is usual to write $SN(R)$ rather than $SN(\to_R)$, we will write Live$(I, R, R^=, G)$ rather than Live$(I, \to_R, \to_{R^=}, G)$.

For an introduction to term rewriting the reader is referred, for instance, to [12].

Now, again after [5], we will introduce the notion of top TRSs, which we are going to use to model liveness problems.

Definition 5 (Top TRSs). *Let Σ be a signature and* top *be a fresh unary symbol in this signature, that is* top $\notin \Sigma$. *A term $t \in \mathcal{T}(\Sigma \cup \{top\}, \mathcal{V})$ is called a top term if it contains exactly one instance of the* top *symbol, at the root of the term. We denote the set of top terms by $\mathcal{T}_{top}(\Sigma, \mathcal{V})$.*

A TRS over $\Sigma \cup \{$top$\}$ is called a top term rewrite system *(top TRS) if for all its rules $\ell \to r$ one of the following holds:*

- *Both ℓ and r are top terms. Then we call this rule a* top rule.
- *Both ℓ and r do not contain an instance of the* top *symbol. Then the rule is called a* non-top rule.

Clearly for top TRSs every reduction starting in a top term only contains top terms. In the remainder we restrict ourselves to liveness with respect to

- reduction relations described by top TRSs,
- the set of initial states consisting of all top terms, and
- the set of good states of the form:

$$G(P) = \{t \in \mathcal{T}_{top}(\Sigma, \mathcal{V}) \mid \neg \exists p \in P, \ \sigma, \ C : t = C[p\sigma]\},$$

for some set $P \subseteq \mathcal{T}(\Sigma, \mathcal{V})$, that is $G(P)$ represents top terms not containing an instance of any of the terms from P.

So we are going to investigate liveness properties of the form:

$$\text{Live}(\mathcal{T}_{top}(\Sigma, \mathcal{V}), R, R^=, G(P))$$

for some top TRSs R and $R^=$. This is equivalent to proving that every infinite fair reduction of top terms contains a term which does not contain an instance of any of the terms from P.

As we will show later this type of question can be transformed to a relative termination question of an ordinary TRS. This allows us to employ the techniques for proving relative termination for TRSs to verify liveness properties. Also, while quite restricted, this setting seems to be general enough to be able to cope with some interesting and practical examples, two of which will be presented at the end of this paper.

3   A New Transformation

3.1   Motivation

We are seeking a transformation with the property that relative termination of the transformed pair of systems implies that the liveness property in question holds (even better if we can have equivalence). In [5] two such transformations were proposed: the first one sound and complete (equivalence between termination and liveness holds) and the second one only sound (termination implies liveness but not the other way around) but significantly simpler. Experiments with them show that the former is so complex that, although it is a nice theoretical result, in practice it leads to TRSs far too complicated for present termination techniques to deal with, especially in an automated way. The sound transformation does not have this disadvantage but in several examples it is not powerful enough, leading to non-terminating TRSs, while the desired liveness property does hold.

In this section we propose a new transformation avoiding the aforementioned problems. But before we do that we will shortly introduce the sound transformation LS from [5] where $P = \{p\}$. As in our presentation also LS can be easily generalized to allow P to contain more than one element, as remarked in [5].

Definition 6 (LS). *Let R be a top TRS over $\Sigma \cup \{\text{top}\}$ and $p \in \mathcal{T}(\Sigma, \mathcal{V})$. We define $\text{LS}(R, p)$ to consist of the following rules:*

$$\ell \rightarrow r \qquad \text{for all non-top rules } \ell \rightarrow r \text{ in } R$$
$$\text{top}(\ell) \rightarrow \text{top}(\text{check}(r)) \qquad \text{for all top rules } \text{top}(\ell) \rightarrow \text{top}(r) \text{ in } R$$
$$\text{check}(f(x_1, \ldots, x_n)) \rightarrow f(x_1, \ldots, \text{check}(x_i), \ldots, x_n)$$
$$\text{for all } f \in \Sigma \text{ of arity } n \geq 1, 1 \leq i \leq n$$
$$\text{check}(p) \rightarrow p$$

While *LS* is sound, it is not complete. This is illustrated by the following TRS $R = \{\text{top}(f(x, b)) \rightarrow \text{top}(f(b, b)), \ a \rightarrow b\}$. Normal forms do not contain symbol a and in every infinite reduction after finitely many steps only term $\text{top}(f(b, b))$ occurs, so liveness for $p = a$ holds. However, $\text{LS}(R, p)$ admits an infinite reduction, namely: $\text{top}(\text{check}(f(b, b))) \rightleftarrows \text{top}(f(\text{check}(b), b))$.

3.2 Definition of the Transformation

We give a new transformation inspired by the sound and complete transformation presented in [5] but significantly simpler so that obtained systems can still be treated with tools for automatic termination proving. It can deal with a much broader class of liveness problems than the sound transformation from [5]. We present it for only one unary top symbol but generalization to more top symbols and/or different arities is straightforward.

Definition 7 (LT). *Let R and $R^=$ be top TRSs over $\Sigma \cup \{\text{top}\}$ and $P \subseteq \mathcal{T}(\Sigma, \mathcal{V})$. The transformed systems $\text{LT}(R)$ and $\text{LT}^=(R^=, P)$ over $\Sigma \cup \{\text{top}, \text{ok}, \text{check}\}$ are defined as follows:*

$$\boxed{\text{LT}(R)}$$

$$\ell \rightarrow r \qquad \text{for all non-top rules } \ell \rightarrow r \text{ in } R$$
$$\text{top}(\text{ok}(\ell)) \rightarrow \text{top}(\text{check}(r)) \qquad \text{for all top rules } \text{top}(\ell) \rightarrow \text{top}(r) \text{ in } R$$

$$\boxed{\text{LT}^=(R^=, P)}$$

$$\ell \rightarrow r \qquad \text{for all non-top rules } \ell \rightarrow r \text{ in } R^=$$
$$\text{top}(\text{ok}(\ell)) \rightarrow \text{top}(\text{check}(r)) \qquad \text{for all top rules } \text{top}(\ell) \rightarrow \text{top}(r) \text{ in } R^=$$
$$\text{check}(p) \rightarrow \text{ok}(p) \qquad \text{for all } p \in P$$
$$\text{check}(f(x_1, \ldots, x_n)) \rightarrow f(x_1, \ldots, \text{check}(x_i), \ldots, x_n)$$
$$\text{for all } f \in \Sigma \text{ of arity } n \geq 1, 1 \leq i \leq n$$
$$f(x_1, \ldots, \text{ok}(x_i), \ldots, x_n) \rightarrow \text{ok}(f(x_1, \ldots, x_n))$$
$$\text{for all } f \in \Sigma \text{ of arity } n \geq 1, 1 \leq i \leq n$$

The idea behind this transformation is that the presence of an ok symbol at the root of the term is intended to indicate existence of an instance of $p \in P$. Every time a top rule is applied this ok symbol is transformed to a check symbol. This check symbol can traverse toward the leaves and upon reaching an instance of some term $p \in P$ is transformed back into an ok symbol. This ok symbol can move up again and allow further top reductions upon reaching the root of the term.

Few remarks concerning the transformation:

- For readability concerns we will write $\to_{LT}$ instead of $\to_{LT(R)}$ and $\stackrel{=}{\to}_{LT}$ instead of $\to_{LT^=(R^=,P)}$.
- In order to apply automatic techniques the set P should be finite, otherwise the TRS $LT^=(R^=, P)$ is infinite.
- If the liveness problem does not involve fairness, so it is modelled by single TRS R, then we define the result of the transformation to be also a single TRS, namely $LT^=(R, P)$.

3.3   Soundness

Now we show soundness, that is relative termination of the transformed system implies liveness of the original one.

Theorem 8 (Soundness). *Let $R, R^=$ be top TRSs over $\Sigma \cup \{top\}$, let $P \subseteq T(\Sigma, V)$. Then:*

$$SN(LT(R)/LT^=(R^=, P)) \implies Live(\mathcal{T}_{top}(\Sigma, V), R, R^=, G(P))$$

Proof. Assume that $SN(LT(R)/LT^=(R^=, P))$ holds and $Live(\mathcal{T}_{top}(\Sigma, V), R, R^=, G(P))$ does not hold. By Theorem 4, $SN(\mathcal{T}_{top}(\Sigma, V), \to_G / \stackrel{=}{\to}_G)$ does not hold as it is equivalent to $Live(\mathcal{T}_{top}(\Sigma, V), R, R^=, G(P))$. That means that there is an infinite $\to_G / \stackrel{=}{\to}_G$ reduction of top terms. We will show that this infinite reduction can be mapped to an infinite $\to_{LT} / \stackrel{=}{\to}_{LT}$ reduction, thus contradicting $SN(LT(R)/LT^=(R^=, P))$. For that purpose it is sufficient to show that:

$$top(t) \to_G / \stackrel{=}{\to}_G top(u) \implies top(ok(t)) \to_{LT} / \stackrel{=}{\to}_{LT} top(ok(u))$$

that is that any step in $\to_G / \stackrel{=}{\to}_G$ can be mimicked by a step in $\to_{LT} / \stackrel{=}{\to}_{LT}$. It easily follows if we can show that:

(i) whenever $top(t) \to_G top(u)$ then $top(ok(t)) \to_{LT} / \stackrel{=}{\to}_{LT} top(ok(u))$, and
(ii) whenever $top(t) \stackrel{=}{\to}_G top(u)$ then $top(ok(t)) \stackrel{=}{\to}^*_{LT} top(ok(u))$.

(i) First observe that if $top(t) \to_G top(u)$ by the application of a non-top rule $\ell \to r$ then the same rule is present in $LT(R)$ so we trivially have $top(ok(t)) \to_{LT} / \stackrel{=}{\to}_{LT} top(ok(u))$.

If on the other hand $top(t) \to_G top(u)$ by application of a top rule then from the definition of top TRSs we have that $t = \ell\delta$ and $u = r\delta$ for some substitution δ and some rule $top(\ell) \to top(r)$ from R. Note that $top(u)$ is part of an infinite

$\rightarrow_G / \xrightarrow{=}_G$-reduction so $\mathsf{top}(u) \rightarrow_G \mathsf{top}(w)$ or $\mathsf{top}(u) \xrightarrow{=}_G \mathsf{top}(w)$ for some term w. Then from the definition of $\rightarrow_G$ we get that $\mathsf{top}(u)$ does contain an instance of some $p \in P$ which means that we have $u = C[p\gamma]$ for some context C and some substitution γ. Then we have:

$$
\begin{aligned}
\mathsf{top}(\mathsf{ok}(t)) &= \mathsf{top}(\mathsf{ok}(\ell\delta)) \\
&\rightarrow_{LT} \mathsf{top}(\mathsf{check}(r\delta)) \\
&= \mathsf{top}(\mathsf{check}(C[p\gamma])) \\
&\xrightarrow{=}{}^*_{LT} \mathsf{top}(C[\mathsf{check}(p)\gamma]) \\
&\xrightarrow{=}_{LT} \mathsf{top}(C[\mathsf{ok}(p)\gamma]) \\
&\xrightarrow{=}{}^*_{LT} \mathsf{top}(\mathsf{ok}(C[p\gamma])) \quad = \mathsf{top}(\mathsf{ok}(u))
\end{aligned}
$$

The reasoning for (ii) is similar, just the first step is from $\xrightarrow{=}_{LT(R)}$ instead of $\rightarrow_{LT(R)}$. $\qquad\square$

3.4 Completeness Results

In the previous subsection we proved that our approach is correct, that is that the proposed transformation is sound. Now we will try to address the question of its power. First we show (Theorem 9) that any liveness problem that could be dealt with using LS can also be dealt with using LT. Then we show that under some restrictions our new approach is even complete.

Theorem 9. *Let R be a top TRS over $\Sigma \cup \{\mathsf{top}\}$ and let $p \in T(\Sigma, V)$. Then* $\mathrm{SN}(\mathrm{LS}(R, p))$ *implies* $\mathrm{SN}(\mathrm{LT}^=(R, \{p\}))$.

Proof. Follows from the observation that any $\mathrm{LT}^=(R, \{p\})$ reduction can be mapped to $\mathrm{LS}(R, p)$ reduction by dropping all ok symbols and the rule for propagating ok symbol is terminating in itself. $\qquad\square$

Note however that there is no 'if and only if' in Theorem 9, which means that LT may succeed in case LS fails. A very simple example showing that is the TRS $R = \{\mathsf{top}(f(x, b)) \rightarrow \mathsf{top}(f(b, b)), \ a \rightarrow b\}$ used at the end of Section 3.1 to show incompleteness of LT. We concluded there that $\mathrm{LS}(R, p)$ is not terminating, however it is not difficult to see that $\mathrm{LT}^=(R, \{p\})$ is terminating. Two more complex and practical examples will be presented in Section 4.

There is a good reason why the sound and complete transformation presented in [5] is so complicated, so clearly enough we cannot hope that a transformation as simple as LT would be complete. The best we can hope for is completeness under some additional restrictions on the shape of TRSs modelling the liveness problem. Indeed that is the case. First we present three such requirements along with examples showing that if they do not hold completeness is lost. However, for the setting of liveness problems, these requirements are quite mild. Then we will prove completeness for the restricted set of systems for which they do hold.

Example 1. Let us begin with a very simple example, namely:

$$
R = \{\mathsf{top}(a) \rightarrow \mathsf{top}(b), \quad b \rightarrow a\} \qquad R^= = \emptyset.
$$

Consider liveness with $P = \{a\}$, meaning that in every reduction eventually a term without a is reached. It is an easy observation that in every infinite reduction of this TRS its two rules have to be applied interchangeably, so after at most one step the term without a is reached and liveness holds. But the transformation yields:

$$\begin{aligned} \mathrm{LT}(R) &= \{\mathsf{top}(\mathsf{ok}(a)) \to \mathsf{top}(\mathsf{check}(b)),\ b \to a\} \\ \mathrm{LT}^=(R^=, P) &= \{\mathsf{check}(a) \stackrel{=}{\to} \mathsf{ok}(a)\}. \end{aligned}$$

The above system allows an infinite $\to_{\mathrm{LT}} / \stackrel{=}{\to}_{\mathrm{LT}}$ reduction, namely:

$$\mathsf{top}(\mathsf{ok}(a)) \to_{\mathrm{LT}} \mathsf{top}(\mathsf{check}(b)) \to_{\mathrm{LT}} \mathsf{top}(\mathsf{check}(a)) \stackrel{=}{\to}_{\mathrm{LT}} \mathsf{top}(\mathsf{ok}(a)) \to_{\mathrm{LT}} \cdots$$

The reason why things go wrong here is that some term from P (being a in this case) can be created, that is there are reductions from terms not containing an instance of p (for any $p \in P$) to terms containing an instance of p (for some $p \in P$). We can mend that by forbidding this kind of behavior. Let us note that this means restricting to liveness problems for which if the desired property holds at some point it will hold from that point onwards.

From now on, for readability concerns, we will assume that rules from R are given as $l \to r$ and rules from $R^=$ as $l \stackrel{=}{\to} r$ and we will just present a set of rules leaving the separation to R and $R^=$ implicit. Now we move on to another example showing another property that can destroy liveness.

Example 2. Consider the TRS over $\{f, g, \mathsf{top}, a, b\}$ consisting of the following rules:

$$\mathsf{top}(g(x, y, a)) \to \mathsf{top}(f(x)), \qquad\qquad f(x) \to g(x, x, x).$$

In any infinite top reduction the second rule is applied infinitely often, and a straightforward analysis shows that after applying the second rule in a top reduction, no infinite reduction from a term containing the symbol b is possible. So liveness with $P = \{b\}$ holds. The transformed system reads:

(1)	$\mathsf{top}(\mathsf{ok}(g(x, y, a)))$	$\to$	$\mathsf{top}(\mathsf{check}(f(x)))$	(7)	$\mathsf{check}(g(x, y, z)) \stackrel{=}{\to} g(x, y, \mathsf{check}(z))$
(2)	$f(x)$	$\to$	$g(x, x, x)$	(8)	$f(\mathsf{ok}(x)) \stackrel{=}{\to} \mathsf{ok}(f(x))$
(3)	$\mathsf{check}(b)$	$\stackrel{=}{\to}$	$\mathsf{ok}(b)$	(9)	$g(\mathsf{ok}(x), y, z) \stackrel{=}{\to} \mathsf{ok}(g(x, y, z))$
(4)	$\mathsf{check}(f(x))$	$\stackrel{=}{\to}$	$f(\mathsf{check}(x))$	(10)	$g(x, \mathsf{ok}(y), z) \stackrel{=}{\to} \mathsf{ok}(g(x, y, z))$
(5)	$\mathsf{check}(g(x, y, z))$	$\stackrel{=}{\to}$	$g(\mathsf{check}(x), y, z)$	(11)	$g(x, y, \mathsf{ok}(z)) \stackrel{=}{\to} \mathsf{ok}(g(x, y, z))$
(6)	$\mathsf{check}(g(x, y, z))$	$\stackrel{=}{\to}$	$g(x, \mathsf{check}(y), z)$		

and allows an infinite reduction, namely:

$$\mathsf{top}(\mathsf{check}(f(\mathsf{ok}(a)))) \stackrel{(2)}{\to} \mathsf{top}(\mathsf{check}(g(\mathsf{ok}(a), \mathsf{ok}(a), \mathsf{ok}(a)))) \stackrel{(6)}{\to}$$

$$\mathsf{top}(g(\mathsf{ok}(a), \mathsf{check}(\mathsf{ok}(a)), \mathsf{ok}(a))) \stackrel{(11)}{\to} \mathsf{top}(\mathsf{ok}(g(\mathsf{ok}(a), \mathsf{check}(\mathsf{ok}(a)), a))) \stackrel{(1)}{\to}$$

$$\mathsf{top}(\mathsf{check}(f(\mathsf{ok}(a)))) \to \cdots$$

This time completeness was harmed by duplicating rules in the original system.

Example 3. Finally consider the following simple TRS consisting of two rules: $top(f(a)) \to top(b)$ and $b \to b$. Clearly liveness with $P = \{a\}$ holds but after transformation we obtain a non-terminating TRS since b can be rewritten to itself. This gives rise to the third, and last, requirement, namely that the signature of the TRS for which we consider liveness problem must contain at least one symbol of arity ≥ 2. This is a really weak requirement: it is not required that this symbol occurs in the rewrite rules.

Now we will prove that if all three restrictions are satisfied, that is there are no duplicating rules, terms from P cannot be created and Σ contains some symbol of arity ≥ 2, then the completeness holds.

Before we state the completeness theorem we need some auxiliary results. First let us denote by $\bar{t}$ the term t after removing all occurrences of ok and check symbols. Formally:

$$\overline{\mathsf{check}(t)} = \bar{t}$$

$$\overline{\mathsf{ok}(t)} = \bar{t}$$

$$\overline{f(t_1,\ldots,t_n)} = f(\bar{t_1},\ldots,\bar{t_n}) \quad \text{for } f \notin \{\mathsf{check},\mathsf{ok}\}$$

We need two lemmas for which the proofs are easy and can be found in [8]. First we will state the lemma which shows that the reduction steps in a transformed system can be mimicked in the original system after removing extra ok and check symbols.

Lemma 10. *Given two TRSs R and $R^=$ over the same signature Σ and arbitrary terms t, u, we have the following implications:*

$$\text{(i) } t \to_{\mathrm{LT}} u \implies \bar{t} \to \bar{u}$$
$$\text{(ii) } t \overset{=}{\to}_{\mathrm{LT}} u \implies \bar{t} \overset{=}{\to}^{*} \bar{u}$$

Later on we will need the following lemma stating that extending TRS with administrative rules for check and ok preserves termination.

Lemma 11. *Given two TRSs R and $R^=$ over Σ (top, ok, check $\notin \Sigma$). Let S consist of the following rules:*

$$\mathsf{check}(p) \to \mathsf{ok}(p) \qquad \text{for all } p \in P$$
$$\mathsf{check}(f(x_1,\ldots,x_n)) \to f(x_1,\ldots,\mathsf{check}(x_i),\ldots,x_n)$$
$$\text{for all } f \in \Sigma \text{ of arity } n \geq 1,\ i = 1,\ldots,n$$
$$f(x_1,\ldots,\mathsf{ok}(x_i),\ldots,x_n) \to \mathsf{ok}(f(x_1,\ldots,x_n))$$
$$\text{for all } f \in \Sigma \text{ of arity } n \geq 1,\ i = 1,\ldots,n$$

Now if $\mathrm{SN}(R/R^=)$ then $\mathrm{SN}(R/(R^= \cup S))$.

Proof. Easy using Lemma 10.

Now we will present the theorem stating that for non-duplicating TRSs relative termination on top terms is equivalent to relative termination on arbitrary terms. We start by an example showing that non-duplication is essential for that.

Example 4. Let us consider the following TRS:

$$\mathsf{top}(f(x)) \rightarrow \mathsf{top}(a) \qquad\qquad f(x) \stackrel{=}{\rightarrow} g(f(x), f(x))$$

Here relative termination on top terms follows from the observation that any $\rightarrow$-step on any top term always yields the normal form $\mathsf{top}(a)$. However, this system admits the following fair reduction:

$$f(\mathsf{top}(f(x))) \stackrel{=}{\rightarrow} g(f(\mathsf{top}(f(x))), f(\mathsf{top}(f(x)))) \rightarrow g(f(\mathsf{top}(a), \underbrace{f(\mathsf{top}(f(x)))}_{\text{initial term}}) \stackrel{=}{\rightarrow} \cdots .$$

Theorem 12. *Let $R, R^=$ be non-duplicating top TRSs over Σ. Then we have:*

$$\mathrm{SN}(\mathcal{T}(\Sigma, \mathcal{V}), R/R^=) \iff \mathrm{SN}(\mathcal{T}_{top}(\Sigma, \mathcal{V}), R/R^=)$$

Proof. The ($\Rightarrow$)-part is trivial. For the ($\Leftarrow$)-part assume we have an arbitrary infinite fair reduction; we have to prove that there is also an infinite fair top reduction. By putting a top symbol around all terms we force that all terms in the infinite fair reduction have top as the root symbol. Next among all infinite fair reductions having top as the root symbol we choose one in which the number N of top symbols occurring in the initial term is minimal. Due to non-duplication in every term in this reduction at most N top symbols occur; due to minimality of N we conclude that each of these terms contains exactly N top symbols. We write $\mathsf{top}(C[\mathsf{top}(t_1), \ldots, \mathsf{top}(t_n)])$ for the initial term in the reduction for a context C not containing the symbol top. Since the number of top-symbols remains unchanged every term in the reduction is of the same shape, having the same number n of holes in the context. Due to minimality every infinite $\rightarrow \cup \stackrel{=}{\rightarrow}$ reduction of $\mathsf{top}(t_i)$ contains only finitely many $\rightarrow$-steps, for $i = 1, \ldots, n$. Due to definition of top TRSs all steps are either in the context C or in descendants of $\mathsf{top}(t_i)$. Since the descendants of $\mathsf{top}(t_i)$ allow only finitely many $\rightarrow$-steps and there are infinitely many $\rightarrow$-steps in total, we conclude that there are infinitely many $\rightarrow$-steps in the contexts. More precisely, we arrive at an infinite top reduction of $\mathsf{top}(C[x, \ldots, x])$ containing infinitely many $\rightarrow$-steps, contradicting $\mathrm{SN}(\mathcal{T}_{top}(\Sigma, \mathcal{V}), R/R^=)$. $\square$

Now we formulate the theorem which states that, under the three extra requirements introduced before, the transformation defined in Sect. 3.2 is complete.

Theorem 13 (Completeness). *Let R, $R^=$ be top TRSs over $\Sigma \cup \{\mathsf{top}\}$. If the following conditions are satisfied:*

(i) if u contains an instance of some $p \in P$ and $t \rightarrow u$ or $t \stackrel{=}{\rightarrow} u$ then t also contains an instance of p,
(ii) both R and $R^=$ are non-duplicating,
(iii) there is at least one function symbol of arity ≥ 2 in Σ.

then:

$$\text{Live}(\mathcal{T}_{top}(\Sigma, \mathcal{V}), R, R^=, G(P)) \implies \text{SN}(\text{LT}(R)/\text{LT}^=(R^=, P))$$

Proof. Assume $\text{Live}(\mathcal{T}_{top}(\Sigma, \mathcal{V}), R, R^=, G(P))$ and conditions (i)-(iii) hold and $\text{SN}(\text{LT}(R)/\text{LT}^=(R^=, P))$ does not hold. Then there is an infinite $\to_{\text{LT}} / \overset{=}{\to}_{\text{LT}}$ reduction. Due to non-duplication of R and $R^=$, $\text{LT}(R)$ and $\text{LT}^=(R^=, P)$ are also non-duplicating and by application of Theorem 12 we get that there is an infinite top $\to_{\text{LT}} / \overset{=}{\to}_{\text{LT}}$ reduction, call it ω.

Assume infinitely many terms in ω contain instances of terms from P. By the observation that an instance of p occurs in $\overline{C[p\delta]}$, Lemma 10 applied to ω gives rise to an infinite top reduction in $R/R^=$ having infinitely many terms containing instances of $p \in P$. Due to (i) all terms in this infinite reduction contain instances of $p \in P$ contradicting $\text{Live}(\mathcal{T}_{top}(\Sigma, \mathcal{V}), R, R^=, G(P))$. Hence only finitely many terms in ω contain instances of terms from P. So removing this finite prefix of ω yields an infinite top $\to_{\text{LT}} / \overset{=}{\to}_{\text{LT}}$ reduction ω' in which no instance of $p \in P$ occurs at all.

Note that non-top rules of R are relatively terminating to non-top rules of $R^=$. Assume they are not. Then there is an infinite $\to / \overset{=}{\to}$ reduction sequence obtained using non-top rules of R and $R^=$. Let $f \in \Sigma$ be a function symbol of arity ≥ 2 (its existence is ensured by (iii)). Put the infinite $\to / \overset{=}{\to}$ reduction in context $\text{top}(f(p, \square, \ldots))$. This yields an infinite, fair top reduction containing p and thus contradicting $\text{Live}(\mathcal{T}_{top}(\Sigma, \mathcal{V}), R, R^=, G(P))$. Now, by application of Lemma 11, we conclude that non-top rules of $\text{LT}(R)$ are relatively terminating to non-top rules of $\text{LT}^=(R^=, P)$.

In ω' top rules are applied infinitely often as non-top rules of $\text{LT}(R)$ are relatively terminating to non-top rules of $\text{LT}^=(R^=, P)$. Note that because of (ii) the only way to create an ok symbol is by application of the rule $\text{check}(p) \overset{=}{\to} \text{ok}(p)$. Every top reduction removes one occurrence of the ok symbol, so the aforementioned rule should be applied infinitely often. But since p does not occur in ω' this rule is not applicable which leads to a contradiction and ends the proof.   □

Examples 1, 2 and 3 show that conditions (i)-(iii) of this theorem are essential.

4   Examples

In this section we present two examples illustrating the applicability of the proposed transformation. None of them could be treated with the use of the LS transformation described in [5]. Both relative termination proofs of the transformed systems were found completely automatically by TPA .

Example 5 (Cars over a bridge). There is a road with cars going in two directions. But on their way there is a bridge which is only wide enough to permit a single lane of traffic. So there are lights indicating which side of the bridge is allowed to cross it. We want to verify the liveness property, namely that every car will eventually be able to cross the bridge. For that clearly we need some assumptions about the lighting system. We want to be as general as possible so instead of assuming some particular algorithm of switching lights we just require them to change in a fair way, that is in the infinite observation of the system there must be infinitely many light switches (or equivalently: no matter when we start watching the road after some, arbitrary, time we will see the change of lights). Also we assume that before a light switches at least one car will pass (otherwise liveness is lost as lights can change all the time without any cars passing).

We model the system with a unary *top* symbol whose arguments start with a binary symbol *left* or *right* indicating which side has a green light. The arguments of *left* and *right* start with unary symbols *new* and *old* representing cars waiting to cross the bridge. The constant *bot* stands for the end of the queue. New cars are allowed to arrive at the end of the queue at any time. What we want to prove is that finally no old car remains.

$$(1) \quad \mathsf{top}(\mathsf{left}(\mathsf{old}(x), y)) \to \mathsf{top}(\mathsf{right}(x, y))$$

$$
\begin{aligned}
(2) \quad & \mathsf{top}(\mathsf{left}(\mathsf{new}(x), y)) \to \mathsf{top}(\mathsf{right}(x, y)) \\
(3) \quad & \mathsf{top}(\mathsf{right}(x, \mathsf{old}(y))) \to \mathsf{top}(\mathsf{left}(x, y)) \\
(4) \quad & \mathsf{top}(\mathsf{right}(x, \mathsf{new}(y))) \to \mathsf{top}(\mathsf{left}(x, y)) \\
(5) \quad & \mathsf{top}(\mathsf{left}(\mathsf{bot}, y)) \to \mathsf{top}(\mathsf{right}(\mathsf{bot}, y)) \\
(6) \quad & \mathsf{top}(\mathsf{right}(x, \mathsf{bot})) \to \mathsf{top}(\mathsf{left}(x, \mathsf{bot})) \\
(7) \quad & \mathsf{top}(\mathsf{left}(\mathsf{old}(x), y)) \overset{=}{\to} \mathsf{top}(\mathsf{left}(x, y)) \\
(8) \quad & \mathsf{top}(\mathsf{left}(\mathsf{new}(x), y)) \overset{=}{\to} \mathsf{top}(\mathsf{left}(x, y)) \\
(9) \quad & \mathsf{top}(\mathsf{right}(x, \mathsf{old}(y))) \overset{=}{\to} \mathsf{top}(\mathsf{right}(x, y)) \\
(10) \quad & \mathsf{top}(\mathsf{right}(x, \mathsf{new}(y))) \overset{=}{\to} \mathsf{top}(\mathsf{right}(x, y)) \\
(11) \quad & \mathsf{bot} \overset{=}{\to} \mathsf{new}(\mathsf{bot})
\end{aligned}
$$

We have the following semantics of the rules:

$$
\begin{aligned}
(1) - (4) \quad & \text{Car passes and the light changes.} \\
(5) - (6) \quad & \text{No car waiting, light can change.} \\
(7) - (10) \quad & \text{Car passes, light remains the same.} \\
(11) \quad & \text{New car arriving.}
\end{aligned}
$$

We want to prove liveness with $P = \{\mathsf{old}(x)\}$. For that purpose we need to show relative termination of the transformed system. It is an easy observation that the following procedure is termination-preserving: if for every rule the number of occurrences of some symbol is bigger or equal in the left hand side than in the right hand side, then remove the rules for which it is strictly bigger. This approach, already presented in [5], corresponds to proving termination with polynomial orderings with successor as interpretation for symbol begin counted and identity for all the other symbols.

The proof of relative termination can be given as follows. First count occurrences of old to remove four rules. Then apply semantic labelling over $\{0, 1\}$ taking constant 1 for old, identity for remaining unary symbols, disjunction for all binary symbols and constant 0 for bot. In the resulting system repeatedly apply counting argument to remove all the $\rightarrow$ rules thus proving relative termination. The details including the proof generated automatically by TPA can be found in [8].

The next example we investigate is commonly known as "the readers-writers problem" and goes back to Courtois et al. [2]. It is considered as a classical synchronization problem.

Example 6 (The readers and writers problem). Some resource is to be shared among a number of processes. There are two types of processes: "readers", which perform only reading operation and "writers" which can perform both reading and writing. The safety requirement is that writers must have exclusive access to the resource (that is when a writer has access to the resource no other process can have it) whereas readers can share the access (as long as there is no writer active at the same time).

It is usual in literature ([11], [10]) to concentrate only on safety requirements and propose a solution with priority for readers (writers) which can clearly lead to starvation of writers (readers). In [7] a fair solution to this problem has been proposed. We will present another variant of this starvation-free solution, where the access to the resource is controlled in a first-come first-served manner and we will verify that indeed starvation is not possible, corresponding to liveness.

To achieve that we introduce a flag indicating which group of processes (either readers or writers) has priority. If only one group claims the resource it is simply allowed to use it. But in case of a conflict, that is two groups interested in use of the resource, the group having priority is allowed to access it and then the priority is changed. Without adding this priority flag obviously the desried liveness property does not hold.

As in example 5 we distinguish between old and new processes and verify that finally there are no old processes in the system. We model reader processes by unary function symbols: RAO, RAN, RIO, RIN where the second character indicates whether the reader is currently **A**ctive (performs reading) or **I**nactive (waits for access to the resource) and the third character indicates whether the reader is **O**ld or **N**ew. The argument is used to organize processes into lists. Similarly for writers we have WAO, WAN, WIO, WIN. However WAO and WAN are constants as there can be at most one active writing process at a time and there is no need to keep a list of such processes.

The whole system is then modelled by means of binary function symbols: sys-r or sys-w indicating priority for readers or writers respectively. The first argument describes all readers in the system and the second one models writers. Readers are modelled by a binary operator read whose first argument contains the list of active processes terminated by constant RT and the second argument contains the list of processes waiting for the resource terminated by constant RB. Similarly, the binary operator write describes writers processes. Its first argument can be either WT (no active writer),WAO (active old writer) or WAN (active new writer). The second argument describes a list of inactive writers.

Due to using lists to represent active processes, we make one additional restriction that simplifies the modelling substantially, namely we assume that reading processes free the resource in the same order as they got access to it. It corresponds to the situation when the reading operation always takes some fixed interval of time. Now we are ready to present the model of the system.

$$
\begin{array}{ll}
(1) \quad \mathsf{RB} \stackrel{\Rightarrow}{=} \mathsf{RIN}(\mathsf{RB}) & (4) \quad \mathsf{RAN}(\mathsf{RT}) \rightarrow \mathsf{RT} \\
(2) \quad \mathsf{WB} \stackrel{\Rightarrow}{=} \mathsf{WIN}(\mathsf{WB}) & (5) \quad \mathsf{WAO} \rightarrow \mathsf{WT} \\
(3) \quad \mathsf{RAO}(\mathsf{RT}) \rightarrow \mathsf{RT} & (6) \quad \mathsf{WAN} \rightarrow \mathsf{WT}
\end{array}
$$

(7) $\mathsf{top}(\mathsf{sys\text{-}r}(\mathsf{read}(r_1, \mathsf{RIO}(r_2)), \mathsf{write}(\mathsf{WT}, \mathsf{WB}))) \stackrel{\Rightarrow}{=} \mathsf{top}(\mathsf{sys\text{-}r}(\mathsf{read}(\mathsf{RAO}(r_1), r_2), \mathsf{write}(\mathsf{WT}, \mathsf{WB})))$

(8) $\mathsf{top}(\mathsf{sys\text{-}w}(\mathsf{read}(r_1, \mathsf{RIO}(r_2)), \mathsf{write}(\mathsf{WT}, \mathsf{WB}))) \stackrel{\Rightarrow}{=} \mathsf{top}(\mathsf{sys\text{-}w}(\mathsf{read}(\mathsf{RAO}(r_1)r_2), \mathsf{write}(\mathsf{WT}, \mathsf{WB})))$

(9) $\mathsf{top}(\mathsf{sys\text{-}r}(\mathsf{read}(r_1, \mathsf{RIN}(r_2)), \mathsf{write}(\mathsf{WT}, \mathsf{WB}))) \stackrel{\Rightarrow}{=} \mathsf{top}(\mathsf{sys\text{-}w}(\mathsf{read}(\mathsf{RAN}(r_1), r_2), \mathsf{write}(\mathsf{WT}, \mathsf{WB})))$

(10) $\mathsf{top}(\mathsf{sys\text{-}w}(\mathsf{read}(r_1, \mathsf{RIN}(r_2)), \mathsf{write}(\mathsf{WT}, \mathsf{WB}))) \stackrel{\Rightarrow}{=} \mathsf{top}(\mathsf{sys\text{-}w}(\mathsf{read}(\mathsf{RAN}(r_1), r_2), \mathsf{write}(\mathsf{WT}, \mathsf{WB})))$

(11) $\mathsf{top}(\mathsf{sys\text{-}r}(\mathsf{read}(\mathsf{RT}, \mathsf{RB}), \mathsf{write}(\mathsf{WT}, \mathsf{WIN}(w)))) \stackrel{\Rightarrow}{=} \mathsf{top}(\mathsf{sys\text{-}r}(\mathsf{read}(\mathsf{RT}, \mathsf{RB}), \mathsf{write}(\mathsf{WAN}, w)))$

(12) $\mathsf{top}(\mathsf{sys\text{-}w}(\mathsf{read}(\mathsf{RT}, \mathsf{RB}), \mathsf{write}(\mathsf{WT}, \mathsf{WIN}(w)))) \stackrel{\Rightarrow}{=} \mathsf{top}(\mathsf{sys\text{-}w}(\mathsf{read}(\mathsf{RT}, \mathsf{RB}), \mathsf{write}(\mathsf{WAN}, w)))$

(13) $\mathsf{top}(\mathsf{sys\text{-}r}(\mathsf{read}(\mathsf{RT}, \mathsf{RB}), \mathsf{write}(\mathsf{WT}, \mathsf{WIO}(w)))) \stackrel{\Rightarrow}{=} \mathsf{top}(\mathsf{sys\text{-}r}(\mathsf{read}(\mathsf{RT}, \mathsf{RB}), \mathsf{write}(\mathsf{WAO}, w)))$

(14) $\mathsf{top}(\mathsf{sys\text{-}w}(\mathsf{read}(\mathsf{RT}, \mathsf{RB}), \mathsf{write}(\mathsf{WT}, \mathsf{WIO}(w)))) \stackrel{\Rightarrow}{=} \mathsf{top}(\mathsf{sys\text{-}w}(\mathsf{read}(\mathsf{RT}, \mathsf{RB}), \mathsf{write}(\mathsf{WAO}, w)))$

(15) $\mathsf{top}(\mathsf{sys\text{-}r}(\mathsf{read}(r_1, \mathsf{RIO}(r_2)), \mathsf{write}(\mathsf{WT}, w))) \stackrel{\Rightarrow}{=} \mathsf{top}(\mathsf{sys\text{-}w}(\mathsf{read}(\mathsf{RAO}(r_1), r_2), \mathsf{write}(\mathsf{WT}, w)))$

(16) $\mathsf{top}(\mathsf{sys\text{-}r}(\mathsf{read}(r_1, \mathsf{RIN}(r_2)), \mathsf{write}(\mathsf{WT}, w))) \stackrel{\Rightarrow}{=} \mathsf{top}(\mathsf{sys\text{-}w}(\mathsf{read}(\mathsf{RAN}(r_1), r_2), \mathsf{write}(\mathsf{WT}, w)))$

(17) $\mathsf{top}(\mathsf{sys\text{-}w}(\mathsf{read}(\mathsf{RT}, r_2), \mathsf{write}(\mathsf{WT}, \mathsf{WIO}(w)))) \stackrel{\Rightarrow}{=} \mathsf{top}(\mathsf{sys\text{-}r}(\mathsf{read}(\mathsf{RT}, r_2), \mathsf{write}(\mathsf{WAO}, w)))$

(18) $\mathsf{top}(\mathsf{sys\text{-}w}(\mathsf{read}(\mathsf{RT}, r_2), \mathsf{write}(\mathsf{WT}, \mathsf{WIN}(w)))) \stackrel{\Rightarrow}{=} \mathsf{top}(\mathsf{sys\text{-}r}(\mathsf{read}(\mathsf{RT}, r_2), \mathsf{write}(\mathsf{WAN}, w)))$

The meaning of the rules is as follows:

$(1-2)$ New inactive process appears in the system and is queued to wait for the resource.

$(3-6)$ Active process finishes reading/writing.

$(7-10)$ Nobody is writing nor waiting for write access — inactive reading process is allowed to start reading; priority does not change

$(11-14)$ Nobody is reading nor waiting for read access and nobody is writing — writer is allowed to start writing; priority does not change.

$(15-16)$ Nobody is writing and priority is for readers — reader is allowed to start reading; priority is switched.

$(17-18)$ Nobody is reading nor writing and priority is for writers — writer is allowed to start writing; priority is switched.

What we want to prove is that finally no old process remains in the system. This corresponds to verifying liveness with the set $P = \{\mathsf{RAO}(x), \mathsf{RIO}(x), \mathsf{WAO}, \mathsf{WIO}(x)\}$.

To prove this liveness property we need to show relative termination of the transformed system. This was done completely automatically by TPA. The proof produced by TPA consists of more than 1000 lines. It proceeds by repeating a number of times the following procedure: apply semantic labelling, remove some rules using polynomial interpretations, unlabel the system to obtain a TRS with few rules less than before labelling. The proof applies semantic labelling with different interpretations 7 times. For a more detailed description we again refer to [8].

5   Conclusions

This paper describes a technique to transform a liveness problem with fairness to the problem of proving relative termination of a transformed TRS. In two presented examples the latter could be done fully automatically. The only human activity in this approach is modelling the original problem in the language of term rewriting. The advantage of this approach compared to standard model checking is that it can easily deal with liveness problems involving infinite state spaces.

In modelling liveness problem as TRS there is usually a lot of choice. This choice can influence the difficulty of the corresponding termination problem. This holds for instance for readers-writers example presented in Section 4 for which we considered a number of variations not all of which could be proved by TPA. Therefore improving TPA to be able to handle the broader class of relative termination problems is an obvious goal. Therefore we consider work on adopting existing termination techniques (like dependency pairs) for proving relative termination as well as developing techniques specifically for proving relative termination to be an interesting subject of further research.

References

1. T. Arts and J. Giesl. Termination of term rewriting using dependency pairs. *Theor. Comput. Sci.*, 236(1-2):133–178, 2000.
2. P. J. Courtois, F. Heymans, and D. L. Parnas. Concurrent control with "readers" and "writers". *Commun. ACM*, 14(10):667–668, 1971.
3. N. Dershowitz. Orderings for term-rewriting systems. *Theor. Comput. Sci.*, 17:279–301, 1982.
4. N. Francez. *Fairness*. Springer-Verlag, 1986.
5. J. Giesl and H. Zantema. Liveness in rewriting. In *Proc. 14th RTA, LNCS 2706*, pages 321–336, 2003.
6. J. Giesl and H. Zantema. Simulating liveness by reduction strategies. *Electr. Notes TCS*, 86(4), 2003.
7. C. A. R. Hoare. Monitors: an operating system structuring concept. *Commun. ACM*, 17(10):549–557, 1974.
8. A. Koprowski and H. Zantema. Proving liveness with fairness using rewriting. Technical Report CS-Report 05-06, Tech. Univ. of Eindhoven, March 2005. Available from http://w3.tue.nl/en/services/library/digilib/tue_publications/reports/.
9. D. S. Lankford. On proving term rewriting systems are noetherian. Technical Report MTP-3, Math. Dept., Louisiana Tech. Univ., Ruston, May 1979.
10. M. Raynal and D. Beeson. *Algorithms for mutual exclusion*. MIT Press, Cambridge, MA, USA, 1986.
11. A. Silberschatz, P. B. Galvin, and G. Gagne. *Operating system concepts*. John Wiley & Sons, Inc., 2004.
12. TeReSe. *Term Rewriting Systems*, volume 55 of *Cambridge Tracts in TCS*. Cambridge University Press, 2003.
13. H. Zantema. Termination of term rewriting by semantic labelling. *Fundamenta Informaticae*, 24(1/2):89–105, 1995.

A Concurrent Lambda Calculus with Futures

Joachim Niehren[1], Jan Schwinghammer[2], and Gert Smolka[2]

[1] INRIA Futurs, LIFL, Lille, France
[2] Programming Systems Lab, Saarland University, Saarbrücken, Germany

Abstract. We introduce a new concurrent lambda calculus with futures, λ(fut), to model the operational semantics of Alice, a concurrent extension of ML. λ(fut) is a minimalist extension of the call-by-value λ-calculus that yields the full expressiveness to define, combine, and implement a variety of standard concurrency constructs such as channels, semaphores, and ports. We present a linear type system for λ(fut) by which the safety of such definitions and their combinations can be proved: Well-typed implementations cannot be corrupted in any well-typed context.

1 Introduction

The goal of this paper is to model the operational semantics of Alice [23,2], a concurrent extension of Standard ML (SML) [17] for typed open distributed programming. Alice is the first concurrent extension of SML where all synchronisation is based on futures rather than channels [22,20,10]. Many ideas in Alice are inspired by and inherited from the concurrent constraint programming language Mozart-Oz [26,13,19].

Futures [5,12] are a restricted form of logic variables, which carefully separate read and write permissions. In contrast to logic variables, futures grant for *static data flow* that can be predicted at compile time. Otherwise, they behave like the logic variables of concurrent logic and concurrent constraint programming [25,24]: A future is a transparent placeholder for a value; it disappears once its value becomes available. Operations that need the value of a future block until the value becomes available. Other operations may simply continue with the placeholder, as long as they do not need its value. This form of *automatic data driven synchronisation* is invoked as late as possible, so that the potential for concurrent and distributed computation is maximised.

Static data flow is an indispensable prerequisite for static typing as in SML, CAML, or Haskell. This fact is well-known, as it led to serious problems in several previous approaches to concurrent programming: It prohibited static typing in programming languages with unrestricted logic variables such as Oz [18,26] and in π-calculus based extensions of SML such as Pict [21]. The problem for π-calculus based channel approaches was solved with the join-calculus [10,11] and the corresponding programming language JoCaml [8] which extends on CAML [7]. The join-calculus, however, does not model futures on which we focus in this paper.

B. Gramlich (Ed.): FroCoS 2005, LNAI 3717, pp. 248–263, 2005.
© Springer-Verlag Berlin Heidelberg 2005

We introduce a new concurrent lambda calculus with futures $\lambda(\mathsf{fut})$ that models the operational semantics of Alice at high level. $\lambda(\mathsf{fut})$ is a minimalist extension of the call-by-value λ-calculus that yields the full expressiveness to define, implement, and combine a variety of standard concurrency constructs, including channels, semaphores, and ports.

Previous λ-calculi with futures by Felleisen and Flanagan [9] were proposed to model the parallel execution of *otherwise purely functional programs*. They too describe a set of parallel threads that communicate through futures. However, our very different perspective on futures as a *uniform mechanism for introducing concurrency* to Alice necessitates a number of nontrivial extensions:

Indeterminism. Standard concurrency constructs are indeterministic, which is incompatible with confluence properties enjoyed by previous λ-calculi with futures. We propose to add indeterminism via reference cells, as these are already available in SML. Furthermore, we propose *handled futures* for single assignment, similarly to the I-structures of Id [4] and promises of [14]. A handled future comes with a handle that can eventually assign a value to a future. Any attempt to use the same handle twice raises a programming error.

Explicit recursion. Similarly to cells, handles permit the construction of cyclic structures. This raises a number of nontrivial technical problems, some of which are known from call-by-need λ-calculi with explicit recursion. Indeed, we can easily extend $\lambda(\mathsf{fut})$ by lazy threads, so that we obtain an elegant model for call-by-need [3,15] mixed with call-by-value computation.

Static typing. We have to add a type system, as previous λ-calculi with futures were untyped.

We show that $\lambda(\mathsf{fut})$ can *safely* express concurrency constructs, so that these cannot be corrupted in any well-typed context, in that their usage never raises handle errors. We prove this kind of safety result on basis of a linear type system we introduce, inspired by [27].

We present $\lambda(\mathsf{fut})$ in Sects. 2 and 3. The linear type system for $\lambda(\mathsf{fut})$ that excludes handle errors is given in Sect. 4. We then express diverse concurrency constructs in $\lambda(\mathsf{fut})$ (Sect. 5) and prove their safety (Sect. 6). Finally, we briefly discuss some implementation issues in Sect. 7.

2 Lambda Calculus with Futures

We present the lambda calculus with futures $\lambda(\mathsf{fut})$. We start with an untyped version, discuss its syntax and operational semantics.

2.1 Syntax

Fig. 1 introduces the syntax of $\lambda(\mathsf{fut})$. This calculus extends the call-by-value λ-calculus with cells (as featured by SML and CAML) and by concurrent threads,

$$x, y, z \in Var$$

$$c \in Const ::= \textbf{unit} \mid \textbf{cell} \mid \textbf{exch} \mid \textbf{thread} \mid \textbf{handle}$$

$$e \in Exp ::= x \mid c \mid \lambda x.e \mid e_1\, e_2$$

$$v \in Val ::= x \mid c \mid \lambda x.e \mid \textbf{exch}\, v$$

$$C \in Config ::= C_1 \mid C_2 \mid (\nu x)C \mid x\, \textsf{c}\, v \mid x\!\Leftarrow\!e \mid y\, \textsf{h}\, x \mid y\, \textsf{h}\, \bullet$$

Fig. 1. Syntax of $\lambda(\textsf{fut})$

$$(C_1 \mid C_2) \mid C_3 \equiv C_1 \mid (C_2 \mid C_3) \qquad\qquad C_1 \mid C_2 \equiv C_2 \mid C_1$$

$$((\nu x)C_0) \mid C_1 \equiv (\nu x)(C_0 \mid C_1) \quad \text{if } x \notin \textsf{fv}(C_1) \qquad (\nu x)(\nu y)C \equiv (\nu y)(\nu x)C$$

Fig. 2. Structural congruence

futures, and handles. Expressions and values of $\lambda(\textsf{fut})$ model sequential higher-order programming; configurations add the concurrency level.

The expressions e of $\lambda(\textsf{fut})$ are standard λ-terms with variables $x, y, \ldots$ and constants ranged over by c. We introduce 5 constants, 3 of which are standard: **unit** is a dummy value, **cell** serves for introducing reference cells, and **exch** for atomic exchange of cell values. The new constants **thread** and **handle** serve for introducing threads, futures, and handles. Values v are defined as usual in a call-by-value λ-calculus.

Configurations C are reminiscent of expressions of the π-calculus. They are built from base components by parallel composition $C_1 \mid C_2$ and new name operators $(\nu x)C$. We distinguish four types of base components: a thread $x\!\Leftarrow\!e$ is a concurrent component whose evaluation will eventually bind the future x to the value of expression e unless it diverges or suspends. We call such variables x *concurrent futures*. Note that a concurrent future x may occur in the expression e whose evaluation computes its future value, i.e., a thread is like a recursive equation $x = e$, but directed from right to left. A cell $x\, \textsf{c}\, v$ associates a name x to a cell with value v. A handle component $y\, \textsf{h}\, x$ associates a handle y to a future x, so that y can be used to assign a value to x. We call x a future handled by y, or more shortly a *handled future*. Finally, a used handle component $y\, \textsf{h}\, \bullet$ means that y is a handle that has already been used to bind its future.

We define free and bound variables as usual; the only scope bearing constructs are λ-binder and new operators (νx). We identify expressions and configurations up to consistent renaming of bound variables. We write $\textsf{fv}(C)$ and $\textsf{fv}(e)$ for the free variables of a configuration and expression, resp., and $e[e'/x]$ for capture-free substitution of e' for x in e.

We do not want the order of components in configurations to matter. Following the presentation of π-calculus in [16] we use a *structural congruence* $\equiv$ to simplify the statement of the operational semantics. This is the least congruence relation on configurations containing the identities in Fig. 2. The first two axioms render parallel composition associative and commutative. The third rule is known as *scope extrusion* in π-calculus and allows to extend the scope of a local variable. The final identity expresses that the order of restricting names does not matter.

2.2   Operational Semantics

The operational semantics of $\lambda(\mathsf{fut})$ is given in Figs. 3, 4 and 5 by a binary relation $C_1 \rightarrow C_2$ on configurations called *reduction*.

The reduction strategy of $\lambda(\mathsf{fut})$ is specified using the evaluation contexts defined in Fig. 3. We base it on standard evaluation contexts F for call-by-value reduction and lift them to threads and configurations. Formally, a context is a term with a single occurrence of the *hole marker* $[\,]$ which is a special constant. Evaluation contexts F are expressions where some subexpression in call-by-value reduction position is replaced by the hole marker. A context E is a thread where a subexpression is left out, and D is a configuration where a subconfiguration is missing. We write $D[C]$, $E[e]$, and $F[e]$ resp. for the object obtained by filling the hole in the context with an expression.

A nontrivial question is *when* to allow to replace futures by their values. The naive approach to always do so once the value becomes available fails, in that it introduces non-terminating unfolding in the presence of recursion. For instance, consider a thread $x\!\Leftarrow\!\lambda y.xy$. The thread's expression contains an occurrence of the future x whose value the thread has computed. Replacing this occurrence of x by its value yields $x\!\Leftarrow\!\lambda y.((\lambda y'.xy')\ y)$ which again contains an occurrence of x because of recursion, so the substitution process can be repeated indefinitely.

Alternatively, one might want to permit future substitution in all evaluation contexts. This approach, however, yields confluence problems. Suppose that x is bound to value 5 by some thread $x\!\Leftarrow\!5$ and that another thread is evaluating the expression $(\lambda y.\lambda z.z)\ x$ which contains an occurrence of x in evaluation position. We could thus first replace x by 5 and then β-reduce, resulting in $\lambda z.5$. Or else, we could β-reduce first, yielding $\lambda z.x$. Now the problem is that the occurrence of x has escaped the evaluation context, so that replacing the future by its value is impossible and we are left with two distinct, irreducible terms.

We propose to replace a future only if its value is needed to proceed with the computation of the thread. In order specify this need, we define *future evaluation contexts* E_f and F_f in Fig. 3 that we will use in the rule (FUTURE.DEREF) of the operational semantics in Fig. 5. In the version of $\lambda(\mathsf{fut})$ presented here, the value of futures x is needed in two situations, in function applications xv and for cell exchange **exch** $x\,v$ in evaluation contexts. Furthermore, note that future evaluation contexts can equally be used to extend $\lambda(\mathsf{fut})$ by lazy threads. The same mechanism has also proved useful to model more implementation oriented issues in [9]. Future evaluation contexts are called *placeholder strict* there.

Every reduction step of $\lambda(\mathsf{fut})$ is defined by an evaluation rule in Fig. 5 which involves either one or two threads of a configuration. These threads can be freely selected according to the two inference rules in Fig. 4: given a configuration C we choose a representation $D[C']$ congruent to C and apply a reduction rule

$$D ::= [] \mid C \mid D \mid (\nu x)D$$

$$E ::= x \Leftarrow F \qquad\qquad\qquad E_\mathsf{f} ::= x \Leftarrow F_\mathsf{f}$$

$$F ::= [] \mid F\,e \mid v\,F \qquad\qquad F_\mathsf{f} ::= F[[]\,v] \mid F[\mathbf{exch}\,[]\,v]$$

Fig. 3. Evaluation contexts D, E, F and future evaluation contexts E_f, F_f

$$\frac{C_1 \equiv C_1' \quad C_1' \to C_2' \quad C_2' \equiv C_2}{C_1 \to C_2} \qquad\qquad \frac{C_1 \to C_2}{D[C_1] \to D[C_2]}$$

Fig. 4. Selection of threads during reduction

to C'. Reduction inside threads $x \Leftarrow e$ means to reduce a subexpression e' in an evaluation context F so that $e = F[e']$. Evaluation inside expressions is call-by-value, i.e., all arguments of a function are evaluated before function application. This by the standard call-by-value beta reduction rule (BETA) in Fig. 5.

Besides β-reduction, there are six other reduction rules in Fig. 5. Concurrent futures are created by rule (THREAD.NEW). Evaluating applications **thread** $\lambda y.e$ has the following effects:

- a new concurrent future y is created,
- a new thread $y \Leftarrow e$ is spawned which evaluates the expression e concurrently and eventually assigns its value to y,
- the concurrent future y is returned instantaneously in the original thread.

Note that the expression e may also refer to y, i.e., our notion of thread creation incorporates explicit recursion.

As an example consider an application $f\,e$ of some function f, where the evaluation of the argument e takes considerable time, e.g., a communication with a remote process or an expensive internal computation. In this case it may be advantageous to use instead

$$f\,(\mathbf{thread}\,\lambda y.e)$$

which applies f to a fresh future y and delegates the evaluation of e to a concurrent thread $y \Leftarrow e$. The point here is that f will only block on y if it really needs the value of its argument, so that the latest possible synchronisation is obtained automatically. The only way we can simulate this effect with channels is by rewriting the function f (even the argument type of f changes). So what futures buy us is maximal concurrency without the need to rewrite existing code.

Rule (FUTURE.DEREF) states when to replaces futures y by their value v. It applies to futures in future evaluation contexts, once the value of the future has been computed by some concurrent thread $y \Leftarrow v$ in the configuration.

Rule (HANDLE.NEW) introduces a handled future jointly with a handle. The idea of handled futures appeared before in the form of I-structures [4] and promises [14]. Evaluating applications **handle** $\lambda x.\lambda y.e$ has the following effects:

(BETA)	$E[(\lambda y.e)\, v] \rightarrow E[e[^v\!/_y]]$	
(THREAD.NEW)	$E[\textbf{thread}\, v] \rightarrow (\nu y)(E[y] \mid y{\Leftarrow}v\, y)$	$(y \notin \mathsf{fv}(E[v]))$
(FUTURE.DEREF)	$E_f[y] \mid y{\Leftarrow}v \rightarrow E_f[v] \mid y{\Leftarrow}v$	
(HANDLE.NEW)	$E[\textbf{handle}\, v] \rightarrow (\nu y)(\nu z)(E[v\, y\, z] \mid z\, \mathsf{h}\, y)$	$(y, z \notin \mathsf{fv}(E[v]))$
(HANDLE.BIND)	$E[z\, v] \mid z\, \mathsf{h}\, y \rightarrow E[\textbf{unit}] \mid y{\Leftarrow}v \mid z\, \mathsf{h}\, \bullet$	
(CELL.NEW)	$E[\textbf{cell}\, v] \rightarrow (\nu y)(E[y] \mid y\, \mathsf{c}\, v)$	$(y \notin \mathsf{fv}(E[v]))$
(CELL.EXCH)	$E[\textbf{exch}\, y\, v_1] \mid y\, \mathsf{c}\, v_2 \rightarrow E[v_2] \mid y\, \mathsf{c}\, v_1$	

Fig. 5. Reduction rules of operational semantics

- a new handled future x is created,
- a new handle y is created,
- a new handle component $y\, \mathsf{h}\, x$ associates handle y to future x,
- the current thread continues with expression e.

Handles can be used only once. According to rule (HANDLE.BIND) an application of handle y to value v reduces by binding the future associated to y to v. This action consumes the handle component $y\, \mathsf{h}\, x$; what remains is a used handle component $y\, \mathsf{h}\, \bullet$. Trying to apply a handle a second time leads to *handle errors*:

$$D[E[y\, v] \mid y\, \mathsf{h}\, \bullet] \qquad \text{(handle error)}$$

We call a configuration C *error-free* if it cannot be reduced to any erroneous configuration, i.e., none of its reducts C' with $C \rightarrow^* C'$ is a handle error.

Evaluating $\textbf{cell}\, v$ with rule (CELL.NEW) creates a new cell y with content v represented through a cell component $y\, \mathsf{c}\, v$. The exchange operation $\textbf{exch}\, y\, v$ writes v to the cell and returns the previous contents. This exchange is *atomic*, i.e., no other thread can interfere. The cell exchange operation $\textbf{exch}$ is strict in its first argument; the definition of strict evaluation contexts E_f expresses this uniformly. Observe that cells introduce indeterminism since two threads might compete for access to a cell.

Programs without handle errors and cell exchange are uniformly confluent [19] and thus confluent. So cell exchange by concurrent threads remains the *sole* source of indeterminism in $\lambda(\textbf{fut})$. Nevertheless, handles are needed together with cells in order to safely express nondeterministic concurrency constructs (see Sect. 5). While handles can be expressed in terms of the other constructs, such an encoding unnecessarily complicates the formal treatment. In order to rule out handle errors by means of the linear type system of Sect. 4 we chose to introduce handled futures as primitive.

2.3 Examples

The first example illustrates concurrent threads and data synchronization. Let I be the lambda expression $\lambda z.z$. We consider the expression below, and reduce it by a THREAD.NEW step followed by a trivial BETA step. In the previous explanation of thread creation we left such BETA steps implicit.

$$x \Leftarrow \underline{(\textbf{thread } (\lambda y.I\,I))}\,(I\,\textbf{unit}) \rightarrow (\nu y)(x \Leftarrow y\,(I\,\textbf{unit}) \mid y \Leftarrow \underline{(\lambda y.I\,I)y})$$
$$\rightarrow (\nu y)(x \Leftarrow y\,(I\,\textbf{unit}) \mid y \Leftarrow I\,I)$$

At this point, we can reduce both threads concurrently, i.e., we have a choice of BETA reducing the left or right thread first. We do the former:

$$(\nu y)(x \Leftarrow y\,\underline{(I\,\textbf{unit})} \mid y \Leftarrow I\,I) \rightarrow (\nu y)(x \Leftarrow y\,\textbf{unit} \mid y \Leftarrow \underline{I\,I})$$
$$\rightarrow (\nu y)(x \Leftarrow y\,\textbf{unit} \mid y \Leftarrow I)$$

In fact, any other reduction sequence would have given the same result in this case. At this point, both threads need to synchronize to exchange the value of y by applying FUTURE.DEREF; this enables a final BETA step:

$$(\nu y)(\underline{x \Leftarrow y\,\textbf{unit}} \mid y \Leftarrow I) \rightarrow (\nu y)(x \Leftarrow \underline{I\,\textbf{unit}} \mid y \Leftarrow I)$$
$$(\nu y)(x \Leftarrow \textbf{unit} \mid y \Leftarrow I)$$

The second example illustrates the power of thread creation in $\lambda(\textsf{fut})$; in contrast to all previous future operators, it can express explicit recursion. Indeed, **thread** can replace a fixed point operator **fix**. Consider for instance:

$$x \Leftarrow (\textbf{thread } \lambda f.\lambda x.(f\ x))\ z$$

Thread creation THREAD.NEW yields a thread assigning a recursive value to f, so that the original thread can FUTURE.DEREF and BETA reduce forever.

$$(\nu f)\ \underline{(x \Leftarrow f\ z \mid f \Leftarrow \lambda x.(f\ x))} \rightarrow (\nu f)\ (x \Leftarrow \underline{(\lambda x.(f\ x))\ z} \mid f \Leftarrow \lambda x.(f\ x))$$
$$\rightarrow (\nu f)\ \underline{(x \Leftarrow f\ z \mid f \Leftarrow \lambda x.(f\ x))}$$

Indeed, rule FUTURE.DEREF simulates the usual UNFOLD rule for fixed point operators.

$$(\text{UNFOLD}) \qquad\qquad \textbf{fix } \lambda f.\lambda x.e \rightarrow \lambda x.e[\textbf{fix } \lambda f.\lambda x.e/f]$$

As a final example, consider how handles can introduce cyclic bindings:

$$x \Leftarrow \underline{\textbf{handle } \lambda z.\lambda y.y\,z} \rightarrow^3 (\nu y)(\nu z)(x \Leftarrow \underline{y\,z} \mid y\,\textsf{h}\,z)$$
$$\rightarrow (\nu y)(\nu z)(x \Leftarrow \textbf{unit} \mid z \Leftarrow z \mid y\,\textsf{h}\,\bullet)$$

by HANDLE.NEW and two BETA steps. The final step by HANDLE.BIND binds the future z to itself. This is closely related to what is sometimes referred to as *recursion through the store*, or implicit recursion.

$\alpha, \beta \in \text{Type} ::= \text{unit} \mid \alpha \to \beta \mid \alpha \, \text{ref}$

$$\frac{}{\Gamma \vdash c : \text{TypeOf}(c)}$$

unit : unit

$$\frac{}{\Gamma, x{:}\alpha \vdash x : \alpha}$$

thread : $(\alpha \to \alpha) \to \alpha$

handle : $(\alpha \to (\alpha \to \text{unit}) \to \beta) \to \beta$

$$\frac{\Gamma, x{:}\alpha \vdash e : \beta}{\Gamma \vdash \lambda x.e : \alpha \to \beta}$$

cell : $\alpha \to (\alpha \, \text{ref})$

exch : $\alpha \, \text{ref} \to \alpha \to \alpha$

$$\frac{\Gamma \vdash e_1 : \alpha \to \beta \quad \Gamma \vdash e_2 : \alpha}{\Gamma \vdash e_1 \, e_2 : \beta}$$

Fig. 6. Typing of $\lambda(\text{fut})$ expressions

3   Typing

Since our intention is to model extensions of the (statically typed) language
ML we restrict our calculus to be typed. Types are function types $\alpha \to \beta$, the
type $\alpha \, \text{ref}$ of reference cells containing elements of type α, and the single base
type unit. Typing of expressions is standard and integrates well with ML-style
polymorphism and type inference. On the level of configurations, types are used
to ensure a number of well-formedness conditions, and allow us to state a type
preservation property during evaluation.

3.1   Typing of Constants and Expressions

According to the operational semantics described in Sect. 2, the constants obtain
their natural types. For instance, **thread** has type $(\alpha \to \alpha) \to \alpha$ for any type α
since its argument must be a function that maps a future of type α to a value
of type α. The operation **thread** then returns the future of type α. The types
of the other constants are listed in Fig. 6 and can be justified accordingly.

Let Γ and Δ range over *type environments* $x_1{:}\alpha_1 \ldots x_n{:}\alpha_n$, i.e. finite functional relations between *Var* and *Type*. In writing Γ_1, Γ_2 we assume that the
respective domains are disjoint. Writing *TypeOf*(c) for the type of constant c we
have the usual type inference rules for simply typed lambda calculus (Fig. 6).

3.2   Typing of Configurations

Every future in a configuration is either concurrent or handled, i.e., its status
is unique. Moreover, the binding of a concurrent future must be unique, and
a handle must give reference to a unique future. Since parallel compositions of
components are reminiscent of (mutually recursive) declarations the following
two configurations are ill-typed:

$$x{\Leftarrow}e_1 \mid x{\Leftarrow}e_2 \quad \text{or} \quad y \, h \, x_1 \mid y \, h \, x_2 \qquad (1)$$

Therefore, in the type system it will be required that the variables introduced
by C_1 and C_2 are disjoint in concurrent compositions $C_1 \mid C_2$.

$$\frac{\Gamma,\Gamma_1 \vdash C_1 : \Gamma_2 \quad \Gamma,\Gamma_2 \vdash C_2 : \Gamma_1}{\Gamma \vdash C_1 \mid C_2 : \Gamma_1, \Gamma_2} \qquad \frac{\Gamma, x{:}\alpha \vdash e : \alpha}{\Gamma \vdash x{\Leftarrow}e : (x{:}\alpha)}$$

$$\frac{\Gamma, x{:}\alpha \, \mathsf{ref} \vdash v : \alpha}{\Gamma \vdash x\,c\,v : (x{:}\alpha\,\mathsf{ref})} \qquad \frac{x, y \notin \mathrm{dom}(\Gamma)}{\Gamma \vdash y\,\mathsf{h}\,x : (x{:}\alpha, y{:}\alpha \rightarrow \mathsf{unit})}$$

$$\frac{\Gamma \vdash C : \Gamma'}{\Gamma \vdash (\nu x)C : \Gamma' - x} \qquad \frac{y \notin \mathrm{dom}(\Gamma)}{\Gamma \vdash y\,\mathsf{h}\bullet : (y{:}\alpha \rightarrow \mathsf{unit})}$$

Fig. 7. Typing rules for components

Types are lifted to configurations according to the inference rules in Fig. 7. The judgment $\Gamma \vdash C : \Gamma'$ informally means that given type assumptions Γ the configuration C is well-typed. The type environment Γ' keeps track of the variables declared by C. In fact, the rules guarantee that $\mathrm{dom}(\Gamma')$ is exactly the set of variables declared by C, and that $\mathrm{dom}(\Gamma) \cap \mathrm{dom}(\Gamma') = \emptyset$.

To type a thread $x{\Leftarrow}e$ we can use the environment Γ as well as the binding $x{:}\alpha$ that is introduced by the component. Note that writing $\Gamma, x{:}\alpha$ in the premise implies that x is not already declared in Γ. Similarly, when typing a reference cell $x\,c\,v$ both Γ and the assumption $x{:}\alpha\,\mathsf{ref}$ can be used to derive that the contents v of the cell has type α. The typing rule for handle components $y\,\mathsf{h}\,x$ and $y\,\mathsf{h}\bullet$ take care that the types of the handled future x and its handle y are compatible, and that they are not already declared in Γ.

A restriction $(\nu x)C$ is well-typed under assumptions Γ if the configuration C is. The name x is kept local by removing any occurrence $x{:}\alpha$ from Γ', which we write $\Gamma' - x$.

The typing rule for a parallel composition $C_1 \mid C_2$ is reminiscent of the circular assume-guarantee reasoning used in compositional verification of concurrent systems [1]. Recall that the combined environment Γ_1, Γ_2 in the conclusion is only defined if the variables appearing in Γ_1 and Γ_2 are disjoint. So the rule ensures that the sets of variables declared by C_2 and C_1 resp., are disjoint. Note how this prevents the ill-formed configurations in (1) to be typed. Moreover, by typing C_1 in the extended environment Γ, Γ_1 the rule allows variables declared by C_2 to be used in C_1, and vice versa. For example, we can derive

$$\vdash (x{\Leftarrow}y\,\mathsf{unit} \mid y\,\mathsf{h}\,z) : (x{:}\mathsf{unit}, z{:}\mathsf{unit}, y{:}\mathsf{unit} \rightarrow \mathsf{unit}) \tag{2}$$

The thread on the left-hand side declares x and can use the assumption $y{:}\mathsf{unit} \rightarrow \mathsf{unit}$ about the handle declared in the component on the right. No further assumptions are necessary.

Theorem 1 (Subject Reduction). *If $\Gamma \vdash C_1 : \Gamma'$ and $C_1 \rightarrow C_2$ then $\Gamma \vdash C_2 : \Gamma'$.*

Program errors are notorious even for a statically typed programming language. Indeed it turns out that the class of *handle errors* is not excluded by the type system just presented.

Multiplicities $\kappa ::= \mathbf{1} \mid \omega$

Linear types $\alpha, \beta \in LinType ::= \mathsf{unit} \mid \alpha \xrightarrow{\kappa} \beta \mid \alpha\,\mathsf{ref}$

Multiplicities of linear types

$$|\mathsf{unit}| \overset{def}{=} \omega, \qquad |\alpha \xrightarrow{\kappa} \beta| \overset{def}{=} \kappa, \qquad |\alpha\,\mathsf{ref}| \overset{def}{=} \omega$$

Typing of constants where $\kappa, \kappa', \kappa''$ arbitrary

> **unit** : unit
>
> **thread** : $(\alpha \xrightarrow{\kappa} \alpha) \xrightarrow{\kappa'} \alpha$ where $|\alpha| = \omega$
>
> **handle** : $(\alpha \xrightarrow{\kappa} (\alpha \xrightarrow{\mathbf{1}} \mathsf{unit}) \xrightarrow{\kappa'} \beta) \xrightarrow{\kappa''} \beta$ where $|\alpha| = \omega$
>
> **cell** : $\alpha \xrightarrow{\kappa} (\alpha\,\mathsf{ref})$
>
> **exch** : $\alpha\,\mathsf{ref} \xrightarrow{\kappa} \alpha \xrightarrow{\kappa'} \alpha$

Operations on type environments

> $\mathsf{once}(\Gamma) \overset{def}{=} \{x \mid x{:}\alpha \text{ in } \Gamma, |\alpha| = \mathbf{1}\}$
>
> $\Gamma_1{\cdot}\Gamma_2 \overset{def}{=} \Gamma_1 \cup \Gamma_2$ provided $\Gamma_1 \cap \Gamma_2 = \{x{:}\alpha \mid x{:}\alpha \in \Gamma_1 \cup \Gamma_2, |\alpha| = \omega\}$

Fig. 8. Linear types

4   Linear Types for Handles

We refine the type system to prevent handle errors. We see this system as a proof tool to facilitate reasoning about the absence of handle errors; we do *not* want to argue that the linear types should be used in practice. We do also not discuss how to deal with handle errors in a concrete programming language.

Most previous uses of linear type systems in functional languages, such as the uniqueness typing of Clean [6], aimed at preserving referential transparency in the presence of side-effects, and taking advantage of destructive updates for efficiency reasons. In contrast, our system rules out a class of programming errors, by enforcing the single-assignment property for handled futures.

The linear type system will be sufficiently expressive to type a variety of concurrency abstractions (Sects. 5 and 6). Moreover, the linear types of the handles implementing these abstractions will be encapsulated. Thus, users of these abstractions need not know about linear types at all.

We annotate types with *usage information* in the sense of [27]. In our case it is sufficient to distinguish between linear (i.e., exactly one) and nonlinear (i.e., any number of times) uses. Multiplicities $\mathbf{1}$ and ω are ranged over by κ. Moreover, for our purposes of ruling out handle errors we annotate only function types, values of other types can always be used non-linearly (recall that handles have functional types $\alpha \to \mathsf{unit}$). In particular, $\alpha \xrightarrow{\kappa} \beta$ denotes functions from α to β that can be used κ times, and so $\alpha \xrightarrow{\omega} \beta$ corresponds to the usual function type. We write $|\alpha|$ for the multiplicity attached to a type α (see Fig. 8).

For a context Γ we write $\mathsf{once}(\Gamma)$ for the set of variables occuring in Γ with linear multiplicity. If Γ can be split into Γ_1 and Γ_2 that both contain all the variables of Γ with multiplicity ω and a partition of $\mathsf{once}(\Gamma)$ we write $\Gamma = \Gamma_1{\cdot}\Gamma_2$.

$$\frac{\mathsf{once}(\Gamma) = \emptyset}{\Gamma \vdash c : \mathit{TypeOf}(c)}$$

$$\frac{\Gamma, x{:}\alpha \vdash e : \alpha \quad |\alpha| = \omega}{\Gamma \vdash x \Leftarrow e : (x{:}\alpha; x{:}\alpha)}$$

$$\frac{\mathsf{once}(\Gamma) = \emptyset}{\Gamma, x{:}\alpha \vdash x : \alpha}$$

$$\frac{\Gamma, x{:}\alpha\,\mathsf{ref} \vdash v : \alpha}{\Gamma \vdash x\,c\,v : (x{:}\alpha\,\mathsf{ref}; x{:}\alpha\,\mathsf{ref})}$$

$$\frac{\Gamma, x{:}\alpha \vdash e : \beta \quad \mathsf{once}(\Gamma) = \emptyset}{\Gamma \vdash \lambda x.e : \alpha \xrightarrow{\omega} \beta}$$

$$\frac{x, y \notin \mathsf{dom}(\Gamma) \quad |\alpha| = \omega}{\Gamma \vdash y\,h\,x : (x{:}\alpha, y{:}\alpha \xrightarrow{1} \mathsf{unit}; x{:}\alpha, y{:}\alpha \xrightarrow{1} \mathsf{unit})}$$

$$\frac{\Gamma, x{:}\alpha \vdash e : \beta}{\Gamma \vdash \lambda x.e : \alpha \xrightarrow{1} \beta}$$

$$\frac{y \notin \mathsf{dom}(\Gamma)}{\Gamma \vdash y\,h\,\bullet : (y{:}\alpha \xrightarrow{1} \mathsf{unit}; \emptyset)}$$

$$\frac{\Gamma_1 \vdash e_1 : \alpha \xrightarrow{\kappa} \beta \quad \Gamma_2 \vdash e_2 : \alpha}{\Gamma_1 \cdot \Gamma_2 \vdash e_1\,e_2 : \beta}$$

$$\frac{\Gamma \vdash C : \Gamma_1; \Gamma_2}{\Gamma \vdash (\nu x)C : \Gamma_1 - x; \Gamma_2 - x}$$

$$\frac{\Gamma, \Delta_2 \vdash C_1 : \Gamma_1; \Gamma_2 \cdot \Gamma_3 \quad \Delta, \Gamma_2 \vdash C_2 : \Delta_1; \Delta_2 \cdot \Delta_3}{\Gamma \cdot \Delta \vdash C_1 \mid C_2 : \Gamma_1, \Delta_1; \Gamma_3 \cdot \Delta_3} \quad \left(\begin{matrix} \mathsf{dom}(\Gamma) \cap \mathsf{dom}(\Delta_1) = \emptyset \\ \mathsf{dom}(\Delta) \cap \mathsf{dom}(\Gamma_1) = \emptyset \end{matrix} \right)$$

Fig. 9. Linear typing rules for $\lambda(\mathsf{fut})$ expressions and configurations

The types of the term constants are now refined to reflect that handles *must* be used linearly. However, we do not want to restrict access to futures through the rule (FUTURE.DEREF). Hence it must be guaranteed that futures will never be replaced by values of types with linear multiplicity. This is done by restricting the types of **thread** and **handle** by the condition $|\alpha| = \omega$. On the other hand, note that no such restriction is necessary for cells which may contain values of any (i.e., multiplicity 1 or ω) type. Intuitively this is sound because cells can be accessed only by the exchange operation. In particular, the contents of a cell (potentially having multiplicity 1) cannot be *copied* through cell access.

The type rules for expressions are given in Fig. 9. The rules guarantee that every variable of type α in Γ with $|\alpha| = 1$ appears exactly once in the term: In the rules for constants and variables, the side-condition $\mathsf{once}(\Gamma) = \emptyset$ ensures that Γ contains only variables with use ω. There are two rules for abstraction, reflecting the fact that we have function types with multiplicities 1 and ω. The condition $\mathsf{once}(\Gamma) = \emptyset$ in the first abstraction rule allows us to derive a type $\alpha \xrightarrow{\omega} \beta$ only if e does not contain any free variables with multiplicity 1. However, with the second rule it is always possible to derive a type $\alpha \xrightarrow{1} \beta$. Finally, the rule for application splits the linearly used variables of the environment. The annotation κ is irrelevant here, but the type of function and argument must match exactly.

The rules for configurations (Fig. 9) have changed: Judgments are now of the form $\Gamma \vdash C : \Delta_1; \Delta_2$, and the type system maintains the invariants (i) $\Gamma \cap \Delta_1 = \emptyset$ and (ii) $\Delta_2 \subseteq \Delta_1$. The intended meaning is the following.

- As before, Γ contains the type assumptions and Δ_1 is used to keep track of the variables which C provides bindings for. In particular, the use of Δ_1 allows to ensure the well-formedness conditions in configurations (cf. the configurations (1) on page 255) by means of invariant (i).

- Variables with multiplicity **1** declared by C may not be used both by a surrounding configuration *and* within C. The environment $\Delta_2 \subseteq \Delta_1$ lists those variables "available for use" to the outside.

The example configuration (2) on page 256 shows the need for the additional environment Δ_2: Although a binding for the handle y is provided in $y\,h\,z$, y is already used *internally* to bind its future, in the thread $x\Leftarrow y$ **unit**.

The rules for typing thread and handle components now contain the side condition $|\alpha| = \omega$ corresponding to the type restriction of the respective constants. Moreover, the type of y in $y\,h\,x$ must have multiplicity **1**. Note that in each case we have $\Delta_1 = \Delta_2$, i.e., all the declared variables are available.

In $y\,h\,\bullet$ the variable y is declared, but not available anymore, i.e. it cannot be used in a surrounding configuration at all. Thus $\Delta_2 = \emptyset$. The rule for restriction keeps declarations local by removing all occurrences of x from Δ_1 and Δ_2.

The rule for parallel composition is the most complex one. Compared to the corresponding inference scheme of the previous section, it splits the linearly used assumptions (in $\Gamma \cdot \Delta$) as well as the linearly used variables available from each of the two constituent configurations ($\Gamma_2 \cdot \Gamma_3$ and $\Delta_2 \cdot \Delta_3$, resp.). A variable with multiplicity **1** declared by C_1 can then either be used in C_2 (via Γ_2), or is made available to a surrounding configuration (via Γ_3) but not both. The environment of declared variables of $C_1 \mid C_2$ is Γ_1, Δ_1 and therefore contains all the variables declared in C_1 (i.e., those in Γ_1) and C_2 (in Δ_1) as before. By our convention, this ensures in particular that C_1 and C_2 do not contain multiple bindings for the same variable. Finally, the side-condition of the rule is necessary to establish the invariant (i).

Theorem 2 (Subject Reduction). *If* $\Gamma \vdash C_1 : \Delta_1; \Delta_2$ *and* $C_1 \rightarrow C_2$ *then* $\Gamma \vdash C_2 : \Delta_1; \Delta_2$.

Error-freeness of well-typed configurations follows by combining the absence of handle errors in the immediate configuration and Subject Reduction as usual.

Corollary 1 (Absence of Handle Errors). *If* $\Gamma \vdash C : \Delta_1; \Delta_2$ *then* C *is error-free.*

5   Concurrency Constructs

We now show how to express various concurrency abstractions in $\lambda(\mathsf{fut})$ which demonstrates the power of handled futures. We use some syntactic sugar, writing **let** $x_1 = e_1$ **in** e for $(\lambda x_1.e)\,e_1$, $\lambda\_.e$ for $\lambda x.e$ where x is not free in e, and $e_1; e_2$ for $(\lambda\_.e_2)\,e_1$. We also extend $\lambda(\mathsf{fut})$ with products and lists.

Mutual Exclusion. When concurrent threads access shared data it is necessary that they do not interfere in order to prevent any data inconsistencies. We can implement an operation **mutex** of type $(\mathsf{unit} \rightarrow \alpha) \rightarrow \alpha$ that applies its argument under mutual exclusion. We use a strict context to synchronize several threads wishing to access a *critical region*.

let $r = \textbf{cell}\,(\lambda y.y)$
in $\lambda a.\textbf{handle}(\lambda x \lambda bind_x.\ (\textbf{exch}\,r\,x)\,(\textbf{unit});$
$\qquad\qquad\qquad\qquad (\text{let } v=a\,(\textbf{unit}) \text{ in } bind_x\,(\lambda y.y); v))$

Before running the function a that is given as argument (the critical region), a handled future (of type unit $\rightarrow$ unit) is stored in the reference cell r. This future is bound (to the identity function) only *after* the argument is evaluated. Moreover, *before* this happens, the previous contents of the cell r cannot be an unbound future anymore since the function application $(\textbf{exch}\,r\,x)\,(\textbf{unit})$ is strict in its arguments. Consequently, threads cannot interfere when evaluating a.

Ports. We assume that there are pairs and a list data type, and write $v :: l$ for the list with first element v, followed by the list l. A *stream* is a "open-ended" list $v_1 :: \cdots :: v_n :: x$ where x is a (handled) future. The stream can be extended arbitrarily often by using the handle of the future, provided each new element is again of the form $v :: x'$, with x' a handled future. We call the elements $v_1, \dots, v_n$ on a stream *messages*.

A function newPort that creates a new *port* can be implemented as follows.

$\lambda\_.\textbf{handle}(\lambda s \lambda bind_s.$
$\quad$ let $putr = \textbf{cell}\,bind_s$
$\qquad put = \lambda x.\textbf{handle}(\lambda s \lambda bind_s.(\textbf{exch}\,putr\,bind_s)\,(x :: s))$
$\quad$ in $(s, put))$

The port consists of a stream s and an operation put to put new messages onto the stream. The stream is ended by a handled future, which in the beginning is s itself. Its handle $bind_s$ is stored in the cell $putr$ and used in put to send the next message to the port. put introduces a new handled future before writing the new value to the end of the stream. The new handle is stored in the cell.

Channels. By extending ports with a receive operation of type unit $\rightarrow \alpha$ we obtain channels, which provide for indeterministic many to many communication. A function newChannel that generates channels is

$\lambda\_.\textbf{handle}(\lambda init \lambda bind_{init}.$
$\quad$ let $putr = \textbf{cell}\,bind_{init}$
$\qquad getr = \textbf{cell}\,init$
$\qquad put = \lambda x.\textbf{handle}(\lambda n \lambda bind_n.(\textbf{exch}\,putr\,bind_n)\,(x :: n))$
$\qquad get = \lambda\_.\textbf{handle}(\lambda n \lambda bind_n.\textbf{case}(\textbf{exch}\,getr\,n))$
$\qquad\qquad\qquad\qquad\qquad \text{of } x :: c \Rightarrow bind_n(c); x)$
$\quad$ in $(put, get))$

Given a stream, applying get yields the next message on the stream. If the stream contains no further messages, get blocks: We assume that the matching against the pattern $x :: c$ is strict. Note how get uses a handled future in the same way as the mutual exclusion above to make the implementation thread-safe.

$$\alpha, \beta \in LinType ::= \ldots \mid \alpha \times^\kappa \beta \mid \alpha\,\text{list}^\kappa \quad \text{such that } |\alpha| = \mathbf{1} \text{ or } |\beta| = \mathbf{1} \implies \kappa = \mathbf{1}$$

$$\frac{\Gamma_1 \vdash e_1 : \alpha \quad \Gamma_2 \vdash e_2 : \beta}{\Gamma_1 \cdot \Gamma_2 \vdash (e_1, e_2) : \alpha \times^\kappa \beta} \qquad \frac{\Gamma_1 \vdash e_1 : \alpha \quad \Gamma_2 \vdash e_2 : \alpha\,\text{list}^\kappa}{\Gamma_1 \cdot \Gamma_2 \vdash e_1 :: e_2 : \alpha\,\text{list}^\kappa}$$

$$\frac{\Gamma_1 \vdash e_1 : \alpha \times^\kappa \beta \quad \Gamma_2, x{:}\alpha, y{:}\beta \vdash e_2 : \gamma}{\Gamma_1 \cdot \Gamma_2 \vdash \text{case } e_1 \text{ of } (x,y) \Rightarrow e_2 : \gamma} \qquad \frac{\Gamma_1 \vdash e_1 : \alpha\,\text{list}^\kappa \quad \Gamma_2, x{:}\alpha, y{:}\alpha\,\text{list}^\kappa \vdash e_2 : \beta}{\Gamma_1 \cdot \Gamma_2 \vdash \text{case } e_1 \text{ of } x{::}y \Rightarrow e_2 : \beta}$$

Fig. 10. Typing rules for products and lists

6 Proving Safety

The three abstractions defined in the previous section are *safe*, in the sense that no handle errors are raised by using them. For instance, we can always send to the port without running into an error. Intuitively, this holds since nobody can access the (local) handle to the future at the end of the stream s, and the implementation itself uses each handle only once.

The linear type system can be used to make this intuition formal: By the results of Sect. 4 typability guarantees the absence of handle errors. Moreover, all three abstractions obtain "non-linear" types with multiplicity ω. The use of handled futures is thus properly encapsulated and not observable from the types. This suggests to provide concurrency abstractions through safe libraries to users.

Mutual Exclusion. The mutual exclusion mutex can be typed as

$$\vdash \text{mutex} : (\text{unit} \xrightarrow{\kappa} \alpha) \xrightarrow{\omega} \alpha$$

in the linear type system. In fact, in a derivation there is no constraint on the multiplicity κ which can be chosen as either $\mathbf{1}$ or ω. More importantly, the type of mutex itself has multiplicity ω, which allows mutex to be applied any number of times.

Ports and Channels. We only sketch how to extend the linear type system to deal with pairs and lists. The details of such an extension are quite standard (see [27], for instance). Just as with function types these new types are annotated with multiplicities. We can devise the inference rules in Fig. 10 for the new types. If the constructs are given the usual operational semantics, the subject reduction theorem can be extended, as can Corollary 1. For the port abstraction, we derive

$$\vdash \text{newPort} : \text{unit} \xrightarrow{\omega} (\alpha\,\text{list}^\omega \times^\kappa \alpha \xrightarrow{\omega} \text{unit}) \qquad (|\alpha| = \omega)$$

for any κ. In particular, both newPort itself and the *put* operation (the second component of the result pair) can be used unrestrictedly. Similarly, for $|\alpha| = \omega$,

$$\vdash \text{newChannel} : \text{unit} \xrightarrow{\omega} ((\alpha \xrightarrow{\omega} \text{unit}) \times^\omega (\text{unit} \xrightarrow{\omega} \alpha))$$

can be derived for the implementation of channels.

7   Implementation View

An implementation of futures has to deal with placeholder objects and dereferencing to obtain the value associated with a future. Further, in the case of lazy futures it must perform the triggering of computations. All these aspects are visible on the level of the compiler only; futures are transparent from the programmer's point of view. Therefore, these *touch* operations are introduced by the compiler rather than the programmer.

With an explicit touch operator "?" the expression $?x$ waits for the value of the future x, forces its evaluation if necessary, and returns the value once available. To improve efficiency, a compiler should be able to remove as many redundant touches as possible. That this can be done by strictness analysis was an important achievement of previous work on futures by Felleisen and Flanagan [9]. In this paper, we did not deal with touches and their optimization. We expect that the analysis of [9] can be extended to our calculus, but leave this for future work.

8   Conclusion

We have presented the lambda calculus with futures $\lambda(\mathsf{fut})$ which serves as a semantics for concurrent extensions of ML where all synchronization is based on futures. We assumed call-by-value evaluation, static typing, and state. We have demonstrated how the handled futures of $\lambda(\mathsf{fut})$ provide an elegant, unifying mechanism to express various concurrency abstractions.

We have proved the safety of these implementations on basis of a linear type system. Hence, handle errors cannot arise when using handles only through safe libraries. As a consequence, handled futures can be safely incorporated into a strongly typed ML-style programming language without imposing changes in the type system. An ML extension called Alice [2] along these lines is available.

In future work, we intend to develop a strictness analysis for improving the efficiency of implementations of $\lambda(\mathsf{fut})$. We plan to investigate operational equivalences as a further tool in reasoning about $\lambda(\mathsf{fut})$ programs.

Acknowledgements. We would like to thank the anonymous referees for their detailed comments and feedback.

References

1. M. Abadi and L. Lamport. Conjoining specifications. *ACM Transactions on Programming Languages and Systems*, 17(3):507–534, 1995.
2. *The Alice Project*. Web site at the Programming Systems Lab, Universität des Saarlandes, http://www.ps.uni-sb.de/alice, 2005.
3. Z. M. Ariola and M. Felleisen. The call-by-need lambda calculus. *Journal of Functional Programming*, 7(3):265–301, 1997.
4. Arvind, R. S. Nikhil, and K. K. Pingali. I-structures: Data structures for parallel computing. *ACM Transactions on Programming Languages and Systems*, 11(4):598–632, 1989.

5. H. Baker and C. Hewitt. The incremental garbage collection of processes. *ACM Sigplan Notices*, 12:55–59, Aug. 1977.
6. E. Barendsen and S. Smetsers. Uniqueness type inference. In *Proc. PLILP'95*, volume 982 of *LNCS*, pages 189–206. Springer, 1995.
7. E. Chailloux, P. Manoury, and B. Pagano. *Developing Applications With Objective Caml*. O'Reilly, 2000. Available online at http://caml.inria.fr/oreilly-book.
8. S. Conchon and F. L. Fessant. Jocaml: Mobile agents for Objective-Caml. In *First International Symposium on Agent Systems and Applications (ASA'99)/Third International Symposium on Mobile Agents (MA'99)*, 1999.
9. C. Flanagan and M. Felleisen. The semantics of future and an application. *Journal of Functional Programming*, 9(1):1–31, 1999.
10. C. Fournet and G. Gonthier. The reflexive chemical abstract machine and the join-calculus. In *Proc. POPL'96*, pages 372–385. ACM Press, 1996.
11. C. Fournet, C. Laneve, L. Maranget, and D. Rémy. Implicit typing à la ML for the join-calculus. In *Proc. CONCUR'97*, volume 1243 of *LNCS*, pages 196–212. Springer, 1997.
12. R. H. Halstead, Jr. Multilisp: A Language for Concurrent Symbolic Computation. *ACM Transactions on Programming Languages and Systems*, 7(4):501–538, 1985.
13. S. Haridi, P. V. Roy, P. Brand, M. Mehl, R. Scheidhauer, and G. Smolka. Efficient logic variables for distributed computing. *ACM Transactions on Programming Languages and Systems*, 21(3):569–626, 1999.
14. B. Liskov and L. Shrira. Promises: Linguistic support for efficient asynchronous procedure calls in distributed systems. *SIGPLAN Notices*, 23(7):260–268, 1988.
15. J. Maraist, M. Odersky, and P. Wadler. The call-by-need lambda calculus. *Journal of Functional Programming*, 8(3):275–317, 1998.
16. R. Milner. The polyadic π-calculus: A tutorial. In F. L. Bauer, W. Brauer, and H. Schwichtenberg, editors, *Logic and Algebra of Specification, Proc. Marktoberdorf Summer School*, pages 203–246. Springer, 1993.
17. R. Milner, M. Tofte, R. Harper, and D. B. MacQueen. *The Standard ML Programming Language (Revised)*. MIT Press, 1997.
18. M. Müller. *Set-based Failure Diagnosis for Concurrent Constraint Programming*. PhD thesis, Universität des Saarlandes, Saarbrücken, 1998.
19. J. Niehren. Uniform confluence in concurrent computation. *Journal of Functional Programming*, 10(5):453–499, 2000.
20. F. Nielson, editor. *ML with Concurrency: Design, Analysis, Implementation, and Application*. Monographs in Computer Science. Springer, 1997.
21. B. C. Pierce and D. N. Turner. Pict: A programming language based on the pi-calculus. In G. Plotkin, C. Stirling, and M. Tofte, editors, *Proof, Language and Interaction: Essays in Honour of Robin Milner*. MIT Press, 2000.
22. J. H. Reppy. *Concurrent Programming in ML*. Cambridge University Press, 1999.
23. A. Rossberg, D. L. Botlan, G. Tack, T. Brunklaus, and G. Smolka. *Alice Through the Looking Glass*, volume 5 of *Trends in Functional Programming*. Intellect, Munich, Germany, 2004.
24. V. A. Saraswat, M. Rinard, and P. Panangaden. Semantic foundations of concurrent constraint programming. In *Proc. POPL'91*, pages 333–352. ACM Press.
25. E. Shapiro. The family of concurrent logic programming languages. *ACM Comput. Surv.*, 21(3):413–510, 1989.
26. G. Smolka. The Oz programming model. In J. van Leeuwen, editor, *Computer Science Today*, volume 1000 of *LNCS*, pages 324–343. Springer, 1995.
27. D. N. Turner, P. Wadler, and C. Mossin. Once upon a type. In *Proc. 7th ICFPCA*, pages 1–11. ACM Press, 1995.

The ASM Method for System Design and Analysis. A Tutorial Introduction

Egon Börger

Università di Pisa, Dipartimento di Informatica, I-56125 Pisa, Italy
boerger@di.unipi.it

Abstract. We introduce into and survey the ASM method for high-level system design and analysis. We explain the three notions—*Abstract State Machine* [37], *ASM ground model* (system blueprint) [7] and *ASM refinement* [8]—that characterize the method, which integrates also current validation and verification techniques. We illustrate how the method allows the system engineer to rigorously capture requirements by ASM ground models and to stepwise refine these to code in a validatable and verifiable way.

1   Scope and Achievements of the ASM Method

An outstanding feature of the ASM method is that within a single *precise yet simple conceptual framework*, it naturally supports and uniformly integrates the following activities and techniques, as illustrated by Fig. 1 (taken from [24]):

- the major **software life cycle activities**, linking in a controllable way the two ends of the development of complex software systems:
  - **requirements capture** by constructing rigorous *ground models*, i.e. accurate concise high-level system blueprints (system contracts), formulated in domain-specific terms, using an application-oriented language which can be understood by all stakeholders [7],
  - **architectural and component design** bridging the gap between specification and code by *piecemeal, systematically documented detailing* of abstract models via stepwise refined models to code [8],
  - **validation** of models by their tool-supported *simulation*,
  - **verification** of model properties by tool-supported *proof techniques*,
  - **documentation** for *inspection*, *reuse* and *maintenance* by providing, through the intermediate models and their analysis, explicit descriptions of the *software structure* and of the major *design decisions*,
- the principal **modeling and analysis techniques**, on the basis of a systematic separation of different concerns (e.g. design from analysis, orthogonal design decisions, multiple levels of definitional or proof detail, etc.):
  - integrating dynamic (*operational*) and static (*declarative*) descriptions,
  - combining validation (simulation) and verification (proof) methods *at any desired level of detail*.

B. Gramlich (Ed.): FroCoS 2005, LNAI 3717, pp. 264–283, 2005.

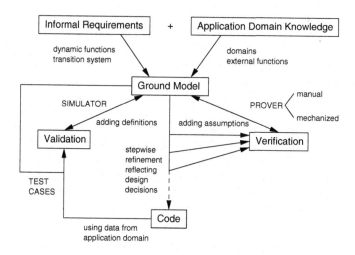

Fig. 1. Models and methods in the ASM-based development process

The integration potential of the ASM method is reflected by the great variety of its successful applications (for references see [24,9]), for example:

- definition of industrial standards for Prolog (ISO), VHDL93 (IEEE), Java and JVM (Sun), SDL-2000 (ITU-T), C# (ECMA), BPEL for Web Services,
- design and reengineering of industrial control systems: software projects related to railway and mobile telephony network components (at Siemens), debugger and UPnP specification (at Microsoft), business systems interacting with intelligent devices (at SAP),
- modeling e-commerce and web services (at SAP),
- simulation and testing: a fire detection system in coal mines, the simulation of railway scenarios (at Siemens), the implementation of behavioral interface specifications on the .NET platform and conformance test of COM components (at Microsoft), compiler testing, test case generation,
- design and analysis of protocols for authentication, cryptography, cache-coherence, routing-layers for distributed mobile ad hoc networks, group-membership etc.,
- architectural design: verification (e.g. of pipelining schemes or of VHDL-based hardware design at Siemens), architecture/compiler co-exploration, combined validation and verification project,
- language design: definition, implementation and analysis of the semantics for real-life programmming languages, e.g. SystemC, Java/JVM—the book [51] contains the up to now most comprehensive non-proprietary real-life ASM case study, covering in every detail ground modeling, refinement, structuring, implementation, verification and validation of ASMs—, C#, domain-specific languages (Union Bank of Switzerland), etc.
- verification of compilation schemes and compiler back-ends.

The ASM method comes with a rigorous scientific foundation (see [24]). The *ASM ground model technique* adds the precision of mathematical blueprints to the loose character of human-centric UML descriptions. The *ASM refinement method* fills a widely-felt gap in UML-based techniques, namely by accurately linking the models at the successive stages of the system development cycle in an organic and effectively maintainable chain of coherent system views at different levels of abstraction. The resulting documentation maps the structure of the blueprint to compilable code, providing a road map for system use and maintenance. The practitioner needs no special training to use the ASM method since Abstract State Machines are a simple extension of Finite State Machines, obtained by replacing unstructured "internal" control states by states comprising arbitrarily complex data, and can be understood correctly as pseudo-code or Virtual Machines working over abstract data structures.

2   Turning FSMs into Abstract State Machines

In this section we explain ASMs as mathematical form of Virtual Machines that extend Finite State Machines and Codesign-FSMs by an enriched notion of state, which in support of modular design is accompanied by a classification of ASM locations defined below.[1]

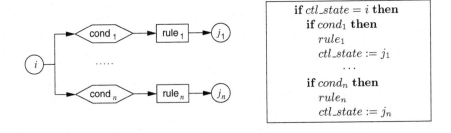

Fig. 2. Viewing FSM instructions as control state ASM rules

An FSM is defined by a program of instructions of the form pictorially depicted in Fig. 2, where $i, j_1, \ldots, j_n$ are internal (control) states, $cond_\nu$ (for $1 \leq \nu \leq n$) represents the input condition $in = a_\nu$ (reading input a_ν) and $rule_\nu$ the output action $out := b_\nu$ (yielding output b_ν), which goes together with the ctl_state update to j_ν. Control state ASMs have the same form of programs, but the underlying notion of state is extended from three locations, namely:

- a single internal ctl_state assuming values in a not furthermore structured finite set
- two input and output locations in, out assuming values in a finite alphabet

---

[1] The original definition in [37] was motivated by an epistemological concern related to the Church-Turing thesis. For historical details see [6]. The practice-oriented approach we follow here is taken from [10].

to a *set of values of whatever types* residing in updatable memory units, so-called *locations*. Any desired level of abstraction can be achieved by permitting possibly parameterized locations to hold values of arbitrary complexity, whether atomic or structured: objects, sets, lists, tables, trees, graphs, whatever comes natural at the considered level of abstraction. As a consequence, the FSM updates of *ctl_state* and of its *out*put location are extended to ASM state changes resulting from updates of the value content of arbitrary many locations, namely via multiple assignments of the form $loc(x_1, \ldots, x_n) := val$.

This simple change of view of what a state is yields machines whose states can be arbitrary *multisorted structures*, i.e. domains of whatever objects coming with predicates (attributes) and functions defined on them, structures programmers nowadays are used to from object-oriented programming. In fact such a memory structure is easily obtained from the flat location view of abstract machine memory by grouping subsets of data into tables (arrays), via an association of a value to each table entry $(f, (a_1, \ldots, a_n))$. Here f plays the role of the name of the table, the sequence $(a_1, \ldots, a_n)$ the role of a table entry, $f(a_1, \ldots, a_n)$ denotes the value currently contained in the location $(f, (a_1, \ldots, a_n))$. Such a table represents an array variable f of dimension n, which can be viewed as the current interpretation of an n-ary "dynamic" function or predicate (boolean-valued function). This allows one to structure an ASM state as a set of tables and thus as a multisorted structure in the sense of mathematics.

In accordance with the extension of unstructured FSM control states to arbitrary ASM structures, the FSM-input *cond*itions are extended to arbitrary ASM-state expressions, which are called *guards* since they determine whether an instruction can be executed.[2] In addition, the usual non-deterministic interpretation, in case more than one FSM-instruction can be executed, is replaced by the parallel interpretation that in each ASM state, the machine executes simultaneously all the updates which are guarded by a condition that is true in this state. This *synchronous parallelism*, which yields a clear concept of *locally described global state change*, helps to abstract for high-level modeling from irrelevant sequentiality (read: an ordering of actions that are independent of each other in the intended design) and supports refinements to parallel or distributed implementations.

As a result of this extension of FSMs we obtain the definition of an ASM as a set of instructions of the following form, called ASM *rules* to stress the distinction between the parallel execution model for ASMs and the sequential single-instruction-execution model for traditional programs:

if *cond* **then** *Updates*

where *Updates* stands for a set of *function updates* $f(t_1, \ldots, f_n) := t$ built from expressions t_i, t and an n-ary function symbol f. The notion of run is the same as for FSMs and for transition systems in general, taking into account the syn-

---

[2] For the special role of *in/out*put locations see below the classification of locations.

chronous parallel interpretation.[3] Similarly to this extension of FSMs by basic
ASMs, asynchronous ASMs extend globally asynchronous, locally synchronous
Codesign-FSMs [42]. Only the notion of mono-agent sequential runs has to be
extended to asynchronous (also called partially ordered) multi-agent runs. For a
detailed definition in terms of ASMs we refer to [24, Ch.6.1].

Thus ASMs provide a rigorous mathematical semantics, which accurately
supports the way application-domain experts use high-level process-oriented descriptions and software practitioners use "pseudo-code over abstract data". For
the sake of completeness we list below notations for some other frequently used
forms of rules, which enhance the expressivity of ASMs.

2.1   Classification of ASM Functions and Locations

In this section we describe how the ASM method supports the separation of
concerns, information hiding, data abstraction, modularization and stepwise refinement by a systematic distinction between basic locations and derived ones
(that are definable from basic ones), together with a read-write-permit classification of basic locations into static and dynamic ones and of the dynamic ones
into monitored (only read), controlled (read and write), shared and output (only
write) locations, as illustrated by Fig. 3.[4]

These distinctions reflect the different roles played in a given machine M
by the auxiliary locations that are used in function updates to compute the
arguments t_i and the new value t. The value of a *static* location never changes
during any run of M because it does not depend on the states of M. The value
of a *dynamic* location depends on the states of M since it may change as a
consequence of updates either by M or by the environment. Static locations can
be thought of as given by an initial system state, so that their definition can be
treated separately from the description of the system dynamics. It depends on
the degree of information-hiding the specifier wants to realize how the meaning
of such locations is determined—by a mere signature ("interface") description or
by axiomatic constraints or by an abstract specification, an explicit or recursive
definition, a program module, etc.

Controlled locations for M are the ones which are directly updatable by and
only by the rules of M, where they appear in at least one rule as the leftmost
location in an update $f(s) := t$ for some s, t. These locations are the ones which
constitute the internally controlled part of the dynamics of M, for example the
location *ctl_state* in an FSM. Locations called *monitored* by M are those read
but not updated by M and updatable by other machines or the environment.

---

[3] More precisely: to execute one step of an ASM in a given state S determine all the
fireable rules in S (s.t. *cond* is true in S), compute all expressions t_i, t in S occuring
in the updates $f(t_1, \ldots, t_n) := t$ of those rules and then perform simultaneously all
these location updates if they are consistent. In the case of inconsistency, the run is
considered as interrupted if no other stipulation is made, like calling an exception
handling procedure or choosing a compatible update set.

[4] A set of locations or a function is called of a kind if all their locations are of that
kind.

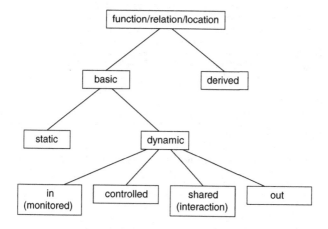

Fig. 3. Classification of ASM locations

They appear in updates of M, but not as a leftmost update location. An example is the input location *in* of an FSM. These monitored locations constitute the externally controlled part of the dynamic state of M. The concept of monitored locations allows one to separate in a specification the computation concerns from the communication concerns. In fact, the definition does not commit to any particular mechanism (e.g. message passing via channels) to describe the exchange of information between interacting agents. As with static locations the specification of monitored locations is open to any appropriate method, a feature that helps the system designer to control the amount of information which he wants to give to the programmer. The only (but crucial) assumption made is that in a given state the values of all monitored locations are determined.

Combinations of internal and external control are captured by *interaction* or *shared* locations that can be read and are directly updatable by more than one machine (so that typically a protocol is needed to guarantee consistency of updates). *Output* locations are updated but not read by M and are typically monitored by other machines or by the environment. An example is the location *out* of an FSM. Locations are called *external* for M if for M they are either static or monitored.

Distinguishing *basic* locations from *derived* locations whose values are defined by a fixed scheme in terms of other (static or dynamic) locations, pragmatically supports defining the latter by a specification or computation mechanism which is given separately from the main machine. Thus derived locations can be thought of as defining a global method with read-only variables.

An important type of monitored functions are dynamic selection functions f, which out of a collection X of objects satisfying a property φ select one element $f(X)$ in a way that may depend on the current state. They are frequently

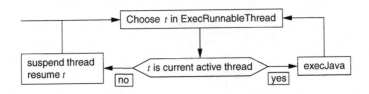

Fig. 4. Multiple thread Java machine

used to abstract from details of scheduling procedures. The following notation denotes $rule(f(X))$ when no specific name of the selection function f is needed:

> **choose** x **with** φ
> $\quad rule(x)$

Also notational variations are frequently used, like **choose** $x \in X$ **in** $rule(x)$. Fig. 4 shows an example from the ASM model for thread handling in Java and C# [51,49].

Similarly the following notation is used to make the synchronous parallelism of ASMs expressable in terms of arbitrary properties:

> **forall** x **with** φ
> $\quad rule(x)$

standing for the simultaneous execution of $rule(x)$ for every element x satisfying φ.

2.2   Some Examples

Many industrial control systems, protocols, business processes and the like come with a concept of *status* or *mode* or *phase* that directs complex state transformations. Such a high-level system structure can be appropriately modeled by *control state ASMs*, introduced in [5] and closest to FSMs, i.e. ASMs all of whose rules are of the form in Fig. 5, written $\text{FSM}(i, \textbf{if } cond \textbf{ then } rule, j)$.

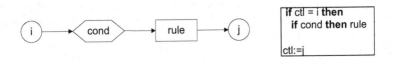

Fig. 5. FSM

A typical example is the top-level DEBUGGER model in Fig. 6, which was defined in [3] as part of a reverse-engineering case study to model a command-line debugger of a stack-based run-time environment. During the reverse engineering

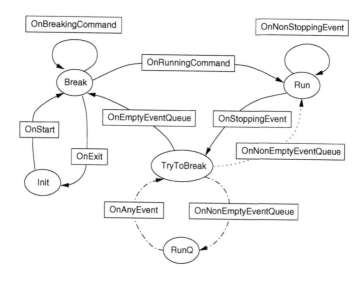

Fig. 6. DEBUGGER control state ASM

process, this simple model led to the discovery of a flaw in the code, namely that the submachine executed during the dotted mode transition could lead to a deadlock and had to be replaced by a transition into a fifth mode $RunQ$ (which was inserted into the implementation by an additional flag).

A business process example with only start/stop and busy mode is illustrated in Fig. 7, which is used in [1] to define the kernel of a web service mediator. The machine delivers for a current request a service answer that is to be compiled from the set of results of an iterative subrequest processing submachine, which in turn sends out further subrequests to – and collects the respective services from – other possibly independent subproviders.

Fig. 8 defines the top-level control structure of a double-phase sender ASM, which appears in the Kermit protocol as ALTERNATINGBITSENDER instance and

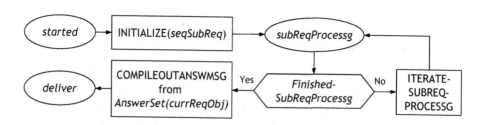

Fig. 7. Virtual Provider PROCESSING the current request

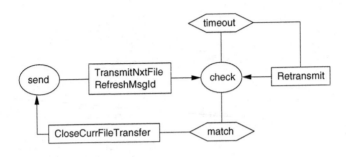

Fig. 8. Kermit protocol sender ASM

as its refinement to a SLIDINGWINDOWSENDER [40]. For a generalization as a service interaction pattern see [4].

Fig. 9 from [23] defines the black-box view of neural nets characterized by two top-level phases: in the input phase the Neural Kernel is activated by the arrival of new input from the environment (transmitted by special input units to dedicated internal units), to perform on that input an internal computation which ends with emitting an output to the environment and switching back to the input mode.

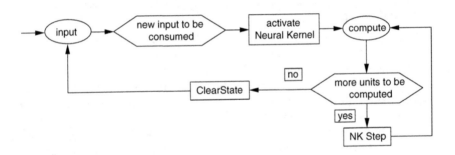

Fig. 9. Neural abstract machine model

2.3　ASM Submachines

The diagrams for control state ASMs enhance similar graphical UML notations by their rigorous semantics, which is formally defined in Fig. 2, 5, based upon the precise ASM semantics of the occurring abstract submachines that typically describe rather complex state transformations. In the examples above these submachines describe a Java interpreter *execJava* in Fig. 4; the Debugger actions *OnStart*, etc. in Fig. 6; the subrequest processing iterator in Fig. 7; the different refinements of the Kermit macros in Fig. 8; the Neural Kernel Step submachine in Fig. 9 whose basic computing units (nodes of a directed data-flow graph) perform a finite sequence of atomic actions propagating their results through the graph until the output units are reached.

Where convenient one can also abstract away the FSM-typical control-state details of an intended sequentiality and encapsulate the execution of a machine M immediately followed by the execution of N into a black-box view M **seq** N, which is supported also by the well-known traditional graphical representations of FSMs that omit labels for intermediate internal states. Iterating such a **seq** operator leads to so-called turbo ASMs that support the standard iteration constructs of programming. In the same way one can define a general ASM submachine concept that fits the synchronous parallel view of ASMs and supports the two abstraction levels defined by the black-box and the white-box view of submachines (see [21]). It also supports the traditional understanding of recursive machine calls (see [12]).

We illustrate ASM submachines by two examples. The first one is the submachine INITIALIZE(*class*) used in the ASM model for a Java interpreter [51], providing a succinct formulation for the intricate interaction of the initialization of classes with other language concepts. In Java the initialization of a class c is done implicitly at the first use of c, respecting the class hierarchy (the superclass of c has to be initialized before c). Thus INITIALIZE(*class*) stores its call parameter *class*, say into a local variable $currInitClass$, and then iterates the creation of class initialization frames until a class is reached which is *Initialized*.[5]

$$
\begin{aligned}
&\text{INITIALIZE}(class) = \\
&\quad currInitClass := class \text{ seq} \\
&\qquad \textbf{while not } Initialized(currInitClass) \\
&\qquad\quad \text{CREATEINITFRAME}(currInitClass) \\
&\qquad\quad \textbf{if not } Initialized(superClass(currInitClass)) \textbf{ then} \\
&\qquad\qquad currInitClass := superClass(currInitClass)
\end{aligned}
$$

The INITIALIZE submachine offers the possibility that the designer works with a black-box view—of an atomic operation that pushes all initialization methods in the right order onto the frame stack, followed by calling the Java interpreter to execute them (in the inverse order)—whereas the programmer and the verifier work with the refined white-box view, which provides the necessary details to implement the machine and to analyze its global properties of interest (see [22]). A refinement of INITIALIZE for a C# interpreter has been defined in [17] and has been used in [32] to investigate problems related to class initialization in C#.

We illustrate the support of recursive submachines by an ASM describing the well-known procedure to quicksort lists L: FIRST partition the *tail* of the list into the two sublists $tail(L)_{<head(L)}, tail(L)_{\geq head(L)}$ of elements $< head(L)$ respectively $\geq head(L)$ and quicksort these two sublists separately (independently of each other), THEN *concatenate* the results placing $head(L)$ between them.[6]

---

[5] The termination happens at the latest at the top of the finite class hierarchy. The submachine CREATEINITFRAME(c) sets $classState(c)$ to $InProgress$ whereby $Initialized(currInitClass)$ becomes true.

[6] See [12] for a formal definition of the **let** $x = R(a), y = S(b)$ **in** M construct.

$\text{QUICKSORT}(L) =$
  if$| L | \leq 1$ then result $:= L$ else
    let
      $x = \text{QUICKSORT}(tail(L)_{<head(L)})$
      $y = \text{QUICKSORT}(tail(L)_{\geq head(L)})$
    in result $:= concatenate(x, head(L), y)$

Computing $tail(L)_{<head(L)}, tail(L)_{\geq head(L)}$ appears in this machine as an external subcomputation. We illustrate in Sect. 5 how to internalize such a subcomputation by a refinement step.

3   ASM Ground Models (System Blueprints)

The role of a system blueprint (ground model) is to capture changing system requirements ("what to build") in a *consistent and unambiguous, simple and concise, abstract and complete* way, so that the resulting documentation "grounds the design in reality" by its being *understandable and checkable* (for correctness and completeness) by both domain experts and system designers. Using ASMs one can cope with ever-changing requirements by building ground models for change which share the above eight attributes, as we will shortly describe here, refering for further explanations to [7].

Understandability implies that domain expert and system designer share the language in which the ground model is formulated, as part of the contract that binds the two parties. In this respect it is crucial that ASMs allow one to calibrate the degree of precision of a ground model to the conceptual frame of the given problem domain, supporting the concentration on domain issues instead of issues of notation.

Checkability means that both reasoning and experimentation can be applied to a blueprint to establish that it is complete and consistent, that it reflects the original intentions and that these are correctly conveyed— together with all the necessary underlying application-domain knowledge—to the designer. Since ASM ground models are formulated in application-domain terms, they are inspectable for correctness and completeness by the application-domain expert; on the other side, due to their mathematical nature, they also support the designer in mathematically checking the internal model consistency and the consistency of different system views. In addition, exploiting the concept of ASM run, one can perform experiments with ASM ground models simulating them for running relevant scenarios (use cases), supporting systematic attempts to "falsify" the model against the to-be-encoded piece of reality. As technical side-effect one can define – prior to coding – a precise system-acceptance test plan, thus turning the ground model into a test model that is to be matched by the tester against executions of the final code.

Understandability and checkability of ASM ground models already help to avoid that a software project fails simply because it does not build the right system, due to a misunderstanding of the requirements. We now shortly characterize the remaining above mentioned six intrinsic properties an ASM ground model has to satisfy, namely to be:

- *precise* (unambiguous and consistent) at the appropriate level of detailing yet *flexible*, to satisfy the required accuracy avoiding unnecessary precision;
- *simple and concise* to be understandable by both domain experts (for inspection) and system designers (for analysis). ASMs allow one to explicitly formulate those abstractions that "directly" reflect the structure of the real-world problem, avoiding any extraneous encoding;
- *abstract (minimal) yet complete.* Completeness means that all and only semantically relevant features are to be made present: parameters concerning the interaction with the environment, the basic architectural system structure, the domain knowledge representation, etc., alltogether making the ASM "closed" modulo some "holes". However, the holes are explicitly delineated, including statements of the assumptions made for them at the abstract level (to be realized through the detailed specification via later refinements). Minimality means that the model abstracts from details that are relevant either only for the further design or only for a portion of the application domain, which does not influence the system to be built.

It is this combination of blueprint properties that made ASM ground models so successful as means to formulate high-level models for industrial control systems, patent documents, standards. See the formulation of the forthcoming standard for the Business Process Execution Language for Web Services [52], for the ITU-T standard for SDL-2000 [35], the ECMA standard for C# [17], the de facto standard for Java and its implementation on the JVM [51], the IEEE-VHDL93 standard [18], the ISO-Prolog standard [14]. Or see the development of railway [13,19] and mobile telephony network components [25] at Siemens. These examples show also that ASM ground models are fit for *reuse.* When the requirements change, these changes can often be directly reflected by blueprint adaptations, typically additions to or refinements of the ground model abstractions.

4   ASM Refinements (Reflecting Design Decisions)

We describe in this section the practice-oriented *ASM refinement notion* [8], which provides a framework to systematically separate, structure and document orthogonal design decisions and thus to effectively relate different system views and aspects. The method supports cost-effective system maintenance and management of system changes as well as piecemeal system validation and verification techniques. Putting together the single refinement steps, typically into a chain or tree of successively more detailed models, allows the designer to rigorously link the system architect's view (at the abstraction level of a blueprint) to the programmer's view (at the level of detail of compilable code), crossing levels of abstraction in a way that supports design-for-change.

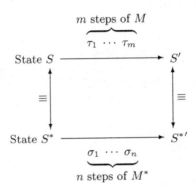

With an equivalence notion $\equiv$ between data in locations of interest in corresponding states.

Fig. 10. The ASM refinement scheme

Refinement is a general methodological principle which is present wherever a complex system or problem is described piecemeal, decomposing it into constituent parts which are detailed in steps to become manageable. Refinement goes together with the inverse process of abstraction. The principle of the ASM refinement method is illustrated by Fig. 10: to refine an ASM M to an ASM M^*, the designer has the freedom to define the following items:

- a notion of *refined state*,
- a notion of *states of interest* and of *correspondence* between M-states S and M^*-states S^* of interest, i.e. the pairs of states in the runs one wants to relate through the refinement, including usually the correspondence of initial and (if there are any) of final states,
- a notion of abstract *computation segments* $\tau_1, \ldots, \tau_m$, where each τ_i represents a single M-step, and of corresponding refined computation segments $\sigma_1, \ldots, \sigma_n$, of single M^*-steps σ_j, which in given runs lead from corresponding states of interest to (usually the next) corresponding states of interest (the resulting diagrams are called (m, n)-diagrams and the refinements (m, n)-refinements),
- a notion of *locations of interest* and of *corresponding locations*, i.e. pairs of (possibly sets of) locations one wants to relate in corresponding states,
- a notion of *equivalence* $\equiv$ of the data in the locations of interest; these local data equivalences usually accumulate to a notion of equivalence of corresponding states of interest.

Once the notions of corresponding states and of their equivalence have been determined, one can define that M^* is a correct refinement of M if and only if every (infinite) refined run simulates an (infinite) abstract run with equivalent corresponding states. More precisely: fix any notions $\equiv$ of equivalence of states and of initial and final states. An ASM M^* is called a *correct refinement* of an ASM M if and only if for each M^*-run $S_0^*, S_1^*, \ldots$ there is an M-run $S_0, S_1, \ldots$ and sequences $i_0 < i_1 < \ldots, j_0 < j_1 < \ldots$ such that $i_0 = j_0 = 0$ and $S_{i_k} \equiv S_{j_k}^*$ for each k and either

- both runs terminate and their final states are the last pair of equivalent states, or
- both runs and both sequences $i_0 < i_1 < \ldots, j_0 < j_1 < \ldots$ are infinite.

Often the M^*-run $S_0^*, S_1^*, \ldots$ is said to simulate the M-run $S_0, S_1, \ldots$. The states $S_{i_k}, S_{j_k}^*$ are the corresponding states of interest. They represent the end points of the corresponding computation segments (those of interest) in Fig. 10, for which the equivalence is defined in terms of a relation between their corresponding locations (those of interest). The scheme shows that an ASM refinement allows one to combine in a natural way a change of the signature (through the definition of states and of their correspondence, of corresponding locations and of the equivalence of data) with a change of the control (defining the "flow of operations" appearing in the corresponding computation segments).

It is important for the practicability of ASM refinements that the size of m and n in (m, n)-refinements is allowed to dynamically depend on the state. Practical experience also shows that (m, n)-refinements with $n > 1$ and including $(m, 0), (0, n)$-steps support the feasibility of decomposing complex (global) actions into simpler (locally describable) ones whose behavior can be verified in practice. Procedural $(1, n)$-refinements with $n > 1$ have their typical use in compiler verification when replacing a source code instruction by a chunk of target code; for numerous examples see [16,15,53,39,36,51]. A convenient way to hide multiple steps of a procedural refinement is to use ASM submachines as discussed above, which allow one to "view" n submachine steps as one step of an overall (here the more abstract) computation.

The ASM literature surveyed in [6] is full of examples of the above definition, which generalizes numerous more specialized and less practical refinements notions in the literature [43,44]. The ASM refinement method integrates declarative and operational techniques and widely used modularization concepts into the design and analysis of ASM models. In particular it supports modularizing ASM refinement correctness proofs aimed at mechanizable proof support, see [43].

5   ASM Analysis Techniques (Validation and Verification)

Based upon the notion of ASM *run*, various tools have been built to mechanically execute ASM models for their experimental validation by simulation and testing, notably: *ASM Workbench* [26], *AsmGofer* [46], ASM2C++ compiler [47], *XASM* [2], *AsmL* [31] and *CoreASM* [30]. Based upon the mathematical character of ASMs, also any standard mathematical verification techniques can be applied to prove or disprove ASM model properties, implying precision at the desired level of rigour: from proof sketches over traditional [20,51] or formalized mathematical proofs [50] to tool supported proof checking or interactive or automatic theorem proving, e.g. by KIV [45], PVS [28,33], model checkers [27,34]. In a comprehensive development and analysis environment for real-life ASMs, various combinations of such verification and validation methods can be supported and can be used for the analysis of compilers [29,41] and hardware [48,38] and in the context of the program verifier challenge [11].

6　Combined Refinement and Verification Example

In this section we illustrate for the mathematically inclined reader how to combine the stepwise refinement technique with piecemeal proving of properties of interest. We use as simple but characteristic examples a refinement of the above QUICKSORT machine and an ASM for the well-known leader election protocol together with its extension by a shortest path computation.

The goal of the leader election protocol is to achieve the election of a leader among finitely many homogeneous agents in a connected network, using only communication between neighbor nodes. The *leader* is defined as $max(Agent)$ with respect to a linear order $<$ among agents. The algorithmic idea, underlying the ASM defined in Fig. 11 together with the macros below, is as follows: every agent proposes to his *neighb*ors his current leader *cand*idate, checks the leader *proposals* received from his *neighb*ors and upon detecting a proposal which improves his leader candidate, he improves his candidate for his next proposal. The protocol correctness to be proved reads as follows: if initially every agent is without *proposals* from his neighbors and will *proposeToNeighbors* him*self* as *cand*idate, then eventually every agent will *checkProposals* with empty set *proposals* and *cand* = $max(Agent)$.

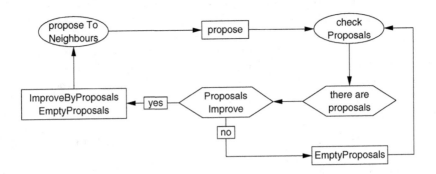

Fig. 11. Basic ASM of LEADERELECTION agents

LEADERELECTIONMACROS =
   $propose$ = **forall** $n \in neighb$ insert $cand$ to $proposals(n)$
   $proposals$ improve $= max(proposals) > cand$
   improve by $proposals = cand := max(proposals)$
   $EmptyProposals = (proposals := empty)$
   there are proposals $= (proposals \neq empty)$

Assuming that every enabled agent will eventually make a move, the protocol correctness can be proved by an induction on runs and on $\sum\{leader - cand(n) \mid n \in Agent\}$, which measures the distances of candidates from the leader.

Assume we now want to compute for each agent also a shortest path to the leader. One has to provide for every agent (except for the leader), in addition to the leader candidate, also a neighbor which is currently known to be closest to the leader, together with the minimal distance to the leader via that neighbor. This is an example of a pure data refinement and consists in enriching $cand$ and $proposals$ by a neighbor with minimal distance to the leader, recorded in new dynamic functions $nearNeighb$: $Agent$ and $distance$: $Distance$ (e.g. $Distance = \mathbb{N} \cup \{\infty\}$), so that $proposals \subseteq Agent \times Agent \times Distance$ (triples of leader $cand$, $nearNeighbor$ and $distance$ to the leader). Initially we assume $nearNeighbor =$ **self** and $distance = \infty$ except for the $leader$ where $distance = 0$.

Thus each agent of the refined async MINPATHTOLEADER ASM executes the properly initialized basic ASM defined in Fig. 11 with the refined macros below. Priority is given to determine the largest among the proposed neighbors (where Max over triples takes the max over the proposed neighbor agents), among the $proposalsFor$ the current $cand$ the one with $minimal$ $distance$ is chosen.

MINPATHTOLEADERMACROS =
   $propose$ = **forall** $n \in neighb$
      insert $(cand, nearNeighb, distance)$ to $proposals(n)$
   $proposals$ improve $=$ **let** $m = Max(proposals)$ **in**
     $m > cand$ **or**
       $(m = cand$ **and** $minDistance(proposalsFor\ m) + 1 < distance)$
   improve by $proposals =$
     $cand := Max(proposals)$
     update PathInfo to $Max(proposals)$
   update PathInfo to $m =$ **choose** (n, d) **with**
     $(m, n, d) \in proposals$ **and** $d = minDistance(proposalsFor\ m)$
      $nearNeighb := n$
      $distance := d + 1$

The leader election correctness property can now be sharpened by the shortest path correctness property, namely that eventually for every agent, $distance$ is the minimal distance of a path from agent to leader, and $nearNeighb$ is a neighbor on a minimal path to the leader (except for the leader where $nearNeighb = leader$). The proof extends the above induction by a side induction on the minimal distances in $proposalsFor\ Max(proposals$.

As second example we illustrate how by a refinement step for QUICKSORT one can internalize the computation of $tail(L)_{<head(L)}, tail(L)_{\geq head(L)}$ into a partitioning submachine PARTITION(l, h, p). This machine works on the representation of lists as functions $L\colon [r, s] \to VAL$ from intervals of natural numbers to a set of values. When $r < s$, $Partition$ is started with the search boundaries $l = r, h = s$ and the list head $pivot = L(r)$. It terminates when reaching $l = h$ with $L(l) = pivot$, all L-elements smaller than the pivot to the left of l, and all the others at l or to the right of l. Until reaching $l = h$, the partitioning procedure alternates between searching from above for list elements $L(h) \leq pivot$ and searching from below for list elements $L(l) \geq pivot$. When such an element is encountered and it is different from the element at the other current search boundary—one of them is the pivot—, then the boundary elements $L(l), L(h)$ are swapped and the search switches to the other boundary. When $L(h) \leq pivot \leq L(l) \leq L(h)$ before $l = h$ is encountered (namely when pivot has multiple occurrences in the list), h can be decreased by one.

PARTITION$(l, h, pivot) =$
    if $L(h) > pivot$ **then** $h := h - 1$
    elseif $L(l) < pivot$ **then** $l := l + 1$
    elseif $L(l) > L(h)$ **then**
        $L(l) := L(h)$
        $L(h) := L(l)$
    elseif $l < h$ **then** $h := h - 1$

7   Conclusion

The ASM method offers no fool-proof button-pushing, completely mechanical design and verification procedure, but it directly supports professional knowledge and skill in "building models for change", stepwise detailing them to compilable code and maintaining models and code in a cost-effective and reliable way. This is the best one can hope for, given the intrinsically creative character of defining the essence of a complex computer-based system.

References

1. M. Altenhofen, E. Börger, and J. Lemcke. A high-level specification for mediators. In *1st International Workshop on Web Service Choreography and Orchestration for Business Process Management*, 2005.
2. M. Anlauff and P. Kutter. Xasm Open Source. Web pages at http://www.xasm. org/, 2001.
3. M. Barnett, E. Börger, Y. Gurevich, W. Schulte, and M. Veanes. Using Abstract State Machines at Microsoft: A case study. In Y. Gurevich, P. Kutter, M. Odersky, and L. Thiele, editors, *Abstract State Machines: Theory and Applications*, volume 1912 of *Lecture Notes in Computer Science*, pages 367–380. Springer-Verlag, 2000.

4. A. Barros and E. Börger. A compositional framework for service interaction patterns and communication flows. In *Proc. 7th International Conference on Formal Engineering Methods (ICFEM 2005)*, Springer LNCS, 2005.

5. E. Börger. High-level system design and analysis using Abstract State Machines. In D. Hutter, W. Stephan, P. Traverso, and M. Ullmann, editors, *Current Trends in Applied Formal Methods (FM-Trends 98)*, volume 1641 of *Lecture Notes in Computer Science*, pages 1–43. Springer-Verlag, 1999.

6. E. Börger. The origins and the development of the ASM method for high-level system design and analysis. *J. Universal Computer Science*, 8(1):2–74, 2002.

7. E. Börger. The ASM ground model method as a foundation of requirements engineering. In N.Dershowitz, editor, *Verification: Theory and Practice*, volume 2772 of *LNCS*, pages 145–160. Springer-Verlag, 2003.

8. E. Börger. The ASM refinement method. *Formal Aspects of Computing*, 15:237–257, 2003.

9. E. Börger. Modeling with Abstract State Machines: A support for accurate system design and analysis. In B. Rumpe and W. Hesse, editors, *Modellierung 2004*, volume P-45 of *GI-Edition Lecture Notes in Informatics*, pages 235–239. Springer-Verlag, 2004.

10. E. Börger. From finite state machines to virtual machines (Illustrating design patterns and event-B models). In E. Cohors-Fresenborg and I. Schwank, editors, *Präzisionswerkzeug Logik–Gedenkschrift zu Ehren von Dieter Rödding*. Forschungsinstitut für Mathematikdidaktik Osnabrück, 2005. ISBN 3-925386-56-4.

11. E. Börger. Linking content definition and analysis to what the compiler can verify. In *Proc.IFIP WG Conference on Verified Software: Tools, Techniques, and Experiments*, Lecture Notes in Computer Science, Zurich (Switzerland), October 2005. Springer.

12. E. Börger and T. Bolognesi. Remarks on turbo ASMs for computing functional equations and recursion schemes. In E. Börger, A. Gargantini, and E. Riccobene, editors, *Abstract State Machines 2003 – Advances in Theory and Applications*, volume 2589 of *Lecture Notes in Computer Science*, pages 218–228. Springer-Verlag, 2003.

13. E. Börger, H. Busch, J. Cuellar, P. Päppinghaus, E. Tiden, and I. Wildgruber. Konzept einer hierarchischen Erweiterung von EURIS. Siemens ZFE T SE 1 Internal Report BBCPTW91-1 (pp. 1–43), Summer 1996.

14. E. Börger and K. Dässler. Prolog: DIN papers for discussion. ISO/IEC JTCI SC22 WG17 Prolog Standardization Document 58, National Physical Laboratory, Middlesex, England, 1990.

15. E. Börger and G. Del Castillo. A formal method for provably correct composition of a real-life processor out of basic components (The APE100 Reverse Engineering Study). In B. Werner, editor, *Proc. 1st IEEE Int. Conf. on Engineering of Complex Computer Systems (ICECCS'95)*, pages 145–148, November 1995.

16. E. Börger and I. Durdanović. Correctness of compiling Occam to Transputer code. *Computer Journal*, 39(1):52–92, 1996.

17. E. Börger, G. Fruja, V. Gervasi, and R. Stärk. A high-level modular definition of the semantics of C#. *Theoretical Computer Science*, 336(2/3), 2005.

18. E. Börger, U. Glässer, and W. Müller. The semantics of behavioral VHDL'93 descriptions. In *EURO-DAC'94. European Design Automation Conference with EURO-VHDL'94*, pages 500–505, Los Alamitos, California, 1994. IEEE Computer Society Press.

19. E. Börger, P. Päppinghaus, and J. Schmid. Report on a practical application of ASMs in software design. In Y. Gurevich, P. Kutter, M. Odersky, and L. Thiele, editors, *Abstract State Machines: Theory and Applications*, volume 1912 of *Lecture Notes in Computer Science*, pages 361–366. Springer-Verlag, 2000.

20. E. Börger and D. Rosenzweig. The WAM – definition and compiler correctness. In C. Beierle and L. Plümer, editors, *Logic Programming: Formal Methods and Practical Applications*, volume 11 of *Studies in Computer Science and Artificial Intelligence*, chapter 2, pages 20–90. North-Holland, 1995.

21. E. Börger and J. Schmid. Composition and submachine concepts for sequential ASMs. In P. Clote and H. Schwichtenberg, editors, *Computer Science Logic (Proceedings of CSL 2000)*, volume 1862 of *Lecture Notes in Computer Science*, pages 41–60. Springer-Verlag, 2000.

22. E. Börger and W. Schulte. Initialization problems for Java. *Software – Concepts and Tools*, 19(4):175–178, 2000.

23. E. Börger and D. Sona. A neural abstract machine. *J. Universal Computer Science*, 7(11):1007–1024, 2001.

24. E. Börger and R. F. Stärk. *Abstract State Machines. A Method for High-Level System Design and Analysis*. Springer, 2003.

25. G. D. Castillo and P. Päppinghaus. Designing software for internet telephony: experiences in an industrial development process. In A. Blass, E. Börger, and Y. Gurevich, editors, *Theory and Applications of Abstract State Machines*, Schloss Dagstuhl, Int. Conf. and Research Center for Computer Science, 2002.

26. G. Del Castillo. *The ASM Workbench. A Tool Environment for Computer-Aided Analysis and Validation of Abstract State Machine Models*. PhD thesis, Universität Paderborn, Germany, 2001.

27. G. Del Castillo and K. Winter. Model checking support for the ASM high-level language. In S. Graf and M. Schwartzbach, editors, *Proc. 6th Int. Conf. TACAS 2000*, volume 1785 of *Lecture Notes in Computer Science*, pages 331–346. Springer-Verlag, 2000.

28. A. Dold. A formal representation of Abstract State Machines using PVS. Verifix Technical Report Ulm/6.2, Universität Ulm, Germany, July 1998.

29. A. Dold, T. Gaul, V. Vialard, and W. Zimmermann. ASM-based mechanized verification of compiler back-ends. In U. Glässer and P. Schmitt, editors, *Proc. 5th Int. Workshop on Abstract State Machines*, pages 50–67. Magdeburg University, 1998.

30. R. Farahbod, V. Gervasi, and U. Glässer. CoreASM: An extensible ASM execution engine. In D. Beauquier, E. Börger, and A. Slissenko, editors, *Proc.ASM05*. Université de Paris 12, 2005.

31. Foundations of Software Engineering Group, Microsoft Research. AsmL. Web pages at http://research.microsoft.com/foundations/AsmL/, 2001.

32. N. G. Fruja. Specification and implementation problems for C#. In B. Thalheim and W. Zimmermann, editors, *Abstract State Machines 2004*, volume 3052 of *Lecture Notes in Computer Science*, pages 127–143. Springer, 2004.

33. A. Gargantini and E. Riccobene. Encoding Abstract State Machines in PVS. In Y. Gurevich, P. Kutter, M. Odersky, and L. Thiele, editors, *Abstract State Machines: Theory and Applications*, volume 1912 of *Lecture Notes in Computer Science*, pages 303–322. Springer-Verlag, 2000.

34. A. Gawanmeh, S. Tahar, and K. Winter. Interfacing ASMs with the MDG tool. In E. Börger, A. Gargantini, and E. Riccobene, editors, *Abstract State Machines 2003– Advances in Theory and Applications*, volume 2589 of *Lecture Notes in Computer Science*, pages 278–292. Springer-Verlag, 2003.

35. U. Glässer, R. Gotzhein, and A. Prinz. Formal semantics of SDL-2000: Status and perspectives. *Computer Networks*, 42(3):343–358, June 2003.
36. G. Goos and W. Zimmermann. Verifying compilers and ASMs. In Y. Gurevich, P. Kutter, M. Odersky, and L. Thiele, editors, *Abstract State Machines: Theory and Applications*, volume 1912 of *Lecture Notes in Computer Science*, pages 177–202. Springer-Verlag, 2000.
37. Y. Gurevich. Evolving algebras 1993: Lipari Guide. In E. Börger, editor, *Specification and Validation Methods*, pages 9–36. Oxford University Press, 1995.
38. A. Habibi. *Framework for System Level Verification: The SystemC Case*. PhD thesis, Concordia University, Montreal, July 2005.
39. A. Heberle. *Korrekte Transformationsphase – der Kern korrekter Übersetzer*. PhD thesis, Universität Karlsruhe, Germany, 2000.
40. J. Huggins. Kermit: Specification and verification. In E. Börger, editor, *Specification and Validation Methods*, pages 247–293. Oxford University Press, 1995.
41. A. Kalinov, A. Kossatchev, A. Petrenko, M. Posypkin, and V. Shishkov. Using ASM specifications for compiler testing. In E. Börger, A. Gargantini, and E. Riccobene, editors, *Abstract State Machines 2003–Advances in Theory and Applications*, volume 2589 of *Lecture Notes in Computer Science*, page 415. Springer-Verlag, 2003.
42. L. Lavagno, A. Sangiovanni-Vincentelli, and E. M. Sentovitch. Models of computation for system design. In E. Börger, editor, *Architecture Design and Validation Methods*, pages 243–295. Springer-Verlag, 2000.
43. G. Schellhorn. Verification of ASM refinements using generalized forward simulation. *J. Universal Computer Science*, 7(11):952–979, 2001.
44. G. Schellhorn. ASM refinement and generalizations of forward simulation in data refinement: A comparison. *Theoretical Computer Science*, 2004.
45. G. Schellhorn and W. Ahrendt. Reasoning about Abstract State Machines: The WAM case study. *J. Universal Computer Science*, 3(4):377–413, 1997.
46. J. Schmid. Executing ASM specifications with AsmGofer. Web pages at http://www.tydo.de/AsmGofer.
47. J. Schmid. Compiling Abstract State Machines to C++. *J. Universal Computer Science*, 7(11):1069–1088, 2001.
48. J. Schmid. *Refinement and Implementation Techniques for Abstract State Machines*. PhD thesis, University of Ulm, Germany, 2002.
49. R. F. Stärk and E. Börger. An ASM specification of C# threads and the .NET memory model. In W. Zimmermann and B. Thalheim, editors, *Abstract State Machines 2004*, volume 3052 of *Lecture Notes in Computer Science*, pages 38–60. Springer-Verlag, 2004.
50. R. F. Stärk and S. Nanchen. A logic for Abstract State Machines. *J. Universal Computer Science*, 7(11):981–1006, 2001.
51. R. F. Stärk, J. Schmid, and E. Börger. *Java and the Java Virtual Machine: Definition, Verification, Validation*. Springer-Verlag, 2001.
52. M. Vajihollahi. High level specification and validation of the Business Process Execution Language for web services. Master's thesis, School of Computing Science at Simon Fraser University, April 2004.
53. W. Zimmerman and T. Gaul. On the construction of correct compiler back-ends: An ASM approach. *J. Universal Computer Science*, 3(5):504–567, 1997.

Matching Classifications via a Bidirectional Integration of SAT and Linguistic Resources

Fausto Giunchiglia

Dept. of Information and Communication Technology,
University of Trento, 38050 Povo, Trento, Italy
fausto@dit.unitn.it

Abstract. Classifications, often mistakenly called directories, are pervasive: we use them to classify our messages, our favourite Web Pages, our files, ... And many more can be found in the Web; think for instance of the Google and Yahoo's directories. The problem is that all these classifications are very different or more precisely, semantically heterogeneous. The most striking consequence is that they classify documents very differently, making therefore very hard and sometimes impossible to find them.

Matching classifications is the process which allows us to map those nodes of two classifications which, intuitively, correspond semantically to each other. In the first part of the talk I will show how it is possible to encode this problem into a propositional validity problem, thus allowing for the use of SAT reasoners. This is done mainly using linguistic resources (e.g., WordNet) and some amount of Natural Language Processing. However, as shown in the second part of the talk, this turns out to be almost useless. In most cases, in fact, linguistic resources do not contain enough of the axioms needed to prove unsatisfiability. The solution to this problem turns to be that of using SAT as a way to generate the missing axioms.

We have started using linguistic resources to provide SAT with the axioms needed to match classifications, and we have ended up using SAT to generate missing axioms in the linguistic resources. We will argue that this is an example of a more general phenomenon which arises when using commonsense knowledge. This in turns becomes an opportunity for the use of decision procedures for a focused automated generation of the missing knowledge.

References

1. F. Giunchiglia and P. Shvaiko. Semantic matching. *The Knowledge Engineering Review*, 18(3):265–280, Sept. 2003.
2. F. Giunchiglia, P. Shvaiko, and M. Yatskevich. S-match: an algorithm and an implementation of semantic matching. In *Proceedings of ESWS'04, Heraklion, Crete, Greece*, LNCS 3053, pages 61–75. Springer, May 2004.
3. F. Giunchiglia, M. Yatskevich, and E. Giunchiglia. Efficient semantic matching. In *Proceedings of ESWS'05, Heraklion, Crete, Greece*, LNCS 3532, pages 272–289. Springer, 2005.

B. Gramlich (Ed.): FroCoS 2005, LNAI 3717, p. 284, 2005.

Connecting a Logical Framework to a First-Order Logic Prover[*]

Andreas Abel, Thierry Coquand, and Ulf Norell

Department of Computing Science, Chalmers University of Technology
{abel,coquand,ulfn}@cs.chalmers.se

Abstract. We present one way of combining a logical framework and first-order logic. The logical framework is used as an interface to a first-order theorem prover. Its main purpose is to keep track of the structure of the proof and to deal with the high level steps, for instance, induction. The steps that involve purely propositional or simple first-order reasoning are left to a first-order resolution prover (the system Gandalf in our prototype). The correctness of this interaction is based on a general meta-theoretic result. One feature is the simplicity of our translation between the logical framework and first-order logic, which uses implicit typing. Implementation and case studies are described.

1 Introduction

We work towards human-readable and machine-verifiable *proof documents* for mathematics and computer science. As argued by de Bruijn [11], dependent type theory offers an ideal formal system for representing reasoning steps, such as introducing parameters or hypotheses, naming constants or lemmas, using a lemma or a hypothesis. Type theory provides explicit notations for these proof steps, with good logical properties. Using tools like Coq [5], Epigram [3], or Agda [9] these steps can be performed interactively. But low level reasoning steps, such as simple propositional reasoning, or equality reasoning, substituting equals for equals, are tedious if performed in a purely interactive way. Furthermore, propositional provers, and even first-order logic (FOL) provers are now very efficient. It is thus natural to create interfaces between logical frameworks and automatic propositional or first-order provers [7,24,18]. But, in order to arrive at proof documents which are still readable, only *trivial* proof steps should be handled by the automatic prover. Since different readers might have different notions of *trivial*, the automatic prover should not be a black box. With some effort by the human, the output of the prover should be understandable.

In this paper, we are exploring connections between a logical framework MLF_{Prop} based on type theory and resolution-based theorem provers. One problem in such an interaction is that resolution proofs are hard to read and understand in general. Indeed, resolution proof systems work with formulæ in clause normal form, where clauses are (the universal closures of) disjunctions of literals, a literal being an atom or a negated

[*] Research supported by the coordination action *TYPES* (510996) and thematic network *Applied Semantics II* (IST-2001-38957) of the European Union and the project *Cover* of the Swedish Foundation of Strategic Research (SSF).

atom. The system translates the negation of the statement to be proved to clause form, using skolemisation and disjunctive normal form. It then generates new clauses using resolution and paramodulation, trying to derive a contradiction. If successful, the system does pruning on the (typically high number of) generated clauses and outputs only the relevant ones.[1]

We lose the structure of the initial problem when doing skolemisation and clausification. Typically, a problem such as

$$\forall x. \exists y. \forall z. R(x, y) \Rightarrow R(x, z) \tag{1}$$

is negated and translated into the two contradictory unit clauses

$$\forall y.\, R(a, y), \qquad \forall y.\, \neg R(a, f(y)), \tag{2}$$

but the connection between the statement (1) and the refutation of (2) is not so intuitive.

We do not solve this problem here, but we point out that, if we restrict ourselves to implicitely universally quantified propositional formulæ, in the following called *open* formulæ, this problem does not arise. Furthermore, when we restrict to this fragment, we can use the idea of implicit typing [4,26]. In this way, the translation from framework types to FOL formulæ is particularly simple. Technically, this is reflected by a general meta-theorem which ensures that we can lift a first-order resolution proof to a framework derivation. If we restrict the class of formulæ further to so-called *geometrical* open formulæ [10,6], then the translation to clausal form is transparent. Indeed, any resolution proof for this fragment is intuitionistically valid and can be interpreted as it is in type theory. This meta-theorem is also the theoretical justification for our interface between MLF$_{\mathsf{Prop}}$ and a resolution-based proof system.

We have implemented a prototype version of a type system in Haskell, with a connection to the resolution prover Gandalf [25]. By restricting ourselves to open formulæ we sacrifice proof strength, but preliminary experiments show that the restriction is less severe than it may seem at first since the steps involving quantification are well handled at the framework level. Also, the proof traces produced by Gandalf are often readable (and surprisingly clever in some cases).

We think that we can represent Leslie Lamport proof style [17] rather faithfully in this system. The high level steps such as introduction of hypotheses, case analysis, induction steps are handled at the framework level, and only the trivial steps are sent to the FOL automatic prover.

One can think also of other plug-in extensions, e.g., rewriting systems and computer algebra systems. We have experimented with a QuickCheck [8] plug-in, that allows random testing of some propositions. In general, each plug-in extension of our logical framework should be justified in the same way as the one we present in this paper: we prove a conservativity result which ensures that the use of this plug-in can be, if desired, replaced by a direct proof in the framework. This way of combining various systems

---

[1] If the search is not successful, it is quite hard to get any relevant information from the clauses that are generated. We have not yet analyzed the problem of getting useful feedback in this case.

works in practice, as suggested by preliminary experiments, and it is theoretically well-founded.

This paper is organized as follows. We first describe the logical framework MLF_{Prop}. We then present the translation from some LF types to FOL formulæ. The main technical result is then a theorem that shows that any resolution and paramodulation step, with one restriction, can be lifted to the framework level. Finally, we present some examples and extensions, and a discussion of related work.

2 The Logical Framework MLF_{Prop}

This section presents an extension of Martin-Löf's logical framework [20] by propositions and local definitions.

Expressions (terms and types). We assume countable sets of variables Var and constants Const. Furthermore, we have a finite number of built-in constants to construct the primitives of our type language. A priori, we do not distinguish between terms and types. The syntactic entities of MLF_{Prop} are given by the following grammar.

Var	$\ni x, y, z$		variables
Const	$\ni c, f, p$		constants
BuiltIn	$\ni \hat{c}$	$::=$ Fun | El | Set | () | Prf | Prop	built-in constants
Exp	$\ni r, s, P, Q$	$::= \hat{c} \mid c \mid x \mid \lambda xr \mid r\,s \mid$ let $x\!:\!T\!=\!r$ in s	expressions
Ty	$\ni T, U$	$::=$ Set | El s | Prop | Prf P | Fun $T\,(\lambda xU)$	types
Cxt	$\ni \Gamma$	$::= \diamond \mid \Gamma, x\!:\!T$	typing contexts
Sig	$\ni \Sigma$	$::= \diamond \mid \Sigma, c\!:\!T \mid \Sigma, c\!:\!T\!=\!r$	signatures

We identify terms and types up to α-conversion and adopt the convention that in contexts Γ, all variables must be distinct; hence, the context extension $\Gamma, x\!:\!T$ presupposes $(x\!:\!U) \notin \Gamma$ for any U. Similarly, a constant c may not be declared in a signature twice. We abbreviate a sequence of context entries $x_1 : T, \ldots, x_n : T$ of the same type by $x_1, \ldots, x_m : T$. Multiple application $r\,s_1 \ldots s_n$ is expressed as $r\,\boldsymbol{s}$. (Capture-avoiding) substitution of r for x in s is written as $s[r/x]$, or $s[r]$ if x is clear from the context of discourse.

For dependent function types Fun $T\,(\lambda xU)$ we introduce the notation $(x\!:\!T) \to U$. Curried functions spaces $(x_1 : T_1) \to \ldots (x_k : T_k) \to U$ are shortened to $(x_1 : T_1, \ldots, x_k : T_k) \to U$, which explains the notation $(\Gamma) \to U$. Non-dependent functions $(\_\!:\!T) \to U$ are written $T \to U$. The inhabitants of Set are type codes; El maps type codes to types. E.g., $(a : \mathsf{Set}) \to \mathsf{El}\,a \to \mathsf{El}\,a$ is the type of the polymorphic identity $\lambda a \lambda x x$. Similarly Prop contains formal propositions P and Prf P proofs of P.

Types of the shape $(\Gamma) \to \mathsf{Prf}\,P$ are called *proof types*. A context $\Gamma := x_1 : T_1, \ldots, x_n : T_n$ is a *set context* if and only if all T_i are of the form $(\Delta) \to \mathsf{El}\,S$. In particular, if $P : \mathsf{Prop}$, then the proof type $(\Gamma) \to \mathsf{Prf}\,P$ corresponds to a universal first-order formula $\forall x_1 \ldots \forall x_n P$ with quantifier-free kernel P.

Judgements. The type theory MLF_{Prop} is presented via five judgements, which are all relative to a (user-defined) signature Σ.

$$\Gamma \vdash_\Sigma \qquad\qquad\qquad \Gamma \text{ is a well-formed context}$$
$$\Gamma \vdash_\Sigma T \qquad\qquad\quad T \text{ is a well-formed type}$$
$$\Gamma \vdash_\Sigma r : T \qquad\qquad r \text{ has type } T$$
$$\Gamma \vdash_\Sigma T = T' \qquad\quad T \text{ and } T' \text{ are equal types}$$
$$\Gamma \vdash_\Sigma r = r' : T \qquad r \text{ and } r' \text{ are equal terms of type } T$$

All five judgements are defined simultaneously. Since the signature remains fixed in all judgements we will omit it. The typing rules are available in the extended version of this paper [2]. Judgmental type and term equality are generated from expansion of signature definitions as well as from β-, η-, and let-equality, the latter of which is given by $(\text{let } x : T = r \text{ in } s) = s[r/x]$. The rules for equality are similar to the ones of MLF_Σ [1], and type-checking of normal terms with local definitions is decidable.

Natural deduction. We assume a signature Σ_{nd} (see the extended version of this paper [2]) which assumes the infix logical connectives $op ::= \wedge, \vee, \Rightarrow$, plus the defined ones, $\neg$ and $\Leftrightarrow$. Furthermore, it contains a set PredSym of basic predicate symbols p of type $(\Gamma) \to \text{Prop}$ where Γ is a (possibly empty) set context. Currently we only assume truth $\top$, absurdity $\bot$, and typed equality Id, but user defined signatures can extend PredSym by their own symbols. For each logical constructs, there are appropriate proof rules, e. g., a constant impl : $(P, Q : \text{Prop}) \to (\text{Prf } P \to \text{Prf } Q) \to \text{Prf } (P \Rightarrow Q)$.

First-order logic assumes that every set is non-empty, and our use of a first-order prover is only sound under this assumption. Hence, we add a special constant $\epsilon : (D : \text{Set}) \to \text{El } D$ to Σ_{nd} which enforces this fact. Notice that this implies that all set contexts are inhabited[2].

Classical reasoning can be performed in the signature Σ_{class}, which we define as the extension of Σ_{nd} by EM : $(P : \text{Prop}) \to \text{Prf } (P \vee \neg P)$, the law of the excluded middle.

The FOL rule. This article investigates conditions under which the addition of the following rule is conservative over $\text{MLF}_{\text{Prop}} + \Sigma_{\text{nd}}$ and $\text{MLF}_{\text{Prop}} + \Sigma_{\text{class}}$, respectively.

$$\text{FOL} \frac{\Gamma \vdash T}{\Gamma \vdash () : T} \quad \Gamma \vdash_{\text{FOL}} T$$

The side condition $\Gamma \vdash_{\text{FOL}} T$ expresses that T is a proof type and that the first-order prover can deduce the truth of the corresponding first-order formula from the assumptions in Γ. It ensures that only tautologies have proofs in MLF_{Prop}, but it is not considered part of the type checking. Meta-theoretical properties of MLF_{Prop} like decidability of equality and type-checking hold independently of this side condition.

Conservativity fails if we have to compare proof objects during type-checking. This is because the rule FOL produces a single proof object for all (true) propositions, whereas upon removal of FOL the hole has to be filled with specific proof object. Hence two equal objects which each depend on a proof generated by FOL could become inequal after replacing FOL. To avoid this, it is sufficient to restrict function spaces $(x : T) \to U$: if T is a proof type, then also U.

In the remainder of the paper, we use LF as a synonym for MLF_{Prop}.

---

[2] Semantically, it may be fruitful to think of terms of type Set as inhabited Partial Equivalence Relations, while terms of type Prop are PERs with at most one inhabitant.

3   Translation from MLF$_{\mathsf{Prop}}$ to FOL

We shall define a *partial* translation from some LF types to FOL propositions. We translate only types of the form

$$(x_1 : T_1, \ldots, x_k : T_k) \to \mathsf{Prf}\ (P(x_1, \ldots, x_k)),$$

and these are translated to *open* formulæ $[P(x_1, \ldots, x_k)]$ of first-order logic. All the variables $x_1, \ldots, x_k$ are considered universally quantified. For instance,

$$(x : \mathsf{El}\ \mathsf{N}) \to \mathsf{Prf}\ (\mathsf{Id}\ \mathsf{N}\ x\ x \land \mathsf{Id}\ \mathsf{N}\ x\ (\mathsf{add}\ 0\ x))$$

will be translated to $x = x \ \land \ x = \mathsf{add}\ 0\ x$. If we have a theory of lattices, that is, we have added

$$
\begin{array}{rl}
D & : \mathsf{Set} \\
\mathsf{sup} : & \mathsf{El}\ D \to \mathsf{El}\ D \to \mathsf{El}\ D \\
\le & : \mathsf{El}\ D \to \mathsf{El}\ D \to \mathsf{Prop}
\end{array}
$$

to the current signature, then $(x, y : \mathsf{El}\ D) \to \mathsf{Prf}\ (\mathsf{sup}\ x\ y \le x \Leftrightarrow y \le x)$ would be translated to $\mathsf{sup}\ x\ y \le y \ \Leftrightarrow \ y \le x$.

The translation is done at a syntactical level, without using types. We will demonstrate that we can lift a resolution proof of a translated formula to a LF derivation in the signature Σ_{class} (or in Σ_{nd}, in some cases).

3.1   Formal Description of the Translation

We translate *normal* expressions, which means that all definitions have been unfolded and all redexes reduced. Three classes of normal MLF$_{\mathsf{Prop}}$-expressions are introduced: (formal) *first-order terms* and (formal) *first-order formulæ*, which are quantifier free formulæ over atoms possibly containing free term variables, and *translatable formulæ*, which are first-order formulæ prefixed by quantification over set elements.

$$
\begin{array}{llll}
t, u & ::= x \mid f\ t & & \text{first-order terms} \\
A, B & ::= p\ t \mid \mathsf{Id}\ S\ t_1\ t_2 & & \text{atoms} \\
W & ::= A \mid W\ op\ W' & & \text{first-order formulæ} \\
\phi & ::= (\Delta) \to \mathsf{Prf}\ W & & \text{translatable formulæ} (\Delta\ \text{set context})
\end{array}
$$

Proper terms are those which are not just variables. For the conservativity result the following fact about proper terms will be important: In a well-typed proper term, the types of its variables are uniquely determined. For this reason, a formal first-order term t may neither contain a binder (λ or let) nor a variable which is applied to something, for instance, $x\ u$.

An example of a first-order formula is $W_{\mathsf{ex}} := \mathsf{Id}\ D\ x\ (f\ y) \Rightarrow (\mathsf{Less}\ x\ (f\ y) \Rightarrow \bot)$, which is well-typed in the extension $D : \mathsf{Set}$, $f : \mathsf{El}\ D \to \mathsf{El}\ D$, $\mathsf{Less} : \mathsf{El}\ D \to \mathsf{El}\ D \to \mathsf{Prop}$ of signature Σ_{nd}.

On the FOL side, we consider a language with equality ($=$), one binary function symbol app and one constant for each constant introduced in the logical framework. Having an explicit "app" allows partial application of function symbols.

Let $\Delta = x_1 : T_1, \ldots, x_n : T_n$ be a set context. A type of the form

$$\phi := (\Delta) \to \mathsf{Prf}\, W$$

is translated into a universal formula $[\phi] = \forall x_1 \ldots \forall x_n [W]$. The translation $[W]$ of first-order formulæ and the translation $\langle t \rangle$ of first-order terms depends on Δ and is defined recursively as follows:

$[W_1 \ op \ W_2] := [W_1] \ op \ [W_2]$		logical connectives
$[\mathsf{Id}\, S\, t_1\, t_2] := \langle t_1 \rangle = \langle t_2 \rangle$		equality
$[p\, t_1 \ldots t_n] := p(\langle t_1 \rangle, \ldots, \langle t_n \rangle)$		predicates, including $\top, \bot$
$\langle x_i \rangle := x_i$		variables in Δ
$\langle x \rangle := c_x$		variables not in Δ
$\langle c \rangle := c$		0-ary functions
$\langle f\, t_1 \ldots t_n \rangle := f(\langle t_1 \rangle, \ldots, \langle t_n \rangle)$		n-ary functions

where we write $f(t_1, \ldots, t_n)$ for $\mathsf{app}(\ldots \mathsf{app}(\mathsf{app}(f, t_1), t_2), \ldots, t_n)$. Note that the translation is purely syntactical, and does not use type information. It is even homomorphic with two exceptions: (a) the typed equality of $\mathsf{MLF_{Prop}}$ is translated into the untyped equality of FOL, and (b) variables bound outside ϕ have to be translated as constants.

For instance, the formula $(y : \mathsf{El}\, D) \to W_{\mathrm{ex}}$ is translated as $\forall y.\ c_x = f(y) \Rightarrow (\mathsf{Less}(c_x, f(y)) \Rightarrow \bot)$. Examples of types that cannot be translated are

$$(x : \mathsf{Prop}) \to \mathsf{Prf}\, x, \quad \mathsf{Prf}\, (F\, (\lambda x x)), \quad (y : \mathsf{El}\, D \to \mathsf{El}\, D) \to \mathsf{Prf}\, (P\, (y\, x)).$$

We shall also use the class of *geometrical formulæ*, given by the following grammar:

$$
\begin{aligned}
G &::= H \mid H \to G \mid G \wedge G \qquad \text{geometrical formula} \\
H &::= A \mid H \wedge H \mid H \vee H \qquad \text{positive formula}
\end{aligned}
$$

The above example W_{ex} is geometrical. As we will show, (classical) first-order proofs of geometrical formulæ can be mapped to intuitionistic proofs in the logical framework with Σ_{nd}.

3.2   Resolution Calculus

It will be convenient to use the following non-standard presentation of the resolution calculus [22]. A *clause* C is an open first-order formula of the form

$$A_1 \wedge \cdots \wedge A_n \Rightarrow B_1 \vee \cdots \vee B_m$$

where we can have $n = 0$ or $m = 0$ and A_i and B_j are atomic formulæ. Following Gentzen [12], we write such a clause on the form

$$A_1, \ldots, A_n \Rightarrow B_1, \ldots, B_m,$$

that is, $X \Rightarrow Y$, where X and Y are finite sets of atomic formulæ. An empty X is interpreted as truth, an empty Y as absurdity.

$$\text{AX} \; \overline{A \Rightarrow A} \qquad \text{SUB} \; \frac{X' \supseteq X \qquad X \Rightarrow Y \qquad Y \subseteq Y'}{X' \Rightarrow Y'}$$

$$\text{RES} \; \frac{X_1 \Rightarrow Z_1, Y_1 \qquad X_2, Z_2 \Rightarrow Y_2}{(X_1, X_2 \Rightarrow Y_1, Y_2)\sigma} \; \sigma = \mathsf{mgu}(Z_1, Z_2)$$

$$\text{REFL} \; \overline{\cdot \Rightarrow x = x} \qquad \text{PARA} \; \frac{X_1 \Rightarrow t = u, Y_1 \qquad X_2[t'] \Rightarrow Y_2[t']}{(X_1, X_2[u] \Rightarrow Y_1, Y_2[u])\sigma} \; \sigma = \mathsf{mgu}(t, t')$$

Fig. 1. Resolution calculus

Resolution is forward reasoning. Figure 1 lists the rules for extending the current set of derived clauses: if all clauses mentioned in the premise of a rule are present, this rule can fire and the clause of the conclusion is added to the clause set.

In our formulation, all rules are intuitionistically valid[3], and can be justified in $\mathsf{MLF_{Prop}} + \Sigma_{\mathsf{nd}}$. It can be shown, classically, that these rules are *complete* in the following sense: if a clause is a semantical consequence of other clauses then it is possible to derive it using the resolution calculus. Hence, any proof in FOL can be performed with resolution[4].

It can be pointed out that the SUB rule is only necessary at the very end—any resolution proof can be normalized to a proof that only uses SUB in the final step.

Let the *restricted* paramodulation rule denote the version of PARA where both t and t' are proper terms (not variables).

3.3 Proof of Correctness

In this section, we show that every FOL proof of a translated formula $[\phi]$ can be lifted to a proof in $\mathsf{MLF_{Prop}} + \Sigma_{\mathsf{class}}$, provided the resolution proof confines to restricted paramodulation. This is not trivial because FOL is untyped and $\mathsf{MLF_{Prop}}$ is typed, and our translation forgets the types. The crucial insight is that every resolution step preserves well-typedness.

Fix a signature Σ. A first-order term t is *well-typed* iff there exists a context Δ, giving types to the variables $x_1, \ldots, x_n$ of t, such that in the given signature, $\Delta \vdash t : T$ for some type T. For example, in the signature

$$D : \mathsf{Set} \qquad\qquad f : \mathsf{El}\ D \to \mathsf{El}\ D$$
$$F : \mathsf{El}\ D \to \mathsf{Prop} \qquad g : (x : \mathsf{El}\ D) \to \mathsf{Prf}\ (F\ x)$$

the proper first-order terms $f\ x$, $F\ y$, and $g\ z$ are well-typed, but $F\ x\ y$ is not. Notice that if a *proper* FOL term is well-typed, then there is only one way to assign types to its variables.

---

[3] In the standard formulation, the AX rule would read $\neg A \vee A$—the excluded middle.

[4] To deal with existential quantification we also need skolemisation.

Lemma 1. *If two proper first-order terms t_1, t_2 over disjoint variables are well-typed and unifiable, then the most general unifier* $\mathsf{mgu}(t_1, t_2)$ *is well-typed.*

For instance, add $x\ 0$ and add $(S\ y)\ z$ are unifiable and well-typed and the most general unifier $\{x \mapsto S\ y, z \mapsto 0\}$ is well-typed. The lemma is proven in the extended version of this paper [2].

Using this lemma, we can lift any FOL resolution step to an LF resolution step. The same holds for any *restricted* paramodulation step, which justifies the translation of Id $S\ t\ u$ as $\langle t \rangle = \langle u \rangle$ in FOL, Indeed, in the paramodulation step between $X_1 \Rightarrow t = u, Y_1$ and $X_2[t'] \Rightarrow Y_2[t']$ we unify t and t' and for Lemma 1 to be applicable both t and t' have to be proper terms. Similar arguments have been put forth by Beeson [4] and Wick and McCune [26].

A clausal type is a formula which translates to a clause.

Lemma 2. *If two FOL clausal types* $(\Gamma_1) \to$ Prf (W_1) *and* $(\Gamma_2) \to$ Prf (W_2) *are derivable, and C is a resolution of $[W_1]$ and $[W_2]$ then there exists a context Γ and a derivable* $(\Gamma) \to$ Prf W *such that $C = [W]$. The same holds if C is derived from $[W_1]$ and $[W_2]$ by restricted paramodulation. Furthermore in both cases, Γ is a set context if both Γ_1 and Γ_2 are set contexts.*

In the next theorems, $\phi, \phi_1, \ldots, \phi_k$ are translatable formulæ of the form $(\Gamma) \to$ Prf W where Γ is a set context.

The following theorem is a consequence of Lemma 2, since an open formula is (classically) equivalent to a conjunction of clauses.

Theorem 3. *If we can derive $[\phi]$ from $[\phi_1], \ldots, [\phi_k]$ by resolution and restricted paramodulation then ϕ is derivable from $\phi_1, \ldots, \phi_k$ in any extension of the signature Σ_{class}.*

A resolution proof, as we have presented it, is intuitionistically valid. The only step which may not be intuitionistically valid is when we express the equivalence between an open formula and a conjunction of clauses. For instance the open formula $\neg P \vee Q$ is not intuitionistically equivalent to the clause $P \Rightarrow Q$ in general. This problem does not occur if we start with geometrical formulæ [6].

Theorem 4. *If we can derive $[\phi]$ from $[\phi_1], \ldots, [\phi_k]$ by resolution and restricted paramodulation and $\phi, \phi_1, \ldots, \phi_k$ are geometric formulæ, then ϕ is derivable from $\phi_1 \ldots \phi_k$ in any extension of the signature Σ_{nd}.*

It is important for the theorem that all set contexts are inhabited: if D : Set and P : Prop (with x not free in P), then both

$$\phi_1 = (x : \mathsf{El}\ D) \to \mathsf{Prf}\ P \quad \text{and} \quad \phi_2 = \mathsf{Prf}\ P$$

are translated to the same FOL proposition $[\phi_1] = [\phi_2] = P$ but we can derive ϕ_2 from ϕ_1 in Σ_{nd}, D : Set, P : Prop only because El D is inhabited.

As noticed above, if we allow paramodulation from a variable, we could derive clauses that are not well-typed. For instance, in the signature

$$N_1 : \mathsf{Set}, 0 : \mathsf{El}\ N_1, h : (x : \mathsf{El}\ N_1) \to \mathsf{Prf}\ (\mathsf{Id}\ N_1\ x\ 0), A : \mathsf{Set}, a : \mathsf{El}\ A$$

the type of h becomes $x = 0$ in FOL and from this we could derive, by paramodulation from the variable x, $a = 0$ which is not well-typed. This problem is also discussed in [4,26] and the solution is simply to forbid the FOL prover to use paramodulation from a variable[5].

We can now state the conservativity theorem.

Theorem 5. *If a type is inhabited in the system* $\mathsf{MLF_{Prop}} + \mathrm{FOL} + \Sigma_{class}$ *then it is inhabited in* $\mathsf{MLF_{Prop}} + \Sigma_{class}$.

Proof. By induction on the typing derivation, using Thm. 3 for FOL derivations.

3.4 Simple Examples

Figure 2 shows an extension of Σ_{nd} by natural numbers, induction and an addition function defined by recursion on the second argument. Now consider the goal $(x : \mathsf{El\, N}) \to \mathsf{Id\, N}\,(\mathsf{add}\,0\,x)\,x$. Using the induction schema and the propositional proof rules, we can give the proof term

$$\mathsf{indN}\,(\lambda x.\ \mathsf{Id\, N}\,(\mathsf{add}\,0\,x)\,x)\,()\,(\lambda a.\ \mathsf{impl}\,(\lambda ih\,()))$$

in the logical framework, which contains these two FOL goals:

$$\vdash_{\mathsf{FOL}} \mathsf{Id\, N}\,(\mathsf{add}\,0\,0)\,0$$
$$a : \mathsf{El\, N},\ ih : \mathsf{Id\, N}\,(\mathsf{add}\,0\,a)\,a \vdash_{\mathsf{FOL}} \mathsf{Id\, N}\,(\mathsf{add}\,0\,(\mathsf{S}\,a))\,(\mathsf{S}\,a)$$

Both goals can be handled by the FOL prover. The first goal becomes $\mathsf{add}\,0\,0 = 0$ and is proved from $\mathsf{add}\,x\,0 = x$, the translation of axiom add0. The second goal becomes $\mathsf{add}\,0\,(\mathsf{S}\,a) = \mathsf{S}\,a$. This is a first-order consequence of the translated induction hypothesis $\mathsf{add}\,0\,a = a$ and $\mathsf{add}\,x\,(\mathsf{S}\,y) = \mathsf{S}\,(\mathsf{add}\,x\,y)$, the translation of axiom addS.

This example, though very simple, is a good illustration of the interaction between LF and FOL: the framework is used to handle the induction step and in the second goal, the introduction of the parameter a and the induction hypothesis.

Here is another simple example which illustrates that we can call the FOL prover even in a context involving non first-order operations. This example comes from a correctness proof of Warshall's algorithm. Let $D : \mathsf{Set}$.

$$F : \mathsf{El\, D} \to (\mathsf{El\, D} \to \mathsf{El\, D} \to \mathsf{Prop}) \to \mathsf{El\, D} \to \mathsf{El\, D} \to \mathsf{Prop}$$
$$F\,a\,R\,x\,y = R\,x\,y \lor (R\,x\,a \land R\,a\,y)$$
$$swap : (a,b,x,y : \mathsf{El\, D}) \to \mathsf{Prf}\,(F\,a\,(F\,b\,R)\,x\,y \Leftrightarrow F\,b\,(F\,a\,R)\,x\,y)$$

The operation F is a higher-order operation. However, in the context $R : \mathsf{El\, D} \to \mathsf{El\, D} \to \mathsf{Prop}$, the goal *swap* can be handled by the FOL prover. The normal form of $F\,a\,(F\,b\,R)\,x\,y \Leftrightarrow F\,b\,(F\,a\,R)\,x\,y$, where all defined constants (here only F) have been unfolded, is a translatable formula.

---

[5] This is possible in Otter. In Gandalf, this could be checked from the trace. Paramodulation from a variable is highly non-deterministic. For efficiency reasons, it was not present in some version of Gandalf, but it was added later for completeness. In the examples we have tried, this restriction is not a problem.

N   : Set   natural numbers

0   : El N   zero
S   : El N → El N   successor

indN : $(P:\text{El N} \to \text{Prop}) \to P\,0$
       $\to ((x:\text{El N}) \to P\,x \Rightarrow P\,(S\,x))$
       $\to (n:\text{El N}) \to P\,n$ induction

add   : El N → El N → El N   addition

add0 : $(x \quad :\text{El N}) \to \text{Id N (add } x\,0)\,x$ axiom 1 of add
addS : $(x,y:\text{El N}) \to \text{Id N (add } x\,(S\,y))\,(S\,(\text{add } x\,y))$ axiom 2 of add

Fig. 2. A Signature of Natural Numbers and Addition

4 Implementation

To try out the ideas described in this paper we have implemented a prototype type checker in Haskell. In addition to the logical framework, the type checker supports implicit arguments and the extensions described in Section 7: sigma types, datatypes and definitions by pattern matching.

4.1 Implicit Arguments

A problem with LF as presented here is its rather heavy notation. For instance, to state that function composition is associative one would give the signature in Figure 3.This is very close to being completely illegible due to the fact that we have to be explicit about the type arguments to the composition function. To solve the problem, we have implemented a mechanism for implicit arguments which allows the omission of arguments that can be inferred automatically. Using this mechanism the associativity example can be written as follows:

$comp : (A, B, C : \text{Set}) \to (\text{El } B \to \text{El } C) \to (\text{El } A \to \text{El } B) \to (\text{El } A \to \text{El } C)$
$comp\ A\ B\ C\ f\ g = \lambda x.\ f\,(g\,x)$

$assoc : (A, B, C, D : \text{Set}) \to$
$\qquad (f : \text{El } C \to \text{El } D,\ g : \text{El } B \to \text{El } C,\ h : \text{El } A \to \text{El } B) \to$
$\qquad \text{Prf (Id (El } A \to \text{El } D)\ (comp\ A\ C\ D\ f\ (comp\ A\ B\ C\ g\ h))$
$\qquad\qquad\qquad (comp\ A\ B\ D\ (comp\ B\ C\ D\ f\ g)\ h))$

Fig. 3. Associativity without Implicit Arguments

$(\circ)(A, B, C : \mathsf{Set}) : (\mathsf{El}\ B \to \mathsf{El}\ C) \to (\mathsf{El}\ A \to \mathsf{El}\ B) \to (\mathsf{El}\ A \to \mathsf{El}\ C)$
$f \circ g = \lambda x.\ f\,(g\,x)$

$assoc\,(A, B, C, D : \mathsf{Set}) :$
$\quad (f : \mathsf{El}\ C \to \mathsf{El}\ D,\ g : \mathsf{El}\ B \to \mathsf{El}\ C,\ h : \mathsf{El}\ A \to \mathsf{El}\ B) \to$
$\quad \mathsf{Prf}\,(f \circ (g \circ h) == (f \circ g) \circ h)$

In general, we write $x\,(\Delta) : T$ to say that x has type $(\Delta) \to T$ with (Δ) implicit. The scope of the variables in Δ extends to the definition of x (if there is one). For every use of x we require that the instantiation of (Δ) can be inferred using pattern unification [19]. Note that when we have implicit arguments we can replace Id with an infix operator $(==)\,(D : \mathsf{Set}) : \mathsf{El}\ D \to \mathsf{El}\ D \to \mathsf{Prop}$

We conjecture that the conservativity result can be extended to allow the omission of implicit arguments when translating to first-order logic if they can be inferred from the resulting first-order term. In this case we preserve the property that for a well-typed FOL term there exists a unique typing, which is an important lemma in the conservativity theorem. The kind of implicit arguments we work with can most often be inferred in this way. It is doubtful, however, that it would work for other kinds of implicit arguments such as implicit dictionaries used for overloading.

Omitting the implicit arguments, the formula $f \circ (g \circ h) = (f \circ g) \circ h$ in the context $A, B, C, D : \mathsf{Set}, f : \mathsf{El}\ C \to \mathsf{El}\ D, g : \mathsf{El}\ B \to \mathsf{El}\ C, h : \mathsf{El}\ A \to \mathsf{El}\ B$ is translated to

$$f \circ (g \circ h) = (f \circ g) \circ h$$

With this translation, the first-order proofs are human readable and, in many cases, correspond closely to a pen and paper proof.

4.2   The Plug-in Mechanism

The type checker is equipped with a general plug-in interface that makes it easy to experiment with connections to external tools. A plug-in should implement two functions: a *type checking function* which can be called on particular goals in the program, and a *finalization function* which is called after type checking.

To control where the type checking function of a plug-in is invoked we introduce a new form of expressions:

$$\mathsf{Exp} ::= \ldots \mid name\text{-}\mathbf{plugin}(s_1, \ldots, s_n) \qquad \text{invoking a plug-in}$$

where $name$ is the name of a plug-in. It is possible to pass arguments $(s_1, \ldots, s_n)$ to the plug-in. These arguments can be arbitrary expressions which are ignored by the type checker. Hence it is possible to pass ill-typed terms as arguments to a plug-in; it is the responsibility of the plug-in to interpret the arguments. Most plug-ins, of course, expect well-typed arguments and in this case, the plug-in has to invoke the type checker explicitly on its arguments.

4.3   The FOL Plug-in

The connection between LF and FOL has been implemented as a plug-in using the mechanism described above. With this implementation we replace the built-in constant () by a call to the plug-in. The idea is that the plug-in should be responsible for checking the side condition $\Gamma \vdash_{\mathsf{FOL}} P$ in the FOL rule.

An important observation is that decidability of type checking and equality do not depend on the validity of the propositions being checked by the FOL plug-in—nothing will break if the type checker is led to believe that there is an $s : \mathsf{Prf}\bot$. This allows us to delay all first-order reasoning until after type checking. The rationale for doing this is that type checking is cheap and first-order proving is expensive.

Another observation is that it is not feasible to pass the entire context to the prover. Typically, the context contains lots of things that are not needed for the proof, but would rather overwhelm the prover. To solve this problem, we require that any axioms or lemmas needed to prove a particular goal are passed as arguments to the plug-in. This might seem a severe requirement, but bear in mind that the plug-in is intended for simple goals where you already have an idea of the proof.

More formally, the typing rule for calls to the FOL plug-in is

$$\frac{\Gamma \vdash \phi \qquad \Gamma \vdash s_1 : \phi_1 \ \ldots \ \Gamma \vdash s_n : \phi_n}{\Gamma \vdash \mathbf{fol\text{-}plugin}(s_1, \ldots, s_n) : \phi} \ \phi_1, \ldots, \phi_n \vdash_{\mathsf{FOL}} \phi.$$

When faced with a call to a plug-in the type checker calls the type checking function of the plug-in. In this case, the type checking function of the FOL plug-in will verify that the goal is a translatable formula and that the arguments are well-typed proofs of translatable formulæ. If this is the case it will report success to the type checker and store away the side condition in its internal state. After type checking the finalization function of the FOL plug-in is called. For each constraint $\phi_1, \ldots, \phi_n \vdash_{\mathsf{FOL}} \phi$, this function verifies that $[\phi]$ is derivable from $[\phi_1], \ldots, [\phi_n]$ in the resolution calculus by translating the formulæ to clause normal form and feeding them to an external first-order prover (Gandalf, at the moment). If the prover does not manage to find a proof within the given time limit, the plug-in reports an error.

5   Examples

The code in this section has been type checked successfully by our prototype type checker. In fact, the typeset version is automatically generated from the actual code. The type checker can infer which types are Sets and which are Props, so we omit El and Prf in the types.

Natural numbers can be added to the framework by three new constants Nat, $zero$, and $succ$ plus an axiom for mathematical induction.

$Nat \in \mathcal{S}et$
$zero \in Nat$
$succ \in Nat \to Nat$
$indNat\,(P \in Nat \to \mathcal{P}rop) \in P\,zero \to ((n \in Nat) \to P\,n \to P\,(succ\,n)) \to$
$$(m \in Nat) \to P\,m$$

Now we fix a set A and consider relations over A. We want to prove that the transitive closure of a symmetric relation is symmetric as well. We define the notion of symmetry and introduce a symbol for relation composition. We could define $R \circ R' = \lambda x \lambda z \exists z.\, x\, R\, y \wedge y\, R'\, z$, but here we only assume that a symmetric relation composed with itself is also symmetric.

$$A \in Set$$
$$sym \in (A \to A \to Prop) \to Prop$$
$$sym\, R \equiv (x, y \in A) \to R\, x\, y \implies R\, y\, x$$

$$(\circ) \in (A \to A \to Prop) \to (A \to A \to Prop) \to (A \to A \to Prop)$$
$$axSymO \in (R \in A \to A \to Prop) \to sym\, R \to sym\, (R \circ R)$$

We define a monotone chain of approximations $R^{(n)}$ (in the source: $R \,\hat{}\, n$) of the transitive closure, such that two elements will be related in the transitive closure if they are related in some approximation. The main lemma states that all approximations are symmetric, if R is symmetric.

$$(\hat{}\,) \in (A \to A \to Prop) \to Nat \to (A \to A \to Prop)$$
$$axTc \in (R \in A \to A \to Prop) \to (x, y \in A) \to (n \in Nat) \to$$
$$((R \,\hat{}\, succ\, n)\, x\, y \Leftrightarrow (R \,\hat{}\, n)\, x\, y \vee ((R \,\hat{}\, n) \circ (R \,\hat{}\, n))\, x\, y)$$
$$\wedge\, ((R \,\hat{}\, zero)\, x\, y \Leftrightarrow R\, x\, y)$$

$$main \in (R \in A \to A \to Prop) \to sym\, R \to (n \in Nat) \to sym\, (R \,\hat{}\, n)$$
$$main\, R\, h \equiv indNat$$
$$\qquad\quad \text{'} \quad \textbf{fol–plugin}\,(h,\; axTc\, R)$$
$$\qquad\quad (\lambda\, n\, ih \to \textbf{fol–plugin}\,(h,\; axSymO\,(R \,\hat{}\, n)\, ih,\; axTc\, R,\; ih))$$

Induction is performed at the framework level, base and step case are filled by Gandalf. Pretty printed, Gandalf produces the following proof of the step case:

(1)	$\forall xy.\ (R^{(n)} \circ R^{(n)})\, x\, y \implies (R^{(n)} \circ R^{(n)})\, y\, x$	
(2)	$\forall mxy.\ R^{(succ\, m)}\, x\, y \implies (R^{(m)} \circ R^{(m)})\, x\, y \vee R^{(m)}\, x\, y$	
(3)	$\forall mxy.\ (R^{(m)} \circ R^{(m)})\, x\, y \implies R^{(succ\, m)}\, x\, y$	
(4)	$\forall mxy.\ R^{(m)}\, x\, y \implies R^{(succ\, m)}\, x\, y$	
(5)	$\forall xy.\ R^{(n)}\, x\, y \implies R^{(n)}\, y\, x$	
(6)	$R^{(succ\, n)}\, a\, b$	
(7)	$R^{(succ\, n)}\, b\, a \implies \bot$	
(8)	$(R^{(n)} \circ R^{(n)})\, a\, b \vee R^{(n)}\, a\, b$	$(2), (6)$
(9)	$(R^{(n)} \circ R^{(n)})\, b\, a \vee R^{(n)}\, a\, b$	$(1), (8)$
(10)	$R^{(n)}\, a\, b$	$(3), (7), (9)$
(11)	$R^{(n)}\, b\, a$	$(5), (10)$
(12)	$\bot$	$(4), (7), (11)$

The transitive closure is now defined as $TC\,R\,x\,y = \exists n.\,R^{(n)}xy$. To formalize this, we add existential quantification and its proof rules. The final theorem demostrates how existential quantification can be handled in the framework.

$Exists\,(A \in Set) \in (A \to Prop) \to Prop$

$existsI\,(A \in Set)(P \in A \to Prop) \in (x \in A) \to P\,x \to Exists\,P$

$existsE\,(A \in Set)(P \in A \to Prop)(C \in Prop) \in$
$\qquad Exists\,P \to ((x \in A) \to P\,x \to C) \to C$

$TC \in (A \to A \to Prop) \to A \to A \to Prop$

$TC\,R\,x\,y \equiv Exists\,(\lambda\,n \to (R\,\hat{}\,n)\,x\,y)$

$thm \in (R \in A \to A \to Prop) \to sym\,R \to sym\,(TC\,R)$

$thm\,R\,h\,x\,y \equiv impI\,(\lambda\,p \to$
$\qquad existsE\,p\,(\lambda\,n\,q \to existsI\,n\,\mathbf{fol-plugin}(q,\,main\,R\,h\,n)))$

See the extended version [2] for an example involving algebra and induction.

6   Related Work

Smith and Tammet [24] also combine Martin-Löf type theory and first-order logic, which was the original motivation for creating the system Gandalf. The main difference to their work is that we use implicit typing and restrict to quantifier-free formulæ. An advantage is that we have a simple translation, and hence get a quite direct connection to resolution theorem provers. Hence, we can hope, and this has been tested positively in several examples, that the proof traces we get from the prover are readable as such and therefore can been used as a proof certificate or as feedback for the user. For instance, the user can formulate new lemmas suggested by this proof trace. We think that this aspect of readability is more important than creating an explicit proof term in type theory (which would actually be less readable). It should be stressed that our conservativity result contains, since it is constructive, an algorithm that can transform the resolution proof to a proof in type theory, if this is needed.

Huang et. al. [13] present the design of Ω-MKRP[6], a tool for the working mathematician based on higher-order classical logic, with a facility of proof planning, access to a mathematical database of theorems and proof tactics (called methods), and a connection to first-order automated provers. Their article is a well-written motivation for the integration of human and machine reasoning, where they envision a similar division of labor as we have implemented. We have, however, not addressed the problem of mathematical knowledge management and proof tactics.

Wick and McCune [26] list three options for connecting type systems and FOL: include type literals, put type functions around terms, or use implicit typing. We rediscovered the technique of implicit typing and found out later that it is present already in the work of Beeson [4]. Our work shows that this can also be used with dependent

---

[6] Markgraf Karl Refutation Procedure.

types, which is not obvious a priori. Our formulation of the correctness properties, as a conservativity statement, requires some care (with the role of the sort Prop), and is an original contribution.

Bezem, Hendriks, and de Nivelle [7] describe how to transform a resolution proof to a proof term for *any* first-order formula. However, the resulting proof terms are hard to read for a human because of the use of skolemisation and reduction to clausal forms. Furthermore, they restrict to a fixed first-order domain.

Hurd's work on a Gandalf-tactic for HOL [14] is along the same lines. He translates untyped first-order HOL goals to clause form, sends them to Gandalf and constructs an LCF proof from the Gandalf output. In later work [15,16] he handles types by having two translations: the untyped translation, and a translation with explicit types. The typed translation is only used when the untyped translation results in an ill-typed proof.

JProver [23] is a connection-based intuitionistic theorem prover which produces proof objects. It has been integrated into NuPrl and Coq. The translation from type theory to first-order logic involves some heuristics when to include or discard type information. Unfortunately, the description [23] does not contain formal systems or correctness arguments, but focuses on the connection technology.

Jia Meng and Paulson [18] have carried out substantial experiments on how to integrate the resolution theorem prover Vampire into the interactive proof tool Isabelle. Their translation from higher-order logic (HOL) to first-order logic keeps type information, since HOL supports overloading via axiomatic type classes and discarding type information for overloaded symbols would lead to unsound reasoning. They claim to cut down the search space via type information, but this is also connected to overloading. The aim of their work is different to ours: while they use first-order provers to do as much automatic proofs and proof search as possible, we employ automation only to liberate the user from seemingly trivial proof steps.

In Coq, NuPrl, and Isabelle, the user constructs a proof via tactics. We provide type theory as a proof language in which the user writes down a proof skeleton, consisting of lemmas, scoped hypotheses, invocation of induction, and major proof steps. The first-order prover is invoked to solve (easy) subgoals. This way, we hope to obtain human-readable proof documents (see our examples).

7 Conclusion and Future Work

We have described the implementation of a logical framework with proof-irrelevant propositions and its connection to the first-order prover Gandalf. Soundness and conservativity of the connection have been established by general theorems.

It is natural to extend LF by sigma types, in order to represent, for instance, mathematical structures. The extension of the translation to FOL is straightforward, we simply add a new binary function symbols for representing pairs. A more substantial extension is the addition of data type and functions defined by case [21]. In this extension, it is possible to represent each connective as a parameterized data type. Each introduction rule is represented by a constructor, and the elimination rules are represented by functions defined by cases. This gives a computational justification of each of the axioms of the signature Σ_{nat}. The extension of the translation to FOL is also straightforward: each defined equations for functions becomes a FOL equality. One needs also to express that each constructor is one-to-one and that terms with distinct constructors are distinct.

We plan to the extend the conservativity theorem to implicit arguments as presented in Section 4.1. We also think that we can extend our class of translatable formulæ, for instance, to include some cases of existential quantification.

One could think of adding more plug-ins, with the same principle that they are justified by a general meta-theorem. For instance, one could add a plug-in to a model checker, or a plug-in to a system with a decision procedure for Presburger arithmetic.

Acknowledgments. We thank all the members of the Cover project, especially Koen Claessen for discussions on implicit typing and the clausification tool Santa for a uniform connection to FOL provers, and Grégoire Hamon for programming the clausifier of the FOL plug-in in a previous version.

References

1. Andreas Abel and Thierry Coquand. Untyped algorithmic equality for Martin-Löf's logical framework with surjective pairs. In Paweł Urzyczyn, editor, *TLCA'05*, volume 3461 of *LNCS*, pages 23–38. Springer, April 2005.
2. Andreas Abel, Thierry Coquand, and Ulf Norell. Connecting a logical framework to a first-order logic prover (extended version). Technical report, Department of Computing Science, Chalmers University of Technology, Gothenburg, Sweden, 2005. Available under http://www.cs.chalmers.se/~ulfn/papers/fol.html.
3. Thorsten Altenkirch, Conor McBride, and James McKinna. Why dependent types matter. Manuscript, available online, April 2005.
4. Michael Beeson. Otter-λ home page, 2005. URL: http://mh215a.cs.sjsu.edu/.
5. Yves Bertot and Pierre Castéran. *Interactive Theorem Proving and Program Development. Coq'Art: The Calculus of Inductive Constructions*. Texts in Theoretical Computer Science. An EATCS Series. Springer, 2004.
6. Marc Bezem and Thierry Coquand. Newman's lemma – a case study in proof automation and geometric logic. *Bulletin of the EATCS*, 79:86–100, 2003. Logic in Computer Science Column.
7. Marc Bezem, Dimitri Hendriks, and Hans de Nivelle. Automated proof construction in type theory using resolution. *JAR*, 29(3–4):253–275, 2002. Special Issue *Mechanizing and Automating Mathematics: In honour of N.G. de Bruijn*.
8. Koen Claessen and John Hughes. QuickCheck: a lightweight tool for random testing of Haskell programs. *ACM SIGPLAN Notices*, 35(9):268–279, 2000.
9. Catarina Coquand and Thierry Coquand. Structured type theory. In *Workshop on Logical Frameworks and Meta-languages (LFM'99)*, Paris, France, September 1999.
10. Michel Coste, Henri Lombardi, and Marie-Françoise Roy. Dynamical methods in algebra: Effective Nullstellensätze. *APAL*, 111(3):203–256, 2001.
11. Niklas G. de Bruijn. A survey of the project Automath. In J. P. Seldin and J. R. Hindley, editors, *To H. B. Curry: Essays in combinatory logic, lambda calculus and formalism*, pages 579–606, London-New York, 1980. Academic Press.
12. Gerhard Gentzen. Untersuchungen über das logische Schließen. *Mathematische Zeitschrift*, 39:176–210, 405–431, 1935.
13. Xiaorong Huang, Manfred Kerber, Michael Kohlhase, Erica Melis, Dan Nesmith, Jörn Richts, and Jörg H. Siekmann. Omega-MKRP: A proof development environment. In Alan Bundy, editor, *CADE'94*, volume 814 of *LNCS*, pages 788–792. Springer, 1994.

14. Joe Hurd. Integrating Gandalf and HOL. In Yves Bertot, Gilles Dowek, André Hirschowitz, Christine Paulin, and Laurent Théry, editors, *TPHOLS'99*, volume 1690 of *LNCS*, pages 311–321. Springer, September 1999.

15. Joe Hurd. An LCF-style interface between HOL and first-order logic. In Andrei Voronkov, editor, *CADE'02*, volume 2392 of *LNAI*, pages 134–138. Springer, 2002.

16. Joe Hurd. First-order proof tactics in higher-order logic theorem provers. In Myla Archer, Ben Di Vito, and César Muñoz, editors, *STRATA'03*, number CP-2003-212448 in NASA Technical Reports, pages 56–68, September 2003.

17. Leslie Lamport. How to write a proof. In *Global Analysis in Modern Mathematics*, pages 311–321. Publish or Perish, Houston, Texas, U.S.A., February 1993. Also appeared as SRC Research Report 94.

18. Jia Meng and Lawrence C. Paulson. Experiments on supporting interactive proof using resolution. In David A. Basin and Michaël Rusinowitch, editors, *IJCAR'04*, volume 3097 of *LNCS*, pages 372–384. Springer, 2004.

19. Dale Miller. Unification under a mixed prefix. *J. Symb. Comput.*, 14(4):321–358, 1992.

20. Bengt Nordström, Kent Petersson, and Jan Smith. Martin-Löf's type theory. In *Handbook of Logic in Computer Science*, volume 5. OUP, October 2000.

21. Bengt Nordström, Kent Petersson, and Jan M. Smith. *Programming in Martin Löf's Type Theory: An Introduction.* Clarendon Press, Oxford, 1990.

22. John Alan Robinson. A machine-oriented logic based on the resolution principle. *JACM*, 12(1):23–41, January 1965.

23. Stephan Schmitt, Lori Lorigo, Christoph Kreitz, and Aleksey Nogin. JProver: Integrating connection-based theorem proving into interactive proof assistants. In R. Gore, A. Leitsch, and T. Nipkow, editors, *IJCAR'01*, volume 2083 of *LNAI*, pages 421–426. Springer, 2001.

24. Jan M. Smith and Tanel Tammet. Optimized encodings of fragments of type theory in first-order logic. In Stefano Berardi and Mario Coppo, editors, *TYPES'95*, volume 1158 of *LNCS*, pages 265–287. Springer, 1995.

25. Tanel Tammet. Gandalf. *JAR*, 18(2):199–204, 1997.

26. Cynthia A. Wick and William McCune. Automated reasoning about elementary point-set topology. *JAR*, 5(2):239–255, 1989.

Combination of Isabelle/HOL with Automatic Tools

Sergey Tverdyshev *

Saarland University, Germany
deru@wjpserver.cs.uni-sb.de

Abstract. We describe results and status of a sub project of the Verisoft [1] project. While the Verisoft project aims at verification of a complete computer system starting with hardware and up to user applications, the goal of our sub project is an efficient *hardware* verification.

We use the Isabelle theorem prover [2] as the major tool for hardware design and verification. Since many hardware verification problems can be efficiently solved by automatic tools, we combine Isabelle with model checkers and SAT solvers. This combination of tools speeds up verification of hardware and simplifies sharing of the results with verification of the whole computer system. To increase the range of problems which can be solved by external tools we implemented in Isabelle several algorithms for handling uninterpreted functions and data abstraction.

The resulting combination was applied to verify many different hardware circuits, automata, and processors.

In our project we use open source tools that are free for academical and commercial purposes.

1 Introduction

In large verification projects such as verification of a complete computer system the linking of verification results from different parts plays a major role. Specifying and proving all theorems within one environment, e.g. a higher order logic (HOL) theorem prover, makes linking a lot easier. Such a combination is also much safer because verification gaps, due to a manual transfer of the results from one system into another, are excluded. This was one of the motivations for this work.

In a long-term project Verisoft we are currently working on verification of a computer system starting with hardware, going through compiler, operating system kernel, operating system and up to end user applications. The main verification tool for all parts of the project is the Isabelle theorem prover for higher order logic. Because many hardware verification problems can be efficiently solved by external automatic tools, we combined Isabelle with the NuSMV model checker [3] and SAT solvers. In this paper we describe the result of the combination and demonstrate applications of this combination for hardware verification.

* Supported by The Verisoft Project under grant 01 IS C38 of the German Ministry for Education and Research (BMBF)

B. Gramlich (Ed.): FroCoS 2005, LNAI 3717, pp. 302–309, 2005.

2 Related Work

The most recent combination external tools into Isabelle was done through input-output automata [4]. In this work the user gives a model and manually defines its abstraction. Then an LTL model checker is used to prove temporal properties of the abstracted model and a μ-calculus model checker is used to check forward simulations between these two models. A drawback is that defining a suitable abstraction for a big model can be a very hard task. On the contrary, our approach does not have this disadvantage because an abstracted model is derived fully automatically.

An interesting ongoing work of L. Paulson's group [5] is the integration of the first oder theorem prover SPASS [6] into Isabelle. A highlight of the integration is that SPASS proofs can be converted into Isabelle proofs and then rechecked by Isabelle. In this approach the user does not have to trust an external tool, and soundness of the translation can be guaranteed. However, at the moment the integration is experimental and has only a very basic functionality.

The UCLID system [7] is another interesting tool that can handle big problems with great automation. It also has a lot of built-in features, e.g. handling of uninterpreted functions, efficient algorithms for term reduction. The UCLID system is mostly used for verification of invariants of a system (safety properties) but liveness properties (directly) are missing [7]. Even though the UCLID system is more powerful than our tool, our approach allows verification of liveness properties directly. Furthermore we believe that *complete* automatic abstraction, as we implemented, is more suitable for an automatic proof tool. Integration with Isabelle increases the domain of application of our tool but we have to pay for that with user's involvement in proof process. Last but not the least: UCLID is distributed as a close source system with a strict license.

The rest of the paper is organized as follows. In the Section 3 we present the used tools. Section 4 provides subset of the HOL we use to specify hardware. In Section 5 the main functionalities of the translation tool are presented. Section 6 reports results of applications of the resulting system to hardware verification.

3 Tools

The Theorem Prover. Isabelle [2] is a generic theorem prover that supports several object logics. We use Isabelle with its instantiation of HOL. We refer to it as Isabelle/HOL.

The Modelchecker. NuSMV [3] is a symbolic model checker for CTL and LTL properties. It can perform bounded model checking using an external SAT solver. We used NuSMV to verify temporal properties of our models and as an external BDD decision procedure.

SAT Solvers. We implemented an algorithm to convert given problems into propositional logic extended by uninterpreted functions and linear arithmetic. Using this algorithm we can easily bind almost any SAT solver.

We bind these tools to Isabelle/HOL through the Oracle interface. Translation of a problem from Isabelle/HOL into language of an external tool is done by the translation tool

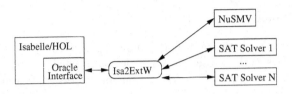

Fig. 1. Isabelle/HOL and External Tools

Isa2ExtW. We implemented Isa2ExtW as a decision procedure in Isabelle/HOL. An overview of the connection is shown in Figure 1. Isa2ExtW performs not only syntax translation but also several semantic transformations, e.g. data abstraction.

4   Subset of HOL for Hardware Design and Verification

Most of our verification problems can be split up into a number of smaller problems which can be solved automatically by one or the other external tool. However as none of these tools can solve our problem entirely, we still need Isabelle/HOL and Isa2ExtW as central instance. To allow translation of our theorems into the language of external tools we need to specify a suitable subset of Isabelle's HOL. Note that this subset has to be translatable into VHDL [8] in order to get synthesizable hardware.

4.1   Types

A fragment of the Isabelle/HOL language to be translated into external tools consists of expressions involving types which are finite. Examples of such types are scalar types, lists of constant length, records constructed from finite types and each other.

4.2   Subtyping

As we have already mentioned we are mostly interested in finite types. However, some infinite data types, namely their subtypes are interesting for us as well[1]. Since there are no subtypes in Isabelle/HOL, we have to define a mechanism for encoding subtype information into our models. For this purpose we created in Isabelle/HOL a library of predicate sets[2]. For the given predicate a *predicate set* defines the set of all elements satisfying this predicate. By means of predicate sets we reduce types in our models to desired finite subtypes. This information is added to the set of assumptions of a theorem we want to prove by external tools. A drawback is that the model will be correct with respect to the specified subtypes. However, the property will be proved automatically. This idea can be easily described by the following example:

Bit vectors in Isabelle/HOL are represented as lists of bits, possibly of infinite length. However, in general we are interested in the lists of a constant length only to allow synthesis of real hardware. Thus, additional information about the length of bit vectors has to be provided. We illustrate our approach on a model of a shifter: suppose

---

[1] Using data abstraction we can handle infinite types (see Section 5.2).

[2] Full description of the library can be found at http://busserver.cs.uni-sb.de

we want to perform an equality test of two functions sh_impl and sh_spec which are implementation and specification of the shifter respectively. The desired lemma could be formulated in Isabelle/HOL as follows:

```
∀ op. ∀ d. ∀ r. ∀ a.
sh_impl(op, d, r, a) = sh_spec(op, d, r, a)
```

This theorem would state that for all bit vectors to be shifted (op), for all shift distances (d), and for all boolean flags r, a the implementation and the specification return the same result. In this theorem the bit vectors op and d can have arbitrary length. However, for our purpose it is enough to show the correctness for op of length 32 and for d of length 5. To describe these subtypes we use parametrized predicate set bv_n from our library. For the given natural number n it defines the set of all bit vectors of the length n. We add an assumption that inputs are from the desired subsets and the theorem in Isabelle/HOL is formulated as follows:

```
∀ op ∈ bv_n(32). ∀ d ∈ bv_n(5). ∀ r. ∀a.
sh_impl(op, d, r, a) = sh_spec(op, d, r, a)
```

This goal is easily discharged by an external tool through a call of Isa2ExtW as a proof method. An advantage of this approach is that the original model is not influenced by any subtyping information, and can be easily reused for other goals. In a similar fashion we handle arrays, records etc., i.e. for each of them we defined a predicate set.

4.3 Operators

There are several operators which are substituted by analogous operators in a target external tool (e.g. boolean connectives) or interpreted by Isa2ExtW (e.g. basic operations on lists as head, tail). The list of such operators can be roughly described as follows: boolean connectives, bit operations, linear arithmetic operators, basic operations on lists, and update of variables of function types.

4.4 Functions

A drawback of the absence of subtypes in Isabelle/HOL is that we can not restrict function inputs to desired subtypes. There are two solutions (i) handle cases of undesirable inputs in the definition of a function; (ii) formally guarantee absence of that inputs.

The first solution allows using functions with any input and functions will return expected results. However, a drawback is that extra handling can be inconvertible into external tools or into VHDL, e.g. in physical sense the behaviour of a circuit for an empty bit vector is unclear. With the second solution the user does not handle undesired input. In this case for some inputs a circuit will have undesired but well-defined behaviour. The absence of undesirable inputs is guaranteed by the use of a function, namely we prove properties about a model for a clearly defined set of inputs (see Section 4.2).

Non-recursive functions will be translated into external tools as they are, i.e. using their definitions. The returned type of a function is computed on the fly by Isa2ExtW and must be one of the supported types, otherwise an error will be raised.

Recursive Functions. For translation of recursive definitions into external tools we support recursions on natural numbers and on the length of a list. Based on earlier experience in hardware design and verification [9,10] these two types of recursion are enough to describe all constructions we need to build and verify a processor. Our translation algorithm unrolls a recursive definition in a set of non-recursive definitions. Initial value for recursion is taken from the current input of a function. Unrolling rules are taken from the original recursive definition.

Uninterpreted Functions. Sometimes it is very useful to abstract a functional unit as an uninterpreted function, e.g. while verifying datapaths of a processor. We defined a simple mechanism to specify uninterpreted functions in our models. To force Isa2ExtW to translate a function as an uninterpreted function, the user has to specify input/output interfaces of the function. It includes the name of the function and predicate sets for inputs and outputs of the function, e.g. "$\forall$ a $\in$ bv_n(32). foo(a) $\in$ bv_n(5)". For the given example Isa2ExtW will not look up the definition of function foo. The tool will replace it by an uninterpreted function foo which takes a bit vector of length 32 and returns a bit vector of length 5. The restriction is that such a function can not be updated. The usage of such a function is controlled by Isa2ExtW.

5 Isa2ExtW

In this section we describe some functionalities of Isa2ExtW.

5.1 Uninterpreted Functions

When verifying processors big storages such as general purpose registers or memories have to be modelled. It is convenient to represent memories as uninterpreted functions. In our library we have a parametrized predicate set which for the two given predicate sets A and B returns the set of functions A $\rightarrow$ B. The only restriction is that the input predicate sets themselves can not be sets of functions. Direct translation of such types into the mentioned external decision procedures is unpractical because of the size. To avoid this limitation we implemented a simple but efficient algorithm for elimination of variables of function types. The idea was taken from [11]. This algorithm consists of three parts: (i) representation of the variables of a function type (memories) as uninterpreted functions, (ii) elimination of memories updates by if-then-else expressions and (iii) elimination of applications of uninterpreted functions by nested if-then-else expressions. For more details we refer the reader to [11].

5.2 Data Abstraction

To counter act the state explosion problem we implemented a data abstraction algorithm based on symmetry reduction [12]. Implementations of Dill's idea usually include a type constructor scalar type, e.g. [7,13]. This constructor defines an abstract type on which the symmetry reduction can be done. In contrast, our implementation works *completely automatically*. For the given model it finds, on the fly, all variables which can be abstracted, exploiting data symmetry of the model. The new reduced model is constructed *automatically* as well.

Often implementations of symmetry reduction can not handle constants, e.g. when we compare a variable with a constant we can not apply symmetry reduction to that variable (a drawback of SMV [13]). We solved the problem by introducing a new unique symbolic value for every constant and adding it to the definition of abstracted type. We exploit advantages of this feature in processor verification. In our models of processors we have bit vectors of length 32 and we use a few constants of this type, e.g. 32 zeroes. Application of our symmetry reduction algorithm reduces the state space of such a variable from 2^{32} just to *number of variables + number of constants*.

Another advantage of our implementation is that uninterpreted functions do not break symmetry of the model. Since the result of the application of an uninterpreted function does not depend on input, then, from the symmetry point of view, such application splits the model into two independent parts. These are: arguments of function and the result of application. We apply the abstraction algorithm independently on both parts. The effect is that even if the result cannot be abstracted then arguments may be abstracted and vice versa. The idea behind this is a combination of algorithms for elimination of uninterpreted functions and symmetry reduction. Consider the following example. In equality (1) f is supposed to be an uninterpreted function. Bryant et. al. [11] proved that (2) holds. After application of symmetry reduction[3] we come to (3). Where variables da', db' and a', b' have abstracted types. By applying the Bryant theorem in reverse direction we can conclude that there exists an uninterpreted function f' with the same domain/range type as the type of a'/da' (4).

```
f(a) = f(b)                                                          (1)
f(a) = f(b)      ↔ da = (if a = b then da else db)                  (2)
                    da' = (if a' = b' then da' else db') (3)
f'(a') = f'(b')                                                      (4)
```

Our implementation abstracts applications of uninterpreted functions in only one step. This feature *increases significantly* the range of models where the abstraction algorithm can succeed. It allows hiding symmetry-breaking functions by declaring them as uninterpreted functions. It leads not only to a reduced state space of the model but also to a reduced number of terms the model consists of. These all will result in faster verification.

5.3 SAT Solving

All problems which are specified according to the rules presented above can be converted to propositional logic and solved by an external SAT solver. If the model contains linear arithmetic, the external tool should have a decision procedure for it. Ourself we do not require from SAT solvers to support uninterpreted functions, since we can handle them. However, native support of them may speed up the verification process[4].

5.4 Model Checking

Models to be model-checked have to be represented as finite state machines (FSM). To define such a machine the user has to provide a next-state function, a set of states and

---

[3] Without support of uninterpreted functions.
[4] E.g. by usage of ModuSAT [14] after solving some performance problems.

a set of initial states. To express temporal properties of FSM's we specified CTL and LTL in Isabelle/HOL. FSM and CTL/LTL are combined in simple interface functions $\models_{LTL}$ and $\models_{CTL}$:

$$\text{for } LTL: \text{(States, Init, NSF)} \models_{LTL} \text{LTL\_formula}$$
$$\text{for } CTL: \text{(States, Init, NSF)} \models_{CTL} \text{CTL\_formula},$$

where States is a predicate set as described earlier, Init is a predicate on the state type and NSF is a next state function. LTL_formula and CTL_formula are properties in LTL and CTL respectively. The user has to take care that the Init predicate holds at least for one state from States. Otherwise the results of verification can be nonsense.

Optionally the user can turn off the algorithm for elimination of applications of uninterpreted functions. In this case such a function will be represented in NuSMV as an additional state variable. The type of that variable is an array of the domain type of the function. The size of the array is computed based on the type of the range of the function. We do not put any transition constraints on the behaviour of that variable and it can change non-deterministically along the time. It captures behaviour of an uninterpreted function. If the abstraction algorithm does not succeed then application of NuSMV may be inefficient because of the size of the state space. However, usually[5] the abstraction algorithm succeeds and we can use model checking technique even for *models containing uninterpreted functions and memories.*

6   Results and Future Work

We used the Isa2ExtW tool for verification of many combinational circuits. For example we automatically verified all hardware components of our processors such as shifters, decoders, encoders, parallel prefix or-operation etc. by an external SAT solver and NuSMV. We automatically verified a simple sequential DLX [15] processor using uninterpreted functions.

Verification of a pipelined DLX processor featuring 3-stage forwarding and stalling was a more challenging task. We took proofs of the processor from [16,10] as a base. We built models of specification and implementation in Isabelle/HOL. Then the proof was started in Isabelle/HOL. We interactively distinguished major cases of the proof and got subgoals which were discharged by a SAT solver. Uninterpreted functions were heavily used to simplify verification of datapaths of the processor. Through instantiation of uninterpreted functions by concrete verified functions in verified datapaths, the correctness proof could be completed. The liveness of the processor was verified completely automatically. Applying our method as front-end to NuSMV, we were even able to model-check models with big storages (e.g. data memory, general purpose registers) and uninterpreted functions (e.g. arithmetic-logical unit). In this manner we got a completely verified processor on the gate level. Our method significantly improves verification of a similar processor in [10] because the user is no longer required to prove "simple" subgoals manually.

---

[5] For the models we verified, see section 6.

We incorporated the NuSMV model checker to verify automata for the memory management unit [17] and automata for a replacing policy in a cache system [9].

In order to get synthesizable hardware we aim towards a tool which will translate our hardware specifications from Isabelle/HOL into VHDL. The next benchmark for our method is verification of an out-of-order DLX processor featuring Tomasulo algorithm, precise interrupts and memory management unit [16,10,9].

References

1. The Verisoft Consortium: The Verisoft Project. http://www.verisoft.de/ (2003)
2. Paulson, L.C.: Isabelle - A generic theorem prover. LNCS **828** (1994)
3. Cimatti, A., Clarke, E.M., Giunchiglia, E., Giunchiglia, F., Marco Pistore, M.R., Sebastiani, R., Tacchella, A.: NuSMV 2: An open source tool for symbolic model checking. In: CAV '02, Springer-Verlag (2002) 359–364
4. Müller, O.: A Verification Environment for I/O Automata Based on Formalized Meta-Theory. PhD thesis, Techn. Univ. Munich (1998)
5. Larry Paulson: Larry Paulson's home page. (http://www.cl.cam.ac.uk/users/lcp/)
6. Weidenbach, C., Brahm, U., Hillenbrand, T., Keen, E., Theobalt, C., Topic', D.: SPASS version 2.0. In Voronkov, A., ed.: Automated deduction, CADE-18. Volume 2392 of Lecture Notes in Artificial Intelligence., Kopenhagen, Denmark, Springer (2002) 275–279
7. Lahiri, S.K., Seshia, S.A., Bryant, R.E.: Modeling and verification of out-of-order microprocessors in uclid. In: FMCAD '02, London, UK, Springer-Verlag (2002) 142–159
8. Ashenden, P.J.: The Designer's Guide to VHDL. Morgan Kaufmann Publishers Inc. (1999)
9. Beyer, S., Jacobi, C., Kröning, D., Leinenbach, D., Paul, W.: Putting it all together formal verification of the VAMP, to appear in STTT, Springer-Verlag (2005)
10. Kröning, D.: Formal Verification of Pipelined Microprocessors. PhD thesis, Saarland University, Computer Science Department (2001)
11. Bryant, R.E., German, S.M., Velev, M.N.: Microprocessor verification using efficient decision procedures for a logic of equality with uninterpreted functions. In: TABLEAUX '99, Springer-Verlag (1999) 1–13
12. Ip, C.N., Dill, D.L.: Better verification through symmetry. Form. Methods Syst. Des. **9** (1996) 41–75
13. McMillan, K.L.: The SMV language. Technical report, Berkeley Labs (1999)
14. Prevosto, V.: ModuProve Developer and User Manual. Max-Planck Institut für Informatik – Verisoft Project. (2005)
15. Patterson, D.A., Hennessy, J.L.: Computer architecture: a quantitative approach. Morgan Kaufmann Publishers Inc. (1995)
16. Müller, S.M., Paul, W.J.: Computer Architecture: Complexity and Correctness. Springer-Verlag New York, Inc. (2000)
17. Dalinger, I., Hillebrand, M., Paul, W.J.: On the verification of memory management mechanisms. Technical report, Saarland University (2005)

ATS: A Language That Combines Programming with Theorem Proving

Sa Cui, Kevin Donnelly, and Hongwei Xi

Computer Science Department,
Boston University
{cuisa, kevind, hwxi}@cs.bu.edu

Abstract. ATS is a language with a highly expressive type system that supports a restricted form of dependent types in which programs are not allowed to appear in type expressions. The language is separated into two components: a proof language in which (inductive) proofs can be encoded as (total recursive) functions that are erased before execution, and a programming language for constructing programs to be evaluated. This separation enables a paradigm that combines programming with theorem proving. In this paper, we illustrate by example how this programming paradigm is supported in ATS.

1 Introduction

The framework *Pure Type System* (*PTS*) [1] offers a simple and general approach to designing and formalizing type systems. However, *PTS* makes it difficult, especially, in the presence of dependent types to accommodate many common realistic programming features, such as general recursion [7], recursive types [11], effects [10] (e.g., exceptions [9], references, input/output), etc. To address such limitations of *PTS*, the framework *Applied Type System* (*ATS*) [14] has been proposed to allow for designing and formalizing (advanced) type systems in support of practical programming. The key salient feature of *ATS* lies in a complete separation of the statics, in which types are formed and reasoned about, from the dynamics, in which programs are constructed and evaluated. With this separation, it is no longer possible for programs to occur in type expressions as is otherwise allowed in *PTS*.

Currently, ATS, a language with a highly expressive type system rooted in the framework *ATS*, is under active development. In ATS, a variety of programming paradigms are supported in a typeful manner, including functional programming, object-oriented programming [3], imperative programming with pointers [16] and modular programming. There is also a theorem proving component in ATS [4] that allows the programmer to encode (inductive) proofs as (total recursive) functions, supporting a paradigm that combines programming with theorem proving [5]. This is fundamentally different from the paradigm of extracting programs from proofs as is done in systems such as Coq [2] and NuPrl [6]. In ATS, proofs are completely erased before execution, while proofs in Coq, for example, are not. In addition, ATS allows the construction of programs involving

B. Gramlich (Ed.): FroCoS 2005, LNAI 3717, pp. 310–320, 2005.

$$
\begin{array}{rl}
\text{sorts} & \sigma ::= b \mid \sigma_1 \rightarrow \sigma_2 \\
\text{static terms} & s ::= a \mid \lambda a : \sigma.\, s \mid s_1(s_2) \mid sc(s_1, ..., s_n) \\
\text{sta. var. ctx.} & \Sigma ::= \emptyset \mid \Sigma, a : \sigma
\end{array}
$$

$$
\begin{array}{rl}
\text{dynamic terms} & d ::= x \mid dc(d_1, ..., d_n) \mid \mathbf{lam}\ x.d \mid \mathbf{fix}\ x.d \mid \mathbf{app}(d_1, d_2) \mid \lambda a : \sigma.d \mid d(s) \mid ... \\
\text{values} & v ::= x \mid dcc(v_1, ..., v_n) \mid \mathbf{lam}\ x.d \mid ... \\
\text{dyn. var. ctx.} & \Delta ::= \emptyset \mid \Delta, x : T
\end{array}
$$

Fig. 1. Abstract syntax for statics and dynamics of ATS

effects (e.g., non-termination, exceptions, references), which on the other hand are difficult to properly address in Coq.

The current implementation of ATS [15] is written in Objective Caml, which mainly consists of a type-checker and an interpreter, and a compiler from ATS to C is under active development. The entire implementation (including source code) is made available to the public, and a tutorial is also provided for explaining a variety of language features in ATS. In this paper, we focus on a unique feature in ATS that combines programming with theorem proving, and illustrate by example how this kind of programming paradigm is supported in ATS.

2   Overview of ATS

Some formal syntax of ATS is shown in Figure 1. The language ATS has two components: the static component (statics) which includes types, props and type indices and the dynamic component (dynamics) which includes programs and proof terms. The statics itself is a simply typed language and a type in it is referred to as a *sort*. For instance, we have the following base sorts in ATS: *addr*, *bool*, *int*, *prop*, *type*, *view*, *viewtype*, etc. Static terms L, B, I of sorts *addr*, *bool* and *int* are referred to as static address, boolean and integer terms, respectively. Static terms T of sort *type* are types of program terms, and static terms P of sort *prop*, referred to as props, are types of proof terms. Proof terms exist only to show that their types are inhabited (in order to prove constraints on type indices). Since the type system guarantees that proof functions are total, we may simply erase proof terms after type-checking. We also allow linear proof terms, which are assigned a view V, of sort *view*. Since it is legal to use non-linear proofs as linear ones, we have that *prop* is a subsort of *view* and *type* is a subsort of *viewtype*.

Types, props and views may depend on one or more type indices of static sorts. A special case of such indexed types are singleton types, which are each a type for only one specific value. For instance, $\mathbf{int}(I)$ is a singleton type for the integer equal to I, and $\mathbf{ptr}(L)$ is a singleton type for the pointer that points to the address (or location) L.

We combine proofs with programs using *proving types* of the form $(V \mid T)$ where V and T stand for static terms of sort *view* and *type*, respectively. A proving type formed with a view is assigned the sort *viewtype*; if V can be assigned a prop then we can assign the proving type the sort *type*. We may

	Assigned To	Purity/Linearity
sort	type/prop/view indices	pure
prop	proof terms	pure
type	program terms	effectful
view	linear proof terms	pure, linear
viewtype	program terms with embedded linear proofs	effectful, linear

Fig. 2. Sorts, props, types, views and viewtypes in ATS

think of the proving type $(V \mid T)$ as a refinement of the type T because V often constrains some of the indices appearing in T. For example, the following type:

$$(\mathbf{ADD}(m,n,p) \mid \mathbf{int}(m) * \mathbf{int}(n) * \mathbf{int}(p))$$

is a proving type of sort *type* for a tuple of integers (m,n,p) along with a proof of the prop $\mathbf{ADD}(m,n,p)$ which encodes $m + n = p$ (as is explained later). In the case of props which are linear constraints on integers, or more precisely, constraints on integers that can be transformed into linear integer programming problems, ATS can handle them implicitly, without proofs. Given a linear constraint C and a type T, we have two special forms of types: asserting types of the form $C \wedge T$ and guarded types of the form $C \supset T$. Note that $C \wedge T$ is essentially the proving type $(C \mid T)$, and $C \supset T$ is essentially the type $(C \mid 1) \rightarrow T$, except that assertions and guards are proved and discharged automatically by a built-in decision procedure. Following is an example involving singleton, guarded and asserting types:

$$\forall a : int.a \geq 0 \supset (\mathbf{int}(a) \rightarrow \exists a' : int.(a' < 0) \wedge \mathbf{int}(a'))$$

The meaning of this type should be clear: Each value that can be assigned this type represents a function from nonnegative integers to negative integers.

3   Data-Classes in ATS

In ATS it is possible to introduce user defined data-classes which can be sorts, types, props, or views. The intended uses and properties of these classes are described in Figure 2. The syntax for data-class introduction is inspired by that of SML. A new base sort for binary trees of integers can be defined by:

```
datasort itr = leaf | node of (int, itr, itr)
```

Sorts may also be higher order. For example, the sort of higher-order abstract syntax (HOAS) for pure lambda calculus is defined by:

```
datasort tm = ap of (tm,tm) | lm of (tm -> tm)
```

Because there is no recursion in the statics we can allow negative occurrences of the sort being declared without sacrificing strong normalization of static terms.

One may also define datatypes similarly to datatypes in SML. The main difference is that in ATS datatypes may be indexed by static terms and the datatype constructors may universally quantify over static term variables. For example, the following is a datatype for lists which has two indices: one for the type of elements of the list and the other for the length of the list.

```
datatype list (type, int) =
  {a:type} nil (a, 0) | {a:type, n:nat} cons (a, n+1) of (a, list (a, n))
```

Sorts are used as type indices and are often universally quantified over in function and data(prop/type/view/viewtype) definitions. The syntax {n:nat} stands for universal quantification of n over the sort *nat*. Universal quantification can also be guarded by one or more constraints, as in {n:int | n >= 0}. The sort *nat* is a subset sort, which is really just a sort with an attached constraint, so {n:nat} is equivalent to {n:int | n >= 0}. Notice that in the definition of the datatype **list**(*type, int*), the second index is of sort *int*, yet the constructors can only create terms whose type has a *nat* in that position. The reason for this is that we do not want well-sortedness of statics to depend on solving constraints. So, there is nothing ill-formed about the type *list*(*a*, −1), though it is uninhabited.

Dataprops may be introduced with syntax similar to that for datatypes. For example, the following is a dataprop for proofs that a given integer is in a tree.

```
dataprop ITR(int,itr) = // the first bar (|) is optional
  | {n:int, l:itr, r:itr} ITRbase(n,node(n,l,r))
  | {n:int, n':int, l:itr, r:itr} ITRleft(n,node(n',l,r)) of ITR(n,l)
  | {n:int, n':int, l:itr, r:itr} ITRright(n,node(n',l,r)) of ITR(n,r)
```

This declaration creates three constructors for forming **ITR** proofs:

$$ITRbase \; : \forall n : int. \forall l : itr. \forall r : itr. \; \mathbf{ITR}(n, node(n, l, r))$$
$$ITRleft \; : \forall n : int. \forall n' : int. \forall l : itr. \forall r : itr. \; \mathbf{ITR}(n, l) \rightarrow \mathbf{ITR}(n, node(n', l, r))$$
$$ITRright : \forall n : int. \forall n' : int. \forall l : itr. \forall r : itr. \; \mathbf{ITR}(n, r) \rightarrow \mathbf{ITR}(n, node(n', l, r))$$

In general we construct dataprops in order to prove constraints on the indices of the prop. The proofs are then erased after type-checking, leaving only program terms to be executed. We need to ensure all proof terms are total in order to allow for this erasure semantics. Because of this requirement we restrict the definition of dataprops and dataviews to not have negative occurrences of the prop or view being defined. Without this restriction one could implement a fixed-point operator on props using a dataprop with a negative occurrence. Dataviews are simply linear dataprops and have essentially the same syntax.

4 Programming with Theorem Proving in ATS

In this section, we illustrate by example how the paradigm that combines programming with theorem proving is supported in ATS.

4.1 Programming with Constraints

The design of the concrete syntax of ATS is largely influenced by that of Standard ML (SML) [12]. Previously, we used following concrete syntax to define a datatype constructor **list** for forming a type for a list:

```
datatype list (type, int) =
  {a:type} nil (a, 0) | {a:type, n:nat} cons (a, n+1) of (a, list (a, n))
```

Given two static terms: a type T and an integer I, we can form a datatype **list**(T, I) for lists of length I in which each element is of type T. The above concrete syntax indicates that two associated list constructors *nil* and *cons* are assigned the following types:

$$nil \quad : \quad \forall a : type. \ \textbf{list}(a, 0)$$
$$cons \quad : \quad \forall a : type. \forall n : nat. \ (a, \textbf{list}(a, n)) \to \textbf{list}(a, n + 1)$$

The type of *cons* means that given a value of type T and a list of length I in which each element is of type T, we can construct a list of length $I + 1$ in which each element is of type T. The function that appends two given lists is implemented as follows:

```
fun append {a:type, m:nat, n:nat}
  (xs: list (a, m), ys: list (a, n)): list (a, m+n) =
  case xs of nil () => ys | cons (x, xs') => cons (x, append (xs', ys))
```

where the syntax indicates that *append* is assigned the following type:
$$\forall a : type. \forall m : nat. \forall n : nat. \ (\textbf{list}(a, m), \textbf{list}(a, n)) \to \textbf{list}(a, m + n)$$
That is, *append* returns a list of length $m + n$ when applied two lists of length m and n, respectively.

When this function is type-checked, two linear constraints on integers are generated. First, when the first given list xs is *nil*, i.e., the length m is 0, the constraint $n = 0 + n$ is generated in order to assign ys the type **list**$(a, m + n)$. Second, in order to assign $cons(x, append(xs', ys))$ the type **list**$(a, m + n)$, the constraint $(m - 1) + n + 1 = m + n$ is generated, since xs' is of length $m - 1$, $append(xs', ys)$ is of type **list**$(a, (m - 1) + n)$ and $cons(x, append(xs', ys))$ is thus of type **list**$(a, (m - 1) + n + 1)$.

In ATS, we also provide a means for the programmer to solve constraints[1] by constructing explicit proofs, supporting a paradigm that combines programming with theorem proving. In Figure 3, we define a datasort *mynat* with two value constructors: Z for the natural number 0 and S for a successor function on natural numbers. Then given three natural numbers m, n, and p, a dataprop **ADD**(m, n, p) represents a proposition $m + n = p$, which is defined inductively. The datatype constructor **mylist** now takes a natural number of sort *mynat* instead of an integer of sort *int*. The syntax $[p : mynat]$ in the *append* function, which stands for an existentially quantified static variable, means that there exists a natural number p of sort *mynat*. Now the *append* function takes two lists of length m and n respectively, and its return type is a proving type of the form (**ADD**(m, n, p) | **mylist**(a, p)), meaning that the return value is a list with a

---

[1] In the current version of ATS, linear constraints on integers can be solved implicitly by a built-in decision procedure based on the approach of Fourier-Motzkin variable elimination [8]. However, the programmer is required to construct explicit proofs to handle nonlinear constraints.

```
datasort mynat = Z | S of mynat

dataprop ADD (mynat, mynat, mynat) =
  | {n:mynat} ADDbas (Z, n, n) // base case
  | {m:mynat, n:mynat, p:mynat} // inductive case
      ADDind (S m, n, S p) of ADD (m, n, p)

datatype mylist (type, mynat) =
  | {a:type} mynil (a, Z)
  | {a:type, n:mynat} mycons (a, S n) of (a, mylist (a, n))

// '(...) : this syntax is used to form tuples
fun append {a:type, m:mynat, n:mynat}
  (xs: mylist (a, m), ys: mylist (a, n))
  : [p: mynat] '(ADD (m, n, p) | mylist (a, p)) =
case xs of
    | mynil () => '(ADDbas | ys)
    | mycons (x, xs') => let
          val '(pf | zs) = append (xs', ys)
      in '(ADDind pf | mycons (x, zs)) end
```

Fig. 3. An example of programming with theorem proving

proof that proves the length of the return list is the sum of the lengths of two
input lists.

4.2   Programming with Dataprops

In this section we briefly outline a verified call-by-value evaluator for pure λ-
calculus. We begin by declaring a static sort to represent λ-terms via higher-order
abstract syntax (h.o.a.s.) [13].

```
datasort tm = lm of (tm -> tm) | ap of (tm, tm)
```

This syntax declares a datasort tm with two term constructors: lm which takes
as its argument a function of sort $tm \rightarrow tm$, and ap which takes as its arguments
two static terms of sort tm. For instance, the λ-term $\lambda x.\lambda y.y(x)$ is represented
as lm (lam x => (lm (lam y => ap (y, x)))) in the concrete syntax of ATS,
where lam is a keyword in ATS for introducing λ-abstraction.

We declare another sort tms to represent environments such that a term of
the sort tms consists of a sequence of terms of the sort tm:

```
datasort tms = none | more of (tms, tm)
```

With these two sorts as indices, we can specify the big-step call-by-value evaluation relation as the dataprop **EVAL**:

```
dataprop EVAL(tm, tm, int) =
  | {f:tm -> tm} EVALlam (lm f, lm f, 0) // λx.e → λx.e
```

```
    | {t1:tm, t2:tm, f:tm -> tm, v1:tm, v2:tm, n1:nat, n2:nat,n3:nat}
        EVALapp (ap (t1, t2), v2, n1+n2+n3+1) of
            (EVAL (t1, lm f, n1), EVAL (t2, v1, n2), EVAL (f v1, v2, n3))
            // if e1 → λx.e1', e2 → v1 and [v1/x]e1' → v2, then e1(e2) → v2

propdef EVAL0 (t1:tm,t2:tm) = [n:nat] EVAL (t1,t2,n) // prop def.
```

The third index of **EVAL**, an integer, is the length of the reduction sequence and it is needed in forming termination metrics to assure proof totality. Additionally we define **EVAL₀** to be an **EVAL** of any length. Now we define another prop constructor **ISVAL** expressing that the static term of sort *tm* it is indexed by is a value. Note that λ-abstractions are the only form of values in this simple language.

```
dataprop ISVAL (tm) = {f: tm -> tm} ISVALlam (lm f)
```

Now we can construct two proof functions: *lemma1* which proves that any value evaluates to itself and *lemma2* which proves that any term which is the result of evaluation is a value.

```
prfun lemma1 {t:tm} .< >. (pf :ISVAL (t)): EVAL0 (t, t) =
    case* pf of ISVALlam () => EVALlam

prfun lemma2 {t1:tm,t2:tm,n:nat} .<n>. (pf: EVAL (t1,t2,n)): ISVAL t2 =
    case* pf of EVALlam () => ISVALlam | EVALapp (_, _, pf') => lemma2 pf'
```

These proof functions make use of two techniques to guarantee totality: the *case⋆* which mandates that the pattern matching following it is exhaustive (an error message is issued otherwise) and the termination metric (written in the form of .<*metric*>.) which specifies a well-ordering (based on the lexicographical ordering on tuples of natural numbers) to guarantee termination of the recursion. Now we create datatypes for terms, values and environments:

```
datatype EXP (tms, tm) = ...

datatype VAL (tm) =
    {ts:tms,f:tm->tm} VALclo(lm f) of (ENV ts, {t:tm} EXP(more(ts,t), f t))

and ENV (tms) =
    | ENVnil (none)
    | {ts:tms, t:tm} ENVcons (more (ts, t)) of (ISVAL t | ENV ts, VAL t)
```

With these sorts, types and propositions, we can now define an evaluation function whose type proves its correctness:

```
fun eval {ts: tms, t: tm} (env: ENV ts, e: EXP (ts, t))
    : [v:tm] '(EVAL0 (t, v) | VAL v) = ...

fun evaluate {t: tm} (e: EXP (none, t))
    : [v:tm] '(EVAL0 (t, v) | VAL v) = eval (ENVnil, e)
```

The concrete syntax indicates that the *evaluate* function is assigned the following type:

$$\forall t : tm.\mathbf{EXP}(none, t) \rightarrow \exists v : tm.(\mathbf{EVAL}_0(t, v) \mid \mathbf{VAL}(v))$$

which means that *evaluate* takes a *closed* term t and returns a value v along with a proof that t evaluates to v. Such proofs can be erased before execution leaving a verified interpreter. Please find the omitted code on-line:

http://www.cs.bu.edu/~hwxi/ATS/EXAMPLE/LF/callByValue.ats

4.3   Programming with Dataviews

A novel notion of *stateful views* is introduced in ATS to describe memory layouts and reason about memory properties. A stateful view is a form of linear prop, which can also be assigned to proof terms. There is a built-in sort *addr* for static terms L representing memory addresses (or locations). Given a type T and an address L, $T@L$ is a primitive stateful view meaning that a value of the type T is stored at the location L. Given two stateful views V_1 and V_2, $V_1 \otimes V_2$ is a stateful view that joins V_1 and V_2 together, and $V_1 \multimap V_2$ is a stateful view which yields V_2 when applied to V_1. We also provide a means to form recursive stateful views through dataviews. For instance, a view for an array is recursively defined below:

```
dataview arrayView (type, int, addr) =
  | {a:type, l:addr} ArrayNone (a, 0, l)
  | {a:type, l:addr, n:nat}
    ArraySome (a, n+1, l) of (a@l, arrayView (a, n, l+1))
```

The stateful view **arrayView**(T, I, L) means that there is an array of length I in which all the elements are of type T stored at addresses $L, L+1, \ldots, L+(I-1)$. The two associated constructors are of the following props:

$ArrayNone : \forall a : type.\forall l : addr.$ **arrayView**$(a, 0, l)$
$ArraySome : \forall a : type.\forall l : addr.\forall n : nat.$
$\qquad\qquad (a@l \otimes \mathbf{arrayView}(a, n, l + 1)) \multimap \mathbf{arrayView}(a, n + 1, l)$

The types of some built-in functions in ATS can be specified through the use of stateful views. For instance, the types of functions for safe reading from and writing to a pointer are given as follows.

```
dynval getPtr :  // read from a pointer
  {a:type, l:addr} (a@l | ptr l) -> (a@l | a)

dynval setPtr :  // write to a pointer
  {a1:type, a2:type, l:addr} (a1@l | ptr l, a2) -> (a2@l | unit)
```

According to the type of *getPtr*, the function can be applied a pointer to L only if a proof term of the view $T@L$ is given, which assures that the address L is accessible. In other words, without specifying a proper proof, *getPtr* is not allowed to be applied. Thus, we can readily prevent dangling pointers from ever being accessed as no proofs for dangling pointers can be provided.

A proof function manipulating views is referred to as a *view change function*. For instance, a view **arrayView**(T, I_0, L) can be changed into two views: a view $T@(L + I)$ where $0 \leq I < I_0$ and a functional view $T@(L + I) \multimap$ **arrayView**(T, I_0, L) which basically means that given a proof of $T@(L+I)$, it returns a proof of **arrayView**(T, I_0, L). This is like taking the Ith element out of an array of size I_0 (described by $T@(L + I)$) and leaving the rest (described by $T@(L + I) \multimap$ **arrayView**(T, I_0, L)). The following view change function *takeOutLemma* implements this idea:

```
prfun takeOutLemma
      {a:type,n:int,i:nat,l:addr | i < n} .<i>. (pf: arrayView (a, n, l))
   : '(a@(l+i), a@(l+i) -o arrayView (a, n, l)) = ...
```

We now introduce an interesting example – an array subscripting function – which makes use of the *takeOutLemma* given above.

```
fun sub {a:type, n:int, i:nat, l:addr | i < n}
   (pf: arrayView (a, n, l) | p: ptr l, i: int i)
  : '(arrayView (a, n, l) | a) = let
    prval '(pf1, pf2) = takeOutLemma {a, n, i, l} (pf)
    val '(pf1 | x) = getPtr (pf1 | p + i)
  in '(pf2 pf1 | x) end
```

In the *sub* function, we use *getPtr* to access the Ith element of an array of size I_0 such that $0 \leq I < I_0$ holds. In order to provide a proof of $T@(L + I)$, we apply the view change function *takeOutLemma* to a proof term *pf* of the **arrayView**(T, I_0, L). At last it recovers the view for the array using linear function application on two proofs pf_2 and pf_1, and then returns the value of the type T as we wish. Note that *sub* can be readily compiled into a function with a body of one load instruction after the proofs in *sub* are erased.

4.4   More Examples

Many more interesting and larger examples can be found on-line [15]. In particular, the current library of ATS alone consists of over 20K lines of code written in ATS, where the paradigm of programming with theorem proving is widely employed.

5   Conclusion and Future Work

The language ATS supports a paradigm that combines programming with theorem proving, and we have illustrated by example that how this paradigm is carried out in ATS. In addition to standard non-linear props, a form of linear props, stateful views, is supported in ATS for reasoning about memory. At present, we know no other programming languages that support the paradigm of programming with theorem proving as is described in this paper. In particular, we emphasize that this paradigm is fundamentally different from the one that extracts programs out of proofs as is advocated in theorem proving systems such as NuPrl [6] and Coq [2].

We believe that programming with theorem proving is a promising research topic. Developing automated theorem proving (rather than constructing proofs explicitly) and combing it in programming is one of our future works. In order to support more programming paradigms, we plan to combine assembly programming with theorem proving, and employ the idea of view change functions to model the computation of assembly instructions and capture program states (including registers, stacks and heaps) at assembly level. We also plan to reason about other interesting properties by building proper logics on top of ATS. For instance, we would like to develop concurrent programming in ATS, supporting formal reasoning on properties such as deadlocks and race conditions.

References

1. H. P. Barendregt. Lambda Calculi with Types. In S. Abramsky, D. M. Gabbay, and T. Maibaum, editors, *Handbook of Logic in Computer Science*, volume II, pages 117–441. Clarendon Press, Oxford, 1992.
2. Y. Bertot and P. Casteran. *Interactive Theorem Proving and Program Development Coq'Art: The Calculus of Inductive Constructions*. Texts in Theoretical Computer Science. An EATCS Series. Springer Verlag, 2004.
3. C. Chen, R. Shi, and H. Xi. A Typeful Approach to Object-Oriented Programming with Multiple Inheritance. In *Proceedings of the 6th International Symposium on Practical Aspects of Declarative Languages*, Dallas, TX, June 2004. Springer-Verlag LNCS vol. 3057.
4. C. Chen and H. Xi. ATS/LF: a type system for constructing proofs as total functional programs, November 2004. http://www.cs.bu.edu/~hwxi/ATS/PAPER/ ATSLF.ps
5. C. Chen and H. Xi. Combining Programming with Theorem Proving, November 2004. (http://www.cs.bu.edu/~hwxi/ATS/PAPER/CPwTP.ps)
6. R. L. Constable et al. *Implementing Mathematics with the NuPrl Proof Development System*. Prentice-Hall, Englewood Cliffs, New Jersey, 1986.
7. R. L. Constable and S. F. Smith. Partial objects in constructive type theory. In *Proceedings of Symposium on Logic in Computer Science*, pages 183–193, Ithaca, New York, June 1987.
8. G. Dantzig and B. Eaves. Fourier-Motzkin elimination and its dual. *Journal of Combinatorial Theory (A)*, 14:288–297, 1973.
9. S. Hayashi and H. Nakano. *PX: A Computational Logic*. The MIT Press, 1988.
10. F. Honsell, I. A. Mason, S. Smith, and C. Talcott. A variable typed logic of effects. *Information and Computation*, 119(1):55–90, 15 May 1995.
11. N. Mendler. Recursive types and type constraints in second-order lambda calculus. In *Proceedings of Symposium on Logic in Computer Science*, pages 30–36, Ithaca, New York, June 1987. The Computer Society of the IEEE.
12. R. Milner, M. Tofte, R. W. Harper, and D. MacQueen. *The Definition of Standard ML (Revised)*. MIT Press, Cambridge, Massachusetts, 1997.
13. F. Pfenning and C. Elliott. Higher-order abstract syntax. In *ACM SIGPLAN '88 Conference on Programming Language Design and Implementation*, volume 23 (7), pages 199–208, Atlanta, Georgia, July 1988. ACM Press.

14. H. Xi. Applied Type System (extended abstract). In *post-workshop Proceedings of TYPES 2003*, pages 394–408. Springer-Verlag LNCS 3085, 2004.
15. H. Xi. Applied Type System, 2005. `http://www.cs.bu.edu/ ~hwxi/ATS`
16. D. Zhu and H. Xi. Safe Programming with Pointers through Stateful Views. In *Proceedings of the 7th International Symposium on Practical Aspects of Declarative Languages*, Long Beach, CA, January 2005. Springer-Verlag LNCS, 3350.

Author Index

Lecture Notes in Artificial Intelligence (LNAI)

Vol. 3508: P. Bresciani, P. Giorgini, B. Henderson-Sellers, G. Low, M. Winikoff (Eds.), Agent-Oriented Information Systems II. X, 227 pages. 2005.

Vol. 3505: V. Gorodetsky, J. Liu, V. Skormin (Eds.), Autonomous Intelligent Systems: Agents and Data Mining. XIII, 303 pages. 2005.

Vol. 3501: B. Kégl, G. Lapalme (Eds.), Advances in Artificial Intelligence. XV, 458 pages. 2005.

Vol. 3492: P. Blache, E. Stabler, J. Busquets, R. Moot (Eds.), Logical Aspects of Computational Linguistics. X, 363 pages. 2005.

Vol. 3488: M.-S. Hacid, N.V. Murray, Z.W. Raś, S. Tsumoto (Eds.), Foundations of Intelligent Systems. XIII, 700 pages. 2005.

Vol. 3487: J. Leite, P. Torroni (Eds.), Computational Logic in Multi-Agent Systems. XII, 281 pages. 2005.

Vol. 3476: J. Leite, A. Omicini, P. Torroni, P. Yolum (Eds.), Declarative Agent Languages and Technologies II. XII, 289 pages. 2005.

Vol. 3464: S.A. Brueckner, G.D.M. Serugendo, A. Karageorgos, R. Nagpal (Eds.), Engineering Self-Organising Systems. XIII, 299 pages. 2005.

Vol. 3452: F. Baader, A. Voronkov (Eds.), Logic for Programming, Artificial Intelligence, and Reasoning. XI, 562 pages. 2005.

Vol. 3451: M.-P. Gleizes, A. Omicini, F. Zambonelli (Eds.), Engineering Societies in the Agents World V. XIII, 349 pages. 2005.

Vol. 3446: T. Ishida, L. Gasser, H. Nakashima (Eds.), Massively Multi-Agent Systems I. XI, 349 pages. 2005.

Vol. 3445: G. Chollet, A. Esposito, M. Faundez-Zanuy, M. Marinaro (Eds.), Nonlinear Speech Modeling and Applications. XIII, 433 pages. 2005.

Vol. 3438: H. Christiansen, P.R. Skadhauge, J. Villadsen (Eds.), Constraint Solving and Language Processing. VIII, 205 pages. 2005.

Vol. 3430: S. Tsumoto, T. Yamaguchi, M. Numao, H. Motoda (Eds.), Active Mining. XII, 349 pages. 2005.

Vol. 3419: B. Faltings, A. Petcu, F. Fages, F. Rossi (Eds.), Constraint Satisfaction and Constraint Logic Programming. X, 217 pages. 2005.

Vol. 3416: M. Böhlen, J. Gamper, W. Polasek, M.A. Wimmer (Eds.), E-Government: Towards Electronic Democracy. XIII, 311 pages. 2005.

Vol. 3415: P. Davidsson, B. Logan, K. Takadama (Eds.), Multi-Agent and Multi-Agent-Based Simulation. X, 265 pages. 2005.

Vol. 3403: B. Ganter, R. Godin (Eds.), Formal Concept Analysis. XI, 419 pages. 2005.

Vol. 3398: D.-K. Baik (Ed.), Systems Modeling and Simulation: Theory and Applications. XIV, 733 pages. 2005.

Vol. 3397: T.G. Kim (Ed.), Artificial Intelligence and Simulation. XV, 711 pages. 2005.

Vol. 3396: R.M. van Eijk, M.-P. Huget, F. Dignum (Eds.), Agent Communication. X, 261 pages. 2005.

Vol. 3394: D. Kudenko, D. Kazakov, E. Alonso (Eds.), Adaptive Agents and Multi-Agent Systems II. VIII, 313 pages. 2005.

Vol. 3392: D. Seipel, M. Hanus, U. Geske, O. Bartenstein (Eds.), Applications of Declarative Programming and Knowledge Management. X, 309 pages. 2005.

Vol. 3374: D. Weyns, H. V.D. Parunak, F. Michel (Eds.), Environments for Multi-Agent Systems. X, 279 pages. 2005.

Vol. 3371: M.W. Barley, N. Kasabov (Eds.), Intelligent Agents and Multi-Agent Systems. X, 329 pages. 2005.

Vol. 3369: V. R. Benjamins, P. Casanovas, J. Breuker, A. Gangemi (Eds.), Law and the Semantic Web. XII, 249 pages. 2005.

Vol. 3366: I. Rahwan, P. Moraitis, C. Reed (Eds.), Argumentation in Multi-Agent Systems. XII, 263 pages. 2005.

Vol. 3359: G. Grieser, Y. Tanaka (Eds.), Intuitive Human Interfaces for Organizing and Accessing Intellectual Assets. XIV, 257 pages. 2005.

Vol. 3346: R.H. Bordini, M. Dastani, J. Dix, A.E.F. Seghrouchni (Eds.), Programming Multi-Agent Systems. XIV, 249 pages. 2005.

Vol. 3345: Y. Cai (Ed.), Ambient Intelligence for Scientific Discovery. XII, 311 pages. 2005.

Vol. 3343: C. Freksa, M. Knauff, B. Krieg-Brückner, B. Nebel, T. Barkowsky (Eds.), Spatial Cognition IV. XIII, 519 pages. 2005.

Vol. 3339: G.I. Webb, X. Yu (Eds.), AI 2004: Advances in Artificial Intelligence. XXII, 1272 pages. 2004.

Vol. 3336: D. Karagiannis, U. Reimer (Eds.), Practical Aspects of Knowledge Management. X, 523 pages. 2004.

Vol. 3327: Y. Shi, W. Xu, Z. Chen (Eds.), Data Mining and Knowledge Management. XIII, 263 pages. 2005.

Vol. 3315: C. Lemaître, C.A. Reyes, J.A. González (Eds.), Advances in Artificial Intelligence – IBERAMIA 2004. XX, 987 pages. 2004.

Vol. 3303: J.A. López, E. Benfenati, W. Dubitzky (Eds.), Knowledge Exploration in Life Science Informatics. X, 249 pages. 2004.

Vol. 3301: G. Kern-Isberner, W. Rödder, F. Kulmann (Eds.), Conditionals, Information, and Inference. XII, 219 pages. 2005.

Vol. 3276: D. Nardi, M. Riedmiller, C. Sammut, J. Santos-Victor (Eds.), RoboCup 2004: Robot Soccer World Cup VIII. XVIII, 678 pages. 2005.

Vol. 3275: P. Perner (Ed.), Advances in Data Mining. VIII, 173 pages. 2004.

Vol. 3265: R.E. Frederking, K.B. Taylor (Eds.), Machine Translation: From Real Users to Research. XI, 392 pages. 2004.

Vol. 3264: G. Paliouras, Y. Sakakibara (Eds.), Grammatical Inference: Algorithms and Applications. XI, 291 pages. 2004.

Vol. 3259: J. Dix, J. Leite (Eds.), Computational Logic in Multi-Agent Systems. XII, 251 pages. 2004.

Vol. 3257: E. Motta, N.R. Shadbolt, A. Stutt, N. Gibbins (Eds.), Engineering Knowledge in the Age of the Semantic Web. XVII, 517 pages. 2004.

Vol. 3249: B. Buchberger, J.A. Campbell (Eds.), Artificial Intelligence and Symbolic Computation. X, 285 pages. 2004.